Beethoven's Conversation Books

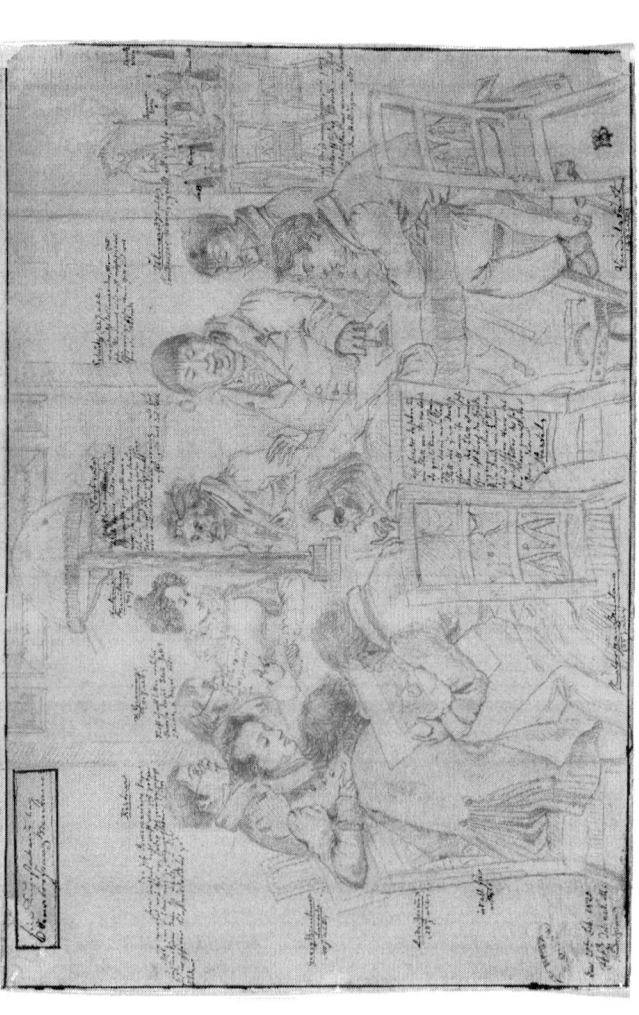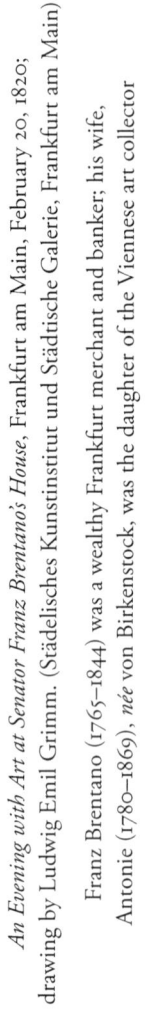

An Evening with Art at Senator Franz Brentano's House, Frankfurt am Main, February 20, 1820; drawing by Ludwig Emil Grimm. (Städelisches Kunstinstitut und Städtische Galerie, Frankfurt am Main)

Franz Brentano (1765–1844) was a wealthy Frankfurt merchant and banker; his wife, Antonie (1780–1869), *née* von Birkenstock, was the daughter of the Viennese art collector Johann Melchior von Birkenstock (1738–1809). Antonie is perhaps the leading candidate for Beethoven's "Immortal Beloved" of 1812 (see Heft 56, Blätter 23r–23v).

Beethoven's Conversation Books

Volume 5: Nos. 44 to 59
(October 1823 to March 1824)

Edited and translated by

Theodore Albrecht

THE BOYDELL PRESS

Translation and editorial matter © Theodore Albrecht 2025

A licensed edition of *Ludwig van Beethovens Konversationshefte, Bd. 4* and *Bd. 5*
edited by Karl-Heinz Köhler, Grita Herre and Dagmar Beck
© 1968 and 1970 by Deutscher Verlag für Musik Leipzig

All Rights Reserved. Except as permitted under current legislation
no part of this work may be photocopied, stored in a retrieval system,
published, performed in public, adapted, broadcast,
transmitted, recorded or reproduced in any form or by any means,
without the prior permission of the copyright owner

First published 2025
The Boydell Press, Woodbridge

ISBN 978 1 83765 102 3

The Boydell Press is an imprint of Boydell & Brewer Ltd
PO Box 9, Woodbridge, Suffolk IP12 3DF, UK
and of Boydell & Brewer Inc.
668 Mt Hope Avenue, Rochester, NY 14620–2731, USA
website: www.boydellandbrewer.com

A catalogue record for this book is available
from the British Library

The publisher has no responsibility for the continued existence or accuracy of URLs for external or third-party internet websites referred to in this book, and does not guarantee that any content on such websites is, or will remain, accurate or appropriate

Typeset by BBR Design, Sheffield

This volume is dedicated to
Susan Lund

Contents

General Introduction to the English Edition ... ix
Acknowledgements ... xxiii
Reader's Guide ... xxvi
Directionality in Vienna (True and Perceived) ... xxxviii
Highlights of Volume 5 ... xl

Heft 44. (ca. October 29 or 30, 1823 – ca. November 2 or 3, 1823) ... 1

Heft 45. (ca. November 4, 1823 – ca. November 20, 1823) ... 17

Heft 46. (ca. November 21, 1823 – ca. November 26, 1823) ... 53

Heft 47. (ca. November 29, 1823 – ca. December 6/7, 1823) ... 75

Heft 48. (December 7, 1823 – December 13, 1823) ... 107

Heft 49. (December 13, 1823 – December 16, 1823) ... 131

Heft 50. (December 20, 1823 – December 25, 1823) ... 143

Heft 51. (December 27, 1823 – ca. January 3, 1824) ... 157

Heft 52. (ca. January 5, 1824 – ca. January 7, 1824) ... 173

Heft 53. (January 16, 1824 – January 21, 1824) ... 179

Heft 54. (January 21, 1824 – February 2, 1824) ... 195

Heft 55. (ca. February 3, 1824 – ca. February 12, 1824) ... 235

Heft 56. (ca. February 13, 1824 – ca. February 20, 1824) ... 249

Heft 57. (February 25, 1824 – March 9, 1824) ... 277

Heft 58. (March 7, 1824 – March 8, 1824) 309

Heft 59. (March 9, 1824 – March 16, 1824) 315

Appendix A: Descriptions of the Conversation Books in Volume 5 329
Appendix B: Nephew Karl's Language Teachers: Pleugmackers and Pulay 331

Bibliography 335
Index of Writers of Conversational Entries 352
Index of Beethoven's Compositions 355
General Index 361

General Introduction to the English Edition

Ludwig van Beethoven (1770–1827) is recognized the world over as one of the greatest composers of all time and is especially known for his musical triumphs in the face of increasing deafness, beginning around 1798.[1]

In 1801 he confided his early hearing loss to Dr. Franz Wegeler in Bonn and schoolmaster/violinist Carl Amenda in Latvia, friends who had lived in Vienna but were now safely far away.[2] By the summer of 1802 others were starting to perceive lapses in his hearing, and his fear and confusion are reflected in the Heiligenstadt Testament in October of that year.[3] With more good days than bad, Beethoven's hearing slowly became weaker, although it had not yet interfered with his performing in public, even with orchestra on the marathon concert of December 22, 1808.[4]

Between 1812 and 1816 he tried using ear trumpets (made for him by Johann

---

[1] There are many medical accounts of Beethoven's deafness. Possibly the most complete and objective in English is by the Australian physician Peter J. Davies, *Beethoven in Person: His Deafness, Illnesses, and Death* (Westport, Conn.: Greenwood Press, 2001), pp. 42–65 and 217–218.

[2] On June 29, 1801, Beethoven wrote to Franz Gerhard Wegeler: "For the last three years my hearing has become weaker and weaker." Two days later, on July 1, he wrote to Amenda: "My most prized possession, my hearing, has greatly deteriorated. While you were still with me, I already felt the symptoms, but I said nothing about them." Amenda had left Vienna shortly after June 25, 1799. See Emily Anderson, transl. and ed., *The Letters of Beethoven*, 3 vols. (London: Macmillan, 1961), Nos. 51 and 53; and (for Amenda's reply) Theodore Albrecht, transl. and ed., *Letters to Beethoven and Other Correspondence*, 3 vols. (Lincoln: University of Nebraska Press, 1996), No. 31.

[3] Ferdinand Ries noted brief lapses while walking with Beethoven in the rural paths around Heiligenstadt, confirmed in the composer's so-called "Heiligenstadt Testament." See Franz Gerhard Wegeler and Ferdinand Ries, *Beethoven Remembered*, transl. Frederick Noonan (Arlington, Va.: Great Ocean Publishers, 1987), pp. 86–87; and Anderson, Vol. 3, Appendix A, pp. 1351–1354 (the Heiligenstadt Testament, actually close to a fair copy, dated October 6 and 10, 1802).

[4] Alexander Wheelock Thayer, *Thayer's Life of Beethoven*, ed. Elliot Forbes (Princeton: Princeton University Press, 1964/67), pp. 446–449. The breakdown in the performance of the *Choral Fantasy*, Op. 80, the last item on the program, was probably caused by orchestral fatigue at the tricky transition between the nocturnal *Adagio, ma non troppo* in 6/8 and the ensuing *Marcia, assai vivace* in 2/4 (*Gesamtausgabe*, p. 22).

Nepomuk Mälzel and possibly his brother Leonhard, also an inventor) with varying, but largely disappointing, degrees of success.[5] Between December 8, 1813, and February 27, 1814, Beethoven conducted (or attempted to conduct) four benefit concerts with an orchestra of ca. 113 professionals, causing considerable commentary about his exaggerated motions, some of which by now were the inevitable result of his weakened hearing.[6] At the performances, which included the premieres of his Symphonies Nos. 7 and 8, as well as *Wellington's Victory*, Beethoven's motions were probably shadowed, much more accurately, by conductor Michael Umlauf. In the fall of 1814, as the Congress of Vienna assembled, Beethoven composed a cantata, *Der glorreiche Augenblick*, for the occasion. On October 10 the Prague pianist and pedagogue Johann Wenzel Tomaschek visited Beethoven, found sketches for the cantata on the piano, and reported that the composer "was especially hard of hearing this day, so that one had to shout, rather than speak, in order to be understood." Tomaschek returned on November 24, just as the parts for the cantata were being copied: "Beethoven received me very politely, but appeared to be very deaf on this day, for I had to exert myself to the utmost to make myself understood." Even though many of his other comments were caustic, Tomaschek did not report that any portion of their conversation took place in writing.[7]

On November 15, 1815, Beethoven's younger brother Carl died, leaving the composer as the contested guardian of his son Karl (b. September 4, 1806). Beethoven soon placed nephew Karl in a boarding school run by Cajetan Giannatasio del Rio, but paid frequent visits, to the extent that Giannatasio's daughter Franziska (Fanny) developed a crush on the composer and reported their spoken conversations in her diary.[8]

The Beginnings of Written Conversations by 1816

In September, 1816, Peter Joseph Simrock (1792–1868), son of the Bonn publisher Nikolaus Simrock (1751–1832), came to Vienna to reestablish his father's earlier close

---

[5] Davies, pp. 50–52, provides a sufficient survey. On April 8, 1823, Beethoven confided his disappointment in such mechanical devices to a chance acquaintance, Herr Sandra, also going deaf. See Heft 28, Blätter 41v–42v.

[6] For a good survey of accounts of the rehearsals and concerts by Louis Spohr and others, see Thayer-Forbes, pp. 564–567.

[7] Oscar George Sonneck, ed., *Beethoven: Impressions by his Contemporaries* (New York: G. Schirmer, 1926; repr. New York: Dover Publications, 1967), pp. 100 and 102–103.

[8] Ludwig Nohl, ed., *Eine stille Liebe zu Beethoven. Nach dem Tagebuche einer jungen Dame* (Leipzig: Ernst Julius Günther, 1875), *An Unrequited Love: An Episode in the Life of Beethoven (from the Diary of a Young Lady)*, transl. Annie Wood (London: Richard Bentley & Son, 1876).

connections with Beethoven[9] and later told biographer Alexander Wheelock Thayer of his activities. Young Simrock often visited Beethoven at Baden (his summer apartment), at his apartment in the Sailerstätte (inside the City walls), and at the restaurant *Zur goldenen Birne* (Hauptstrasse 42 in the nearby suburb of Landstrasse), where Beethoven often ate midday dinner.[10]

Simrock told Thayer that "he had no difficulty in making Beethoven understand him if he spoke into his left ear; but anything personal or confidential had to be communicated in writing." Thayer continues: on one occasion the composer handed him [Simrock] paper and pencil, remarking that his servant was an eavesdropper, etc. A few days afterwards, when Simrock visited again, Beethoven said: "Now we can talk because I have given my servant 5 Gulden, a kick in the rear, and sent him to the devil!" Everywhere in public, said Simrock, Beethoven complained about Emperor Franz because of the reduction of paper money,[11] but he was known and the police officials let him do what he pleased.[12]

Simrock probably departed Vienna on September 29 or 30, 1816, after having spent approximately a month in the Austrian capital.[13]

From roughly November, 1816, through April, 1817, Beethoven reportedly gave

---

[9] Peter Joseph Simrock had been born in Bonn on August 18, 1792, and therefore had reached his majority of 24 years only on August 18, 1816. As such, he probably could not have made any legally binding business agreements before that date. Thus he must have arrived in Vienna sometime in early September, 1816. For young Simrock's dates, see Lothar Niefind and Walther Ottendorff-Simrock, "Simrock," *MGG*, 2nd ed., *Personenteil*, vol. 15, cols. 835–838. While Beethoven still lived in Bonn, Nikolaus Simrock had been second (low) hornist in the Electoral orchestra, and the young composer (whose lower lip, from portraits and the life mask, seems appropriate to a low hornist) seemingly took lessons from him.

[10] Beethoven's City address during this time was on the 3rd floor [4th floor, American] of Count Lamberti's building, Sailerstätte Nos. 1055–1056 [renumbered as 994 in 1821]. Beethoven's surviving letter to Simrock during this period indicates that the visitor was staying at Landstrasser Hauptstrasse No. 40 [renumbered as 50 in 1821], only two buildings north of the *Birne*, No. 42 [renumbered as 52 in 1821], on the east side of the street. See Anderson, Nos. 647, 661, and 662; Brandenburg, No. 977, 979, and 982; Behsel, pp. 30 and 71.

[11] At this point, the English-language editions by Krehbiel (who *may* have seen Thayer's original notes) and Forbes (copying Krehbiel) quote Beethoven concerning Emperor Franz: "Such a rascal ought to be hanged to the first tree." Thayer's original publication and Thayer-Deiters-Riemann omit this sentence and, instead, drop to a footnote, saying (in German), "We shall pass over the very severe expressions imparted by Simrock."

[12] Thayer (1879), III, pp. 402–403; Thayer-Deiters-Riemann, III, p. 566; Thayer-Krehbiel, III, pp. 343–344; and Thayer-Forbes, p. 647; also excerpted in Davies, p. 52.

[13] Unfortunately, Simrock's name does not appear among the selective daily Arrivals and Departures listed in the *Wiener Zeitung* during this period. Simrock later told Ludwig Nohl that he had eaten midday dinner with Beethoven at the *Mehlgrube* on Neuer Markt (in the City) every day for two weeks (Kopitz and Cadenbach, II, p. 915). Added to the locations reported to Thayer, this suggests a month's stay. Fanny Giannatasio del Rio reported in her diary that Beethoven brought Simrock with him for a visit on September 28, and letters to German destinations that Simrock took with him

harmony lessons to Carl Friedrich Hirsch (1801–1881), a grandson of his own teacher Georg Albrechtsberger. In summer 1880 Hirsch told Theodor Frimmel that Beethoven's deafness had advanced to a point where one had to speak to him very loudly. During his lessons Beethoven watched the student's hands closely and was able to detect his mistakes. Frimmel does not report Hirsch's mentioning any written conversations.[14]

On June 19, 1817, Beethoven wrote to his old friend and patron, Countess Anna Marie Erdödy, who seems to have been living in Paucovecz (Paukovec), Croatia, that he had been ill since mid-October, 1816, adding: "Although my health has improved a little, […] my hearing has become worse."[15]

The Beginnings of Conversation Books by 1818

By 1818 Beethoven's deafness had progressed to such an extent that, with increasing frequency, he began to carry blank books with him, so that his friends and acquaintances, especially when in public, could write their sides of conversations without being overheard, while Beethoven himself customarily replied orally.[16] He wrote in them, too, however: shopping lists, errands to run, or books advertised in the local newspapers.[17] He also used them for the conversations and draft memoranda

---

suggest that Simrock departed Vienna on September 29 or 30 (Ludwig Nohl, *Eine stille Liebe*, p. 129; Nohl, *An Unrequited Love*, p. 125; Kopitz and Cadenbach, I, pp. 313–314; Anderson, Nos. 660 and 661; Brandenburg, Nos. 978 and 979).

[14] Theodor von Frimmel, "Carl Friedrich Hirsch," in his *Beethoven-Studien* 2 (Munich: Müller, 1906), pp. 53–69, especially pp. 61–62; Kopitz and Cadenbach, I, pp. 443–454; summarized in Thayer-Forbes, pp. 664–665. Although Frimmel reported Hirsch to be sound of mind and body in 1880, many details in the old man's account are mildly or even wildly inaccurate in light of later research, and Frimmel himself was the first to question them.

[15] Anderson, No. 783; Brandenburg, No. 1132 (with more details concerning Erdödy's whereabouts). Paukovec is 10 miles northeast of Zagreb.

[16] Much of this material appeared in Theodore Albrecht, "Time, Distance, Weather, Daily Routine, and Wordplay as Factors in Interpreting Beethoven's Conversation Books," *Beethoven Journal* 28, No. 2 (Winter, 2013), pp. 64–75.

[17] Heft (booklet) 1, a brief booklet of only 12 pages, filled between ca. February 26 and shortly after March 2, 1818, is almost a chronological anomaly and does not exhibit many of the practices of making entries found in later Hefte. It was seemingly not in Schindler's possession and found its way independently to the Beethoven-Haus, Bonn. Heft 2, a much longer book of 210 pages, was filled between March 17 and after May 15/16, 1819. It is the earliest of the booklets that Schindler deposited in the Royal Library in Berlin in 1846. Here we find some of Beethoven's friends (notably Franz Oliva) making horizontal lines between their conversational entries, and Beethoven himself jotting down specific advertisements from recognizable newspapers. There is another chronological break before Heft 3, 136 pages, filled between November 20 and ca. December 6, 1819. Probably three long or several shorter Hefte are missing between May and November, 1819, but beginning with Heft 3, on November 20, Beethoven's use of conversations books seemingly becomes relatively constant.

pertaining to the protracted negotiations, hearings, and lawsuits surrounding the guardianship of his nephew Karl.[18]

The first surviving conversation book, the relatively impromptu Heft 1, dating from February–March, 1818, demonstrates only the earliest phases of the little formalities that would characterize the conversation books in their more mature phases: the writers placing a horizontal line after their entries as a signal for Beethoven to reply, and so forth.

On Monday, November 16, 1818, Beethoven visited the Giannatasio del Rio family, whom he had not seen in a long time, and stayed for three hours. Daughter Franziska (Fanny), who had earlier been smitten with the composer, noted in her diary, "Since his hearing was especially bad on this day, we wrote everything."[19] The conversational entries for this visit must have been extensive—covering nephew Karl's progress in school, the Giannatasio family's activities, Beethoven's latest works, and general gossip around town—but no conversation book survives.

Thus Beethoven must have had associates write down portions of their conversations on individual pieces of paper by ca. 1816, and if his hearing deteriorated during the winter of 1816–1817, he must have begun using gatherings of leaves to make impromptu conversation books (such as Heft 1) by the winter of 1817–1818. Thereafter, the first surviving *systematic* booklet, Heft 2 (from mid-March to mid-May, 1819), presumably a commercially manufactured blank book, dates from only four months after Beethoven's visit to the Giannatasio family.

Preservation and Loss, 1819–1822

From May 1819 until roughly September 1820 Beethoven apparently set aside the conversation books with major references to Karl's guardianship in one pile, while the others probably went into a trunk or box with most of the rest of the correspondence that he had received over the years. Then, around November 1, 1822, as Beethoven was moving from his summer residence in Baden to an apartment in the suburb of Windmühle, back in Vienna, the trunk or box with the correspondence

---

[18] Karl-Heinz Köhler, *"... tausendmal leben!": Konversationen mit Herrn van Beethoven* (Leipzig: VEB Deutscher Verlag für Musik, 1978). A good English-language summary of this 200-page book can be found in Köhler's "The Conversation Books: Aspects of a New Picture of Beethoven," in *Beethoven, Performers, and Critics: The International Beethoven Congress, Detroit, 1977*, ed. by Robert Winter and Bruce Carr (Detroit: Wayne State University Press, 1980), pp. 147–161. An even briefer overview of the topic may be found in Nicholas Marston, "Conversation Books," in *The Beethoven Compendium*, ed. Barry Cooper (New York: Thames & Hudson, 1991), pp. 164–167.

[19] Ludwig Nohl, *Eine stille Liebe zu Beethoven*, p. 198, and *An Unrequited Love*, p. 185; Kopitz and Cadenbach, I, p. 331. Fanny's description—that Beethoven's hearing "was especially bad that day"—is remarkably similar to Tomaschek's observations in October and November, 1814, above.

and all but sixteen of his conversation books up to that point probably fell off of the wagon transporting his possessions and was lost.[20] This, rather than any other factor, probably accounts for the gap in the surviving conversation books between 1820 and 1822.

Continuity, 1822–1827

In November 1822 Beethoven simply continued his practice of using blank conversation books on a regular basis, as he needed them. Most often he again squirreled them away in some box or trunk, and this time most of them were *not* lost, though he himself probably lost a few or even gave a few away as souvenirs, as he did to Maurice Schlesinger on September 9, 1825. By the end of the first week in March 1827, his supply of purchased blank booklets may have run out as his health sharply declined, leaving the last three weeks of his life without a systematic record of his conversations.

Posterity and Publication

When Beethoven died on March 26, 1827, his unpaid secretary and future biographer Anton Schindler deemed the nearly 140 surviving conversation books of no particular monetary value to Beethoven's estate, and took them with the intention of using them to document his projected biography of the composer.[21] At first Schindler probably went through them, identifying every author of conversational entries that he could—and in that he has proven to be remarkably accurate, although a few identifications did elude him. He also probably began jotting in reminders to himself about conversations that did take place, and then—getting

---

[20] Johann Chrysostomus Sporschil, "Musikalischer Wegweiser," *Allgemeine Theater-Zeitung* (Vienna) 17, No. 137 (November 15, 1823), p. 548, signed "S ... l." Corresponding from Vienna, Sporschil (1800–1863) had recently published the article in the *Stuttgarter Morgenblatt für gebildete Stände*, No. 265 (November 5, 1823). The Viennese publication has been reprinted (among others) in Albert Leitzmann, ed., *Ludwig van Beethoven: Berichte der Zeitgenossen ...*, 2 vols. (Leipzig: Insel-Verlag, 1921), I, pp. 264–267. It was cited in Köhler *et al.*, *Beethovens Konversationshefte*, Vol. 4 (1968), p. 372 (endnote 492).

On July 12, 1823, seemingly when writing about the previous summer, Beethoven noted that "an unfortunate accident robbed me of a considerable portion of my papers," independently confirming what Sporschil would report in November. See Anderson, *Letters*, No. 1207; Brandenburg, *Briefwechsel*, No. 1698.

[21] Schindler explained that Stephan von Breuning, Beethoven's executor, had given the conversation books to him as a token payment for his efforts on the composer's behalf, and this seems credible enough.

into dangerous territory—commandeered blank pages and partially filled pages to write or reflect his own opinions or conversations that may or may not have taken place while the composer was alive. Fortunately, once we know that these "falsified" entries exist, we can see that most of them have a tone all their own and can safely regard or disregard them as circumstances warrant.

In 1842 Schindler wrote that he possessed many more than a hundred ("viel über hundert") conversation books.[22] Three years later, in the seldom cited 1845 second edition of his *Biographie*, the publisher wrote of the conversation books: "There are 138 of them in Prof. Schindler's possession."[23]

In 1846 Schindler, who probably lacked a pension from his earlier employers,[24] sold his Beethoven documents—including 137 conversation books—to the *Königliche Bibliothek*, the Prussian Royal Library in Berlin, for what amounted to a pension stipend. This number corresponds almost exactly to the 138 estimated a year before and certainly fits the description of "many more than a hundred" that Schindler had written four years earlier.

A few years later the American Alexander Wheelock Thayer, working on a modern, scientifically based biography of Beethoven, spent months going through the conversation books in Berlin, extracting notes to be used in his work.[25] In the process, in 1854, he also went to Frankfurt, where Schindler now lived, and asked him about the conversation books. Consistent with his earlier reports, Schindler probably told him that there were "viel über hundert" (many more than a hundred) booklets, which Thayer, as proficient as his German was, probably misheard as "vier hundert" (four hundred). Thus began the erroneous perception that there were 400 conversation books present when Beethoven died and that Schindler had destroyed

---

[22] Anton Schindler, *Beethoven in Paris: Ein Nachtrag zur Biographie Beethoven's* (Münster: Aschendorff, 1842), p. 31.

[23] The original German reads: "Es befinden sich davon 138 im Besitz des Herrn Prof. Schindler." Anton Schindler, *Biographie von Ludwig van Beethoven*, Zweite mit zwei Nachträgen vermehrte Ausgabe (Münster: Aschendorff, 1845), p. 275.

[24] Pensions, when they existed at all, were often based on full decades of employment. Therefore, an employee who had worked for 10 full years would receive a pension equal to 25% of his normal salary; an employee who had worked for 20 full years would receive a pension of 50%, and so on. Schindler had never worked for any theater, either in Vienna, Aachen, or Münster, for the requisite ten years, and so would probably not have been eligible for any pension.

[25] Grant W. Cook, "Alexander Wheelock Thayer: A New Biographical Sketch," *Beethoven Journal* 17, No. 1 (Summer, 2002), pp. 2–11. Thayer spent from October, 1849, to spring, 1851; November, 1854, to February, 1856; September, 1858, to May, 1859; and December, 1859, to February, 1860 (among other periods) working in Berlin.

perhaps two-thirds of them.[26] The answer is plain and simple: Schindler didn't do it! *Nobody* did!

Just as researchers were assembling and editing ever larger compilations of Beethoven's correspondence, so they began to perceive the desirability of having a printed edition of the conversation books. Around the time of World War I, Walther Nohl (b. 1866) began to publish them but was overwhelmed by the amount of editing that they needed as well as by the economics in post-War Germany.[27] In the late 1930s and into the 1940s Georg Schünemann (1884–1945), head of the Music Department at the Prussian State Library, began a much more organized effort with better transcriptions and annotations and published three volumes, a job that took him to July 1823, before World War II and his own death put an end to his project.[28]

In 1943 the conversation books, along with many of the Library's other valuable holdings, were transferred to rural bunkers, but at war's end they came back to Berlin to find that their Unter den Linden home had survived the bombings but was now on the Communist east side of the city.[29] Then, on May 1, 1951, Joachim Krüger, the forty-year-old head of the Music Department of the Deutsche Staatsbibliothek, stole a number of boxes of rare materials—including all of the Konversationshefte— from the Library and took them to the West, claiming that he had saved them from transport to the Soviet Union. The theft caused a worldwide scandal, especially when Krüger established himself as an antiquarian book dealer. In 1956 Karl-Heinz Köhler (1928–1997), Krüger's successor as head of the Music Department in East Berlin, learned that the stolen conversation books were in the Beethoven-Haus, Bonn, and

---

[26] Even hypothetically filling in the gaps that occur between March, 1819 (when continuous use seems to have begun), and March, 1827, would only bring the total number to ca. 300. For a slightly different estimate, see Theodore Albrecht, "Anton Schindler as Destroyer and Forger of Beethoven's Conversation Books: A Case for Decriminalization," in *Music's Intellectual History*, ed. Zdravko Blažeković and Barbara Dobbs Mackenzie (New York: RILM, 2009), pp. 169–181, specifically 173–174.

[27] In addition to several essays based on various later conversation books, Nohl systematically published booklets (today termed Hefte 2 and 3) covering from March, 1819 to March, 1820. Walther Nohl, ed., *Ludwig van Beethovens Konversationshefte* (Munich: O.C. Rech/Allgemeine Verlagsanstalt, 1923–1924). By 1935, Nohl had transferred the publication rights to the Akademische Verlagsgesellschaft Athenaion in Berlin-Potsdam, which sought subscriptions for the *Konversationshefte*. In a "Beethoven-Sonderheft" of its *Athenaion Blaetter* 4, No. 1 (1935), pp. 2–29, the press published a descriptive essay about the conversation books (pp. 2–6), an essay by Nohl about how he became interested in the conversation books and his experiences in editing them (pp. 6–8), noteworthy quotes from the conversation books, as well as illustrations of Beethoven's own handwriting in them.

[28] Georg Schünemann, ed., *Ludwig van Beethovens Konversationshefte*, 3 vols. (Berlin: Max Hesse, 1941–1943).

[29] Horst Kunze, "Geleitwort," in Köhler *et al.*, *Beethovens Konversationshefte*, Vol. 4, pp. 5–6.

called for their return. Finally, in August 1961, a decade after they were stolen, the conversation books were restored to their rightful owners in East Berlin.[30]

Almost immediately, Köhler organized an editorial team including Grita Herre (in 1963) and Dagmar Beck (added in 1971),[31] to make state-of-the-art diplomatic transcriptions with a more sophisticated scholarly apparatus, and to continue editing the conversation books where Schünemann had left off. But now, increasingly isolated behind the Berlin Wall, they enlisted the aid of their counterparts at Vienna's Austrian National Library and other Viennese institutions to help with the documentation needed for dating, identification, and other annotations, and they published Volume 4 in 1968 and Volume 5 in 1970. At the same time, they began replacing Schünemann's now outdated volumes, starting with a new Volume 1, published in 1972.[32] Then, in 1977, Peter Stadlen (1910–1996), a Viennese-born music critic living in London, created virtually a criminal sensation when he detected that Schindler had falsified many of his (Schindler's) entries in the conversation books and implied that the East Berlin team had been negligent in not making such an obvious discovery.[33] The Berliners, who themselves had begun to suspect this problem as they worked ahead on the project, published a list of these falsified entries already with Volume 7 in 1978 and continued to identify them in subsequent volumes. But their swift forward momentum was broken by this distraction, and Grita Herre finally published Volume 11, taking the 139 surviving booklets[34] through early March 1827, only in 2001.[35]

---

[30] Köhler, *"tausendmal leben,"* pp. 186–188; and especially Martin Hollender, "Joachim Krüger ... Bücherdieb ...," *Bibliothek* 30, No. 1 (2006), pp. 69–75. While Köhler discreetly declined to name names, the investigative reporter Hollender openly revealed that the conversation books had been in the Beethoven-Haus, Bonn, and that Joseph Schmidt-Görg, then its Director, had denied that the stolen goods were there. The demeanor of that venerable institution has changed remarkably in the ensuing half century.

[31] Köhler, *"tausendmal leben,"* p. 200.

[32] Therefore, the material in the present Volumes 1–3 (Hefte 1–31) is based on the "second wave" of the East Germans' experience, as published in 1972, 1976, and (post-Stadlen) 1983.

[33] For Stadlen's possible motivation, see Albrecht, "Anton Schindler as Destroyer and Forger," pp. 171–172.

[34] In addition to Schindler's 137 conversation books in the Staatsbibliothek zu Berlin—Preussischer Kulturbesitz, two more booklets, Hefte 1 and 95, are in the collection of the Beethoven-Haus Bonn, making a total of 139 that survive reasonably intact.

[35] This standard German-language edition is Karl-Heinz Köhler, Grita Herre, and Dagmar Beck, eds., *Ludwig van Beethovens Konversationshefte*, in collaboration with Ignaz Weinmann, Peter Pötschner, Renate Bormann, Heinz Schöny, and Günther Brosche, 11 volumes to date (Leipzig: VEB Deutscher Verlag für Musik, 1968–2001). The three primary editors were based in Berlin, their numerous collaborators in Vienna. More recently, Heft 95 has seen a separate facsimile publication: *Beethoven im Gespräch: Ein Konversationsheft vom 9. September 1825*, transcription and commentary by Grita Herre, with English translation by Theodore Albrecht (Bonn: Verlag Beethoven-Haus, 2002).

Therefore, when set against more than a half century of war and political division, theft and recovery, ideological and geographical isolation, and attempts to discredit it, the East Berlin edition of *Beethovens Konversationshefte* remains one of the true miracles of modern musicology, and no one can reasonably diminish the accomplishment of its editors!

The Quest for an English Edition of the Konversationshefte

As early as 1977, *Konversationshefte* editor Karl-Heinz Köhler announced that "a translation of this edition into English is being contemplated by a press in the United States."[36] During the 1980s a British team including author-researcher Susan Lund and Dr. Robert Terence (Terry) Llewellyn (1933–2013) began negotiations with Oxford University Press for such an edition. Llewellyn was on the German faculty of Christ's College, Cambridge, with research interests in Beethoven and Goethe.[37] In 1985, however, Oxford University Press announced, "A complete English translation of the Conversation Books is being prepared by Professor Lewis Lockwood of Harvard University."[38] Nothing came of that project, but Lockwood teamed up with the Trieste-born Dr. Piero Weiss of Peabody Conservatory with the idea of compiling a one-volume English-language anthology of the most significant entries in the conversation books and made selections through Volume 2 of the German edition.

Meanwhile, I had published my three-volume *Letters to Beethoven and Other Correspondence* in 1996 and was researching Beethoven's orchestral colleagues. I had included draft letters from the conversation books in my *Letters* collection so was aware of Lockwood's involvement. By 1998, however, he indicated that he was no longer interested in the project. Sometime later he made his materials available to me,[39] and I tentatively embarked on the present complete edition in

---

[36] Köhler, "The Conversation Books: Aspects of a New Picture of Beethoven," p. 148. Köhler's paper, delivered in Detroit in 1977, may have been revised, with this parenthetical statement added, shortly before its publication in 1980.

[37] Susan Lund (London), personal communication, August 16, 2015. A third participant in the project was to have been Llewellyn's Viennese-born wife Gudrun, who predeceased him. See Geoffrey Ingham, "In Memoriam," *Christ's College Magazine* (2014), pp. 93–94.

[38] The announcement appeared in Martin Cooper, *Beethoven: The Last Decade, 1817–1827*, revised edition (Oxford/New York: Oxford University Press, 1985), p. 470 (at the end of Cooper's bibliography).

[39] Lewis Lockwood, personal communication with files, Cambridge, Mass., January 27, 2004. Lockwood's files consisted of 128 double-spaced typed pages, seemingly generated between ca. 1985 and 1989/1991. The selection of entries seems to have been Lockwood's work, while the translations

English.[40] By 1998, however, it was also obvious that the *Konversationshefte* (which, after all, had begun to appear three decades before) would need a major revision in conjunction with any translation into English.

The Present English Edition of the Conversation Books

The German editors were diligent in establishing a rough chronology for the entries at the beginning of each *Heft* (or booklet) and provided ample endnotes to identify individuals and explain those entries. Even so, the inexperienced user (and especially the English speaker) was likely to view the unadorned diplomatic transcriptions as a virtual stream of consciousness without any immediately perceptible relationship to specific place or time. As a result, many misunderstandings and misinterpretations arose from even these published conversation books—problems that a closer identification of their organization, chronology, and contents might clarify.

Translations

When I began this project, several colleagues warned me that translation would be especially difficult because many of the conversational entries were "in the Viennese dialect." At the time of writing this General Introduction, I have drafted translations and annotations through Heft 79 (more than halfway through the project) and have encountered very few entries in *Wienerisch*, something of a Viennese counterpart to London's Cockney.[41] Instead there are often regional terms used by the normal population: *Kren* (rather than *Meerrettich*) for horseradish, *Semmel* (rather than

---

into facile, colorful, and idiomatic English were Piero Weiss's work. The final entry in the material that I received was from Heft 22, Blatt 61v (February, 1823), from the very end of Vol. 2 of the *Konversationshefte*.

[40] Although the Staatsbibliothek zu Berlin—Preussischer Kulturbesitz had granted me permission to make a translation and edition in 1999, and the Beethoven-Haus, Bonn, did likewise in 2001, I concentrated my work on the period surrounding the premiere of the Ninth Symphony in 1824. Only in 2007, as Boydell & Brewer undertook negotiations to license the published material from Breitkopf und Härtel, did I embark on a systematic translation and edition, starting with Heft 1, Blatt 1, and with strong encouragement from Lewis Lockwood.

[41] To this end, however, there is a vast literature on the subject, including Peter Wehle, *Sprechen Sie Wienerisch?* (Vienna: Ueberreuter, 1981/2003); Hans Eidherr, *Also fåhr ma Euer Gnadn: Wiener Redensart—Wiener Musik*, book with 4 CDs (Vienna: Edition Wien/Pichler, 1996); and Susanne Finsterl-Lindlar, *Lilliput Wienerisch* (Berlin/Munich: Langenscheidt, 2011). For the last-named dictionary of 381 pages, I am grateful to Herr Franz-Josef Schmiedl (Wiener Stadt- und Landesarchiv) and Frau Gertraud Heindl (Archiv, Allgemeines Krankenhaus, Vienna).

Brötchen) for rolls, *Fisolen* for green beans,[42] *Licitation* for an auction, and so on. These examples might be similar to using couch, sofa, or davenport for the same (or similar) piece of furniture in the English language.

German spelling was not yet fully standardized in Beethoven's time, and so B could be phonetically interchangeable with P, and C with G or K, or D with T, and even F with V. Haydn could be spelled Haidn or Heiden. A "tz" sound could be represented as a "z" or a "c." The name Joseph in Beethoven's time would frequently be spelled "Josef" as the century progressed and Germans sought to distance their language from foreign influences.

Compared to many of his contemporaries, Beethoven was a tolerably good writer. His handwriting was an extension of late Baroque style, more akin to Johann Sebastian Bach's than to an early nineteenth-century clerk's. His variable phonetic spelling was more standardized than that of most musicians of his time,[43] and when he copied an advertisement from a newspaper, it was usually remarkably accurate.[44] By comparison, his brother Johann (1776–1848), a trained apothecary and landowner whose entries are frequent in the *Conversation Books*, was a less advanced writer than Ludwig. On an understandably lower level, Beethoven's favorite copyist Wenzel Schlemmer (1758–1823) and his housekeeper-cook Barbara Holzmann (1755–1831) wrote almost exclusively in a phonetic and ungrammatical style, and one must often read their entries aloud to "hear" how they sounded and understand what they meant.

The conversational entries themselves have largely been translated into modern conversational American English, to include contractions that might not otherwise be proper to scholarly English. There has been no attempt at rendering them into "a sort of timeless English," as Emily Anderson characterized her translation of Beethoven's letters.[45]

---

[42] See the menu in "Das himmlische Leben," the fourth movement of Gustav Mahler's Symphony No. 4.

[43] Brandenburg, *Beethoven: Briefwechsel*, I, pp. xxi–xxxiv; and Harald Süss, *Deutsche Schreibschrift* (Augsburg: Augustus Verlag, 1995), pp. 11–13.

[44] Judging from his letters from ca. 1802 to 1805, Beethoven's younger brother Carl (1774–1815) was probably the best writer of the three surviving siblings.

[45] Anderson, *Letters*, Introduction, Vol. 1, p. xix, circularly terming it "an English translation that would stand the test of time."

Dictionaries

My home library includes almost two dozen German dictionaries in varying degrees of depth and focus. For everyday translation I have used a *Cassell's German–English, English–German Dictionary* from the 1970s, but also editions in Gothic lettering as far back as Cassell and Heath in 1909. One of my major criteria for any such dictionary was that the English translations of the German word *Kur* had to include an Elector or some historical Electoral function.

In addition, I have regularly used the two-volume *Muret-Sanders Enzyklopädisches englisch-deutsches und deutsch-englisches Wörterbuch* from 1910, and the four-volume *Muret-Sanders encyclopädisches Wörterbuch der Englischen und Deutschen Sprache* from 1899.

Among specialty dictionaries, *Lang's German–English Dictionary of Terms Used in Medicine* (1924)[46] and the *Illustriertes Landwirtschafts-Lexikon* (1884)[47] have proven helpful, as has, occasionally, the *Österreichisches Wörterbuch* (2006). Various German-language dictionaries by Wahrig, Duden, or Grimm have been potentially helpful, although the 32-volume Grimm (like the Oxford English Dictionary) is a bit excessive for our purposes.

One of translationdom's relics, the *Thieme-Preusser: Neues vollständiges kritisches Wörterbuch der Englischen und Deutschen Sprache* (1859),[48] once widely used, contains some amusing and archaic definitions, but also mistranslations that are misleading or even unintentionally harmful in the area of musical terminology.

For translation of occasional French terms, I have used Cassell's (1960–1980s), the original two-volume Clifton and Grimaux (ca. 1880), and the two-volume Harrap (1940/1961). Other languages have followed similar patterns.

While the translations are overwhelmingly my own work, I have occasionally sought assistance from colleagues, including Dr. Michael Lorenz, Ing. Walther Brauneis, Dr. Helmut Weihsmann, Karl Misar, Dr. Karen Wilde, Josef Bednarik, Thomas Gröger, Dr. Bernhard Paul, Dr. Ernst Kobau, Dr. Rita Steblin, Klaus George Roy, Dr. Irving Godt, Dr. Alan Krueck, and my wife, Dr. Carol Padgham Albrecht. For mistranslations or misinterpretations (and there may be many in these volumes), I alone am responsible.

---

[46] *Lang's*, ed. Milton K. Meyers (Philadelphia: K. Blakiston's Son, 1924), although it (like other dictionaries) does not list or define the term *Schleimschlag*.

[47] *Landwirtschaft*, ed. Guido Krafft (Berlin: Paul Parey, 1884).

[48] *Thieme-Preusser*, ed. H. Breithaupt (Hamburg: Haendcke & Lehmkuhl, 1846/1859). This dictionary was probably used for the century-old English translation of Richard Wagner's *Mein Leben*.

Conclusion

There have been several editions of Beethoven's correspondence in both German and English over the past 150 years, and so a succession of editors and translators has had the opportunity and good fortune to learn from the mistakes of others.[49] The East Berlin edition of Beethoven's *Konversationshefte*, which appeared from 1968 to 2001, was roughly the third edition of the conversation books to be begun but only the first to be completed.

This edition of the *Conversation Books* is likewise only the first in English, and yet it has had the privilege, after the four-decade gestation period of the German edition, to enlarge upon and clarify it. As with my *Letters to Beethoven* (1996), I have tried to do so in an appropriately objective manner[50] and in the interest of scholarly progress, knowing full well that errors in my own translations and annotations will naturally be corrected by scholars in the future.[51] I merely beg my successors' indulgence with the same perspective in mind. Music research is still a cumulative effort, over the years and across national and linguistic boundaries. If I have made these conversation books more useful to scholars, performers, and admirers of Beethoven for even a moment in that continuum, then my efforts will have been richly rewarded.

Theodore Albrecht
Vienna, Austria
Kent, Ohio
August 30, 2015

---

[49] In fact, Emily Anderson was highly critical or dismissive of virtually all of her predecessors, German or English, in compiling and editing collections of Beethoven's letters. See Anderson, *Letters*, Introduction, Vol. 1, pp. xii–xix and *passim*.

[50] When I detect minor inaccuracies in the German edition of the *Konversationshefte*, I usually correct them silently, without further commentary.

[51] Subsequent volumes in the English-language *Conversation Books* will provide an opportunity to correct substantive mistakes made here.

Acknowledgements

A project as massive as this one could not have come even this far—the publication of the first three of a projected twelve volumes—without the assistance of a great number of individuals, both known and unknown to me. For the source materials themselves, I am most grateful to Dr. Helmut Hell, Frau Grita Herre, and Dr. Martina Rebmann (Staatsbibliothek zu Berlin–Preussischer Kulturbesitz) and to Dr. Sieghard Brandenburg, Dr. Bernhard Appel, and Dr. Michael Ladenburger (Beethoven-Haus, Bonn), as well as to Breitkopf und Härtel/VEB Deutscher Verlag für Musik (Wiesbaden and Leipzig), who negotiated with Dr. Bruce Phillips and, most recently and effectively, Dr. Michael Middeke of Boydell & Brewer (Martlesham, Suffolk) to secure the rights for this English translation, adaptation, and new edition.

This project has become one developed in Vienna (and indeed in suburban Josefstadt) as much as in the United States, and in that I am grateful to Dr. Otto Biba, Dr. Ingrid Fuchs, and Frau Ilse Kosz (Library/Archive, Gesellschaft der Musikfreunde), as well as Herr Karl Misar (Handschriften-Sammlung, Wiener Stadt- und Landesbibliothek, Rathaus) and his wife Edith. Herr Misar's gift for imitating and clarifying accents and dialects as used in the conversation books has proven invaluable.

Much of my work has been done in non-musical libraries and archives such as the Wiener Stadt- und Landesarchiv, where Dr. Michaela Laichmann, Dr. Klaralinda Ma-Kircher, Dr. Susanne Pils, Dr. Heinrich Berg, Dr. Brigitte Psarakis, and Dr. Andreas Weigl, as well as their reading-room colleagues, Herr Mehmet Urhan, Herr Franz-Josef Schmiedl, Herr Edmund Knapp, Herr Alfred Prohsmann, Herr Erich Denk, and Frau Silvia Ableidinger (among others), have provided continued assistance over the years.

At the Haus-, Hof- und Staatsarchiv, I am grateful to Dr. Joachim Tepperberg, as well as its retired director, Dr. Leopold Auer, and its retired librarian, Dr. Clemens Höslinger. At the world-renowned Musical Instrument Collection of the Kunsthistorisches Museum (whose future and location are currently seriously threatened), its director Dr. Rudolf Hopfner has been especially encouraging of this project, which has, in turn, benefited from his research.

The Österreichisches Theatermuseum is located in the Lobkowitz Palace. Three rooms east of its famed *Eroica*-Saal is the Library where, for over two decades, Herr Othmar Barnert has provided what is possibly the most expert (and the most effortless) reference service in Vienna, including answering questions about various details from across the Atlantic.

Most of Vienna's church records (for baptisms, marriages, and funerals) have now been placed online, but before they were, the following representative churches were particularly generous with access to these *Matriken*: Stephansdom, archivist Dr. Reinhard H. Gruber; Augustinerkirche, Frau Ursula Lechner, but also P. Matthias Schlögl and P. Albin Scheuch (welcoming us non-Catholics, especially on Sundays); Michaelerkirche, Frau Constanze Gröger; Paulaner Kirche, Frau Monika Bauer and Msgr. Franz Wilfinger (who often stopped, pipe in hand, to ask researchers about their projects); St. Joseph ob der Laimgrube, Frau Maria Doberer; and the Karlskirche, with Herr Josef Macháček, P. Milan Kučera, and especially Frau Stella Pfarrhund.

For over a decade the Gesellschaft der Freunde der Wiener Oboe has kindly supported my study of orchestral instrumentalists in Beethoven's time with a grant, and has encouraged the edition of the *Conversation Books* as an extension of it, especially in connection with the Ninth Symphony. Josef Bednarik, Bernarda Bobro, Thomas Gröger, Dr. Bernhard Paul, Dr. Ernst Kobau, and Dr. Rudolf Führer deserve special recognition in this connection.

Likewise, the Wiener Beethoven-Gesellschaft has always been encouraging through Ing. Walther and Frau Vera Brauneis, Frau Rosemarie and Prof. Martin Bjelik. I am especially grateful for the tour of Beethoven's apartment in the Laimgrubengasse that Ing. Brauneis and Frau Bjelik provided my wife Carol and me. On the American side, Dr. William R. Meredith, Patricia Stroh, and Dr. William George of the American Beethoven Society and the Ira. F. Brilliant Center for Beethoven Studies at San Jose State University in California have been friends and supporters since the 1980s.

At the University of Vienna, Dr. Gerhard Kubik and Dr. Regine Allgayer-Kaufmann (ethnomusicology) have been supportive, as has Dr. Michael Lorenz (musicology), who probably knows more about archival work in Vienna than anyone and is always generous in offering many details as he discovers them. Dr. Rita Steblin and the professional bass tubist Mag. Gerhard Zechmeister are also active archival researchers and helpful, as well. The violinist and conductor Dr. Eduard Melkus and artist Frau Marlis Melkus deserve special thanks for their encouragement and generosity.

Living accommodations and meals were important to Beethoven, and Carol and

I have learned firsthand the Viennese concept of a *Stammlokal* from Frau Elisabeth Schmid (Pension Columbia), Frau Grazyna Gierlichs and Frau Maria Ribar (Pension Lehrerhaus), Frau Sushma Sood (Oliva Verde), Frau Ernestine Rathgeber and Rudi (*Zur goldenen Schale* [Josephstadt No. 96] and *Berg'l Wirt*), and, for the past decade, Mag. Werner Kremser, Frau Dika Masić, Frau Leila Masić, and Frau Ana Mostić (*Weinhaus Sittl, Zum goldenen Pelikan* [Neulerchenfeld No. 1]). The *Pelikan* was first mentioned in documents by ca. 1740, and it is possible that Beethoven and Franz Oliva walked by it (or even stopped in for a glass of wine) on an excursion to or from the more distant Gallizinberg.

Several colleagues at Kent State University (some no longer living) have been encouraging and helpful over the years: Dr. F. Joseph Smith (musicology), Dr. Kazadi wa Mukuna (ethnomusicology), Mary Sue Hyatt (director), Raymond DiMattia (flute), David DeBolt (bassoon), Harry Herforth (trumpet), Ma Si-Hon (violin), Dr. Moshe Amitay (violoncello), Lois Ozanich and Dr. Robert Palmieri (piano), Dr. John Lee and Dr. Ralph Lorenz (directors), Scott Curfman (bands), Jack Scott (music librarian), and especially former orchestra director John Ferritto, with whom I happily shared an office for nine years.

Over fifty years and even now, Dr. Dika Newlin (formerly of North Texas State University) has provided the inspiration for my work. More recently, Dr. Nita Heard Hardie (Assistant Dean emerita, Western Michigan University) read every emerging Heft with eager anticipation.

In Vienna, these are well-matched by our engaging and perceptive colleagues Prof. Eugenie Russo (piano, Akademie der Musik, Wiener Neustadt) and her husband Dr. Helmut Weihsmann (architecture historian).

Several scholars around the world have read and commented upon my rough drafts as they have emerged over the years: Dr. Barry Cooper (University of Manchester), Susan Lund (London), Dr. Susan Kagan (Hunter College), Dr. Bathia Churgin (Bar-Ilan University), and especially this project's most enthusiastic and encouraging supporter, Dr. Lewis Lockwood (Harvard University).

Since 2015, the Boydell Press has assembled a cooperative and communicative team who understand the nature of this complicated project and the unusual means necessary to bring it to fruition: Dr. Michael Middeke (editorial director), Nick Bingham (production coordinator), Phil Dematteis (Columbia, South Carolina, copy editor), Amanda Thompson and Chris Reed (BBR Design, Sheffield, typesetters, book designers), John Duggan (music typesetter), and Catherine Watts (marketing, publicity). My gratitude to them all!

But the final and most appreciative word must be reserved for my wife, Dr. Carol Padgham Albrecht, who has walked every one of Beethoven's Viennese miles with me.

Reader's Guide

Beethoven's Vienna

BEETHOVEN'S DAILY ROUTINE

Except for unusual circumstances (clearly presented in the German edition), the entries in most of Beethoven's conversation books start at the beginning of a Heft and continue to its end. Internally, the entries essentially reflect the composer's daily routine, even though it changed periodically, depending upon whether he employed a cook at home or ate his meals at a restaurant, whether he lived in Vienna or in a summer apartment in the country, and so on.

In the third edition of his biography,[1] Anton Schindler described Beethoven's routine, as he knew it from roughly November 1822 through May 1824. Moreover, the young journalist Johann Chrysostom Sporschil became acquainted with Beethoven in late 1822 or early 1823, and in November 1823 published essentially a feature story about Beethoven that corroborates many of Schindler's observations.[2] From these, and random comments like Franz Oliva's that Beethoven got up at 5 o'clock in the morning,[3] we can reach a composite daily routine that would, of course, vary from time to time and place to place:

---

[1] Anton Felix Schindler, *Biographie von Ludwig van Beethoven*, third edition, 2 vols. (Münster: Aschendorff, 1860), Vol. 2, p. 192, translated as *Beethoven As I Knew Him*, ed. Donald W. MacArdle, trans. Constance S. Jolly (Chapel Hill: University of North Carolina Press, 1966; repr. Mineola, N.Y.: Dover, 1996), pp. 385–386.

[2] Sporschil, "Musikalischer Wegweiser," p. 548.

[3] Heft 7, Blatt 66r (February 11, 1820), in Köhler *et al.*, *Konversationshefte*, Vol. 1, p. 259. Oliva (1786–1848) was a bank official and friend of Beethoven's, who helped the composer in financial and practical affairs until he moved to Russia in late December, 1820. For a chart comparing Schindler's, Sporschil's, and Oliva's accounts, see Albrecht, "Time, Distance, Weather, Daily Routine," p. 65.

Early morning (ca. 5 a.m.)	Beethoven rose early and, while fresh, worked as long as he could (composing and/or writing letters) without distractions, often jotting lists of errands and shopping items along the way.
ca. 12 noon	He might wash and leave his apartment about noon and run a few errands before dinner.
ca. 2 p.m.	He ate his midday dinner at 2 p.m. or so (often with friends).[4] If he ate at his apartment, he might invite friends to arrive about 1:30 p.m.
ca. 3:30 p.m.	After dinner, more errands and shopping.
ca. 5 p.m.	A late afternoon visit to a coffee house to drink coffee, perhaps smoke a pipe, read current newspapers, and make notes of advertisements that interested him.
until ca. 7 p.m.	Perhaps a late errand or a meeting.
Evening	Perhaps a light supper, possibly some reading, and then to bed by 10 o'clock.

In getting around Vienna, except for special occasions such as major performances of his own works, Beethoven *walked* virtually everywhere, and so distance and time must also be factored into his daily routine and other activities.

DIRECTIONS OF THE COMPASS

Directions in Vienna can be difficult. As any map of Europe will show, the Danube River generally flows from west to east across Austria, with the left bank on the north side and the right bank on the south side. A dozen miles upstream from Vienna, however, the Danube turns to the southeast and when it reaches the City, its Channel (*Canal*) decidedly flows from northwest to southeast, with the Inner

---

[4] On May 6, 1803, Ferdinand Ries in Vienna reported to Nikolaus Simrock in Bonn that he received three lessons a week from Beethoven from 1 to 2:30 p.m., suggesting that the composer ate dinner after that on those days, consistent enough with Schindler's observation that Beethoven ate at 2 or 3 o'clock, and a few instances in the conversation books (1820–1824) where Beethoven met someone for dinner at 1:30 p.m. It suggests a routine consistent with Viennese practice at the time, but without rigidity. See Albrecht, *Letters to Beethoven*, No. 58.

City on the right bank to the southwest and suburban Leopoldstadt on the left bank to the northeast. A century ago Bertha Koch had problems of directionality in her volume of photographs of surviving Beethoven residences and attempted to solve them by designating views as northeast and southwest, but also as north, south, east, and west.[5]

This edition of the *Conversation Books* adopts a more Vienna-specific orientation and views the Danube as more of a north-to-south axis when it reaches the City, with the sun rising over the Leopoldstadt to the east and setting in the vicinity of the Gallizinberg or the Schmelz in the west (please see the maps on pp. xxxviii–xxxix). Suburban Rossau is therefore north, and suburban Landstrasse south, with the Burgtor looking west. All of these directions still remain approximate (and even open to individual interpretation), depending upon the season of the year, but once the Danube has passed Vienna, it can safely turn again toward Pressburg (Bratislava) to the east.

HOUSE NUMBERS

Vienna enjoyed three separate *Haus* (house or general building) numberings during Beethoven's lifetime there. These are often called *Konskriptions-Nummern*, whereby every building in the walled City and every building in each of the suburbs had its own individual number in addition to its street location. When Beethoven arrived in 1792 he found a numbering system that had been in effect since 1770. In the ensuing years new buildings would have been built, or two smaller old buildings might have been torn down to make room for a single larger building. Thus a new numbering was needed by 1795.

This numbering of 1795 was in effect in 1818 when the conversation books began, and remained so until still another renumbering, generally called the "renumbering of 1821," although several parts of the City had received their new numbers by late 1820. In the walled City and most suburbs, the renumbering of 1821 remained in effect until 1862, although several of the growing suburbs (most notably Landstrasse, Wieden, Mariahilf, and Gumpendorf) needed another renumbering by 1830.

In this edition of the *Conversation Books*, buildings mentioned in or associated with entries before 1821 (i.e., in Hefte 1–16) are also identified by their future numbers in the renumbering of 1821 supplied in brackets, for instance: City, Seilergasse No. 1154 [renumbered as 1088 in 1821]. This is done so as to avoid confusion of

---

[5] Bertha Koch, *Beethovenstätten in Wien und Umgebungen, mit 124 Abbildungen* (Berlin: Schuster & Loeffler, 1912), for instance pp. 9, 18, 20, 22–23, 27–29, 33–35, 38, 40–41, 53–54, 65–66, 72, 81, 83–84, 90, 94, and 96.

numberings and in an effort to make the renumbering of 1821 the consistent identification of houses throughout the conversational entries.

The best contemporary source for comparing house numbers is Anton Behsel, *Verzeichniss aller in ... Wien mit ihren Vorstädten befindlichen Häuser*, dating from 1829. This guide, arranged by the 1821 house numbers, also provides the 1795 and 1770 numberings; the name of the building's owner in 1829; its house sign, if any (e.g., Golden Dragon or St. Florian); the street or square where the building was located; the administrative unit handling its affairs (usually the *Magistrat*, but also possibly an ecclesiastical division such as the Cathedral Chapter); its Police district; and its parish.

Behsel's *Verzeichniss* is located in several libraries in Vienna and is now available online, but the copy used for this edition of the *Conversation Books* is located in the Wiener Stadt- und Landesarchiv, and is also latterly supplied with the house numberings of 1830 (as applicable).[6]

MAPS

One of the most helpful attributes of Sieghard Brandenburg's *Beethoven: Briefwechsel* (1996) was the inclusion, as a Supplement to Volume 3, of a separate folder containing two full-sized maps of Vienna and its suburbs: one published by J.V. Degen in 1809, the other published by Artaria in 1824. The Degen map includes the house numberings used from 1795 to 1821, the Artaria map those initiated in 1820–1821. The most accurate modern maps of the Inner City and selected suburbs are found as folded supplements to the historical/topographical studies by Robert Messner, dating from 1962 to 1998.

Virtually all of the addresses mentioned in this edition of the *Conversation Books* have been verified (usually without further source citation) in Behsel's *Verzeichniss* and the Degen and Artaria maps, often supplemented by Messner. The reader may wish to consult them as well for the additional perspectives that they may offer.

---

[6] Some readers will be disappointed that I have not also added today's street numberings for these locations, but that seemed a separate activity and could have created potential confusion. Readers can readily find these later parallels in the guides to the buildings of the Inner City (1996–1998), as well as the Leopoldstadt (1962), Landstrasse (1978), Wieden (1975), Josefstadt (1972), and Alsergrund (1970) by Robert Messner, all cited in the Bibliography.

CURRENCY VALUES

The lowest practical value in Austrian coinage and currency in Beethoven's time was the *kreuzer* (sometimes spelled *kreutzer*).[7] Other values included:

1 groschen	=	ca. 3 kreuzer
1 gulden	=	60 kreuzer
1 gulden	=	1 florin, abbreviated as fl., but still pronounced "gulden"
1 fl.	=	60 kreuzer (kr.)
1 ducat (#)	=	ca. 4½ gulden (or 4½ florins)
10 gulden	=	ca. £1 (British)

After Austria officially went bankrupt as a result of inflation during the Napoleonic Wars, the government initiated a *Finanz-Patent* on February 20, 1811, and ultimately a number of reforms in currency values, with figures given in *Conventions-Münze* (C.M., convention coinage) and in local paper currency, *Wiener Währung* (W.W., Viennese currency).[8] Under this system, in effect during the entire period covered by the conversation books,

1 fl. C.M.　　=　　2½ fl. W.W.

Beethoven never forgave Emperor Franz for allowing the devaluation of paper money, and said so, loudly, in public in 1816.[9] Shortly thereafter he began using conversation books.

Guide to the Conversational Entries

GERMAN TERMS

The English-language reader who uses this edition of the *Conversation Books* must still learn two German terms, most often used for locating conversational entries within the texts:

---

[7] Some writers used upper case while others used lower case for currency values (e.g., Kreuzer *versus* kreuzer or Ducats *versus* ducats). In the service of sanity in these and similar situations, I have not attempted any standardized form for this edition.

[8] A concise view of the whole subject appears in Barry Cooper, "Economics," *Beethoven Compendium*, ed. Cooper (London/New York: Thames and Hudson, 1991), pp. 68–70.

[9] As reported by Peter Joseph Simrock, visiting from Bonn in September, 1816. Thayer (1879), III, pp. 402–403; Thayer-Deiters-Riemann, III, p. 566; Thayer-Krehbiel, III, pp. 343–344; and Thayer-Forbes, p. 647.

Heft: a booklet, the individual *Konversationsheft* (conversation book); its plural is *Hefte*.

Blatt: a sheet, page, double-sided page (front: *recto*; back: *verso*; abbreviated r and v); its plural is *Blätter*.

In addition, a few other German terms may occasionally be helpful:

Stadt: City, generally meaning the walled City of Vienna.
Haus: house or building.
Stiege: stairway.
Wohnpartei: apartment.

CONVERSATIONAL ENTRY FORMATS

In this English edition of the *Conversation Books*, the names of the writers of conversational entries appear in CAPITAL LETTERS in normal typeface, followed (to the extent that they can be determined) by **place, day of the week, date, and time of day** in bold face and brackets. Sometimes this designation will include other elements—religious holidays, for instance—where these might affect Beethoven's environment.[10]

In many cases the method of determining a date and time for conversational entries will be found in an explanatory footnote, although in general it will be assumed that Beethoven loosely followed a daily routine, as described above.

The entries themselves are presented in a paragraph format, with a new paragraph for every apparent change in conversational topic. This largely clarifies the problem of a cluttered stream-of-consciousness format found in diplomatic transcriptions. Even so, the reader should be aware that, given the ambiguous nature of some entries, this system is susceptible to error.

As noted elsewhere, when Beethoven's conversational partners place a horizontal line at the ends of their entries for him to reply, this line is represented by // in the present paragraph format. Where there is no horizontal line in the original, but a pause of some sort seems apparent in context, that pause is represented as [//]. In early conversation books, where the horizontal line had not yet become a standard division in conversation, pauses in the entries are already designated editorially as [//]. A Blatt number in brackets pertains to the material following the designation;

---

[10] Beethoven very seldom attended church services, and his acquaintances often had to remind him that a certain day in the future was a religious holiday. Therefore, he was still affected by closed businesses, school visitation days, etc. Even so, his lawyer Johann Baptist Bach often held office hours on Sunday mornings, the same time frame when Matthäus Andreas Stein might come to his apartment to regulate his piano.

therefore, [Blatt 33v] indicates that the following material appears on the verso of Blatt 33.

External movements during conversations—for instance, the **arrival** or **departure** of correspondents, the **continuation of conversations** that might be unclear, or the **ending of long conversations**—are given in **bold print** and brackets, in order to clarify what is happening in Beethoven's immediate environment.

The result is very much like the script of a play, with character designations, dialogue, and stage directions. With this almost three-dimensional quality, it might bring Beethoven's world to life to an unprecedented degree.

SCHINDLER'S FALSIFIED ENTRIES

When excerpted entries from Beethoven's conversation books began appearing in Schindler's *Biographie* (especially the third edition of 1860) and then Thayer's *Leben* (1866–1911), musicologists thought that they had discovered the mother lode, from compositional processes (*Zwei Principe*) to nicknames for compositions (*Tempest* Sonata). They embellished these terms, titles, and slogans into seminal articles and books that helped to build major careers and influential positions within the field.[11] Then in 1977 Peter Stadlen demonstrated that many of Schindler's conversation book entries were *fingierte*, falsified, forged, fictitious—in any case entered into the conversation books (often at improper places, reflecting improbable subject contexts or chronology) long after Beethoven's death.

Scholars who had set their hopes on Schindler's slogans now felt betrayed by their unlikable hero and turned on him with a vengeance, virtually vying with each other to assassinate him, using the most vitriolic names and epithets. Gradually, however, it began to emerge that at least some of Schindler's falsified entries, if viewed in a reasonable and adjusted context, might contain a grain of historically useful truth.[12]

When I began translating and editing Beethoven's *Conversation Books*, several respected scholars in the field (still under Stadlen's spell) advised me to omit Schindler's falsified entries altogether. Ultimately we agreed that the entries had a certain function in the surviving documents and that I would retain them, generally with the sufficiently visible designations: [falsified entries begin→] and

---

[11] See, for instance, Arnold Schmitz, *Beethovens Zwei Principe; ihre Bedeutung für Themen- und Satzbau* (Berlin: F. Dümmler, 1923).

[12] See, for instance, Theodore Albrecht, "Beethoven and Shakespeare's *Tempest*: New Light on an Old Allusion," *Beethoven Forum* 1 (1992), pp. 81–92; his "Anton Grams: Beethoven's Double Bassist," *Bass World* 26 (October, 2002), pp. 19–23; and especially his "Anton Schindler as Destroyer and Forger … Decriminalization," pp. 177–181.

[←falsified entries end].¹³ Posterity may be glad that the "falsified" entries remain, as there is still a great deal to be learned from them about both Schindler and Beethoven.

EXTRA CONVERSATION BOOK BLÄTTER

Many individual Blätter were ripped out of Beethoven's conversation books while he was alive. In fact, he probably did so himself: he might send his housekeeper, his nephew Karl, or an acquaintance on an errand and jot the address on a blank conversation book page before tearing it out and giving it to the person. At least one of the individual Blätter preserved at the Beethoven-Haus, Bonn, served this function.¹⁴ If there were entries already on the other side of the sheet that was removed, that might have been immaterial to Beethoven at the moment. The German editors often indicated where a sheet may have been removed from a conversation book, and I have designated several more, often in bold print in between entries. Dozens of such sheets survive in libraries and private collections worldwide.¹⁵ Frau Grita Herre will include them in a Volume 12 of her Berlin edition, and so this English edition of the *Conversation Books* will not duplicate or "scoop" that project in any way.

FOOTNOTES

In the German edition, a diplomatic transcription with annotations and explanatory endnotes, footnotes were used to note technical variants or visual anomalies within the transcribed texts: the mistaken upper- or lower-case beginning of a German word; other mistakes in starting or spelling a German word; reinforced words or letters in them (sometimes covering a penciled word in ink), corrected on the spot; and routine flourishes or other doodles. These notes have generally been omitted as not pertinent to an English-language edition.

Occasionally, in the early years, young nephew Karl drew profile heads and other cartoons into the conversation books; these are noted in German footnotes and largely retained in the present edition. Karl also used the pages for calligraphic and spelling practice, footnoted in the German edition; these are selectively retained here. The German footnotes also indicate editorially how the authorship of an entry has been authenticated; these are largely retained in the present edition

---

[13] Very brief falsified entries, possibly only a word or two, might have a commensurately brief designation of the fact.

[14] My gratitude to Dr. Michael Ladenburger for making these materials available to me when I visited the Beethoven-Haus in September, 2014.

[15] Some of these are available as illustrations on the internet.

as one of the English-language footnotes and generally designated KH (meaning Konversationshefte).

Explanatory notes (which had appeared almost exclusively as endnotes in the German edition) generally appear as footnotes at the bottom of the appropriate page in the English language edition. Notes simply translated from the German edition (*Konversationshefte*) with virtually no change are "signed" at the end of the note as KH. Notes from the German edition that have been significantly updated, corrected, or otherwise changed in the English edition are noted as KH/TA. Footnotes that are new to the present edition are designated TA.[16]

STANDARD FOOTNOTE SOURCES

As consistent with scholarly practice, sources are not cited for material that is available in multiple sources. The German edition cited articles in the encyclopedia *MGG* (*Die Musik in Geschichte und Gegenwart*) without providing the names of the authors of individual articles. This edition provides the names of those authors and abbreviated titles of their articles in the footnotes, but (in the name of economy) cites only *MGG* (under M) in the Bibliography. English-language users will know to consult *The New Grove Dictionary of Music and Musicians* for parallel articles, and so these will not be given here. For the most part, this edition will eschew citing the second editions of *MGG* and *New Grove* as editorially and often factually problematical. Similarly, this edition retains references to Frimmel's *Beethoven-Handbuch*[17] but largely avoids the most recent Beethoven encyclopedias and compendia in German. For relatively recent biographical articles concerning Beethoven's contemporaries, however, Peter Clive's *Beethoven and His World* (2001) provides a convenient, if not exhaustive, source in English.[18]

Oddly enough, there are materials collected by Alexander Wheelock Thayer and available in the German editions of his biography that have never been included or translated in full in its English-language editions. The names of the members of the Bonn orchestra in the 1780s or Stumpff's account of visiting Beethoven in September 1824—and its direct application to interpreting the conversation book entries—are just two of many such instances. Therefore the German edition's

---

[16] If I have inadvertently misattributed the authorship of any footnote among the 4,800 in these first three volumes, I apologize.

[17] An abridged English translation of the Frimmel *Handbuch* (1926), along with a few items translated from Wurzbach, appeared as *Beethoven Encyclopedia*, ed. Paul Nettl (New York: Philosophical Library, 1956).

[18] Clive's articles are often based on the first edition of *MGG*, but also include more unusual sources.

references to Thayer-Deiters-Riemann have been retained, usually paired with references to corresponding passages in the English-language Thayer-Forbes.

Fortunately, modern editions of Beethoven's correspondence by Anderson, Albrecht, and Brandenburg largely supersede their predecessors and are cited almost exclusively here.[19]

COMMON ABBREVIATIONS

Whenever possible this edition prefers full words, rather than any system of cryptic initials or acronyms, no matter how standardized. Thus the source of a death or estate record is given as "Wiener Stadt- und Landesarchiv" rather than "WStLA." Fully written out surnames such as Anderson, Behsel, Brandenburg, Clive, Thayer, Wurzbach, and so forth are probably recognizable, but in any case will send the less experienced reader to the appropriate item in the Bibliography, as will the abbreviation *MGG*. The few abbreviations used are mostly common sense. There may be a few inconsistencies through these many volumes, but the intention should still be relatively clear.

CROSS-REFERENCING AND INDEXES

The amount of detail in the *Conversation Books* is enormous and almost impossible to control without an index as voluminous as the volumes themselves. A cumulative index for the entire set of *Conversation Books* is almost unthinkable. Therefore, during the translating and editing processes, cross-references from one subject to another, sometimes across Hefte and volumes, were made using Heft and Blatt numbers to identify the location of the reference. After the pagination was applied, an Index of Persons, an Index of Beethoven's Compositions, and a General Index could be made, with page numbers used to designate the location of a reference.

MISCELLANEOUS EDITORIAL MATTERS

Names are generally given in their original languages. The Austrian emperor during this period was Franz rather than Francis; his military younger brother was Archduke Carl (or occasionally Karl), rather than Charles. Most cities like Vienna and Munich, however, are given in their English forms, but Wagner's *Meistersinger* still sang in Nürnberg (with an Umlaut and only two syllables).

---

[19] Even so, *New Beethoven Letters*, transl. and ed. Donald W. MacArdle and Ludwig Misch (Norman: University of Oklahoma Press, 1957), remains valuable for its extensive and lively commentaries and explanations.

The capitalized word City generally refers to within the walled city alone. When used from a distant location, it can refer to metropolitan Vienna as a whole.

Because the translator/editor is an American, spellings and editorial practice will follow American style. One of the few exceptions is that the editor prefers the monosyllabic "bar" rather than "measure" when referring to locations in a piece of music.

This edition transliterates the German ess-zet (ß) as "ss" or rarely "sz" (so as to avoid the novice's temptation to render it as "B"), but retains the vowels with Umlauts, as having some counterpart in English orthography.

Translations may vary: titles such as *Wellingtons Sieg* and *Wellington's Victory*, for instance, are used interchangeably.

When referring to a building, *Stock* generally designates the *Oberstock*, the number of the floor *above* the ground level. Therefore, the 1st *Stock* or floor in Viennese terminology would be called the 2nd floor in America. In an effort to achieve accuracy and clarity (but not pedantry), this edition will identify the floor in Viennese terms, with the American designation in brackets: "3rd floor [4th floor, American]."

In this edition of the *Conversation Books* the abbreviations p. (page) and pp. (pages) are used more extensively than usual, in the interest of clarity and completeness. This is true in other instances, as well, including library sigla.

Editorial Conventions

In most cases, the following symbols or editorial directions are based, for relative consistency, on the common-sense practice followed by the German edition:

//	Signifies a pause in the conversation where Beethoven's conversational partner drew a horizontal line as a signal for Beethoven to reply. This practice took some time to be standardized, and always remained open to variations. Few conversationalists wrote a line under the final entry on a page, for instance. Conversationalists new to Beethoven's circle (or merely passing through) often did not follow the practice. Sometimes Beethoven himself used the horizontal line to divide advertisements copied from newspapers, items to buy, or errands to run.
[//]	Signifies a place in a conversation where a pause seems to have occurred, but the conversationalist did not insert a horizontal line for Beethoven to reply. This editorially supplied "line" is very common throughout the early conversation books.

[Blatt __]   Indicates that the text that follows was taken from a particular Blatt in the manuscript, as indicated in the German edition. Thus, a bracketed [Blatt 35r] indicates that the following text came from Blatt 35r. Retaining these locations is especially helpful in locating editorial cross-references.

[written vertically→] [←written vertically]
         Indicates that part (or all) of the designated text was written vertically (or at least diagonally) as opposed to the customary horizontal entries.

[falsified entries begin→] [←falsified entries end]
         Points out Schindler's falsified entries at the point where they are found in the manuscript. Brief falsified entries have commensurately brief designations.

<crossed out>   Indicates a text that has been crossed out in the manuscript, and generally follows the German editors' attempts to read or reconstruct it.

[illegible word]   Signifies what it says. This and similar phrases in editorial brackets occur frequently throughout the conversation books.

Directionality in Vienna (True and Perceived)

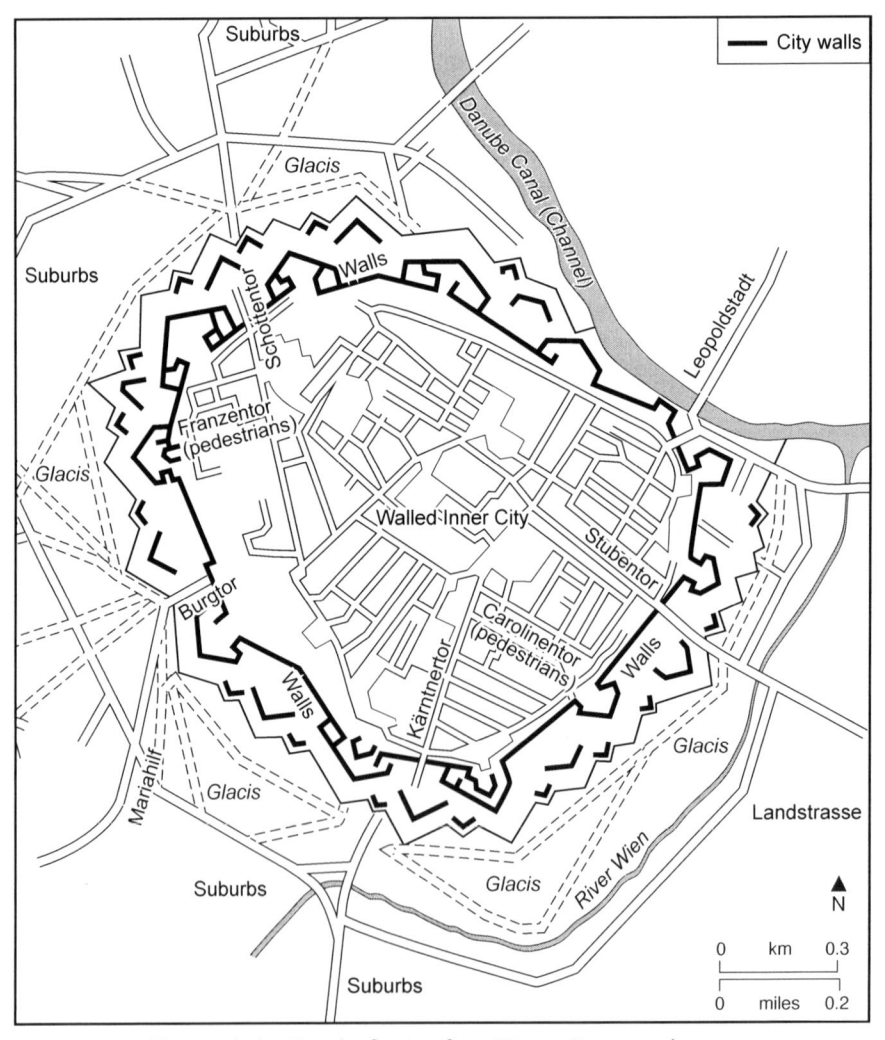

True, with the Danube flowing from West to East at 45 degrees

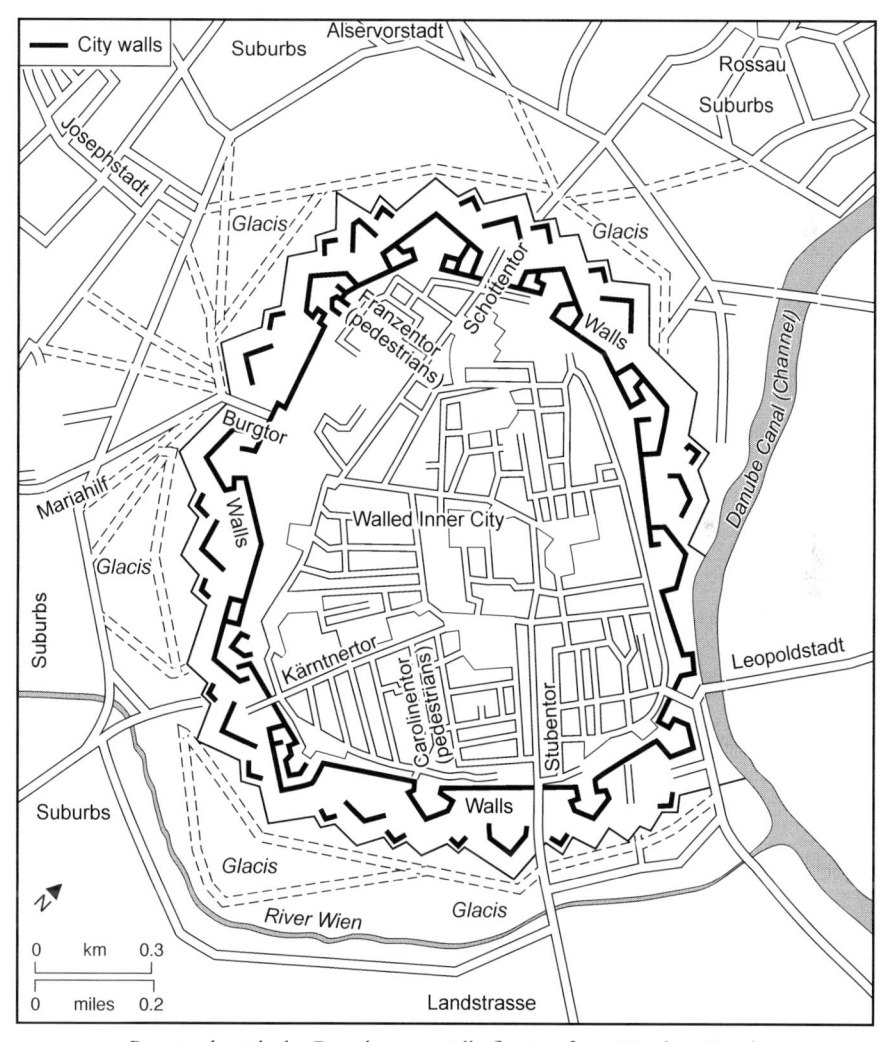

Perceived, with the Danube essentially flowing from North to South

Highlights of Volume 5

October – December 1823

October 29/30: Nephew Karl: "Only mediocre people can become rich." (Heft 44, Blatt 4r)

October 30/31: A last sheet withheld from Gloria of *Missa solemnis* score as security measure during copying. (Heft 44, Blatt 4v)

November 1: Count Lichnowsky invites Beethoven to *hear* how bad Weber's *Euryanthe* is; also expressed earlier to Karl. (Heft 44, Blätter 9r and 12r)

November 1: Karl sets up Beethoven's library in the Ungargasse apartment. (Heft 44, Blatt 18r)

November 1: Karl warns against police surveillance. (Heft 44, Blätter 20v–21r)

November 2: Karl goes to church on All Souls' Day. (Heft 44, Blatt 20r)

November 3: Karl begins at the university. (Heft 44, Blätter 3r and 17v)

November 5: Visit by Berlin concertmaster Henning to obtain *Consecration of the House* Overture and music for a theater opening there. (Heft 45, Blatt 5v)

November 11: Shopping for complete works of Schiller. (Heft 45, Blätter 13e and 41v)

November 11: Maid exposes her chest to nephew Karl. (Heft 45, Blatt 13v)

November 16: References to language teachers Joseph Pleugmackers and Paul Pulay. (Heft 45, Blatt 25r, fn.)

November 16: Karl goes to confession on the anniversary of his father's death. (Heft 45, Blatt 16r)

November 16: Joseph Ries repairs Beethoven's Broadwood piano. (Heft 45, Blätter 27v–29r)

November 16:	Karl encounters Schindler, who wants to reconcile with Beethoven. (Heft 45, Blatt 29v)
November 16:	Beethoven drowsy at a coffee house. (Heft 45, Blatt 30v)
November 18:	Sporschil's interview article (mentioning Beethoven's lost "correspondence," including conversation books) in the *Theater-Zeitung*. (Heft 45, Blatt 32r)
November 18:	Karl describes Hauschka's conducting style on November 16. (Heft 45, Blatt 38r)
November 20:	Beethoven's pipe repaired. (Heft 45, Blatt 39r)
November 20:	Shopping for dinnerware for 5 or 6 persons. (Heft 45, Blatt 42v)
November 20:	Count Kollowrat reportedly denied Jeitteles, poet of *An die ferne Geliebte*, a house physician's position because he was a Jew. (Heft 45, Blatt 9r)
November 21:	Beethoven reads Littrow's biographical sketch of astronomer Johannes Kepler with nephew Karl. (Heft 46, Blatt 1v)
November 21:	Schindler reconciled with Beethoven but remains gossipy. (Heft 46, Blatt 2r)
November 21:	First plans for concert (*Akademie*) to premiere Ninth Symphony and *Missa solemnis*. (Heft 46, Blätter 2r–5v)
November 21:	Ailing Salieri's position not to be filled. (Heft 46, Blatt 7r)
November 22:	Moscheles includes first movement of Beethoven's Symphony No. 2 on his concert. (Heft 46, Blatt 16r)
November 23:	Karl reports: "Salieri has cut his throat, but is still alive." (Heft 46, Blatt 18r)
November 24:	Copying of *Missa solemnis* continues. (Heft 46, Blatt 22v)
November 23:	Beethoven's Mass in C performed at the Augustiner Church for St. Cecilia's Day. (Heft 46, Blatt 23v)
November 25:	Schuppanzigh recommends that Beethoven revise earlier piano works and comments negatively about Moscheles as a Jew. (Heft 46, Blätter 34v–35r)
November 29:	Karl describes lectures at the university and living conditions of the faculty. (Heft 47, Blätter 6r–7v; 9v–10r)
November 29:	Karl alludes to Prince Kaunitz's taste for young ballet students. (Heft 47, Blatt 8r)

November 29/30:	Beethoven shops for macaroni and Parmesan cheese. (Heft 47, Blatt 8r)
December 1/3:	Beethoven presumably donates to the poorhouse and a blind woman, collecting alms door-to-door during Advent. (Heft 47, Blätter 15r and 27r)
December 3:	Moscheles: long conversation; mentions Johann Reinhold Schultz; biographical details. (Heft 47, Blätter 28r–33r)
December 3:	Moscheles mentions Count Troyer, possibly Ferdinand, chamberlain and procurer for Archduke Rudolph. (Heft 47, Blatt 32v)
December 4:	Joseph Linke noted as the best cellist in Europe for string quartets. (Heft 47, Blatt 38r)
December 4:	Sketch for "Freude" theme in finale of Ninth Symphony. (Heft 47, Blatt 38r)
December 7:	Beethoven improvises impressively at Count Lichnowsky's. (Heft 48, Blatt 4r)
December 10:	Karl writes complete and correct address of the Ungargasse apartment. (Heft 48, Blatt 17v)
December 11:	Beethoven lends Moscheles his Broadwood piano for concert on December 15. (Heft 48, Blatt 23v)
December 14:	Brother Johann takes Beethoven and Karl to see *Figaro* at Kärntnertor Theater. Karl, unsure of date, wishes Beethoven a happy birthday. (Heft 49, Blätter 3r and 6r–8r)
December 15/17:	Beethoven seemingly attends Moscheles's concerts. (Heft 49, Blätter 7v and 10v–11v)
December 20:	Schindler reports that Zips, Archduke Rudolph's valet, had died on September 25. (Heft 50, Blatt 3v)
December 23:	Lichnowsky becomes intrusive with his advice. (Heft 50, Blatt 9r)
December 24:	Schindler reports Salieri's deteriorating health. (Heft 50, Blätter 13r–14r)
December 25:	Schindler predicts that Lichnowsky's support will run its course. (Heft 50, Blatt 20r)
December 27:	Beethoven reads "Notice" by Anton Weidinger concerning keyed trumpets and keyed horns. (Heft 51, Blatt 1r)

January – March 1824

January 2:	Karl comments on High vs. common German language and Beethoven's using vocabulary that servants do not understand. (Heft 51, Blatt 16r)
January 21:	Beethoven dissatisfied with amount of light in his Ungargasse apartment. Schindler confirms. (Heft 53, Blatt 21v)
January 21:	Schindler advises planning for upcoming *Akademie* and identifies potentially helpful friends. (Heft 53, Blätter 22r–23v)
January 22/24:	Karl reports: Salieri confesses that he poisoned Mozart. Schindler confirms rumor. (Heft 54, Blätter 2v and 6r)
February 7:	Long conversation with Grillparzer concerning *Ottokar*, *Melusine*, and *Drahomira*. (Heft 55, Blätter 2v–5v)
February 8:	Schindler on Salieri's confused confession. (Heft 55, Blatt 6r)
February 8:	Czerny plays Piano Sonatas, Opp. 106, 110, and 111, and *Diabelli Variations* on house concert. (Heft 55, Blatt 6v)
February 3/8:	Karl discusses string portamento. (Heft 55, Blätter 1v and 8r)
February 11:	Schickh and Schindler comment on Salieri's confession. (Heft 55, Blätter 11r–12r)
February 15:	Schindler suggests *Consecration of the House* Overture with large orchestra, foreshadowing May, 1824, concerts. (Heft 56, Blätter 7v–8r)
February 15:	Karl explains the idiosyncratic *Ludlamshöhle* group to a seemingly skeptical Beethoven. (Heft 56, Blätter 11r–11v)
February 15:	Glöggl(?): Beethoven understands him when he speaks loudly. (Heft 56, Blatt 12v)
February 15:	Brother Johann projects profit of 3,000 fl. from upcoming concert. (Heft 56, Blatt 17r)
February 15:	Brother Johann had wanted nephew Karl to become an apothecary. (Karl wanted to become a French teacher.) (Heft 56, Blatt 17v)
February 17:	Schindler dissuades Beethoven from buying a house, especially in Landstrasse/Erdberg, where Antonie Brentano had lived. (Heft 56, Blätter 23r–23v)
February 18:	Schuppanzigh's negative opinion of dilettantes as taking income from professionals. (Heft 56, Blatt 28v)

February 25:	Sonnleithner offers himself, Schuppanzigh, and Piringer to help organize upcoming concert. (Heft 57, Blatt 2r)
February 25/26:	Attempt to deliver the *Ludlamshöhle* Petition on 25th, succeeds on 26th. (Heft 57, Blätter 4r and 11v)
February 26:	Beethoven and Karl visit copyist Josepha Schlemmer. (Heft 57, Blatt 7r)
February 27:	Karl reports: Mozart's fingers bent by incessant playing. (Heft 57, Blatt 11v)
February 27:	Karl asks if Beethoven learned a wind instrument. (Heft 57, Blatt 11v)
February 29:	Progress on the program and performers for the May concerts. (Heft 57, Blätter 18v–20r)
March 1:	Beethoven (briefly) on musical ideas and working them out. (Heft 57, Blatt 23r)
March 1:	Josepha Schlemmer as copyist for *Missa solemnis* scores. (Heft 57, Blätter 23v–24r)
March 4:	Schindler talks about his early life and schooling in Moravia. (Heft 57, Blätter 25r–25v)
March 4:	Schindler reports an uprising in the Josephstadt Theater's orchestra. (Heft 57, Blätter 25v–26v)
March 4:	Schindler's second falsified entry regarding the "*2 Principe.*" First in Heft 35, Blatt 9r. (Heft 57, Blatt 26v)
March 4:	Repairs to Beethoven's Broadwood piano. (Heft 57, Blätter 28r–28v)
March 4/5:	Karl observes clarinetist/violinist Caroline Schleicher Krähmer attending a *Concert spirituel*. (Heft 57, Blätter 31v–32r)
March 5:	After several substitutes, housekeeper Barbara Holzmann returns. (Heft 57, Blatt 32r)
March 7:	Meeting with Schuppanzigh, Haslinger, and Lichnowsky to plan the upcoming *Akademie*. Schuppanzigh introduces his violin students Joseph Böhm and Karl Holz to Beethoven. (Heft 58, Blätter 1r–2v)
March 7:	Brother Johann and nephew Karl attend oboist Ernest and wife, clarinetist/violinist Caroline Krähmer's, concert. (Heft 58, Blatt 3r)

March 8:	Schindler finally reads the *Ludlamshöhle* petition. (Heft 57, Blatt 39v)
March 8:	Beethoven may have decided upon Michael Umlauf to conduct the upcoming *Akademie*. (Heft 57, Blatt 39v)
March 12/13:	Schindler's long falsified entry about Beethoven's changing tempos in performing orchestral works. (Heft 59, Blätter 9v–10r)
March 13:	Paul Maschek copies orchestral and choral parts for the *Missa solemnis*. (Heft 59, Blätter 10v–11v)
March 14:	Beethoven hosts embarrassing Sunday dinner for Sontag, Unger, and Schindler. (Heft 59, Blätter 11v–13v)
March 16:	Schindler brings questionable gossip about Sontag's and Unger's reactions to Beethoven's wine. (Heft 59, Blätter 15r–15v)

Theodore Albrecht
Kent, Ohio
Feast of St. Crispin
October 25, 2024

Heft 44

(ca. October 29 or 30, 1823 – ca. November 2 or 3, 1823)

[Blatt 1r]

NEPHEW KARL [seemingly while unpacking at Beethoven's new apartment in the Ungargasse;[1] either Wednesday, October 29, or Thursday, October 30]:[2] Because eating in restaurants no longer tastes good to us, we can directly observe the difference between the cooking of the old woman [temporarily retired housekeeper Barbara Holzmann][3] and this one.[4] // A good cookbook has come out and is available for 2 fl.; she should buy it. She could get it for that price from the cook who wrote it, since it would surely be more expensive elsewhere. //

---

[1] In drafting an advertisement for a housekeeper or cook in the second week of December 1823, nephew Karl described the apartment's location: "Ungargasse No. 323, 1st floor [2nd floor American], up the back stairway, door [apartment] no. 12." See Heft 48, Blatt 17v.—TA

[2] The second performance of Weber's *Euryanthe* took place on Monday, October 27, 1823. Reportedly the next day, Weber's assistant, Julius Benedict, went to the shop of Steiner and Haslinger, in the Paternostergasse at the northeast corner of the Graben, to discuss details of the opera's publication. Beethoven came in and asked Haslinger how the performances had gone. Haslinger reportedly wrote in Beethoven's conversation book: "Outstanding! A great success!" After asking about Henriette Sontag's performance, the elder composer exchanged a few pleasantries, then left quickly. See Max Maria von Weber, *Carl Maria von Weber: Ein Lebensbild*, 3 vols. (Leipzig: E. Keil, 1864–1866), II, p. 534; quoted in John Warrack, *Carl Maria von Weber*, 2nd ed. (Cambridge: Cambridge University Press, 1976), p. 308.
This encounter, presumably on Tuesday, October 28, is not recorded in the current Heft 44, and so it probably took place in a conversation book that did not survive but was filled by a day or two beforehand, therefore between surviving Hefte 43 and 44. This encounter also supports the conclusion that the entry concerning Czerny and Mayseder on Blatt 1v refers to the upcoming small-scale evening's entertainment at Haslinger's on Thursday, October 30.—TA

[3] After a period of increasing dissatisfaction on both sides, Barbara Holzmann (ca. 1755–1831) left Beethoven's employ at the end of September 1823. She later returned and—off and on—worked for the composer until she finally retired in ca. March 1826.—TA

[4] The names of Beethoven's domestic employees, their precise duties, and the duration of their employment are only occasionally given in the conversation books and other literature. For a sample of them, see Rita Steblin, "Beethoven's Name in Viennese Conscription Records," *Beethoven Journal* 24, No. 1 (Summer 2009), pp. 4–13. Steblin provides biographical details on housekeeper Barbara Holzmann (July 1, 1822, to March 1826), pp. 9 and 13. Others include the maid Anna Zimenska, born Vienna, 1800 (fall 1822 – summer 1823), p. 9; and maid Katherina Josephy, born Budweis, Bohemia, 1801 (fall 1824), pp. 8–9.—TA

[NEPHEW KARL, *continued*]

At a [foreign] legation—the newest one is the best.—Thank God! //

[looking at a letter from 1815:]

This letter from the office to my father was also written in a very unkind way.[5] //

A blind woman from the Kothgasse is here; she declares that she has always received alms, perhaps from the old woman [housekeeper Barbara Holzmann].[6] //

Today I must laugh about my composition in which I entered the number according to Mälzel's metronome in every movement. //

Obstinate. [//] [Blatt iv] Your brother [Johann] is sick.—Presumably—10 fl. *monthly*? // That is at 120 percent. //

Her father's educational method, however, was also like that. I remember that she often told me that, whenever she wanted money, her father said: "I'm not giving you any. But if you can take some money without my knowing about it, then it belongs to you." Naturally, she learned to steal in this way, quite unpunished.[7] //

Very much meat. //

---

[5] See the letter from Count Joseph von Herberstein-Moltke, Imperial Royal Treasury Office, to Carl van Beethoven, October 23, 1815. The letter essentially reprimanded brother Carl for his absenteeism and negligence owing to health. Carl died of tuberculosis less than a month later, on November 15, 1815. Beethoven annotated it: "This miserable bureaucratic product caused the death of my brother…. A fine monument to these uncouth high officials." See Albrecht, *Letters to Beethoven*, No. 211, and Brandenburg, No. 842.—TA

[6] Obere Pfarrgasse, the relatively narrow street where Beethoven's old apartment was located, was only one building north of Kothgasse, a wider street. Even so, Beethoven and his friends often referred to his living in the Kothgasse as a generality. Therefore, it seems that this conversation takes place in the new Ungargasse apartment. In any case, it is notable that a blind woman would walk such a distance to seek alms. Occasionally there had been comments when Barbara Holzmann's household allowance did not tally with the receipts; in such cases, she may have been giving a few kreuzer to the indigent (such as this blind woman) in Beethoven's name. See Heft 45, Blatt 34, for an indication that the housekeeper had given some woman 30 kr. per day—possibly this blind woman. She came calling again on ca. December 2 or 3, 1823; see Heft 47, Blatt 27v.—TA

[7] This paragraph may concern former housekeeper Barbara Holzmann and may be a continuation of the discussion about the blind woman on Blatt 1r.—TA

[NEPHEW KARL, *continued*]

Czerny[8] and Mayseder[9] will play.[10] // Czerny, though, has spread *his* art fairly widely.[11] [//] [Blatt 2r]

I don't find any objection to this rabbit and am washing my hands. // In *my opinion*, it might even be older. // In any case, we cannot eat very much *this evening*. // Schiller, though. // Usually Austrian [literature]. //

Only well-cooked. // We have *never* before bought such a one [rabbit] for 3 fl. // Today, though, you should take Hungarian tobacco wrapped in *paper*. [//] [Blatt 2v] Also a product of Baden. //

This passage is from *Fidelio*, from the Prisoners' Chorus. //

I consider them collectively to be weak people as *human beings*, but they are all good-natured. // Like Piringer,[12] for example. Limited, but good-natured. [//] Journey. // Nature. //

---

[8] Carl Czerny (1791–1857), formerly Beethoven's piano student. Now a teacher to wealthy and fashionable pupils as well as well-connected talents such as Franz Liszt, he visited Baden in August 1823 and stayed in the expensive *Sauerhof*. See his long dinner conversation with Beethoven on Sunday, August 24 (Heft 39, Blätter 6r–21v).—KH/TA

[9] Joseph Mayseder (1789–1863), significant violinist and composer, member of the Hofkapelle since 1816 and the Kärntnertor Theater's orchestra since 1821. He had been a student of Ignaz Schuppanzigh, who probably introduced him to Beethoven in ca. 1800. He was handsome and a favorite teacher for wealthy pupils. See Böckh, 1822, p. 375; Frimmel, *Handbuch*, I, pp. 397–399; Wurzbach, vol. 17, pp. 195–197; Ziegler, *Addressen-Buch*, p. 78; and Clive, pp. 231–232.—KH/TA

[10] During this period, Mayseder played frequently in public or important semiprivate venues. On November 15, 1823, he played his own "Variations" (typically with no further identification) at a potpourri Public Charities benefit concert at the Kärntnertor Theater. Two weekends later, on November 30, he similarly played a Polonaise of his own on a concert at Court celebrating the Investiture of the Order of the Golden Fleece. Perhaps Czerny accompanied him on one or more of such appearances, but see the note immediately below. See *Allgemeine musikalische Zeitung* 25, No. 52 (December 24, 1823), col. 865; and Hofmusikkapelle, K. 12 (1821–1823), No. 160 (Haus-, Hof- und Staatsarchiv).—TA

[11] Most of Czerny's frequent performances were before private and semiprivate audiences. Exaggerating for effect, he wrote to Beethoven on ca. May 20, 1824, that he had not played to Vienna's public at large for 14 years. See Albrecht, *Letters to Beethoven*, No. 366.

In a letter of November 1, 1823, Weber reported to his wife that, on the evening of Thursday, October 30, he had attended a "quartet [concert] at Haslinger's, where Moscheles and Mayseder played excellently." This, then, is probably the event to which Karl refers.

Moscheles had arrived in Vienna from London, via Munich, on October 19 and then "was taken seriously ill" with a long recovery (presumably akin to the possible case of kidney stones that he suffered upon his arrival in Prague in early January 1824). See *Wiener Zeitung*, No. 243 (October 21, 1823), p. 984; and Emil Smidak, *Isaak-Ignaz Moscheles: The Life of the Composer* (Aldershot: Scolar Press, 1989), pp. 31–32; and Heft 54, Blätter 16v and 23v.

Thus, whether Czerny or Ignaz Moscheles played at Haslinger's on Thursday, October 30, remains open to question. See *Reise-Briefe von Carl Maria von Weber an seine Gattin Carolina*, ed. grandson Carl von Weber (Leipzig: Alphons Dürr, 1886), p. 65.—TA

[12] Ferdinand Piringer (1780–1829), assistant to the director in the accounting office of the I.R. Court Commission of Commerce and member of the Board of Representatives of the Gesellschaft der Musikfreunde, lived in the City, Schlossergasse No. 598. He was a good violinist and had played in

[NEPHEW KARL, *continued*]
I am having him grow like the Greek heroes. [//] [Blatt 3r]
She[13] prepared the preserved veal and leftover cauliflower in a broth. //
It [the university's semester] begins on Monday [November 3].[14] //
Do you want the remaining rabbit tomorrow [Friday, October 31]? // We should never eat meat in the evening. //
I don't understand how they can sell the wine for 2 fl., in comparison with other wine dealers. // It is better than the Vöslauer wine from Count Fries.[15] // It is also probable that if a harmful mixture [of wines] is not present, then the district medical officer has nothing to say. [//] [Blatt 3v]
We, who live in cultivated circumstances, cannot say, as can be said of the old soldiers: *per quatuordecim annos tecta non subiere* (for fourteen years they lived under the open sky).[16] // Because not a single raindrop fell on them. // But it is. //
I would just like to make a journey to Nova Zemblia [*sic*] or the Spitzbergen [*sic*] or Siberia;[17] then I could also walk around in summer clothes during the severest winter, the way the English Sea Admiral[18] does. [//] [Blatt 4r]

or led many amateur performances. As such, he belonged to Beethoven's circle of friends. See Böckh, 1822, p. 376; Frimmel, *Handbuch*, II, pp. 21–23; *Hof- und Staats-Schematismus*, 1823, I, p. 255; Ziegeler, *Addressen-Buch*, pp. 115 and 138; and Clive, pp. 267–268.—KH/TA

[13] The current interim housekeeper, mentioned on Blatt 1r.—TA

[14] November 3 was the Monday after All Souls' Day (Sunday, November 2). For a similar chronology, see the events in early November 1822 (Heft 18, Blätter 1r–2r, 4v–5v, 6v, 25v–27r, and especially 27v).—TA

[15] Protestant banker Count Moritz von Fries also dealt in wines. See Heft 41, Blatt 17v, and Clive, pp. 120–121.—KH/TA

[16] Hyginus Gromaticus and Polybius Megalopolitanus, *De castris Romanis quae exstant: Cum notis ... de ... militari populi Romani* (Amsterdam: Pluymer, 1660), p. 113. The actual source of Karl's quote is unclear.—TA

[17] Nephew Karl originally writes *Novazemblia* and *Spitzbergen*. Novaja Semlja is an archipelago in the Arctic Ocean and Barents Sea, west of the Russian mainland and north of Norway. Spitsbergen (a Dutch name often given as the German Spitzbergen or even Spitzenbergen) is the largest and only permanently populated island of the Svalbard archipelago, north of Norway. It had been a whaling center and was the launching point for Parry's recent expedition (see immediately below) as well as for those of Roald Amundsen (1872–1928) or Ernest Shackleton (1874–1922), several generations later. For a description of the Svalbard reindeer, not including a red-nosed variety, see (Martin) Theodor von Heuglin, *Beiträge zur Fauna, Flora und Geologie: Von Spitzenbergen und Novaja Semlja* (Braunschweig: Westermann, 1874; repr. St. Albans [U.K.]: Wentworth Press, 2019).

As if to confuse matters, in 1818, Parry had been a member of Captain John Ross's unproductive expedition to Baffin Bay in Canada, with an area called Nova Zembla. Geographical distinctions courtesy Phil Dematteis.

Siberia is in eastern Russia. All three areas are noted for being remote and extremely cold. Karl means that if he were to visit one of these places, his body would become acclimatized to the cold, and then he would not have to worry about heavy clothing in Vienna's winters.—TA

[18] The second polar expedition by Sir William Edward Parry (1790–1855) had just ended on October 18, 1823. Viennese newspapers had reported about it during 1823, and Beethoven had mentioned him humorously in a letter to Schindler, ca. April 21, 1823 (Anderson, No. 1223; Brandenburg, No. 1633).

Only mediocre people can become rich, because they seldom reject a means to success.[19] //

[presumably Thursday, October 30, considering purchases for meatless Friday (or the holiday weekend in general):]

The pike costs 45 kr. The carp, 42. Both fish, 1 fl. 27 kr. // The carp weighs 1½ pounds; the pike, 1¼ pounds. // Is she to make something from the lentils? // Potatoes. //

He asked 7 fl. for the jacket, but noted the small size of the dress coat, which would become even smaller through turning. [//]

[Blatt 4v]

BEETHOVEN:
+ 3 pots
+ Coffee
+ Sugar, large bag

NEPHEW KARL: 1 fl. 12 [kr.] with lid. // Another 7 fl. 30 [kr.] on top of that. //

[written vertically→] One sheet is also missing from the last gathering of the Gloria.[20] You could give them to her to take along; so that Wunderl copies them.[21] [←written vertically] [Blatt 5r]

I consider it almost for the better if, for the sake of his five children, one were to give the pieces to Wunderl [for copying]; one would get more thanks for it. // She [Frau Schlemmer] can also farm it out. //

No good wine is to be drunk with water. //

On September 28, Karl had spent some time conversing with English visitor Johann Reinhold Schultz, and Parry's adventures could easily have come up then. See Heft 43, Blätter 39v–44v.—KH/TA

[19] The source of this cynical proverb is unidentified.—TA

[20] The German edition reads "vom letzten *Ternion* des *Gloria*." A ternion is a quire or gathering of three sheets, each folded in two. (An ordinary quire is made up of four sheets.) For security purposes, Beethoven initially omitted the final page or sheet from one or two movements of the *Missa solemnis* so that they would not be copied and distributed by unauthorized hands; he explains this in earlier conversation-book entries and in his letter to Prince Galitzin, December 13, 1823, to which the prince replied on December 30, 1823. See Anderson, Nos. 1195 and 1244; MacArdle & Misch, *New Beethoven Letters*, No. 374; Albrecht, *Letters to Beethoven*, No. 340; and Brandenburg, Nos. 1652, 1757, and 1763.—TA

[21] Mathias Wunderl (1771–1833) had collaborated with Wenzel Schlemmer and Wenzel Rampl in copying Beethoven's score to the *Consecration of the House* Overture in late September 1822. As such, he is Alan Tyson's so-called Copyist E. After Schlemmer's death in August 1823, Wunderl was employed by Schlemmer's widow, Josepha, to make at least one of the subscription copies of the *Missa solemnis*. For details concerning Wunderl's own wife and five children, see Heft 40, Blatt 10v. For more details concerning Copyist E, see Heft 41, Blatt 1v, and Heft 47, Blatt 11r.—KH/TA

[NEPHEW KARL, *continued*]

Must Truth always have a white beard, so that one believes it? // One is not as skilled as the other. [//] [Blatt 5v]

She still had the colic yesterday. // She did not dare. //

The other one is whole. //

In my opinion, there is not a wench who cannot have rye [bread]. // Many throw it away. // It was a very little bit, and she did not know that …. //

She has very severe diarrhea and sweats a great deal, and is weak. // There is also a physician here. // [Blatt 6r]

2 fl. 40 [kr.]
Coffee
Sugar?
1 fl. 36 [kr.]

        1 fl. 40 [kr.]
        1 fl. 36 [kr.]
        4 fl. 16 [kr.][22]

1 fl. 15 [kr.]

        7 fl. 30 [kr.]

1 fl. 45 [kr.]
1 fl. 45 [kr.]
   90
[therefore:]
3 fl. 30 [kr.]

[written vertically→] Monday. Tomorrow is Friday [October 31].[23] [←written vertically] [Blatt 6v]

48 kr. per pound.[24] //

[possibly Friday, October 31:]

If I were a composer, I would far prefer to write operas. // I thought that

---

[22] The correct sum is 3 fl. 16 kr. Karl had originally written "3," but then wrote "4" over it.—KH/TA

[23] Thus, today would be Thursday, October 30; and Monday would be November 3, 1823. For another reference to that coming Monday, see Blatt 3v above. Given the two holidays—All Saints' Day on Saturday, November 1, and All Souls' Day on Sunday, November 2—Beethoven and Karl seem to be grocery shopping for the entire weekend.—TA

[24] Relating to the figures above, 2 x 48 kr. = 96 kr. = 1 fl. 36 kr., the amount shown below "sugar."—TA

[NEPHEW KARL, *continued*]
immediately when I heard that the opera [*Euryanthe*] by Weber[25] had a serious subject, [and] that it doesn't measure up to that of *Der Freischütz*.[26] [//] [Blatt 7r] He [Weber] holds himself strictly to his principles; that's what he *said* in Baden.[27] //

She already used it at midday for the hot boiled carp; it was very small, however. // By Albrechtsberger.[28] //

Very serious subject, but the music [is] outstanding. He [probably publisher Haslinger] enjoyed it in a heavenly way, and will go again, every time that it [*Euryanthe*] is given. // He also considers himself to be a composer. [//] [Blatt 7v] Surely to a *narrow circle* of the artistically inclined, but not to the general public. // But I almost believe that beautiful music must have more effect upon totally *unmusical people* than upon the connoisseur who only looks for *Art*. //

"The *fine arts* breathe *life*; I ask for *spirit* from the *poet*, but *Polyhymnia* only expresses the *soul*."[29] [//] [Blatt 8r]

For feeling and especially *discernment*, though, an opera like *Fidelio* has a theme that cannot be compared with the devilish tale in *Der Freischütz*. Because the theater is not merely to touch a person fleetingly, it is also to form and awaken noble sentiments— and that is only possible by means of a *true* subject or at least a subject that *appears* to be true. //

How is the music? // Italian music is like refined cooking that certainly gratifies, but does harm [sentence ends] [//] [Blatt 8v] I know it merely from Rossini.[30] //

---

[25] The premiere of Weber's opera *Euryanthe* (to a libretto by Helmine von Chezy) took place under the composer's baton at the Kärntnertor Theater on Saturday, October 25, 1823. The Viennese reports in the *Allgemeine musikalische Zeitung* (Leipzig) were polite, indicating that the composer received four curtain calls after the premiere but that the libretto prevented it from being successful overall. See *Allgemeine musikalische Zeitung* 25, No. 47 (November 19, 1823), cols. 764–765; and No. 52 (December 24, 1823), cols. 861–865.—TA

[26] Karl writes the noun as *Freyschütze*, the way it appeared on contemporary Viennese theater *Zettel* (posters).—TA

[27] On Sunday, October 5, Weber and his assistant, Julius Benedict, had visited Beethoven in Baden. See Sonneck, *Beethoven: Impressions by His Contemporaries*, pp. 159–161, for Weber's full account, but Thayer-Forbes, p. 872, for corrected details of dating and context. The conversation book recording that visit (which would appear chronologically between Hefte 43 and 44) has seemingly not survived.—TA

[28] (Johann) Georg Albrechtsberger (1736–1809), composer, teacher, organist at St. Stephan's Cathedral; and Beethoven's teacher, ca. 1793–1795. See Frimmel, *Handbuch*, I, p. 8, and II, p. 479; Clive, pp. 3–4; as well as Julia Ronge, *Beethovens Lehrzeit: Kompositionsstudien bei Joseph Haydn, Johann Georg Albrechtsberger und Antonio Salieri* (Bonn: Verlag Beethoven-Haus, 2011).—KH/TA

[29] From "*Tonkunst*," a proverb by Friedrich von Schiller from the *Votivtafeln*, appearing in the *Musenalmanach für 1797*.—KH

[30] After Domenico Barbaja leased the Viennese Court Opera in late 1821, he began importing popular Italian operas (including those by Gioacchino Rossini) and singers, seemingly to the exclusion of customary German works. The revival of Beethoven's *Fidelio* in November 1822 and the premiere of

[NEPHEW KARL, *continued*]

Weber surely knows Prince Radziwill[31] from Berlin, though he doesn't know *what* he is and where he has a palace *here*. // Should one .... //

[shopping for meat at a butcher shop or market stand:]

1 rabbit for 1 fl. 54 kr. 3 pounds of beef [*Rindfleisch*] for today and tomorrow. The beef costs 20 kr. [//] [Blatt 9r]

Beef loin [*Lungenbraten*], 20 kr. 2 pounds [cost] 40 kr. // 3 pounds of beef [cost] 1 fl. 24 kr. C.M. // Those are the intestines [*Gedärme*, tripe]. //

He [Lichnowsky][32] railed terribly against Weber's opera and only wishes that you would go with *him* [and sit] in the parterre near the orchestra in order to observe the nonsense by means of the music itself. // Full of terrible dissonance. //

Anyhow, the maid is not eating. //

Herr Professor Stein[33] is a terrible pedant. [//] [Blatt 9v] He has adopted Reuchlin's[34] pronunciation, which is rejected by most of the most intelligent philologists and supported only by the New Greeks and their friends, and he demands this horribly hard-sounding pronunciation from all of his pupils, instead of allowing each person his own preference. Beyond this, he demands the translation of Greek classics (which is impossible) with those words that he uses, and as he has interpreted them. [//]

[written vertically→] He is a little *Wunder* [miracle], therefore a *Wunderl*.[35] [←written vertically] [//]

Weber's *Euryanthe* in October 1823 were calculated to appease the opposition among Vienna's German-loving operagoers.—TA

[31] Prince Anton Heinrich Radziwill (1775–1833), the Prussian governor in Posen since 1815. Cellist, singer, and generous patron in whose Berlin palace chamber music concerts with contemporary compositions were organized. He himself was also a composer (music for Goethe's *Faust*). See Frimmel, *Handbuch*, II, pp. 48–49; Reinhold Sietz, "Radziwill," *MGG*, vol. 10, cols. 1859–1860; Clive, p. 275.—KH/TA

[32] Karl must have encountered Count Moritz Lichnowsky earlier and heard his reaction to *Euryanthe*. In any case, Lichnowsky himself visited Beethoven on Blätter 10r–13r below and repeated many of the same things.—TA

[33] Anton Joseph Stein (1759–1844), professor of Latin literature and Greek philology at the University of Vienna, lived in suburban Landstrasse, Ungargasse No. 329 (only six houses south of Beethoven's new apartment). See *Hof- und Staats-Schematismus*, 1823, II, p. 97; Meusel, *Gelehrtes Teutschland*, vol. 8, p. 592.—KH/TA

[34] Johann Reuchlin (1455–1522), the most significant humanist after Erasmus of Rotterdam. He especially supported the propagation of Greek and Hebrew languages. In contrast to Erasmus, who desired the phonetically correct pronunciation of the Greeks, he propagated the pronunciation of the vowels according to the model of the New Greeks (iotacism).

The difference seems to be classical Greek versus modern Greek pronunciation. Karl draws the parallel with Latin and modern Italian on Blatt 14v below.—KH/TA

[35] Probably a sarcastic reference to Professor Stein, but also a pun on the name of music copyist Matthias Wunderl, who was active in copying for Beethoven during this period and was Tyson's so-called Copyist E. See Blatt 4v above.—TA

[Blatt 10r]

LICHNOWSKY [presumably at Beethoven's apartment in the Ungargasse; Saturday, November 1 (All Saints' Day)]: I am also moving into the City.[36] // Because of my little [daughter].[37] //

Yesterday [Friday, October 31], I heard your Quartet in A major at Schuppanzigh's concert.[38] //

The music [of Weber's *Euryanthe*] is not at all [appropriate] for the text; it is much too tragic, contains nothing but dissonances, unnatural transitions, and far-fetched difficulties. [//] [Blatt 10v] People will no longer come to hear the opera, and thus it will not endure. // The opera. //

BEETHOVEN [filling the rest of the page, perhaps later]:

$$
\begin{array}{rr}
60 & 120 \\
6 & 120 \\
& 60 \\
& 70 \\
& 70 \\
& \underline{70} \\
& 510
\end{array}
$$

[Blatt 11r]

---

[36] Beethoven's friend Count Moritz Lichnowsky had spent the summer in Hietzing, about a mile northwest of Beethoven's first summer residence in Hetzendorf. See Heft 36, Blatt 1r.—TA

[37] Josepha Maria Stummer (b. June, 1814), Lichnowsky's illegitimate daughter; she is mentioned again in Heft 48, Blatt 2r. See Clive, pp. 306–308; and Ziegler, *Addressen-Buch*, p. 52.—TA

[38] Ignaz Schuppanzigh (1776–1830), prominent violinist. Initially a violinist in the resident quartet of Prince Karl von Lichnowsky (Count Moritz's elder brother), he was first violinist in Count/Prince Rasumovsky's quartet from 1808 to early 1816. He then toured Germany and the Baltic countries, settling in Russia (mostly dividing his time between St. Petersburg and Lemberg/Lvov), returning to Vienna in mid-April 1823. As soon as possible, he reestablished his own quartet with Karl Holz (second violin), Franz Weiss (viola), and Joseph Linke (violoncello). When they played quintets, Ferdinand Piringer often played second viola.

The second of Schuppanzigh's series of six midday subscription concerts at the hall of the *Musik-Verein* (*Gesellschaft der Musikfreunde*), three blocks north of the cathedral, took place on Friday, October 31, 1823. The program consisted of George Onslow, Quartet No. 11 in D minor; Mozart, Quartet No. 6 in D (K. 465); and Beethoven, Quartet in A, Op. 18, No. 5.

See Frimmel, *Handbuch*, II, pp. 161–163; Wurzbach, vol. 32, pp. 215–217; Clive, pp. 329–331; *Allgemeine musikalische Zeitung* 25, No. 47 (November 19, 1823), cols. 764 and 766; *Wiener AmZ* 7, No. 98 (December 6, 1823), cols. 783–784.—KH/TA

LICHNOWSKY [continuing from above]: Believe me then that if you write the opera,[39] the administration will not give you everything that you always demand. // I would guarantee the sum that you desire for the opera. [//] [Blatt 11v] If you would state your wish [concerning] what you wish for the opera. // Certainly, in addition to merely selling the opera to the administration, you can also reserve [Blatt 12r] the rights to sell it in *foreign countries* and domestically. //

If you want to go to Weber's opera the next time, I'll get 2 reserved seats in the orchestra. [//] [Blatt 12v]

I only had her [a servant] in the country. //

How's it going with the Greek?[40] //

Indeed, one now has the most confidence in the bankrupt.[41] // [Blatt 13r]

I'll certainly come again in a few days. //

Were you satisfied in Baden? //

She [Therese van Beethoven] already has *half* of his property now; and after his [Johann's] death, she'll have *all* of it.[42] [//]

[Blatt 13v]

NEPHEW KARL [after Lichnowsky's departure; Saturday, November 1]: The sound of metal [coins?] is doubtless far louder, but also very unclear. //

Otherwise, [Stein is] a very learned man. // One can still adapt to *his* peculiarities, but I must confess before the professor of religion that I am afraid, because he has [the students] memorize the book word for word; I already know [the book], and it is absolutely nothing but empty stuff; and that is too distressing, though. [//] [Blatt 14r] Then it sets Second Class. // Because we cannot talk in the way that you believe; one makes enemies not of *one*, but of *all* the professors, and afterward is hindered in all things and with all of these people. // There is *no* objecting against his arguments *except* that the old Greeks *certainly* did not speak this way. He, however, cites communication with the New Greeks, to whom one can surely bring the sacrifice and against whom nothing can be said. [//] [Blatt 14v] One cannot cite one *name*. // It is *exactly* the case as with the Italian language; even *it* is Latin, but a bowdlerized Latin; the pronunciation is quite different in *that* way. //

---

[39] The never-realized setting of Grillparzer's libretto *Melusine*, a potential collaboration possibly initiated by Lichnowsky. See Heft 43, Blatt 40r.—KH/TA

[40] See Karl's discussion about Stein and Greek study (above and below).—TA

[41] Probably a reference to the Lobkowitz family, from whom Beethoven still drew a stipend. His patron Prince Franz Joseph Maximilian Lobkowitz (1772–1816) had died so close to bankruptcy that his holdings had to be administered by relatives after June 1813. See Clive, pp. 212–215; and Heft 43, Blatt 32v.—TA

[42] Lichnowsky's wife and Therese van Beethoven were friends. Beethoven believed that Therese was already having love affairs. In the event, Therese died in 1828, and Johann outlived her to 1848.—TA

[NEPHEW KARL, *continued*]
[possibly showing Beethoven a Greek book with the word "Odysseus":]
It reads *this* way, but is not *pronounced* in this way, but rather "Ozisseus" ["Odsisseus"] according to the New Greek pronunciation, according to which [Blatt 15r] Stein also speaks. In the future, I shall therefore have to say "Odsisseus" when I translate Homer. // Also the various methods of writing are rooted in this pronunciation; for example the word *Zeus*, which many authors write as "Zevs." // There exist at present only 2 men who, as *truly* great philologists, possess a *credible* voice about this matter: Buttmann[43] and Thiersch.[44] [//] [Blatt 15v] So what is someone like *Stein* compared to the great philologists? // Otherwise, Stein is a good Greek specialist, who has also written in Greek, but he has only recently adopted the New Greek pronunciation. // He may be *far* less in order to be a professor in Vienna. [//] [Blatt 16r] [The situation in] *The Ruins of Athens* will still remain *true* for a *long time*. But if it ever becomes untrue, and if Minerva needs to find her Old Athens, then *I'll* write a sequel to Kotzebue's play, and *you* can likewise set it to music.[45] //

The maid eats too much. A healthy diet will do the most in the case of such situations.[46] [//] [Blatt 16v]

The people *here* are dreadfully naive. // Good for *him*. // The whole family. // If one reads their letter, one sees the way that they were educated in their youth; they cannot write orthographically [correctly] even once, and their *style*!!! I am saying *only* what I know; I don't know [Blatt 17r] how the *others* are. One can conclude, however, that they are pretty similar, with a *few* exceptions. [//]

Something, though, needs to be said about Napoleon. // At one time, the region

---

[43] Philipp Carl Buttmann (1764–1829), philologist and librarian, wrote, among others, *Kurzgefasste griechische Grammatik* [Brief Greek Grammar] (Berlin, 1792); *Lexilogos, oder Beiträge zur griechischen Worterklärung, hauptsächlich für Homer und Hesiod* [Contributions to Greek Word Interpretation, Primarily for Homer and Hesiod], 2 vols. (1818–1825); and *Mythologos, oder gesammelte Abhandlungen über die Sagen des Alterthums* [Collected Documents concerning the Epics of Antiquity], 2 vols. (1828–1829). See *Allgemeine Deutsche Biographie*, vol. 3, pp. 656–658; Kayser, I, p. 400.—KH/TA

[44] Friedrich Thiersch (1784–1860), philologist and pedagogue, active as a *Gymnasium* teacher in Munich. See Meusel, *Gelehrtes Teutschland*, vol. 9, pp. 49–50.—KH

[45] August von Kotzebue (1761–1819) wrote his occasional play *Die Ruinen von Athen* in 1811, to be set by Beethoven for the opening of the new German Theater in Pesth in 1812. It initially portrays Athens in ruins and overrun by the Turks. Minerva (Athena), the goddess of wisdom and war, laments the loss of her cultural home but is reassured that a new Temple of the Arts has been built in Pesth, and she is immediately transported there to witness the glory of the new theater. Kotzebue had been assassinated for his promonarchical sympathies in 1819 and so would not be present to write a sequel if and when the Turks were run out of Greece by Lord Byron and his fellow revolutionaries. See Clive, pp. 191–192.—KH/TA

[46] They have the maid examined by a doctor; see Blätter 19r–19v below.—TA

[NEPHEW KARL, *continued*]
around Laibach and Krain[47] was *French*, during Napoleon's time. University education looked entirely *different* then. // At the examination, [Blatt 17v] everyone who excelled in a subject received 20 *francs* on a neck chain and was kissed on the forehead by the principal. //

From Monday [November 3] on, I shall be a [university] student in philosophy, or "Philosoph" as they call it *here*; therefore please honor me appropriately. [//] [Blatt 18r] I believe and I believe not. //

If it doesn't disturb you, I'll set up the library[48] now. // I can dispense with the key, because I can also unlock the white *Schrank* [cabinet] with my key to the chest. //

It would be sad if an error—like the time that you thought that I had laughed—could have caused conflict; only your fierceness made an immediate [Blatt 18v] explanation impossible. Now, however, I believe that I can do that so much the better, because I certainly am completely innocent. As you yourself will remember, you said, namely, that I was to go out there and have the door opened because of the odor from the toilet. I went out there, but since the smell of the [cologne] water (or whatever it was with which she had perfumed the entire room) was unbearable, when I went through it I held out the handkerchief, and [Blatt 19r] told her again (as the maid must also have heard) that I would still prefer the odor from the toilet to that which her [cologne] water or perfume would cause. // Although I didn't see it, it is possible that she laughed about the fact that I called the excellent smell that she made an odor. // But the cologne water is far more expensive. //

[after a physician visits to examine the maid; possibly late afternoon of Saturday, November 1:]

The physician appears to be very skillful.[49] He asked her very clearly about everything possible. But it is of no significance. [//] [Blatt 19v] The maid understood him; she feels that it is the better food allotment that she now receives, and which she has enjoyed a little too abundantly. The difference between her present and former food allotment was so sudden and pronounced that it had an effect on her. // What she ate *there* is quite understandable, because, as she says, the people themselves had a roast only extremely seldom. [//] [Blatt 20r]

---

[47] The province of Krajina (formerly Krain) and its capital, Ljubljana (formerly Laibach), in Slovenia. Until 1918, the region belonged to the Austrian monarchy. Through the Treaty of Schönbrunn (October 14, 1809), however, it came under French rule until 1814.—KH/TA

[48] Beethoven's musical library and a few nonmusical books (as they existed at the time of the composer's death) are detailed in Thayer-Forbes, pp. 1061–1070. An additional estate inventory sheet with mostly nonmusical books is found in Albrecht, *Letters to Beethoven*, No. 483.—TA

[49] Several remarks concerning the maid's health and eating habits lead up to Blatt 16r above.—TA

[NEPHEW KARL, *continued*]

Tomorrow [Sunday, November 2, All Souls' Day], I must spend a little time in church because a grand service will be held.[50] // *Veni, sancte Spiritus* will be sung.[51] //

I'll have to take my boots in for new soles, because I now have only one pair that I must wear every day. //

Medicine, powder, and tea cost 1 fl. 20 kr.

    1670
    <u>1513</u>
      157 years old.[52] //

[possibly before a light evening meal; Saturday, November 1:]

[written vertically→] It would surely be safer if she made soft eggs, because then we could see whether all the eggs are good, which is not as easy in the case of dishes made with eggs. *Quid dicis?* [What do you say?] [←written vertically] // [Blatt 20v]

I am curious about the treatment of philosophy, since there is no kind of regular textbook here; otherwise, the professor is said to be skilled, as witnessed by Giannatasio,[53] at whose school he taught the A-B-Cs. //

It is not good that you express yourself so openly; for example, when you recently spoke about the arrangement for my studies, he [presumably Lichnowsky] made a face. He will not keep it to himself, and then it will be said that you are making me

---

[50] In some cases, when All Souls' Day (November 2) fell on a Sunday, the observation would be postponed until Monday, November 3. Since the *Wiener Zeitung* appeared on that Monday as usual, it appears likely that the holiday was celebrated on Sunday.

There are very few references to Beethoven's or Karl's ever attending church services. In this case, however, one of the purposes of the feast was to pray for souls in purgatory, and Karl may have felt a need to pray on behalf of his father, Carl, as the seventh anniversary of his death approached in two weeks.—TA

[51] *Veni, sancte Spiritus* (Come, Holy Spirit) is the sequence for Pentecost, but it may have been used for one of the three *Requiem*-like Masses said on All Souls' Day. Karl may have mentioned it in connection with Beethoven's idea of composing a Mass with several proper movements in the taste preferred by Emperor Franz. In today's Vienna, a half dozen of the city's churches, including St. Stephan's Cathedral, are likely to perform Mozart's *Requiem* in its liturgical setting on this day.

Beethoven's new apartment was in the St. Rochus Parish, but Karl may have intended to go to one of the other churches, including the aforementioned cathedral.—TA

[52] This historical computation remains unclear. In 1513, Leo X succeeded Julius II as pope. Unlike most of his predecessors, Leo tolerated and even defended Jewish writings. In 1670, however, Emperor Leopold I expelled the Jews from Vienna, destroying their synagogue in the Leopoldstadt and laying the cornerstone for a new St. Leopold Church on the site. In 1675, he allowed 250 Jewish families to return. See also *Stadt Chronik Wien: 2000 Jahre in Daten, Dokumenten, und Bildern* (Vienna: Verlag Christian Brandstätter, 1986), pp. 102 and 125; and *Die Chronik Wiens* (Dortmund: Chronik-Verlag Harenberg, 1988), pp. 64 and 86–88.—TA

[53] Cajetan Giannatasio del Rio, in whose private school Karl studied from January 1816 to January 1818.—KH

[NEPHEW KARL, *continued*]
into someone who scorns the Fatherland, [Blatt 21r] and even more about such fine things. //

[Professor] Stein thinks just the same way. //

Rothschild is an important man in the present age.[54] // He really didn't need to make many difficulties, since the pope also has him honored. // I find it extraordinarily humiliating that [in] all of Christendom (in which there are many people who differ with His Holiness), these people kiss his slipper; and the glorification of *God* and of the *pope* are differentiated merely with the words *worship* and *adore*. [//] [Blatt 21v]

At the time of the campaign against Austria, a commander of several Napoleonic regiments, by the name of Mandl,[55] came over to our side with a couple of companies of soldiers, and excused his lack of loyalty to Napoleon by saying that he had not been able to watch his atrocities. Specifically, that right after a battle, Napoleon had quite calmly eaten his midday dinner on the *battlefield* amid the death rattles of the seriously wounded, and when someone asked him whether he could enjoy his meal, surrounded by the [Blatt 22r] dead and wounded who had fallen in his name, he replied: "What do these dogs mean to me?" //[56]

In the first place, who would have dared to *ask* him how he could *enjoy* it? // That Mandl had crossed the lines is true; his excuses, however, were made up. //

Blöchlinger has a book on Napoleon, which I have read, that is full of the most dreadful defamation, [written] by a professor in Bavaria. Obviously not written until *after* Napoleon's downfall; but that's not the point. [//] [Blatt 22v]

---

[54] Jewish banker Salomon Mayer Rothschild (1774–1855) had arrived in Vienna from the familial home in Frankfurt in December 1819 and immediately curried favor with the Viennese nobility, often to the disadvantage of Vienna's established Jewish banking families of Biedermann, Arnstein, Eskeles, etc. The five Rothschild brothers rapidly built financial empires throughout Europe, with influence extending to the Americas. The popes during this period were Pius VII (August 14, 1742 – August 20, 1823), pope from 1800, and Leo XII (reigned from October 1823 until his death in 1829). Emperor Franz and his Empress Caroline had made an official visit to Pope Pius VII in 1819, but there is no record of a Rothschild having done so.—TA

[55] Brigadier General Eugène-Charles-Auguste-David de Mandeville (b. Avesnes, Pas-de-Calais, June 11, 1780; d. Neuwiller-lès-Saverne, Bas-Rhin, January 28, 1850). From a family of military officers, he attended the Royal School and joined the staff of General Emmanuel de Grouchy. He fought in the French army through the Napoleonic Wars until August 29, 1813, then entered the Prussian army before the Battle of Leipzig (October 1813). He was captured by the French but was released in September 1814 under the Treaty of Paris. He served Napoleon again during the Hundred Days and remained in responsible French military positions until his retirement in 1831.

Karl may have told this story directly after the discussion about Rothschild because he may have thought the name Mandl (as he understood it) was Jewish.—TA

[56] Beethoven may have expressed annoyance or disbelief at this story, prompting Karl's own seeming disbelief, following.—TA

[preparing a shopping list, presumably to be used on Monday, November 3:]
Coffee cups.
Coffee mill.

BEETHOVEN [adding to the shopping and to-do list; possibly Sunday, November 2 (All Souls' Day), or Monday, November 3]:
Potato sack.
+ Oil the stove and window.
+ Tiefer Graben, [under the] supporting arch.[57]

[heavily crossed out→]

1 fl.	1 fl.	1 fl.	
1 __	1 __	1 20	3 fl.
1 __	1 30	1 40	2 fl. 33
	1	1 8	8

End of Heft 44

N.B. The redating of problematical Heft 45 proposed in this English edition begins as early as Tuesday, November 4, 1823. Thus, there is little or no break between Hefte 44 and 45.

---

[57] [Unter dem] *Schwibbogen*: this was the location of a shop that sold inexpensive Austrian wines. See Heft 48, Blatt 17r.—TA

Heft 45

(ca. November 4, 1823 – ca. November 20, 1823)

N.B. The entries in Heft 45 were not made in the chronological order suggested by the subsequent pagination in Blatt numbers. A chronological contents (immediately below), similar to what was done with Hefte 19–21, may prove helpful, though several entries still cannot be dated precisely.

If Schindler was back in Beethoven's good graces on ca. Friday, November 21 (Heft 46, Blatt 2r), then the *concert* in Heft 45, Blatt 29v, has to be that of the Gesellschaft der Musikfreunde on Sunday, November 16.

A new reverse chronology from Blatt 29v works fairly well back to (and including) Blatt 16r.

Konversationshefte editor Grita Herre (Berlin) kindly sent corrected information that Blätter 8–9, 14–15, 26–27, and 38–39 are on light blue paper in two sizes slightly smaller than the normal paper. Blatt 25v (normal) contains a sentence finished on 26r (blue), and there is similar continuity in Kirchhoffer's entries from Blatt 27v (blue) to 28r (normal), suggesting that the various papers were already bound when Beethoven used the book.

Using the new reverse chronology and working forward from Tuesday, November 4, there are still no specifically datable entries for Thursday, November 6, through Monday, November 10; Wednesday, November 12 (possibly blue Blätter 14r–15v); or Monday, November 17. Once the semester begins on Monday, November 3, entries by nephew Karl on Mondays and Wednesdays are relatively rare. It is possible that some "undated" entries from Blätter 12r or 14r–15v (blue) **might fit those gaps.**

* * * * *

NEW CHRONOLOGY BASED ON BLATT 29r AS SUNDAY, NOVEMBER 16

Bold print = customary paper; normal print = light blue paper.

1r–4r (continuous): no precise chronology, but Karl's reference to dinners on Tuesdays, Thursdays, Saturdays points to organizing routine for the semester. Therefore, it could be Tuesday, November 4, ca. 2 p.m.

4v–5r: facing pages, left blank earlier, filled by Carbon, possibly Wednesday, November 19.

5v–7v (continuous): Schuppanzigh and Henning: Wednesday, November 5, or later.

8r–9v and 10r–11v: probably Tuesday, November 18, through Thursday, November 20 (with rabbit, 8v) (with *Theater-Zeitung* in hand, Blatt 10r).

12r: rabbit; Karl eats at home tomorrow; date *unknown*.

12v–13v: Tuesday, November 11 (datable from advertisements).

14r–15v: KARL: maid, Bach, Philosophy & Logic, shopping list; ARTISAN: barometer; KARL: Seidl; dates *unknown*.

16r–19r: Thursday, November 13 (top of 19r = Thursday).

19r (lower)–26r–26v: Friday, November 14 (a business day), continuing to Saturday, November 15 (a holiday).

26v–27v and 28r–31v (and a stray entry on 38r): Sunday, November 16 (with the premise that the concert is by the Gesellschaft der Musikfreunde).

38r (lower): Sunday, November 16 (after the Gesellschaft der Musikfreunde's concert).

32r: Tuesday, November 18.

37v and 38r–39v: Karl and Beethoven shopping; 41v to the end in a coffee house. To end on Blatt 42v (ca. November 20).

[Therefore, Hefte 44, 45, and 46 (despite some remaining questions concerning the entry order in Heft 45) follow each other in normal sequence and without significant break.—TA]

* * * * *

[Blatt 1r]

NEPHEW KARL [presumably at Beethoven's apartment in the Ungargasse; possibly as early as Tuesday, November 4, at ca. 2 p.m.]:[1]

	1 fl. 40 [kr.]
1 fl.	2 fl. 30 [kr.]
	2 fl.
	4 fl. 30 [kr.] //

15
24.
They don't have anything that large. //

On the days when I have *Collegium* in the afternoon, I can certainly eat *at home* and avoid all the confusion. // One needn't say anything to her [housekeeper Barbara Holzmann]. Then we eat together on Tuesdays, Thursdays, and Saturdays.[2] [//] [Blatt 1v] But that wouldn't be different if I were here.[3] //

Doubtless the district policeman. //

Even more to be admired is the multitude of fish, in spite of the number that are caught daily. // But have they *all* escaped? // People assert that fish [Blatt 2r] do not have the sense of hearing; I can't believe that. // They have examples that fish in ponds, etc., come to a call from their master. //

What does a pound of wax candles cost? // How many candles? // I almost believe that you should only burn wax. When you add it up, [Blatt 2v] it doesn't cost any more than tallow, because the candles burn a long time; and then there is the damage that tallow candles make to the *chest*, and [it] also says in the Hufeland [*Makrobiotik*][4] that one is not to burn any tallow lights. //

---

[1] In Heft 44, Blatt 3r, Karl had indicated that the new semester at the university began on Monday, November 3. Blätter 1r–1v and Blatt 35r (below) suggest that Karl may have been rooming elsewhere part-time, seemingly confirmed on Blätter 19r and 33v–34r below. Tuesdays and Thursdays are common to the varying estimates of when he would be able to eat midday dinner at home with Beethoven, so this entry could be as early as Tuesday, November 4, at ca. 2 p.m.—TA

[2] On ca. September 23, Karl had projected that he would be able to eat with Beethoven on Sunday, Tuesday, and Thursday afternoons (see Heft 43, Blätter 23v–24r), but he also seems to have eaten with Beethoven on Friday, November 14, and possibly Friday, November 21.—TA

[3] This suggests that Karl may be rooming elsewhere part of the time, seemingly confirmed on Blatt 35r below.—TA

[4] Christoph Wilhelm Hufeland (1762–1836), famous physician, author of such writings as *Makrobiotik, oder die Kunst, das menschliche Leben zu verlängern* (Macrobiotics, or the Art of Prolonging Human Life), published in Berlin in 1805. On June 20, 1820, Beethoven made a note to look at its new third, expanded edition at Gräffer's Bookshop (see Heft 14, Blatt 53r). There are several subsequent references to Hufeland, his work, and recommendations in the conversation books; see, for instance, Heft 24, Blatt 7r (February 13, 1823). By May 18, 1823, Part 2 of Beethoven's copy was missing

Dried sausage in the soup. [//] 33 [kr.]. // [Blatt 3r] [Soup at] 24 kr. and ½ beer [at] 9 kr. makes 33 kr. //

In the beginning, [school director] Blöchlinger gave his tutors coffee, which, however, in order to provide them with a good example, he drank *without sugar*. Hereupon, naturally, the tutors could also not wish for sugar; thus everyone drank unsugared coffee until finally Köferle,[5] who became tired of it, bought a quarter pound of sugar and [Blatt 3v] brought it with him in his briefcase and sugared his coffee in Blöchlinger's presence. From that time on, presumably because he didn't want to incur this expense, Blöchlinger drank coffee with his wife (who, however, sugared her coffee), and the tutors got [hot] chocolate. //

Two groschen for a sugar-drop candy. // [//] [Blatt 4r]

However, he must. //

I am finished [with one class] after 10 o'clock; if I had the Mass [*Missa solemnis*] right with me, I could take it to him and to the other places because I must be back to the university by 11:45 for English class.[6] //

You could pay 5 fl. Then she has to get 1 fl. 50 [kr.] [//]

[chronology probably continues on Blatt 5v:]

* * * * *

[Blatt 4v]

CARBON[7] **[filling two pages left blank earlier, at Beethoven's apartment; presumably no later than ca. Wednesday, November 19, when nephew Karl was not present]**:[8] My wife is on her way to recovery. // Türkheim is treating her. // An old friend of my wife's. //

I have a request. // D[octo]r at Archduke Rudolph's. // Hubertus[9] has this

---

(Heft 33, Blarr 2v). When he died, Beethoven's library still contained a copy of Hufeland's *Übersicht der Heilquellen Teutschlands* (Survey of the Mineral Baths in Germany), published in Berlin in 1815; see Albrecht, *Letters to Beethoven*, No. 483.—TA

[5] Teacher of geography, history, and religion at Joseph Blöchlinger's Institute; see Heft 39, Blatt 36v.—KH

[6] Karl possibly went to copyist Wenzel Rampl's; see a similar errand on Blatt 8r below.—TA

[7] From his handwriting and context (including his wife's illness and physician), this writer can be identified as Franz Ludwig Carbon, community leader and property owner in Mödling. See Heft 20, Blatt 5r.—TA

[8] In Heft 46, Blätter 7v–8r (probably late afternoon of Friday, November 21), Karl comments negatively about Carbon's visit out of the blue, merely to request Beethoven's help.—TA

[9] Dr. Johann Hubertus (b. 1752), staff physician and personal physician of Archduke Rudolph, Beethoven's longtime patron, who had been archbishop-cardinal at Olmütz since March 1820. Hubertus maintained an apartment in the Bürgerspital No. 1100. See Conscriptions-Bogen, Stadt, No. 1100 (Wiener Stadt- und Landesarchiv); Groner, 1922, p. 60; *Hof- und Staats-Schematismus*, 1823, I, pp. 120 and 193, and II, p. 126.—KH/TA

apartment, without using it. [//] [Blatt 5r] [He is] always in Olmütz with the archduke and the quarters are always empty. // But it will give you a great deal of inconvenience. // As long as I have lived in the Bürgerspital, which has been 1½ years now, Hubertus has always been at Rudolph's in Olmütz. //

Is he [Karl] finished with his studies? [//]

* * * * *

[Blatt 5v]

BEETHOVEN [ca. November 4/5 or November 19?]: + Karl: washbasin.[10] [//]

[Visit from the violinist Ignaz Schuppanzigh, bringing the Berlin concertmaster Carl Wilhelm Henning; possibly Wednesday, November 5, when nephew Karl was not at home.][11]

SCHUPPANZIGH: The Prussian concertmaster Henning[12] wants to make his [= your][13] acquaintance.

HENNING: I have long wished the honor of making your personal acquaintance, since, as both a violinist and composer, I belong among your innumerable admirers, and now, since I have taken over the music direction [i.e., the concertmaster's position] [Blatt 6r] of the newly built theater in Berlin, I believe that its opening could not take place with anything more worthy than if I request you kindly to provide us your

---

[10] The washbasin remained on Beethoven's shopping list in Heft 46, Blatt 20v (Monday, November 24), so this entry could have been made before Schuppanzigh and Henning's visit or after Carbon's.—TA

[11] As noted below, Henning and Bethmann arrived in Vienna on Tuesday, November 4. One of their intended purposes seems to have been to obtain *Die Weihe des Hauses* for the upcoming opening of the Königstädtisches Theater in Berlin. Therefore, Henning would not have tarried in visiting Beethoven, which might have taken place the next day, Wednesday, November 5, or soon thereafter. Nephew Karl's apparent absence points to the likelihood of a Wednesday.—TA

[12] Carl Wilhelm Henning (1784–1867), concertmaster at the Royal Opera in Berlin. From 1823 to 1826, he was music director of the Königstädtisches Theater, which would open on August 4, 1824 (see continuing conversation). He arrived in Vienna on Tuesday, November 4, 1823; see Blatt 6v below.

Henning also writes entries in Heft 47, Blatt 1v (November 29, 1823), as if it were his first meeting with Beethoven; or perhaps he had to reintroduce himself. He notes there that Schuppanzigh had played one of his (Henning's) quartets on November 28 and that he would remain another ten days in Vienna. See *Allgemeine musikalische Zeitung* 26, No. 39 (September 23, 1824), cols. 633–635; Frimmel, *Handbuch*, I, p. 209; Ledebur, pp. 233–235.—KH/TA

[13] Schuppanzigh (as "Mylord" Falstaff) always jokingly addressed Beethoven (a "commoner") in the third person.—KH/TA

Prologue for the Josephstadt Theater.[14] // I am interested *only* in the music, because our theater poet[15] will make the necessary alterations. //

SCHUPPANZIGH: H[err] Bethmann[16] from Berlin is the director of this new theater; he is [Blatt 6v] here [in Vienna] at the moment, and wishes to speak with him [= you] about this subject. [//]

HENNING: 14 days [= two weeks].[17] [//]
  I hope to perform your music as well as is worthy of your Muse. [//]
  Spontini[18] has somewhat removed the apathy from her [Wilhelmine Schröder].[19] [//]

SCHUPPANZIGH: She is terribly lazy. [//]

[Blatt 7r]

---

[14] *Die Weihe des Hauses* (Consecration of the House), the play by Carl Meisl (after Kotzebue) that opened the remodeled Theater in der Josephstadt on October 3, 1822. Beethoven's music was a reworking of his score for Kotzebue's *Ruins of Athens* that had opened the German Theater in Pesth on February 9, 1812. The 1822 reworking featured a new Overture, Op. 124, and chorus "Wo sich die Pulse," WoO 98. See Kinsky-Halm, pp. 366–367.—KH

[15] Probably Carl von Holtei (1798–ca. 1878). In 1823, as the result of a theater scandal, he had lost his position as theatrical poet and secretary in Breslau and turned to Berlin, where he was engaged as administrative secretary, stage poet, and dramatic director of the new Königstädtisches Theater. See Wurzbach, vol. 9, pp. 233–234.—KH

[16] Heinrich Eduard Bethmann (1774–1834), actor, stage director, and theater poet in Berlin. See *Allgemeine Deutsche Biographie*, vol. 2, p. 573. Bäuerle's *Allgemeine Theater-Zeitung* 16, No. 142 (November 27, 1823), p. 568, noted: "Herr Bethmann, the director of the *Volkstheater* in Berlin, is in Vienna with his music director Herr Henning, to make acquisitions for their new theater. Earlier, he was in Munich, where he made some good business arrangements." Even before the new Königstädtisches Theater opened on August 4, 1824, Bethmann was forced out of his position by March; see Heft 60, Blätter 35v–36r.—KH/TA

[17] This may indicate that Bethmann and Henning had visited Munich for two weeks. They had arrived from Munich on Tuesday, November 4. The *Wiener Zeitung*'s "Arrivals" column indicated that they were staying at City No. 822. When Henning visited Beethoven again on November 29, however, he indicated (with more details of the address) that he was staying at *Zum ungarischen König*, in the Schullerstrasse, but at 852. Thus, the *Wiener Zeitung*'s "822" was probably a typographical error.
  On November 29, Henning indicated that he would remain another ten days in Vienna. He and Bethmann actually departed on December 11, 1823. See the *Wiener Zeitung*, No. 256 (November 6, 1823), p. 1035, and No. 286 (December 13, 1823), p. 1162; Behsel, p. 25; and Heft 47, Blatt 1v.
  In any case, Henning's purpose in Vienna was to meet and negotiate with Beethoven for *Consecration of the House*, so they probably did so without delay on Wednesday, November 5.—TA

[18] Gaspare Spontini (1774–1851). In his day, he was a famed opera composer and, from 1820 to 1842, general music director of the Royal Opera in Berlin. See Wilhelm Pfannkuch, "Spontini," *MGG*, vol. 12, cols. 1078–1090.—KH/TA

[19] Wilhelmine Schröder (1804–1860) had sung Leonore in the Viennese revival of *Fidelio* on November 3, 1822. She sang the role in Dresden from April 29, 1823, and in Berlin from July 22, 1823. See Heft 43, Blätter 41v–42r.—TA

HENNING: In *Fidelio*, in spite of all discussion, she also omitted half of your beautiful aria. She began at the reentry of the theme.[20] She cannot be convinced that she is hurting herself the most in the eyes of the musical connoisseur. //

Insurance Society with Royal Protection.[21] //

SCHUPPANZIGH: But the operas from the Royal Theater will not be given [at the new Königstädtisches Theater].[22] [//]

[Blatt 7v]

HENNING: Romantic operas and, generally, any opera containing a comic element. //

SCHUPPANZIGH: It is very warm in his [= your] room; I think it is heated too much. //

HENNING: Bethmann is a very charming man, who cannot possibly deny himself the joy of making your personal acquaintance. [//]

[End of Schuppanzigh and Henning's visit to Beethoven.]

[Break in continuity of subject:]

* * * * *

[Blatt 8r—light blue paper]
[Blätter 8 and 9 on light blue paper; most possibly written after Karl's entries on Blätter 32r–32v.]

---

[20] In Leonore's recitative and aria "Abscheulicher! … Komm Hoffnung," at the Allegro con brio, the horn fanfares and the text "Ich folg' dem innern Triebe" occur twice, once on p. 120 and again on p. 123 of the Breitkopf und Härtel *Gesamtausgabe*, Series 20, No. 106. Presumably, Schröder made a cut from "die Liebe wird's erreichen" at the end of the Adagio (p. 120) to the second statement of "Ich folg'" (p. 123).—TA

[21] Possibly Berlin's counterpart of Vienna's *Tonkünstler-Societät* (Society for the Protection of Widows and Orphans of Musicians), established under Imperial sponsorship in 1771.—TA

[22] Königstadt (called Königsstadt until 1873) was a near northeastern suburb of Berlin, located beyond the Königstor. The new "Theater in der Königstadt," facing the Alexanderplatz, was a privately financed and directed theater, modeled after the Boulevard Theatre in Paris and the Theater an der Wien in Vienna, and was to be devoted almost entirely to singspiels, farces, melodramas, comedies, and pantomimes. Operas and tragedies were expressly prohibited. Therefore, it would function more like Vienna's Theater in der Leopoldstadt or Theater in der Josephstadt than any of the Court-sponsored theaters.

By the time the theater opened on August 4, 1824, its directorship had been transferred to Karl Friedrich Carl, where it remained until his death in 1845. The building was turned to different purposes in 1851 and was torn down in 1932. See Thomas Ludewig, *Berlin: Geschichte einer deutschen Metropole* (Munich: C. Bertelsmann Verlag, 1986), pp. 48, 113–115, and 246.—TA

BEETHOVEN [presumably at his apartment; ca. Tuesday, November 18, but no later than Thursday, November 20]:
+ Pencil;[23] bookbinder.
+ Gray curtain. //

NEPHEW KARL [at Beethoven's apartment; probably Thursday, November 20, bringing some copying work and possibly the previous Saturday's *Theater-Zeitung*;[24] probably just before midday dinner, ca. 2 p.m.]:
This has been sent by Rampl's wife.[25] //
Today, old Weinmüller performs for the last time at the close of a 40-year career. // As Leporello.[26] //
Saturday evening [November 22], Moscheles is giving a concert.[27] // The curiosity [of the public] helps for a good income. [//] [Blatt 8v—light blue paper]

---

[23] The pencil was still on Beethoven's shopping list in Heft 46, Blatt 22r (Monday, November 24, 1823).—TA

[24] This means that certain entries in the first half of Heft 45 need to be inserted chronologically into the second half. These entries might fit chronologically after Karl's entries on Blatt 32v.—TA

[25] Rampl's older wife, Anna Ettmann (1768–1826). Copyist Wenzel Rampl (1783–1851) was working on subscription copies of the *Missa solemnis*. See also Blatt 4r above for what may have been a similar errand.—KH/TA

[26] Carl Friedrich Clemens Weinmüller (1764–1828), Court chamber singer in the Kärntnertor Theater, made his farewell appearance as Leporello in Mozart's *Don Giovanni* (Don Juan) on Friday, November 21, 1823. See *Wiener AmZ* 7, No. 93 (November 19, 1823), col. 744; Frimmel, *Handbuch*, II, p. 411.

The customary large theater *Zettel* [poster] for Thursday, November 20, advertised that evening's performances but in addition announced that there would be a performance of *Don Giovanni* for the benefit of "Herr Karl Weinmiller," the next day, as well as an *Akademie* (concert) by Herr Moscheles before a ballet on Saturday, November 22.

In addition, there was also a smaller, vertical poster advertising Mozart's *Don Giovanni* alone, noting that it was for the benefit of "Weinmiller," on the occasion of the 40th anniversary of his theatrical career and noting "bey seinem bevorstehenden nahen Austritte aus diesem k.k. Hoftheater," which implied a last performance. Courtesy librarian Othmar Barnert, Bibliothek, Österreichisches Theatermuseum, Vienna.

Thus, Karl probably saw these two posters on Thursday, November 20, misread the *Don Giovanni* performance as "today," but got the date of Moscheles's concert correctly and termed it "Saturday," instead of "tomorrow."—KH/TA

[27] Ignaz Moscheles (1794–1870), Prague-born pianist and composer, who came to Vienna in 1808 and studied with Salieri, toured widely between 1815 and 1825. He gave his first Viennese concert of this visit at the Kärntnertor Theater on Saturday, November 22, 1823. The program (the first half of the evening) consisted of the first movement of Beethoven's Symphony No. 2 in D; Moscheles's Piano Concerto in E major, Op. 64; and a fantasy on a motive from Rossini's opera *Die diebische Elster* (*La gazza ladra*) and the Hunters' Chorus from Weber's *Euryanthe*; as well as an Italian aria sung by Caroline Unger. A brief advertisement for Moscheles's first concert appeared just under the note for Weinmüller's in the *Wiener AmZ* 7, No. 93 (November 19, 1823), col. 744.

His second Viennese concert took place there on Saturday, November 29, 1823, with the following program: Cherubini, Overture to *Lodoiska*; Moscheles, Piano Concerto in G minor, Op. 60; Variations on "Au Claire de la lune"; and a Fantasia on Themes by Mozart and Beethoven. In between were vocal works sung by Henriette Sontag, Anton Haitzinger, and Joseph Seipelt.

She is still cutting up the rabbit with the side sides. // I've had an egg made for myself. // Excuses. [//]

BEETHOVEN [at a coffee house; possibly Thursday, November 20, late afternoon, probably reading the *Intelligenzblatt*; accompanied by Karl]:
+ The late Mößle's widow, on the Graben, No. 1144.[28] //

NEPHEW KARL: You have only paid 1 fl. C.M. [//]

[Blatt 9r—light blue paper]

WILDFEYER [encountering Beethoven and Karl at the coffee house; possibly Thursday, November 20, late afternoon]:[29] I had sprained my foot and was at home for 9 days.[30] //

His third concert, on December 15, had to be repeated on December 17 and consisted of Beethoven, [*Namensfeier*] Overture in C, Op. 115; Moscheles, Piano Concerto in E-flat, Op. 56; Variations on the "Alexander March"; and a Fantasia on Haydn's "Gott erhalte Franz den Kaiser" on the Broadwood piano lent to him by Beethoven. In between were vocal works sung by Theresia Grünbaum, Henriette Sontag, and Anton Haitzinger; and Joseph Mayseder (the theater's "solo violinist") played a solo.

Beethoven was kindly, even generously, disposed toward Moscheles; Czerny (see Heft 39, Blatt 13r) and nephew Karl (here) are relatively neutral about him; but Schuppanzigh (Heft 46, Blatt 34v) seemingly disliked him. In 1840, while living in London, Moscheles would translate the first edition of Schindler's biography; he would publish it with his own name alone on the title page in 1841. Schindler, in turn, reacted to the plagiarism in the third edition of the *Biographie* in 1860.

See *Wiener AmZ* 7, No. 97 (December 3, 1823), cols. 772–774; No. 100 (December 13, 1823), cols. 793–795; and No. 104 (December 27, 1823), cols. 829–830.—KH/TA

[28] Johann Georg (*Edler*) von Mösle's widow, Elisabeth von Mösle, book dealer, lived on the Graben No. 1144. She specialized in publishing collections of laws and legal writings. The shop's two most recent advertisements had been for a 15-volume collection of *Volkspredigten und Homilien* (Popular Sermons and Homilies), also advertised, on a different day, by Mayer in the *Deutsches Haus*; see the *Intelligenzblatt*, No. 264 (November 17, 1823), p. 1037; and No. 267 (November 20, 1823), p. 1063. Beethoven must not have been interested in these particular books but may simply have reminded himself to visit that shop.

Mösle's next advertisement, No. 268 (November 21, 1823), p. 1074, featured ten miscellaneous practical books, including J.C. Adelung's *Kleines Wörterbuch* of the German language. See also Böckh, 1822, p. 400; Redl, p. 74.—KH/TA

[29] Wilhelm Wildfeyer/Wildfeuer (b. 1783), who, in 1820, was tutor to the three sons and two daughters of Count Franz Xaver Kollowrat (1783–1855), who lived in a large apartment at Dorotheergasse 1116 [numbering of 1821]. See Heft 7, Blatt 19v, for fuller information. Wildfeyer seems to have been friendly with the Bernard-Peters-Janschikh circle, from which Beethoven distanced himself after ca. March 1820.

Wildfeyer writes again on Blätter 9r and 9v, and Karl mentions him again on Blatt 25r below. He is someone whom Beethoven might have encountered irregularly on his errands; but not recently, because of Wildfeyer's sprained foot. He mentions Tomaschek, and, himself, seems to play the guitar.—TA

[30] If this was Wildfeyer, who presumably lived with his employers, the Kollowrat family, in the Dorotheergasse, and if he were recovering from a sprain, it is much more likely that he encountered Beethoven in the City, near the Dorotheergasse, rather than in suburban Landstrasse.—TA

NEPHEW KARL [**seemingly writing for Wildfeyer**]: What's the name of the poet of the song *An die ferne Geliebte*?[31] // He [Jeitteles] was supposed to have become the physician to Count Kolowrat,[32] but because he was a *Jew*, was not accepted.[33] //

WILDFEYER: Tomaschek.[34] //

NEPHEW KARL [**seemingly writing for Wildfeyer**]: Herr W[ildfeyer] has heard Tomaschek. [//] [Blatt 9v—light blue paper] A considerable theoretician. //
Have you written something for the guitar? [//]

WILDFEYER: A French scholar said: The nobleman thinks finer because he eats a great number of partridges.[35] //
[**Wildfeyer departs.**]

NEPHEW KARL: These letters are just as little lost as *I* am. *He has them*, I'd swear to that.[36] [//]
[presumably the end of entries on light blue paper; possibly Thursday, November 20.]

[Break in continuity of the subject. N.B. The reference on Blatt 10r seems to be *after* Blätter 31–32:]

[Blatt 10r]

---

[31] Alois Jeitteles (b. Brünn/Brno, Moravia, 1794; d. Brünn, 1858) was a physician with a strong literary-poetic bent. Beethoven composed the song cycle, Op. 98, in 1816. Johann Schickh had often published poems by members of the Jewish Jeitteles family in his *Wiener Zeitschrift*, much to the annoyance of one-time partner Joseph Carl Bernard. After his medical studies in Vienna, Alois had returned to Brünn in 1819, so the origins of this smug story might have been several years old by November 1823.—KH/TA

[32] Presumably a member of the noble family of Kolowrat (or Kollowrat), one of the oldest lines of nobility in Austria. See Wurzbach, vol. 12, p. 371. Karl spells the name phonetically as *Collobrad*.—KH/TA

[33] Joseph Carl Bernard was an avowed anti-Semite, and the members of his circle might have been, as well. Beethoven now kept them at some distance. This entry might have been Karl's reminder to the composer that he did not want to extend the conversation with Wildfeyer for very long.—TA

[34] Johann Wenzel (Jan Václav) Tomaschek (Tomášek), 1774–1850, Prague-based organist, pianist, and composer; teacher of Jan Václav (Johann Hugo) Voříšek. He visited Vienna in 1801 (meeting Haydn) and 1814 (meeting Beethoven). See Frimmel, *Handbuch*, II, pp. 325–327.—KH/TA

[35] See Karl's mention of partridges during a shopping trip on Blatt 19r below.—TA

[36] Karl may be referring to Beethoven's correspondence, lost in the move from Baden back to Vienna, late October/early November 1822, and possibly implying some treachery on the part of brother Johann.—TA

NEPHEW KARL [**possibly late afternoon, Thursday, November 20 (Blatt 37r), after getting the *Theater-Zeitung***]:[37]

The *Pythagoreans*[38] may not eat any beans; in general, few vegetables. //

We must go, because a few drops are beginning to fall—a heavy rain could easily take us by surprise.[39] //

3 fl. 36 [kr.][40] //

The author [Sporschil] knew very well who was "commissioned with bringing in the *Geräthschaften* [implements]."[41] // One may complain in that way. // Where does it come out?[42] [//] [Blatt 10v]

<That would have ….>

[illegible word] *humanum*. [//]

You didn't shave yourself very well.[43] //

It is natural that she is crying because she feared losing her servant's job, because she

---

[37] This group of entries was probably written between Tuesday, November 18, when Karl learned of the *Theater-Zeitung*'s article about Beethoven (Blatt 32r) and Thursday, November 20 (Blatt 37r), when Beethoven noted a razor on his shopping list.—TA

[38] Pythagoreans, an extinct sect founded by Pythagoras (ca. 580–500 B.C.) in southern Italy. It assumed a politically conservative attitude, was active scientifically and mathematically, and was characterized by peculiar clothing and eating habits (often based on old taboos).—KH

[39] The weather of Monday, November 17, had been clear, but Karl's description could be consistent with Tuesday, November 18: clear at 8 a.m., overcast at 3 p.m., and cloudy at 10 p.m. Wednesday, November 19, was clear. After a foggy day, Vienna experienced rain and heavy wind by 10 p.m. on Thursday, November 20 (therefore even more consistent with Karl's comment). By 8 a.m. on Friday, November 21, the winds were "stormy," and the skies were overcast. At 3 p.m. (nearer another time when this entry may have been made), it was still cloudy with heavy winds. By 10 p.m. on Friday, however, the winds had moderated and the skies were clear. See the *Wiener Zeitung*, No. 267 (November 20, 1823), p. 1079; No. 268 (November 21, 1823), p. 1083; No. 269 (November 22, 1823), p. 1090; and No. 270 (November 24, 1823), p. 1093.—TA

[40] The amount of the bill at the coffee house or restaurant.—TA

[41] This remark is a reference to (but not an exact quote from) the essay about Beethoven that appeared in Bäuerle's *Allgemeine Theater-Zeitung* 16, No. 137 (November 15, 1823), p. 548, which says: "It was very painful for him that, last year [1822], when moving from the country into the city—perhaps through carelessness or perhaps through the treachery of those commissioned with the transfer of his effects (because this man, who is occupied with his art, is frequently cheated)—all of his correspondence was lost." The person who arranged Beethoven's move (ca. October 31/November 1, 1822) was his brother Johann. See Theodore Albrecht, "Anton Schindler as Destroyer and Forger of Beethoven's Conversation Books: A Case for Decriminalization," in *Music's Intellectual History*, ed. Zdravko Blažeković and Barbara Dobbs Mackenzie (New York: RILM, 2009), pp. 175–176; and Blätter 31v–32r below.—KH/TA

[42] The aforementioned article was by journalist Johann Chrysostomus Sporschil but signed only as "S …… l." Beethoven did not yet seem to know who the author was. Vienna's *Allgemeine Theater-Zeitung* gave the source for the article as the *Morgenblatt* of November 5, 1823. That journal appeared in Stuttgart, but its Viennese correspondent was Beethoven's friend Friedrich Wähner.—TA

[43] Beethoven placed a razor on his shopping list on Blatt 37r (probably Thursday, November 20).—TA

doesn't want to exchange with that of the countess.⁴⁴ // She only wrote that because she believed that it would make an impression on you (I believe so, too), if she said that you had taken her out of the countess's service and into your own, and already wanted to send her away. [//] [Blatt 11r] It was obviously her wish, but it is natural that she prefers service at the countess's, all the more so now, when there is a profusion of so-called *facierenden* (unemployed) people, and it is therefore difficult to get work. // Before the new year, *every woman* seeks to keep her place, and takes *all* pains to please her employers; she would certainly not get any work now. [//] [Blatt 11v] That was a devilish attempt by the old woman [former housekeeper Barbara Holzmann], though, to provoke the maid. // Envious. //

Am I to buy the *Psychologie* by Feder?⁴⁵ [//] Otherwise, *another* [person] will take it, because there is only one of everything at the used-book dealer's. [//]

BEETHOVEN:
+ Wine spirits,   1 fl. 36 kr. per measure
                   48 kr. per ½ measure
                   48⁴⁶

SCHINDLER IMPERSONATING NEPHEW KARL [falsified entry at the bottom of the page→]: Schindler knows and can say more about that than I can.⁴⁷ [←falsified entry ends] [//]

* * * * *

[Blatt 12r] **[Possible break in chronology here.]**

NEPHEW KARL: The woman *also* ate, took the *whole* poor rabbit, since the h[ouse-keeper]⁴⁸ doesn't eat rabbit, and wants 30 kr. more. // Does she do it? //

---

⁴⁴ A domestic servant, formerly in the employ of Countess Morzin; she had interviewed with Beethoven on ca. September 23 but presumably came to work for him only in mid-October. See Heft 43, Blatt 23r, and Heft 46, Blätter 21v–22r.—KH/TA

⁴⁵ Johann Georg H. Feder (1740–1821) wrote, among others, books about human will and natural law, practical philosophy, and the fundamentals of logic and metaphysics, many published in several editions in Göttingen in the 1780s and 1790s. See Kayser, II, pp. 195–196, and Blätter 14v and 29r below.—KH/TA

⁴⁶ In reverse, Beethoven adds 48 + 48 (= 96 kr. or 1 fl. 36 kr.) to reassure himself that the price per unit is the same.—TA

⁴⁷ Schindler's self-serving attempt to write as if he were Karl at this point (among a series of authentic entries by the nephew) might be viewed as malicious but is really just a pitiful act.
In fact, Beethoven had probably not associated with Schindler since ca. August 7, 1823 (see Heft 38, Blatt 39r). Karl encountered Schindler at the Gesellschaft der Musikfreunde's concert of November 16 (Blatt 29v below), but Schindler himself does not resume authentic entries until Heft 46, Blatt 2r (ca. November 21, 1823).—TA

⁴⁸ Barbara Holzmann.—TA

HEFT 45 (CA. NOVEMBER 4 – CA. NOVEMBER 20, 1823), BLATT 12V

BEETHOVEN: + Karl's certificate.
By Shakespeare. //

NEPHEW KARL: Are you eating at home tomorrow? [//] 33 kr. // *Effectus philosophiae* [The Effect of Philosophy]. [//]

[written vertically→] The people *live* this way. Everyone helps to the best of his ability; just as *these people*, for example. [←written vertically]

[Blatt 12v]

BEETHOVEN [**reading the *Intelligenzblatt* of Tuesday, November 11; probably late afternoon or early evening of that day**]:
+ Stoneware crockery;[49] Cöllnerhofgasse No. 739. Dinner service for 6 persons.

White	20 fl. W.W.	With blue rim	24 fl.
With serving dishes	10		12 <W.W.>
With coffee service	4		5
	34		41

[on the same page:]
Punch, cold and warm;[50] Josephstadt, Glacis No. 40; warehouse on the Franziskanerplatz No. 912. 24 per measure; the half, and so on, proportionately. Viennese punch essence: 1 fl. 24 kr. C.M. per half measure. [//] [Blatt 13r]

[his own reminder:]
+ Diploma.[51] //

[**back to the *Intelligenzblatt* of Tuesday, November 11, six pages later, looking at an advertisement for Schiller's collected works:**]
2nd, most complete pocket edition by the Tanzer Brothers, in <XXX> 30 volumes, the most complete of all editions; unaltered, etc. Subscription: stock paper [for] 5 fl. C.M.; vellum paper [for] 10 fl. C.M., in 4 quarterly installments, which will be

---

[49] *Intelligenzblatt*, No. 260 (November 11, 1823), p. 995 (Advertisements). This concerns the shop of Joseph Winkler, Cöllnerhofgasse No. 739. The narrow block-long street runs between Lugeck and Alter Fleischmarkt; No. 739 was on the south side. Beethoven and Karl considered the costs of a *different* dinner service in their computations on Blatt 42v below.—KH/TA

[50] *Intelligenzblatt*, No. 260 (November 11, 1823), p. 995 (Advertisements). Josephstadt, Glacis No. 40 was on the northern corner with Kaiserstrasse (today's Josephstädter Strasse). That section of the Glacis is now Lenaugasse. Franziskanerplatz No. 912 faced the Platz and extended to Singerstrasse to the east; Camillo Bellonci, a hornist at the Kärntnertor Theater, had lived in that building until recently.—KH/TA

[51] Possibly the diploma from the Royal Swedish Music Academy, Stockholm, dated December 28, 1822, and sent to Beethoven on January 31, 1823. See Albrecht, *Letters to Beethoven*, Nos. 301 and 306. Beethoven needed Austrian permission to accept such a foreign honor.—TA

available, complete, in 1824. One subscribes at Mayer and Comp[any], Singerstrasse, Deutsches Haus.[52] [//] [Blatt 13v]

Louise Brachmann, best German woman poet.[53] [//]

NEPHEW KARL [**possibly referring to the vellum-paper edition of Schiller, noted above**]: 10 fl. C.M., I think.[54] //

With beer and bread, midday dinner costs 33 kr.[55] //

She [the maid] lay in bed; that was *at 5:30*. I believed that she was sick, but she said that she [just] lay *in this way*. // Just in general. // But I just wasn't pleased with her because she spoke very arrogantly and, moreover, had bared her whole chest without covering herself; but on the contrary she displayed it even more.[56] [//]

[Break in continuity, chronology, and color of paper:]

---

[52] *Intelligenzblatt*, No. 260 (November 11, 1823), p. 1001: "Jacob Mayer and Comp.; Singerstrasse, Deutsches Haus: News of the reprint of Schiller's *Sämtliche Werke* [Collected Works]. Second, most complete, very beautiful pocket edition by the Tanzer Brothers, in XXX volumes … which is the most complete of all editions appearing up to now, in that it contains everything unaltered, that came from the hand of this immortal poet. Subscription prices:

"Stock paper edition … 5 fl. C.M. (12 fl. 30 kr. W.W.)

"Vellum paper edition … 10 fl. C.M. (25 fl. __ kr. W.W.)

"All thirty small volumes … will be available, complete, in four quarterly installments in 1824. Through the bookstore of Jacob Mayer and Comp., Singerstrasse, Deutsches Haus."

Beethoven still seems intent on purchasing a complete works of Schiller for Karl or for himself, especially as he is presently composing the Ninth Symphony, whose Finale will use Schiller's *An die Freude*.

For Jacob Mayer, see Böckh, 1822, p. 400; Redl, p. 24. Mayer's shop was only a few doors north of (and across Singerstrasse) from the location of Beethoven's potential source for punch. The *Deutsches Haus* (House of the Teutonic Order) has a bookshop at this location even today.—KH/TA

[53] The original German reads: "Beste deutsche Dichterin." Louise Brachmann, a lyric poet and novelist, was born in Rochlitz, Saxony, in 1777. Her father was a civil servant and her mother the daughter of a clergyman. Her mother was also a friend of the Hardenberg family, including the poet Novalis, who, in turn, introduced the fledgling writer Louise to Friedrich von Schiller. Schiller published her writings in his various journals, but in 1800, suffering from depression, she attempted suicide. She continued writing in the sentimental style popular at the time, but on September 17, 1822, jumped into the Saale River in Halle and drowned herself. See *Allgemeine Deutsche Biographie*, vol. 47, pp. 157–159.

There are no mentions of Brachmann in Viennese newspapers in November 1823, so Beethoven's jotting the foregoing advertisement for Schiller's works may have conjured up her name by free association. It is also possible that, because the chronology of this Heft is so uncertain, Beethoven may have seen a volume of Brachmann's works while visiting Mayer's bookshop.—TA

[54] This figure could reflect the price of the Schiller edition on Blatt 13r above, or it could represent the slightly discounted rate of a contract for 20 dinners at 33 kr. at the boardinghouse, immediately below.—TA

[55] Probably the cost of an individual dinner at Born and Paumgarten's boardinghouse in the *Rother Igel*, between Tuchlauben and Wildpretmarkt, where Karl probably ate on days when university classes prevented his coming to Beethoven's apartment. See also Blatt 19r below.—TA

[56] Karl, very restrained for age 17, makes a similar complaint about the maid in Heft 46, Blatt 8v (ca. Friday, November 21, 1823).—TA

HEFT 45 (CA. NOVEMBER 4 – CA. NOVEMBER 20, 1823), BLATT 14R

[Blatt 14r—light blue paper]

[Blätter 14 and 15 have light blue paper; Blatt 14 is bound in differently.]

She [presumably a housekeeper applicant] would be satisfied. // Concerning the housekeeping, she said: At the beginning of every month, the *gentleman* who might wish to employ her must give her a sum with which she would maintain the housekeeping for the entire month. // I said that the arrangement is *different* at this gentleman's. [//] Has she calculated the money? //

One must send the money to the Dr. [presumably lawyer Bach]; otherwise he'll believe that one [might] want him to withdraw it. [//] [Blatt 14v—light blue paper, upside down]

[discussing his current university curriculum:]
Merely the propaedeutic [introductory material]. // Preparation for philosophy. // In the whole *first* year, there is still *absolutely no* philosophy. *Psychology* in the first semester; *logic* in the second.[57] // He has also written a *Psychologie* that we shall probably have to read.[58] // Latin. // [Blatt 15r—light blue paper] *That* is merely the "business" of *logic*, as he said. //

BEETHOVEN **[making a shopping and to-do list; possibly Wednesday, November 12, or Thursday, November 13]**:
+ Nails.
+ Blotting paper.
+ Sugar.
differ. [?]
Small machine [device] for the iron coffee machine.[59]

[Blatt 15v—light blue paper]

UNKNOWN ARTISAN[60] **[possibly at Karl Joseph Rospini's optical shop on the north side of Stephansplatz]**: I cannot make any use of it and also cannot repair it. [//] If he will take it, then the barometer maker in the Wallnerstrasse [Franz Rospini][61] could do it. Perhaps he will exchange with you for another one. [//]

---

[57] As late as the 1960s, some American universities laid the basis for their philosophy requirements with general psychology and logic.—TA

[58] Possibly the textbook by Johann Georg H. Feder (1740–1821); see Blatt 11v above.—TA

[59] The next entry may find Beethoven shopping for such a device.—TA

[60] This artisan writes phonetically but intelligently.—TA

[61] Franz Rospino [*sic*], a "maker of mathematical, optical, and scientific instruments," Wallnerstrasse No. 262 (east side of the street, two buildings north of the Esterházy palace). See Böckh, 1822, p. 417. Both Böckh and this artisan spell Wallnerstrasse as "Wallerstrasse"; contemporary estate and census records give the family name (probably correctly) as "Rospini."

NEPHEW KARL [written vertically→] *Seidl*, 24 kr.[62] [←written vertically]
[End of entries on light blue paper.]

[Break in continuity of subject:]

[Blatt 16r]

[Seemingly Thursday, November 13:]
Today [the lecture] was about the viscous humidity in the nose (*psychology*). //
It should not, indeed *can* not be all there is; there must be annotations about the prescribed textbook. // Likawetz, *Elementa philos*[*ophiae*].[63] //
Sunday, I shall also have to go to confession.[64] //
It is not seldom that two [individuals or businesses] get the *same Privilegium* [license], if the second imitated the first one. //
Where I ate. [//]
In the church where he was consecrated [at death], one person cried quite loudly about this desecration, that a person who has hanged himself, a suicide, [Blatt 16v] should have as magnificent a funeral as W. had. // Because several people had been poisoned by one of the medicines that he had made. // He made the medicine for *himself*, a house porter took a bottle of it, thinking that it was wine, and gave everyone some of it. // He was said to have been so very distressed because he hoped to become chief surgeon at Court.[65] // [Blatt 17r]
Cherubini himself is said to have become foolish, because when awarding a prize, he preferred the opera of another [composer] over *his own*. // Too *much*. // He, however, he is no longer foolish. // He may already be old. // Just wait another 20 years; then you will also no longer write as quickly. [//]

[Blatt 17v]

Beethoven owned a thermometer supposedly made by Rospini; perhaps that was the device that needed repair. See Heft 12, Blatt 1v; Heft 34, Blatt 11r; and Heft 42, Blatt 5v.—KH/TA

[62] The price for a small glass or mug (ca. 9 ounces) of wine or beer.—TA

[63] Joseph Calasanz Likawetz, *Elementa philosophiae in usum auditorium philosophiae adumbrata*, 5 parts (Graz, 1818–1820). See Kayser, III, p. 556.—KH

[64] The "also" here implies that Beethoven had said something about going to confession, possibly in observance of the anniversary of the elder Carl van Beethoven's death on November 15, 1815. If this entry was written on Thursday, November 13, then the coming Sunday would be the day following the anniversary of his death.—TA

[65] A cursory survey of death notices in the *Wiener Zeitung*, extending back to ca. November 1, fails to reveal a doctor or even an apothecary who committed suicide. Similarly, a survey in the *Hof- und Staats-Schematismen*, 1821–1825, for Court apothecaries, Court physicians, and medical faculty of the university, fails to reveal any Viennese physician or apothecary whose name begins with "W" or "V" who committed suicide during this period.—TA

HEFT 45 (CA. NOVEMBER 4 – CA. NOVEMBER 20, 1823), BLATT 18R

LICHNOWSKY [**at Beethoven's apartment in the Ungargasse; possibly Thursday, November 13, or early on Friday, November 14**]:
You must ask for it back. //
I certainly don't know whether he is here, too. //
The Italian Opera is to come back in April.[66] [//] [Blatt 18r] If you don't compose the opera [Grillparzer's libretto to *Melusine*], then German opera is finished anyway—everybody is saying that. After Weber's failed opera [*Euryanthe*], many [patrons] sent the books back. // *Freischütz* is actually no opera. [//] [Blatt 18v] If you can use me for anything, *you* know how I honestly think. //
Haven't you attended the Schuppanzigh Quartet [concerts] yet?[67] [//] [Blatt 19r] I'll come again in a few days. //

NEPHEW KARL [**grocery shopping with Beethoven, probably in the walled City; afternoon of Friday, November 14**]:[68] At the *Brotsitzer*'s,[69] as they are called here; they buy bread in quantity from the baker [for resale at a profit]. // 68 [?] //
She said that she would have been able to buy partridges, but the large ones were at no other [price] than 1 fl. 54 kr., the small ones at 1 fl. 15 [kr.]; but they were as thin as birds.[70] //
At the people's place, I have already spoken about a housekeeper; they will take all possible pains [to find one].[71] I promised that we would be grateful, and so they will procure someone soon. //

---

[66] The first performance of Barbaja's Italian Opera Company, which remained longer in Vienna in 1824 than in previous years, took place on April 1, 1824, in the Kärntnertor Theater. See Bäuerle's *Allgemeine Theater-Zeitung* 17, No. 43 (April 8, 1824), p. 170.—KH

[67] Ignaz Schuppanzigh's Quartet had begun its fall series of six midday concerts on Wednesday, October 22, and continued on Fridays: October 31 and November 7, 14, 21, and 28. Each concert consisted of three chamber works (not always string quartets); all the concerts except November 7 and 14 included one work by Beethoven.
The program for Friday, November 21, consisted of a String Quartet in D by the Schuppanzigh Quartet's violist, Franz Weiss; a Trio in G [String Trio, Op. 9, No. 1] by Beethoven; and a Quartet in F [K. 590] by Mozart.
See *Wiener Allgemeine musikalische Zeitung* 7, No. 98 (December 6, 1823), cols. 783–784.—KH/TA

[68] This shopping excursion took place at some time after Schuppanzigh's noon-hour concert of Friday, November 14. The fact that there is no discussion of the event suggests that Karl (in classes) and Beethoven (home working) did not attend. These entries were almost surely made on Friday, a business day, because Saturday, November 15 (St. Leopold's Day) was a national holiday.—TA

[69] *Brotsitzer*, an intermediate dealer who bought bread from a baker at a discount and resold it for a profit. See Loritza, p. 31.—KH

[70] See Wildfeyer's mention of partridges on Blatt 9v above.—TA

[71] German original "bei den Leuten." Karl probably writes without specific names so that no one (especially the current maid, whom he does not like) might read them accidentally, and also because they are obviously still in the middle of shopping. On Blätter 33v–34r below, Karl says that he has made such a request "at the place where I eat." Karl is eating midday dinner with Beethoven three times per week (see Blätter 1r–1v above), and so he may have been eating at the boardinghouse of Baroness von

It will probably have been 1½ pounds. [//] [Blatt 19v] The wild pig[72] was 1 pound and ¼. At 48 kr. per pound, that makes exactly 1 fl. //

I believe that, in all respects, one is better off on the Kohlmarkt[73] than at the *Kamehl*.[74] // But we have already experimented and found that it was not correct in *many things*; what people do in *one place* may be expected in *all*. // For example, the fact that someone complained about the adulterated *Piccolit* [wine][75] was only a roguish trick by the waiter (certainly not by the *old man*, but instead by another) who brought a totally different bottle in which there was no *Piccolit* at all. [//] [Blatt 20r] If he had looked at the seal, he would not have been deceived. //

Wine may be far less expensive in Italy. // To Pavia; I [would like to] study there.[76] // A clergyman is also there.[77] //

[possibly at the Born and Paumgarten boardinghouse in *Zum rothen Igel*:]
The two people would be happy to come to see us.[78] //

[Blatt 20v]

BEETHOVEN **[possibly reading a flyer posted in the courtyard of *Zum rothen Igel* or nearby]**: *Joseph Hauffen*, dressmaker,[79] *Gar*[illegible]. //

Born and Frau Paumgarten in the *Rother Igel* (where Franz Oliva and Joseph Carl Bernard ate in 1820) on other days. Beethoven seems to have asked for the ladies' advice on such matters in the past. See Blatt 20r below for a projected visit from "the two people"; and confirmation that they will act on Beethoven's behalf on Blatt 24v below.—TA

[72] The discussion about the wild pig here, as well as the partridges above, suggests that Karl and Beethoven may have been shopping in the *Wildpretmarkt*, the Wild Game Market (adjoining the Kammerhof), in front of the back entrance of *Zum rothen Igel*.—TA

[73] This refers to the Grocery Shop of Ignaz Spöttl's Late Widow's Son [!] on the Kohlmarkt, *Zum grünen Fassel* [At the Little Green Barrel], No. 260; on the north side of the street, two buildings west of Wallnerstrasse. See Groner, 1922, p. 102; Redl, p. 39.—KH/TA

[74] The grocery and wine shop *Zum schwarzen Kameel* [At the Black Camel], Bognergasse No. 312, dating back to the 1600s and owned, since 1818, by Joseph Stiebitz, Joseph Söhnel, and Ignaz Arlet. Associated with the store was a wine restaurant that Beethoven frequented; it survives today as a fashionable café and catering service. See Frimmel, *Handbuch*, I, pp. 160 and 245–247; Groner, 1922, p. 210.—KH/TA

[75] *Piccoléto* or *Piccolét*, Italian wine from Friuli and the province of Gorizia, ca. 40 miles northwest of Trieste.—KH/TA

[76] The University of Pavia (Lombardy) was founded in 1361.—TA

[77] Karl would have needed a priest who knew him to write a brief testimonial that he was "alive" in order to collect his pension based on his late father's civil service.—TA

[78] German original "Die beiden Leute." "The two people," mentioned in circumlocution, may be potential candidates for the housekeeper's position, referred by Baroness von Born and Frau Paumgarten; see Blatt 19r above and Blatt 24v below.—TA

[79] A *Kleidermacher* (dressmaker) by the name of Joseph Hauffen cannot be traced, but one Joseph Hauffe (b. 1801), a journeyman tailor from the Salzburg region, lived in the City, Landskrongasse No. 547 (apartment no. 5), with the municipal master tailor Anton Fischer. The location was just around the

NEPHEW KARL [presumably stopping in a coffee house[80] with Beethoven, during their shopping errands; mid-to-late afternoon of Friday, November 14]: To give you an idea of what kind of men are among the gentlemen in philosophy, I can, for example, tell you that one man, *thinking* that he had an *overcoat*—although he presumably had none—considered another one to be *his*, and left with it. The perpetrator is still being sought. // The overcoat, which hung at the entrance to the [lecture] hall, is gone. Therefore, only a student could have taken it.[81] That is very difficult. [//] [Blatt 21r]

Where is Meyer's [*sic*] bookshop?[82] //

[He] is no relation to me. [//]

[Karl may have left for Mayer's bookshop.]

BEETHOVEN [presumably left alone in the coffee house, reading the current *Intelligenzblatt*; the afternoon of Friday, November 14]:

Viennese water:[83] whoever buys 6 in a small crate pays 5 fl. 30 kr. W.W.; to be had at Wieshofer's, Singerstrasse No. 898.

Pfann's Spa[84] with curative and drinking waters in Untermeidling may now be used even in winter (with suitable warmth), because it is heated, etc., as well as a

---

corner from the rear entrance (Kammerhof No. 550) to *Zum rothen Igel* and the Born and Paumgarten boardinghouse. See Conscriptions-Bogen, Stadt, No. 547 (Wiener Stadt- und Landesarchiv); Guetjahr, p. 26.

In Heft 47, Blatt 13r (ca. December 1, 1823), Beethoven jotted the word *Kleider* (dress) into his list of errands, possibly a repeat reference to Hauffe. Many employers of domestic help in Vienna provided a standard dress or apron for their staff. Perhaps Beethoven had this in mind. See Wolfgang Kos, ed., *Wiener Typen: Klischees und Wirklichkeit*, exhibit catalogue (Vienna: Wien Museum and Christian Brandstätter Verlag, 2013), pp. 155–156, 191, and 204.—KH/TA

[80] See Karl's note concerning an Imperial proscription against students' assembling in coffee houses on Blatt 22v below.—TA

[81] On ca. November 30, after a scuffle in a history class at the university, Karl noted to Beethoven that the vice-director of the Faculty of Philosophy would also be investigating the theft of overcoats, hats, and books. See Heft 46, Blätter 9v–10r.—TA

[82] Karl may have been interested in the collected works of Schiller, available through subscription at Mayer's bookshop in the *Deutsches Haus* in the Singerstrasse, one block west of the Stephansdom. See Blatt 13r above. Schiller was a relatively frequent topic of conversation; see, for instance, Heft 44, Blatt 2r.—TA

[83] *Intelligenzblatt*, No. 263 (November 14, 1823), p. 1021 (Advertisements). See Heft 38, Blatt 37r (August 1823), when the advertisement ran every Saturday. In November, it ran on Saturday the 8th and Saturday the 22nd but appeared here on Friday the 14th, because there was no issue on Saturday, November 15, as it was St. Leopold's Day, a holiday, the name day of the most recently deceased monarch.—KH/TA

[84] *Intelligenzblatt*, No. 263 (November 14, 1823), p. 1022 (Advertisements); Groner, 1922, pp. 304 and 356. Laimgrube No. 97 was at the corner of Kanalgasse and Kothgasse, several blocks farther west from Beethoven's former residence in the Windmühle suburb; see Behsel, p. 140.

On ca. November 25, Lichnowsky, formerly an advocate for Beethoven's use of Pfann's spa, now warned the composer that it caused coughing (see Heft 46, Blatt 29v).—KH/TA

boardinghouse, also the baths, [waters taken] to the City. [Blatt 21v] Reservation for a bath, Kothgasse, No. 97; a bath costs 1 fl. 15 kr. C.M. [//]

+ Pay the physician.[85] [//]

NEPHEW KARL [writing vertically on the page, presumably later, computing the cost of swimming in Joseph Pfann's heated pool for himself and Beethoven]:
1 fl. 15 [kr.]
1 fl. 15
$\underline{42}$
3 fl. 12

[Blatt 22r]

BEETHOVEN [continuing to read the *Intelligenzblatt* on November 14]:
Chemical lighters and matches,[86] across from the Kärntnertor Theater (at the New Kärntner Gate). //

+ Candles, soap, etc., Wipplingerstrasse, No. 386.[87] //

[single item, from another source:]
Gerold's Book Shop, Stephansplatz, No. 625: + *Multiplication in Its Most Complete Form*, etc., octavo, 1 fl. C.M.[88] //

[Blatt 22v]

---

[85] Possibly the physician who examined the maid on ca. November 1, 1823; see Heft 44, Blätter 5v and 19r–19v.—TA

[86] *Intelligenzblatt*, No. 263 (November 14, 1823), p. 1023 (Advertisements). In 1808, to accommodate increasing traffic, a second Kärntnertor (the New Carinthian Gate) was opened through the city walls, about even with the front entrance of the Kärntnertor Theater. Several small buildings existed along the bastion's base at that point. See Groner, 1922, p. 221.—KH/TA

[87] Excerpt from an advertisement in the *Intelligenzblatt*, No. 263 (November 14, 1823), p. 1025 (Advertisements). "Candles, Soap, and Tallow Products. In the tallow-melting establishment of the undersigned, *unter den Weissgärbern* No. 3, one can obtain all types of poured and ordinary candles, soap, and molded-tallow products of excellent quality and at reasonable prices. In the City, these products may be had at Herr Johann Mayer's, Wipplingerstrasse No. 386, and in the Tobacco and Lottery Shop, Roten Turmstrasse in the large Weighing House, No. 641. [signed:] Salomon Preisach, Leopoldstadt, Grosse Fuhrmannsgasse, No. 478."

Beethoven will copy more extensive excerpts from Preisach's advertisement on Blätter 30v–31r below; see also Blatt 37r below. Candles will still be on his shopping list in Heft 46, Blatt 22r (Monday, November 24).—KH/TA

[88] Carl Gerold, book publisher and dealer, Stephansplatz, No. 625. The textbook in question was *Multiplication in ihrer vollkommensten Gestalt, oder Beschreibung einer neuerfundenen, einfachen und untrüglichen Rechnen-Maschine für die Multiplication* (Dresden, 1823). It does not appear in any of Gerold's contemporary advertisements in the *Intelligenzblatt*. Its abbreviated title was copied accurately, either by Beethoven glancing at another newspaper, or by Karl, jotted at Gerold's during his errands, and then recopied by Beethoven into this conversation book. See Kayser, IV, p. 178; Redl, 1823, p. 73.—KH/TA

NEPHEW KARL [rejoining Beethoven at the coffee house; later in the afternoon of Friday, November 14]: He didn't want anything to do with the advance payment, because it was inconvenient for them; otherwise, it doesn't make any difference at all whether a buyer comes, because they do not make the tallow themselves, but instead only lease the space to the producer.[89] //

Now I am no longer going anywhere before real lectures. In general, as a student, according to Imperial decrees, I may no longer go into any coffee house, but no one will inquire about it, especially if I go with *you*, and therefore would immediately have a defense. //

The music paper is not *soft* enough for this use; therefore already protected from itself. [//] [Blatt 23r]

I absolutely did not know that you wanted that, especially since they already said at the Prussian legation that it was not at all necessary. //

From Vöcklabruck in Upper Austria.[90] // Her parents. [//]

BEETHOVEN [continuing to read the *Intelligenzblatt* on Friday, November 14]:
+ The toilet that removes all odor.[91]
+ The prevention of smoke and the danger of fire connected with it.
+ To dry out wet walls; to coat the whole building, etc., without odor, by Jos[eph] Bened[ict] Withalm, proprietor of the varnish factory, Graz in Steyermark. [//]

[Presumably the end of entries for Friday, November 14.]

* * * * *

[Reverse chronology (positing Blätter 29r–30r as Sunday, November 16) begins here:]

[Blatt 23v]

KIRCHHOFFER[92] [probably at Beethoven's apartment; probably St. Leopold's Day, Saturday, November 15, with nephew Karl present]: He [Ferdinand Ries] sent me 4 harps, with which I will have had much vexation; because they cost a high tariff, I had to lay out the money and could not sell them.[93] //

---

[89] This seems to be about the advertisement for "Candles, Soap, and Tallow Products" that Beethoven had partially jotted two entries earlier.—TA
[90] Vöcklabruck, Upper Austria, about halfway between Linz and Salzburg.—KH
[91] Three advertisements in the *Intelligenzblatt*, No. 263 (November 14, 1823), p. 1023 (Advertisements).—KH
[92] Franz Christian Kirchhoffer (1785–1842), cashier and bookkeeper with the firm of Hofmann and Goldstein in Vienna, advised Beethoven in financial matters and acted as intermediary in sending letters, money, and packages to Ferdinand Ries in London. For the identification of him as the writer of these entries, as well as those on Blätter 26v–28v below, see Heft 34, Blatt 8v.—TA
[93] These may have been harps made by Johann Andreas Stumpff (1769–1846), mentioned by Moscheles in Heft 47, Blatt 29r.—TA

Have you looked through his two concertos? The last movements are worked out in a fairly frivolous way, and [I] have scolded him on that account. [//] [Blatt 24r] Moscheles is going to London next month. Hasn't he been to see you. //
Aren't you giving an *Akademie*?—and when?[94]
Are you writing an opera or oratorio?[95] //
Weber was unlucky with his opera [*Euryanthe*]. //

NEPHEW KARL [**Saturday, November 15; initially writing on Kirchhoffer's behalf**]: [written vertically on Blatt 24r→] He is sending Ries's brother, the piano maker,[96] to see you. [←written vertically on Blatt 24r] [//] [Blatt 24v]
[presumably alone with Beethoven:]
It will certainly be done by the people themselves.[97] //
1 fl. C.M. for a saucepan. //
What of yours will be done?[98] //
I think that we would reserve the postal coach, make our preparations, and depart in a few days. // Who was it, though, who always wrote you letters from Italy, when he was on a journey there?[99] //

---

[94] Concerning the frequent mentions of an upcoming *Akademie* (concert), ultimately on May 7, 1824, see Heft 43, Blatt 3r.—KH

[95] Discussions of Beethoven's writing an opera to Grillparzer's *Melusine* or an oratorio to Bernard's *Der Sieg des Kreuzes* did not come to fruition.—TA

[96] The piano maker Joseph Franz Ries (1792–1862). In ca. 1821, he lived in the Alter Fleischmarkt No. 739 [probably the building that would be renumbered as 695 in 1821]. Coincidentally, the City No. 739 in 1823 was in tiny Cöllnerhofgasse, mentioned on Blatt 12v above. Presumably by fall 1822 he lived at either Leopoldstadt No. 314 (as Franz); or Landstrasse, Hauptstrasse No. 106 (as Nicolaus). See Böckh, 1822, p. 420; Breuning, *Aus dem Schwarzspanierhause*, p. 10; Breuning, *Memories of Beethoven*, ed. Solomon, p. 27; Hopfner, *Wiener Musikinstrumentenmacher, 1766–1900*, p. 402; Behsel, pp. 21–22; Ziegler, *Addressen-Buch*, p. 258. See also Heft 34, Blatt 17v; Heft 46, Blatt 16r; and Heft 94, Blatt 42r.—KH/TA

[97] Karl and Beethoven also use the circumlocution "people" (seemingly referring to Born and Paumgarten's search for a housekeeper) on Blatt 20 above.—TA

[98] In Austria, the name day of the most recently deceased emperor was observed as a holiday: thus St. Leopold's Day, November 15, in memory of Emperor Leopold II (d. 1792). The customary St. Leopold's Day benefit concert at the Kärntnertor Theater on the evening of Saturday, November 15, featured a typical potpourri program in which Beethoven's *Fidelio* Overture was the seventh item and had to be repeated. Beethoven had composed the horn solo in it for the Kärntnertor's senior low hornist Friedrich Hradetzky in 1814. This may have been the last time that Hradetzky played it in that orchestra before being dismissed as part of Barbaja's cost-cutting measures in January 1824. See the *Allgemeine musikalische Zeitung* 25, No. 52 (December 24, 1823), col. 865; the evening hour specified in the *Wiener Zeitung*, No. 261 (November 12, 1823), p. 1056; and No. 263 (November 14, 1823), p. 1064.—TA

[99] This could mean the Lobkowitz family tutor, Karl Peters, who chaperoned young Prince Joseph (Pepi) Lobkowitz on a tour to Italy, beginning on March 9, 1820, and sent many letters home. At about that time, he nominally became Karl's co-guardian (with Beethoven), but the composer later distanced himself from the circle that included Peters, Bernard, and Janschikh. For details, see Hefte 8 and 9, among others.—TA

[NEPHEW KARL, *continued*]

We are now living in the Ungargasse and have not yet seen the honorable Frau von Streicher.[100] // [Blatt 25r]

Tomorrow [Sunday, November 16] is really somewhat awkward, since we are going to the concert and therefore he[101] must be expecting us. //

A son of Schiller's is still living. // He's a judge at a public court.[102] //

[at Beethoven's apartment; ca. 11 a.m. on Sunday, November 16:]

Don't you want to go and read the newspaper?[103] //

If you absolutely don't want to go [to the Gesellschaft's concert], I would like to take my teacher from Blöchlinger's[104] with me; he has done me a great many favors,

---

[100] Anna (Nannette) Stein Streicher (1769–1833), a member of the prominent piano-building family, lived at Ungargasse No. 371, about three blocks farther south from Beethoven's new apartment. In 1817, Beethoven had written over 40 letters to her about household matters; in 1818, he wrote ca. 20, and then the matter seems to have died down as Beethoven sought other arrangements. In any case, by this time, Nannette Streicher might have regarded Beethoven as something of a pest and might have feared resuming such a close personal acquaintance. Karl essentially asked the same question on Blatt 41v below.—KH/TA

[101] This probably refers to Joseph Carl Bernard, whom Karl eventually encountered at the concert. Because Beethoven was about to reject his libretto for the oratorio *Der Sieg des Kreuzes* (commissioned from them both by the Gesellschaft der Musikfreunde), the composer himself obviously did not wish to encounter Bernard at the concert.

The event was the season's first subscription concert of the Gesellschaft der Musikfreunde, held at the Grosser Redoutensaal at the "midday hour" (12:30 p.m.) on Sunday, November 16, 1823. The program consisted of a new Symphony in D by Krommer (termed "quite brilliant, clear, and comprehensible"); a vocal duet by Rossini; a Concertante for two flutes by Berbiguier; a chorus by Voříšek; and the Overture to *Abrahams Opfer* by Lindpaintner. Vincenz Hauschka conducted. See *Allgemeine musikalische Zeitung* 25, No. 52 (December 24, 1823), col. 865.—TA

[102] At that time, both of poet Friedrich von Schiller's sons were alive: Karl von Schiller (1793–1857), high forester in Württemberg, and Ernst von Schiller (1796–1841), Prussian appellate court councillor. Karl obviously meant the latter.—KH

[103] Since November 15 was a holiday, there was no new issue of the *Wiener Zeitung* that day.—TA

[104] Two teachers seem distinct possibilities here: (Peter) Joseph Pleugmackers (b. 1774), Karl's former French teacher, and Paul (Wolfgang) Pulay (1777–1836), Karl's former Greek teacher. Their biographical sketches in Appendix B may provide clues.

Karl had a special rapport with his French teacher Pleugmackers, who might seem the obvious choice. Pleugmackers, however, was married and evidently had independent means. The comparison with Wildfeyer (whom Beethoven seems to have suggested), immediately below, indicates that Karl meant to give the ticket to a former teacher without significant means. Paul Pulay, although not as personally close to Karl as Pleugmackers, seems to have been unmarried and dependent upon his teaching for his entire livelihood. The fact that Pulay had roomed at the Institute likewise suggests that he might not have been able to buy a ticket otherwise. Pulay seems to have obtained at least one book for Karl but needed to press for reimbursement. While the question must remain open (especially since there were other teachers at Blöchlinger's Institute not considered here), it is possible that the recipient of the extra ticket was Paul Pulay.—TA

and I still have books of his. [//] Wildfeyer[105] is not as poor and can buy one [a ticket] for himself. [//] [Blatt 25v]

Her sister and a (female) friend of hers. //

If a hero performs an extraordinary deed and a poet takes this as a subject of a theatrical piece, then this play, if it pleases, will be performed often, even though the *hero* has not done such a deed more than once. In just this way, it is the case with you, because [Blatt 26r—light blue paper] since you assailed the housekeeper *one time*, then you cannot complain that I remind you of it so often, because it is just the same as can be seen in the theater. [//] *Read*, and *marvel* at my *genius*. [//] [Blatt 26v—light blue paper]

What kind of calendar do you want to buy for next year? //

Do you want to go with me [to the concert], or shall I take him the ticket? //

[Karl departs Beethoven's apartment, ca. 11:00–11:30 a.m., in time to meet his former teacher and give him the extra ticket for the Gesellschaft der Musikfreunde's concert at the Grosser Redoutensaal, beginning at 12:30 p.m.]

KIRCHHOFFER **[at Beethoven's apartment; ca. noon on Sunday, November 16]**: Whom do you have instead of Schlemmer?[106] //

The Quartets are specified. Three.[107] [//] That is not too well paid.[108] // That is more than 325 fl. 20 kr. // First the wares, then the money. [//] [Blatt 27r—light blue paper]

100 £	=	1,000 fl.
150 # [ducats]	=	675 fl.
		325

| 100 [ducats] | = | 450 fl. |
| 50 | = | 225 |

<at that time>

<at that time> 9 fl. 57 [kr.]—but it was also 10 fl. 18 [kr.] already.

---

[105] Karl writes "Willfeyer," but means Wilhelm Wildfeyer (or Wildfeuer), b. 1783, the tutor to Count Kollowrat's children. See their encounter with Wildfeyer on Blätter 9r–9v above.—TA

[106] After copyist Wenzel Schlemmer's death on August 6, 1823, Beethoven worked with his widow, Josepha; Wenzel Rampl; and Matthias Wunderl.—TA

[107] On November 9, 1822, Prince Nicolas Galitzin wrote from St. Petersburg, commissioning Beethoven for "one, two, or three new quartets." Beethoven replied on January 25, 1824, specifying a fee of 50 ducats per quartet. Although Beethoven eventually composed three Quartets, Op. 127, 130, and 132, for Galitzin, the number of works was not fixed in Beethoven's initial correspondence with the prince; moreover, Galitzin's banking contact in Vienna was Henikstein, not Kirchhoffer's employers. See Albrecht, *Letters to Beethoven*, No. 299 (English); and Anderson, No. 1123 (original French); and MacArdle & Misch, No. 347 (English).—KH/TA

[108] Kirchhoffer is commenting on the 50 ducats that Beethoven asked for each quartet.—TA

Now. // Anyway, it takes 6 weeks for an answer to come [from St. Petersburg]. [//] [Blatt 27v—light blue paper] In any case, begin [composing the Quartets]; he [Galitzin] will certainly take them. // There is already mistrust on your part. // Last year. // But [you] must write to him earlier. //

No one can read that. //

By Erard.[109] [//] [Blatt 28r]

The customs fee for *mus*[incomplete/illegible ending] is 160 fl., and the pass[port] 800 fl.[110] // I'll have them declared as "speculation," so that they are left at the Customs Office. // It is not divided equally.

He is getting along well, by giving lessons. // Only as a tuner; he also makes instruments for himself.[111] [Blatt 28v]

Are you going [to the Gesellschaft's concert] today [Sunday, November 16]?[112] //

I shall ask you for a couple of lines of your handwriting. // To raise up as a relic.[113] //

If you have a piece of wood, he'll do it right away. // A light [candle]. // He will glue it; he has it with him.[114] [//]

[Blatt 29r]

JOSEPH RIES[115] [at Beethoven's apartment, joining Kirchhoffer; shortly after noon on Sunday, November 16]:

H[err] v[an] Beethoven. Behind the bass there is an opening. If it [is] too much, it will be pulled toward the discant [upper register]. [//]

---

[109] The well-known Parisian piano firm founded by Sébastian Erard (1752–1831) and his brother Jean-Baptiste sent Beethoven one of its instruments in 1803. See Frimmel, *Handbuch*, I, p. 267.—KH/TA

[110] Kirchhoffer may be discussing the import fees on the four harps mentioned on Blatt 23v above.—TA

[111] Presumably piano maker Joseph Ries (brother of Ferdinand), who arrives on Blatt 29r below, to make quick repairs to Beethoven's piano, as later entries suggest. For another reference to his giving lessons, see Heft 51, Blatt 2r.—TA

[112] On Blatt 29v below, it becomes clear that Beethoven did not attend the 12:30 p.m. concert.—TA

[113] On Blatt 27v, Kirchhoffer had already commented about the illegibility of Beethoven's handwriting. Here he asks for a sample, possibly to establish authenticity for business purposes. Knowing that visitors seek handwriting samples as souvenirs, Kirchhoffer likens the practice to holding up a sacred relic for veneration in church.—TA

[114] Matthäus Andreas Stein appears periodically in Beethoven's conversation books, also coming on Sunday mornings, and providing maintenance for his Broadwood piano, so the repairs mentioned here (possibly a crack in the sounding board under the bass strings) were probably applied to the composer's Erard piano, now two decades old.—TA

[115] In Heft 97, Blatt 17v, this entry is confirmed as written by Joseph Franz Nikolaus/Klaus Ries (bapt. Bonn, March 3, 1792; d. Vienna, October 4, 1861), who sometimes signed himself "Joseph Riß." A younger brother of Beethoven's former student Ferdinand Ries, Joseph had come to Austria in 1814 and by 1821 or 1822 had moved to Vienna, where he became an instrument builder.

Probably mentioned on Blatt 28r above, he is barely literate and writes with phonetic spelling, at

By Maria Trost, at the *12 Himmelzeichen*, No. 15, on the 2nd floor [3rd floor, American]. //

NEPHEW KARL [at Beethoven's apartment, having returned from the Gesellschaft der Musikfreunde's concert; Sunday, November 16, probably ca. 3:00 p.m.]:[116]

Feder must surely be acquired. Therefore I ordered Feder's *Logik und Metaphysik* for 2 fl. several days ago.[117] [//] [Blatt 29v]

[reporting on the midday concert:]

Schindler was at the concert. He still has books of yours that he will send very soon.[118] // Bernard was also there, but he was very cold to me. Naturally because of the oratorio.[119] //

She [presumably the maid] doesn't know where it comes from. // She says: from the bones in the meat. //

There weren't very many at the concert. //

It all depends upon the composition [Krommer's symphony or Lindpaintner's

best. He calls the composer "Behhoffen." From the elements of his address presented here, it can be determined that he lives in the near-western suburb of St. Ulrich, whose parish church is called *Maria Trost* (Comfort of Mary); that he lives in No. 15 (in the Kirchengasse, just east of the church, and one building south of the rectory or parish offices); that his building bears the sign *12 Himmelszeichen*; and that he lives on the 2nd [American 3rd] floor.

The census records for this address include the instrument maker Joseph Kossen (b. 1796). See Conscriptions-Bogen, St. Ulrich, No. 15 (Wiener Stadt- und Landesarchiv); Behsel, p. 155.

Ries returns on Saturday, December 27, or Sunday, December 28, 1823; nephew Karl identifies him as "Herr von Ries" (Ferdinand's brother), who may have moved to an instrument factory on the Alter Fleischmarkt; see Heft 51, Blatt 2r. See a fuller identification with contributions by Michael Lorenz in Heft 94, Blatt 42v.—KH/TA

[116] The 12:30 p.m. concert would have ended by ca. 2:15 p.m., and the walk from the Grosser Redoutensaal to Beethoven's apartment in the Ungargasse took ca. 30 minutes.—TA

[117] Either Feder's *Grundsätze der Logik und Metaphysik* or his *Logik und Metaphysik im Grundrisse*, both of which went through several editions in the 1780s and 1790s; see Kayser, II, pp. 195–196, and Blatt 11r above.—KH/TA

[118] This and the entry on Blatt 30r below provide evidence of a significant rift between Beethoven and Schindler, beginning on ca. August 7, 1823 (Heft 38, Blatt 29r), or shortly thereafter. On August 23, Beethoven, writing from Baden, instructed Karl in Vienna to pay Schindler 50 fl. for various expenditures and services (presumably his secretarial assistance in soliciting subscriptions for the *Missa solemnis*) and to obtain a specifically worded receipt for the money. He also admonished Karl not to engage in any gossip at Schindler's expense (Anderson, No. 1233; Brandenburg, No. 1735). It now becomes evident that the composer intended a permanent break with Schindler. The rift lasted until shortly after November 16: authentic conversation-book entries by Schindler do not resume until Heft 46, Blatt 2r (ca. Friday, November 21).—TA

[119] Several years before, Beethoven had agreed to set an oratorio libretto, *Der Sieg des Kreuzes* [The Victory of the Cross], by Joseph Carl Bernard, editor of the *Wiener Zeitung*. From November 1819 through March 1820 (see conversation books for this period), as Beethoven got to know Bernard better, he gradually distanced himself from his would-be librettist.—TA

overture]. Even the best execution is without effect in the case of bad compositions; that was the case today. [//] [Blatt 30r] They took all pains with it.[120] //

I find it quite natural. He [Schindler] wants to get into [your] good graces again. // You are quite right. //

It [presumably Feder's *Psychologie*][121] can be had at a used book dealer's. // What [school director] Kudlich[122] sent along with me [in 1819] is still here. // Haslinger gave it to me, I think. //

Though not with *cash* money. //

Capisco. [I understand.] //

The maid says that it's all right. [//]

[Blatt 30v]

BEETHOVEN [**seemingly in a coffee house, dozing off while reading Friday's newspapers and jotting notes; late afternoon of Sunday, November 16**]:[123] <every>

Taller-melting, *unter den Weissgräben*, No. 3, in the City, Tobacco and Lottery Shop, [Blatt 31r] roten Turnstrasse, No. 386. Salomo Preisach, Leopoldstadt, grosse Fuhrmannsgasse, No. 478.[124] [//]

+ Little foot-warmers, __ fl. C.M. //

+ Staudenheim. Give [him] the above. [No.] 249.[125]

[top of Blatt 31v]

---

[120] See Blatt 25r above for the full program. Since the Krommer symphony seems to have been well received, Karl's negative judgment might refer to the Lindpaintner overture. For a comment concerning Hauschka's conducting, seemingly also made on Sunday, November 16, see Blatt 38r below.—TA

[121] See Karl's mention of the book on Blatt 11v above.—TA

[122] Johann Baptist Kudlich (1786–1831), manager of an educational institution at Erdberggasse No. 91 in the Viennese suburb of Landstrasse, which Karl had attended for a short time in 1818–1819. See Kysselak, "Todesnachrichten aus Zeitungen 1814–1839," Blatt 109 (Handschriften 3.4.A.112.1–8, Wiener Stadt- und Landesarchiv); Böckh, 1822, p. 533; Frimmel, *Handbuch*, I, p. 308; Clive, p. 138.—KH/TA

[123] Beethoven is copying other details of the advertisement for candles and soap that he began copying on Blatt 22r above (see footnote there for pertinent full text of the ad). Usually, Beethoven copies advertisements relatively accurately. Here, however, there are misspellings, elided words, a confused address, and so on that suggest either that he had had too much to drink or, more likely, that he was drowsy after dinner and was dozing off as he read the newspapers in a coffee house near his apartment. This English translation attempts to reflect that confusion.—TA

[124] Excerpt from an advertisement in the *Intelligenzblatt*, No. 263 (November 14, 1823), p. 1025 (Advertisements), as drowsily (and inaccurately) copied by Beethoven. See Blatt 22r above for the text of the advertisement.—KH/TA

[125] Dr. Jacob Staudenheim (1764–1830) lived in an apartment in the Harrach Palace, Freyung No. 239, but had lived near Beethoven in Baden the previous summer. Sundry references in the conversation books indicate that Staudenheim was ill for most of his time in Baden and often bundled up against a chill. It appears here that Beethoven wants to buy some padded foot-warmers to give him as a present. Even though Beethoven wrote over the "4" in "249" several times, Staudenheim's address was still 239. See Heft 38, Blatt 36v.—TA

+ Stove, knife and scissors, above, far out in the Landstrasse.
+ Also carpenter's things. //

[No apparent entries on Monday, November 17.]

[Blatt 32r]

NEPHEW KARL [**presumably at Beethoven's apartment, probably at midday dinner; ca. 2:00 p.m. on ca. Tuesday, November 18**]:[126] I spoke with my Greek teacher [at the university?] today.[127] He told me that in the *Theater-Zeitung* of Saturday, there is a *description* of your domestic life, in which I am also mentioned.[128] // The signature of the author is S____l, S .... l. // [back to Blatt 31v] He presumes that it is Schlegel.[129] // It corresponds to the signature S_____l. [//] [continuing with

---

[126] On Blatt 1r above, Karl said that he could eat dinner with Beethoven on Tuesdays, Thursdays, and Saturdays. If these entries follow those after the Gesellschaft's concert of Sunday, November 16, they could have been made at dinner on Tuesday, November 18.

In any case, Karl's conversation seems to begin on Blatt 32r (for two entries); then he fills in the remaining space on Blatt 31v, before returning to Blatt 32v and continuing on. The entries below reflect that logical ordering (also suggested, but not carried out, by the German editors).

As for the time, Karl notes on Blatt 32v that it will soon be 2:30, so this conversation may have begun at ca. 2:00 p.m.—TA

[127] This seems to be a Greek teacher at the university and not Paul Pulay (1777–1836), who had been Karl's Greek teacher at Blöchlinger's Institute, although issues concerning religion and the state, which had been sticking points with Pulay, surface in the continuation of Blatt 32r below. For details about Pulay, see the footnote to Blatt 25r above.

More likely, it was Anton Joseph Stein (1759–1844), professor of Latin literature and Greek philology at the University of Vienna; see Heft 60, Blatt 30r.—TA

[128] An article on Beethoven in Bäuerle's *Allgemeine Theater-Zeitung* 16, No. 137 (November 15, 1823), p. 548, mentions Karl: "Other than to his art, he is attached with his entire soul to his nephew Carl. For the orphan, he assumed the father's place in the full sense of the word." The essay, signed "S ...... l," had already appeared in the *Stuttgarter Morgenblatt für gebildete Stände*, No. 265. Its author, the historian and journalist Johann Chrysostomus Sporschil (1800–1863), acknowledged his authorship only in a footnote in an obituary of Beethoven in 1827. See Theodore Albrecht, "Anton Schindler as Destroyer and Forger of Beethoven's Conversation Books: A Case for Decriminalization," in *Music's Intellectual History*, ed. Zdravko Blažeković and Barbara Dobbs Mackenzie (New York: RILM, 2009), pp. 175–176; and Blatt 10v above.—KH/TA

[129] Friedrich von Schlegel (b. Hanover, 1772; d. Dresden, 1829), philosopher, historical researcher, and poet; younger brother of August Wilhelm von Schlegel. He came from a Lutheran family of pastors and poets and married Dorothea Veit (the eldest daughter of Moses Mendelssohn) in 1804. In 1808, he converted to Catholicism and lived in Vienna in the Imperial service (court secretary, later legation councillor). In 1823, he was prematurely pensioned because he stood in opposition to Metternich. For a reference to both Schlegels, see Blatt 41v below.—KH/TA

Blatt 32r] If it is he.[130] // In the coffee house.[131] // It is also available in the "first" coffee house here.[132] //

My Greek teacher[133] was just amazed that someone did not ask you for permission, as is appropriate. // Things that are not against religion and the state are all right. // Also about your life in the country. // It will probably not say anything beyond that you take long walks, love Nature, and compose while walking, etc.[134] // [Blatt 32v]

I was called upon today in mathematics class.[135] //

If I am still to get the *Theater-Zeitung*, I must go now—because it's nearly 2:30.[136] If not, then I can also bring it with me later. [//]

BEETHOVEN [presumably in a coffee house, reading the *Intelligenzblatt*'s issues of Monday, November 17, and Wednesday, November 19; making notes from them on the afternoon of Wednesday, November 19]:[137]

+ *Die Schiesskunst* [The Art of Shooting], etc. by Forest M[aster] Thon; octavo; Sondershausen, 2 fl. C.M.; [Blatt 33r] Kohlmarkt, No. 257.[138] //

---

[130] On Sunday, November 23 (Heft 46, Blatt 18r), Karl posited that the article was by postal official Joseph von Seidl. Only later did Beethoven and Karl realize that the author was Johann Chrysostomus Sporschil.—TA

[131] Beethoven must have asked where the teacher had read the article.—TA

[132] As early as 1804, a coffee house was located in the building Landstrasse No. 42 (southeast corner of Gärtnergasse and Landstrasse Hauptstrasse); its proprietor was Felix Anselm. When one left the City through the Stubentor [gate] in the direction of suburban Landstrasse, this establishment was the first coffee house that he encountered, one block beyond the Glacis. For this reason, it was popularly known as the "first" coffee house. From Beethoven's apartment, it was a long block east on Bockgasse (today's Beatrixgasse), and across Landstrasse Hauptstrasse. See Conscriptions-Bogen, Landstrasse No. 42 (Wiener Stadt- und Landesarchiv); and Fink.—KH/TA

[133] Possibly Anton Joseph Stein, Karl's Greek teacher at the University, rather than his former Greek teacher at Blöchlinger's Institute, Paul Pulay (1777–1836); for a biographical sketch of Pulay, see Appendix B.—TA

[134] In this essay (see above), Sporschil wrote: "Above all, however, he loves the wide-open spaces of Nature. Even in the worst weather of winter, it is not easy for him to spend an entire day in his room, and when he is in the country in the summer, he is usually in the blossoming garden of God already before sunrise."—KH

[135] Therefore written on a weekday, as posited above.—TA

[136] If Karl planned on trying to get a copy at the "first" coffee house, he had perhaps a 5-minute walk. If, however, he intended to get a copy from the *Allgemeine Theater-Zeitung*'s own offices (which seems more likely), they were in the Leopoldstadt, Weintraubengasse No. 510 (next to the Theater in the Leopoldstadt), probably a 45-minute walk from Beethoven's apartment. See Böckh, 1822, pp. 67–68.—TA

[137] It is also possible that these entries represent not one, but two afternoon visits to a coffee house and that Beethoven jotted down *Die Schiesskunst* on Tuesday, November 18, and "Mountain potatoes" and the "Piano" on Wednesday, November 19.—TA

[138] Excerpt from an advertisement in the *Intelligenzblatt*, No. 264 (November 17, 1823), p. 1037: "Notice. To be had at Mörschner and Jasper, book dealers on the Kohlmarkt, No. 257: *Die Schiesskunst*, or Complete Instructions for Shooting with a Rifle, Shotgun, and Pistols … by Forest Commissioner [Theodor] Thon; octavo; Sondershausen, 2 fl. C.M."

Mountain potatoes; Kohlmessergasse, No. 476.[139]
Piano for 300 fl. W.W.; Wipplingerstrasse, No. 386, 1st floor [2nd floor, American].[140]
All these flannel [clothes] still don't warm enough.—*Lamb's skin.* [//]
[End of Beethoven's own entries of Wednesday, November 19.]

[Blatt 33v]

NEPHEW KARL **[presumably at Beethoven's apartment; late afternoon or evening, Wednesday, November 19, making a note for Beethoven to read later]**: There was no lack of meat, but she had it roasted at the baker's,[141] and it got ruined there. //

Because we are *so* far, I must tell you in all sincerity that I am convinced about the honesty of the h[ousekeeper][142] throughout the time that she is here; and what is *more*, I am convinced that she lost account of more than you think she pocketed. // Otherwise, I am not saying thereby that I want to have her here;—*no*, get rid of her today yet—it is all the same to me. I have already put out a summons at the place where I eat,[143] [Blatt 34r] and shall ask again, about getting another woman. When I discussed with you about taking *her*, I should have foreseen that you would *never* believe in her eagerness or honesty—as many pains as she might take—because you already employed her with the preconceived opinion to the contrary. //

That is not the point! I am only saying that, because she expressed the view only yesterday (*therefore I could not say it any earlier*), she has already lost money more often than—as you believe—she would have pocketed something. I have already written *one* such case out for you; [Blatt 34v] therefore—*because you don't believe it*—you cannot say that I *remained silent* about it; specifically with the 3 bundles of straw[144] that she bought then and added 20 kr. per bundle, since I myself inquired about the matter at the shopkeeper's, and he told me that they cost 21 kr. I learned about the second case

---

In these three advertisements, Beethoven again copies the pertinent points with his customary relative accuracy.—KH/TA

[139] See the *Intelligenzblatt*, No. 266 (November 19, 1823), p. 1051 (Advertisements).—KH

[140] Excerpt from an advertisement in the *Intelligenzblatt*, No. 266 (November 19, 1823), p. 1051 (Advertisements): "*Ein überspieltes Fortepiano* [A played-out fortepiano] with six octaves and pedals, and a pure tone, is for sale at a reasonable price of 300 fl. W.W., and can be seen daily in the Wipplingerstrasse, No. 386, in the first floor [second floor, American]." Note that Beethoven uses the term "piano" rather than the archaic "fortepiano."—KH

[141] Johann van Beethoven's brother-in-law, the baker Leopold Obermayer (1784–1841), on the corner of Kothgasse and Pfarrgasse in suburban Windmühle, next to Beethoven's old apartment. It was indeed far from Beethoven's current apartment in the Ungargasse, although the distance of which Karl speaks seems to imply that they are far apart in their opinions about the domestic servants.—TA

[142] From Karl's note and the ensuing conversation, it appears as if Beethoven employed a genuine housekeeper for a period—even if only four days—in November, 1823.—TA

[143] Probably the boardinghouse of Baroness von Born and Frau Baumgarten in *Zum rothen Igel*; see Blatt 19r above for another circumlocutious reference to them.—TA

[144] Straw would have been used for sack mattresses and changed periodically.—TA

[NEPHEW KARL, *continued*]

only *yesterday*, specifically that she gave the woman 30 kr. per day, and did not dare to write it down. // For that reason she also did not write it down.[145] [//] [Blatt 35r]

[Beethoven must have asked Karl about the housekeeper, causing Karl to answer:]

I *just* wrote down for you that I learned about it only yesterday; therefore I could not tell you earlier.[146] //

I did not say one word of reproach; I only wanted to indicate that she *had* to be honorable. // Because she worked for the maid. // Washed, got wine from the City, carried water and wood, and got the medicines, and helped with the cooking—which the maid would do otherwise. // She was here 4 days. It's 2 fl. [//] [Blatt 35v]

She has her calculation, and therefore needs only to write it down. She did not write down the 2 fl.; I *myself* have so much to do that I forgot about the money and thought that she would deal with the woman, and did *not* give the 30 kr., <yesterday> since, at that time—as I wrote down for you—you said that it was much too much. She told me about it only yesterday; I therefore did what I could, in that I am telling you today. // [Blatt 36r]

I only want to show that she must not be as completely corrupt as you believe, since she never ventured to write down what she really paid, because she feared that what she paid would appear to you to be too much. //

I cannot judge about the letter because I didn't read it. You must obviously know what she wrote in it; therefore I cannot say anything about it. //

I don't know how [it] stands with the two different kinds of lung; meanwhile it wouldn't be difficult to obtain information about it. // [Blatt 36v]

I am not saying anything about such a thought; I cannot even think about such a thing; I just think that you are carrying your mistrust too far. //

As long as she is here. // A woman who would like to be employed as a housekeeper is here. She learned by accident that you need someone and is therefore inquiring. //

[written vertically→] You have cleaned enough, if you consider her.[147] [←written vertically] [//] [Blatt 37r]

6/2 .12/3
   18
   —
   32

---

[145] This may even refer to the alms given to a blind woman in the Kothgasse, mentioned in Heft 44, Blatt 1r.—TA

[146] This seems to confirm that Karl is rooming elsewhere and not sleeping consistently at Beethoven's apartment. See also Blatt 1v above.—TA

[147] Written in second-person, familiar "du" form.—TA

BEETHOVEN [probably the morning of Thursday, November 20, after Blätter 33–37]:
+ Candles[148]   + Razor[149]
+ Coffee cups.
+ Glasses. [//]

HOUSEKEEPER [?]: He only has 4 pounds. [//] Should I cut a schnitzel now for another meal? [//]

BEETHOVEN:
$$\begin{array}{r}28\\28\\\underline{28}\\28\end{array}$$
1 fl. 52 [kr.]

* * * * *

[Blätter 8r–11v, including a reference to the *Theater-Zeitung* article on Blatt 10r, and that Beethoven had not shaved well, seem to belong here chronologically.]

[Blatt 37v]

NEPHEW KARL [presumably Thursday, November 20]:[150] I asked this woman who sent her; she didn't want to say; instead, she mentioned a [woman] friend who heard that you needed someone, and this one in turn learned it from someone else who had told *her*. //
  [presumably at a carpenter's shop:]
  The chairs are pretty. //
  [presumably back at Beethoven's apartment:]
  You have seen what the carpenter asked for one stand of thin, breakable wood—varnished—without cushions, 6 fl.; [made] from a better kind, 7 fl. // One chair for 5 fl. is not expensive. // What do you want to bet? [//] [Blatt 38r—light blue paper] With all the shoes. //

---

[148] On Blatt 22r above, Beethoven had copied an advertisement for soap and candles. They are still on his shopping list of Monday, November 24 (Heft 46, Blatt 22r).—TA

[149] On Blatt 10v above (possibly Tuesday, November 18), Karl had noted that Beethoven had not shaved himself well.—TA

[150] Based on the general reference to Hauschka's conducting style on Blatt 38r below, Karl's entries would have been made after the Gesellschaft der Musikfreunde's concert on Sunday, November 16, which he attended.—TA

HEFT 45 (CA. NOVEMBER 4 – CA. NOVEMBER 20, 1823), BLATT 38V

[NEPHEW KARL, *continued*]

<I> She says that she needs a knife for the kitchen. // Because she roasted it herself. //

I already asked at the *Tandelmarkt* [secondhand shops].[151] You get the same thing there. //

[possibly after the Gesellschaft der Musikfreunde's concert on the afternoon of Sunday, November 16:]

Hauschka[152] has a peculiar way of beating time; I have never seen its like.[153] // That is the case with most state officials. Everything *mechanical*, like a machine—which he did today, he will also do tomorrow, and so it goes on and on forever. [//]

[possibly back to entries of Thursday, November 20:]

[Blatt 38v—light blue paper]

They are not of any use to me for school, since the professor approaches the works completely differently and always concerns himself with interpretations. // The lecture is quite nice, but I would like to have a *compendium* as a *recapitulation* of what he has said, agreed, because he does not limit himself to the textbook, which is also useless. [//] [Blatt 39r—light blue paper]

We will get the money; we just have to wait at the Tuscan legation until around the middle of December; there is no use hoping for it any earlier because nothing

---

[151] Located on the Glacis, south of the City walls, between the *Carolinentor* and the *Heumarkt*.—KH

[152] Vincenz Hauschka (1766–1840), treasury official, a friend of Beethoven's (with whom the composer used the "du" form of address). He had trained to be a professional violoncellist and even worked in that capacity; but by 1792, he had entered the civil service, rising to a senior position. He still played as an amateur and was a prominent member of the Gesellschaft der Musikfreunde. He lived at Schottengasse No. 103. On December 26, 1819, Beethoven, Bernard, and possibly Johanna von Weissenthurn had eaten St. Stephan's Day dinner at his apartment; see Heft 5, Blätter 54r–56r. See also Frimmel, *Handbuch*, I, p. 201; Clive, pp. 153–154; and Ziegler, *Addressen-Buch*, p. 112.—KH/TA

[153] On Sunday, November 16, 1823, Vincenz Hauschka had conducted the first concert of the season sponsored by the Gesellschaft der Musikfreunde and held in the Grosser Redoutensaal. The program included Franz Krommer's Symphony in D; a Pacini duet; a movement from a Concerto for Two Flutes by Berbiguier; Voříšek's *Gott im Frühlinge*; and Lindpaintner's Overture to *Abrahams Opfer*. Nephew Karl attended and encountered Bernard and Schindler there (see Blätter 25r and 29v–30r above).

There were no works by Beethoven, who would be represented by his Symphony No. 2 in D and the *Egmont* Overture on the second Gesellschafts-Concert on December 14, but that concert would be conducted by Johann Baptist Schmidl. See *Allgemeine musikalische Zeitung* 25, No. 52 (December 24, 1823), cols. 865–866; 26, No. 3 (January 15, 1824), col. 43; and Perger, *Gesellschaft der Musikfreunde*, I, p. 288.

When Karl writes "today … tomorrow, and … forever," he may be speaking metaphorically and not implying that he heard the concert "today"; but given the ambiguities in dating this Heft, a literal interpretation cannot be ruled out.—TA

[NEPHEW KARL, *continued*]
will arrive from Tuscany before three weeks, and it also takes a letter three weeks to get from here down to there.[154] //

A *good* oaf otherwise. //

Necessary repairs were made to the pipe, for 15 kr.[155] [//] [Blatt 39v—light blue paper] Who was the man who sat at the table in the coffee house? //

Don't you remember the woman whom we visited in Mödling when we lived there, and who also had a son who was a student? // What was her name? // Her son studies at the university, and I seem to know him. // One boy who was also in the *Theresianum*[156] and whom I knew from the [Piaristen] *Gymnasium* in the Josephstadt, has also left now and certainly because of the priests. //

What does a pound cost? [//] [Blatt 40r]

It is strange that when a person wants to complain about a clergyman, he tells a *Pfaff* [priest], who, on the contrary, is a very honorable *Epitheton*, because this designation as a Shepherd of the Soul was borrowed from a gravestone in the earliest era of Christendom, where it says: *P. F. A. F.* (*Pastor Fidelis Animarum Fidelium*) [Faithful Shepherd of the Faithful Souls], and is therefore nothing less than insulting. // Especially the *Domherren* [canons]! // Here, only a nobleman can become a canon (unless a special miracle occurs). [//] [Blatt 40v]

$$\begin{array}{r} 28 \text{ [kr.]} \\ \underline{4} \\ 112 \text{ [kr.] [=] 1 fl. 52 kr.} \end{array}$$

How did you like the essay by Frau Helmine v[on] Chezy?[157] // But there is a great difference between such necessary supplements and totally overruling a story line, such as Weber did. // He is too *apathetic* about it. // A *dull* person. // [Publisher Sigmund Anton] Steiner will have nothing good to say about Weber now. [//] [Blatt 41r]

---

[154] Probably a reference to the correspondence with the grand duke of Tuscany concerning a subscription to the *Missa solemnis*. See Frimmel, *Handbuch*, I, p. 416.—KH

[155] For Eduard Klosson's frequently reproduced line drawing of Beethoven in a coffee house, smoking a pipe and reading newspapers, in 1823, see Siegfried Kross, ed., *Beethoven, Mensch seiner Zeit* (Bonn: Ludwig Röhrscheid Verlag, 1980), p. 25 (and dust jacket).—TA

[156] An educational institution for young noblemen in the Wieden, Favoritenstrasse No. 156. See Heft 39, Blatt 25r.—TA

[157] Helmina von Chezy (1783–1856), librettist of Weber's *Euryanthe* and Schubert's *Rosamunde*. In Bäuerle's *Allgemeine Theater-Zeitung* 17, No. 134 (November 8, 1823), p. 536, one week after a review of Weber's *Euryanthe*, there appeared an article by Chezy entitled "Another Word about *Euryanthe* by the Librettist, to Contest the Review, signed 'Th.,' in No. 131 of This Magazine." In it she discussed, among other things, the history of the libretto and its various revisions requested by the composer, including eleven revisions for one particular passage, and signed it "Helmina von Chezy, Vienna, November 3, 1823." See also Lichnowsky's discussion in Heft 46, Blatt 25r (possibly Tuesday, November 25).—KH

HEFT 45 (CA. NOVEMBER 4 – CA. NOVEMBER 20, 1823), BLATT 41V

When I first saw him,[158] I greeted him first, but he didn't answer or even tip his hat. I haven't looked at him again since that time, and we pass each other like statues as often as we encounter one another, which happens rather often, because he mostly walks into the City when I am coming out. // He speaks to no one, like the *Raizen*.[159] // Nothing except the most necessary. // A compiler. // [Blatt 41v]

But with whom do we even get together?[160] // He is even more of a merchant than other people. // For example, if we were to go to Carbon's,[161] don't you think that nothing would be played as often there?[162] // It's amazing to me that Frau Nannette Streicher *née* Stein has not yet honored us [with a visit].[163] //

That is August Wilhelm Schlegel. Friedrich Schlegel is here, I believe.[164] //

BEETHOVEN [in a coffee house, reading newspapers; probably the afternoon or evening of Thursday, November 20]:

+ Supplement volumes for the pocket edition of Schiller's Works, 6 vols., [Blatt 42r] (are available for *four* Thaler 16 gr.) at Friedrich Christ. Wilh[elm] Vogel in Leipzig.[165]

Ordinary	16 [kr.]
English beer	22
Double	26

[158] This conversation must refer to someone who lives in suburban Landstrasse but goes into the walled City frequently, presumably through the Stubentor.—TA

[159] The *Raizen* were Serbs of the Greek Orthodox religion, whose name was derived from Ras Castle. Coming from Slovenia and south Hungary, a small colony of them lived to the west of Baden.—KH

[160] During this period, Beethoven evidently feels a need to get together socially with people and considers buying furniture, dishes, etc. as preparations.—TA

[161] Franz Ludwig Carbon owned property in Mödling but now lived in the Bürgerspital apartment complex between Kärntnerstrasse and the Lobkowitz Palace.—TA

[162] Beethoven seems anxious to avoid the playing of his own music and of parlor games, as well as other social customs.—TA

[163] Karl introduces the same conversational point as he did on Blatt 24v above (q.v.), but in a slightly different context.—TA

[164] August Wilhelm von Schlegel (b. Hanover, 1767; d. Bonn, 1845), poet, journalist, and famous translator of Shakespeare's plays; elder brother of Friedrich von Schlegel (b. Hanover, 1772; d. Dresden, 1829). Although August Wilhelm had given important lectures on literary criticism in Vienna in 1808, most of his life was spent elsewhere. This remark may have been prompted by association with Friedrich von Schiller (see the very next entry); in 1797, August Wilhelm had had a major falling-out with Schiller.

See also Blatt 31v above, where Karl's teacher thought that Friedrich Schlegel was the author of Sporschil's article on Beethoven, signed only "S . . . . l."—TA

[165] A six-week-old advertisement in the *Intelligenzblatt*, No. 233 (October 9, 1823), p. 779: "To be had in the bookshop of the late Anton Doll's Widow and Son, in the Bischofsgasse, next to the Lichtensteg, across from the large Federlhof: Friedrich Schiller's *Ergänzungen* [*Supplements*] in 6 volumes, with copperplates and engraved title pages, size: 12mo, 1819. Subscription price for each volume, 3 fl. W.W."

Beethoven probably saw this *Supplement* advertised (with variants in wording) in another newspaper more recently and copied it here.—KH/TA

+ Asioli, *Klawier-Instrumente ... auf die leichteste Art zu stimmen*, 2 fl. W.W., at Artaria's.[166] [//]

[Blatt 42v]

NEPHEW KARL: The ones with roses, 1 fl. 15 kr.; the ones with little flowers, 1 fl. 40 kr. 3 fl. C.M. = 7 fl. 30 kr. W.W.

BEETHOVEN [**calculating 5 items with little flowers**]:

1 fl. 40 [kr.]
1   40
1   40
1   40
1   40
8 fl. 20 kr.

NEPHEW KARL:

  1 fl. 40 for one
10 fl.   for a half dozen
  1 fl. 15
17 fl. 50 kr. for a service of porcelain.[167]

End of Heft 45

---

[166] Bonifazio Asioli (1769–1832), composer and author of several pedagogical writings. This note concerns his *Anleitung, Clawier-Instrumente zu temperieren, und auf die leichteste Art ohne Beihülfe eines Meisters ... rein und richtig zu stimmen*, published by Artaria in Vienna on July 22, 1818, for 2 fl. W.W. Beethoven presumably made this note about the do-it-yourself tuning method from the *Wiener Zeitung*, No. 266 (Wednesday, November 19, 1823), p. 1076 (bottom of col. 1).—KH/TA

[167] For an advertisement of a *different* dinner service, possibly on November 11, 1823, see Blatt 12v above.—TA

Heft 46

(ca. November 21, 1823 – ca. November 26, 1823)

[Blatt 1r]

NEPHEW KARL [**presumably at Beethoven's apartment in the Ungargasse; ca. Friday, November 21, possibly at midday dinner**]:[1] I have already found sheep's-wool stockings; she offered them to me for 1 fl. 36 kr., but I immediately went to leave, and then she gladly wanted to let me have them for 1 fl. 24.[2] [//]

BEETHOVEN [**calculating the cost of three pairs of stockings**]:
  1 fl. 24 [kr.]
  1   24
  1   24
  ―――――――
  4 fl. 12 kr.

+ Beer.
+ Music paper. // [Blatt 1v]
+ Karl, this evening, to read *Keplers Leben* by Litrov,[3] with a small glass of punch in the coffee house.

---

[1] With the start of the new semester at the university on Monday, November 3, Karl seems to have roomed somewhere in the City on most nights. In Heft 45, Blatt 1r, Karl also projected that he could eat dinner with Beethoven on Tuesdays, Thursdays, and Saturdays. With the entry on Blatt 13r, seemingly on Saturday, November 22, pacing backward suggests that today could be Friday, November 21. See Heft 44, Blatt 3r; and Heft 45, Blätter 1r, 19r, 33v–34r, and 35r.—TA

[2] What Karl describes may be tactics at the *Tandelmarkt* (secondhand shops) rather than a customary new-clothing shop.—TA

[3] Johannes Kepler (b. Weil, west of Stuttgart, December 27, 1571; d. Regensburg, November 15, 1630) was a Protestant mathematician, astronomer, philosopher, and sometime writer on (mathematical) music theory. He studied at Tübingen, then taught in Graz (1594–1600), and became assistant to the astronomer Tycho Brahe in Prague (1600), continuing at the liberal and eccentric Court of Emperor Rudolph II after Brahe's death (1601) until 1612. Thereafter, he was active in Linz until ca. 1626, and then led a nomadic lifestyle. He was considering an offer from Rostock in northern Germany when he died on a business trip to Regensburg on November 15, 1630, and was buried there.

Joseph Johann Littrow (1781–1840), professor of scientific astronomy; had been director of the University of Vienna's observatory since 1819 and was ennobled in 1837. He wrote numerous works on astronomy. An earlier article by Littrow (in Schickh's *Wiener Zeitschrift*, 1820) had been the source of

+ Unger, singer.[4] [//]

[Blatt 2r]

SCHINDLER [presumably at Beethoven's apartment; ca. Friday, November 21]:[5] Weigl[6] is lamenting that you have never visited him, [even though] he has visited you so often. Therefore he no longer ventures to come, since you have not done the same. //

Beethoven's oft-cited quote, "The Moral Law in us and the starry Heaven above us … Kant" (Heft 7, Blatt 17r). See also *Hof- und Staats-Schematismus*, 1823, II, p. 96; Wurzbach, vol. 15, p. 286; and Franz Michael Maier, "Beethoven liest Littrow," in *Beethoven liest*, ed. Bernhard R. Appel and Julia Ronge (Bonn: Verlag Beethoven-Haus, 2016), pp. 251–288.

The work mentioned here is Littrow's article "Kosmologische Betrachtungen über die Bahnen der Himmelskörper," *Wiener Zeitschrift* 8, No. 138 (November 18, 1823), pp. 1134–1137; No. 139 (November 20, 1823), pp. 1145–1148; No. 140 (November 22, 1823), pp. 1154–1157; and No. 141 (November 25, 1823), pp. 1161–1164. The first two installments (published closest to the anniversary of Kepler's death) dealt with the movements of the sun, moon, and earth in philosophical and practical terms. The third installment included a biographical sketch of the wealthy English mathematician, physicist, and astronomer Sir Isaac Newton (1642–1727), leading to the fourth installment (November 25, 1823; pp. 1161–1164), devoted exclusively to Kepler, who influenced Newton. The sketch portrayed Kepler as a German who had overcome poverty and malnutrition to become a brilliant and influential scientist but who still suffered from periods when he was paid little or nothing, even by the Imperial Court in Prague. Nonetheless, Kepler's work extended to the "Laws of Nature, inscribed in the starry heavens."

In addition to copying Littrow's Kantian quote about the "starry Heaven" on February 2, 1820, Beethoven had composed his *Abendlied unterm gestirnten Himmel* (Evening Song under the Starry Heaven; text by Count Otto Heinrich von Loeben), WoO 150, for publication in Schickh's *Wiener Zeitschrift* in late March of that year. Therefore, the presence of another article by Littrow, referring to Kepler's "starry heavens," suggests that Schickh provided Beethoven with either a copy of the whole article ahead of time, or at least an advance copy of the fourth installment, by ca. November 21, several days before its publication. These issues of Schickh's *Wiener Zeitschrift* also contain extensive coverage of the recent premiere of Weber's opera *Euryanthe* at the Kärntnertor Theater.—TA

[4] In May 1824, the alto Caroline Unger (1803–1877) would sing in the first performances of Beethoven's Ninth Symphony.—TA

[5] In Heft 45, Blätter 29v–30r, nephew Karl reported that Schindler was at the Gesellschaft der Musikfreunde's midday concert of Sunday, November 16, and wanted to get back into Beethoven's good graces. These are the first surviving entries by Schindler since ca. August 7, 1823. Already there is a certain element of gossip in them.—TA

[6] Joseph Weigl (1766–1846), opera composer, Kapellmeister at the Court Theaters, at the time director of the Court Opera. Perhaps Weigl used a slate at Beethoven's apartment or was among those who could make themselves heard by the composer; otherwise, there is not a single surviving entry by Weigl in the conversation books up to this point. In fact, Beethoven may have believed that Weigl was complicit in designating which orchestra members were to be dismissed as part of opera lessee Barbaja's cost-cutting in 1822–1823 and therefore maintained a certain distance from him. See Böckh, 1822, p. 383; Frimmel, *Handbuch*, II, p. 410; Wurzbach, vol. 13, pp. 279–281; Clive, pp. 391–392. See also Theodore Albrecht, "Picturing the Players in the Pit: The Orchestra of Vienna's Kärntnertor Theater, 1821–1822," *Music in Art, International Journal for Music Iconography* 34 (Spring–Fall 2009), pp. 203–213.—KH/TA

[SCHINDLER, *continued*]

We must wait a few days, though, [to see] what Duport[7] will decide; then I shall <most urgently> ask you to ask H[err] D[uport] what he has decided. [//] [Blatt 2v] But Weigl appears to leave everything only to H[err] D[uport]. // Gottdank[8] and Forti[9] were also present and resoundingly affirm that they often saw me at the Josephstadt [Theater] and bore witness that I am in a position to lead their orchestra [at the Kärntnertor Theater] as well,[10] by the time that I had practiced for it. //

It can't last long in the Kärntnertor.[11] // [Blatt 3r]

and in the [sentence ends] //

In a few days. // Because he [Duport] will certainly write you earlier if he receives word. // In the meantime, I shall nose around, and perhaps I'll hear what is happening. // Because he wants to write about the opera [Grillparzer's proposed *Melusine*] at the same time, as he assures me. // He asked me whether you had already begun with the opera's plot, but unfortunately I could not answer him; therefore, he will surely inquire at the Source itself. // [Blatt 3v]

What have you decided concerning the Mass [*Missa solemnis*]? Will you not have it performed in public?[12] I can assure you, upon my honor, that *everyone* is anxiously awaiting it, and that you won't have any difficulties with it. // Then it will be protracted again, and perhaps nothing will come of it. // Do you really believe that skilled people will have to be pressured to do it? Everyone will very gladly work together [Blatt 4r] to do what needs to be done. // That way, you'll be placed in a position where you can work comfortably the whole winter through, without having to worry about anything more. // Just believe otherwise that you could have someone make a rough estimate [of the costs] even now. // Sonnleithner[13] won't be able to tell

---

[7] Louis Antoine Duport (1783–1853), former ballet dancer and currently Domenico Barbaja's administrator of the Court Opera at the Kärntnertor Theater. See Castelli, I, p. 226.—KH/TA

[8] Joseph Gottdank (1779–1849), singer at the Kärntnertor Theater. See Verlassenschafts-Abhandlung, Fasz. 2: 6637/1849 (Wiener Stadt- und Landesarchiv); and Ziegler, *Addressen-Buch*, p. 73.—KH/TA

[9] Anton Forti (1790–1859), baritone singer at the Kärntnertor Theater. See Frimmel, *Handbuch*, I, p. 145; and Ziegler, *Addressen-Buch*, p. 73.—KH/TA

[10] Since its reopening in October 1822, Schindler had been concertmaster (a position different from "solo player") at the Theater in der Josephstadt. He lived one block east and one block south of the theater at Josephigasse No. 15, a lot currently occupied by Vienna's English Theater and the rear wing of Pension Lehrerhaus. Schindler applied for one of the conductor's positions at the Kärntnertor Theater but did not obtain it until 1825. See Joseph Schmidt-Görg, "Schindler," *MGG*, vol. 11, cols. 1728–1729; and Ziegler, *Addressen-Buch*, p. 95.—KH/TA

[11] Probably a reference to the decline in number and quality of performances outside the imported Italian repertoire.—TA

[12] This and the following remarks concern Beethoven's plans to give an *Akademie* (concert), which ultimately took place in the Kärntnertor Theater on May 7, 1824. See Heft 43, Blatt 3r.—KH

[13] Probably Leopold Sonnleithner (1797–1873), who held several offices in the Gesellschaft der Musikfreunde. His uncle Joseph Sonnleithner (1766–1835), librettist of the first version of Fidelio

[SCHINDLER, *continued*]

you what is necessary concerning the Akademie; I believe Piringer[14] [can do] more. [//] [Blatt 4v] He [Seyfried or Zmeskall?][15] is sickly and may not. // Just make up your mind soon; everything can be arranged very quickly, without your being very inconvenienced. //

<With your permission, I'll place myself as the first violin and will occupy the position well.[16]> // I absolutely never see him [Schuppanzigh]. //

Weber also forgot variety in *Euryanthe*. [//] [Blatt 5r]

In God's name, the least stressful thing for you would be to hand *Der Sieg des Kreuzes* back to the [Musik-]Verein and give up on it, because you will still have a thousand annoyances with it. // Give the finished libretto back to the Verein, and *Amen!*[17] //

No one will dispute his [Schuppanzigh's] right to this position, because the Verein has none. [//] [Blatt 5v] All the orchestra members who have that much time would certainly be happy to participate. // On my honor, I can assure you that Sonnleithner did not say a word about it to me. //

The Akademie will indeed give them [the Verein] the opportunity to place a commissary in the box office, who will immediately take the 400 fl. back.[18] [//] [Blatt 6r]

[Schindler momentarily turns to domestic matters:]

You can look at the other [candidate for housekeeper] if you wish. // Otherwise, one cannot entirely pay attention to [Count Moritz] Lichnowsky, but you could allow

---

(1804–1805), was cofounder and secretary of the Society. See Frimmel, *Handbuch*, II, p. 219; Wurzbach, vol. 36, pp. 9–10; Ziegler, *Addressen-Buch*, pp. 112, 118; and Clive, p 342.—KH/TA

[14] Ferdinand Piringer (1780–1829), a good amateur violinist and one of the conductors of the Gesellschaft der Musikfreunde's concerts. Ultimately he provided several accomplished players and choral singers for Beethoven's *Akademie* on May 7, 1824. See also Heft 44, Blatt 2v.—KH/TA

[15] Ignaz von Seyfried, conductor at the Theater an der Wien, was known to be sickly. Amateur violoncellist Nikolaus Zmeskall von Domanowecz suffered from arthritis and gout; see also Blatt 30v below.—TA

[16] This sentence is, as indicated above, crossed out. Beethoven probably told Schindler in no uncertain terms that he intended Schuppanzigh to be concertmaster at the *Akademie*, prompting Schindler's next entry, and then quickly moving to another topic.—TA

[17] As early as April 27, 1816, Beethoven had contracted with the Gesellschaft der Musikfreunde to compose an oratorio for a fee of 300 ducats. Ultimately, Beethoven was not happy with the projected librettist Bernard, the subject of *Der Sieg des Kreuzes*, or the partially antisemitic text itself, and on January 23, 1824, wrote to the Gesellschaft, withdrawing from the agreement (Anderson, no. 1260). See Frimmel, *Handbuch*, I, pp. 36 and 472; Perger, pp. 16–18; Heft 39, Blatt 8r; and many of Bernard's conversation-book entries in the period from December 1819 through March 1820.—KH/TA

[18] At this point, Beethoven seems to be projecting the *Akademie* as a joint production of the Kärntnertor Theater and the Gesellschaft der Musikfreunde, using the occasion as his opportunity to repay the 400 fl. that the Gesellschaft had advanced him for composing Bernard's *Der Sieg des Kreuzes*.—TA

[SCHINDLER, *continued*]
her a probationary period, because there is no other woman available right now. //
She is outstanding as a cook. // For many years, she worked all alone for a Baron
Wetzlar,[19] where she had everything to herself. [//] [Blatt 6v]

[probably through Wetzlar's association with Mozart, the topic returns to music:]

One speaks [of Mozart's *La clemenza di Tito*] as a grand *classical* work. //

Twelve operas that the [Barbaja] administration had taken over are missing in the Archive [i.e., theater library]; they must have loaned *Titus* out recently; this is how they are said to have managed their affairs. // *Lodoiska, Die Tage der Gefahr*, and other great operas [are missing].[20] [//] [Blatt 7r]

Fidelio is there. // Even so, you should have it copied. // People want to blame the late Stegmayer[21] and Weigl for having [allowed] them to be carried off. //

They say that Salieri's position is not to be filled, and that Eybler[22] alone is to reign. //

---

[19] Barons Raimund and Alexander von Wetzlar numbered among the wealthiest art lovers in Vienna and had been friends of Mozart's. See Frimmel, *Handbuch*, II, p. 430.—KH/TA

[20] The three operas named are Mozart's *La clemenza di Tito* (1791) and Cherubini's *Lodoiska* (1791) and *Les deux Journées, ou le Porteur d'eau* (1800), known in German as *Der Wasserträger* (H.G. Schmieder's translation), *Die Tage der Gefahr*, or *Graf Armand*. Indeed, all three operas were probably German-language versions, often with considerable adaptation. See Frimmel, *Handbuch*, I, p. 93; Loewenberg, I, col. 552.—KH/TA

[21] Matthäus Stegmayer (b. Vienna, April 29, 1771; d. Vienna, May 10, 1820), actor, composer, theatrical poet, and choral director of the Court Opera. See Totenbeschauprotokoll, 1820, S, fol. 45r (Wiener Stadt- und Landesarchiv); Wurzbach, vol. 37, pp. 327–329.—KH/TA

[22] Antonio Salieri (1750–1825), composer and *Hofkapellmeister*, living in the City, house between Spiegelgasse and Seilergasse (formerly Krautgasse), at their intersection with narrow Göttweihergasse, House No. 1154 [renumbered as 1088 in 1821], actually belonging to his late wife's Helferstorfer family. His health, especially mental, took a steep decline in fall 1823, and Leipzig's *Allgemeine musikalische Zeitung* 25, No. 47 (November 19, 1823), col. 766, reported, "Court *Kapellmeister* Salieri is seriously ill, such that his recovery is in doubt. Age has had its detrimental effect upon his body as well as his mind. The lot of all Mankind. *Senectus ipsa est morbus!* [Old age itself is a disease!]"

After Salieri's pensioning on June 1, 1824, Vice-*Kapellmeister* Joseph Eybler (1764–1846), who had worked in the Court establishment for decades, took over the position of first *Kapellmeister*. See Frimmel, *Handbuch*, II, p. 95, and I, p. 131; Angermüller, "Salieri," *MGG*, vol. 11, cols. 1295–1298; Zieger, *Addressen-Buch*, pp. 61 and 113; Alexander Wheelock Thayer, *Salieri, Rival of Mozart*, ed. Theodore Albrecht (Kansas City: Philharmonia, 1989), pp. 151–154; Volkmar Braunbehrens, *Maligned Master: the Real Story of Antonio Salieri* (New York: Fromm International, 1992), pp. 227–231. Indeed, Beethoven's conversation books and the Viennese reports in the *AmZ* provide the most accurate cumulative account of the decline in Salieri's health.—KH/TA

Joel[23] bought it from him for a song. // He has managed it in such a way that this building ultimately was left to him *gratis*.[24] [//]

[Blatt 7v]

NEPHEW KARL [**presumably resuming after Schindler's departure**]: You indicated Frauendorfer [wine][25] at 48 kr; that is the same *Most* [wine] that we always drank at the *Birne*,[26] red. //

One can have Honor and Money. // In the book that I bought today, every time that gold is the subject, it says "yellow filth" [filthy lucre]. Because the expressions are somewhat "Old German"—from the times when people knew Latin better than German. //

Even Carbon,[27] except for his farming, is nothing extraordinary. // [Blatt 8r] Nothing annoys me so much as when I see that people [who] have lived a whole year as if they were on the other side of the world, suddenly come, just because they *need* something. If Carbon's dilemma about his furniture had not come up, then you could surely have waited a long time until you would have seen him. //

Nothing more today. // If I only knew the approximate price, how the old woman [Barbara Holzmann] had bought it, then I would know how far I can get involved. //

---

[23] Probably Carl Joel *Ritter* von Joelson (1762–1827), Court and Justice attorney, notary, member of the law faculty of the University of Vienna and of the Gesellschaft der Musikfreunde, who lived at Seilerstatt No. 992. Probably *not* his brother Felix Joel (1776–1856), doctor of law, member of the Gesellschaft der Musikfreunde, who lived on the Kohlmarkt No. 1147.
See Conscriptions-Bogen, Stadt, No. 992/1; and Stadt, No. 1147 (Wiener Stadt- und Landesarchiv); Kysselak, Memorabilien Österreichs, Verstorbene 1814 bis 1839, Blatt 84 (Tresor, Wiener Stadt- und Landesarchiv); *Allgemeine Theater-Zeitung* 50, No. 266 (November 18, 1856), p. 1078; *Hof- und Staats-Schematismus*, 1823, I, p. 702, and II, p. 112; Wurzbach, vol. 10, pp. 224–225; Ziegler, *Addressen-Buch*, p. 169.—KH

[24] Karl *Ritter* von Joelsohn owned City, Seilerstatt No. 992 (noted above as his residence), which was a composite of four houses numbered as 1052–1053 and 1274–1275 before 1821, all abutting the south wall of the City. Variant spelling in Behsel, p. 30.—TA

[25] Wine from Frauendorf in the Steyermark. See Raffelsperger, vol. 2, p. 522.—KH

[26] Possibly the restaurant *Zur goldenen Birne* (At the Golden Pear) in the suburb of Landstrasse, Hauptstrasse No. 52, that Beethoven often visited when he lived virtually across the street and four houses north from it and from October 1817 to October 1819, except for summers in the country. But it could also mean the coffee house *Goldene Birne*, in the Josephstadt No. 5 [renumbered as 6 in 1821], at the corner of the Glacis and Schwibbogengasse, in the building where Beethoven had an apartment more recently, from October 1819 to May 1820. See Frimmel, *Handbuch*, I, p. 160; Groner, 1922, p. 42; and Klein, *Beethovenstätten*, pp. 99–100, 108–110.—KH/TA

[27] Franz Ludwig Carbon, landowner in Mödling and one of the town's leading lights. Karl spells his name "Carbonne," which provides a clue to its pronunciation. Carbon's visit is recorded in Heft 45, Blätter 4v–5r; he asked Beethoven's assistance in securing an apartment in the Bürgerspital complex. Karl mentioned him again in Heft 45, Blatt 41v. See also Heft 38, Blatt 40r.—KH/TA

HEFT 46 (CA. NOVEMBER 21 – CA. NOVEMBER 26, 1823), BLATT 8V 59

BEETHOVEN: 40
               30
              <u><24></u>
              1 fl. 34 kr.

[Blatt 8v]

NEPHEW KARL: The maid is also an arch-sow; she goes to bed in the evening with her clothes on, just so she won't have to put anything on in the morning.[28] // She *can* cook well, if only she *wants to*. // She says that what the maid says, that she waited for her with the cooking, is not true. // It hasn't cost as much as veal for a long time. //

Today I was talking with someone who was with me as a pupil of the pastor at Mödling,[29] and who now studies philosophy. He said that the pastor now has a benefice in Upper Austria and has become a dean. // [Blatt 9r]

Violoncello. // In accompaniment with Violoncello?[30] [//]

Carpet. //

BEETHOVEN [**probably in a coffee house; late afternoon of Friday, November 21, looking at newspapers from the two days before, in reverse order**]:

Styrian capons, Kleine Schulerstrasse, Domherrn Hof, No. 872, from 8 o'clock in the morning until 7 o'clock in the evening, at the most reasonable price.[31] //

Two vacant apartments, with or without furniture, Landstrasse Hauptstrasse No. 50.[32]

[Blatt 9v: No writing, and crossed out with red pencil.]

[Blatt 10r]

NEPHEW KARL [**probably still Friday, November 21, in the evening**]: More than a pastor. He is still *pastor*, but now a dean, in addition, as a special honor. //

It ought to be simmered more. //

One would prefer to ring one time for the maid, because one wishes the h[ouse-keeper] less frequently, and it would make less trouble. //

---

[28] Karl made a similar complaint, including that the maid exposed herself unduly, in Heft 45, Blatt 13v (possibly two days earlier).—TA

[29] During Beethoven's summer stay in Mödling in 1818, Karl took a month of instruction from the town's pastor, Johann Baptist Fröhlich. See Frimmel, *Handbuch*, I, p. 156; Thayer-Deiters-Riemann, IV, p. 97; Thayer-Forbes, pp. 700–701. Karl's wording here suggests that this entry was made later in the day.—KH/TA

[30] This could refer to the Cello/Contrabass recitatives in the Fourth Movement or the entrance of the bass vocal soloist. See Heft 47, Blatt 38r (ca. December 6, 1823) for a sketch for the *Freude* theme.—TA

[31] See *Intelligenzblatt*, No. 266 (Wednesday, November 19, 1823), p. 1059 (Advertisements).—KH/TA

[32] See *Intelligenzblatt*, No. 265 (Tuesday, November 18, 1823), p. 1040 (Advertisements).—KH/TA

[NEPHEW KARL, *continued*]

The merchant on the Kohlmarkt appears to be more honorable than the gentlemen at the *Kamehl*.[33] // The merchant is incurably deaf in one ear. [//] [Blatt 10v] I shall still go to the Wildpretmarkt[34] and shop. // One can have rabbit with the fur for 3 fl.; but I think that it's all the same whether one takes the fur or has it skinned *before one's eyes*—the people do everything that way. // A pretty fur costs 1 fl. // As frugal as they might be otherwise, people pay like crazy. I saw that just today.—*This year* it is nothing like last year. // [Blatt 11r]

Tomorrow [presumably Saturday, November 22], if you want, I will have plenty of free time to see if I can bring a wild duck. // I need only go there and order it at 7:30 a.m., and pick it up at 1 o'clock. // If you don't need it [a wild duck]. // I'll already leave early. // If anyone opens the shutters, then I would get right up; but this way, I won't until someone awakens me. //

It's not exactly the housekeeper, it's the people in the Bischofhof,[35] who have taken the money from the maid. [Blatt 11v] The housekeeper took it to them.—By means of the *housekeeper*, otherwise *not*. // The housekeeper can protest against it, because *she* did not take the money from her; *she* is *not* indebted to *her*; rather the maid *knowingly* and *intentionally* lent it to the people in the Bischofhof. // The maid has neither a trunk, nor any other place to keep her money; she is also happy if someone takes it from her.[36] [//] [Blatt 12r]

It has now become the fashion among the servants to dress like ladies; they told me at Frau von Reinlein's[37] that whenever the daughter of the house got a new dress, the chambermaid had one *exactly like it* made for herself. The cook misused Frau von Reinlein's kindness, or weakness, so much that when she had to ask her for something, she would actually ask Frau von Reinlein to come to her in the kitchen. //

She said that the commissioner said that the wine-spirits cost so much, but I wrote too little [about it]. [//] [Blatt 12v] The maid has been told that she should not get the wine-spirits there, but rather in the Riemerstrasse. What can I do about it if she didn't do it? // The woman said that it [the wine-spirits] cost 46 kr.—she doesn't

---

[33] For the proprietors of the two grocery shops, see the difficult-to-date entries in Heft 45, Blatt 19v.—KH/TA

[34] Wildpretmarkt, a small square in the inner city, to the north of the cathedral, between Bauernmarkt and Tuchlauben. The *Rother Igel* essentially backed up on the Wildpretmarkt. See Groner (1922), p. 210.—KH/TA

[35] The archbishop's residence, across the street from and to the east of the cathedral. See Groner (1922), p. 43.—KH/TA

[36] The story continues on Blatt 19v below.—TA

[37] A well-off middle-class family, living at the southwest corner of Obere Breunerstrasse and the Graben, City No. 1134; Karl had been school friends with son Jacob Reinlein. See Heft 39, Blätter 25r–25v, among others.—KH/TA

[NEPHEW KARL, *continued*]
know what she wrote down. // She says that the man wrote it, and the woman paid it and said that the *spirits* cost 46 kr. // [Blatt 13r]

[presumably still at Beethoven's apartment; the morning of Saturday, November 22:]

Since he [Moscheles] is himself a composer, it would really be shame on him if he played compositions by others; he is therefore playing a concerto *of his own* [tonight], and a free Fantasia, likewise of his *own*.[38] // For those who like speed. //

I could go there [Blöchlinger's] tomorrow evening [Sunday, November 23]. // At that time, Giannatasio told me: "You have broken the ice; bring your uncle with you soon, because my whole family longingly wishes to see him."[39] [//] [Blatt 13v] I shall say that you will appear there sometime, quite unexpectedly:

Thus, as from High Heaven,
The Hour of Joy appears. //

Schiller. // I shall quote the song to you right away where this verse is. It is called *Die Erwartung*[40] and begins:

Hört' ich das Pförtchen nicht gehen?
Hat nicht der Riegel geklirrt?
Nein, es ist des Windes Wehen,
Der durch diese Pappeln schwirrt.[41] [Blatt 14r]

It goes like this through several stanzas, where the yearning man always believes that his beloved is coming and deceives himself. Finally, it says:

Und wie aus dem himmlischen Höhen
Die Stunde des Glückes erscheint,

---

[38] The surviving *Theaterzettel* (poster) confirms that Moscheles's concert took place at the Kärntnertor Theater on the evening of Saturday, November 22; the second half of the evening was devoted to a ballet. See also Heft 46, Blätter 16r–17r.—KH/TA

[39] Cajetan Giannatasio del Rio (1764–1828) lived and operated an educational institute in suburban Landstrasse, Glacis No. 426, perhaps a 10-minute walk from Beethoven's apartment in the Ungargasse. Indeed, if Beethoven walked into the walled City through the Carolinentor, his path would have taken him within a couple minutes of Giannatasio's place. Nephew Karl had attended the school from January 1816 to January 1818. Giannatasio's daughter Fanny was smitten with Beethoven and noted in her diary that Beethoven's own visits had become rare and that the last time the family had visited the composer was on April 19, 1820. See her excerpted and annotated diary in *Eine stille Liebe zu Beethoven: Nach dem Tagebuche einer jungen Dame* by Ludwig Nohl (Leipzig: Ernst Julius Günther, 1875), pp. 209–213; translated into cautious Victorian English as *An Unrequited Love: An Episode in the Life of Beethoven (from the Diary of a Young Lady)*, trans. Annie Wood (London: Richard Bentley & Son, 1876), pp. 197–201.—KH/TA

[40] With only a few discrepancies, nephew Karl cites the first and last stanzas of Friedrich Schiller's poem *Die Erwartung* (1799) from the *Musenalmanach auf das Jahr 1800*.—KH/TA

[41] Roughly translated: "Didn't I hear the garden gate move? / Didn't the latch clink? / No, it is the grief of the wind / That rustles through these poplars."—TA

So war sie genaht, ungesehen,
Und weckte mit Küssen den Freund.[42] //

Even if this poem is not one of Schiller's most beautiful, in this way, my good fellow, you can see that I am well-read. [//] [Blatt 14v]
    I must take that to Blöchlinger.[43] //
    She [the maid] has already made my bed. //

SCHINDLER [**presumably at Beethoven's apartment; later on Saturday, November 22**]: I didn't encounter Weigl yesterday. //
    Also yesterday I really wished that you had requested Duport to give you an answer, so that, if it was favorable, I would have had something in my hands, so that I could have proceeded. // I shall ask him about it, but orally. // [Blatt 15r] I am now going *directly* to Duport. //

[**presumably returning relatively early the next day, Sunday, November 23:**]
    Today I am going to a house where I am meeting the woman who was at Lichnowsky's. // Count Lichnowsky himself confirms that she is quite an excellent cook. // She has already been a cook for 15–16 years; therefore it may be expected that she is capable of running such a small household. [//] [Blatt 15v] Lichnowsky complains that she makes everything too well, but just too little of it. //
    I told him [Duport] that only the distance of your apartment is to blame that you don't visit his theater more often. //

NEPHEW KARL [**Beethoven's apartment; Sunday, November 23, no earlier than ca. 6 p.m., and probably continuing into the evening**]: Extraordinary man, [Blatt 16r] [smudged passage] from 4–5 o'clock. Easily manipulated and charmed by Rossini. The young people are good and show great promise.[44] //
    From his father to here. Godsberg. // It won't do.[45] //

---

[42] Roughly translated: "And so, as from High Heaven, / The Hour of Joy appears, / And so she approached unseen / And awakened her friend with a kiss."—TA

[43] Joseph Blöchlinger, proprietor of another, more enlightened educational institute in the Josephstadt, where Karl had studied until graduating in summer 1823.—KH/TA

[44] This may refer to the twelve-year-old pianist Johann Promberger, who gave a concert at the Landständischer Saal at midday (12:30 p.m.) on Sunday, November 23. He played Hummel's Concerto in A minor, as well as music by Spohr, Weber, and Assmeyer. See *Allgemeine musikalische Zeitung* 25, No. 52 (December 24, 1823), cols. 865–866. It might also refer to a concert by pupils of the conservatory of the Gesellschaft der Musikfreunde. See also Blatt 23v below.—TA

[45] Godsberg: presumably Godesberg, a spa town, ca. two miles south of Bonn. Ferdinand Ries's father, the former Bonn Court concertmaster Franz Ries (1755–1846), had presumably moved there. In 1824, Ferdinand Ries would buy an estate there and move back from London, where he had spent eleven years and amassed considerable wealth. Perhaps Franz Ries had sent something to his younger son, Joseph Franz (1792–1862), active as a piano maker in Vienna, that proved unsuccessful. See Heft 45, Blatt 23v (ca. November 13).—TA

[NEPHEW KARL, *continued*]

Moscheles presented the first movement of your Symphony in D, yesterday evening [Saturday, November 22].[46] // Fantasie. // From his head. [//] [Blatt 16v]

As you know, I have a great natural inclination to genius, and therefore, in connection with my erudition, it is easy for me to take delight in delighting people with interesting conversational exchanges.[47] In this sense, I've just told [people] that a bad actor from Flanders, who debuted in Paris, acted in a tragedy by a famous poet, where he portrayed [Blatt 17r] a fugitive, and said to his friends: "*Mais pour ma fuite, amis, quel parti dois-je prendre?*" (Which way shall I flee?). A wit in the parterre replied quite loudly: "*Ami, prenez la poste, et retournez en Flandre.*"[48] (He was from Flanders!) How do you like that? //

Herr von Kirchhoffer[49] says that it is very beautiful. [//] [Blatt 17v] The C-sharp Minor Concerto[50] is said to be not bad. // He asked if I didn't play billiards and smoke. // I said that I knew the name. // Merely suspicions. // Pangs of conscience. // How many cups? [Blatt 18r] Linz. *Capisco* [I understand]. //

Do you know Seidel? // He wrote the essay in the *Theater-Zeitung*. // Postal officer.[51] //

Salieri has cut his throat, but is still alive. [//] [Blatt 18v] He didn't know Haydn's

---

[46] Karl is reporting on Moscheles's concert of Saturday, November 22, 1823, constituting the first half of an evening at the Kärntnertor Theater, with the second half occupied with a ballet—a customary pairing of events. Moscheles's concert consisted of the first movement of Beethoven's Symphony No. 2 in D, Op. 36; a Piano Concerto in E major by Moscheles; a Phantasie on themes by Rossini and Weber, played on a piano made by Wilhelm Leschen (1781–1839) of Vienna; and Mlle Unger sang an Italian aria. See the *Allgemeine musikalische Zeitung* 25, No. 52 (December 24, 1823), cols. 865–866; and *Wiener AmZ* 7, No. 97 (December 3, 1823), cols. 771–774.—TA

[47] Karl is speaking with tongue in cheek here.—TA

[48] "My friends, take the post-coach and return to Flanders." Other than the omission of "My friends," the first French sentence is fairly fully translated in Karl's remarks.—TA

[49] Franz Christian Kirchhoffer, bookkeeper with the banking firms of Oppenheimer, as well as Hofmann & Goldstein, in Vienna. He facilitated Beethoven's transactions with Ferdinand Ries in London but seemingly carried on some of his own business with Beethoven's former student. See Heft 38, Blatt 49v, as well as Kirchhoffer's latest conversation concerning Ries in Heft 45, Blatt 23v (seemingly on Saturday, November 15).—KH/TA

[50] Presumably Ries's Piano Concerto in C-sharp Minor, Op. 55.—KH

[51] Joseph *Edler* von Seidl was an "I[mperial] R[oyal] High Postal Official," living at Stephansplatz, No. 627. See *Hof und Staats-Schematismus*, 1823, vol. 1, p. 530. Actually, Johann Chrysostomus Sporschil (1800–1863) wrote the feature story about Beethoven (signed "S ...... l") that appeared in Bäuerle's *Allgemeine Theater-Zeitung* on November 15. See Heft 45, Blätter 32r and 31v. For potential confusion, see also Scheidl (Blatt 22r below).—KH/TA

Quartets. // Only last year, he had them (Haydn's Quartets) played for him, so he could become acquainted with them.[52] // Umlauf.[53] [//] [Blatt 19r]

Not less. // By St. Stephan's.[54] Applications.[55] //

People are saying that I am a *Pfifficus* [sly dog]. // In everything. //

This evening the maid came to me and lamented that she would like to have shoes made for herself, but doesn't have so much as a kreuzer in money. I said: "How did that happen?" She replied that [Blatt 19v] the housekeeper had taken all of her savings, amounting to 29 fl. 30 kr., and had already failed to pay her bread money two times. // She has promised the maid 2 fl. percent [sic] monthly. //

100 : 12[56] =

20	100	X	2	10
1	12	2̶0̶	100	12
2	X	1̶	12	

//

You ignore all of that. She has just promised the maid to pay her [Blatt 20r] everything tomorrow. So we'll see whether she keeps her word. // As she says, the money is in the Bischofhof.[57] //

One writes a very brief notice: "A housekeeper of moral character is sought. For details, inquire at Wollzeil No. so-and-so." //

"Housekeeper sought; she must be a widow, draw a pension, and possess a moral character. Inquire concerning further attractive details at No. so-and-so." [//]

BEETHOVEN: "A widow as housekeeper, who [has] a little pension or ...." [//]

[Blatt 20v]

---

[52] In October 1823, Antonio Salieri's (1750–1825) health declined severely, and his daughters had him taken to the *Allgemeines Krankenhaus* for treatment. By early 1824, he slipped into dementia and never recovered. Salieri had participated in performances of Haydn's *Creation* during the composer's lifetime, but it is conceivable that he did not know the String Quartets well until the early 1820s.—TA

[53] Michael Umlauf (1781–1842), who had conducted the revival of *Fidelio* at the Kärntnertor Theater in November 1822 and would conduct the premiere of Beethoven's Ninth Symphony there on May 7, 1824. Umlauf was also a fine violinist, and it is possible that he participated in Salieri's private readings of the Haydn String Quartets.—KH/TA

[54] This could refer to Seidl's address; see Blatt 18r above.—TA

[55] Original German *Einkamen* could mean "income" or "applications." Since Beethoven was occupied with soliciting applications from prospective domestic servants, I have adopted the latter meaning.—TA

[56] Computations for the maid's earnings. Originally a "5" instead of "1" in "12," probably thinking of 52 weeks in a year.—KH/TA

[57] See Blätter 11r–11v for earlier aspects of this concern.—TA

NEPHEW KARL [**still the evening of Sunday, November 23, or possibly the morning of Monday, 24**]: Was Schindler here? //

Enough women will apply; we can surely choose the right one. //

Englishmen write "Beefsteake" and pronounce it "Bihfstähk"; Viennese write and say "Biftek." [//]

BEETHOVEN [**at his apartment; Monday, November 24, probably in the morning**]:

+ Washbasin[58]

+ Sugar

+ A *Binde* [necktie] of flannel, [Blatt 21r] but first ask Schindler.

+ Write Count Browne[59] concerning an apartment. //

NEPHEW KARL [**possibly adding items to Beethoven's list, later in the day**]:

Frau von Schulz.

Get water. //

[written vertically→] This week, yet. // That is the cook from the 3rd floor [4th floor, American], from whom she borrowed a cake pan. [←written vertically] [//] [Blatt 21v]

There was no one there today.[60] //

I am just now telling her that she should moderate her speech a little; because she says that you take her to be a fool in that you took her away from the countess. // She is close to spitting at us; she has already said, "Pfui Teufel!" about it that you didn't leave her [Blatt 22r] at the countess's.[61] // One must determine from the woman what she wants. //

BEETHOVEN:

+ Tallow[62] candles.

Bootjack.[63] //

---

[58] This was for Karl; see Heft 45, Blatt 5v.—TA

[59] Count Johann Georg Browne (1767–1827), patron of the arts, was in the Russian service. Beethoven had dedicated to him his String Trios, Op. 9 (of which No. 1 had been performed on Schuppanzigh's concert of Friday, November 21, 1823); the Piano Sonata, Op. 22; and the Gellert *Lieder*, Op. 48. See Frimmel, *Handbuch*, I, pp. 70–72.—KH/TA

[60] If Karl was out for classes and errands early, this could have even been written in late morning.—TA

[61] Countess Louise Morzin (b. 1777), living in Wieden, Alleegasse No. 60, the servant's previous employer. See also Heft 43, Blatt 23r.—KH/TA

[62] Candles were on the shopping list in Heft 45, Blatt 37r (probably Thursday, November 20), and in an advertisement of November 14 in Heft 45, Blatt 22r.—TA

[63] An iron tool consisting of a hook and wooden handle, to assist in pulling on tight boots. See Campe, IV, p. 655. Nephew Karl mentions Campe's dictionary in Heft 40, Blatt 26v.—KH

    56 kr.
    <u>56 kr.</u>
1 fl. 52 kr. //

NEPHEW KARL: How will we entertain Lord Falstaff [Schuppanzigh]?[64] //

She wants to be happy when she goes shopping; therefore a new basket must also be purchased, so that she looks good with it. //

BEETHOVEN [writing over Karl's previous group of entries and his own monetary computations above]:[65]

+ Pencil.[66]

   Scheidl.[67]

+ Frankfurt.[68]

+ Olmütz.[69]

+ Pencils.

[Blatt 22v]

NEPHEW KARL [possibly continuing the above, but in the afternoon, presumably Monday, November 24]: When I came out this morning, she had not yet completed the letter, and I looked at it. She immediately took the paper from my hand and said that it was to a good [female] friend; therefore a sign that she wants nothing to do with me. // Seems dear to me. //

COPYIST[70] [at Beethoven's apartment; presumably the afternoon, Monday, November 24]: I ask that you indicate where this part/voice belongs within it [the *Missa solemnis*]. // I believe in around 4 weeks. [//]

---

[64] See the long conversation among Beethoven, Karl, and Schuppanzigh (either Tuesday, November 25, or Wednesday, November 26) on Blätter 30r–36r.—TA

[65] In addition, an unknown hand later wrote "4 November" at a point to the right of the monetary figures; thus, three layers of entries at this point. This page is illustrated in *Konversationshefte*, vol. 4, facing p. 240.—KH/TA

[66] Beethoven had already needed to buy pencils by ca. Friday, November 21 (see Heft 45, Blatt 8r), had evidently gotten one or two, but now needed to stock up.—TA

[67] Johann Maximilian Scheidl, municipal bookbinder, living in the Leopoldstadt, Kleine Ankergasse No. 14. See Böckh (1822), p. 395. For potential confusion, see also Seidl (Blatt 18r above).—KH/TA

[68] Probably a reminder to write Franz Brentano, who was acting as financial intermediary in his dealings in Germany.—TA

[69] A reminder to write Archduke Rudolph in Olmütz.—KH

[70] See Alan Tyson, "Notes on Five of Beethoven's Copyists," *Journal of the American Musicological Society* 23, No. 3 (Fall 1970), pp. 439–470, especially pp. 450–454, discussing Wenzel Rampl to see who copied parts for the *Missa solemnis* (presumably the subject here). It could also concern Matthias Wunderl, who was at times associated with Rampl and who was Tyson's "Copyist E." See Heft 40, Blatt 10v; Heft 41, Blatt 1v; Heft 44, Blätter 4v–5r; and Heft 45, Blatt 26v.—TA

[Blatt 23r]

NEPHEW KARL [**presumably while the copyist is making annotations**]: The woman wants 5 fl. for ironing and pressing every day; *coffee, meals, and wine*. It is good that you deal with her right away, because otherwise there will be stories at the end. // She says that when she is finished, there is still time enough to come in here. //

COPYIST [**concluding his visit**]: I can only copy it alone, and have to take care of several *Lektionen* [recriminations].[71] [//] I will try to do what I can. [//]

[Blatt 23v]

LICHNOWSKY [**at Beethoven's apartment; possibly the morning of Tuesday, November 25; Karl is not present**]:[72]

Last Friday [November 21], a Trio of yours was performed.[73] // This past Sunday [November 23], your Mass [in C] was performed at the Augustiners'[74] for the Feast of St. Cecilia,[75] and it came together badly. //

Half of the popular theater. [//] [Blatt 24r] If you want to read the book, I can leave it here for a week. // You would surely get considerably more without a contract. // If you want, the administration [of the Kärntnertor Theater] will immediately make a contract, and with pleasure. [//] [Blatt 24v] Talk to Grillparzer about it; he will also know all about it. // A few days ago, Duport asked about the opera [*Melusine*]. // Your Overture to *Fidelio* [Blatt 25r] was stormily applauded in the last Akademie, and was repeated.[76] //

Almost nobody goes to the Weber opera [*Euryanthe*]. // <the following defense

---

[71] The original *Lektionen* means "rebukes," "recriminations," "scoldings," or "lessons." Its translation is not entirely clear from this context.—TA

[72] See Blätter 26v–28r, where Karl is the subject of conversation, obviously in his absence.—TA

[73] Schuppanzigh and his colleagues performed Beethoven's String Trio, Op. 9, No. 1 in G at their concert on Friday, November 21, 1823. See *Wiener AmZ* 7, No. 98 (December 6, 1823), col. 783. Schuppanzigh himself will report about the performance on Blatt 33v (November 25 or 26) below.—KH/TA

[74] The Cloister Church of the Augustinian Order that served as the Court's parish church and still maintains a thriving parish and musical program. It fronts onto Josephsplatz in the Hofburg complex. On Sunday, May 7, 1820, the Augustiner church had witnessed what was probably Vienna's first performance of Beethoven's Mass in C in a liturgical setting (see Heft 12, Blatt 74r). It still remains in the church's repertory today.—KH/TA

[75] The Feast of St. Cecilia, the patron saint of music, takes place on November 22. In 1823, November 22 was a Saturday, and so the musical observation with a large-scale Mass (in this case Beethoven's Mass in C, Op. 86) was postponed until the next day, Sunday, November 23.—KH/TA

[76] The Overture to *Fidelio* opened the second half of the Grand *Akademie* that was given at the Kärntnertor Theater on November 15, 1823, "to benefit the Public Charity Institutions." November 15, St. Leopold's Day, was the name day of the most recently deceased emperor, Leopold II, and was customarily the occasion for benefit concerts. See *Allgemeine musikalische Zeitung* 25, No. 52 (December 24,

[LICHNOWSKY, *continued*]
has> The following review has been written in defense of the poet [Helmina von Chezy].[77] [//] [Blatt 25v]

As I hear it, *Fidelio* will be revived with [Henriette] Sonntag [*sic*]. // Sonntag [*sic*] is better in singing, but [Wilhelmina] Schröder is better in acting and power. // [Blatt 26r] Sonntag [*sic*] has a considerable high range // and very accurate intonation. // I assure you that it [presumably Beethoven's *Akademie*] is absolutely a universal wish.[78] //

A fine but lazy person. // She was a cook at my place. [//] [Blatt 26v] If I hear of such a person, I'll send her here. //

How's it going, then, with dear Karl? If you visit me with him sometime, I'll introduce him to an interesting man [Blatt 27r] who is deeply involved in Greek history. He was once a professor in Poland, but, because he was something of a freethinker, left there. [Blatt 27v] <This B .... Sometime .... So, on ....[79]> Would you like to have dinner at my place on Sunday [November 30], and bring Karl? Give me that pleasure; then he can converse with the gentleman [Blatt 28r] in Greek to his heart's content. // In the Wieden, at the sign of the *Burned-down House*.[80] //

He [brother Johann] is the manager and she [wife Theresia] the squanderer. [//] [Blatt 28v] If he reads that page in the *Theater-Zeitung*, he will be angry that there is *no other* mention of him, except that he is an apothecary.[81] [//] [Blatt 29r]

This gentleman was professor of history, and is a learned and enlightened man. // <or in Brühl in the> Or in the Brühl. It is always dry there.[82] [//] [Blatt 29v] Convulsive. // The Baths in Meidling cause coughing.[83] //

[Blatt 30r]

1823), col. 865; *Wiener AmZ* 7, No. 95 (November 26, 1823), cols. 753–755; *Zettel*, Kärntnertor Theater, November 15, 1823 (Bibliothek, Österreichisches Theatermuseum); *Allgemeine Theater-Zeitung* 16, No. 144 (December 2, 1823), p. 575; and Weinzierl, p. 238.—KH/TA

[77] Helmina [Wilhelmina] von Chezy, the amateurish librettist for Weber's opera *Euryanthe*, which premiered at the Kärntnertor Theater on October 25, 1823, with Weber conducting. See, among others, Heft 44, Blätter 6v–7r, and Heft 45, Blatt 40v.—KH/TA

[78] Ultimately, Henriette Sontag (1806–1854) would sing in the Ninth Symphony on Beethoven's *Akademie* of May 7, 1824.—TA

[79] Three unsuccessful attempts to interject, probably while Beethoven continued to speak.—TA

[80] In suburban Wieden, the house with the sign *Abgebranntes Haus* was in the Altwiedener Hauptstrasse No. 242 [renumbered as 447 in 1830], on the west side of the street, between Grosse Neue Gasse and Klagbaumgasse.—KH/TA

[81] This remark concerns a reference to brother Johann in Sporschil's article about Beethoven in the *Allgemeine Theater-Zeitung* of November 15, 1823: "Other than his nephew, a brother of his lives in Vienna: Johann van Beethoven, an apothecary by profession." See also Heft 45, Blatt 32r.—KH

[82] Brühl, the picturesque valley of the Mödling Brook. See Frimmel, *Handbuch*, I, pp. 77–78.—KH

[83] Joseph Pfann's recently developed mineral spring and bathing establishment in Meidling. Schindler and brother Johann had recommended it on May 15, 1823, as had Lichnowsky on July 23 or 24, even offering to take Beethoven there himself (see Heft 36, Blätter 2r–2v). Beethoven had recently made note that Pfann's spa, now heated, could be used even in winter (see Heft 45, Blätter 21r–21v).—TA

SCHUPPANZIGH [at Beethoven's apartment or possibly at dinner in a restaurant, with Karl present; probably beginning ca. 2 p.m. but lasting into the late afternoon or early evening, probably Tuesday, November 25;[84] through Blatt 36r]:

Bethmann[85] [visiting from Berlin] said that he [= you] are free either to designate the price yourself or to leave it to their own generosity. // He [= You] can be assured that they will certainly treat you generously. // He [Weber] was more successful with *Der Freischütz*. [//] [Blatt 30v]

In the future, I shall give my Quartet concerts on Sunday afternoons at 4:30.[86] // On Friday [November 28], I am playing the 3rd *Rasumovsky* Quartet.[87] // He [Zmeskall?][88] will carry on with difficulty, I have been told, he is very weak. [//]

[Blatt 31r]

NEPHEW KARL: How shall we let him know? //

SCHUPPANZIGH: That's it, as I feared, because to play a [set of] Variations is not Art.[89] // Concerning my [application], Duport told me that making me concertmaster would not go so quickly, because one would have to break some contracts first.[90] //

NEPHEW KARL: He [Barbaja] is no longer here. // Naples. //

SCHUPPANZIGH: Menzel,[91] at the Court, has now died. // Now the position is vacant. //

---

[84] Tuesdays were among the days of the week when Karl was available for dinner with Beethoven. He presumably had classes in the morning.—TA

[85] Heinrich Eduard Bethmann (1774–1834), theater director in Berlin, came to Vienna with concertmaster Henning to obtain Beethoven's Overture and incidental music to *Consecration of the House* for the upcoming inauguration of their own new theater.—KH/TA

[86] The *Wiener AmZ* 7, No. 103 (December 24, 1823), col. 824, announced that Schuppanzigh's new series of String Quartet concerts would begin on Sunday, December 28, 1823.—KH/TA

[87] This concerns the Schuppanzigh Quartet's sixth noon-hour (12:30 p.m.) concert in the hall of the Musikverein on Friday, November 28, 1823. The program consisted of a "Quartet by Herr Henning, concertmaster in Berlin," performed "in the presence of the composer," as well as Mozart's Quartet No. 1 in G, K. 387 (first of the Quartets dedicated to Haydn), and Beethoven's Quartet in C, Op. 59, No. 3 (dedicated to the Russian ambassador, Count Andreas Kyrillowich Rasumovsky). See *Wiener AmZ* 7, No. 98 (December 6, 1823), cols. 783–784.—KH/TA

[88] See also Blatt 4v above for a similar possible reference to Nikolaus Zmeskall von Domanowecz.—TA

[89] Perhaps a reference to Moscheles's Fantasy on themes by Rossini and Weber, played on Saturday, November 22; see Blatt 16r above.—TA

[90] Indeed, the position was already honorably occupied by Joseph Katter (1770–1841), who had assumed it when Anton Wranitzky died in August 1820.—TA

[91] Longtime violinist in the Opera orchestra and *Hofkapelle* Zeno Franz Menzel (b. 1757) had died on November 19, 1823. He had lived in suburban Laimgrube, *bei den 14 Nothelfern*, Dreyhufeisengasse [today's Lehárgasse] No. 14 (two buildings west of the stage entrance of the Theater an der Wien). See

[Blatt 31v]

NEPHEW KARL [**writing, in part, on Schuppanzigh's behalf**]: There's no use. It's already been done. [//] The archduke [Rudolph] could do it. One word from him would be enough. // He *ought to* apply first, Dietrichstein said.[92] // Is already .... // Herr Schuppanzigh says that you could impress the archduke from 2 directions, that is to say, by providing him this position, he [Rudolph] would be doing two good deeds; *first*, that Herr Schuppanzigh would no longer have to make his living elsewhere; [Blatt 32r] and *second*, that the music would benefit greatly if he got the position. //

SCHUPPANZIGH [**continuing**]: Beethoven, he [= you] must eat at my place one of these days. // I can now get him [= you] a very fine housekeeper and at the same time a very good cook, a wife of a *Sollicitator* [justice of the peace] who just died a few days ago. [//] [Blatt 32v] How much is he [= are you] paying his [= your] housekeeper, then? // Yes, eggs are now in a bad way; most of them smell and one can easily determine that. // Where is she, then? // Strong. //

One of these days, my brother-in-law, the doctor, will send him [= you] a red wine. He told me that he already [Blatt 33r] sent him [= you] one—whether that is true, I don't know—with the advice that this wine would be very beneficial for his [= your] health. // One of these days, he will again send him [= you] one from Hungary. //

To hell with the stuff [you've] saved. // It's too bad that this person is so arrogant. [//] [Blatt 33v] If he [= you?] lost it, then the lucky finder will be able to make very little use of it because of its lack of clarity.[93] //

Last Friday [November 21], we played the Trio. // G major.[94] //

What is he [= are you] actually writing now? [//] [Blatt 34r] Weber says, "As God wills"; Beethoven says, "As Beethoven wills."[95] //

Totenbeschauprotokoll, 1823, M, fol. 41v (Wiener Stadt- und Landesarchiv); and Ziegler, *Addressen-Buch*, p. 64.—KH/TA

[92] Count Moritz Dietrichstein-Proskau-Leslie (1775–1864), *Hofmusikgraf* [Court musical administrator], managed the *Hofkapelle*. On February 12, 1821, he had been named manager of the Court Theaters and in November 1823 was succeeded in this office by Count Johann Rudolph Czernin. See *Hof- und Staats-Schematismus*, 1823, I, p. 5; and Frimmel, *Handbuch*, I, p. 111.—KH/TA

[93] This could refer to the lost materials mentioned in Sporschil's article. He indicated that all of Beethoven's correspondence had been lost, but it is quite possible that several sketchbooks were also in the box or trunk that disappeared during the move. It is possible that self-satisfied brother Johann arranged for inexpensive transportation of Beethoven's belongings back from Baden in late October 1822 and that Beethoven blamed him for the loss. In this case, Schuppanzigh might be saying that if someone found the sketches, he could not use them because their meaning was so unclear.—TA

[94] Schuppanzigh (with violist Weiss and cellist Linke) played Beethoven's Trio in G, Op. 9, No. 1, on Friday, November 21. See *Wiener AmZ* 7, No. 98 (December 6, 1823), col. 783.—KH

[95] This bon mot alludes to a proverb by Carl Maria von Weber. His portrait by Carl Christian Vogel von Vogelstein, engraved by C.A. Schwerdgeburth, appeared in Weimar and Leipzig in 1823 with the facsimile signature: "As God wills! Carl Maria von Weber."—KH

HEFT 46 (CA. NOVEMBER 21 – CA. NOVEMBER 26, 1823), BLATT 34V

Do me the favor of writing to the archduke on my behalf tomorrow; if it doesn't do any good, at least it can't hurt anything. The archduke would have to write to Dietrichstein about it; nothing else can do any good. [//] [Blatt 34v]

The Jew Moscheles is here again; the Jews are making a terrible commotion [over him].[96] //

Beethoven, he [= you] could make a great monetary speculation if he [= you] would publish all his [= your] works by subscription in revised versions. // [Blatt 35r] If he wants [= you want], I will give him [= you] a hand, and he [= you] will become a rich man with his [= your] old works. // Steiner is a damned Jew.[97] // He himself [= You yourself] must make it known that he [= you] want to issue a splendid edition of all his [=your] works. [//] [Blatt 35v]. But he [= you] would have to promise to make some small alterations. [//] Only *pro forma*. // I assure him [= you] that it would bring him [= you] great capital. // I already know how it is to be begun. [//] [Blatt 36r] Unfortunately we live in an age where one must deal with works [of art] like a businessman. // Steiner has made fine capital with his [= your] compositions. //

[End of the conversation with Schuppanzigh, presumably late in the afternoon or even in the early evening.]

NEPHEW KARL **[probably having supper at a restaurant; probably evening and late night**[98] **after having dinner with Schuppanzigh on Tuesday, November 25, through Blatt 39r]**:

Schindler hopes to become <not a 1st violinist, but> 2nd concertmaster instead of Hildebrand;[99] Duport told him so. Today he auditioned, which was entirely to Duport's satisfaction. [//]

---

[96] As noted on Blätter 13r and 16r above, pianist-composer Ignaz Moscheles gave a half-evening's concert at the Kärntnertor Theater on Saturday, November 22, 1823. Several in Beethoven's circle considered him to be facile and superficial, thus Schuppanzigh's remarks here.—TA

[97] Schuppanzigh writes "Stein," but surely means the publisher Sigmund Anton Steiner (1773–1838), who was not Jewish but, in the stereotypical context here, had acted in the capacity of a banker (a "Jew") in loaning money to Beethoven and in profiting from his works. See also Heft 41, Blätter 9r–9v. Nephew Karl expressed a similar sentiment, but in less emphatic terms, in Heft 43, Blatt 43v [*sic*].—KH/TA

[98] See Blatt 38r below, where Karl refers to having seen Professor Stein that morning, so this must be much later (possibly the day after their dinner with Schuppanzigh); Karl's admonition that Beethoven's loud speech might waken people suggests that this conversation might have lasted well into the night of the same day that they dined with Schuppanzigh.

With the new semester, Karl seems to have roomed in the City, at least part-time, from ca. November 3 on. Even so, he often eats midday dinner with Beethoven and refers to coming "*hinaus*" (out) to the Ungargasse, etc. Heft 44, Blatt 3r (semester); and Heft 45, Blätter 19r, 33v–34r, and 35r, suggest that Karl roomed elsewhere.—TA

[99] Violinist Johann Hildebrand (b. 1790) had not been in any of Vienna's theater orchestras in fall 1822, when Ziegler's *Addressen-Buch* was compiled, and so seems to be a very recent addition in fall 1823. He became one of the concertmasters at the Kärntnertor Theater and lived, unmarried,

[NEPHEW KARL, *continued*]

We paid 4 fl. 24 kr.—2 fl. for the kitchen candles, and 2 fl. 24 kr. for the molded ones. [//] [Blatt 36v]

A sweet inquiry! [//] They have just come. Oysters are here. [//] 9 kr. [//] It's quite the same to me. // I haven't arranged anything. [//] Joke. // It's all the same to me. //

He will be that anyway, good fellow! // Schindler was quite beside himself with joy. // Now he will soon be in better standing. //

Did you already calculate how much you spent? [//] 4 fl. 24 kr. [for candles]. [//] [Blatt 37r]

Eel. // Mussels. // Patience, good fellow! //

Schuppanzigh appears to be a good man. // Not *entirely too much spirit*, but a good man.[100] // Caesar said: "I do not fear fat men; I fear lean ones."[101] (If Caesar *can* be afraid.) He [Antony?] would have preferred that the [knife] blow had struck him. //

Antiochus[102] had a soldier—who was very brave, but [Blatt 37v] looked bad—restored to health, but found that afterward, when his health was restored, he was no longer as brave as he had been before. It may have been the same with Caesar. Once he had attained the highest power, life became all the more dear to him. // They offered him the crown. //

It [the wine] is no longer good. The other Italian wines are good. // Costs 1 fl. 30 kr. [//] [Blatt 38r]

This morning, I walked to the university with Professor Stein.[103] //

Taceas, amici [Be silent, my friends]. Good fellow! You are awakening the people.[104] // In any case, the people do nothing but sleep. // *Animalia ruminantia* [Bovines]. [//]

---

in the City, Kärntnerstrasse No. 1005. See Conscriptions-Bogen, Stadt, No. 1005 (Wiener Stadt und Landesarchiv).—KH/TA

[100] Nephew Karl had been too young to know Schuppanzigh before he set out on tour and eventually a prolonged residency in Russia early in 1816. Thus he is commenting on someone who, to him, is a recent acquaintance.—TA

[101] Karl is quoting Shakespeare's play *Julius Caesar*, act 1, scene 2. This segment of Caesar's conversation with Antony runs from lines 192 to 212, including, "Let me have men about me that are fat … Yond Cassius has a lean and hungry look … Would he were fatter! But I fear him not." Karl seems to be paraphrasing the Schlegel and Tieck translation, rather than the Eschenburg version that Beethoven had known from his youth.—TA

[102] Antiochus, the name of several kings of Syria (4th–1st centuries B.C.). Plutarch reports the same anecdote that Karl tells here, but about Antigonus. Therefore, Karl may have confused Antiochus for Antigonus. See Plutarch's *Vitae parallelae, Pelopidas I*.—KH

[103] Anton Joseph Stein (1759–1844), professor of Latin and Greek, lived in the Ungargasse No. 359, only six houses south of Beethoven's apartment. Four weeks before, Karl had described him as "a terrible pedant" and had provided compelling reasons for his opinion (see Heft 44, Blätter 9r–9v).—KH/TA

[104] Something, possibly the reference to Stein, irritated Beethoven (who, late at night, may have had too much wine), and Karl spent the rest of this conversation book trying to calm him down.—TA

[NEPHEW KARL, *continued*]

2 fl. per pound. // ¼ pound costs 30 kr. // Almonds are always more expensive than raisins. // Good fellow! You don't need anything. // You are already satisfied with *me*! [//] [Blatt 38v] Good fellow! You could <carry something away; drink up!> // Good fellow! I have already made a report of all of today's happenings. //

To bed. // That is always my last wish at the end of the day.[105] [//] [Blatt 39r]

7 fl. 15 kr. [total of evening expenses].

3 fl. 51 kr. for the late supper
3 fl. 24 kr. for the sugar
7 fl. 15

[probably at Beethoven's apartment; perhaps the next morning, Wednesday, November 26, drafting an extensive reaction to the previous evening's conversation:]
<You speak of ....> [//] [Blatt 39v]
I believe that at this moment, I have demonstrated not only that I do not take any improper measures against you, but also that I love you more than I would have loved my father if he were still alive. But you cannot take me amiss (since so *much* depends upon it, as you yourself know that I have *consideration* for the servants—for how would it be otherwise?) that *I* considered the subject from the maid's point of view to be a disturbing remark of yours, and left, [Blatt 40r] as if you had advised me, to go to sleep, because I knew that if I remained in there, you would continue telling me about your dissatisfaction with my stubbornness, as it certainly only *appeared* to provide you with evidence, at least at *this* moment. //

Concerning the confusion with the keys, it is certainly a rare case that I left them here; it could only have happened in my haste and worry about taking all the written materials that I needed; and concerning the 2 pocket handkerchiefs, I don't know at all how they could have gotten *there*, since [Blatt 40v] I certainly remember having placed at least the *blue one* in my chest.—Thus you have also reproached me today that I should be taking care that your underpants fit you. As you know, I have too little time to do things that you yourself can do the best, since you know what is wrong with them.

End of Heft 46

---

[105] Karl is probably reassuring Beethoven that he prays for him at the end of the day, or some similar sentiment.—TA

Heft 47

(ca. November 29, 1823 – ca. December 6/7, 1823)

[Blatt 1r]

NEPHEW KARL [**presumably at Beethoven's apartment in the Ungargasse; ca. Saturday, November 29, presumably in the morning**]:[1]
Good fellow! We study, we sleep, we eat, we drink, we laugh—what more could you want?[2] //
She[3] is dreadfully angry at the old woman [former housekeeper Barbara Holzmann], because, as she says, she [Holzmann] must have indulged you very much, since you were not like that earlier. I say *ditto*. // If I *would have to be* a fish, then I would like to be a swordfish.[4] [//]

$$\begin{array}{r} 13 \\ \times\ 4 \\ \hline 52 \end{array}$$ //

A priest, a lawyer, a philosopher, etc.[5]

$$\begin{array}{r} 13 \\ \times\ 4 \\ \hline 52 \end{array}$$ //

90 ÷ 2 = 45   45   90 ÷ 7 = 12, with 6 left over. [//] [Blatt 1v]

The pound [weight] is reckoned at 51 kr., i.e., 17 Groschen. [//]

---

[1] If Henning came at a normal calling hour on Saturday, November 29, then Karl's entries are surely earlier in the day.—TA

[2] Nephew Karl may be parodying Shylock's speech in Shakespeare's *Merchant of Venice* (act 3, scene 1) here. It also suggests that Karl may be rooming part-time elsewhere.—TA

[3] Beethoven's "new" housekeeper was evidently Maria Pamer (b. 1807), who had worked for the composer as a very young maid before June 1822 and had now returned. See Heft 42, Blatt 24v.—TA

[4] Beethoven may have mentioned Karl's rapier-like opinion of Barbara Holzmann, followed by this parry from Karl.—TA

[5] It almost seems as if Karl is setting up a joke: "A priest, a lawyer, and a philosopher walk into a bar …."—TA

HENNING[6] **[at Beethoven's apartment; Saturday, November 29, possibly late morning or early afternoon]**: I have to bring you the very best regards from Privy Chamber Councillor Duncker.[7] //

Schuppanzigh played one of my Quartets quite superbly yesterday [November 28].[8] //

In the Schullerstrasse, in the *König zum Ungarn*,[9] in the second [American third] floor, No. 15. My name is Henning.[10] // We're staying here another 10 days. [//]

[Blatt 2r]

BEETHOVEN: + Beer.
+ 23.
+ Mustard.
+ Cut hair. //

HENNING: From ancient times, your [Austrian] government has unfortunately already distinguished itself in this respect, and it is sad to see what consequences it retains in this respect. // In that way, people in Berlin are fortunate, because we live in complete freedom, and the arts and sciences flourish ever more and more, and would develop further *if* Spontini's egotism[11] did not create an obstacle. [//] [Blatt 2v]

Decorations do not honor the artist; rather his art does. //

He [Radziwill][12] is alternately in Berlin and in Posen, where he is governor. He plays your Quartets superbly; we've passed the time with several works, 2 or 3 times each, at his place, with ever-increasing pleasure, until 3 o'clock at night. [//]

---

[6] Carl Wilhelm Henning (1784–1867), the Berlin concertmaster seeking to acquire Beethoven's *Die Weihe des Hauses* for the upcoming opening of his new theater there, had arrived in Vienna on Tuesday, November 4, and may have visited Beethoven in the company of violinist Schuppanzigh on the next day. See Heft 45, Blätter 5v–7v; Clive, pp. 159–161.—KH

[7] Johann Friedrich Leopold Duncker (1768?–1842), first chamber secretary to the king of Prussia and privy high government councillor. His acquaintance with Beethoven went back to 1814, when he was in Vienna for the post-Napoleonic Congress. Beethoven wrote four pieces, WoO 96, for his presumably unperformed tragedy *Leonore Prohaska*, initially projected for the suburban Leopoldstadt Theater. See Frimmel, *Handbuch*, I, p. 117; Kinsky-Halm, pp. 553–554.—KH/TA

[8] A string quartet of Henning's had been performed on Schuppanzigh's midday concert of Friday, November 28, 1823. See Heft 44, Blatt 10r; and Clive, p. 96.—KH

[9] Henning was staying at the hotel *Zum ungarischen König* [At the (Sign of the) Hungarian King], in the (Grosse) Schulerstrasse No. 852. See Schmidl, *Wien*, 1833, pp. 273 and 332; Pezzl, p. 240; and Heft 45, Blatt 6v.—KH/TA

[10] Henning may not have had to reintroduce himself completely but probably had to remind Beethoven of his name, which Schuppanzigh had written once when he initially introduced them in Heft 45, Blatt 6v.—TA

[11] Gaspare Spontini (1774–1851), general music director at the Royal Opera in Berlin; see also Heft 45, Blatt 6v.—KH

[12] Prince Anton Heinrich Radziwill (1775–1833); see also Heft 44, Blatt 8v; Clive, p. 275.—KH

He has successfully set several scenes from Goethe's *Faust* for orchestra. // It would be very fine if you sometime want to carry out these ideas,[13] and [Blatt 3r] designate them to be performed at our theater. I wish that you would be so kind as to write out these ideas and your entire concept, so that it would serve the poet [librettist] as a model. // At our theater we have a very talented young poet;[14] he would certainly agree to your demands. // That is why we have engaged this poet full-time. //

They were amazed here how a Berliner could be so musical [and] compose a rational quartet. // [Blatt 3v]

If you would, please allow me to call upon you one more time, and I hope that you will then give me your ideas about *Faust*. //

BEETHOVEN [at a coffee house; late afternoon of Saturday, November 29, reading current and retrospective newspapers]:

+ This evening, hire one or the other as housekeeper. [//] [Blatt 4r]

+ *Die Heizung mit erwärmter Luft* [Heating with Warmed Air], etc., by P.J. Meissner, with 20 copperplates, 2nd edition, Vienna, at Gerold's, 1823.[15] //

+ Plankengasse, [No.] 1063: snuffing tobacco tins.[16] [//]

[Blatt 4v]

NEPHEW KARL [presumably at Beethoven's apartment; evening of Saturday, November 29; long conversation through Blatt 8r]: The housekeeper told the maid that she is to receive 25 fl. per month from you. // I won't say another word to her; also not *in front of* you. // She crossed that out herself, because she already gave her 6 fl. 30 [kr.] // I myself don't know how I forgot to tell you, because yesterday evening, it was no longer a topic of conversation, and the maid told me about it. I didn't consider it so important; otherwise you can surely see that, because of this, I didn't mention

---

[13] For Beethoven's plans to set *Faust*, extending back to 1808, see Frimmel, *Handbuch*, I, p. 469; Max Unger, *Ein Faustopernplan Beethovens und Goethes* (Regensburg: G. Bosse, 1952); and Clive, p. 135.—KH/TA

[14] Probably Carl von Holtei; see Heft 45, Blatt 6r.—KH

[15] Excerpt from an advertisement in the *Intelligenzblatt*, No. 237 (October 14, 1823), p. 814: "To be had at C. Gerold's bookshop on Stephansplatz, on the left corner of Goldschmidgasse No. 625, *Die Heitzung mit erwärmter Luft* ... by P.J. Meissner, Master of Pharmacology ... [and] Professor at the I.R. Polytechnic Institute; second, very expanded ... edition with 20 copperplate illustrations; octavo, ... 3 fl. C.M." The same advertisement had also appeared on October 6 and 10, 1823.

Beethoven was obviously looking at a six-week-old copy of the *Wiener Zeitung*'s *Intelligenzblatt* that he probably found among older papers in a coffee house. In any case, his excerpting and copying of the advertisement were accurate or within customary variants. Gerold's shop was, as described, on the northwest corner of Stephansplatz and Goldschmidgasse.—KH/TA

[16] See the *Intelligenzblatt*, No. 275 (November 29, 1823), p. 1131 (Advertisements). The same announcement had appeared on November 22 and would appear again on December 6 (three successive Saturdays).—KH/TA

[NEPHEW KARL, *continued*]
anything about the housekeeper's salary, etc., [Blatt 5r] which was to be given to the maid. If she knows it, then she knows it from the maid herself. //

The postal coach to Frankfurt departs every Saturday.[17] //

In the house where I eat, I have in any case done everything that I could. The people have spread the word and have promised to find a good one.[18] // How does it stand with the one whom [Count Moritz] Lichnowsky[19] wanted to bring you? // One must consider that when the old woman [housekeeper Barbara Holzmann] was here, we didn't need anyone [else], because the old woman did everything herself, etc. Now, however, everything is difficult, since she does absolutely *nothing*, and therefore leaves a gaping hole there. // I continually hear her calling outside, but when I am studying, I can't hear what she is saying. [//] [Blatt 5v] The maid will probably know it, if she will only *tell*! // She is ill-tempered. // We'll want to ask her. // She has made it a principle to conduct herself quite roughly with us, because, she says, "if I behave timidly, then it is only more annoying." "You were able to make amends with the old woman with a glass of wine, but not *her*.["] And more of the *same*. // Among the many other things that the maid reeled off, she said that it would do *her* no honor if she had been released from service after so short a time. [//]

[Blatt 6r][20]

The pike *surely* did not cost so much. // That is over 20 kr. in silver. How is that possible? !?!?? *O Tempora, o mores!* [O the times, o the customs!][21] //

What I noticed about her, among other things, is that, when you scold her, she remains quite indifferent, and even makes motions as if she wanted to leave, etc., as you yourself have seen. But she is *completely different* when someone is here and she is scolded in his presence—for example, when you scolded her in front of Schuppanzigh, she was quite beside herself about the humiliation of her offended dignity. //

At one time, I gave you a description of the goings-on in the philosophy lecture halls, but that was only true [Blatt 6v] if no professor was there. Today, however, it was so noisy after the professor[22] had issued a warning, that the whole class raised

---

[17] "The departure ... of the postal coach at the I.R. Chief Transport Office is established as follows: Saturdays, evenings at 7 o'clock: Via Linz, Schärding and Passau, to Regensburg, Nürnberg, Würzburg, Frankfurt ...." See Pezzl, pp. 630–632. Franz and Antonie Brentano lived in Frankfurt; and a copy of the *Missa solemnis* was destined for the *Cäcilien-Verein* there; see Blatt 24v below.—KH/TA

[18] Karl ate at the boardinghouse of Baroness von Born and Frau Baumgarten ("the people") in the *Rother Igel* in the Tuchlauben. As evidenced by earlier conversation books, he and Beethoven had evidently asked them to help find a new housekeeper.—TA

[19] Several of Beethoven's friends were on the lookout for servants on his behalf.—TA

[20] If there is a missing Blatt between Blätter 39 and 40 near the end, its counterpart might be a Blatt missing before 6r, here, though no missing material is immediately apparent.—TA

[21] A quote from Cicero, who did not use an exclamation point.—TA

[22] Dr. Martin Johann Wikosch, professor of history; see Blatt 7r below.—TA

[NEPHEW KARL, *continued*]
a loud commotion against him. There was a *scuffle* in one corner of the hall during the period, so that he himself had to rise from the lecturer's seat in order to separate the combatants. He asked one of them what his name was (in order to make note of him), and he got *nothing* for an answer. *Angrily*, he asked him *again* what his name was, and again *no answer*. Finally the boy said: "What concern is my name to you? I am no delinquent," until finally the professor threw him out of the door. [Blatt 7r]

He can never write down the bad types (in the roll), because he does not know the names of those who created the disturbance. // They would only laugh him out. // That he does not know enough to gain a reputation.

In Stein's lectures,[23] on the contrary, you can hear a mouse stirring; everything is *that* quiet. // Everything depends upon the professor. If he behaves passively, he is already lost. //

The one at whose lecture this happened today (Wikosch,[24] professor of history) knows no other means of creating quiet than, at the beginning of the class, [Blatt 7v] praising to the heights the quietness that prevailed in the previous class (even if it had been noisy). *In this way*, he believes, he would influence the students to take more care to earn his praise; but unfortunately, his belief is false! // He is knowledgeable; even the *book* is by him, but he is already very old. // I believe 1,200 fl. C.M. [or] 3,000 [fl. W.W.].[25] // The professors all have wretched lodgings. [//] [Blatt 8r]

You heard about the infamous Kaunitz, though. He is said to have shot himself in Paris.[26] //

---

[23] Anton Joseph Stein (1759–1844), Karl's professor of Greek literature; Karl considered him "a terrible pedant." See Heft 44, Blätter 9r and 9v.—KH/TA

[24] Dr. Martin Johann Wikosch (1751–1826), professor of general and Austrian state history, diplomacy, and heraldry at the University of Vienna. He wrote the book *Grundriss der Universal-Geschichte* (Vienna, 1812). Wikosch lived with his sister in the City at Jakobergasse (the far southern extreme of Schullerstrasse) No. 807. See *Hof- und Staats-Schematismus* (1823), II, pp. 96 and 120. Karl spells his name "Vikosch."—KH/TA

[25] Probably the professor's annual salary.—TA

[26] Prince Aloys Wenzel Kaunitz (1774–1848), grandson of Chancellor Prince Wenzel Anton Kaunitz, had served as Austria's ambassador to Madrid from 1815 to 1817. During that time, Francisco Goya painted his portrait. On July 6, 1822, however, Kaunitz was arrested in his palace in the Dorotheergasse in Vienna. At his trial, it was revealed that he had abused and shamed no fewer than 200 girls between the ages of 11 and 14. He supposedly "only kissed" the future ballet star Fanny Elssler (then 11), but he did have sexual relations with her older sister, ballet student Therese (then 14). He paid token reparations to many of the parents, repaired to his country estate near Brno, and died in Paris at age 75 in 1848.

Beethoven had known the Elssler family through his connections with Haydn, had hired oboist Joseph Elssler (1767–1843), the brother of Johann Elssler (1769–1843) and uncle of Fanny (1810–1884) and Therese Elssler (1808–1878) and two other dancing daughters [probably Johann's], for his 1813–1814 benefit concerts and was probably enraged at the revelation of Kaunitz's sexual improprieties.

Similar activities on the part of the reigning Prince Nikolaus Esterházy (1765–1833), who had commissioned Beethoven's Mass in C, Op. 86, in 1807, had been known for years. See Gustav Gugitz,

BEETHOVEN [Saturday evening, November 29, or Sunday morning, November 30]:
+ Macaroni.[27]
+ Mustard.[28]
+ Parmesan cheese.
+ Dumpling forms.[29] //

NANNETTE BAUER[30] [at Beethoven's apartment; presumably Sunday, November 30, answering typical questions concerning employment history and residence]: [I worked] for 10 years for a Hungarian nobleman, until he died. [//] [I was] a cook at Maier's.[31] [//] My employer was 81 years old. [//] [I live] with my married sister [Blatt 8v] in the Josephstadt in the Ledererstrasse, at the *Unicorn*, No. 353 [*sic*]. //

Die Ehetragödie Ferdinand Raimunds, nach den unveröffentlichten Akten des Wiener Stadtgerichtes in Archiv der Stadt Wien (Vienna: Wiener Bibliophilien-Gesellschaft, 1956), pp. 26 and 30; summarized with additional material in H.C. Robbins Landon, *Haydn: Chronicle and Works*, vol. 4 (Bloomington: Indiana University Press, 1977), pp. 45–48.

From March 21 through August 20, 1822, John Russell (ca. 1796–1846), a young Scottish lawyer, had visited Vienna and left an extensive description of the City, including: "Nor are mothers ashamed to be the brokers of their daughters. There is no want of purchasers. The most famous, or rather infamous, is Prince Kaunitz … An incensed father … complained directly to the Emperor. The Emperor instantly ordered Kaunitz to be imprisoned, and proceeded against criminally." See John Russell, *Tour in Germany and … the Austrian Empire in 1820, 1821, 1822*, new ed., 2 vols. (Edinburgh: Constable and Co., 1828), 2: 199–201; facsimile with Introduction by William Meredith, *Beethoven Journal* 29, No. 2 (Winter 2014), pp. 67 and 74–75.—TA

[27] Macaroni and cheese (Parmesan also listed below) was one of Beethoven's favorite dishes. Schindler commented: "It had to be particularly bad for him not to like it." See Schindler-MacArdle, pp. 386–387.—TA

[28] Mustard is carried over from his shopping list on Blatt 2r above.—TA

[29] German original, *Knöpfformen*; literally "button-forms," but in this context, more likely forms for shaping foods, perhaps *Knödel*, large Viennese dumplings. If smaller, they might make dumplings like gnocchi. Larger ones could also be used for meatballs or lending shape to the macaroni and cheese mentioned elsewhere in this list. Even today, Viennese restaurants often serve rice or a mixture of rice and peas portioned and shaped in a similar form.—TA

[30] The name Nannette is a diminutive form of the name Anna. Nephew Karl provides the name of this applicant for the housekeeper's position in Heft 48, Blatt 6r. Unlike many of Beethoven's domestic servants, Nannette Bauer could write reasonably well. In ca. 1819/1820, one Joseph Bauer (b. 1790), an "authorized carpenter" from "Schwarzwald in Baden" and his wife, Anna (b. ca. 1791), were living in the Josephstadt, at the sign of the *Goldenes Einhorn* (Golden Unicorn), Ledererstrasse No. 153 (not 353), apartment 9. The building was on the west side of the street, two buildings south of Florianigasse. In 1824, Magdalena Zing (b. 1782), a "baker's widow from Passau," also lived in apartment 9. About the same time, Anna Bauer (b. ca. 1788), a "handworker from Passau"—and certainly identical with the Anna Bauer above—lived there with three other people. By 1830, all of them had moved away. See Conscriptions-Bögen, Josephstadt, No. 153, new collations 153/26, 153/70, and 153/71 (Wiener Stadt- und Landesarchiv); Behsel, p. 154.—KH/TA

[31] German original *Maierin* could also mean a female steward, in addition to the proper surname Maier (with the female suffix -*in*).—TA

NEPHEW KARL [**immediately following; probably as Bauer or another candidate cooks some samples**]: She has commissioned a [woman] friend, who in turn learned about it from another woman. // Like the candidates for an official's position. // Only nothing too hasty. We also want to see a sample of her cooking, for that is probably [Blatt 9r] the only way that one can be sure that her claims are honorable. //

[calculating salary:]

  18 [fl. per month]
 x 12 [months]
  ―――――
  36
  18
  ―――――
 216 fl. is the yearly salary, figured from monthly.
  12 fl. for laundry, if one needs a large wash done monthly.

  56 [kr. per week]
 x 52 [weeks per year]
  ―――――
  112
  280
  ―――――
 2912 [kr.] ÷ 60 = 44 fl. 48 kr. is the *Brotgeld* [bread money].[32] //

The salary at 18 fl. monthly is	216 fl.
Washing at 1 fl. monthly	12
Bread money	44
Total of 272 fl. 48 kr.	272

[Blatt 9v]

She can do nothing for it; she did not immediately let Marie [Pamer?] go, because she still needed her for something. // My portion is too salty. //

Tomorrow [Monday, December 1], the vice-director of the philosophy faculty[33] will come to the class, in order to investigate yesterday's incident and to dismiss the perpetrators. He will also investigate the theft of the overcoats and hats and *books*, committed up to now.[34] // There are guards there, but no one pays any attention to them. // This week is the election of a *Rector magnificus*.[35] [//] [Blatt 10r]

---

[32] Karl includes the remaining calculations in the long division, omitted here.—TA

[33] Vice-director of the broadly-defined philosophical faculty was Franz Xaver Wilde, doctor of philosophy, living in the City, Graben No. 1094. See *Hof- und Staats-Schematismus* (1823), II, p. 96.—KH

[34] In Heft 45, Blatt 20v, perhaps two weeks before these entries, Karl had told Beethoven about the theft of an overcoat hung at the entry to the lecture hall. See also Blatt 12v below.—TA

[35] The *Wiener Zeitung*, No. 286 (December 13, 1823), p. 1159, reported that on November 6 and 7, there had been a selection of four new *Nations-Procuratoren* [procurators], and that they, in turn, met in the university's Consistorial Hall on November 19 and elected Carl Joseph Pratobevera from among three candidates for rector. Pratobevera (1769–1853) was a doctor of laws, vice president of the

[NEPHEW KARL, *continued*]

But no one knows it yet; therefore it will not be long before the perpetrators are caught. //

I am curious how the heiress[36] from Pressburg will get ready if she is to provide some samples of her cooking. // She worked for the nobleman for 10 years. // At the grocer's. Today she got only 3 kr.; the h[ousekeeper] always writes on the bill if she got 3 times as much, thus 9 kr. //

When Bürger[37] translated *The Iliad*, he wanted—as he says in his preface—to translate the [Blatt 10v] Greek honorary titles, such as (for example) *dios Achilleus* (Godly Achilles), etc., as [German] *highly-noble born*, or *well-born*, and that Homer had used these honorary titles as customary formulas of courtesy. We don't want to look into how much of that is true, but this much is certain: that the Greek honorary titles, [Blatt 11r] such as (for example) the "Power of Hercules," would be very poorly reproduced with our words, "His Majesty, Hercules."[38] //

Sometime, we should go back to the Optical Armchair Journeys; they are showing only new presentations on various regions and cities.[39] //

Imperial Appellate and Criminal Court, and a member of the Court Commission for Laws of Justice. On December 1, in the Great Hall of the university, he was publicly inaugurated as rector, succeeding Court Councillor Joseph Aloys Jüstel, Knight of the Imperial Order of St. Leopold.—KH/TA

[36] Nannette Bauer (see Blätter 8r–8v above), who was often termed "the heiress" or "the one with the Testament."—KH

[37] Gottfried August Bürger (b. Molmerswende, Harz, 1747; d. Göttingen, 1794), the poet of Beethoven's pair of songs "Seufzer eines Ungeliebten" and "Gegenliebe" in the 1790s. The latter Lied had served as Beethoven's model for the Choral Fantasy, Op. 80, in 1808, and it, in turn, would serve as a model for the finale of Symphony No. 9, which was presently on Beethoven's work desk. A sketch for the "Freude" theme, datable as ca. December 4/5, 1823, appears on Blatt 38r below.—TA

[38] Bürger had translated Books 1–6 of Homer's *Iliad* into hexameters in the 1770s. Karl's discussion here reflects Bürger's introductory material as it later appeared in his *Sämtliche Werke*, ed. Karl von Reinhard (Berlin, 1823), 4:17–19. In Heft 44, Blätter 9r and 9v, nephew Karl had noted his differences with Greek literature professor Stein.—TA

[39] Karl's report is confirmed in Bäuerle's *Allgemeine Theater-Zeitung* 16, No. 147 (December 9, 1823), p. 588: "New *Zimmerreise* [Armchair Journeys]. During the upcoming inclement days of winter, every excursion into the picturesque and idyllic environs of Vienna will be cold and cruel to friends of Nature and Art. Therefore they will certainly welcome the pleasant country excursions through this pleasant and successfully artistic surrogate, the panoramas by Josef Lixa and Anton Wild, the academic art-painters from Prague. The theater-in-the-round, set up in Müller's Building, is a faithful representation of Nature."

The Müller Building, a long two-storied structure [three-storied, American] between the Adlergasse and the Bastion near the Rotenturm Gate [essentially occupying most of today's Schwedenplatz], was built and owned by Count Joseph Deym von Stritetz (1750–1804), who had lost his status as a nobleman for a period of time as the result of a duel, and who then stylized himself as "Court Statuary Müller." He brought his comprehensive art collection (which included musical clocks and even strange, exotic exhibits) to the building and opened them as a museum to the paying public. Count Deym is best known in the Beethoven literature as the husband of Countess Josephine von Brunsvik (1779–1821),

[NEPHEW KARL, *continued*]

It burns like fire in my mouth.[40] [//] [Blatt 11v]

The physician must still be paid by the maid. // I'll take it to him tomorrow, if you want. //

[Brother Johann arrives at Beethoven's apartment; presumably midafternoon, Sunday, November 30; Karl writes in part on his behalf:]

Do you want to take a little drive with him? He brought his coach with him and is *alone*.[41] [//] [Blatt 12r]

How is it going with the opera? //

Your brother is going to *Euryanthe* [this evening],[42] and asks whether you'd like to go with him. //

The country is the best medicine.[43] //

If you deliver it, you can prepay several fl. // [Blatt 12v]

Time hangs heavy on your hands in the opera. // One doesn't know at all what it actually is; I [Karl] did not comprehend the relationship at all, because one hears *nothing* because of the music. // As [he did] in *Der Freischütz*, Herr Weber has also taken passages from *Fidelio* here.[44] //

Just recently arrived. //

[written vertically→] Permitted theft.[45] [←written vertically] [//]

[Blatt 13r]

---

with whom the composer enjoyed a close relationship between 1805 and 1807. See Frimmel, *Handbuch*, I, p. 433; Groner (1922), p. 318.—KH/TA

[40] Doubtless a reference to the samples being cooked by candidate Nannette Bauer.—TA

[41] Meaning that Johann was not accompanied by his wife, Therese, or her illegitimate daughter, Amalie Waldmann.—TA

[42] Between October 25 and December 15, 1823, Weber's opera *Euryanthe* was performed in the Kärntnertor Theater on October 25, 27, and 29; November 1, 14, 19, 23, and 30; as well as December 5 and 12. From November 14, the opera was given only in an abbreviated version. See *Allgemeine musikalische Zeitung* 25, No. 52 (December 24, 1823), col. 861. Given the dating of the surrounding entries, Johann's invitation was for that evening, November 30.—KH/TA

[43] Brother Johann had been ill before he went to Gneixendorf to oversee his estate sometime between July 13 and 23, 1823 (see Heft 35, Blätter 36r and 40v; and Heft 36, Blatt 1r). Johann had seemingly returned only recently but had evidently recovered from his illness. He was not among the selective departures for the July period noted above or the arrivals listed in the *Wiener Zeitung* for November 23 through December 2, 1823.—TA

[44] Weber's *Euryanthe* also contains passages that imitate Beethoven's oratorio *Christus am Ölberge* and (by extension) Salieri's *Les Danaïdes*, which had served as a model for Beethoven.—TA

[45] This presumably refers to items taken from the entry of the lecture hall of the university; see also Blätter 9v–10r above. This vertical entry may have been made after the visit from the vice-director of the philosophy faculty on Monday, December 1.—TA

BEETHOVEN [at his apartment in the Ungargasse; Monday morning, December 1]:

Dress[maker].[46]

+ Broom.

+ Pencil.

Bookbinder. //

NEPHEW KARL [presumably at Beethoven's apartment; Monday afternoon, December 1]: A woman acquaintance, who heard that you need a woman. // Marianne Neuwirth, Alstergasse, Feldgasse, No. 136.[47] I was just saying that we would need to set a time for a cooking sample. //

I am not here on Wednesday. [It could be] Thursday or Friday. <Tomorrow at 3 o'clock.> //

She has parents here. // [Blatt 13v]

On Thursday, I am eating in the City, but not on Wednesday.[48] //

5 fl. give 60 fl.[49]

5	300
20	18

None of the women without a [cooking] sample! // The one with the Testament [Nannette Bauer] could make her cooking sample already on Wednesday. // *Quite fine*; I don't know, but probably pastry. [//] [Blatt 14r] She is already past her prime; otherwise also more ugly than pretty, so there is nothing to fear. //

I know the wholesaler very well, because I have studied with his sons. He doesn't deal like grocery merchants, etc.; for the most part only monetary business is done there and wares handled in great quantities; he is making a great house. //

---

[46] Original German: *Kleider*. On ca. November 15, Beethoven had jotted down the name and occupation of *Kleidermacher* (dressmaker) Joseph Hauffe (or Hauffen), living in the vicinity of the *Rother Igel*; see Heft 45, Blatt 20v. Perhaps Beethoven occasionally had the idea of standardizing the attire of his domestic help, as some wealthy Viennese did.—TA

[47] In suburban Alsergrund, Feldgasse No. 136 (corner of Alstergasse), apartment 17, lived one Georg Neuwirth, a journeyman stonemason from Jamnitz, Prussian Moravia (b. 1773) and his wife, Petronella/Petronilla (b. 1771), with four sons: Leopold (b. 1800), in the infantry; Franz (b. 1805), a stonemason with his father; Carl (b. 1813); Anton (b. 1816); and two daughters, Margarethe (b. 1813/14) and Rosalia (b. 1818).

Presumably that is where Marianne Neuwirth lived upon occasion; the final entry on Blatt 13r seems to indicate that Georg and Petronella might have been her parents. All had seemingly moved by 1830. See Conscriptions-Bogen, Alsergrund, No. 136, new collation 136/7 [third layer between 1818 and 1824] and 136/72 (Wiener Stadt- und Landesarchiv).—KH/TA

[48] The entries here about when Karl will eat at Beethoven's apartment contradict each other and further contradict his projections in early November (see Heft 44, Blatt 3r, and Heft 45, Blatt 1r).—TA

[49] Essentially: 300 fl. divided by 5 gives [equals] 60 fl.—TA

HEFT 47 (CA. NOVEMBER 29 – CA. DECEMBER 6/7, 1823), BLATT 14v

She [Nannette Bauer] would even accept for a trial period of 4 weeks, after which we could keep her or send her away. [//] [Blatt 14v] Her sister gives lessons in music. // We shall look closely at the food dishes in the samples, as the critics do a new work. //

SCHINDLER [falsified entries begin→]: A thousand thanks for the great pains that you have taken with my education. I shall value it my whole life long. // It would be more important to me if you would deal with the Piano Sonata, Op. 10, D major, concerning the *Largo*,[50] and whether I have remembered it exactly. Since Karl is present, I could also profit from it immediately. // I have practiced all 3 [Piano] Sonatas [Op. 10] well, but the first one the most. [←falsified entries end]

[Blatt 15r]

SCHINDLER [**authentic entries; possibly the afternoon of Monday, December 1**]:
I heard yesterday that it was already decided for the 3rd chair. // Between today and tomorrow, I'll probably learn something specific. // When are they to come? //

NEPHEW KARL [**interrupting**]: A man is here, [collecting] for the poor.[51] // It is the overseer of the poorhouse. //

SCHINDLER [**resuming**]: I was greatly amazed yesterday that Duport[52] made absolutely no mention of it [the *Akademie*], in that so much depends upon him, to know whether you should write to him about it. //

How, then, do you like [singer Henriette] Sontag? [//] [Blatt 15v] In acting, she still has some work to do. //

I encountered your brother on the street, the day after his arrival, and had a conversation with him, in that he wanted to go and see you immediately, to discuss with you that you should compose no more operas, because the opera must lead to ruin.—He *certainly* let you know about that. [//] [Blatt 16r]

She is in Amsterdam.[53] //

---

[50] Beethoven's three Piano Sonatas (C minor, F major, and D major), Op. 10, date from between 1796 and 1798. See Kinsky-Halm, pp. 23–25.—KH/TA

[51] Sunday, November 30, would have signaled the beginning of Advent, therefore a time when charities might come calling for contributions.—TA

[52] Louis Antoine Duport (1785–1853), former ballet dancer and Domenico Barbaja's resident manager of the Kärntnertor Theater in Vienna. See Clive, pp. 97–98.—KH/TA

[53] Amalie Schütz was a singer at the Theater an der Wien and had given her farewell benefit performance in Rossini's *Armida* on August 28, 1823, then gave her final Viennese performance in Conradin Kreutzer's opera *Cordelia* at the Kärntnertor Theater on August 31, 1823, departed Vienna on September 3, and went to the German Opera in Amsterdam, appearing there for the first time as Rosina in Rossini's *Barber of Seville* on October 5. See *Wiener Zeitung*, No. 205 (September 5, 1823), p. 831 (Departures); *Allgemeine musikalische Zeitung* 25, No. 40 (October 1, 1823), cols. 650–651, and No. 51 (December 17,

[SCHINDLER, *continued*]

He [Duport] told me long ago that he is afraid to give you free tickets, so as not to impose quite so many miserable works of the same sort upon you; therefore, he would consider it the greatest honor if you came to the [theater's] loges very often. // What's more, it would be inevitable that Karl would have many a profitable evening of entertainment by doing so. [//] [Blatt 16v]

Moscheles[54] told me that in London and Paris, even the least important artist receives free admission to the Royal Theatre. // He asked me to convey his most courteous <and sincere> request that he might pay you his respects, since he must return to London soon.[55] //

[falsified entries begin→] Please—you must do it for my sake, and receive him, and yet in a very friendly way. [←falsified entries end] [Blatt 17r]

He [Moscheles?] arrived just a short time ago and regrets that there was no way that he could get access to the king.[56] Even Esterhazy[57] has turned to Conyngham, the king's mistress,[58] but he is said to be a <shithead;>[59] therefore, *partout comme chez nous* [everywhere the same as here]. //

1823), col. 837; and Bäuerle's *Allgemeine Theater-Zeitung* 16, No. 111 (September 16, 1823), p. 443, and No. 143 (November 29, 1823), p. 572.—KH/TA

[54] Pianist Ignaz Moscheles (1794–1870) had arrived in Vienna from London on October 19, 1823, but then took ill and did not give his first concert until Saturday, November 22 (see Heft 44, Blatt 1v, and Heft 45, Blatt 8r). On December 27, 1823, he played his own Piano Concerto in E, Op. 64, on violinist Joseph Mayseder's benefit concert at the Kärntnertor Theater, and then bade farewell to the Viennese public with a newspaper notice dated December 30. He departed Vienna for Prague on January 2, 1824. See *Wiener Zeitung*, No. 243 (October 21, 1823), p. 984, and No. 3 (January 5, 1824), p. 13; *Wiener AmZ* 7, No. 105 (December 31, 1823), col. 840; *Allgemeine Theater-Zeitung* 17, No. 2 (January 3, 1824), p. 7; and Clive, pp. 237–240. See also Carl Czerny's perceptions of Moscheles in Heft 39, Blätter 13r and 20r.—KH/TA

[55] Moscheles will visit Beethoven for a long and cordial conversation, presumably in the afternoon, after dinner, on Wednesday, December 3, 1823; see Blätter 28r–33r below.—TA

[56] After serving as prince regent from 1811, George IV (1762–1830) became king of England and Ireland (but also of Hannover) from 1820 to 1830. He was often shamefully neglectful of his duties, and Beethoven had not been successful in getting his attention concerning *Wellington's Victory*, Op. 91, and now sought his subscription to the *Missa solemnis*.—KH/TA

[57] Prince Paul Esterházy von Galantha (b. March 11, 1786; d. May 21, 1866), son of Beethoven's sometime patron Nikolaus II (1765–1833). Paul was Austrian ambassador in Dresden from 1810; thereafter in The Hague; from 1814 in Rome; and finally in London until 1842. See *Hof- und Staats-Schematismus*, 1823, I, pp. 22 and 221; Wurzbach, vol. 4, pp. 105–106.—KH/TA

[58] Lady Elizabeth Conyngham, *née* Denison (1769–1861), wife of Marquess Henry Conyngham, was the last mistress of England's King George IV (1762–1830), beginning in 1819.—KH/TA

[59] German original: *Scheiskerl* or *Scheisskerl* [literally: shit-fellow].—TA

Bauer[60] told me that the *Capitain*[61] had already prepared his whole house to receive you, because he read in the London newspapers [Blatt 17v] that you had already arrived in Munich. Therefore it was the general talk of London that you were on a journey there. //

<He is said to be> [//] He [Moscheles] is an operator,[62] that much is true, but he has received considerable amounts [in fees]. He has acquired tolerably good manners; [falsified entries begin→] don't be so severely judgmental. [←falsified entries end] [//] [Blatt 18r]

<He> Moscheles could not assure me enough, indeed to excess, how much that people *in all of England* adore you, and he did not dare to go [back] to London without being able to say that he had seen you. [//]

BEETHOVEN: + Beef, 17½ kr. W.W. [or] 7 kr. C.M.

[Blatt 18v]

SCHINDLER [**resuming**]: At the end of November, 1824, this [theater] administration retires, and probably H[err] Moritz [Dietrichstein?] and Court Councillor M. takes its place. // One hears that plays will also be given then in the opera house. // The present administration appears to have horribly defrauded the Court,

---

[60] Caspar Bauer (ca. 1775/76 – after 1842), a *Hauptmann* (captain) and secretary in the Austrian embassy in London, when Prince Nikolaus Esterházy was ambassador there. Beethoven seemingly met him through Schindler in February 1823, and he occasionally acted as a courier on the composer's behalf. See also Heft 39, Blatt 7v, among others.—KH/TA

[61] Presumably the "English Captain Reigersfeld" [*sic*] who was mentioned by Caspar Bauer in February 1823 (Heft 24, Blatt 21v) in connection with a Beethoven quartet to be sent to him. At the end of July 1826, the *Wiener Zeitung* reported the arrival of "Baroness Maria von Raigersfeld, wife of a Royal British Navy Captain" in Vienna, and on this occasion, Schindler speaks of the "Ship's Captain" to whom Beethoven "had already often written." *Capitän* Raigersfeld is easily confused with *Hauptmann* Bauer in these accounts.

Johann Chrysostom Sporschil's 1823 interview article about Beethoven says: "One time, when he was having a light evening supper in a small restaurant, the waiter called him by name. Overhearing this, an English ship captain approached him, and exhibited the most extraordinary joy to see the man whose splendid symphonies he had admiringly heard even in the East Indies. The Briton's pure and unaffected outburst of admiration sincerely gladdened him." See Sporschil, "Musikalischer Wegweiser: Biographische Notiz über Beethoven," in Bäuerle's *Allgemeine Theater-Zeitung* 16, No. 137 (November 15, 1823), p. 548.

See also Heft 24, Blätter 21v–22r (Bauer writing on February 15, 1823); Heft 47, Blatt 17r (Schindler on ca. December 1, 1823); Heft 81, Blatt 9v; Heft 116, Blätter 24r–25r (Schindler on ca. July 31, 1826); and *Wiener Zeitung*, No. 173 (July 31, 1826), p. 729.—TA

[62] Schindler uses the term *Mäkler* (a broker, but in this case an "operator"). For Moscheles's self-serving distortions of the truth, see Blätter 29r–30r below.—TA

in that, in addition to the 14,000 fl.,⁶³ it wanted another 25,000, but when it heard that the [Blatt 19r] termination date is approaching, then it let the 25—along with 60,000 fl.—slip, and declared that it also wanted to retain ca. 40,000 fl. C.M. But Franz I said *No*, and it remained *No*. Perhaps he believed that he would profit greatly by doing so. [//] [Blatt 19v]

In the ballet, the dances are extraordinarily fine; in general, just as good as in Paris, one says. [//]

Duport is extremely active; he is already down to business daily at 8 in the morning, either in the theater or in the office. //

[Blatt 20, if ever numbered, seems to be missing.]

[Blatt 21r]

NEPHEW KARL [**presumably at Beethoven's apartment; possibly late on Monday, December 1**]: I believe, though, that we will not fare very well with the qualification: she *must* have a pension. It can happen that a very honorable woman would have *no* pension. // For example, the woman who was here today has no pension, and the woman who was here a moment ago has just as little. //

I find that one should employ far more ceremony than took place at the election of a head of the university. Everything took place in a terribly boring way. // The attorney Schönauer⁶⁴ sat next to Bach,⁶⁵ with whom he carried on a conversation. [//] [Blatt 21v] Both gentlemen behaved rudely, in that they sat themselves in the *front* seats reserved for the professors, so that the professors, when they came, had to seat themselves in the second row. // But it wasn't that way today; the professors had to sit behind. // He belongs to the university as a *Doctor Juris*. //

Castelli⁶⁶ wrote a poem, in which a Grenadier extols the common man's nature [Blatt 22r] of Emperor Joseph,⁶⁷ and says, among other things:

---

⁶³ In late 1821, the Italian impresario Domenico Barbaja (1778–1841), from Naples and Milan, leased the Kärntnertor Theater (the Court Opera) and, at the same time, the Theater an der Wien (which held an Imperial license). The Imperial Court made an annual contribution of 140,000 (not 14,000!) fl. Barbaja's first lease in Vienna ran until March 31, 1825.—KH/TA

⁶⁴ Johann Michael Schönauer, Imperial Court and trial attorney, lived in the City, Schwertgasse No. 327. In his testament, Beethoven's brother Carl (d. November 15, 1815) had named him as executor of his estate. See Frimmel, *Handbuch*, II, p. 139; *Hof- und Staats-Schematismus*, 1823, I, p. 702, and II, p. 110.—KH

⁶⁵ Beethoven's lawyer, Johann Baptist Bach.—KH

⁶⁶ Ignaz Castelli (1781–1862), Austrian poet and theatrical author (including musical subjects). The original German lines read: "Ich denke hin, ich denke her: / S'kommt doch kein Kaiser Joseph mehr." See Wurzbach, vol. 2, pp. 303–305.—KH/TA

⁶⁷ Emperor Joseph II (1741–1790), still remembered for his promotion of the Enlightenment in the Holy Roman Empire during his co-regency with his mother, Maria Theresia (1765–1780), and especially in his final decade of life, when he ruled alone. His younger brother, Leopold II, succeeded him until

My thoughts roam here, my thoughts roam there,
But no longer Emperor Joseph anywhere.

This could not remain, otherwise it would have been struck out immediately. //

To a woman who complained that the nobility needed to mingle among the common people, and *not* just remain among their *equals*, he [Joseph] said: "If I wanted to associate *only* with *my* equals, then I would have to go to the catacomb of the Capuchins."[68] [//]

[Blatt 22v]

BEETHOVEN [**at his apartment; probably Tuesday morning, December 2**]:
+ Ordinary paper.
+ [no item noted.] //

NEPHEW KARL [**at Beethoven's apartment; probably late morning, Tuesday, December 2**]: Not all the wash is ready yet, so I think that I'd better not shut *this*, until everything is gathered. // She must have run around quite a bit, since she didn't buy anything but *Nierenbraten* [loin roast],[69] and it takes two and a half hours [to cook]. //
The heiress [Nannette Bauer][70]

$21 \div 2 = 10½$

$$\begin{array}{r} 21 \\ \times 2 \\ \hline 42 \end{array}$$

[Blatt 23r]
3 pounds make 21 kr. in silver, or 52 kr. ½. //
What kind of roast have you ordered? // When the maid showed her the note that you wrote, she didn't reply with anything except "All right!"[71] // The h[ousekeeper] always has the key to the woodbin outside; I don't know whether she asked you for it; enough, she says, the wood is already almost all gone. //

1792 (and began a reversal of many of Joseph's reforms), and thereafter Leopold's son Franz, whose unsmiling conservatism reigned until 1835.—KH/TA

[68] The Imperial family's burial vault beneath the Capuchin monastery and church on Vienna's Neuer Markt. His parents, Maria Theresia and Franz Stephan, share a large ornate baroque sarcophagus. Joseph's much smaller and simpler sarcophagus is placed directly in front of theirs, a reminder that Joseph practiced something approaching egalitarianism even in death. His joke here, however, was that his only social equals were his Imperial predecessors buried in the *Kapuzinergruft*.—KH/TA

[69] The part of the loin of beef or veal nearest the kidney. See also the reference on Blatt 23v below. Styra Avins and Josef Eisinger (New York and Vienna) kindly pointed out this distinction.—TA

[70] Applicant for the housekeeper's position; see Blätter 8r–8v and 10r above.—TA

[71] Original: *Schon recht*, also used on Blatt 30r below.—TA

If you perhaps want to add an already finished case around the pencils, then I can [Blatt 23v] bring it with me. It cannot cost more than 15–18 kr. and is [made] of wood. //

There are two pieces [of meat]: one leg[72] and one loin roast. // Yesterday, three men made the rounds, and took it to the people who sold the meat. [//]

BEETHOVEN:
+ C[um] gloria dei Patris; All° maestoso e moderate [sic].[73] [//]

[Blatt 24r]

NEPHEW KARL: The sons of Appellation Councillor Schmerling[74] are also ill-mannered boys; they study philosophy at the university. [//]

BEETHOVEN:
26
25
10
18

+ Roasting spit.[75]
+ Hen coop.
+ Pencils.
Bookbinder.
Beer, ordinary.
English   22
Double   26
[Blatt 24v]

---

[72] This could have been leg of veal, haunch of venison, etc.—KH

[73] Beethoven either recalls the incorrect preposition or abbreviates the text of "cum sancto spiritu in gloria Dei patris, Amen" at the end of the text of a Gloria. In his Mass in C, Op. 86, the tempo designation is "Allegro ma non troppo," while in the *Missa solemnis*, Op. 123, it is "Allegro, ma non troppo e ben marcato." Therefore, Beethoven may have been envisioning another Mass, possibly one to be composed to the tastes of Emperor Franz.—TA

[74] Joseph (Ritter) von Schmerling (1777–ca. 1827), doctor of law, Imperial steward and Lower Austrian appellate councillor, lived with his wife, Elisabeth (b. 1784), and his seven children in the Kärntnerstrasse No. 968. Karl's entry deals with his two sons: Anton (1805–1840), who became president of the Supreme Court of Justice, and Joseph (b. 1807), later Imperial master of ordinance. See Conscriptions-Bogen, City 968 (Wiener Stadt- und Landesarchiv); *Hof- und Staats-Schematismus*, 1823, I, pp. 88 and 554; and Wurzbach, vol. 30, p. 187.—KH

[75] See *Spiess* [spit] in Beethoven's list on Blatt 26v.—TA

+ Mass [*Missa solemnis*] to Frankfurt.[76]
+ Scales. //

NEPHEW KARL [**presumably at Beethoven's apartment; possibly midday dinnertime, Tuesday, December 2**]:[77] She has already received 5 fl. C.M. in advance payment from the Russian employer. // I just asked the maid about who owned the money that I just recently saw on the table.[78] //

She doesn't want [a trial period] of 1 day; she says that [Blatt 25r] 2 weeks is more generally useful, because first she must become acquainted with everything. I think that she should either submit [to a trial] for *one* day, like the other one, or not at all. //

Too many women have applied; if we gave each one a trial period of 2 weeks, then months would be lost. I think that you could get involved for 2–3 days, to see how she makes *roast, venison, fish*, etc., but not more. [//] [Blatt 25v]

She certainly wants to come on Saturday [December 6]; but she fears that she will still find *this woman* here, and therefore merely wanted to allow 2 weeks. But if this woman leaves already on Friday, then she wants to make her sample on Saturday. // In the morning. Sample. // Everything. // [Blatt 26r]

Which ones will come yet? //

Is she to make lettuce salad? The maid understood this to be so. //

He [brother Johann] has 4,000 fl. at his place, which he must pay, because he did not pay for the estate all at once, but instead in installments. Therefore the receipts for it must be written *with care*; that's why it is taking so long. //

How much have you paid? //

I am not leaving [the house] until 9 o'clock, since I have *Correpetition* [a tutoring session], and then, from 12 to 1, Italian. [//]

[Blatt 26v]

BEETHOVEN [**presumably in his apartment, drafting a letter to brother Johann; before 9 a.m. on Wednesday, December 3**]: For sale for 100 # [ducats], engraving and everything together, where I pay the copyist 50 #, you receive 50 for the Overture, etc.[79]

---

[76] Either to Frankfurt's Cäcilien-Verein, or elsewhere through Franz Brentano in Frankfurt. See also Blatt 5v above and a drawing of Brentano in the frontispiece of this volume.—TA

[77] Later in this conversation, on Blatt 25v, Karl mentions Saturday, presumably December 6. Since he does not refer to it as "tomorrow," that suggests that these entries were made no later than Thursday, December 3, 1823. Similarly, Blatt 25v also speaks of Friday; it suggests that this conversation actually took place no later than Wednesday, December 3. On Blätter 13r and 13v, Karl's projections concerning when he will visit and/or eat with Beethoven contradict each other, so this conversation could have taken place on Tuesday (posited here), Wednesday, or even through Thursday.—TA

[78] See also Blatt 27r below about something (possibly this money) left on the table.—TA

[79] This is the draft of a letter to his brother Johann, to whom he had ceded the publication rights of the *Consecration of the House* Overture, Op. 124. See Thayer-Forbes, p. 835; Brandenburg, No. 1754.—TA

+ [Roasting] spit for sale.[80]

+ Green houseplants. [//]

[Blatt 27r]

NEPHEW KARL [**presumably at Beethoven's apartment; before leaving at 9 a.m., probably Wednesday, December 3**]:

Your brother's wife has also seen nothing. //

Saturday. // Does *not* read and write.[81] //

The tailor. //

Anyway, I am not here on Saturday. //

A blind woman is outside, who [is asking for] alms.[82] [//]

With sauce? //

Did she leave it on the table?[83] //

If only we had a maid who could write. //

[Blatt 27v]

SCHINDLER [**presumably at Beethoven's apartment; probably mid-afternoon of Wednesday, December 3**]: <If we had known that you were still eating, we would have been able to wait.[84]> //

[falsified entries begin→] Here, dear Master, I introduce Moscheles to you. If the housekeeper had just said that you were still at table, then we would have waited. // We ate together in the City. [//] [←falsified entries end]

[Blatt 28r]

---

[80] See Blatt 24r above.—TA

[81] Probably pertains to the candidate for housekeeper/cook whom they will observe as a trial on Saturday. See Karl's final entry on this page.—TA

[82] The word *Alm* under the next line, probably meaning *Almosen* (alms). This blind woman had also come for alms on October 29 or 30, 1823; see Heft 44, Blatt 1r. Presumably former housekeeper Barbara Holzmann had repeatedly given her small amounts of money in Beethoven's name when he lived in the Windmühle suburb. Her calling again suggests that Beethoven had given her some money the month before.—KH/TA

[83] Possibly the money, noted as on the table, on Blatt 24v above.—TA

[84] Moscheles's account in his diary does not mention Schindler as an intermediary, and so it is possible that this sentence might also have been falsified, and that Schindler did not arrive until shortly before Moscheles departed. Moreover, Moscheles had prepared the piano score to Beethoven's *Fidelio* several years before, so would not have needed Schindler's introduction, below.—TA

MOSCHELES [**at Beethoven's apartment, a long conversation through Blatt 33r; presumably midafternoon**[85] **of Wednesday, December 3,**[86] **the final day of the 5-day trial period of one of the housekeeper candidates. Karl is not present**]: I have often seen [Ferdinand] Ries [in London], and he is certainly very devoted to you, as am I, and place myself at your service. //

Your [*Consecration of the House*] Overture in C went superbly (in London).[87] //
For Englishmen, the name Beethoven represents the highest ideal. // [Blatt 28v]
49 // You want to economize too much. //
Doesn't your nephew live with you?[88] //
Poor Maelzel[89] is in Paris and sends you a thousand greetings. He is now making dolls that say "Papa" and "Mama." [//] [Blatt 29r] He is serious about it. // Money more than progress. [//] Perhaps the latter will still come. //

---

[85] On Blatt 31v below, Moscheles states that Beethoven was still eating his dinner when he and his brother arrived. Beethoven customarily ate midday dinner at ca. 2 p.m., so these entries probably began between 2:30 and 3:00 p.m.—TA

[86] Moscheles recounted the visit in his diary: "Having arrived at the front door, I remembered with some degree of sadness how shy of people Beethoven was, so I asked my brother to wait downstairs until I had tested the water. However, as soon as I asked Beethoven, after greeting him briefly, whether he would be prepared to meet my brother, he inquired hastily, 'Where is he?' 'Downstairs,' I replied. 'What? Downstairs?' he cried out even more hastily. He then rushed down the stairs, grabbed my astonished brother by the arm, and pulled him right into the middle of the room, demanding, 'Do you really think of me as a rough, unapproachable barbarian?' He then showed great kindness toward my brother, but unfortunately, on account of his deafness, we were able to converse with him only in writing." See Smidak, *Moscheles*, p. 32.

Moscheles's conversation-book entries suggest that he did not mention his brother until considerably into his visit; but otherwise, they correspond reasonably closely to his account, which fails to indicate any presence whatsoever of Schindler.—TA

[87] In early February, Beethoven sent his new *Consecration of the House* Overture in C, Op. 124 (not to be confused with the *Namensfeier* Overture in C, Op. 115), to Ferdinand Ries through an intermediary (probably Caspar Bauer) in the embassy. It was then performed on the fifth concert of the London Philharmonic Society on April 21, 1823. See *Allgemeine musikalische Zeitung* 25, No. 35 (August 27, 1823), cols. 563–564; and Beethoven's letter to Ries, February 5, 1823 (Anderson, No. 1133).—KH/TA

[88] This suggests that Karl was not present when Moscheles arrived.—TA

[89] Johann Nepomuk Mälzel (1772–1838), I.R. Court mechanical engineer, inventor of several mechanical musical instruments (the *Panharmonikon* and the mechanical trumpeter). His acquaintance with Beethoven extended back to at least 1813 with their collaboration in (and later proprietary litigation over) *Wellington's Victory*, Op. 91. He and/or his brother Leonhard (1783–1855) had made several ear trumpets for Beethoven. Between 1818 and 1825, he essentially divided his time between London and Paris, where he earned a great deal of money through exhibitions of his mechanical works. In Paris, he patented a metronome, assisted by the Amsterdam mechanic Dietrich Nikolaus Winkel (ca. 1780–1826). See Alfred Orel, "Mälzel," *MGG*, vol. 8, cols. 1456–1457; Thayer-Deiters-Riemann, II, pp. 385–387; Thayer-Forbes, pp. 836–838; Wurzbach, vol. 16, pp. 248–250; and Albrecht, *Letters to Beethoven*, No. 248.—KH/TA

[MOSCHELES, *continued*]

[Kirchhoffer?] has not had any luck.[90] Stumpff in London.[91] //

Toward New Year, I am going to London and could take messages from you with me.[92] [//] [Blatt 29v] I am not stopping very much.[93] // I can take care of everything with the greatest dispatch, because if I spend some time in Paris, then I'll send everything anyhow through a secure private hired coach. Faster than with the courier. [//] [Blatt 30r] It's better in January than in October and November. // This year [1823], I myself made the [Channel] crossing in January.[94] //

[entries with ink begin→]

Will your C-major Symphony[95] perhaps be finished soon? //

Is it all right with you that I am having your [*Namensfeier*] Overture in C (in 6/8) performed at my next concert on the 11th of this month?[96] And would you grace this

---

[90] On ca. November 15, 1823, Franz Christian Kirchhoffer (Ries's business contact in Vienna) mentioned four harps that Ries had sent him from London but that he could not sell; see Heft 45, Blatt 23v.—TA

[91] Johann Andreas Stumpff (1769–1846), German-born musician and harp maker who lived for decades in London. See Frimmel, *Handbuch*, II, p. 271; and Clive, pp. 359–361.—KH/TA

[92] Moscheles departed Vienna on January 2, 1824, but, as noted below, did not reach London until May, 1825. See Blatt 16v above.—TA

[93] Moscheles may have intended a speedy trip back to London, but he departed Vienna for Prague on January 2, 1824, arriving there on January 3. With a side trip to Karlsbad in July, he remained there until late summer, when (still accompanied by his brother), he went to Dresden to see Weber, then to Leipzig, where he gave two concerts in late October 1824; then a side trip to Dessau, before arriving in Berlin on October 31 to visit Mendelssohn. He departed Berlin on ca. December 23, 1824, traveling through Potsdam, Magdeburg, Brunswick, Hannover, and Celle, arriving in Hamburg on January 16, 1825. There he married Charlotte Embden on March 1, with a wedding trip to Bremen and Aachen, with a concert appearance in Paris in April, arriving in London at the beginning of May 1825. See Smidak, *Moscheles*, pp. 33–37.—TA

[94] Moscheles seems to be playing loose with the facts here. He had arrived in London on tour in July 1821, then spent the rest of the summer with pianist Friedrich Kalkbrenner (1785–1849) in northern France before going to Paris, essentially remaining there until spring 1822, returning to London by May 9. He remained there until August 1823, when he went to France (becoming seasick while crossing the English Channel), to Paris, Belgium, and Aachen (by late summer). In early September, he left Aachen, traveling through Frankfurt, Offenbach, and Darmstadt to Munich (where he gave a concert on October 10) and arrived in Vienna on October 19, 1823. See Smidak, *Moscheles*, pp. 26–31. At no time does he seem to have crossed the English Channel in January. On Blatt 17v above, Schindler had called him a *Mäkler* (an operator), and these entries bear out that assessment.—TA

[95] Moscheles means the Symphony No. 9 in D Minor, which Beethoven had projected sending to England. Even so, the composer would have insisted upon a first performance under his own control, so he could have made revisions in the details before publication.—KH/TA

[96] Moscheles's concert at the Kärntnertor Theater did not take place until Monday, December 15, 1823, but it did include Beethoven's *Namensfeier* Overture in C. See *Allgemeine musikalische Zeitung* 26, No. 3 (January 15, 1824), col. 43; *Zettel*, Kärntnertor Theater, December 15, 1823 (Bibliothek, Österreichisches Theatermuseum; courtesy Othmar Barnert).—KH/TA

[MOSCHELES, *continued*]
concert by your presence? [//] They will get it together all right.[97] [//] [Blatt 30v] Hildebrand.[98] //

Schulz is a fine man.[99] //

I am thinking about going there. // Not often.—last time his C-minor Concerto.[100] // This year, he,[101] Cramer,[102] and I could not reach an agreement with the [London] Philharmonic Society. [//] Because they do not want to pay the pianists living there anything.[103] // Neate[104] and Potter[105] happily play without payment. [//] [Blatt 31r] No genius. //

---

[97] Original *schon recht*; also used on Blatt 23r above. Beethoven had probably expressed some concern that the *Namensfeier* Overture, a relatively difficult score to perform well, might not work with the limited amount of rehearsal time that Moscheles could expect.—TA

[98] Violinist Johann Hildebrand (b. 1790) had recently become one of the Kärntnertor Theater's concertmasters (see Heft 46, Blatt 36r). Probably still concerned about the preparation of the difficult *Namensfeier* Overture, Beethoven probably asked who would be conducting, and received this answer.—KH/TA

[99] Johann Reinhold Schultz, a Prussian merchant living in London, who had visited Beethoven in Baden on Sunday, September 28, 1823; see Heft 43, Blatt 33r.

Schultz/Schulz had been born in Marienau (today's Marynowy), West Prussia (today's Poland), in ca. 1787. Marienau is ca. 10 miles north-northeast of Marienburg (today's Malbork), 25 miles southeast of Danzig (Polish Gdańsk). His family had always lived in the region. He entered the University of Königsberg (today's Kaliningrad) in the winter semester, 1805–1806, as a law student, and completed his studies there. By ca. 1814, he moved to London, where he worked as a language teacher and music dealer. In 1818, the visiting composer Weber noted his address as 49 Lime Street. In 1831, he lived at 90 Portland Street (Sir George Smart lived at No. 91). In 1835, he sold what was possibly his parents' house and land in Marienau. From 1843 to 1848, he was listed at 20 Princes Street, Cavendish Square. He was noted as a professor of German with a Ph.D. In 1850, he traveled abroad and returned to London on November 18 of that year. His death date remains unknown. This paragraph of new biographical information (and extensive supporting documentation, not quoted here) courtesy the British researcher "Neville Churchill," emails, May 17 and July 2, 2022.—TA

[100] Presumably Ferdinand Ries's Piano Concerto in C Minor, Op. 115, dedicated to Ignaz Moscheles.—KH

[101] "He" presumably refers to Ferdinand Ries. According to a report concerning the London Philharmonic concerts in the *Allgemeine musikalische Zeitung* 25, No. 35 (August 27, 1823), cols. 558–559, "men like Cramer, Kiesewetter, Moscheles, and Ries" were not appearing this year because of financial considerations.—KH/TA

[102] Johann Baptist Cramer (1771–1858), German-born pianist, composer, pedagogue, publisher, and cofounder of the Philharmonic Society. See Frimmel, *Handbuch*, I, p. 100; Clive, pp. 77–79.—KH/TA

[103] On September 9, 1825, the visiting conductor Sir George Smart would report to Beethoven about the contrabassist Domenico Dragonetti's recent refusal to participate in Philharmonic concerts because the organization would not meet his (possibly unreasonable) salary demands. See Heft 95, Blatt 1v.—TA

[104] Charles Neate (1784–1877), British pianist. He played a composition by Carl Czerny on the fourth concert of the Philharmonic Society in London on April 7, 1823. See *Allgemeine musikalische Zeitung* 25, No. 35 (August 27, 1823), col. 558. See also Heft 43, Blatt 39v; Clive, pp. 245–246.—KH

[105] (Philip) Cipriani (Hambly) Potter (1792–1871), called "Little Chip," English pianist, conductor, and composer; in 1817, he had met Beethoven in Vienna. On March 3, 1823, he played a Mozart piano concerto in the second Philharmonic concert, and he directed the fourth Philharmonic concert on

[MOSCHELES, *continued*]

No wine, but not for certain reasons. // In London, because of digestion, the wine is mixed with rum. //

In the months of March, April, May, and June, every artist hunts for money. In the other months, there is enough work to fill the time. //

My apartment is in Oxford Street, No. 343, consists of 2 rooms and a small sleeping chamber, and costs 2½ guineas per week. [//] [Blatt 31v]

More than one 20th of a part. A pound has 20 shillings; a guinea has 21 shillings. //

I beg your permission that my brother from Prague (who has visited me for several days) might have the good fortune of making your acquaintance. He is waiting outside. // Because you were eating dinner. //

[Beethoven presumably rushes downstairs and brings Moscheles's brother up to his apartment:][106]

You are known for all of your great attributes. [//] [Blatt 32r]

I saw your brother [Johann] for the first time at Artaria's[107] today. // They [Steiner & Co.] have given life to *The Ruins of Athens*.[108] //

An der Wien.[109] //

But now the goodwill is no longer lacking [at the Kärntnertor Theater]. Your Symphony in D went very well in my first concert.[110] //

How is your English piano doing? [//] [Blatt 32v] An English [instrument] now costs 100 guineas, [i.e.,] 220 ducats. // Alternating between Broadwood[111] and Clementi.[112] //

April 7, 1823. See *Allgemeine musikalische Zeitung* 25, No. 35 (August 27, 1823), cols. 561–562; Clive, pp. 269–270.—KH/TA

[106] See Moscheles's account of this scene in his diary, given in a footnote to Blatt 28r above.—TA

[107] Artaria's art and music dealership on the south side of the Kohlmarkt No. 1151, just east of the Michaelerhaus. The business (now restricted to art prints) remains there today.—KH/TA

[108] Beethoven's *Ruins of Athens* Overture had been published by S.A. Steiner in the Paternostergassel (corner of Kohlmarkt and the Graben) in February 1823. See Kinsky-Halm, p. 327, and Heft 41, Blatt 9v.—KH/TA

[109] Presumably the Theater an der Wien or a business close by, like Anton Strauss's printing establishment.—TA

[110] Moscheles's first concert during this visit was a half evening at the Kärntnertor Theater on Saturday, November 22, 1823, and included the first movement of Beethoven's Symphony No. 2 in D, Op. 36. Programming such random movements was not unusual in the potpourri makeup of such concerts. See Heft 45, Blatt 8r.—KH/TA

[111] In 1818, Beethoven had received the gift of a piano from the English firm of Broadwood; Moscheles borrowed that instrument and improvised on it at his Viennese concert of December 15, 1823. See Heft 45, Blatt 8r.—KH

[112] Muzio Clementi (1752–1832), Italian-born British pianist, publisher, and (in this context) piano manufacturer. See also Heft 39, Blatt 13v; Clive, pp. 74–76.—KH

HEFT 47 (CA. NOVEMBER 29 – CA. DECEMBER 6/7, 1823), BLATT 33R   97

He is in very good health; is working on a musical encyclopedia.[113] //

I'll send them [compositions] here and receive a double fee. [//] [Blatt 33r] It must strictly be observed that the works appear on the same day in various places. // If it comes out later here, then the publisher can no longer have proprietary rights to it.[114] //

Count Troyer is coming tomorrow.[115] //

SCHINDLER: He made a gift of 200 fl. to Schoberlechner.[116] //

MOSCHELES: I am staying here at most until Christmas and will come [to see you] again if you'll permit it. [//] [←entries with ink end]
[End of Moscheles's conversation with Beethoven.]

[Blatt 33v]

---

[113] This is probably a reference to London publisher and enthusiastic musical amateur John S. Sainsbury (d. 1844 or later) who would edit and publish a two-volume *Dictionary of Musicians* in 1825. In addition to over a hundred British musicians, Sainsbury may have sent Beethoven one of his questionnaires, because (unlike in then-current Continental lexica) Beethoven's correct birth year and parentage do appear in Sainsbury's *Dictionary*, I, p. 68. See Henry George Farmer, "British Musicians a Century Ago," *Music and Letters* 12, No. 4 (1931), pp. 384–392; reprinted as "Introduction" to John S. Sainsbury, ed., *Dictionary of Musicians, from the Earliest Ages to the Present Time*, 2 vols. (London: Sainsbury and Co., 1825; repr. New York: Da Capo Press, 1966), 1:ix–xi; and Albrecht, *Letters to Beethoven*, No. 422.—TA

[114] Before international copyright in music, successful composers would protect themselves by selling their works to publishers in multiple national or marketing areas, such as Vienna, London, Leipzig, Paris, and Mainz. In 1802–1803, Gottfried Christoph Härtel (Breitkopf und Härtel, Leipzig) had repeatedly lectured Beethoven about the evils of pirate reprinting and then himself conspired to "go halves" with publisher Muzio Clementi (London) in the purchase of Beethoven's works in 1804. See Albrecht, *Letters to Beethoven*, Nos. 42, 47, 48, 61, 65, 68, and 80.—TA

[115] In 1823, there were three brothers from the noble family of Troyer (originally from Luxemburg) living in Vienna: Johann Baptist (1776–1837), Ferdinand (1780–1851), and Franz Anton (1783–1854). Ferdinand eventually became high chamberlain to Archduke Rudolph. He was a student of the Theater an der Wien's principal clarinettist Joseph Friedlowsky (1777–1859) and a practicing member of the Gesellschaft der Musikfreunde. On November 8 or 9, 1825, violinist Carl Holz told Beethoven: "Troyer was previously the *Kuppler* [procurer] of His Eminence [Archduke Rudolph]." Rudolph suffered from epilepsy and was evidently homosexual. See Heft 98, Blatt 21r.

The subject of homosexuality may possibly have come up on September 27, 1823, in conjunction with a proposed day trip from Baden to Vöslau with Johann Baptist Jenger (1793–1836) and Marie Pachler-Koschak (1794–1855). Jenger suffered from "corruption" (presumably homosexuality), was reconciled to it, and was also a close friend of Franz Schubert's. See Heft 43, Blätter 37a-r – 37a-v.

See *Hof- und Staats-Schematismus*, 1823, I, pp. 71–72 and 75; Wurzbach, vol. 47, pp. 246–248; and Peter Clive, *Schubert and His World: A Biographical Dictionary* (Oxford: Clarendon Press, 1997), pp. 89–91.—KH/TA

[116] Franz Schoberlechner (1797–1843), pianist and composer, lived in Vienna until 1823. See Albrecht, *Letters to Beethoven*, No. 324; and Eva Badura-Skoda, "Schoberlechner," *MGG*, vol. 12, cols. 1–2.—KH/TA

SCHINDLER [possibly at Beethoven's apartment; later on Wednesday, December 3]: Yesterday I spoke to Mayseder,[117] who already knew *for certain* concerning me,[118] as did the whole orchestral personnel [at the Kärntnertor Theater]. Now would be the time to ask you most sincerely to write just a few lines to Duport and ask, merely *for yourself*, if he has decided something (and what) in this matter; he will certainly answer. Also you can [Blatt 34r] tell him that in the [Theater in der] Josephstadt one can be convinced of what I can achieve on a daily basis. Mayseder complained very much about the performance of the violins, and said that there was no strength in the bowing.[119] //

NEPHEW KARL [possibly at Beethoven's apartment; possibly on Thursday, December 4]: She gets 3 fl. for the 5 days[120] [and] leaves tomorrow. We have the other woman make her trial period, and with that, *enough*. // [Blatt 34v]

It will be made first. [//] Warmed up. //

Gläser[121] *always* conducts when the music is by him; if it were so difficult and by another master, then you would surely not see him conduct. // The second play was strictly popular, but the first one was a very fine satire on the use of animals at the Theater an der Wien.[122] // Sometimes it [the satire] is excellent; sometimes it is less successful. // [Blatt 35r]

---

[117] Joseph Mayseder (1789–1863), violinist at the Kärntnertor Theater since 1821 and former student of Ignaz Schuppanzigh (1776–1830), who himself now desired employment in that orchestra. See Heft 44, Blatt 1v; and Clive, pp. 231–232.—KH/TA

[118] Schindler had applied for a position at the Kärntnertor Theater; see Heft 46, Blätter 1r–2r.—KH

[119] It is possible that Mayseder complained about the Kärntnertor Theater's string section with 13 violins, 4 violas, 4 cellos, and 4 contrabasses, all of whom were seasoned professionals, with the virtuoso Schuppanzigh actively seeking a position there.

The strings at the smaller, suburban Josephstadt Theater, however, numbered 8 violins, 2 violas, 2 cellos, and 2 contrabasses. Concertmaster Schindler was 28, and of the other five violinists whose ages are known, their average age was 20. One of the violists was 27; a cellist was 34; and a contrabassist was 58 (probably the oldest member in this relatively young orchestra). See Ziegler, *Addressen-Buch* (1823), pp. 78–80 and 95–96; and various supporting conscription, death, and estate records.—TA

[120] Monday, December 1, through Friday, December 5.—TA

[121] Franz Joseph Gläser (1798–1861), son of the copyist Peter Gläser, composer, conductor at the Theater in der Josephstadt since 1822. Here he played a significant role at performances of Beethoven's works. He lived in suburban Josephstadt, Kaiserstrasse [today's Josefstädter Strasse] No. 34. See Böckh (1822), p. 368; Frimmel, *Handbuch*, I, pp. 169–170; Ziegler, *Addressen-Buch*, p. 94; Clive, pp. 130–131.—KH

[122] Fall 1823 witnessed the performance of "animal plays" in the Viennese theaters, with such titles as *Adler, Frosch und Bär* (Eagle, Frog and Bear), *Die Affenkomödie* (Comedy of the Apes), *Der Rehbock* (The Stag), *Die beyden Füchse* (The Two Foxes), *Nachtigall und Rabe* (Nightingale and Raven), *Der Leopard und der Hund* (The Leopard and the Dog), and *Der Hund des Aubri* (The Dog of Aubri), among others. Bäuerle's *Allgemeine Theater-Zeitung* (November 29), p. 572, printed the following notice: "To parody the present theatrical pieces in which animals play major roles, Herr Meisl has written a political parody, *Die vierfüssigen Künstler*, for the Theater in der Josephstadt." This play, a "farce with singing," received its first performance in that theater on December 3, 1823. In the *Allgemeine Theater-Zeitung*

<Schindler says that Moscheles is mean-spirited. He could> see other people die, without helping them with a penny. Who knows whether this is true? // Moscheles will send us tickets to his next concert. // Without a doubt he can play fast. He played one of his sonatas that is very brilliant. //

1 fl. 30 [kr.]
1 fl. 15 [kr.] //

The [mechanical] clock plays a piece from *Fidelio*. [//] "Gut Söhnchen Gut."[123]

[Blatt 35v]

BEETHOVEN:
    36
    36
    36
    36
    36
 2 fl. 30
  + 30
   3 fl.   //

---

on December 16, this farce was called a "crude satire on all animal comedies." It constituted one half of the fare of an evening, and *Der Feuerberg, Schuster Sebastian,* or *Der Feldtrompeter* were alternately performed as the other half. See *Allgemeine Theater-Zeitung* 16, No. 143 (November 29, 1823), p. 572; No. 150 (December 16, 1823), *Supplement*, p. 2.

Karl had attended a performance of the aforementioned *Hund des Aubri* in Baden on September 28, 1823; see Heft 43, Blätter 41r and 42r–42v.—KH/TA

[123] The mechanical clock mentioned here was located in the restaurant *Zum goldenen Strauss*, Kaiserstrasse No. 102, owned by Wolfgang Reischl and located just east of the Theater in der Josephstadt. It probably had several discs or cylinders with various compositions and played, among others, Cherubini's Overture to *Medea*. According to this account, it also played the trio "Gut, Söhnchen, gut, hab' immer Mut" from *Fidelio*, although another report said that the mechanical arrangement from *Fidelio* was actually the Overture. While Beethoven applauded the Overture to *Medea*, he supposedly did not want to hear the Trio from *Fidelio* because its tempo was somewhat too slow. See Frimmel, *Handbuch*, I, p. 94; and Heft 18, Blatt 12r.

Karl begins the third word in the title with an upper case, possibly making the adjective "gut" (good) into a noun "Gut" (estate), possibly a teasing wordplay on the fact that brother Johann owned a "Gut," an estate, in Gneixendorf. The restaurant's main hall still exists and is used as a reception, refreshment, and banquet room for the Josephstadt Theater.—KH/TA

NEPHEW KARL [presumably at Beethoven's apartment; before 5 p.m. on Thursday, December 4, interviewing the next candidate for housekeeper/cook]: She can write.[124] // She heard that you …. // She has several testimonials, but doesn't have them with her. // Wholesaler.[125] // She wants to have a tryout. // [Blatt 36r]

At 5 today, I want to look for the Spenglergasse, and go to see Schuppanzigh, if you want.[126] // 30 kr. //

He presumably fears that it would seem strange to you if, in his customary way, he would speak in a manner different from the *general* style. In this way, he would probably also have written (for example), *das Teller* or *das Zettel*, because one generally *speaks* this way here, even in educated homes. // You have to go a long way to hear *die Butter*.[127] //

[Blatt 36v]

BEETHOVEN: + Music in the case of Judas Iscariot.[128]

NEPHEW KARL [**presumably walking through the City; ca. 5 p.m. on Thursday, December 4**]: Schuppanzigh was supposed to be outside today. // Do you want to go to Wirschmidt's in the Kärntnerstrasse?[129] Schuppanzigh is there. // [Blatt 37r]
   [finding Schuppanzigh at Wirschmidt's and, in part, writing on his behalf:]
You ought to eat here sometime. // S[chuppanzigh] doesn't think that your brother did anything here. // [He] has no objection. // He is going to see Henning tomorrow in order to learn what it is. //

---

[124] Being able to write was a distinct advantage in working for the deaf Beethoven; see Karl's wish for a maid who could write on Blatt 27r above.—TA

[125] Original *Grosshändler*, a wholesaler, but also meaning a banker in common parlance. In this case, probably the applicant's former employer.—TA

[126] Spenglergasse (or Spänglergasse) is the extension of the Kohlmarkt, eastward from the Graben, until it becomes Tuchlauben. It contained, among other buildings, the police headquarters and the *Sparrkasse* (Savings Association), but Karl's destination remains unclear. At least in later years, Schuppanzigh (1776–1830) lived with his wife, Barbara, *née* Killitschky (b. 1776), and his daughter, Theresia (b. 1819), in the nearby Schultergasse No. 395, *Wohnpartei* No. 10. Schultergasse ran north from the east end of Tuchlauben, at about the point that it entered the Hoher Markt. See Conscriptions-Bogen, City, Schultergasse, No. 395; Totenbeschauprotokoll, 1830, S, fol. 17v; Verlassenschafts-Abhandlungen, Fasz. 2: 2313/1830 (all Wiener Stadt-und Landesarchiv).—KH/TA

[127] In German, the grammatical gender of "plate" and "poster" are masculine (i.e., *der Teller* and *der Zettel*), while the gender for "butter" is feminine (i.e., *die Butter*). Karl is evidently talking about someone who is advocating that inanimate objects such as plate, poster, and even butter be assigned neuter gender and the article *das*. He says that his acquaintance would speak in this linguistically revolutionary way but, at the same time, asserts that the common people would also not render the gender of butter as feminine.—TA

[128] Possibly Beethoven was momentarily considering some *Passion* music.—TA

[129] Joseph Wirschmidt (1759–1833), owner of a spacious coffee house at Kärntnerstrasse No. 1046 that backed onto the Neuer Markt. See Heft 38, Blatt 3v. Karl calls him "Werschmidt."—KH

[NEPHEW KARL, *continued*]

You must write to the archduke [Rudolph] tomorrow;[130] otherwise it will be too late; it will already be decided in a few days.[131] [//] Consider. // [It] is not so advantageous for you. [//] [Blatt 37v] He wants to tell him [you?][132] that he is coming to see us tomorrow morning. // At 9. // Should he come out today yet? [//]

[Blatt 38r][133]

S[chuppanzigh] says that you receive a yearly income of 2,000 fl. [//] Guaranteed. // Wolfmeyer.[134] //

The best violoncellist in Europe *in quartets*.[135] //

He must go. //

About your brother. // [Blatt 38v] We are speaking about your brother. //

---

[130] Beethoven to Archduke Rudolph on Sunday, December 7, 1823; see Albrecht, No. 339; Brandenburg, No. 1756.—TA

[131] Schuppanzigh wants Beethoven to write to Rudolph, persuading him to intercede on his behalf for the violinist's position in the Kärntnertor Theater's orchestra.—TA

[132] Karl may be reflecting Schuppanzigh's custom of addressing Beethoven in the third person.—TA

[133] In the right margin, in Beethoven's hand, is a sketch for the "Freude" theme for the finale of Symphony No. 9, partially covered by nephew Karl's entries.

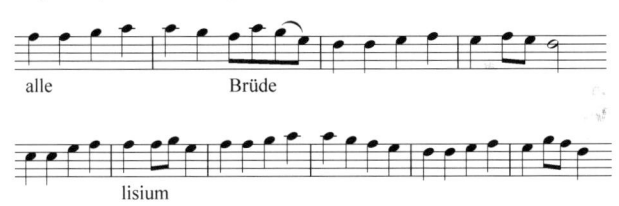

It is possible that Karl's notes about the "Violoncello" in Heft 46, Blatt 9r (ca. November 20–22, 1823), represent current work on the recitatives in the Finale of the Ninth and that Beethoven did not reach the "Freude" theme until ca. December 4, 1823.—KH/TA

[134] Johann Nepomuk Wolfmayer (1768–1841), Viennese cloth dealer and music lover, admirer and friend of Beethoven, whom he frequently supported. He wanted to commission a *Requiem* from Beethoven. Beethoven's reference to Judas Iscariot on Blatt 36v above might have been inspired by Wolfmayer's tastes. See Frimmel, *Handbuch*, II, p. 465; Clive, p. 401.—KH/TA

[135] Joseph Linke (b. Drachenberg/Trachenberg, Prussian Silesia, June 8, 1783; d. Vienna, March 26, 1837), violoncellist in Count Rasumovsky's Quartet, 1807–1816; joined the Theater an der Wien's orchestra as principal cellist in June 1818; moved to the Kärntnertor Theater by the time of his death. He also played in Schuppanzigh's reorganized Quartet from ca. April–May 1823 until 1830. On September 8, 1825, violinist Karl Holz told Beethoven that "his tone in the bass is incomparable, as if one heard a contrabass" (see Heft 44, Blatt 41r). Nearly three years later, Franz Schubert would write the pizzicato second cello part in the slow movement of his String Quintet in C, D. 956, for Linke.—TA

Hütter[136] or Leidesdorf,[137] his business partner, would like to see you.[138] //
Sunday. //

[presumably back at Beethoven's apartment:]

A servant of Lichnowsky's is here and says that the count certainly wishes to have the pleasure of seeing us tomorrow.[139] //

BEETHOVEN **[presumably at his apartment; possibly some time before midday dinner on Friday, December 5]**: + I need a housekeeper, where I [Blatt 39r] take everything that I need; housekeeper and cook will satisfy our requirements. [//]

APPLICANT:[140] Frau v. Frank am she where t .... //

JOHANN VAN BEETHOVEN: I already know 3 new theaters that have been erected within one year, namely one in Munich, one in Frankfurt, and one in Hamburg. It would therefore be good if one stipulated that it [a new opera] not be published immediately. [//] [Blatt 39v] The best would be an opera that you could sell 5 or 6 times.[141] // Right away in March, give an Akademie with it; this is absolutely necessary for your fame // and Schuppanzigh is good for directing it [i.e., serving as concertmaster]. // You must speak with him ahead of time [about] what you are giving him.[142] //

---

[136] Franz Hüther was manager of the Neuer Musikverlag of Anton Pennauer, in the Leopoldstadt, Praterstrasse No. 525, advertised in 1822. From 1825, the firm was located in the City, on the Graben No. 1122. See Alexander Weinmann, *Wiener Musikverleger*, p. 30.—KH

[137] Max Joseph Leidesdorf (1787–1840), composer and partner of the music publisher Sauer & Leidesdorf, Kärntnerstrasse No. 941. See Frimmel, *Handbuch*, I, p. 333; Alexander Weinmann, *Wiener Musikverleger*, p. 31; Clive, pp. 304–305.—KH

[138] If Beethoven was still at Wirschmidt's coffee house, it was essentially across Kärntnerstrasse from Sauer and Leidesdorf's music publishing business. In 1823, Sauer and Leidesdorf printed a collection of Beethoven's songs, including the *Abendlied unterm gestirnten Himmel*, WoO 150, that had appeared in Schickh's *Wiener Zeitschrift*. See Kinsky-Halm, p. 621.—TA

[139] Tomorrow is seemingly Friday, December 5, 1823, but Beethoven was evidently trying out a candidate for housekeeper/cook that day, so probably declined. Ultimately, the messenger called again (Blatt 42r below) on Saturday, December 6, inviting Beethoven for Sunday, December 7, and this time, the composer accepted; see Heft 48, Blatt 1r.—TA

[140] The German editors designated the author as "unknown," but the writer seems to be the applicant for the housekeeper's position who said, through Karl on Blatt 35v, that she could write. If so, her writing was so poor as to be nonfunctional.—TA

[141] Even though there was no international copyright law yet to protect composers, brother Johann's suggestion bordered on the unethical.—TA

[142] There were difficult section violin parts in the Symphony No. 9 and the *Missa solemnis*, but also—if the whole *Missa solemnis* is projected—especially the six-minute violin solo in the Benedictus, with the pun between "in nomine Domini" and "in the name of the Lord/Mylord," meaning Mylord Falstaff (Schuppanzigh).—TA

HEFT 47 (CA. NOVEMBER 29 – CA. DECEMBER 6/7, 1823), BLATT 40R

Is this for the poor citizens?[143] //

I believe the best would be to publish the Mass [*Missa solemnis*] for general subscription, since much [money] could be made. [//]

[Because Blatt 40r begins in the middle of a sentence, a page may be missing between Blätter 39 and 40.[144] This might correspond to a possibly missing page between Blätter 5 and 6.]

[Blatt 40r]

SCHINDLER [presumably at Beethoven's apartment; either Friday, December 5, or Saturday, December 6; entry begins in mid-sentence]: … for the reason that they take a rest and have enough strength for his [Gläser's?] music. //

He recently made it all too painful. I had already decided long before to do your [Second] Symphony in D [Op. 36] when a good occasion came along. Now it did, and the Symphony was very well rehearsed with 12 violins, 4 violas, [3 violoncellos, and] 3 contrabasses.[145] I went to [manager] Hensler and asked him to make note of it on the poster, so that the audience be given notice of it. But he replied "No," and "No!" and even so, it was done,[146] [Blatt 40v] in spite of Gläser's attempt to prevent it, and we earned great applause. //

---

[143] Presumably the customary "Grand Musical *Akademie* in the I.R. Large Redoutensaal, December 25, 1823, for the benefit of the Poor Citizens and Children at St. Marx." At this *Akademie*, Moscheles improvised on the songs "Es waren mir selige Tage" and "Es ist nur eine Kaiserstadt, es ist nur ein Wien," the latter from *Aline, oder Wien in einem anderen Weltteile*, a romantic magic-opera with text by Anton Bäuerle (1768–1859); music by Wenzel Müller (1767–1835). See *Allgemeine musikalische Zeitung* 26, No. 3 (January 15, 1824), cols. 44–45; and Bäuerle's *Allgemeine Theater-Zeitung* 17, No. 2 (January 3, 1824), p. 6.—KH

[144] This, in turn, could complicate the dating at this point.—TA

[145] Schindler does not mention violoncellos, probably a slip of the pencil, hypothetically corrected here. In Ziegler's *Addressen-Buch*, pp. 95–96 (reflecting fall 1822, about the time that the Theater in der Josephstadt reopened with Schindler as concertmaster), the string sections included 8 violins, 2 violas, 2 violoncellos, and 2 contrabasses. The violin and contrabass sections for Schindler's concert are 150 percent of the sizes given in Ziegler, and the violas are doubled. Therefore, it seems safe to assume that Schindler's concert would have included at least 3 violoncellos.—TA

[146] There is no record of a concert at the Josephstadt Theater on December 6, 1823, or at any of the other times when Schindler indicates that Beethoven's music was done in a "concert" there (at least through May 4, 1824).

What *is* consistent for these occasions is the appearance (on a double bill) of Hensler's one-act play *Der Feldtrompeter, oder Wurst wieder Wurst!* It had been adapted into a singspiel for the Leopoldstadt Theater by Joachim Perinet in 1808 and provided with music by Ferdinand Kauer, that theater's concertmaster. It is set in a Hussar regiment's winter quarters in Pesth and features Melko, a trumpeter; his wife, Evchen; several of his fellow trumpeters; a tavern keeper, Speck (who plays horn); as well as a complementary couple in Hansel and Gretchen (Gretl). A mounted rider is appropriately named Blech (brass), and Hansel plays cymbals in the final chorus, which includes hornist Speck and all of the trumpeters playing their instruments.

There is always a large audience at dramas. // But he [Hensler] does not mean it sincerely. // It would go much easier and better, if he did not have as many gossips around him, and were not so headstrong. // You would be astonished to hear how he [Hensler] speaks in public with Drechsler and also often with Gläser. [//] [Blatt 41r] Always in the case of his music. // But he is merely an entrepreneur out of greed, although he really *could not* be such a thing only from love. // Indeed he is rich and doesn't have to care for anyone. // Besides, she [Hensler's daughter][147] has a rich husband. // Scheidlin is one of the most important bankers here. // I have to say this with justification. //

NEPHEW KARL [at Beethoven's apartment; later on Saturday, December 6]: How does it stand with Ries? // [Blatt 41v] With the Mass [*Missa solemnis*].[148] // Write the opera. If well received it would bring you 5,000 fl. in *Conventions Münze*. // Have you written to the cardinal about Schuppanzigh?[149] // In case that this housekeeper also doesn't appear to be good, your brother knows of a good one for whom he could vouch. // How much have you paid for a lemon? // The Akademie. // [Blatt 42r] The Akademie can bring in 3,000–4,000 fl.[150] [//]

Now the play was being revived at the Josephstadt Theater, where Hensler was manager, with at least some of the music provided by resident composer/conductor Franz Gläser, possibly adapted from Kauer's earlier scores. It appears that the December 6 performance included some or all of Beethoven's Symphony No. 2 in D (the first movement, with its double-dotted figure in the introduction and joyously raucous suspensions in the trumpets in the coda, would certainly have been appropriate). On February 15, 1824, *Der Feldtrompeter* would be performed again, this time including Beethoven's *Consecration of the House* Overture (with its trumpet fanfares after the slow opening march). On May 4, 1824, it was done again, this time apparently including Beethoven's *Fidelio* Overture.

As noted above, Hensler would not allow the projected inclusion of Beethoven's music to be placed on the *Zettel* (playbills or posters), but in any case, these important documents for the Josephstadt Theater during this period have not survived. Similarly, Beethoven's music is not mentioned in the occasional reports of these performances in Bäuerle's *Allgemeine Theater-Zeitung*, but at least a daily calendar of performances can be reconstructed from this periodical.

See Karl Friedrich Hensler, *Der Feldtrompeter, oder: Wurst, wieder Wurst!*, arranged as a singspiel in one act for the Theater in the Leopoldstadt by Joachim Perinet, music by Ferdinand Kauer (Vienna: Wallishausser, 1808); 75 pp.; and *Allgemeine Theater-Zeitung* 16, No. 151 (December 18, 1823), p. 604; as well as Heft 56, Blätter 5r, 7v–8r, and 15r; and Heft 65, Blatt 1r.—TA

[147] Karl Friedrich Hensler (1759–1825) was manager of the Theater in the Josephstadt. His daughter Josepha (b. 1796) had married the wholesaler/banker Sigmund von Scheidlin (b. 1785) at St. Stephan's Cathedral in 1814. See also Heft 39, Blatt 9v; Clive, pp. 159–161.—KH/TA

[148] After and under this, Karl's calligraphic doodlings with "Bthvn" and then "Lact" and "Lactantius."—KH

[149] See Schuppanzigh's earlier request on Blätter 37r–37v. Beethoven ultimately wrote the letter on Sunday, December 7, 1823 (Albrecht, No. 339; Brandenburg, No. 1756).—TA

[150] Beethoven's *Akademie* (with the premiere of the Ninth Symphony and first Viennese performance of three movements of the *Missa solemnis*) eventually took place on May 7, 1824, with a modified repeat on May 23. Because of the high costs of hall rental and, especially, copying, Beethoven's profits were far lower than projected.—TA

An opera! In addition to the [commission] payment, you would certainly receive a full evening's income from Duport.[151]

[presumably interrupted by Count Lichnowsky's messenger:]

The servant said: The count certainly wishes thereupon[152] wishes to see us tomorrow [Sunday, December 7], and thereupon sends his regards, and we thereupon certainly should not fail to appear.[153] // Another sister-in-law. //

He has spoken with Moscheles, who told him that he would vouch that in 2 years in England you would get 6,000 # [ducats] in gold. // I am speaking of the End of the World. [//] [Blatt 42v] Opera? // Don't worry at all. //

The new [*Consecration of the House*] Overture made a great sensation.[154] // It has been done very well in London. // *Per se* [Of course.] [//]

Schuppanzigh. [//]

He is giving you 2,600 fl. net and wants to defray [all expenses], [Blatt 43r] and earn still another 400 fl. //

Opera. // He would pay you 12,000 fl. for the opera when it is finished. *Cash*. // The Italian singers are performing in Italian during the next year. [//]

BEETHOVEN: + Coffee. [//]

[Blatt 43v]

SCHINDLER **[presumably at Beethoven's apartment; probably later on Saturday, December 6]**: Presently Duport is making 3-year contracts with the dubious individual. [//] It says that the emperor will not assume it himself; therefore he leaves it to Barbaja, but only for 100,000 fl. C.M., which he then condescended to pay. // [Blatt 44r]

We now have cause to be satisfied with the *Fratello* [brother Johann]; he very seldom allows his wife to drive out anymore; eats mostly away from home, and says that the first time that he has proof of the suspicion that he bore, then he will have her shut in. He cannot seek a divorce, because, according to our laws, he would have to give her half of his property, but he will show the intruder the door from now on. [//]

[Blatt 44v]

---

[151] This and the following references to Beethoven's possibly composing an opera probably refer to Grillparzer's libretto for *Melusine*. If an opera were successful, the composer would generally receive the profit from the fourth performance.—TA

[152] The repetition of the word *alsdann* (thereupon) must represent some quirk in the speech of either Count Lichnowsky or his servant.—TA

[153] Beethoven and Karl had previously been invited on Blatt 38v. This time, they accepted the invitation; see Heft 48, Blatt 1. The gossipy and potentially meddling Lichnowsky lived at Bauernmarkt No. 581 when he died in 1837, and may have lived there as early as 1823; see Heft 21, Blatt 9v.—TA

[154] See Blatt 28r above.—TA

NEPHEW KARL [**presumably at Beethoven's apartment; possibly already on Sunday morning, December 7, evidently writing on behalf of visiting Josepha Schlemmer, who was trying to continue her late husband's copying business**]:[155]
The *last man* copies the fastest, but he would have to copy *here*, since he cannot rightly be trusted. //

She [Frau Schlemmer] could not vouch for it. // She says that one can absolutely not trust him, and has to cut the beginning and the end of *every* piece.[156] // When is he to come tomorrow? Are you eating at home? //

[**writing vertically on three pages, working backward from the end:**]
You must not forget to tell the person who comes tomorrow that he is to copy in the room at Frau Schlemmer's. [//] [Blatt 45r] She will send the copyists to you tomorrow afternoon. [//] [Blatt 45v] You should give her something as a sample, so you can see how he writes. // She asked me to thank you again for the 5 fl. [//] The boy is to go to the orphanage.

End of Heft 47

---

[155] Josepha Schlemmer was assisted in this effort by copyist Mathias Wunderl, who had worked with her husband. This edition (Volume 4) has since identified Wunderl as Alan Tyson's "Copyist E."—TA

[156] Beethoven held back the first and last pages of some of the movements of the *Missa solemnis* when they were sent for copying, in order to prevent theft.—TA

Heft 48

(December 7, 1823 – December 13, 1823)

[Blatt 1r]

NEPHEW KARL [**presumably at Count Moritz Lichnowsky's apartment, probably in the City, possibly at Sterngasse No. 451;**[1] **probably midafternoon, Sunday, December 7**]:
In the program.[2] [//]

LICHNOWSKY:[3] Today at Court there was a public banquet and concert. // For the Festival of the Golden Fleece.[4] //

---

[1] In fall 1822, "Fräulein Jeanette Stummer" (presumably Lichnowsky's daughter) was living in the City at Sterngasse No. 451, a relatively remote dead-end street between the north end of the Hoher Markt and the Danube Canal. When he died on March 17, 1837, Lichnowsky lived in the City at Bauernmarkt No. 581 (a building that faced both the Bauernmarkt and the Kammerhof/Wildpretmarkt).

Along with his elder brother, Prince Karl Lichnowsky, Count Moritz had been close to Beethoven earlier in his career in Vienna. Indeed, he may have been the family member (rather than Prince Karl), who supplied the refreshments at the difficult rehearsal of Beethoven's oratorio *Christus am Ölberge*, probably on April 4, 1803, occasioning the dedication of the composer's so-called *Eroica* Variations for piano, Op. 35. His renewed close, often potentially meddling, friendship with Beethoven during this period lasted only from ca. January 1823, until ca. April 1824. See Heft 21, Blatt 9v; and *Wiener Zeitung*, No. 66 (March 21, 1837), p. 406.—TA

[2] Probably a program from the Golden Fleece ceremony and concert.—TA

[3] Perhaps because this gathering is at Lichnowsky's apartment or possibly because the countess is present, it seems more socially awkward than Lichnowsky's often garrulous, gossip-laden visits at Beethoven's apartments or elsewhere. It is also quite possible that those present could speak their parts of the conversation loudly enough for Beethoven to hear (see Blatt 4r below).—TA

[4] Alarmed by the rise of Islam in Turkey, the dukes of Burgundy and their allies established the Order of the Knights of the Golden Fleece in 1430, with the avowed purpose of defending Christianity. By ca. 1450, they had adopted "L'homme armé" (The Armed Man) as their marching song. Until the Council of Trent discouraged secular influences on Church music in 1562–1563, the Order of the Golden Fleece commissioned prominent composers (such as Dufay, Josquin, and even Palestrina) to write Mass ordinaries based on the "L'homme armé" tune for their annual gatherings. See William F. Prizer, "Music and Ceremonial in the Low Countries: Philip the Fair and the Order of the Golden Fleece," *Early Music History* 5 (1985), pp. 113–153.

In Vienna, the annual festival of this order was set for the first Sunday after St. Andreas's Day (November 30). In 1823, the festival took place on December 7. The *Wiener Zeitung* of December 9

NEPHEW KARL: Weber wrote under his portrait, "As God wills."⁵ One wit said: "Other composers write as *they* will; but Weber writes 'as God wills,' and Rossini, 'as the *Viennese* will.'" // That notwithstanding, this is the best [place in the] world. // [Blatt 1v] No one wants to leave it. //

From the *Travestied Aeneas* by Blumauer.⁶ //

[Brother Johann seems to have driven Beethoven and Karl to Lichnowsky's, stayed briefly, then continued on.]⁷

The countess [Lichnowsky's wife, Johanna] says that your brother may not lead you away.

[writing, in part, on Johann's behalf:]

reported that "the Investiture of the new Knights of the Golden Fleece was postponed from November 30 until December 7."

The ceremony began at 10:30 a.m. The typical potpourri concert by the *Hofkapelle* that followed the noontime banquet consisted of (1) Overture by Mozart; (2) Aria from *Sigismondo* by Rossini, sung by Madame Grünbaum; (3) Polonaise for violin, composed and played by [Joseph] Mayseder; (4) Aria from *Semiramide* by Rossini, sung by Demoiselle Unger; (5) Variations for flute, composed and played by Aloys Khayll; (6) Duet from *Torwaldo e Dorliska* by Rossini, performed by Madame Grünbaum and Herr Seipelt; (7) Trio from *Ciro in Babilonia* by Rossini, performed by Madame Grünbaum, Demoiselle Unger, and Herr Seipelt. Held in reserve in case the program needed to be extended or in case a member of the Imperial family suddenly did not want to hear one of the above seven works, were (1) Duet from *Riciardo e Zoraide* by Rossini, sung by Madame Grünbaum and Demoiselle Unger; and (2) Overture to *Der Schauspieldirector* by Mozart. The five soloists each received 108 fl. C.M. for their appearance.

At just about this time, Beethoven had jotted "türkische Musik" in Sketchbook Autograph 8, Bundle 2—sketches for the finale of the Ninth Symphony. Beethoven would have recognized the name Aloys Khayll (1791–1866) on the Court's program. Khayll, now principal flutist at the Burgtheater, had played Beethoven's piccolo parts from Symphony No. 5 in 1808 through *Der glorreiche Augenblick* in 1814, and so Beethoven probably composed the piccolo parts in the Ninth Symphony with Khayll in mind. See Douglas Johnson, Alan Tyson, and Robert Winter, *The Beethoven Sketchbooks: History, Reconstruction, Inventory* (Berkeley: University of California Press, 1985), pp. 408–410.

See the *Wiener Zeitung*, No. 282 (December 9, 1823), p. 1143; Hof-Musikkapelle, Akten, K. 12 (1821–1823), Nos. 160–162, 188, 194, 196, and 200 (Haus-, Hof- und Staatsarchiv, Vienna); and Pezzl, p. 190.—TA

⁵ On ca. November 25 (Heft 46, Blätter 33v–34r), Schuppanzigh alluded to this proverb on a portrait of Weber published in 1823 and mentioned a potential parallel as coming from Beethoven. In this version, Karl adds Rossini to the quote from Weber, a sentiment that must often have been expressed in Vienna at the time, as reflected in an anecdote in Kanne's *Wiener Allgemeine musikalische Zeitung* 8, No. 14 (April 13, 1824), p. 56.—KH/TA

⁶ Aloys Blumauer (1755–1798); the remark concerns his *Abenteuer des frommen Helden Aeneas, Travestiert* (Adventure of the Pious Hero Aeneas, as a Travesty), produced in Vienna, 1783–1786, a parody on Virgil's *Aeneid*. See Kayser, I, p. 290; and Blätter 3v–4r below.—KH/TA

⁷ On November 1, 1823 (Heft 44, Blatt 10r), Lichnowsky had visited Beethoven and noted that he was planning to move back into the City from his summer apartment in Hietzing (west of Schönbrunn). The logistics of this visit suggest that brother Johann, who liked Sunday afternoon pleasure drives in the Prater, picked Beethoven and Karl up in the Ungargasse, took them to the Sterngasse, then returned later to pick them up (see Blatt 2v). Even though the day was cloudy, the temperature had reached 41 degrees Fahrenheit by 3 p.m., very acceptable for such an outing. See *Wiener Zeitung*, No. 283 (December 10, 1823), p. 1149.—TA

So he still wants to go for a little drive and then come back. // The coachman is gone.[8] //

The countess. //

LICHNOWSKY: Italy. //
Since the letter is to the archduke [Rudolph], he is probably already here.[9] //

[Blatt 2r]

NEPHEW KARL: *Eine Meisterinn; Hörni* [a woman teacher; hears nothing].[10] Also plays [works] by you. // You should tell that to the count, so he gets a good piano teacher for the little girl [Lichnowsky's daughter Josepha Maria].[11] // By this gentleman's brother.[12] //

LICHNOWSKY: My late mother.[13] //

NEPHEW KARL: The count ought to get Czerny.[14] // [Blatt 2v]
[Brother Johann seemingly returns to Lichnowsky's to pick up Beethoven and Karl;[15] Karl writes, in part, on his behalf:]
Your brother will have his evening meal here now, because he has something to do afterward and therefore cannot accompany us. [//]

---

[8] Johann van Beethoven employed a coachman for the horse and carriage that he owned. See Heft 49, Blatt 3r.—TA

[9] As a Knight of the Golden Fleece and a member of the Imperial family, Archduke Rudolph would indeed probably have been in Vienna for the ceremonies on December 7. On that day, but accidentally(?) giving the month as November, Beethoven wrote Rudolph an almost embarrassingly submissive and excuse-laden letter, requesting that he intercede on Schuppanzigh's behalf to secure the position left vacant by the death of violinist Zeno Franz Menzel on November 19, 1823. Time was of the essence, because replacements in the *Hofkapelle* were generally made within a few weeks of an incumbent's death. For Beethoven's letter to Rudolph of December 7, 1823, see Albrecht, *Letters to Beethoven*, No. 339; Brandenburg, No. 1756.—TA

[10] Original German *Hörni* seems to be a wordplay. It could also be the name of the teacher, but there is no match in either Böckh's *Merkwürdigkeiten* (1822) or in Ziegler's *Addressen-Buch* (1823). The closest phonetic approximation is Haydn's old student Katharina von Hohenadel/Hochenadel (1785/86–1861), living in the Bürgerspital No. 1100, Courtyard 5, Stairway 10 (Ziegler, *Addressen-Buch*, p. 132).—TA

[11] Josepha Maria Stummer, born illegitimately in June 1814. Lichnowsky also mentions her briefly in Heft 44, Blatt 10r. See Clive, pp. 206–208; Ziegler, *Addressen-Buch*, p. 52.—TA

[12] Probably a reference to Lichnowsky's nephew Prince Eduard Maria (1789–1845), who had a flair for writing and who signed the February 1824 petition to Beethoven. See Albrecht, *Letters to Beethoven*, No. 344; Blätter 3v–4r below; and Heft 63, Blatt 11r.—TA

[13] Countess Carolina Lichnowsky, *née* Countess Althann (1742–1800). See Clive, p. 202.—TA

[14] Probably Carl Czerny (1791–1857), a very popular teacher among the nobility, but possibly also the unrelated Joseph Czerny (1785–1831), also a very successful piano teacher.—TA

[15] In December, it begins to grow dark in Vienna by 4:15 or 4:30 p.m. Therefore, Johann may have returned from his drive shortly after 5 p.m. or so.—TA

[NEPHEW KARL, *continued*]

60 ÷ 6 = 10 fl.   90 ÷ 6 = 15[16] [//]

[Presumably, Johann's coachman drives Beethoven and Karl back to suburban Landstrasse, either to the composer's apartment in the Ungargasse or possibly his favorite restaurant, the *Goldene Birne*, for a light supper:]

He [the waiter] says that fresh Erlauer [wine] has arrived.[17] // Your brother is more closely acquainted with Herr Kaufmann's financial circumstances;[18] he says that he is a horrible tightwad, to the extent that he puts paper in his shoes, [Blatt 3r] because they are without soles. // He buys his wares *per pound* from other merchants. //

But your brother has been enlightened by the most recent events. He says that he didn't really get to know her [his wife, Therese] until his illness, and now he treats her very patriarchal. If he buys something good, she doesn't get any of it; rather, he eats it with us, as was the case yesterday with the oysters, etc. They eat their plain meals at home. *He*, then, is out of the house all day, and comes back merely to eat and sleep. // It particularly pleases him that she is now old, and no cock will crow after her anymore, and she must remain inactive. [//] [Blatt 3v] Special contracts that he now regrets probably exist, but cannot be changed. [//]

A big braggart.[19] // He [presumably Prince Eduard Lichnowsky] himself, after the model of the *Travestied Aeneid* of Blumauer (which he praised highly), has begun an epic poem, which, very much according to Blumauer, begins:

> There was a great Hero,
> Whom they called Napoleon.
> He took to his heels from Moscow,
> As they burned the city down. [//]

He is also not publishing it at all; I can only say it is impossible that anyone who displays himself in such a way [Blatt 4r] can be a great one. // At every opportunity he parades what he knows; and one can already gather from it that there is not very much to him, because a truly learned man *certainly* does *not* do that. //

---

[16] This may be reckonings for the carriage fares. The figure "6" may represent round trip for three people.—TA

[17] Erlauer: red wine from Erlau in Hungary. For the *Kellner* (here possibly meaning a wine cellarer, rather than just a waiter), see Blatt 7v below.—KH/TA

[18] Herr Merchant, in this case, is Heinrich Seelig, owner of *Zur Stadt Triest*, now (1823) located at the northeast corner of Rauhenstein Gasse and Himmelpfort Gasse. The oysters mentioned on Blatt 3r must have come from Seelig, who supplied them to Beethoven and his friends in the winter of 1819–1820.—TA

[19] The previous two entries may represent a transition from brother Johann to the literary Prince Eduard Lichnowsky (1789–1845) as the subject of conversation. See Albrecht, *Letters to Beethoven*, No. 344.—TA

HEFT 48 (DECEMBER 7 – DECEMBER 13, 1823), BLATT 4V

[NEPHEW KARL, *continued*]

[presumably back at Beethoven's apartment; the evening of Sunday, December 7:]

All of the other housekeepers failed to appear; proof of the connection among all these people. // Only through gossip. //

If you improvise at your Akademie[20] the way you did today,[21] you would have a splendid success. // That is proper to someone who is more than simply a good piano player. [//] [Blatt 4v] I'll be happy to hear Moscheles improvise. //[22] I also don't believe one bit that Moscheles's improvisation, if one may even call it that, is the work of the moment. // I believe that he prepares himself ahead of time. // The main characteristics. [//] [Blatt 5r]

[at Beethoven's apartment; probably the morning of Monday, December 8 (Feast of the Immaculate Conception; therefore, Karl has no classes):]

$$\begin{array}{r} 35 \\ -26 \\ \hline 9 \end{array}$$ //

A scales must be obtained, so that she gets precisely 1 *Loth* of sugar in the coffee; that way there is also a standard here as well. //

[apparently during or after a brief visit by Schuppanzigh, seemingly writing on his behalf:][23]

Think about it. Later I'll give you my opinion of what he told me. //

Must S[chuppanzigh] go to see Henning? *Going with him?* // It only has 7 numbers.[24] [//] [Blatt 5v]

You have expressed the wish to have a sum [of money] all at once; he didn't say anything against it other than that it would be disadvantageous *to you*. I believe that the whole plan would be advantageous to you, but the people don't have enough money, and every other person will press for it just as soon as he hears that you are ready to do it. //

---

[20] Beethoven's projected concert to premiere the *Missa solemnis* and the Ninth Symphony, ultimately on May 7, 1824.—TA

[21] Beethoven must have extemporized extensively at Lichnowsky's. None of the conversations surrounding that event is preserved here, suggesting that the environment allowed the participants to engage in loud spoken conversation.—TA

[22] Under the dividing line are the words "Ticket" and "Thicket."—KH

[23] See Blatt 8r below for the suggestion that Schuppanzigh had visited earlier in the day.—TA

[24] Presumably the Overture and incidental music to *Consecration of the House*, which Henning wanted to take to Berlin for his theater's opening.—TA

[topic changes away from Schuppanzigh and Henning:]
Your brother is going to pick us up with his carriage this afternoon.[25] [//]

[Blatt 6r]

BEETHOVEN: At the end, the trombones, along with the horn quartet, could cease, and open the introduction.[26] //

NEPHEW KARL [**ca. midday on Monday, December 8**]: The woman from Hungary. // She needs her references. [//] Testimonial. // Josephstadt, Lederergasse, at the *Unicorn*, No. 353, the last door [apartment] above the passageway. Nannette Bauer. [//] Passau.[27] [//] She always prepared wild game; he [the Hungarian employer] only ate roasts. [//] She can come back. // [written vertically→] A woman relation of hers likewise worked for a nobleman who added her as an heir.[28] [←written vertically] [Blatt 6v] She could cook tomorrow [Tuesday, December 9]. //

<To say it directly.> She is making faces and told me a short time ago that a cook came to apply, but added that if she [Bauer] wanted it, she need only enter, because "I'm getting out of here."

She has made a salad. She bought vinegar. //

She doesn't want to. // She wants to act like the lady of the house and has already begun to show her capriciousness. Also, I suspect connections with the previous one. // I think that we say that she has now demonstrated how she cooks, and that we have seen enough with what she has demonstrated until now, [Blatt 7r] and now want to propose a trial to another woman. If she is needed further, she will learn of it. // If she should contradict that, one can remind her of her statement: "She is getting out of there, and the other woman could come in." There is nothing to be said after that. [//] I'm amazed that she didn't ask for the *letter* back.[29] //

Concerning Steiner, I believe that you should make use of the law, because he deserves it; he has swindled you enough. // Like the attorneys consulting together. //

---

[25] Monday, December 8, a holiday, was a little cooler than cloudy Sunday but sunny and pleasant all day, certainly a good day for a carriage ride. See *Wiener Zeitung*, No. 284 (December 11, 1823), p. 1153.—TA

[26] This may refer to the 6/8 statement of the "Freude" theme and text (in which Beethoven ultimately retained the horns, trumpets, and timpani), followed by "Seid umschlungen, Millionen," as introduced by the trombones. It may also refer to the aria with prominent horn quartet ("Will unser Genius") in Beethoven's *Ruins of Athens* [*Consecration of the House*], which Henning was about to take with him to Berlin.—TA

[27] Applicant Nannette Bauer, who had worked for a Hungarian nobleman for 10 years; see Heft 47, Blätter 8r–8v, where these details are explained.—TA

[28] Presumably this meant that, after 22 years, the relative received a percentage of her salary as a pension.—TA

[29] At age 17, Karl had already learned how to express himself authoritatively.—TA

HEFT 48 (DECEMBER 7 – DECEMBER 13, 1823), BLATT 7V

[NEPHEW KARL, *continued*]

A stupid peasant. //

She [Therese] will not last much longer, but if she stops, then she will stop [Blatt 7v] *only* with a complete separation. He [brother Johann] is too *very* convinced. // Probably he still found her attractive up to now, though; all of that has ceased now, for she is becoming old. // For a long time he has not been as much a skinflint as before—I have already noted that. // But he was far ruder.[30] //

Yesterday [Sunday evening, December 7], the waiter told me that a *new* and especially good Erlauer [wine] had come; presumably only that we will be less surprised by the changes.[31] [Blatt 8r]

<Tomorrow. [Tuesday, December 9] at 8:30, you ought to send the work [*Consecration of the House*] to your brother,> not to give it out further, but just to have it for himself. //

If you send the work [*Consecration of the House*] to Schuppanzigh tomorrow, it would be better, because he has arranged the whole deal; even Henning knows him better. // You send S[chuppanzigh] a receipt with it. // It is good that they don't want to spread it around any further. // You have already paid him, in that you got him the [orchestra] seat.[32] // S[chuppanzigh] said it himself today, there is still time.[33] [Blatt 8v]

<Has Anton> // Griesinger also told your brother that the Saxon Court is not taking the Mass [*Missa solemnis*], but then he assumed something quite different, as he heard the contrary.[34] //

[possibly at a coffee house:]

This other man has stated in public that he wants to cure you.[35] // People are saying nothing more than that they are hoping for an opera; absolutely no one speaks of your deafness; you will see this for yourself when you give an Akademie. [//] [Blatt 9r]

The chestnuts are old. //

---

[30] This paragraph concerns brother Johann; his wife, Therese; and her proclivity for taking lovers on the side.—TA

[31] Karl uses the term *Kellner*, usually a waiter but possibly a true wine cellarer here. See also Blatt 2v above.—TA

[32] Beethoven's letter to Archduke Rudolph, December 7, 1823, mentioned on Blatt 1v; see Albrecht, *Letters to Beethoven*, No. 339; Brandenburg, No. 1756.—TA

[33] This adds perspective to the references to Schuppanzigh on Blatt 5r above.—TA

[34] Georg August Griesinger (1769–1845) was now a councillor in the Saxon embassy. The Saxon Court initially rejected Beethoven's invitation (January 23, 1823) to subscribe to the *Missa solemnis* but then, upon Archduke Rudolph's intercession, accepted in September 1823. See Heft 40, Blatt 10v; and Heft 41, Blatt 16v.—KH/TA

[35] Probably to this end, Andreas Schulz visited Beethoven on Blatt 16v below to bring him the address for obtaining Dr. G. Schmidt's hearing balm.—TA

[probably back at Beethoven's apartment; evening of Monday, December 8; brother Johann presumably visits; Karl writes, in part, on his behalf:]

He [presumably Johann] is coming to eat on Thursday [December 11]. // Tuesday [tomorrow, December 9], he [Johann] is picking you up with his carriage at 12:30 p.m. // He won't be sick. //

He [Johann] thinks that you should make a deal to give [publisher] Leidesdorf the Mass [*Missa solemnis*] for *nothing more* than 200 copies, which he would have to deliver to you, and which we could sell on subscription for 5 # [ducats] per copy. The 200 would bring in 1,000 # [ducats]. [//] [Blatt 9v] Just like Galitzin advised: Germany, France, England, Russia.[36] // 50 overall. Does it work? It works. // He'll go to see [publisher] Leidesdorf, and all will be well. // Do you want that? He'll pay you the 4500 # [ducats] for 200 subscription copies, and that's it. [//] [Blatt 10r] But that belongs with it. // He wrote out what he has to do. //

[Johann leaves.]

Schuppanzigh must get the corrected copies tomorrow [Tuesday] at 8:30 a.m., because he won't be at home later; also, after 9 o'clock, Henning is also no longer available. //

If only he'll do it! Engraving alone costs 4–5,000 fl.; the paper another couple of thousand, and no publisher would give us what we earn from it. // But not 200 copies. What are 1,000 fl. against that? [//] [Blatt 10v] In your name. //

We also don't need anything from the dogs.[37] //

Today, I brought you less than 24 kr., because the maid got 1 pound of rice without paying for it, which I therefore also paid. //

[End of entries for Monday evening, December 8 (Immaculate Conception).]

[Blatt 11r]

BEETHOVEN:

    <75   <110

    75   140>

    75

    75>

HOUSEKEEPER APPLICANT **[writing phonetically; probably afternoon, Tuesday, December 9]**:[38] I am a gud cook fer everthing. I .... //

---

[36] In a letter of August 3, 1823, Prince Galitzin in St. Petersburg had suggested that Beethoven have the *Missa solemnis* printed and sell the printed copies at 4–5 ducats each. See Thayer-Deiters-Riemann, IV, p. 372; Thayer-Forbes, pp. 830–831; Albrecht, *Letters to Beethoven*, No. 333; Brandenburg, No. 1724.—KH/TA

[37] Perhaps someone came to the door offering to have dogs sniff out the apartment for rats.—TA

[38] For scheduling the cooking tryout, see Blatt 6v above.—TA

NEPHEW KARL [**possibly testing the applicant; probably afternoon, Tuesday, December 9**]:
How many cost 10 fl. C.M.
20 fl. C.M.?
How many 5 fl. C.M. //

[Copyist Matthias] Wunderl[39] was just crossing the Universitätsplatz[40] as I came out of class. So I told him how many errors that you found. He said, "Then there must also have been that many in the *original*." [//]

[Blatt 11v]

SCHINDLER [**at Beethoven's apartment; probably afternoon, Tuesday, December 9**]: At the beginning, Moscheles was embarrassed to ask you about your [Broadwood] piano. He said that it would make an extraordinarily big sensation in London if they hear that he had played on your instrument, because he would be asked everywhere, whether he knew the instrument and whether you still have it. [//]

[Blatt 12r]

NEPHEW KARL: Is the housekeeper already advanced in years? //
The [woman] in our house is horribly made up. It is impossible to deal with that kind of people who wash themselves with good-smelling waters, because for the most part they probably also use any possible means to satisfy such conditions. Marie [Pamer?] is the same way. // Wasn't she here today, too? //
These old women with hats, etc., are for the most part gossips and overly pious. //
Her parents send her linen from which she makes dresses for herself. // In Bohemia. [//] 20 //

Baking flour[41] 1 fl. 4 kr.
Fine flour 1 fl. 30 [kr.] [//]

[Blatt 12v: No writing; crossed through with red pencil.]

[Blatt 13r]

---

[39] Wunderl was assisting copyist Wenzel Schlemmer's widow as she attempted to continue her husband's business after his death on August 6, 1823. He has been identified as Alan Tyson's "Copyist E."—TA

[40] The Universitätsplatz was bordered by the old university, the Jesuit Church (or Universitätskirche), and the *Konvikt*. Today, it is called Dr. Ignaz-Seipel-Platz.—TA

[41] Original *Mundmehl* (flour used in baking) and *Auszugmehl* (an especially fine flour).—KH

STEIN[42] **[at Beethoven's apartment; probably the morning of Wednesday, December 10]**:[43] When is Moscheles playing? // Come to see me, though; I've made a piano that I'd like for you to try out. // I've heard that you are giving a concert. // Do you still have your [Broadwood] piano at home? // The piano maker [Conrad] Graf will not give him [Moscheles] one of his, because he played his concerts [on November 22 and 29] on a Löschen.[44] // If you play in public sometime, then I would like for you to play on one of my pianos. [//] [Blatt 13v]

They cannot last long. // I hope that I can still make you one that you can use; that would make me very happy. // I am curious to hear your [Broadwood] piano in the theater. // But you *should* play sometime. Many people wish for that. // Nobody asks about that.[45] // Moscheles's improvisation was very superficial, especially for anyone who had heard Beethoven. // [Blatt 14r] Come and see me soon, in order to hear what I have just now made for myself. // Don't you have time now?[46] // One must never stand still. //

NEPHEW KARL **[at Beethoven's apartment; probably the afternoon of Wednesday, December 10]**:

    4 fl. 30 kr. : 1 # [ducat]   = 225 fl.: 50 #
       7 kr. : 1 #   = 350 kr.: 50 #
       7 kr. : 1 #   = 5 fl. 50 kr.: 50
    4 fl. 37 [kr.] : 1   = 230 fl. 50 kr. = 50 # //

Since she must have taken something especially bad. // [Blatt 14v]
You have spoken with Stein? //
Everything is bitter like medicine. // The water is not hot enough. //
I was prepared every day. But without money, I cannot have an [advertisement for a housekeeper] placed [in the newspaper]; otherwise you stopped the other day, because

---

[42] (Matthäus) Andreas Stein, the piano maker who most frequently worked on Beethoven's instruments, especially his Broadwood.—TA

[43] On Blatt 14r below, Stein invites Beethoven to his shop, only a short distance away, but the composer seemingly refuses, suggesting that these entries were made in the morning, Beethoven's customary time for working—in this case on the Finale of the Ninth Symphony.—TA

[44] Wilhelm Löschen/Leschen (b. Graue, Hannover, October 27, 1781; d. Vienna, March 1, 1839), piano builder, lived in the Wieden, Alleegasse No. 93, from 1820. Moscheles had played on a Leschen piano at both his November 22 and November 29 concerts. See the *Wiener AmZ* 7, No. 97 (December 3, 1823), col. 771; and No. 100 (December 23, 1823), col. 794; Böckh, 1822, p. 402; Hopfner, p. 301.—KH/TA

[45] Probably concern about whether Beethoven's deafness prevented his playing in public; see nephew Karl's assurance on Blatt 8v above.—TA

[46] Stein's shop in the Rauchfangkehrergasse No. 78 was only a 12–14-minute walk from Beethoven's apartment in the Ungargasse. Even so, Beethoven probably replied that he had work to do. See Ziegler, *Addressen-Buch*, p. 253.—TA

HEFT 48 (DECEMBER 7 – DECEMBER 13, 1823), BLATT 15R

you believe that you will get a woman from Schuppanzigh or from Lichnowsky or from your brother. //

He [Stein] asked right from the beginning whether Moscheles had already gotten the piano. //

[Blatt 15r][47]

Remainder. // Cream. //

$$\begin{array}{r} 46 \\ -39 \\ \hline 7 \end{array}$$ //

[beginning to draft an advertisement, then interrupted by the woodcutters:]
<Is the expression right to you? *A pensionierte Widow.*>

The people get 12 fl. in all. // This time, others have already beaten us to it. Our wood must be cut in the side street. [//] [Blatt 15v] The transport people have gotten 3 fl. They are coming out for the remaining 7 fl. of the [total] 10 fl. [//] [Blatt 16r] It was reported by a woodcutter who chops wood in the house and who learned that we get wood. For a *Klafter* [cord], the following prices are generally assessed:

To the woodcutter	1 fl. 30 [kr.]
Cutting once	1 fl. 30
Cutting once more	1 fl. 30
Laying & carrying	1 fl. 30
Total	6 fl.

For stacking, it is doubled at 12 fl. //

For what time did you reserve her? //
Every transport man at 1 fl. 30 [kr.] //

[Blatt 16v]

ANDREAS SCHULZ[48] **[presumably at Beethoven's apartment, accompanied by his two sons; the afternoon of Wednesday, December 10]**: The other day,[49] an

---

[47] Scribblings in the upper half of the page, and, at right, calligraphic "N," "Pythagoras," and three times "Stuart."—KH

[48] R. Andreas Schulz (b. ca. 1786; d. 1861), bookkeeper at a factory in Meidling (east-southeast of Schönbrunn), violist and guitarist. He lived with his wife, Anna (b. 1784), and his four children in the inner City, Riemerstrasse No. 817. The two children named here are the pianist Eduard (b. February 18, 1812) and guitarist Leonhard (b. November 12, 1813). Andreas is not to be confused with the German-British businessman Johann Reinhold Schultz. See Pfarre St. Peter, Trauungsprotokoll, 1810, Tom. 73, fol. 58 (housed at Pfarre St. Michael); Wurzbach, vol. 32, p. 202; Ziegler, *Addressen-Buch*, p. 46.—KH/TA

[49] This probably refers to the mention of "curing" Beethoven on Blatt 8v above, probably made on Monday, December 8 (Immaculate Conception).—TA

acquaintance of yours promised you the Schmidt hearing balm,[50] and has given me the pleasure of delivering the address for it to you.

Both of these boys are my children and both of them concertize—the bigger one on the piano, the smaller one on the guitar. For both of them it is certainly an interesting occasion when they have the good fortune to meet in person the great man whose works the elder studies, and is still too young to comprehend the great worth of your compositions. [//]

[Blatt 17r]

BEETHOVEN: In the Tiefer Graben, Unter dem Schwibbogen [supporting arch]: Austrian wine, very inexpensive; even Gumboldskirchner for 2 fl. per measure.[51] [//]

[Blatt 17v]

SCHINDLER [**presumably at Beethoven's apartment; afternoon of Wednesday, December 10**]: I mean 50,000 fl. W.W. [plus] 25,000 fl. C.M. make <75,000> 62,500 fl. W.W.; *etiam bene* [certainly, good]. //

NEPHEW KARL [**drafting a newspaper advertisement; afternoon of Wednesday, December 10**]: A professional man's widow, Who has already worked as a housekeeper or cook, can read and write well, and draws a pension, will be employed as a housekeeper under advantageous conditions. Details may be learned in the Ungargasse

---

[50] Dr. G. Schmidt's *wahrer und unverfälschter Gehörbalsam* (true and unadulterated hearing balm), available at the notary Schmidt's in the Schuhmachergässchen No. 569 in Leipzig; also available through the mail. This was advertised in the *Allgemeiner Anzeiger der Deutschen*, No. 248 (September 12, 1822), col. 2666, and other newspapers. Closer to this date of December 10, 1823, an abbreviated version of Schmidt's advertisement for hearing balm had appeared in Bayreuth's *Baireuther Zeitung*, No. 58 (March 23, 1823), p. 264, along with a separate advertisement for Schmidt's tooth powder, also at Schuhmachergässchen No. 569 in Leipzig and also available through the mail. Leipzig's Schuhmachergässchen is perhaps 200 feet northwest of the famed Nikolaikrche, for whose music Johann Sebastian Bach (1685–1750) had also been responsible. Furthermore, the 1823 advertisement specified that Dr. G. Schmidt's tooth powder at the aforementioned address was not to be confused with still another Schmidt's tooth powder, also available in Leipzig. And, of course, the two Leipzig Schmidts are not to be confused with Beethoven's former physician in Vienna, Dr. Johann Adam Schmidt (1759–1808).

What Andreas Schulz was bringing Beethoven was the *address* for obtaining Schmidt's hearing balm in Leipzig, or perhaps even a Viennese address where it could be obtained. As with so many salves and ointments of that era, it was probably ineffective medically. This updated information, courtesy the British researcher "Neville Churchill," November 15 and 18, 2021.—TA

[51] Gumpoldskirchen, a market village between Mödling and Baden, famous as a wine-producing area. Beethoven also refers to the Tiefer Graben/Schwibbogen address in Heft 44, Blatt 22v.—TA

No. 323, in the 1st floor [2nd floor, American], up the rear stairway, door [apartment] no. 12,[52] daily at two o'clock. // [Blatt 18r]

Today you will have to give me a few lines to take with me, saying that I was absent from the mathematics class this morning. It has nothing to do with my learning [the material]; it is only because of the professor; then it doesn't matter. //

This Psychology by Kiesewetter[53] is the best that now exists, only it does not come separately, because it is a part of a large work [edited] by Funke, entitled *Bildungsbibliothek*; this whole work is aimed at *self*-instruction, as is also this Psychology. //

For me, it is even better if I write it, because I think about it at the same time. [//] [Blatt 18v] All branches of knowledge that are necessary for an educated person to know: mathematics, philosophy, philology, etc. // <The work is published here, at least in commission it certainly is; in this way the edition in the [Funke] *Bibliothek* is also from here.> // I think that it was published in Helmstädt. // The *good thing* is that a person would get *everything* in the [Funke] *Bibliothek*.[54] //

[interrupted by the maid:]
The woodcutters need tallow to smear on their saws. She should take them a piece of kitchen candle. [//] [Blatt 19r]

[resuming:]
I went in the *Bibliothek*,[55] as usual, and asked for the best Psychology that is there, and thereupon I was given this. //

You said that someone was eating here. // Again we don't know how the eggs will be this evening. I could bring 2 pounds of chestnuts beforehand. // Fear would also be very much out of place. // As much as I [sentence ends] [//] [Blatt 19v]

I'll subscribe immediately today.[56] [//]

SCHINDLER [filling up the remainder of Blatt 19v with falsified entries→]: I cannot write well with this pencil. //

---

[52] Beethoven's complete and correct address in the Ungargasse. The floor where he lived is often cited or described incorrectly in the literature.—TA

[53] Johann Gottfried Christian Karl Kiesewetter (b. Berlin, 1766; d. Berlin, 1819), *Fassliche Darstellung der Erfahrungsseelenlehre* (Hamburg: Sammer, 1806); part 1 of *Bildungsbibliothek für Nichtstudierte*, ed. L.P. Funke (4 vols.). The Kiesewetter book went through several subsequent reprintings in 1814, 1817, etc. See Kayser, III, p. 273. This Kiesewetter does not seem to be directly related to Vienna's musical amateur Raphael Georg Kiesewetter.—KH/TA

[54] Karl would need to be a skilled salesman to persuade Beethoven to buy Funke's complete *Bildungsbibliothek*.—TA

[55] Karl's meaning is unclear, but perhaps he means *Bibliothek* here as the library—that he went into the library to find a book.—TA

[56] Probably for a complete copy of Funke's *Bildungsbibliothek*, but at least for the Kiesewetter volume.—TA

I believe that, with some indulgence, you will be satisfied with me. I have diligently practiced all three Sonatas, Opus 29,[57] and therefore request an audience [with you]. //

What do you say about this classification? [Piano Sonatas], Op. 2, F Minor; Op. 10, C Minor; then the *Pathétique*, Op. 23 [actually 13]; Op. 29 [actually 31], D Minor; Op. 57.[58] // The representation of similar states of mind, but I find a gradation within them.[59] // Op. 10, D Major—the Largo[60] and the following. // Should the first movement be a preparation? // I beg your pardon. // You said recently that the motive in the 4th movement signified a question—namely "Am I still melancholy?" // Joy and merriment speak in the following passage. // I ask [you]—very soon, because I am on my way. [//] [←falsified entries end]

[Blatt 20r]

NEPHEW KARL [at Beethoven's apartment; probably Thursday morning, December 11]: If we were to see everything that transpires in the kitchen, we would often lose our hunger. //

[turning back to drafting the advertisement:]

Should we designate a particular day and time in the newspaper? [//]

A pensioned widow, of moral character, who can cook, read, and write well, will be employed as a housekeeper under advantageous conditions. Details may be sought in the Ungargasse No. 323, in the 1st floor [2nd floor, American], door [apartment] no. 12, daily at two o'clock.[61] //

I'll bring 2 boxes of tooth powder with me today when I come out of the City.[62] //

I just don't know whether one can say of women that they are "pensioned"; it would be better to say "who draws a pension." //

None of them is tall. // That doesn't concern us. //

---

[57] Beethoven's three Piano Sonatas, Op. 31 (which initially appeared from Nägeli in Zürich), were reprinted by Giovanni Cappi in Vienna in 1803–1805 with the erroneous opus number of 29. See Kinsky-Halm, pp. 77–79.—KH

[58] This concerns the following Piano Sonatas by Beethoven: Op. 2, No. 1, in F Minor; Op. 10, No. 1 in C Minor; *Sonate pathétique*, Op. 13, in C Minor; Op. 31, No. 2, in D Minor; and Op. 57, in F Minor (all composed between ca. 1795 and 1804). Schindler's designation of a sonata as Op. 23 may be a slip of the pencil for Op. 13, or it may actually indicate the Violin Sonata, Op. 23, in A Minor. He seems, however, to be assembling a group of *piano* sonatas in minor keys, so a violin sonata (albeit in minor) may be out of place here.—KH/TA

[59] Schindler often wished to apply poetic interpretations to Beethoven's works, especially the Piano Sonatas; see Schindler, *Biographie* (1860); part 2, pp. 212–222; Schindler-MacArdle, pp. 400–408.—KH/TA

[60] The second movement of Beethoven's Piano Sonata, Op. 10, No. 3, in D Major is a Largo in D Minor.—KH/TA

[61] See also the earlier draft on Blatt 17v above, as well as Karl's partial reversion to the original wording, the second entry below.—TA

[62] On Blatt 29r below, Karl notes that he has brought the tooth powder.—TA

[Karl leaves the house by ca. 12:30 p.m.][63]

[Blatt 20v]

(MARIA) THERESIA HALM **[at Beethoven's apartment; at noon or shortly thereafter, Thursday, December 11 (see below)]**: I am Frau Halm,[64] a fellow countrywoman of yours. [//] [From] Trier. [//] Would you please be so kind as to visit us? I live in the First Coffee House in the Gärtner Gasse, 2nd floor [3rd floor, American], door [apartment] no. 15. //

I was at Zmeskall's;[65] he sends you best greetings. [//]

[Blatt 21r]

SCHINDLER **[at Beethoven's apartment; afternoon of Thursday, December 11]**: The same fate. // I hardly believe that he did not know it, but Karl is very reserved. // He doesn't entirely trust himself to act independently without having consulted with you beforehand; but he *must* do so without restraint—then he would be all right. [//] [Blatt 21v] They probably learn the practical matters of life the hard way, because you probably had to learn them that way the first time. // I was just going to say that you should turn the greatest part of the household management over to him, but it would not work because he has too much to do. Difficult, therefore difficult—have patience, however, he will soon learn it. [//] [Blatt 22r] Young people learn absolutely nothing there, because everything there is handled in a *scholastic* way. I know this from those who have studied with me. // *Monarchist*, and this is the crux of the whole thing. // In the 2nd year of physics it is even harder. // [It] will always cost more. //

---

[63] On Blatt 26r below, Karl reports that he was at the *Zeitung*'s office in the inner City, Rauhensteingasse, at 1 o'clock. The walk would have taken him roughly 25–30 minutes.—TA

[64] (Maria) Theresia Halm, *née* Sebastiani (1782–1843), born in Trier and wife of the composer Anton Halm (1789–1872), with whom Beethoven enjoyed friendly relations. She writes reasonably well but spells phonetically. At that time, the Halms lived in the Viennese suburb of Landstrasse, Hauptstrasse No. 42 (at the corner of Gärtner Gasse), where the "first" Coffee House was located. It was only a long block east of Beethoven's apartment. See Conscriptions-Bogen, Landstrasse, No. 53 [renumbering of 1830], Wohnpartei 18 [became 8]; new collation 53/6; Totenbeschauprotokoll, 1843, H, fol. 37v; Verlassenschafts-Abhandlung (Sperrs-Relation), Fasz. 2: 1847/1843 (all Wiener Stadt- und Landesarchiv); Frimmel, *Handbuch*, I, p. 192, and II, p. 173; Clive, pp. 146–147; and also Heft 45, Blatt 32r. The census records call her "Theresia"; the death record calls her "Maria"; therefore, her name was probably Maria Theresia, and she went by Theresia. She was noted as 69 at her death of *Lungenschwüren* (ulcerated lungs) on September 16, 1843. The house was in the Schlossergassel No. 598 and was owned by her husband, Anton.—KH/TA

[65] The German editors transcribed the phonetic spelling as "Schmesske" but questioned it. It probably refers to Beethoven's longtime friend Nikolaus Zmeskall von Domanowecz, living in the Bürgerspital and largely incapacitated by gout.—TA

[Blatt 22v] To pass down Karpe[66] (from which no smart fellow can become smart) as a philosophical textbook is a blemish on the state of our schools. //

Tomorrow morning, I'll go to the cook myself and send her to you, if you want me to. //

Franz I is not at fault, but instead his servants, because they left it, and not until through <a kind acquaintance and ....>[67] [Blatt 23r]

General Kutschera[68] was quickly dispatched in the cabinet last week. //

Moscheles confirms that the *Accademie* in Amsterdam really still exists, therefore the diploma that it sent could <still> be made known to the public.[69] // I'll get it from the embassy today. //

Monday [December 15] is the concert.[70] [//] [Blatt 23v] Your [Broadwood] instrument is so state-of-the-art that it will be epoch-making in the highest. It is a true joy to hear <this fellow of a> Moscheles play on it. Leschen has strung it entirely with Berlin strings, and you will convince yourself by the way it now sounds. [//] [Blatt 24r] All English pianos will be strung with Berlin strings. // The importation of these strings costs horribly much; but they last 10 times longer than those from here. // Moscheles asks you most courteously to tell him where you would like to sit. // Therefore I have already arranged it in this way. [//]

[Blatt 24v]

BEETHOVEN [**at his apartment; afternoon of Thursday, December 11**]: Ridler,[71] professor of history, now dean of the university. //

---

[66] Franz Samuel Karpe (1747–1806), Slovenian philosopher, professor of philosophy at the university, 1786–1806, wrote *Darstellung der Philosophie ohne Beinamen* (Vienna, 1802–1803). See Kayser, III, p. 308.—KH/TA

[67] Sentence trails off; its meaning is unclear.—TA

[68] Baron Johann Nepomuk von Kutschera (b. Prague, 1766; d. Vienna, 1832), lieutenant field marshal, was adjutant general to Emperor Franz I. In 1823, he was made a privy councillor. See Franz Kysselak, "Todesnachrichten aus Zeitungen 1814–1870," manuscript (Wiener Stadt- und Landesarchiv, Handschriften 3.4.A.112.1–8), fol. 115; and *Hof- und Staats-Schematismus*, 1823, I, p. 30.—KH/TA

[69] This concerns the question whether Beethoven could be designated as "Honorary Member of the Accademies of Stockholm and Amsterdam, etc." on programs and in newspaper advertisements. See Frimmel, *Handbuch*, I, p. 121; Thayer-Deiters-Riemann, V, pp. 88–90.—KH/TA

[70] Moscheles's third Viennese concert had been postponed from Thursday, December 11, to Monday, December 15. It was then repeated on Wednesday, December 17. See Heft 45, Blatt 8r, as well as most of Heft 49.—KH/TA

[71] Johann Wilhelm Ridler (1772–1834), doctor of philosophy, director of the library of the University of Vienna, former professor of universal history; was *Dekan* (dean) of the Faculty of Philosophy in 1824. See *Hof- und Staats-Schematismus*, 1824, II, p. 90; and Franz Kysselak, "Todesnachrichten aus Zeitungen 1814–1870," Manuscript (Wiener Stadt- und Landesarchiv, Handschriften 3.4.A.112.1–8), fol. 128.—KH/TA

HEFT 48 (DECEMBER 7 – DECEMBER 13, 1823), BLATT 25R   123

SCHINDLER [falsified entries begin→] Noble Master—don't be mistrustful! This hinders my effectiveness in your affairs. [←falsified entries end]

[Blatt 25r]

SCHINDLER [**resuming authentic entries; afternoon of Thursday, December 11**]: There is no question of losing here; rather only if he has a loge that is not subscribed, then it would certainly give him the greatest pleasure to be able to demonstrate his respect for you with it. // Again, he was in agreement and—in order not to appear forward—I have given the letter to the secretary. However, he has certainly received it. // [Blatt 25v]

Tomorrow [we] shall hear your Symphony in D.[72] [//] [falsified entries begin→] Another rehearsal would be necessary in your presence; however, I believe that everything has come together securely. After the performance, let's get together; then I'll ask you to tell me whether you were in agreement with everything. // Your seats are the usual ones behind my chair. // [←falsified entries end]

[Blatt 26r]

NEPHEW KARL [**at Beethoven's apartment; later in the day, but seemingly before 4 p.m., Thursday, December 11, and bringing tooth powder with him**]: I was at the *Zeitung*'s office at 1 o'clock. There they said that nothing may be printed that doesn't carry the *Imprimatur* of the High Police Direction. Therefore I went there in the afternoon; there they said that you must first sign your name to it. Then they will let it pass. // [Blatt 26v]

The housekeeper is horribly impertinent. // She gives a lot of lip about everything, even if one does not speak with her. The same way as when we took the maid to task today, she also immediately began to stop scolding. It initially came to my mind that she is also not unalloyed, because that is usually the style of those who reprimand [others] about something that they [themselves] have otherwise committed. // [Blatt 27r]

---

[72] The German editors believed that this entry concerned the second concert of the Gesellschaft der Musikfreunde, which took place in the Grosser Redoutensaal at 12:30 p.m. on Sunday, December 14, 1823, and on which Beethoven's Symphony No. 2 in D, Op. 36, and *Egmont* Overture, Op. 84, were performed. Schindler, however, seems not to have participated in the Gesellschaft's concerts. See the *Allgemeine musikalische Zeitung* 25, No. 3 (January 15, 1824), col. 43.

At the Theater in the Josephstadt, where Schindler was concertmaster, Meisl's play *Das Gespenst in Krähwinkel* (with music by Gläser) was premiered on December 11, 1824, with further performances on December 12 and 13. December 14 saw *Der Bär und das Kind*. It is possible that Beethoven's Symphony No. 2 in D, Op. 36, was performed as an intermission feature on Friday, December 12. Schindler mentions their preparations of Beethoven's Symphony in D from time to time but also indicates elsewhere that theater manager Hensler would not allow such items to be placed on the *Zettel* (playbill). See Bäuerle's *Allgemeine Theater-Zeitung* 16, No. 153 (December 23, 1823), pp. 611–612; and No. 154 (December 25, 1823), pp. 615–616.—KH/TA

[NEPHEW KARL, *continued*]

Recently you wanted to ask the maid[73] why she remained silent that there was still some beef there. // She still always cries about the flatiron. // She took [it that] it was certainly not taken in her presence. // She is also partly afraid. // If the child lives, she will have to feed it. // I am amazed that she didn't give the letter back. // She believed that we had it, because you have looked into everything. // I had to laugh how she writes to her lover about *education*. [//] [Blatt 27v] Don't you want—as you write—to keep the money *here*, and leave it *to her* to pick it up at 4 [o'clock]? // She is to give the receipt to her maid along with it. // Do you also want to write out another one [advertisement] concerning the housekeeping right away tomorrow? // It would be good if we got everything in order; either in the *Zeitung* or the woman that you have seen. [//] [Blatt 28r]

Today there was another prank in class. During the lecture, a firecracker exploded with a very powerful bang. These are balls filled with powder; which someone places on the ground, so that if someone steps on them, the bang results. This was in the afternoon in the history professor's class.[74] The same thing happened in the morning in Stein's class.[75] [//] All investigation is in vain, for how is one to discover the perpetrator? Then the history professor gave them a talking-to, in which, among other things, he said that the perpetrators wouldn't receive any prize for having treated a 70-year-old man in such a way. // He is already old and weak. // It is also probably happening. // Because it is of no use. Who can discover the person who threw around the balls that exploded when another person stepped on them? [//] [Blatt 28v]

[Beethoven may have become angry over Karl's obvious amusement, possibly extended it to ingratitude for his university education, the blame extending to his mother, Johanna, and Karl responds:]

Naturally, I cannot prove to you that I have not have had anything in the least to do with her [Johanna van Beethoven]; I also cannot *prove* that is completely true when I say that I don't know at all where she lives. Meanwhile, if I also want to have even more things that should be quite different, so I don't believe that I have given you occasion to believe this through my behavior, all the more so since you know how we spoke about this matter long ago and also—thank God!—agreed upon it. // That is a simple reproach. // Since no one in the world may distinguish himself, because he must fear that other people, [Blatt 29r] who emulate him, cannot come close to him. //

---

[73] As this topic progresses, it seems apparent that it concerns the maid who was reportedly already pregnant by her boyfriend in the late summer in Baden; see Heft 41, Blatt 24a.—TA

[74] The history professor was Dr. Martin Johann Wikosch (1751–1826); see Heft 47, Blatt 7r.—KH

[75] Anton Joseph Stein (1759–1844), professor of Latin Literature and Greek philology at the University of Vienna; see also Heft 44, Blatt 9r.—KH/TA

HEFT 48 (DECEMBER 7 – DECEMBER 13, 1823), BLATT 29v

[easing the tense situation:]

I brought tooth powder.[76] It is not as strong, and also not nearly as expensive as the last kind, but I don't know whether it will be the right kind for you. //

Schindler. [//]

Receipt [//]

That would be several Sonatas. //

[entries in ink begin→] Veal, 1 pound, that she wanted to preserve. //

Today she encountered the old woman [former housekeeper Barbara Holzmann], whom she knows from the Kothgasse, and who told her that neither she nor any other person would be in your service for long; that you would soon run her off again. [←entries in ink end] [//]

[presumably the end of entries for Thursday, December 11.]

[Blatt 29v]

UNKNOWN [FRANZ LACHNER?][77] [at Beethoven's apartment; probably the afternoon of Friday, December 12; nephew Karl is present]: Would you be so kind

---

[76] Earlier that day, Karl noted (Blatt 20r) that he would bring tooth powder when he came from the City.—TA

[77] The previously unidentified writer is reasonably skilled in grammar and spelling but often omits the curly lines for umlauts. He is familiar with Protestant and liberal Catholic philosophy; he has at least an educated amateur's knowledge of music and may be a church choir director himself, possibly Protestant, and possibly from a rural area. He assumes that Beethoven is acquainted with the Viennese church that he has in mind; he knows Rococo Masses (Brixi) and asks Beethoven to recommend more like them. He is acquainted with conservative Catholic practices (presumably at the cathedral) in Frankfurt, where the slight majority of the population is Protestant. He seems either to have lived earlier in the rural region of Tabor, the Hussite town in Bohemia, 55 miles south of Prague, and performed two of Beethoven's (presumably string) Quartets there, or to have been simply acquainted with Bohemian Protestants and to have performed the Beethoven quartets for them.

One might be tempted to speculate that this conversation was a record of a visit to Anton Halm's apartment, but Halm does not fit the profile above.

A more likely candidate would be Franz Lachner (b. Rain am Lech, Upper Bavaria, April 2, 1803; d. Munich, January 20, 1890). Lachner learned to play organ and piano from his father, Anton Lachner (1756–1820), a watchmaker and organist at the Catholic St. Johannes Church in Rain, ca. 48 miles northwest of Munich. The family was large, with a son, Theodor (1795–1877, from a first marriage), and five other children (from a second marriage): Franz Paul (1803–1890), Ignaz (1807–1895), Vincenz (1811–1893), Thekla (1801–1869), and Christiane (b. 1805), all of whom (including the girls) became musicians. In ca. 1814, Franz attended the *Gymnasium* in Neuburg on the Danube, ca. 12 miles east-northeast of Rain. When father Anton died in 1820, Theodor, at 25, probably became the guardian for all the other children until they reached the majority age of 24, and some sources note him as their "father."

After Anton died, Franz first went to Munich in 1822, where (typical of talented youngsters coming out of the last phases of the Counter-Reformation), he worked as a teacher, violinist, violoncellist, contrabassist, and hornist. In 1823, he won the position as organist at the Evangelical (Lutheran) Church in Vienna, where he then studied with Simon Sechter and Abbé Stadler. He remained there, taking on increasing responsibilities and developing friendships, including with Schubert, Moritz von Schwind, and Anton Schindler, until he left for Mannheim in 1834. In 1836, he became conductor at

[UNKNOWN, *continued*]
as to look over the music of my cousin? She is 10 years [old] and is learning *Generalbass*. // Then does the girl have some aptitude? // She is only 10 years [old]. // Shouldn't she also be writing melodies from her own head? // Förster[78] published a quintet setting from your Symphony in his Works. [//] [Blatt 30r]

He [Karl] indicated that you are right. // He ought to read Salat[79] or Tieftrunk.[80] // Doesn't he have the volumes here? //

But when will you go to England? I heard about this from you long ago. //

What are you doing this evening?[81] // In the case of diarrhea, massage your abdomen with your hands. [//] [Blatt 30v]

What do you think of Schicht's *Harmonie* method, according to the inversion-system?[82] // I only want her to learn the rules in order to understand musical works better, and in any case to play pieces from her own head for herself. // She has a piano teacher for whom she plays daily, and indeed [music] by several composers. [//] [Blatt 31r] She has Handel, Haydn, Mozart, Beethoven, also Clementi. // So you consider the study of *Generalbass* to be good for children? //

What Masses would you advise for me? For example, by Brixi.[83] // Haven't you

---

the Munich Court Opera, until he was deposed through political strife with Richard Wagner and Hans von Bülow in 1864. After their departure, he regained some of his early status and died an honored citizen of Munich. Among his compositions were many Masses and pieces of chamber music. While in Vienna, Lachner variously lived at Landstrasse, Rennweggasse No. 476 [renumbered as 548 in 1830]; and City, Komödiengassel No. 1040, and Untere Bräunerstrasse No. 1127. See Andrea Harrandt, "Lachner," *MGG*, 2nd ed., *Personenteil*, vol. 10, cols. 977–982; Horst Leuchtmann, "Lachner," *New Grove II*, vol. 14, pp. 96–97; Frimmel, *Handbuch*, I, pp. 317–319; Clive, p. 201; and Gugitz, "Conscriptions-Bögen," p. 154.—TA

[78] Emanuel Aloys Förster (1748–1823), composer who was especially known as a teacher. He may have counseled Beethoven concerning his String Quartets, Op. 18, although their relationship later cooled, and he had died on November 12, 1823. This entry deals with Förster's *Anleitung zum Generalbass* (Leipzig: Breitkopf & Härtel, 1805); another edition appeared in 1823.—KH/TA

[79] Jacob S. Salat (1766–1851), theologian, professor of philosophy at the liberal University of Landshut (where Beethoven hoped to send Karl in 1819), wrote numerous works about moral and religious philosophy. See *Allgemeine Deutsche Biographie*, vol. 30, p. 194.—KH

[80] Johann Heinrich Tieftrunk (1760–1837), professor of philosophy in Halle from 1792, wrote works about problems in theology, logic, and natural philosophy. See *Allgemeine Deutsche Biographie*, vol. 38, p. 286; Meusel, *Gelehrtes Teutschland*, vol. 8, pp. 68–70.—KH

[81] Beethoven must have been quite wary of such questions of potential entrapment, but at least he was in his own apartment and could use several excuses, including a case of diarrhea, to escape.—TA

[82] Johann Gottfried Schicht (1753–1823), *Thomaskantor* in Leipzig, wrote *Grundregeln der Harmonie nach dem Verwechslungssystem* (Leipzig: Breitkopf & Härtel, 1812). By "Verwechslung," Schicht meant the invertability of chords in the continuation of their functional relationship. See Gunter Hempel, "Schicht," *MGG*, vol. 11, cols. 1694–1697.—KH

[83] Franz Xaver Brixi (1732–1771), *Kapellmeister* at St. Vitus's Cathedral in Prague, composer of many Masses, including some of relative simplicity. The Brixi family was also intermarried with the Benda family, part of which was Protestant, and part of which remained Catholic.—KH/TA

written anything like that? // The [Mass] has no figured bass.[84] // In Frankfurt, they don't play the organ at Mass. [//] [Blatt 31v] For short Masses in the country it is often missing. //

Once, in the vicinity of Tabor,[85] I had 2 Quartets of yours performed *in the country*, and the people listened to them with the greatest joy. //

JOHANN VAN BEETHOVEN [at Beethoven's apartment; possibly afternoon of Friday, December 12]: Nani[86] knows a fine young woman who can write very well, also loyal. She believes that, because she can write well, that she will be able to get along well [with you]. // So, tomorrow [Saturday?] you can speak with her about it. [//]

[Blatt 32r]

SCHINDLER [at Beethoven's apartment; Saturday, December 13]: That [Frau] Schütz[87] very much pleased [audiences] in Amsterdam. //

NEPHEW KARL: The maid found it, not she. //

SCHINDLER: She has become sickly, therefore she herself had to leave him in order to take care of herself. //

NEPHEW KARL [continuing at Beethoven's apartment; Saturday, December 13]: Graf wanted to give Moscheles his piano [for his concert], but with the condition that he *only* play on *his* instrument. But Moscheles wanted to play first on Graf's and *then* on *yours*, so that the contrast would be stronger. Then Graf revoked his offer of the piano from him. // [Blatt 32v] Now he will play on one by Löschen, and *then* improvise on yours. //

SCHINDLER [continuing at Beethoven's apartment; Saturday, December 13]: Lithographed.[88] // If only you stuck to the point! // It has gone through the embassy. // Engraved. //

---

[84] Beethoven may have shown him the *Missa solemnis* and even indicated that a copy was designated for Schelble's *Cäcilien-Verein* in Frankfurt.—TA

[85] Established in 1420, Tabor (ca. 55 miles south of Prague) was a stronghold of the proto-Protestant Hussites.—TA

[86] Nani, Nanni, Nannerl, etc. were diminutives of the name Anna.—TA

[87] Amalie Schütz, formerly a singer at the Theater an der Wien, had begun singing at the German Opera in Amsterdam on October 5, 1823. See also Heft 47, Blatt 16r.—KH

[88] This and the following entries refer to the diploma sent by the Accademie (i.e., Royal Institute of Sciences, Literature and Fine Arts) in Amsterdam in August 1809, mentioned on Blatt 23r above. See Albrecht, No. 149.—TA

[SCHINDLER, *continued*]

I spoke with him the last time at my audition.[89] // [Blatt 33r]

Among other things, I hear that Herr Bernard has already married and is a landlord.[90] // She has it.[91] Moreover, she is a first-class cook for good homemade meals.[92] //

I am extraordinarily happy with the new [*Namensfeier*] Overture [in C].[93] [//] I hope that it will be *more* effective with this [Kärntnertor Theater] orchestra than previously on Moscheles's concert.[94] // [Blatt 33v]

This Overture in C [actually *Egmont* Overture in F Minor] that will be done tomorrow is not difficult, but great, sublime. // I mean this one.[95] //

---

[89] This refers to Schindler's audition for a position in the Kärntnertor Theater's orchestra, where he would have seen the resident manager Duport. Brother Johann notes that Duport was satisfied with it in Heft 49, Blatt 3v. See also Heft 46, Blätter 1r–2r, and Heft 47, Blatt 33v.—TA

[90] Beethoven's former friend (now a passing acquaintance) Joseph Carl Bernard (1786–1850), editor of the *Wiener Zeitung*, married Magdalena Grassl (or Grassel) at the Paulanerkirche in the Wieden on November 25, 1823. Magdalena's father, Franz Grassl, was dead, but her mother, Theresia (*née* Hammerschmid), now had ownership of the building, the *Eiserner Mann*, Wieden No. 257, directly across Wiedener Hauptstrasse from the back of that church, and retained ownership in 1829. The building immediately south, No. 256, was owned by Joseph Hammerschmidt. See Pfarre Wieden (Paulanerkirche), Trauungs-Register, Tom. 5 (1817–1826), fol. 137; and Behsel, p. 94.—TA

[91] Possibly meaning that Bernard's new mother-in-law actually owns the house.—TA

[92] German original: *Hausmannskost*, home cooking. Even today, one looks for neighborhood restaurants in Vienna that serve such fare.—TA

[93] There is potential confusion here, not entirely of Schindler's making. Beethoven's newest "new Overture" would be the *Consecration of the House* Overture in C, Op. 124, premiered at the Josephstadt Theater on October 3, 1822, but it is not meant in this particular conversation.—TA

[94] The Overture that appeared "*damahls*" (previously) on Moscheles's concert was the so-called *Namensfeier* Overture in C, Op. 115, performed at three concerts given jointly by Moscheles, violinist Joseph Mayseder, and guitarist Mauro Giuliani at the Landständischer Saal, probably with a composite orchestra, on April 16, April 23 (Thursdays), and May 10 (Sunday), 1818, at 12:30 p.m. The *Allgemeine musikalische Zeitung* called it the *Jagd-Ouverture*, but the three notices in the *Wiener AmZ* simply called it Overture in C, noting the conductor as "Hänsel"—Peter Hänsel (1770–1831), violinist and Kapellmeister to Prince Lubomirsky in Vienna. See the *Allgemeine musikalische Zeitung* 20, No. 25 (June 24, 1818), col. 455; the *Wiener AmZ* 2, No. 17 (April 25, 1818), cols. 149–150; No. 18 (May 2, 1818), cols. 158–159; No. 21 (May 23, 1818), col. 183; Schickh's *Wiener Zeitschrift* 3, No. 48 (April 21, 1818), pp. 386–387; No. 56 (May 9, 1818), pp. 450–451; and Weinzierl, pp. 232–233.

The "Overture in C" that would be performed at Moscheles's concert at the Kärntnertor Theater on Monday, December 15, and again on his repeat concert of Wednesday, December 17, 1823, was therefore the *Namensfeier* Overture in C, Op. 115. It is difficult to perform effectively and could never be called "sublime."—TA

[95] The *Egmont* Overture, which would be performed at the Gesellschaft der Musikfreunde's concert on Sunday, December 14, could be described as "not difficult, but great, sublime." See the footnote to Heft 49, Blatt 3r. The *Egmont* Overture is not in C Major but rather in F Minor, probably resulting in Schindler's final word of confirmation, possibly pointing to a copy of the music at hand in Beethoven's apartment. See *Allgemeine musikalische Zeitung* 25, No. 3 (January 15, 1824), col. 43.—TA

Doesn't Steiner still have two Overtures that have not been heard?[96] //

Little Tobias[97] is already bragging about having shipped off 9 copies of the Weber opera.[98] [//] [Blatt 34r] Your brother says that, for the money that he received from the archduke for your works,[99] Little Tobias bought the musical plates from Riedel[100] that are his property. // Little Tobias is supposed to give you 50,000–60,000 fl. for the collected edition, and then you make over everything to him in God's name.[101] [//]

[Blatt 34v]

BEETHOVEN:

2500

2500

2581

2500

2500

End of Heft 48

[96] Sigmund Anton Steiner had publication rights to the Overtures to *The Ruins of Athens*, Op. 113 (actually published in February 1823), and *King Stephan*, Op. 117 (not published until July, 1826). See Kinsky-Halm, pp. 327 and 339.—TA

[97] Original *Tobiesl*, a diminutive of Tobias, meaning publisher Tobias Haslinger (1787–1842). See also Heft 42, Blatt 4r.—KH/TA

[98] S.A. Steiner & Co. (of which Haslinger was a partner) published the piano-vocal score to Carl Maria von Weber's *Euryanthe* on November 8, 1823, two weeks after its premiere in Vienna's Kärntnertor Theater.—KH

[99] In Ziegler's *Addressen-Buch*, assembled in fall 1822 and published early in 1823, there is a section "Libraries for the Purpose of Music," which contains the following listing:

"The Musical Library of Herr Tobias Haslinger, partner in an art and music dealership, consists of almost 500 volumes, for the most part theoretical works .... One laudable undertaking of the owner is that he has assembled the collected works of Ludwig van Beethoven in score in large folio format, and has had them copied on fine English drawing paper. An expert man (Herr Math. Schwarz) has copied on this project for several years, and each individual line of music is drawn cleanly and sharply with his rice-pen. The skilled calligrapher Herr Friedrich Warsow has made the title pages and the inscriptions for it. This work consists of 61 large folio volumes and 4,000 sheets of music ...."

Archduke Rudolph paid 4,000 gulden for this magnificent work, and, after his death, it finally went to the Gesellschaft der Musikfreunde, whose *Archiv* owns it today.

See Böckh, 1822, p. 98; Böckh, 1823, p. 140; Ziegler, *Addressen-Buch*, pp. 221–222.—KH/TA

[100] Joseph Riedl, music dealer in Vienna, on the Hoher Markt No. 541. Riedl's printing activity ceased in May 1823; his products were transferred to S.A. Steiner & Co. See Alexander Weinmann, *Wiener Musikverleger*, p. 15.—KH

[101] Haslinger had already prepared such a list of extant and projected works for Steiner on ca. June 5, 1822. See Albrecht, *Letters to Beethoven*, No. 288.—TA

Heft 49

(December 13, 1823 – December 16, 1823)

[Blatt 1r]

NEPHEW KARL [**presumably at Beethoven's apartment in the Ungargasse; probably late Saturday afternoon, December 13**]:[1]

               50 xr.
                57
           6/107   1 fl. 47 xr.   4 fl. 47

     60 xr.
       47
3 fl. 107   4 fl. 47 xr.
1 fl.   50   1 fl. 50
1 fl.   57
//

SCHINDLER: <I believe that I have to ask you that we not speak about this matter until we are alone; *certainly, for a reason.*> [//] [Blatt 1v]

She might wait until tomorrow to rub out the [stain][2] for Karl, because it is not dry today. //

I fear that he is getting a headache.[3] // His family is his greatest asset, but it is also unfortunate because his mother went bankrupt several years ago and the son had to help her back on her feet. [//] [Blatt 2r]

---

[1] This Heft (and indeed this conversation) seems to be a direct continuation from Heft 48. The sequence of events beginning on Blatt 3r below suggests that Blätter 1 and 2 of this Heft were not filled on the morning of Sunday, December 14, but, rather, late on Saturday, December 13, 1823. As was his habit, Beethoven probably worked through much of the morning of Sunday, December 14.—TA

[2] Because of repairs to the page, this word is illegible, but it is possible that Karl had a mud stain on his clothing that had not yet dried.—KH/TA

[3] This and the following may concern nephew Karl's school friend Joseph Niemetz. See Blätter 5r–5v below.—TA

Be so good as to write a little note to Odelga[4] now; he will already have taken care of further developments, because he himself told me that his grand duke[5] often wants to be admonished and reminded. // Odelga. // I would rather stand security for you for this money, than from Radziwill.[6] // But it is remarkable that there has been no word at all from Sweden.[7] // [Blatt 2v]

He is her Messiah. //

Do not doubt about his [Karl's] sincerity; but that is again his quiet demeanor and reserve.[8] //

That is the usual gift from the emperor.[9] //

Karl has just entered his so-called *Flegeljahren* [awkward age];[10] therefore one looks after him to a certain extent, though he ought to be watchful on his own behalf. //

[presumably the end of entries on Saturday, December 13.]

[Blatt 3r]

NEPHEW KARL **[at Beethoven's apartment; ca. noon, Sunday, December 14]**: Your brother's coachman is here.[11] //

---

[4] Carl von Odelga (1767–1844) had represented the legations of both Nassau and Tuscany in Vienna since at least 1807 and was the intermediary for the grand duke of Tuscany's subscription to a manuscript copy of the *Missa solemnis*. He lived in Vienna, Kärntnerstrasse No. 1073. In 1807, his family included his wife, Josepha (b. 1779); son, August (b. 1804); and daughters Caroline (b. 1801), Josepha (b. 1802), and Pauline (b. 1807). See Franz Kysselak, "Todesnachrichten aus Zeitungen 1814–1870," manuscript (Wiener Stadt- und Landesarchiv, Handschriften 3.4.A.112.1–8), fol. 44; *Hof- und Staats-Schematismus*, 1823, I, pp. 222 and 225; Thayer-Deiters-Riemann, IV, pp. 357 and 370; Thayer-Forbes, pp. 822 and 829–830; Conscriptions-Bogen, Stadt 1127 [1193 before 1821], Wohnpartei 9 [new collation 1127/4] (Wiener Stadt- und Landesarchiv).—KH/TA

[5] Ferdinand III (1769–1824), grand duke of Tuscany from 1790 to 1801 and again from 1814 to 1824, a son of Emperor Leopold II (himself a grand duke of Tuscany until ascending the Imperial throne in 1790). Ferdinand was among the subscribers to the *Missa solemnis*. See Thayer-Deiters-Riemann, IV, pp. 357 and 370; Thayer-Forbes, pp. 822 and 829–830.—KH/TA

[6] Prince Anton Heinrich Radziwill (1775–1833), Prussian governor in Posen since 1815, violoncellist, singer, generous patron. In his Berlin palace, frequent chamber music concerts featuring contemporary composers were organized. Prince Radziwill also numbered among the subscribers to the *Missa solemnis*. See Thayer-Deiters-Riemann, IV, p. 358; Thayer-Forbes, pp. 822–823; and Clive, p. 275.—KH/TA

[7] Beethoven's invitation to the king of Sweden to subscribe to the *Missa solemnis* remained unanswered. See Thayer-Deiters-Riemann, IV, p. 370; Thayer-Forbes, pp. 829–830.—KH/TA

[8] In Heft 48, Blatt 21r, Schindler had noted Karl's reserve.—TA

[9] Perhaps this refers to the modest subsidy that the Court usually gave to concert presenters.—TA

[10] Usually the teenage years from 14 to 17; Karl was actually nearer the end of that period. Jean Paul (actually Johann Paul Friedrich Richter, 1763–1825) wrote a popular novel, *Flegeljahre*, in 1804–1805.—TA

[11] Brother Johann arrives to pick up Karl to go to the Gesellschaft der Musikfreunde's concert in the Grosser Redoutensaal, starting at 12:30 p.m. The program, with the Gesellschaft's orchestra largely of talented amateurs, consisted of Beethoven, Symphony No. 2 in D Major; Rossini, Aria [possibly with bass Anton Forti]; Bernhard Romberg, Capriccio for Violoncello on Swedish Folksongs; Beethoven,

HEFT 49 (DECEMBER 13 – DECEMBER 16, 1823), BLATT 3v

[Karl departs for the 12:30 p.m. concert of the Gesellschaft der Musikfreunde.]

JOHANN VAN BEETHOVEN **[returning to Beethoven's apartment with Karl after the concert; ca. 2:30 p.m., Sunday, December 14]**: Today [Sunday, December 14] is *Figaro* at the Kärntnertor Theater;[12] I would be pleased if you would go with me.[13] It will be out by 9 o'clock;[14] then we can go to the *Fassl*.[15] //

NEPHEW KARL **[writing in part on Johann's behalf]**: Herr von Duport sent you a letter today.[16] // The emperor is here.[17] //

[written vertically→] It says "by Broadwood,"[18] because, in any case, the whole city knows that only you have an English piano by Broadwood. [←written vertically] [//] [Blatt 3v]

He said that he will write an opera again soon. //

There is no separate playbill [for Moscheles's concert] there. //

Overture to *Egmont*; Mozart, Chorus "Dir Herr der Welten" ["Dir Seele des Weltalls," K. 429]. The concert would have been finished by ca. 2 p.m. See the *Allgemeine musikalische Zeitung* 26, No. 3 (January 15, 1824), col. 43.—TA

[12] After a long pause, Mozart's opera *The Marriage of Figaro* [*Le nozze di Figaro*, in German translation as *Die Hochzeit des Figaro*] was performed at the Kärntnertor Theater on Sunday, December 14, 1823. Further performances took place on December 16 and 19, 1823. See Bäuerle's *Allgemeine Theater-Zeitung* 16, No. 154 (December 25, 1823), pp. 615–616; No. 154 (December 27, 1823), pp. 618–619; and a brief notice in the *Allgemeine musikalische Zeitung* 26, No. 3 (January 15, 1824), col. 43.—KH

[13] With Beethoven's birthday approaching, brother Johann might have considered this outing as something of a celebration, although it becomes clear on Blatt 6r below that the composer himself no longer made any obvious outward occasion of it. It is significant, however, that Beethoven, resistant to invitations on other occasions, seems to have accepted Johann's invitation this time.—TA

[14] On Sunday, December 14, 1823, Mozart's *Marriage of Figaro* began at 7 p.m. and would have taken between 2 hours, 45 minutes and 3 hours to perform, exclusive of intermissions. It would not have been finished by 9 p.m. unless it were severely cut. See *Zettel*, Österreichisches Theatermuseum, Bibliothek (courtesy Othmar Barnert).—TA

[15] The grocery dealership of Ignaz Spöttl's Late Widow's Son at *Zum grünen Fassel*, at Kohlmarkt No. 260, also sold fine wine and schnapps. Beethoven and nephew Karl occasionally shopped there for groceries. Spöttl owned the building and evidently had an area where customers could sit and enjoy a glass. See Groner (1922), p. 102; Redl, p. 39; Behsel, p. 8; and Heft 45, Blatt 19v.—KH/TA

[16] Louis Antoine Duport (1783–1853), resident manager of the Kärntnertor Theater. See Castelli, I, p. 226; Cooper, *Beethoven Compendium*, p. 45; and Clive, pp. 97–98.—KH/TA

[17] Probably meaning that the emperor was present in Vienna. He certainly would have been in the capital for the celebration of the Order of the Golden Fleece on the previous Sunday, December 7.—TA

[18] This is probably a reference to the concert poster promoting Ignaz Moscheles's upcoming concert at the Kärntnertor Theater on Monday, December 15. Moscheles used a piano by Viennese piano maker Wilhelm Leschen for most of it but also improvised using Beethoven's English Broadwood piano, received as a gift from the London firm in the first months of 1818. See *Wiener AmZ* 7, No. 104 (December 27, 1823), cols. 829–830; Albrecht, *Letters to Beethoven*, Nos. 246 and 252.—KH/TA

JOHANN VAN BEETHOVEN: Duport told me that he is very satisfied with Schindler's audition.[19] //

[Johann presumably departs.]

NEPHEW KARL: The horns played some wrong notes, then [bass singer] Forti[20] shouted loudly at them: "Good job!" [//]

BEETHOVEN **[on Sunday afternoon, waiting for dinner]**:
+ Nails
+ Drawing paper
+ Bookbinder
+ Pencil [//]

[Blatt 4r]

NEPHEW KARL **[at Beethoven's apartment; ca. 3 p.m. on Sunday, December 14]**: Kirchhoffer was at the [Gesellschaft's] concert and reminded me of the debt.[21] // I find that Forti is better with such [comic] roles than with serious ones. [//]
Boeuf a la mode.[22]
Veal.
Wine. //

He has only calculated 1 fl. [//] 1 *Seidl*.[23] [//]

BEETHOVEN: Inkwell. //

---

[19] Anton Schindler, concertmaster at the Josephstadt Theater since fall 1822, mentions his audition in Heft 48, Blatt 32. In the event, Schindler did not get an appointment at the Kärntnertor Theater until 1825 (possibly not taking real effect until ca. March 1826).—KH/TA

[20] Anton Forti (b. Vienna, June 8, 1790; d. Vienna, July 16, 1859), bass and baritone singer at the Kärntnertor Theater, began his career playing viola in the Theater an der Wien's orchestra, ca. 1806–1807. Forti may have been the soloist in the Rossini aria on the Gesellschaft's program that day. See his Totenbeschauprotokoll, 1859, F, folio unnumbered, death on July 16 (Wiener Stadt- und Landesarchiv); Ziegler, *Addressen-Buch*, p. 73; Frimmel, *Handbuch*, I, pp. 145–146; and Clive, p. 113. The German editors cite his estate record as Verlassenschafts-Abhandlung (Sperrs-Relation), Fasz. 2: 6637/1849 [*sic*].—KH/TA

[21] Franz Christian Kirchhoffer (1785–1842), bookkeeper in the Offenheimer banking house (among others) in Vienna, often acted as Beethoven's financial advisor and, especially, business intermediary with England and especially with Ferdinand Ries in London. Beethoven and Kirchhoffer had discussed Ries and Moscheles on ca. November 15, 1823, in Heft 45, Blätter 23v–24r, 26v–28v. See Frimmel, *Handbuch*, I, p. 263.—KH/TA

[22] This dish, made of beef or ox, is also mentioned in Heft 41, Blatt 1v.—TA

[23] About a third of a liter.—TA

NEPHEW KARL [**still at dinner, Sunday afternoon, December 14**]: Archduke Rudolph's letter[24] changed his [Duport's?] mind right away. //

How did you like the maid who applied today? [//] [Blatt 4v]

It also displeased me that Moscheles did not announce [on his poster] that the piano was *yours*.[25] There appears to be a special intention in doing so. // I believe that he is playing the *Phantasie* [improvisation] on the English [instrument] to direct their attention more to the tone of the piano. //

Your brother says that he is leaving in two weeks. That doesn't agree, however, with what Moscheles himself said.[26] He [Moscheles] said that he would remain here even longer. //

The best restaurant meal is nothing compared to a well-cooked meal at home. [//] [Blatt 5r] One doesn't notice it on the first day; but on the following days one would not stand it very long. //

I have a request for you today. // Namely, I have to run an errand to see the assistant in philosophy[27] concerning the philosophical booklets. He lives on the

---

[24] Beethoven's patron and student, Archduke Rudolph (1788–1831), now cardinal at Olmütz, Moravia, but presumably in Vienna for the Order of the Golden Fleece's ceremonies of December 7, the date on which Beethoven belatedly wrote him a letter on behalf of Schuppanzigh's application (Albrecht, *Letters to Beethoven*, No. 339).—KH/TA

[25] The following works were performed on Ignaz Moscheles's third (half-evening) concert at the Kärntnertor Theater on Monday December 15, 1823: Beethoven, [*Namensfeier*] Overture in C, [Op. 115]; Moscheles, Piano Concerto in E-flat; Rossini, Aria, sung by Madame [Theresia] Grünbaum; Moscheles, Variations on the *Alexander Marsch*; Rossini, Duet from *Moses*, sung by Demoiselle [Henriette] Sontag and Herr [Anton] Haitzinger; Joseph Mayseder, Variations for Violin on a Danish song, played by Mayseder; Free *Phantasie* [improvisations] on Haydn's Volkslied ["Gott erhalte"] paired with the grand chorus from Handel's *Alexander's Feast*. This was an ambitious concert, considering that it was paired with a ballet, *Die Amazonen*. See the *Allgemeine musikalische Zeitung* 26, No. 3 (January 15, 1824), cols. 43–44; and *Wiener AmZ* 7, No. 104 (December 27, 1823), cols. 829–830.

The *Wiener AmZ* did not mention Beethoven's name in conjunction with the Broadwood piano but noted (in comparison with Viennese pianos) that it had a pleasant tone in soft, singing passages but lost its effect in more powerful ones, and also that the bass was too weak.

The Viennese correspondent to the Leipzig *AmZ*, on the other hand, noted: "It is the same instrument that Beethoven received from London as a gift several years ago, and for which he had to pay more in customs, tax, and transport fees than the instrument is actually worth, because this instrument truly cannot be compared with our local products."—TA

[26] Moscheles left Vienna for Prague (his hometown) on January 2, 1824; see *Wiener Zeitung*, No. 3 (January 5, 1824), p. 13. Probably Beethoven did not send any messages via Moscheles in any case, but the touring pianist did not get back to London until May 1825.—KH/TA

[27] Karl uses the term *Supplent*, a teacher's assistant. Among the personnel of the university was Friedrich Socher, an adjunct to the philosophy faculty, living in the Vordere Schenkenstrasse No. 35, a street that leads into the Herren Gasse at the rear of the Harrach Palace, which, in turn, fronts on the Freyung. See *Hof- und Staats-Schematismus*, 1823, II, p. 97.—KH/TA

[NEPHEW KARL, *continued*]

Freyung.[28] Since this is very near the Josephstadt,[29] I would like to go to Blöchlinger's[30] and get Niemetz,[31] to bring him with me to the [theater] loge, which cannot disturb you at all, since it has seats for 6–8 persons. I would like for him to come to the theater even once, because he very seldom has any recreation at Blöchlinger's because he is too poor for his mother to be able to pay for it, and anyway is very busy. If [Blatt 5v] you don't like it, I won't say anything more about it; meanwhile, I don't believe that it could make any trouble for us; it naturally depends only upon you.[32] //

[preparations to attend *Marriage of Figaro*; late afternoon of Sunday, December 14:]

He is supposed to come to see you tomorrow [Monday, December 15] morning. //

[presumably preparing to visit the assistant in philosophy before going to the Kärntnertor Theater:]

You don't know where he lives. // Then I will come directly to the theater. // You and your brother go into the loge as soon as it is time, and I shall come afterward or I'll already be there. //

But he [Johann] said that if he is not here at 6 or 6:30, then he'll come directly to the theater. [//] [Blatt 6r]

[Johann arrives early, before Karl departs on his errand:]

You brother has already come. In any case, I'll be at the entrance to the theater when you come. //

[Karl evidently leaves Beethoven's apartment, probably on his errand. Beethoven and brother Johann drive to the Kärntnertor Theater together; they all meet there for the performance of Mozart's *Marriage of Figaro* at 7 p.m.

---

[28] The *Freyung* is an irregularly shaped square formed, in part, by the Schotten Church and the Harrach Palace, with a wide street leading to another square, *Am Hof*.—TA

[29] To get to suburban Josephstadt, to the west of the Glacis, Karl could have left the walled City through the Franzentor (between the Löwel Bastion and the Schotten Bastion), made a half-left turn, and walked to the foot of Kaiserstrasse (today's Josephstädter Strasse).—KH/TA

[30] For four years, until August 1823, Karl had lived and studied at Joseph Blöchlinger's enlightened and Pestalozzi-influenced Institute for Boys, in the former Strozzi/Czernin Palace, Strozzigrund No. 26, facing Kaiserstrasse, about four long blocks up the hill from the Glacis. See Frimmel, *Handbuch*, I, pp. 50–52; Frimmel, *Studien*, II, pp. 107–109; and Clive, pp. 36–37.—KH/TA

[31] Karl's former fellow student Joseph Niemetz (b. January 20, 1808), of whom Karl was fond and protective. In early September 1823, Karl evidently brought Niemetz to Baden with him and proposed to Beethoven that he spend the vacation months with them there. The composer, working on the middle movements of the Ninth Symphony and not wanting the distraction of a third resident in their crowded summer lodgings, turned down the idea, leading to several quarrels with Karl. Therefore, in proposing that Niemetz join them for a performance, Karl was treading on sensitive ground. See Heft 33, Blatt 19v, and Heft 42, Blätter 8r–11r, among others.—TA

[32] Beethoven probably replied in anger; see Karl's reference to the "disagreement" on Blatt 6v below.—TA

on Sunday, December 14.³³ With encores, the performance would have lasted considerably later than Johann's projected 9 p.m., and they may not have found a restaurant open for anything but late carryout.]³⁴

NEPHEW KARL [presumably at Beethoven's apartment, at midday dinner; ca. 2 p.m. on Monday, December 15]: I already went and looked, and wanted to tell you already this morning what I feel upon this occasion, but I didn't want to awaken you,³⁵ and saved it until this afternoon. // Today is the 15th of December, and the day when you were born, as far as I could see; although I could not be sure whether it is the 15th or 17th, since one cannot rely on the baptismal certificate; and at one time, when I was still at your place, I also read it in the *Janus*.³⁶ I also thought about it yesterday, and [did so] for a long time, [Blatt 6v] but the disagreement [presumably about Niemetz] that took place yesterday did not permit me. // I hope that you accept what I have said to you, even today, although it is contrary to custom. But I must confess to you just now, because, on such days, everything that I enjoy from you occurs to me and I recall all the previous situations, I really don't know where to

---

³³ The performance featured the guest debuts of Johann Michael Wächter as Count Almaviva and his wife, Therese Wächter, as Cherubino. They had come from Pesth, would travel to the Königstadt Opera in Berlin in 1825, and were both engaged in Dresden in 1827.
  The cast also included Anton Forti (1790–1859) as Figaro. Much to Beethoven's satisfaction, Forti had taken over the role of Pizarro from Michael Vogl in the 1814 production of *Fidelio* and had retained it in its November 1822 revival. Henriette Sontag (1806–1854) sang Susanna; and Ignaz Dirzka (1779–1827) sang Dr. Bartolo; and Joseph Gottdank (1779–1849) sang Basilio. The audience was large; the Overture and several numbers (including Forti's "Non più andrai" in its German version) had to be repeated. Three of these would play a role in Beethoven's concert of May 7, 1824, to premiere the Ninth Symphony: Sontag as soprano soloist; Dirzka as choral director; and Gottdank as a personnel manager. See Bäuerle's *Allgemeine Theater-Zeitung* 16, No. 154 (December 25, 1823), pp. 615–616; Clive, pp. 113 and 343–345. For the starting time of the performance, see Blatt 3r (footnote 14) above. For the given names of the Wächter couple, see Otto Erich Deutsch, *The Schubert Reader: A Life of Franz Schubert in Letters and Documents*, trans. Eric Blom (New York: W.W. Norton, 1947), pp. 358–359 and 387.
  There are no conversation-book entries during this occasion, suggesting that Beethoven, Johann, and Karl spoke loudly to one another and were understood, but also that Beethoven could hear well enough to enjoy the performance itself. A similar situation occurred, with very few conversation-book entries, at the premiere of the Ninth Symphony in the same theater on May 7, 1824 (see Heft 66, Blätter 9v–10r).—TA
³⁴ The fatty food mentioned on Blatt 7r below may have been a leftover from takeout the night before or something cooked at Beethoven's apartment earlier.—TA
³⁵ After a late night at the opera on Sunday, Beethoven probably slept later than usual on Monday morning.—TA
³⁶ *Janus*, a magazine edited by Friedrich Wähner at Schrämbl's in Vienna, in 1818/1819. In Nos. 1 and 2 (October 3 and 7, 1818), there appeared an essay, "Ludwig van Beethoven," probably by Wähner, which contains a biographical sketch and characterizes Beethoven's art but specifies no birth date. Following the year given earlier by Choron & Fayolle and the Brockhaus *Conversations-Lexicon*, it says only: "He was born in Bonn in 1772, and therefore, according to the customary measure of human life, we hope to possess him for a long time."—KH/TA

begin first; and *as often as your name- or birthday comes around again,* I will have to say the same thing over again, as [Blatt 7r] I have often said it; only with the difference that, with every passing day, I can better conceive of and understand everything that you have done for me. //

Moscheles is playing Variations on the *Alexandermarsch* of his own composition.[37] // I am most curious about his *Fantasie* [improvisation].[38] //

The other one [housekeeper-cook] is already gone. //

There is only ½ [of Sunday night's supper?] here. In any case, I have to leave right away. // Everything is so fat, that I am already quite full. [//] [Blatt 7v]

NEPHEW KARL [possibly at a restaurant close to the Kärntnertor Theater, now *after* Moscheles's concert; evening of Monday, December 15]:[39]

Everything is expensive here. // The least that a meal costs is 30 kr. //

You believed today that I applauded so out of delight, but that was only because, when they called him back, a part of the audience, presumably enemies, hissed. // When they called him back out. // On the theme "Gott erhalte Franz den Kaiser"; therefore everyone applauded when he began with this theme. // He has a great deal of confidence. // The people said that the [Broadwood] piano really had *tone*! // [Blatt 8r] Not enough power. //

Mayseder plays well.[40] // The piece had no action and coherence at all. //

The least expensive, 30 kr. //

That was nothing more than rehearsed material.—He sought to make the lack of ideas less noticeable by means of brilliant passages. // In the parterre, next to us, you were mentioned; the people said that you are the foremost composer. [Blatt 8v] They

---

[37] This sentence is written over a pencil drawing of a head in profile and scribbles. In the left margin, written calligraphically, is "Pidoll." Pidoll was the name of an old family in Lorraine that had settled briefly in Austrian territory in the 18th century; it was also the name given to a thrown top, invented by an ancestor in the 15th century.—KH/TA

[38] Moscheles was to play the Variations on a Leschen piano and this *Fantasie* on Beethoven's Broadwood piano.—TA

[39] This does not appear to be the *Grünes Fassel* on the Kohlmarkt but instead a similar establishment nearer the Kärntnertor Theater, especially if the piano mover was able to locate them there. From Karl's entries here, on Blatt 7v ("You believed today") and Moscheles's later question on Blatt 10v ("How was the tempo?"), it seems as if Beethoven attended the concert with nephew Karl and then discussed it at a restaurant or coffee house afterward.—TA

[40] Joseph Mayseder (1789–1863), "solo player" (but not concertmaster) in the Kärntnertor Theater's orchestra, also a composer and a member of the Hofkapelle. In about 1800, Beethoven had become acquainted with him through Schuppanzigh, in whose quartet Mayseder occasionally played second violin. On Moscheles's concert of December 15, 1823, Mayseder played his own Variations on a Danish song. See Böckh, 1822, p. 375; Ziegler, *Addressen-Buch*, p. 78; Frimmel, *Handbuch*, I, pp. 397–399; Wurzbach, vol. 17, pp. 195–197; Clive, pp. 231–232; and Blatt 4r above.—KH/TA

HEFT 49 (DECEMBER 13 – DECEMBER 16, 1823), BLATT 9R

should have rolled the piano. [//] Authority. [//] To make a place. // *My* authority, my good fellow! // *I! I! I!* [//]

BEETHOVEN: + A pound of macaroni, to be paid. //

NEPHEW KARL [**written vertically out of sequence, at Beethoven's apartment; probably the next day, Tuesday, December 16→**]: I have come, but only for a moment, to tell you about a newly added hour in philosophy, in which there will only be discussion, every Tuesday from 2 to 3 (tutoring session), compels me to eat in the City. [**←end of vertically written entry**] // [Blatt 9r]

> [**Karl continues on the evening of Monday, December 15:**]
> 2 fl. 15 kr. [//]
> He *is taking care of* that. [//]

PIANO MAKER LESCHEN [?][41] [**after Moscheles' concert**]: I'll take it with me, and send it directly home. [//]

NEPHEW KARL: He will already [sentence ends]

PIANO MAKER LESCHEN [?]: The transport man is taking it right with him. //

NEPHEW KARL: He is sending it today yet. [//] He is sending it. [//] He has people to [sentence ends]. [written vertically→] He says that carrying is better; he will tell the people to take care. // It causes more trouble; it can be transported for 10 fl. [**←written vertically**] [//] [Blatt 9v]
[end of entries of Monday, December 15.]

NEPHEW KARL [**presumably at Beethoven's apartment; afternoon of Tuesday, December 16**]:
> Chestnuts. //
> The maid, whom she knows, is here. // The maid asks for her testimonial, so she can seek a servant's position. //
> The drawing [paper] costs 10 fl. //
> Today, in the presence of the emperor (or in the presence of his portrait, which is about the same thing), was a debate by a student in the *Konvikt*, who acquired

---

[41] The German editors could not identify the writer positively but reasoned (on the basis of Moscheles's remark on Blatt 10v below) that it was probably a piano maker, possibly Wilhelm Leschen, who had supplied Moscheles with his own piano for much of the evening's performance on December 15. Since Leschen lived and worked in the Alleegasse in the Wieden, transporting Beethoven's Broadwood piano back to the Ungargasse would not have taken him and his crew, probably of two or three men, far out of their way. The writer is reasonably literate in these two brief entries.—KH/TA

the doctoral degree;[42] he received a ring, and his parents the Gold Medal and 2,000 fl. C.M. //

[Blatt 10r]

MOSCHELES [at Beethoven's apartment; afternoon of Tuesday, December 16]: Young fellows in the Violins. // Hildebrand[43] took unending pains at the rehearsal. He studied the score. // Katter[44] spoke in support of you at the rehearsal. // That, however, can never do harm to *you*; your works will now be performed much better elsewhere. // [Blatt 10v]

Tomorrow [December 17], it [your Overture in C][45] will be given again, and hopefully in a more secure manner. // How was the tempo of the Allegro?[46] //

I thank you most sincerely for your piano. Hopefully Leschen[47] brought it back undamaged. [//] [Blatt 11r]

I ask that you get your messages for England ready, because I am thinking about departing, at most, in 2 weeks. // Around 3 weeks at most.[48] // I will consider it as a relic.[49] // By my honor, I guarantee that. // I therefore ask you, if possible, to leave it to the aforementioned. I'll come back to see you about this again. [//]

[Blatt 11v]

SCHINDLER [at Beethoven's apartment; afternoon of Tuesday, December 16, possibly while Moscheles was still there]: Moscheles has to repeat the whole concert

---

[42] Karl is speaking of a graduation "sub auspiciis imperatoris" [under the auspices of the emperor], which was conferred upon those receiving doctoral degrees who had completed their studies at the higher schools and university with particular distinction.—KH

[43] Johann Hildebrand/Hildenbrand (b. 1790), second musical director (second concertmaster) at the Kärntnertor Theater, lived at Kärntnerstrasse No. 1005. See Conscriptions-Bogen, Stadt, No. 1005 (Wiener Stadt- und Landesarchiv).—KH

[44] Joseph Katter (ca. 1771–1841), I.R. Court violinist and concertmaster of the opera and Court ballet. See Böckh, 1822, p. 370; *Hof- und Staats-Schematismus*, 1823, I, p. 111; *Portrait-Katalog*, p. 346.—KH

[45] Beethoven's Overture [*Zur Namensfeier*] in C, Op. 115, was performed at Moscheles's Kärntnertor Theater concert of December 15 that was repeated on December 17. During this period in Beethoven's life, it was often called the *Jagd-Overtüre*. It remains a difficult work to pace and balance properly.—KH/TA

[46] This suggests strongly that Beethoven had attended Moscheles's concert with nephew Karl.—TA

[47] Piano maker Wilhelm Leschen lived and had his shop at Wieden, Alleegasse No. 93. See Böckh, 1822, p. 402.—KH

[48] Moscheles left Vienna for Prague on January 2, 1824 and continued his tour of Europe, not returning to England until May 1825. See Blatt 4v above.—TA

[49] Beethoven may have offered Moscheles some token gift.—TA

tomorrow; he asks you to select a loge that pleases you; he believes that you won't refuse it.[50] //

That's how it is on the 3rd floor [4th floor, American]. // She will never give way. [//]

[Blatt 12r]

NEPHEW KARL [at Beethoven's apartment, interviewing another candidate for cook]:[51] She bought a little *Polakel* [spring chicken][52] for 36 kr. // Key to the woodpile. //

BEETHOVEN:[53] Printing paper, 3 fl. 30 kr. W.W., our calendar. //

NEPHEW KARL: She might at least be more skillful. // From Silesia. She has served at a medical doctor's house. // She has served in two places. // She is already an artful cook.[54] // I'll write the receipt [for the spring chicken] right away. //

[Blatt 12v]

SCHINDLER [at Beethoven's apartment; on Tuesday, December 16, with the cook still present]: I don't fear the wrong turn, but being short of money won't hurt him. // The *Konvikt*[55] is the strictest educational institution for higher studies. //

But the white one is quite excellent. //

It is necessary that one knows the needs of the house in general. //

Tomorrow [Wednesday, December 17], in addition to the spring chicken, she would like to make the young rabbit, if you request it.

End of Heft 49

---

[50] Beethoven seemingly accepted Moscheles's invitation; see Schindler's apparent confirmation in Heft 50, Blatt 1r.—TA

[51] This cook presumably stays until December 30, 1823. See the calculations for her pay on that date (Heft 51, Blätter 13r–13v).—TA

[52] A folk word for *poularde* or spring chicken.—KH

[53] The following two sentences written over Karl's calligraphic "Beethov," "I am still," "Son," "I am."—KH

[54] Next to this, twice: "*Stier*" (bull or Taurus).—KH

[55] The Imperial Royal *Konvikt* (or *Convict*), the educational institution at Universitätsplatz No. 750 in Vienna, was also called the "City *Konvikt*," to differentiate it from the older Löwenburg *Konvikt*, run by the Piarist priests in the Josephstadt, a school that was reserved exclusively for the sons of noble houses. The City *Konvikt*, founded in 1802, however, accepted gifted students without financial means but with a stipend. They attended the *Gymnasium* across the square from the university and were brought up in the *Konvikt* according to specific rules and under the strictest supervision. Franz Schubert was among the students there. See *Hof- und Staats-Schematismus*, 1823, II, pp. 148–149; Pezzl, pp. 291–292.—KH

N.B. Heft 50 begins on Saturday, December 20, 1823. It is possible that a small Heft was filled between December 17 and 19 but just as possible that Beethoven stayed largely in his apartment (working on the Finale of the Ninth Symphony) with illiterate domestic servants and an occasional raised-voiced or chalkboard encounter with nephew Karl and did not use a conversation book at all between Heft 49 and Heft 50.

Heft 50

(December 20, 1823 – December 25, 1823)

[Blatt 1r]

SCHINDLER [presumably at Beethoven's apartment in the Ungargasse; presumably the afternoon of Saturday, December 20]:[1] Nothing but rehearsals, the whole week until today; then we are at the end. [//] Today's work costs more than a grand opera. //

Were you in the theater recently?[2] // The *Phantasie*[3] was said to have been very *poor*— the general opinion. // Moscheles is merely a so-called *routine composer* and player. //

NEPHEW KARL: He is a person who is only interested in eating. [//]

[Blatt 1v]

SCHINDLER: I have heard from very reliable people that the administration would have written to you about it [composing an opera] long ago, but certain individuals wanted to declare, with certainty, that nothing more could be expected from you, in that you no longer wrote great works, etc. [//] <Infamy.> //

<I> He is said to have been so flattered by the directors [of the opera] that he has the leading voice among the *Kapellmeisters* [conductors]. He is also usually the only one summoned to all the candidates' auditions.[4] [//] [Blatt 2r]

---

[1] Schindler's most recent entries in the conversation books (Heft 49, Blatt 12v) were presumably written on Tuesday, December 16, and possibly during a hasty visit. The present entries partially explain the chronological gap of three or four days between Hefte 49 and 50. On Blatt 4v below, Schindler notes a performance of *Regulus* at the Burgtheater, confirming that today is Saturday, December 20.—TA

[2] Beethoven had attended Mozart's *Marriage of Figaro* at the Kärntnertor Theater the previous Sunday, December 14, with brother Johann and nephew Karl, as well as Moscheles's concerts there on Monday, December 15, and Wednesday, December 17. Schindler's next entry seems to confirm that Beethoven's reply concerned Moscheles's concert on December 17.—TA

[3] Moscheles's improvisation on Haydn's "Gott erhalte Franz den Kaiser," played on Beethoven's Broadwood piano on Monday night and presumably again on Wednesday.—TA

[4] Possibly Conradin Kreutzer (1780–1849), a peripatetic composer who joined the Kapellmeister staff of the Kärntnertor Theater in spring 1823. He is probably responsible for the appointments of Theobald Hürth (1795–1858) as the new principal bassoonist and Elias Lewy (1796–1846) as the new principal hornist, from outside the normal circles of orchestral recruitment, probably by mid-January 1824. See Theodore Albrecht,

[SCHINDLER, *continued*]

Weigl[5] suddenly has a powerful rival as competitor for the *Kapellmeister*'s position at St. Stephan's [Cathedral]. It is First Lieutenant Gänsbacher[6] from Innsbruck, who is a composer and also has Imperial protection. // He has composed *one* Mass that he earlier performed at the Augustiners;[7] otherwise, the world has never heard of him. *But!* He was a Tyrolese volunteer and earned the favor of the Imperial family. [//] [Blatt 2v] Weigl doesn't have to fear the others. // Eybler[8] has inclined to Gänsbacher, and, in order to give importance to his protection, has the impudence to proclaim him as one of the greatest composers. //

Arsenius,[9] grand comic opera, music by Gläser,[10] libretto by Meisl.[11] // Counterpart to

"Elias (Eduard Constantin) Lewy and the First Performance of Beethoven's Ninth Symphony," *Horn Call (International Horn Society)* 29, No. 3 (May, 1999), pp. 27–33 and 85–94; and Clive, pp. 194–195.—TA

[5] Joseph Weigl (1766–1846), opera composer, conductor, and part-time administrator at the Kärntnertor Theater since 1792. In 1823, he retired from the opera and applied for the cathedral Kapellmeister's position upon the death of Joseph Preindl on October 26, 1823. The position, however, was given to Johann Baptist Gänsbacher. See Böckh, 1823, p. 383; Frimmel, *Handbuch*, II, p. 410; Franz Grasberger, "Weigl," *MGG*, vol. 14, cols. 377–384; Wurzbach, vol. 53, pp. 279–281; and Clive, pp. 391–392.—KH/TA

[6] Johann Baptist Gänsbacher (1778–1844), composer, fought in a volunteer division for the liberation of the Tyrol in 1813. Since 1814, he had been active in military service as a first lieutenant (later as a captain) and had spoken for the improvement of musical life, especially in Innsbruck. Upon his application for the cathedral Kapellmeister's position at St. Stephan's in Vienna, he was especially supported by the archbishop, Count Leopold Maximilian Firmian (1766–1831), who came from an old family of South Tyrolean counts and had been archbishop since January 28, 1822. Gänsbacher had known Firmian's family for many years. The appointment decree, however, was not dated until September 26, 1824. Gänsbacher assumed his duties on November 11, 1824. See *Wiener AmZ* 8, No. 96 (December 1, 1824), pp. 381–382, and subsequent issues; Conrad Fischnaler, *Johann Gänsbacher* (Innsbruck, 1878), pp. 36–37; Walter Senn, "Gänsbacher," *MGG*, vol. 4, cols., 1230–1236; Wurzbach, vol. 5, p. 48; and Franz Loidl and Martin Krexner, *Wiens Bischöfe und Erzbischöfe* (Vienna: Verlag Dr. A. Schendl, 1983), p. 70.—KH/TA

[7] Johann Gänsbacher's Mass in B-flat was performed in the Augustiner Church on Epiphany (Three Kings' Day), January 6, 1822. The Gloria from it had already been performed at the sixth concert of the *Concerts spirituels* on December 20, 1821. See *Wiener AmZ* 6, No. 17 (February 27, 1822), col. 131.—KH

[8] Joseph Eybler (1764–1846), Court vice-Kapellmeister. When Kapellmeister Antonio Salieri's health declined suddenly in fall 1823, Eybler stepped in, and when Salieri was officially pensioned on June 15, 1824, Eybler was promoted to his position. See Alexander Wheelock Thayer, *Salieri, Rival of Mozart*, ed. Theodore Albrecht (Kansas City: Philharmonia, 1989), pp. 151–153.—KH/TA

[9] *Arsenius, der Weiberfeind* (Arsenius, the Woman-Hater), magical tale with song and dance in two acts by Carl Meisl, with music by Franz Gläser, was premiered at the Theater in der Josephstadt on Saturday, December 20, 1823. See Bäuerle's *Allgemeine Theater-Zeitung* 16, No. 156 (December 30, 1823), p. 623.—KH

[10] Franz Joseph Gläser (1798–1861), son of the copyist Peter Gläser, composer, Kapellmeister at the Theater in der Josephstadt (since October 1822), where he played a significant role in performances of Beethoven's music. He lived in the Josephstadt, Kaiserstrasse (today's Josephstädter Strasse) No. 34. See Böckh, 1822, p. 34; Frimmel, *Handbuch*, I, pp. 169–170; Ziegler, *Addressen-Buch*, p. 94; and Clive, p. 130.—KH/TA

[11] Carl Meisl (1773–1853), I.R. marine war commissioner and the author who, in 1822, refashioned Kotzebue's libretto for *The Ruins of Athens* into *The Consecration of the House*. He lived in the

HEFT 50 (DECEMBER 20 – DECEMBER 25, 1823), BLATT 3R

[SCHINDLER, *continued*]

Arsena.[12] // Within a period of 4 weeks, 3 new [theatrical] pieces [Blatt 3r] by him have been given; all of them have been fiascos, but that doesn't scare these authorities away. //

The position at St. Stephan's pays about 10,000 fl. W.W. // Preindl[13] has exploited them in such a way that they have given him their support. // He had several [wealthy] houses where he sent the boys to sing and he got paid 2 fl. per head. I myself have seen an accounting sheet of it that he maintained. [//] [Blatt 3v]

Zips has died.[14] //

The Bourbons have securely established their rule through the Spanish campaign. One actually hears the kindliness of old Louis[15] glorified from all sides. // This lesson, however, was noted and well taken. But what doesn't this miserable Ferdinand VII[16] do now? // [Blatt 4r] They are only the priests and general flatterers. // He has proven it after he named a priest to be prime minister. // Even the king of Portugal,[17] who has reigned despotically for years, has behaved very wisely in the present crisis. [//]

Leopoldstadt, Praterstrasse No. 415. See Böckh, 1822, p. 34; *Hof- und Staats-Schematismus*, 1823, I, p. 376; and Clive, p. 232.—KH

[12] *Arsena, die Männerfeindin* (Arsena, the Man-Hater), magical tale with song and dance by Carl Meisl, with music by Franz Gläser, had been premiered at the Theater in der Josephstadt on September 20, 1823. Its great success caused Meisl to write *Arsenius* as its counterpart. See Bäuerle's *Allgemeine Theater-Zeitung* 16, No. 120 (October 7, 1823), p. 478; and No. 152 (December 20, 1823), p. 608.—KH

[13] Joseph Preindl (1756–1823), composer, and, from 1809 until his death on October 26, 1823, Kapellmeister at St. Stephan's Cathedral. See Ernst Tittel, "Preindl," *MGG*, vol. 10, cols. 1607–1609.—KH

[14] Franz Joseph Zips (b. 1770), personal chamber servant (valet) to Cardinal Archduke Rudolph, had died in Kremsier, seat of the archbishops of Olmütz, on September 25, 1823, leaving two minor-aged sons. On July 26, 1822, Zips had written a letter to Beethoven on Rudolph's behalf, postponing a lesson owing to illness (Albrecht, *Letters to Beethoven*, No. 298; Brandenburg, No. 1484), and Beethoven had mentioned Zips in a letter to Rudolph of February 27, 1823 (Anderson, No. 1146; Brandenburg No. 1586).

Zips may have taken over many of the duties of Rudolph's decade-long secretary and librarian, Joseph *Edler* von Baumeister, who died at age 70 from *Harnblasenbrand* (inflammation of the bladder) at his home in the Strauchgasse No. 252 [renumbered as 244 in 1821] on October 6, 1819. Baumeister was a doctor of law and a pensioned Lower Austrian *Regierungs-Rat*. See Susan Kagan, *Archduke Rudolph*, pp. 6–13; *Wiener Zeitung*, No. 233 (October 11, 1819), p. 931; and Behsel, p. 8

For Zips, see *Hof- und Staats-Schematismus*, 1823, I, p. 193; and "Convoc. Zips's Nachlassansprecher," dated Kremsier, September 27, 1823, in the *Wiener Zeitung*'s *Intelligenzblatt*, No. 248 (October 27, 1823), p. 900.—TA

[15] The Bourbon Louis XVIII (1755–1824), king of France from 1814/15 until his death. The remark concerns the suppression of the Spanish liberal revolution of 1820 by French forces, with which Spanish reactionaries allied themselves, in summer 1823.—KH

[16] Ferdinand VII (1784–1833), king of Spain from 1814 until his death, appointed many ministers of questionable qualifications and spoke with cruel severity for the preservation of absolutism. He was supported by Louis XVIII's troops, who entered Spain on April 7, 1823.—KH/TA

[17] João [John] VI (1769–1826), king of Portugal since 1816. After the liberal revolution of 1820, he had to acknowledge the constitution of the *Cortes* [Assembly] in 1822/23. Strongly influenced to

[SCHINDLER, *continued*]

Haven't you read the work by Dr. O'Meara about Napoleon?[18] It contains quite extraordinary issues concerning the high leaders and the European *Cabinette*. [//] [Blatt 4v] It is put together like a diary and is noteworthy for every century and [all] history. // At the last, there was despair without consideration. //

Today is *Regulus* at the Burgtheater[19]—a fairly rare appearance. //

[At the Theater] an der Wien, an opera by Schubert—with a libretto by [Frau] Chezy.[20] // Admittedly a vulgar fellow in his morality, but on the stage a man in the right place. [//] [Blatt 5r] 1,000 # [ducats]. // It is to wonder how he can still sing with such a lifestyle. // The education is lacking.[21] //

Have you <not> spoken with Grillparzer[22] already? // He has a great deal to do, because Count Stadion[23] is still very sick. // He has really given the libretto to Wallishausser,[24] but I don't believe that he will do it before everything is settled. [//] [Blatt 5v] Grillparzer had to do this, as he himself assured me, because he is indebted to Wallishausser for many obligations.

---

absolutism by his wife, Carlotta, and his son Dom Miguel, he suspended the constitution in 1823. After the exile of his wife and son, he put it in place again in June 1824.—KH

[18] Barry E. O'Meara, *Napoleon in der Verbannung, oder eine Stimme aus St. Helena: Die Ansichten und Urtheile Napoleons über die wichtigsten Ereignisse seines Lebens und seiner Regierung mit seinen eigenen Worten*, 2 vols., translated from the English (Stuttgart, 1822); the original publication was *A Voice from St. Helena* (London, 1822). See Kayser, IV, p. 270.—KH/TA

[19] *Regulus*, tragedy in five acts by Heinrich von Collin (1771–1811), was first performed in a new production at the Burgtheater on Saturday, December 20, 1823. See Bäuerle's *Allgemeine Theater-Zeitung* 16, No. 156 (December 30, 1823), p. 622; and Clive, pp. 76–77.—KH/TA

[20] *Rosamunde, Fürstin von Cypern*, grand Romantic drama in four acts by Helmina von Chezy (1783–1856), music by Franz Schubert, was first performed at the Theater an der Wien on December 20, 1823. In October 1823, Chezy had been the librettist of Weber's *Euryanthe* and was credited with that opera's failure. At *Rosamunde*'s first performance, the Overture and the Choruses of Shepherds and Hunters had to be repeated. See Bäuerle's *Allgemeine Theater-Zeitung* 16, No. 156 (December 30, 1823), pp. 622–623; Otto Erich Deutsch, *The Schubert Reader*, trans. Eric Blom (New York: W.W. Norton, 1947), pp. 308–313.—KH/TA

[21] It is unclear to whom Schindler refers—possibly Schubert, his friend the bass Johann Michael Vogl (1768–1840), or someone else. A Madame Vogl acted and sang in this production, but she was unrelated to the baritone Michael.—TA

[22] Franz Grillparzer (1791–1872), Austrian poet. Probably working through Count Moritz Lichnowsky, he wrote an opera libretto, *Melusine*, intended for Beethoven, in 1822. Although much discussed over the next years, nothing came of the plan. See Frimmel, *Handbuch*, I, p. 181; Thayer-Deiters-Riemann, IV, pp. 396–398; Thayer-Forbes, pp. 841–843; and Clive, pp. 140–141.—KH/TA

[23] Count Johann Philipp zu Stadion (1763–1824), minister of finance from 1815, patron and supervisor of Grillparzer in his position as a clerk in the ministry. See *Hof- und Staats-Schematismus*, 1823, I, p. 246; and 1824, I, pp. 248–249.—KH

[24] Johann Baptist Wallishausser, the Younger (1790–1831), a well-known book dealer and publisher, on the Hoher Markt No. 543, published Grillparzer's collected works. The firm published Grillparzer's opera libretto *Melusine* in 1857. It is also available in *Grillparzers Werke*, ed. Friedrich Schreyvogel, 2 vols. (Salzburg: Bergland-Buch, 1958), vol. 2, pp. 973–1000. See Böckh, 1822, p. 400; Frimmel, *Handbuch*, I, p. 185.—KH/TA

HEFT 50 (DECEMBER 20 – DECEMBER 25, 1823), BLATT 6R 147

You can also use [Henriette] Sontag[25] well, because the girl has rare diligence and rare good breeding. [//] She has long wanted to take the liberty of visiting you, but she ventures that it is not right. // Sontag is a model of rare morality. God grant [sentence ends].[26] [//]

[Blatt 6r]

NEPHEW KARL: She [a domestic servant] had to leave your brother because of his wife, who presumably supposed a secret agreement between him and her. // He[27] is the lord of the house in the highest degree; quite the opposite of your brother. // He will probably come; meanwhile, I'll go there if you believe that [sentence ends]. [//]

BEETHOVEN: 5 fl. 30 [kr]
                     1 fl. 17

KIRCHHOFFER[28] **[presumably at Beethoven's apartment; presumably Sunday, December 21]**: I shall inquire at the state chancellery, or at Esterházy's.[29] Just get finished. // Aren't you giving an Akademie? //

[Blatt 6v]

NEPHEW KARL **[at Beethoven's apartment, writing, in part, on behalf of visiting brother Johann; probably by midafternoon of Sunday, December 21]**: Today he [Johann] spoke with [bass singer] Forti, who also spoke with [resident manager] Duport, and in his presence, Duport declared that you are the only composer who could write a *German* opera; therefore he would, with pleasure, let in every stipulation; only *soon*, because there is now a great shortage and they have not placed their confidence in anyone except you. //
    Don Juan [*Don Giovanni*].[30] //

---

[25] Henriette Sontag (1806–1854), soprano, lived in Vienna from 1823 until 1825, appearing in German and Italian operas, and sang in the premiere of Beethoven's Ninth Symphony on May 7, 1824. See Frimmel, *Handbuch*, II, pp. 223–224; Wurzbach, vol. 27, pp. 68–70.—KH/TA

[26] She was still projecting this visit in Heft 51, Blatt 14v, and in Heft 52, Blatt 3r (now with Caroline Unger).—TA

[27] Possibly Leopold Obermayer (1784–1841), a master baker, brother Johann's brother-in-law, and owner of Windmühle No. 61, corner of Obere Pfarrgasse and Kothgasse, where his bakery was located. See Behsel, p. 144.—TA

[28] For the identity of his handwriting, see Heft 34, Blatt 8v.—TA

[29] These inquiries were presumably about potential subscriptions to the *Missa solemnis*. Prince Nikolaus Esterházy was not among the subscribers. The principal Esterházy palace in the City was at Wallnerstrasse No. 276; see Behsel, p. 9.—KH/TA

[30] Mozart's *Don Giovanni* was performed in German at the Kärntnertor Theater on December 21, 1823, and January 15, 1824. The December performance was for the benefit of the recently engaged guests from Pesth, Johann Michael Wächter as Don Juan and his wife, Therese Wächter, as Zerline.

[NEPHEW KARL, *continued*]

Today is his [Schuppanzigh's] Quartet [concert].[31] // Business people can only attend on Sundays. //

I shall inquire tomorrow. //

What has [Ferdinand] Ries written?[32] //

He asked whether it wouldn't be possible to have the opera finished in April. [//] [Blatt 7r]

Your brother believes that you drink too much water; that may also be part of your diarrhea. // *In part.*—He says that he could not drink that much water.[33] //

Lichnowsky[34] was at his place today and told him with great joy that he would come to see you in 2 days[35] and talk to you about the opera, which everyone is awaiting. // Grillparzer also told the count [Lichnowsky] that he is prepared to make any alterations. // *Libussa* has been given at the wedding festival in Berlin, but did not satisfy, of course;[36] until *Carneval* comes, what better is there to hear? //

If you tell me what you want, I'll copy it in the library. [//] [Blatt 7v] Tell me right away, good fellow! I want to know it. //

When the opera is finished, he promises to come. //

He encountered the *old woman* [former housekeeper Barbara Holzmann],[37] and

---

In the January performance, the company's regulars, Anton Forti and Henriette Sontag, appeared as Don Juan and Zerline

See Bäuerle's *Allgemeine Theater-Zeitung* 16, No. 156 (December 30, 1823), p. 623; and 17, No. 14 (January 31, 1824), p. 55; as well as the footnote to the performance of *The Marriage of Figaro* on December 14, 1823 (Heft 49, Blatt 6r).—KH/TA

[31] In Heft 46, Blatt 30v, Schuppanzigh noted that his future series of subscription concerts would take place on Sunday afternoons at 4:30.—TA

[32] Ferdinand Ries (1784–1838), Beethoven's former student, now living in London. There is no surviving letter from Ries to Beethoven during this time.—KH/TA

[33] This lends credence to Schindler's assertion that Beethoven's "favorite beverage was fresh spring water, which he drank in large quantities in the summertime." See Schindler-MacArdle, p. 387.—TA

[34] Count Moritz Lichnowsky (1771–1837), gossipy younger brother of Beethoven's earlier friend and patron Prince Karl Lichnowsky (1756–1814). See Frimmel, *Handbuch*, I, pp. 349–351; Clive, pp. 206–208; and especially Heft 21, Blatt 9v.—KH/TA

[35] At the end of this conversation (Blatt 8v below), Karl notes that Lichnowsky plans to come on Tuesday, December 23.—TA

[36] *Libussa*, Romantic opera by Conradin Kreutzer, text by Joseph Carl Bernard, was performed in Berlin on December 1, 1823, on the occasion of the wedding of the Prussian crown prince and later King Friedrich Wilhelm IV to Princess Elisa of Bavaria. See the *Allgemeine musikalische Zeitung* 26, No. 2 (January 8, 1824), cols. 17–18.—KH

[37] Barbara Holzmann (b. Vienna, 1755; d. Vienna, October 25, 1831), Beethoven's housekeeper, off and on, from ca. July 1, 1822, to March 1826. Seemingly urged by Karl, who had taken a dislike to her, Beethoven had dismissed her, or she resigned, at the end of September 1823, but the composer found that her potential replacements were largely unsatisfactory. See Heft 17, Blatt 15v; Heft 55, Blatt 1r; and Rita Steblin, "Beethoven's name in Viennese Conscription Records," *Beethoven Journal* 24, No. 1 (Summer 2009), pp. 9 and 13.—TA

[NEPHEW KARL, *continued*]

she looked *quite young*; with *black hair*.³⁸ // I think that one must tell her. //

Grand opera. // They have 7,000 fl. in losses with Weber's *Euryanthe*.³⁹ // Müller is looked upon as the people's Homer.⁴⁰ Long, incomprehensible, and not popular, therefore it [*Euryanthe*] failed. [//] [Blatt 8r]

[writing on behalf of the cook and brother Johann:]

She believed that you wanted it dried, as it also was recently. //

He says that the princesses also go to the market. //

She says that there isn't a drop of butter or fat in the *Boudin* [blutwurst; blood sausage].⁴¹ // Is she also to add broth?

[the domestic crisis having passed, Karl continues on Sunday, December 21, or Monday, December 22:]

Soon the days will become longer again. // Today is *Winteranfang* [the winter solstice].⁴² // You are *das Blümlein Immergrün* [the Evergreen Little Flower].⁴³ //

I am demonstrating wisdom to him. //

Der Taucher by Schiller has been made into an opera, and [Conradin] Kreutzer is setting it to music.⁴⁴ [//] [Blatt 8v]

He [probably Johann] is coming here with Lichnowsky on Tuesday [December 23]. //

[writing on Johann's behalf on Monday, December 22:]

What is your brother [Johann] to say to Duport today [Monday, December 22] about the opera [Grillparzer's libretto for *Melusine*]? He believes that one should tell him that you will give him your reply in two days. [//]

---

³⁸ In a conversation book of April 13, 1823 (Heft 29, Blätter 24r–24v), nephew Karl had commented that brother Johann had dyed his hair black and opined that Beethoven might try it, as well. On May 8, 1823 (Heft 32, Blatt 34v), Karl even wrote a four-line poem about Johann's looking younger with black hair, but that it did not deceive Death.—TA

³⁹ Weber's opera *Euryanthe* had been premiered at the Kärntnertor Theater on October 25, 1823, and repeated several times. From November 14, however, it was given only in a shortened version. See the *Allgemeine musikalische Zeitung* 25, No. 52 (December 24, 1823), col. 861.—KH

⁴⁰ Original German *Volkshomer*. Probably a reference to Wenzel Müller (1759–1835), composer of numerous magic operas, farces, and Singspiele; Kapellmeister at the Theater in der Leopoldstadt. See Ziegler, *Addressen-Buch*, p. 90; and Rudolph Angermüller, *Wenzel Müller und "sein" Leopoldstädter Theater* (Vienna: Böhlau, 2009).—KH/TA

⁴¹ See similar remarks on Blatt 19v below.—TA

⁴² Although the winter solstice fell on Monday, December 22, in 1823, Karl may still be writing on Sunday, December 21.—KH/TA

⁴³ Probably a reference to the poem *Das Blümchen Wunderhold* [The Wondrously Lovely Little Flower] (1789) by Gottfried August Bürger (1747–1794), which Beethoven set to music in ca. 1792 and was published as Op. 52, No. 8, in 1805.—TA

⁴⁴ Samuel Gottlieb Bürde (1753–1831) fashioned the libretto for Conradin Kreutzer's opera *Der Taucher*, premiered on January 24, 1824.—KH

JOHANN VAN BEETHOVEN [**at Beethoven's apartment, probably with Lichnowsky; Tuesday, December 23**]: In all, this opera must bring in 12,000 fl. in paper money [W.W.] // People are telling Duport that he should come to an agreement with Grillparzer. //

[Blatt 9r]

LICHNOWSKY [**at Beethoven's apartment, probably with Johann; presumably Tuesday, December 23, as projected above**]: In your answer, give your estimate of how much time you'll need for the opera and when it will be finished. // Grillparzer is prepared to alter anything that you'd like. // [**conversation continues on Blatt 9v**]

BEETHOVEN [**probably filling this page later, at a coffee house**]:
    Ziper wine at 5 fl. W.W.
    Ditto   3 fl.
    Ditto   4 fl.   per *Maass* [measure]; and many other wines, etc., *Zu den 3 Laufern*, Michaelerplatz No. 255.[45] [//]

[Blatt 9v]

LICHNOWSKY [**continuing from Blatt 9r**]: Give me the letter to Count Neuperg;[46] I'll certainly enclose it. // [Blatt 10r] I shall give you an answer to it in a few days. // Also, I think that the Mass [*Missa solemnis*] should be offered to Marie Louise.[47] // If you want, I will write to Count Neuperg, because I know him. [//] [Blatt 10v]

---

[45] Original term *Cyperwein* (Cyprus wine), which Beethoven spelled *Ziperwein*. A *Maass* was slightly less than 1½ liters. See the *Intelligenzblatt*, No. 292 (December 20, 1823), p. 1284 (Advertisements). The grocery and wine dealership of Mathias Czermack was located in the house *Zu den drey Laufern*, Michaelerplatz No. 253 (on the north side of the street, across from the Michaelerkirche and the western portion of the Michaelerhaus). The same advertisement appeared in No. 296 (December 27, 1823). See also Behsel, p. 8.—KH/TA

[46] Count Albert Adam von Neipperg (1775–1829), Imperial royal lieutenant field marshal, whose name was a phonetic rendering of Neuberg. Since August 7, 1821, he had been in a morganatic marriage with Archduchess Marie Louise, Emperor Franz's daughter, who was now the duchess of Parma and the widow of Napoleon. He had the official function of a Cavalier of Honor to the duchess. A later generation adopted the Italian translation Montenuovo and supported Gustav Mahler as director of the Vienna Court Opera. See *Hof- und Staats-Schematismus*, 1823, I, p. 309; Wurzbach, vol. 20, pp. 146–148.—KH/TA

[47] Marie Louise (1791–1847), daughter of Emperor Franz I, had been consigned to a political marriage to Napoleon in 1810 and quickly bore him a son, initially called the king of Rome. After Napoleon's downfall in 1814–1815, she was given the administration of the dukedom of Parma (1816), where she reigned relatively creditably with the assistance of her new husband, Count Neipperg. Ultimately, she was not among the subscribers to the *Missa solemnis*. See *Hof- und Staats-Schematismus*, 1824, I, p. iv.—KH/TA

Several Masses and a finely developed Requiem.[48] // He was Albrechtsberger's best student, however his compositions are without effect and passion. [//] [Blatt 11r] You will know the fugues of Friedemann Bach?[49] [Blatt 11v] How do like the tragedy *Roderich* by my nephew?[50] //

[end of Lichnowsky's visit, Tuesday, December 23.]

NEPHEW KARL **[at Beethoven's apartment, writing, in part, on behalf of the maid; probably Tuesday, December 23]**: The maid said that on the occasion when you reminded her of being honest, the others who were driven away would not have opened their baskets, so that she could have seen whether anything was in them. She herself, however, certainly didn't take anything. [//] [Blatt 12r]

The maid says that she was extraordinarily happy when you wanted to retain her; she also wants to do everything that you want. In any case, it would be unpleasant for her to take other service that is bad; only it is fatal with the deposit money; I think that she sent us the one whom we have employed; it will also be right *with her* and with the people[51] as well. //

As it appears, they didn't figure in the charge for the bottles, because the maid brought about 12 kr. more than we wrote out. // She said that she has used that much for the pastry. [//] [Blatt 12v] The other one is here, and she can go. //

JOHANN VAN BEETHOVEN **[seemingly at dinner with Beethoven, Karl, and Schindler; possibly on Christmas Eve, Wednesday, December 24]**: How would it be, then, if you were to eat in a restaurant? //

SCHINDLER: Have you already had it placed in the *Zeitung*?[52] It would be good if it happened soon, because now, over the New Year, you might find someone. // Have they already replied? //

---

[48] The subject of conversation is presumably Johann Gänsbacher (see Blatt 2r above), who was a student of (Johann) Georg Albrechtsberger in 1806 and who composed several Masses, including a *Requiem* in C Minor, Op. 15. See Walter Senn, "Gänsbacher," *MGG*, vol. 4, cols. 1230–1236.—KH

[49] Wilhelm Friedemann Bach (1710–1784), eldest son of Johann Sebastian Bach. Of his eleven keyboard fugues or three organ fugues, only eight Fugues for Keyboard (C, C Minor, D, D Minor, E-flat, E Minor, F Minor, and B-flat) had appeared in print by 1823, and those had been published Berlin in 1788. See Martin Falck, *Wilhelm Friedemann Bach* (Leipzig, 1919), pp. 90–92.—KH/TA

[50] Prince Eduard Maria Lichnowsky (1789–1845), son of Beethoven's old friend and patron, Prince Karl Lichnowsky (1761–1814), estate administrator, author, and art historian. His tragedy *Roderich* was published in Breslau in 1823. See *Allgemeine Deutsche Biographie*, vol. 18, p. 533; Kayser, *Schauspiele*, p. 59.—KH

[51] The "people" might be the sisters Baroness Born and Frau Paumgarten, proprietors of a boardinghouse in the *Rother Igel* on Tuchlauben, who helped Beethoven find domestic servants. Some of the pronominal references in this discussion remain unclear.—TA

[52] This refers to the advertisement prepared by nephew Karl (see Heft 48, Blatt 17v) to appear several times in the *Wiener Zeitung*'s *Intelligenzblatt*: "*A Widow* of moral character, who can cook, read,

[SCHINDLER, *continued*]

Specifically, Moscheles departs on January 2nd. He very much asks you to prepare the [Ninth] Symphony by then. [//] [Blatt 13r]

She probably takes her nourishment from the steam coming from the dishes.[53] //

The Cross already castigates the people again, instead of the other way around. // [They] don't know history thoroughly. //

Sand and stone![54] Salieri.[55] // He had to be taken to the hospital by force, because he did not want to bear the costs himself. Then, on the second day, while the guards ate their midday meal, he began to slash away with the table knife, [Blatt 13v] but was restrained from it. // At home, he would absolutely take no medicine, and had to be brought. // His daughters[56] are now already 30 years old, and he still won't allow them to marry, so that he doesn't have to give them anything [as a dowry]. [//] [Blatt 14r]

[probably interrupted by a domestic question:]

We were already diligent, because there is nothing more here. //

[resuming:]

His *Axur* still brings him a good percentage every year.[57] // [Which is] why in Germany they are introducing this fine French custom concerning authors. //

---

and write well, and who draws a small pension, will be employed as a housekeeper under very advantageous terms. Inquire for details in the Ungargasse No. 323, first floor [second floor, American], door [apartment] no. 12, at 2 o'clock daily." See the *Intelligenzblatt*, No. 297 (December 29, 1823), p. 1327; No. 299 (December 31, 1823), p. 1346; and No. 2 (January 3, 1824), p. 14.—KH

[53] This probably indicates that the cook was very thin and seemed not to eat much.—TA

[54] Probably an allusion to Matthew 7:24–27, where Christ taught about the man who built his house on a rock and it withstood the storm, compared to the man who built his house on sand and it could not withstand the storm, "and great was the fall of it." Thus Schindler characterizes the career and decline of Antonio Salieri.—TA

[55] Antonio Salieri (Legnago, 1750 – Vienna, 1825), composer and Court Kapellmeister, lived in the City No. 1088, between Spiegel and Seilergasse (also called Krautgasse), on the western side of Koch Gasse, a narrow street running between them. For a report on his sudden decline in health, including "detrimental effects on his mind as well as his body," probably in October 1823, see the *Allgemeine musikalische Zeitung* 25, No. 47 (November 19, 1823), col. 766. The hospital would simply have been Vienna's state-of-the-art *Allgemeines Krankenhaus*, not its *Narrenturm* (mental ward). See also Ziegler, *Addressen-Buch*, pp. 61 and 113; and Thayer, *Salieri, Rival of Mozart*, pp. 151–154.—KH/TA

[56] From his marriage to Therese von Helferdorfer (the orphaned daughter of a baron) in 1775, Salieri had eight children: one son and seven daughters. Upon his death on May 7, 1825, only four daughters survived him. Franziska (b. 1778), Anna (b. 1784), and Katharina (b. 1788) were still single and lived with their father in the Spiegelgasse, while the eldest, Josepha (b. 1777), was married to Franz Thrier, an adjunct in the field war ministry, living on the Mölkerbastei, No. 1166. See Verlassenschafts-Abhandlung, Fasz. 2: 4385/1825; Conscriptions-Bogen, Stadt, No. 1088 (both Wiener Stadt- und Landesarchiv); Wurzbach, vol. 28, p. 99.—KH/TA

[57] Salieri's *Tarare* (1787) was first produced in Paris, became his most popular opera, and was revised in Italian as *Axur, re d'Ormus* for Vienna in 1788. Composers of operas premiered in Paris received not

Karl is telling a *bon mot* by Hoppe,[58] and your brother says that is [typical of] the Englishman. [//] [Blatt 14v]

He has just now made clear to us that in 40 years we will not bring it as far as he has. //

I am to eat at Stockhammer's,[59] though I would certainly prefer doing so with you; I shall see .... // I'll tell you his specific apartment tomorrow. [//] [Blatt 15r]

Karl wants to write an opera entitled *Der Onkel Johann* [Uncle Johann], and the uncle is supposed to buy it from him for 30,000 fl. // If they do it, the title will have to be changed to *Der arme Onkel Johann* [Poor Uncle Johann]. [//]

[Blatt 15v]

NEPHEW KARL: He also told the housekeeper that she was to do *more*. If you also said that, then it did not come from *him*. //

We aren't getting any rice today. // Dumplings, crackers, noodles. Cauliflower. //
[presumably the end of this get-together on Wednesday, December 24.]

SCHINDLER [**presumably at Beethoven's apartment; afternoon of Thursday, December 25, Christmas Day**]: I beg forgiveness, for my watch is running poorly. [//] [Blatt 16r]

I spent some time at Stockhammer's. The whole family sends you their sincerest regards, with the assurance that they will help with everything in the matter of the sister-in-law in order to demonstrate their respect for you. // [Blatt 16v]

Today, at the Augustiner Church, I met Court Councillor Kiesewetter[60] and

---

only their original fees but also annual royalties based on subsequent performances. *Tarare* had 131 performances in Paris during its composer's lifetime. See Alfred Loewenberg, *Annals of Opera* (3rd ed., 1978), cols. 443–444.—KH/TA

[58] Given Karl's interest in languages and Johann's reference to an Englishman, this was probably Sir Thomas Hope (1774–1831), an English writer, author of *Anastasius, or Memoirs of a Modern Greek*, a novel that appeared in 1819, packed full of humor and fancy. Less likely is Friedrich Ernst Hopp (1789–1869), actor and director at the Theater in der Josephstadt, who was known for his crude jokes and humorous improvisations. See Thayer-Deiters-Riemann, IV, p. 312; Thayer-Forbes, p. 809; Wurzbach, vol. 9, p. 259. For Vienna's Hopp, however, see Heft 51, Blatt 3r.—KH/TA

[59] Presumably Count Ferdinand Stockhammer (1790–1845), official in the Imperial treasury, member of the body of representatives of the Gesellschaft der Musikfreunde; in February 1824, he would be one of the signers of the petition to Beethoven. He lived in the City, Unter den Tuchlauben, *Kleeblatt* No. 434/437. See Albrecht, *Letters to Beethoven*, No. 344; Brandenburg, No. 1784; Ziegler, *Addressen-Buch*, p. 117; Czeike, vol. 3, pp. 525–526; Robert Messner, *Der Innere Stadt Wien im Vormärz*, I, pp. 121–122; Behsel, p. 14; *Hof- und Staats-Schematismus*, 1823, I, p. 78.—KH

[60] Raphael Georg Kiesewetter, *Edler* von Wiesenbrunn (1773–1850), Court councillor and chancellery director of the Court Ministry of War; known as a fine amateur musical scholar and collector of musical autographs. At that time, he was vice president of the Gesellschaft der Musikfreunde. He lived at Salzgries, No. 184. In February 1824, he would be one of the signers of the petition to

[SCHINDLER, *continued*]

Dr. Sonnleithner,[61] who told me to report directly to you about the Akademie—as you heard from Schuppanzigh[62]—that, however you want the whole thing organized, they will arrange it with the participation of the Verein and all the performing artists [of the Verein]. [Blatt 17r] Kiesewetter, who is now the single director of the Verein, just asks that you kindly communicate to the Verein your most gracious letter of intention. Herewith I fulfill this pleasant charge. //

Otherwise, don't believe for a minute that Kiesewetter or anyone else has spoken so much as a word on its behalf. [//] [Blatt 17v]

Little Kanne[63] recently made a gaffe. In the review of Moscheles's concert in the *Theater-Zeitung*, he said: "It opened with a Symphony in C by Beethoven"! I presume that he didn't know what he was writing and that he wasn't even in the hall. // <That

---

Beethoven; see Albrecht, *Letters to Beethoven*, No. 344; Brandenburg, No. 1784. See also Böckh, 1822, p. 351; *Hof- und Staats-Schematismus*, 1823, I, p. 288, and II, p. 340; Wurzbach, vol. 11, p. 252; Ziegler, *Addressen-Buch*, p. 111.—KH/TA

[61] Dr. Leopold Sonnleithner (1797–1873) came from a prominent family of lawyers, amateur musicians, and literary figures. He sang, played viola and violoncello, and was a member of the committee for the Gesellschaft der Musikfreunde's concerts. In February 1824, he would be one of the signers of the petition to Beethoven; see Albrecht, *Letters to Beethoven*, No. 344; Brandenburg, No. 1784. See also Frimmel, *Handbuch*, II, pp. 219–221; Wurzbach, vol. 36, pp. 5–7; Ziegler, *Addressen-Buch*, pp. 107, 112, 116, 118,130, 143, 146, and 193; as well as Clive, pp. 340–343.—KH/TA

[62] Beethoven's longtime friend and collaborator, violinist Ignaz Schuppanzigh (1776–1830), had returned to Vienna from seven years on tour and in Russia on ca. April 15, 1823, and had soon begun a series of string quartet concerts, at first on Thursdays, then on Fridays, and now (beginning with December 28, 1823) on Sunday afternoons. Schuppanzigh was also Beethoven's preferred concertmaster in the premieres of his orchestral works and would serve in that capacity at the Akademie of May 7, 1824. See the *Wiener AmZ* 7, No. 56 (July 12, 1823), col. 447; No. 98 (December 6, 1823), cols. 783–784; No. 102 (December 20, 1823), col. 816; 8, No. 12 (March 27, 1824), col. 45.—KH/TA

[63] Born in Saxony, Friedrich August Kanne (1778–1833), here called "Kannerl," a fond diminutive, was a versatile composer, author, and music critic who had lived in Vienna since 1808. Eventually, he and Beethoven became "Du" friends. In 1823, he was editor of the *Wiener Allgemeine musikalische Zeitung* but also wrote reports for Bäuerle's *Allgemeine Theater-Zeitung* and Schickh's *Wiener Zeitschrift für Kunst, Literatur, Theater und Mode*. Concerning Moscheles's third concert in the Kärntnertor Theater on December 15, 1823, Kanne reported in the *Allgemeine Theater-Zeitung* of December 20: "The Akademie began with Beethoven's Symphony in C. The performance of this musical work was diligent, but the public appeared to have a mixed reaction to its nervous tastes." The following issue of the journal, on December 23, contained a correction by one D[üpree]: "The interestingly laid-out Akademie began with a splendid, still seldom-heard Overture by Beethoven, in which the great master of tones demonstrated his genius in all its individuality. The performance was not very precise, and it would be very interesting to hear this splendid piece of music again soon if it were well rehearsed." See *Allgemeine Theater-Zeitung* 16, No. 152 (December 20, 1823), p. 607, and No. 153 (December 23, 1823), p. 610; Böckh (1822), p. 69; and Wurzbach, vol. 10, pp. 438–440.

In defense of Kanne, he may have used the term *Symphonie* more in the eighteenth-century sense of an overture, because his comment about the work is much more appropriate to Beethoven's *Namensfeier* Overture in C (which was actually performed) than it is to his Symphony No. 1 in C, Op. 21.—KH/TA

[SCHINDLER, *continued*]
is nothing new.> [//] [Blatt 18r] The following issue corrected him, however, so he must have noticed it. //

Kanne laments about the poor success of his magazine, but that's no wonder, since he produces essays full of untruths, when there really are so many facts to the contrary. He writes without having heard things for himself. [//] [Blatt 18v]

Vogler's Mass was performed today, miserably badly, in the Augustinerkirche.[64] One really misses Gebauer in church music.[65] //

Something more about the performance of the Mass [Beethoven's *Missa solemnis*]. Kiesewetter assures that it will do the Verein credit if you place Messrs. Weigl and Schuppanzigh at the head. However, the Verein cannot be of help with the soloists; therefore [Blatt 19r] it will be very good if [Henriette] Sontag or [Caroline] Unger[66] and the foremost male soloists from the opera were invited. //

At present they only have H[err] von Hauschka [as conductor].[67] // Who, then, can [conduct], if not you?? // Kiesewetter says that he himself would prefer no one above Weigl, who unites authority in himself. [//] [Blatt 19v] Weigl. [//] and certainly gives you his honest opinion, of which, however, one is not assured in the case of others. // Weigl certainly directed today's [Christmas benefit] concert splendidly; he himself also organized it.[68] //

---

[64] The performance of a Mass by Abbé Georg Joseph Vogler (1749–1814) in the Augustinerkirche on December 25, 1823, cannot be traced.—KH/TA

[65] Franz Xaver Gebauer (1784–1822) had been Kapellmeister and choral director at the Augustinerkirche, a board member of the Gesellschaft der Musikfreunde, and founder of the *Concerts spirituelles*, which presented liturgical works in a serious concert setting in conjunction with their performances as part of the church's religious services. See Böckh (1822), pp. 352 and 367; *Wiener AmZ*, 6, No. 103 (December 25, 1822), cols. 821–822 (obituary); Frimmel, *Handbuch*, I, p. 160; Wurzbach, vol. 26, p. 383; and Clive, pp. 123–124.—KH/TA

[66] Soprano Henriette Sontag (1806–1854) and alto Caroline Unger (1803–1877), both young operatic stars at Vienna's Kärntnertor Theater, sang the female solos in the premiere of Beethoven's Ninth Symphony on May 7, 1824. Unger lived in the City, Hintere Schenkenstrasse, at the northwest corner with Rosengassel, No. 55. In 1825, she went to Italy with impresario Domenico Barbaja and later married the Frenchman François. See Frimmel, *Handbuch*, I, p. 201; Guetjahr, p. 5; and Wurzbach, vol. 2, pp. 66–68.—KH/TA

[67] Vincenz Hauschka (1766–1840), official in the Court accounting office, talented amateur cellist, prominent member of the Gesellschaft der Musikfreunde, and one of the few friends with whom Beethoven was on familiar "Du" terms. He lived in the Schottengasse No. 103. See Ziegler, *Addressen-Buch*, p. 112; Frimmel, *Handbuch*, I, p. 201; and Clive, pp. 153–154.—KH/TA

[68] On December 25, 1823, Joseph Weigl conducted the traditional potpourri Christmas concert (to benefit the Bürgerspital) in the Grosser Redoutensaal. The dozen numbers included an improvisation by Ignaz Moscheles. See *Allgemeine musikalische Zeitung* 26, No. 3 (January 15, 1824), cols. 44–45.—KH/TA

NEPHEW KARL: Afraid of cooking with too much fat, she did not add a single drop of butter; therefore, she is frugal. // Butter is left out.[69] //

SCHINDLER: *Fidelio* is now going to be performed again. Sontag will sing [the role of] Fidelio.[70] [//] [Blatt 20r] I know, though, that she[71] is very envious of Sontag's fame. // She [Sontag] would have visited you long ago,[72] but she doesn't want to do it alone, and she is afraid to come off second-best in the company of others. But how shortsighted! //

Perhaps he [possibly Count Moritz Lichnowsky][73] will evaporate earlier; but he will doubtless come for the concert ticket. [//] [Blatt 20v]

Was this Stubbornness or Consequence? A philosophical question that inquires too much.

BEETHOVEN:

$$\begin{array}{r} 230 \\ 50 \\ \underline{30} \\ 310 \\ \underline{1} \\ 410 \end{array} \quad \begin{array}{r} 30 \\ 21 \\ \underline{51} \\ 6 \\ \underline{57} \end{array}$$

$$\begin{array}{r} 51 \\ \underline{51} \\ 230 \\ \underline{50} \\ 4 \text{ fl.} \end{array}$$

End of Heft 50

---

[69] See similar remarks on Blatt 8r above. Whoever the current housekeeper/cook was, she certainly had a "modern" healthy outlook, two centuries before it became fashionable. See also Heft 46, Blatt 6r.—TA

[70] See also Heft 46, Blatt 25v. If projected, such performances did not come to fruition in the foreseeable future.—KH/TA

[71] Perhaps soprano Wilhelmine Schröder (1804–1860); see Clive, pp. 325–326.—TA

[72] See a similar report on Blatt 5v above and Heft 52, Blatt 3r.—TA

[73] After becoming increasingly intrusive with Beethoven's compositional plans (see Blätter 9r–11r above) and the preparations for his *Akademie* of May 7, 1824 (to the point of meddling), Count Moritz Lichnowsky suddenly became offended at the publication of the *Ludlamshöhle* petition (of ca. February 24, 1824) and withdrew his participation after April. On April 25, 1824, nephew Karl had already commented that "Count Lichnowsky really is an old lady." See Heft 62, Blätter 2r–7v; and Heft 63, Blätter 10v–11r.—TA

Heft 51
(December 27, 1823 – ca. January 3, 1824)

[Blatt 1r]

BEETHOVEN [presumably at a coffee house; late afternoon of Saturday, December 27, reading that day's issue of the *Intelligenzblatt*]:[1]
  + Waidlinger [*sic*], Imperial High Court trumpeter, maker of the keyed trumpet and keyed horn.[2] (Important.) //

NEPHEW KARL [probably at Beethoven's apartment; later on Saturday, December 27]: In the theater, as everywhere, there are also intrigues; there are some people who begin to hiss out of pure malice as soon as the public applauds, and that, of course, damages Hensler.[3] // A woman-hater [*Weiberfeind*],[4] whose beloved finally compels him to believe in womanly virtue. [//] [Blatt 1v]
  Moscheles was also with Steiner in the shop today.[5] //

---

[1] In addition to Beethoven's reading the *Intelligenzblatt* of Saturday, December 27, nephew Karl reports on Blatt 1v that he was in Steiner's shop earlier that day, which must have been a business day.—TA

[2] On December 27, 1823, Anton Weidinger (1766/67–1852), Imperial High Court and ceremonial trumpeter, living in the Josephstadt, north side of Kaiserstrasse (today's Josefstädter Strasse) No. 105 (one building west of Lange Gasse), published an extensive notice (dated December 18) in the *Intelligenzblatt*, in which he recommended several instruments of his own invention: five keyed trumpets and a keyed horn, some with new crooks (in addition to the keys), and, as a maker of these instruments, "neatly made, after the original of the inventor," recommended the "trumpet and horn maker August Bayde [*sic*]," living in Neulerchenfeld (beyond the *Linie*). Haydn had written his Trumpet Concerto for Weidinger in 1796; in the ensuing quarter century, his one-time astounding invention was being passed by through experiments in valves on horns and trumpets.
  The ensuing comment "*wichtig*" ("important") was Beethoven's own.
  See *Intelligenzblatt*, No. 296 (December 27, 1823), pp. 1318–1319; *Hof- und Staats-Schematismus*, 1823, I, p. 142; Ziegler, *Addressen-Buch*, p. 262. For August Johann Friedrich Beyde (b. Leipzig, 1789; d. Vienna, 1869), see Hopfner, pp. 49–50.—KH/TA

[3] Karl Friedrich Hensler (1761–1825), manager of the Theater in der Josephstadt.—KH/TA

[4] *Arsenius, der Weiberfeind* [Arsenius, the Woman-Hater], premiered at the Theater in der Josephstadt on Saturday, December 20, 1823. See Heft 50, Bl. Blatt 2r.—KH/TA

[5] Pianist Ignaz Moscheles (1794–1870) and music publisher/dealer Sigmund Anton Steiner (1773–1838), whose shop was in the Paternostergässchen No. 572, in the northeast corner of the Graben.—KH/TA

The housekeeper is a terrible gossip; as often as she finds the opportunity, she likes to begin talking. // For example, when the occasion presented itself, she would begin to talk about the housekeeping at Lichnowsky's, etc. I always left right away, but she used every opportunity to gossip. // As it happened at Lichnowsky's. // *House friend.* // Forget it.

[Blatt 2r]

JOSEPH RIES[6] [**at Beethoven's apartment; probably on the morning of Sunday, December 28**]:
Done in vain[7] //

NEPHEW KARL [**taking over writing for the nearly illiterate repairman**]:[8] He absolutely doesn't want to take anything. //
Maria Trost, at the *12 Himmelszeichen*, No. 15, 2nd floor [3rd floor, American]. [//] H[err] v. Ries.[9] [//]
Not entirely. //
On New Year's Day. [//] A week from today.[10] //
Therefore he has devoted himself to lessons. [//] Beginners. [//] Because there is nothing happening in the piano-making business. //
[written vertically→] He can no longer play with speed, because of hard work. // Not since 2 years ago. [←written vertically] [//] [Blatt 2v] He wants to play for you someday, when you have time. // Pleyel.[11] //

[presumably alone with Beethoven after the repairman leaves:]

---

[6] Joseph Franz Nikolaus/Klaus Ries (bapt. Bonn, March 3, 1792; d. Vienna, October 4, 1861), who sometimes signed himself "Joseph Riß." A younger brother of Ferdinand Ries, he had come to Austria in 1814, and by 1821 or 1822, had moved to Vienna as an instrument maker, technician, and piano teacher. He was noted as giving lessons in Heft 45, Blatt 28r and, as a repairman, wrote in Heft 45, Blatt 29r, on Sunday, November 16, 1823. By now he may have had a small instrument factory at Alter Fleischmarkt, No. 739 (old numbering; renumbered as 695 in 1821). Ries was semiliterate, so Karl largely wrote on his behalf. For a fuller biographical note, see Heft 94, Blatt 42v.—KH/TA

[7] Original German: *murgen mahen*, could be "murksen machen," to do something in vain or (probably not in this case) to do something badly, possibly a description of the quick repair made to Beethoven's piano (presumably the Erard) in November 1823, or the prospects for success of any repair made on this visit. See Heft 45, Blätter 27v–28r.—TA

[8] See Karl's perceptive thoughts on Viennese vocabulary and phonetic spelling, Blatt 16r below.—TA

[9] Karl confirms that the visiting technician is Joseph Franz Ries, living in St. Ulrich No. 15, possibly with a shop in the Alter Fleischmarkt. See Blatt 2r above, and Heft 45, Blatt 29r, footnote, and especially Heft 94, Blatt 42v, for details.—KH/TA

[10] It seems that Ries offered to return on New Year's Day, but Beethoven preferred another day, presumably Sunday, January 4, 1824.—TA

[11] Original: Pleyl; the name Pleyel is pronounced very much like the English word "pile," but with an extra "l," and not "play-*ell*," as most Americans pronounce the name. Presumably the Austrian-born pianist Ignaz Pleyel (1757–1831), a composer and piano maker living in Paris since 1795, or his son,

[NEPHEW KARL, *continued*]

It is undeniable that Hensler takes all pains to satisfy the public; he also doesn't lack for anything that results in magnificence and extravagance. In this respect, he incontestably surpasses all the other theaters. Because of the people, however, he can give dramas only seldom, but instead must also call upon *fairies* for help; therefore he always has the bottom [financial] line in mind. // There are always ingenious minds that think up something new. // It also remains fundamentally the same, only with variations. // For the box office, he really couldn't find any better man than Meisl. // The complementary piece, *Die Männerfeindin* [The Man-Hater],[12] likewise by Meisl, was given some 20 times, one after another, always to [Blatt 3r] increasing applause. // Gläser has so many thoughts that aren't bad; he especially doesn't set comedic lyrics to music badly at all; it's just that he doesn't do much that's *original*. Weber and Rossini are his inspirations. // Otherwise, Hensler can be very glad that he has him; he works *diligently*, but Drechsler[13] does nothing. //

Hensler's Theater [in der Josephstadt] is doing great damage to the [Theater an der] Wien and [Theater in der] Leopoldstadt.[14] That's why I think that the people who are hissing are from there, in order to alienate the audience. // As your brother says, Duport [of the Kärntnertor Theater] has certainly distributed very *many* free tickets, so that their owners might applaud performances. //

Pauli, who wrote *Der Weiberfeind* [The Woman-Hater], acts very well. // Herr Fischer.[15]—The comedian's name is Hopp.[16] // These actors are not that way. [//] [Blatt 3v]

It[17] is somewhat floury; boiled too soft. //

---

the piano maker Camille Pleyel (1788–1855), both of whom had met Beethoven in Vienna in 1805. See Frimmel, *Handbuch*, II, pp. 23–24; Rita Benton, "Pleyel," *New Grove*, vol. 15, pp. 6–11.—KH/TA

[12] *Arsena, die Männerfeindin*, libretto by Carl Meisl (1773–1853), set to music by Franz Gläser (1798–1861). See Heft 50, Blatt 2v.—KH/TA

[13] Joseph Drechsler (1782–1852), composer and conductor, was teacher at the Normal School of St. Anna and, from October 1822, upon the reopening of the Josephstadt Theater, was also a conductor there. He later became conductor at the Leopoldstadt Theater. In 1821, he had lived in the Leopoldstadt No. 255, but by the end of 1822 had moved to the City, Brandstadt No. 629 (across from the front of St. Stephan's Cathedral). See Böckh, 1822, p. 366 (reflecting 1821); Ziegler, *Addressen-Buch*, p. 94 (reflecting late 1822); Wurzbach, vol. 3, pp. 380–381; Alfred Orel, "Drechsler," *MGG*, vol. 3, cols. 743–744.—KH/TA

[14] In other words, Hensler's success is hurting the other suburban theaters financially.—KH

[15] Ernst Pauli was an actor, and Matthäus Fischer an actor and stage director, both of them at the Josephstadt Theater. See Bäuerle's *Allgemeine Theater-Zeitung* 16, No. 156 (December 30, 1823), p. 623; Bauer, pp. 44 and 60–62; *Fortuna*, pp. 167–168.—KH

[16] Friedrich Ernst Hopp (1789–1869), actor and stage director at the Josephstadt Theater since 1822. See *ÖBL*, vol. 2, p. 416; Thayer-Deiters-Riemann, IV, p. 312; Thayer-Forbes, p. 809; Wurzbach, vol. 9, p. 259; and Heft 50, Blatt 14r.—KH/TA

[17] The original pronoun is the masculine *er*, probably referring to a *Knödel* (also a masculine noun), a round dumpling about which the Viennese are very particular.—TA

160 HEFT 51 (DECEMBER 27, 1823 – CA. JANUARY 3, 1824), BLATT 4R

[seemingly joined by brother Johann, and writing, in part, on his behalf; during or immediately after midday dinner on Sunday, December 28:]

Has Schuppanzigh sent tickets?[18] //

You should write a few lines to the Musikverein and send the Mass [*Missa solemnis*]; they will have it copied out and perform it in 2 months,[19] since that will be Lent.[20] // They want to defray the costs of everything, if only they receive something from you. // You must write to Kiesewetter, or Sonnleithner.[21] // The whole city is already talking about the new opera [projected *Melusine*]. Duport [Blatt 4r] has already said that he doesn't know why Beethoven hasn't replied to him. // He [Johann?] is coming here tomorrow [presumably Monday], and with that, will write to Duport and to the Verein. At 5 o'clock. // The Verein is defraying the expenses, which amounts to 1500. // Verein of the Austrian Music-.[22] // He spoke with Schindler. Even Duport told him that he doesn't know why you are not answering, since they await it so ardently. //

JOHANN VAN BEETHOVEN [briefly writing for himself]: In your Akademie, you should perform an aria from the new opera [*Melusine*]; that will be terribly effective. //

NEPHEW KARL [still writing, in part, on Johann's behalf]: The Italian Opera will not take place next year.[23] [//] [Blatt 4v]

He [Johann] thinks that he will provide tickets to Kiesewetter, Sonnleithner,

---

[18] The first concert of the Schuppanzigh Quartet's third subscription series, beginning on Sunday, December 28, 1823, at 4:30 p.m. included Haydn's Quartet in G minor (Apponyi No. 6) [Op. 74, No. 3]; Mozart's Grand Quartet in D major, K. 499 or 575; and Beethoven's Quintet in E-flat, Op. 4. See Schickh's *Wiener Zeitschrift* 9, No. 15 (February 3, 1824), p. 128, for a detailed list of the entire series.—KH/TA

[19] *Musikverein*, common parlance for the Gesellschaft der Musikfreunde. Although a number of its singers participated in the premiere of the Ninth Symphony and movements from the *Missa solemnis* on May 7, 1824, the organization itself would not undertake the *Missa solemnis* until March 17, 1861, conducted by Johann Herbeck. See Richard von Perger, *Geschichte der k.k. Gesellschaft der Musikfreunde in Wien* (Vienna, 1912), p. 300; Pohl, *Die Gesellschaft der Musikfreunde* (Vienna, 1871), p. 73.—KH/TA

[20] In 1824, Lent began on Ash Wednesday, March 3.—KH/TA

[21] Kiesewetter and Sonnleithner held influential positions in the Gesellschaft der Musikfreunde; see Heft 50, Blätter 16v–17r.—KH/TA

[22] The organization's official name was *Gesellschaft der Musikfreunde des österreichischen Kaiserstaates* (Society of the Friends of Music of the Austrian Imperial State). See *Hof- und Staats-Schematismus*, 1824, II, p. 340.—KH

[23] The source of this rumor cannot be determined. The spring 1824 season of Barbaja's Italian Opera company at the Kärntnertor Theater began with Michele Carafa's *Gabriella di Vergi* on April 1, 1824. One year later, however, Barbaja's lease expired at the end of the winter season of 1825, and he departed for Italy. Thus, the Kärntnertor Theater remained essentially dark (and its musicians and staff unemployed) until the lease was renegotiated for the spring 1826 season. See Schickh's *Wiener Zeitschrift* 9, No. 48 (April 20, 1824), p. 410.—KH/TA

HEFT 51 (DECEMBER 27, 1823 – CA. JANUARY 3, 1824), BLATT 5r 161

Winter[24] on your behalf. // President of the Musikverein.[25] // He wants to drive with you to see Breuning.[26] // He says that coachman and horses and carriage are freezing. // She is full of caprices. //

A *new* coffee house has been established in the Josephstadt, across the street from the theater, very beautiful and long;[27] it was also quite full. [//] [Blatt 5r] The *other* [proprietor] is losing quite a bit [of business] because of it.[28] //

[writing for himself:]
I told you that I am satisfied with soup, beef and potatoes; therefore I don't know why I am getting a reprimand. // They ought to save that. //

UNKNOWN **[at Beethoven's apartment; probably 2 p.m. on Monday, December 29]:**[29] A *widow* is here, 29 years old, from Prague, gets 500 fl. as a pension and has capital of 11,000 fl. W.W.—along with a farm and garden in Dornbach;[30] [she] can cook and [write][31] well. Also courteous. She is in the building below. //

NEPHEW KARL: [written vertically→] She is below. [←written vertically] [//] [Blatt 5v]
Too aristocratic, I fear. [//] War commissioner's widow. // Do you even want to know any more? //

---

[24] No one by this name appears among the prominent members of the Gesellschaft der Musikfreunde in either Böckh's or Ziegler's directories.—KH/TA

[25] The president of the Gesellschaft der Musikfreunde was Count Friedrich Egon von Fürstenberg, Imperial privy councillor and high master of ceremonies. See Böckh (1822), p. 351; *Hof- und Staats-Schematismus*, 1823, I, p. 5, and II, p. 340.—KH

[26] Beethoven had known the Breuning family since his youth in Bonn. Stephan von Breuning (1774–1827) moved to Vienna in 1800 and became a Court war councillor. After 1806 or so, he and Beethoven saw one another less frequently. At this time, he was living in Esterházy's *Rothes Haus*, Alservorstadt No. 197, facing the Glacis, northwest of the walled City, whereas Beethoven's apartment in the Ungargasse was also near the Glacis, but southeast of the City. Beethoven probably wanted to pay a New Year's visit to Breuning, but the walk, in the raw weather, would have taken almost an hour either way. See Frimmel, *Handbuch*, I, pp. 65–66; and *Hof- und Staats-Schematismus*, 1823, I, p. 288.—KH/TA

[27] Joseph Bäcker's coffee house opened in the suburban Josephstadt, Kaiserstrasse No. 100, on December 24, 1823, across the street from the Theater in der Josephstadt at Kaiserstrasse No. 102. Many such properties featured deep lots leading to courtyard gardens. See the *Intelligenzblatt*, No. 290 (December 18, 1823), p. 1265 (Announcements); *Wanderer*, No. 14 (January 14, 1824).—KH/TA

[28] Wolfgang Reischl, whose restaurant, *Zum goldenen Strauss*, was located at Kaiserstrasse No. 102, to the immediate east of the Theater in der Josephstadt. Today it serves as the theater's refreshment and relaxation hall. See Groner (1922), p. 484; Czeike, vol. 5, p. 374; and Ziegler, *Josephstadt*.—KH/TA

[29] Beethoven's newspaper advertisement directed applicants to come at 2 p.m., and the group of four of them here suggests that they are responding to that instruction.—TA

[30] Dornbach, a village to the northwest of the walled City of Vienna, beyond suburban Alservorstadt and Hernals. It had many country villas of the nobility and upper middle class, and bordered on the wine-growing hills of the Vienna Woods. See Groner (1922), pp. 82–83; Czeike, vol. 2, p. 82.—KH/TA

[31] The original word is illegible here, but "read" or, especially, "write" would make sense in context. Otherwise, the entire entry by this unknown person is difficult to read in the original.—KH

On the Graben No. 619; *Goldne Krone* in the wax shop,[32] Anna Rinn. // In the summer she would have 4–5 rooms that you could occupy.—for 100 fl. C.M., in Dornbach. // She would already be satisfied with the apartment. [//] Superior. // She gets an income of 50–60 fl. per month. // [Blatt 6r]

The woman from Erdberg[33] already has a job. // It would be very easy to get her back, however not before two weeks; because she is said to be dissatisfied at the place where she now serves. // Otherwise, everything is in order. It therefore depends upon *when* they begin. //

APPLICANT ANNA GOTTSCHEDT [at Beethoven's apartment; ca. 2:15 p.m., Monday, December 29]: In Mariahilfer Strasse, at the *Goldener Engel*, No. 85, 1st floor [2nd floor American], door [apartment] no. 13; Anna Gottschedt, at Frau v. Mayer's. //

NEPHEW KARL [writing, in part, for Anna Gottschedt]: Fine bakery products, pastries, all sweet dishes, but no cakes. [//] [Blatt 6v] Earlier she played piano a great deal; her husband was in the Musikverein in Graz;[34] she is *very happy* to meet you. // 100 fl. C.M.[35] // She says that she is primarily concerned with her good name and with being treated well. //

The poster. //

[another applicant, possibly ca. 2:30 p.m.:]

Alservorstadt, Wittenburggasse [*sic*][36] No. 21, 2nd floor [3rd floor American], [door] no. 15; Susanna Krupka, lives at Countess Rosa v. Collet's. // She is already half dead. // [Blatt 7r]

[evidently interrupted by a carpenter or cabinetmaker, possibly ca. 2:45 p.m.:]

---

[32] Thomas Mathias Stregček owned a wax-bleaching and candlemaking factory in suburban Landstrasse No. 250. His shop in the walled City was located on the Graben in the building *Zur goldenen Krone*, No. 619. See Redl, 1823, p. 212.—KH

[33] Erdberg, originally a village on the Danube about two miles southeast from Vienna, documented already in the 12th century. During the Third Crusade, it served as a staging area for troops and supplies. England's Richard the Lionheart taken captive here as he returned from the Holy Land. It has officially been a suburb of Vienna since 1850 and is now incorporated into the suburb of Landstrasse. See Groner (1922), p. 96.—KH/TA

[34] Officially the "*Musikverein in Steyermark zu Grätz*," the Graz Musical Society was founded in 1819 under the protection of Archduke Johann. It was led by Johann Kalchegger von Kalchberg, and in ca. August 1823 awarded Franz Schubert an honorary membership. In 1824, the Verein numbered 145 musically active and 197 supporting (nonperforming) members. See Gräffer-Czikann, III, p. 744; *Hof- und Staats-Schematismus*, 1824, II, p. 353; and Deutsch, *The Schubert Reader* (New York: Norton, 1947), pp. 290–291.—KH/TA

[35] Presumably the annual amount of her widow's pension.—TA

[36] Actually the Wickenburggasse, technically in the suburb Alsergrund, one block west of the Glacis. The names supplied here cannot be found in the surviving *Conscriptions-Bögen* (census sheets) in the Wiener Stadt- und Landesarchiv. See Guetjahr, p. 325; Behsel, p. 196.—KH/TA

[NEPHEW KARL, *continued*]
    He says that for 7 fl. he will make every chest like new.[37] //
    [resuming the discussion about the housekeeper applicants:]
    The one [woman employer] was a countess. // [Woman] friend. //
    Up to now, I like the previous one [presumably Anna Gottschedt] the best. // She has a married daughter in Graz. //
    [after the arrival and departure of the fourth applicant, probably shortly after 3 p.m.:]
    The last one who was here [Leonore Gross] is a worn-out, downtrodden person, who is not suitable for us. And the first one [Anna Rinn] is an aristocratic woman who wants to be treated like a princess, and likewise isn't suitable for us. The one who came second [Anna Gottschedt], however, is sincere and cried when I told her your name, since it aroused a strange feeling in her, because her husband had so often participated in your compositions,[38] and she herself played [pieces] of yours. //
    As a coffee brewer's widow, she [presumably Susanna Krupka] has no pension but has some [income] of her own; she already worked for two households. [//] [Blatt 7v]
    She can bring references. // When is she to come back? //
    Publish the Symphony [No. 9] and the Mass [*Missa solemnis*] by subscription, and then sell the plates to Haslinger.[39] //
    I'll write the letter to Duport now. // Like Lichnowsky wrote. // We must write immediately, because it has already been several days since you received the letter. Plus you already promised Duport a week ago that you would answer him. // This answer was already given to the [theater] administration a year ago. [//] [Blatt 8r]
    [listing the four candidates for housekeeper:][40]
    Anna Rinn, lives on the Graben No. 619, in the wax shop, at the *Goldne Krone*. //
    Anna Gottschedt, Mariahilfer Strasse, at the *Goldner Engel*, No. 85, in the 1st floor, door no. 13, at Frau v. Mayer's. //
    Susanna Krupka, Alservorstadt, Wittenburggasse [*sic*] No. 21, in the 2nd floor, at Frau Rosa von Collet, née Countess von Galler's. //

---

[37] See another reference to cabinetry on Blatt 16v below. Here the German reads *Kasten*; there it reads *Schrank*, but they may refer to the same household item.—TA

[38] While visiting Teplitz in summer 1811, Beethoven had met Joseph von Varena (1769–1843), a music-loving lawyer living in Graz. Starting in December 1811, Beethoven began sending Varena copies of his yet-unpublished orchestral works to be performed on concerts organized by the Ursuline nuns to benefit the poor there, continuing through 1813 and possibly beyond. In 1815, he recommended a piano purchase for them. Varena was among the founders of the Graz Musikverein in 1819. See Anderson, Nos. 334 and 428, among others.—TA

[39] Tobias Haslinger (1787–1842), a partner in the music publishing firm of S.A. Steiner since 1814, took over sole ownership on May 2, 1826. See Frimmel, *Handbuch*, I, p. 197; and Alexander Weinmann, *Wiener Musikverleger*, p. 32.—KH/TA

[40] At this point, Anna Gottschedt seems to have been the strongest candidate, but Beethoven may actually have hoped for the return of Barbara Holzmann as housekeeper.—TA

Leonore Gross in the Trattnerhof,[41] 5th floor [6th floor American], at Madame Rosiza's, a hatmaker. //

SCHINDLER [presumably at Beethoven's apartment; presumably Monday, December 29, possibly ca. 4 p.m.]: Ehlers[42] is stage director at Bethmann's [theater in Berlin],[43] subject to 6-week terms. //

[falsified entries begin→] I am now considering rehearsing the *Pastorale* [Symphony] with the orchestra; before doing so, I still have to study it. // You will support me in this way again; oh yes, please.[44] [←falsified entries end]

[Blatt 8v]

BEETHOVEN [presumably at a coffee house, reading the day's newspapers, seemingly accompanied by nephew Karl and brother Johann; probably late afternoon of Monday, December 29]:

+ Montegre, <A.J., *die Hämeroiden*, etc., etc.> at Mörschner a[nd] Jasper, 2 fl. C.M.[45] //

---

[41] The Trattnerhof, one of Vienna's largest and most fashionable apartment buildings, was built on the east side of the Graben No. 618 in 1773–1776 by the Court printer Johann Thomas von Trattner. A room or small apartment so many flights up would not have been considered a desirable address, but it was convenient for a simple handworker. See Groner (1922), p. 513; Czeike, vol. 5, pp. 470–471; Guetjahr, p. 29.—KH/TA

[42] Wilhelm Ehlers (b. Weimar [or Hannover], 1774; d. Mainz, 1845), tenor at several theaters, including Vienna from 1805 to spring 1814, when he sang in Treitschke's singspiel *Die gute Nachricht*. By fall 1814, he was singing in Breslau, remained there two years, then went on tour. By 1822, he was manager of the United Theaters at Ofen (Buda) and Pesth, and, on ca. January, 25, 1823, visited Beethoven in that capacity. He moved to Berlin as stage director at the Königstädtisches Theater by fall 1823 and remained there until 1826, after which he continued his peripatetic life in Stuttgart, Frankfurt, and ultimately Mainz. See Schilling, vol. 2, pp. 559–560; Fétis, 2nd ed. (1883), vol. 3, p. 119; Conscriptions-Bögen, Laimgrube, Nos. 26/3 and 68/2 (Wiener Stadt- und Landesarchiv); Ledebur, p. 128; *Portrait-Katalog*, p. 349; Heft 19, Blätter 24v and 31v–32r.—KH/TA

[43] Heinrich Eduard Bethmann (1774–1857), actor, stage director, and theater director in Berlin. During a visit to Vienna beginning on November 4, 1823, he and concertmaster Carl Wilhelm Henning (1784–1867) had acquired Beethoven's unpublished music to *Die Weihe des Hauses* for the opening of the new Königstädtisches Theater in Berlin on August 4, 1824. See Heft 45, Blatt 5v; and Heft 52, Blätter 1r–1v, among others.—KH/TA

[44] While Schindler was the concertmaster (but not solo player) at the Theater in der Josephstadt from fall 1822 until 1825, he seems to have conducted several concerts with the theater's orchestra, perhaps including Beethoven's by-then accessible Symphony No. 2 in D (or movements from it). There is no record of a performance of Beethoven's *Pastorale* Symphony in F during this period, and these entries, made after Beethoven's death, seem to be Schindler's attempt to provide evidence that he had discussed the score with the composer.—KH/TA

[45] Excerpt from an advertisement in the *Intelligenzblatt*, No. 297 (December 29, 1823), p. 1333. Beethoven copied the advertisement accurately except for *Haemorrhoiden*. He did not copy the subtitle or the bookshop's address, Kohlmarkt, Count Clary's house, No. 257; translated from the French by Count Wilhelm Becker; Leipzig, 1821, octavo.—KH/TA

JOHANN VAN BEETHOVEN: Duport and the administration would *lose all confidence* if we give them an unspecific answer again, like last year. The best answer is the one [suggested] by Lichnowsky. [//]

[Blatt 9r]

NEPHEW KARL [**writing, in part, on Johann's behalf**]: With pleasure I have [missing verb] the proposition …. // He was at [lawyer] Bach's and showed him the letter, and he [Bach] said that you should make the proposition, and designate the price, then wait for the reply. He cannot make the contract *before* they know the conditions. //

JOHANN VAN BEETHOVEN: I ask you for Lichnowsky's letter. //

NEPHEW KARL [**continuing**]: The administration must know where it is. //

JOHANN VAN BEETHOVEN: You have carried it so far that no one believes you anymore, and you can be assured that they are saying that nothing can be gotten from you. //

[Blatt 9v]

NEPHEW KARL [**continuing, in part, on Johann's behalf**]: Duport told him that he wished to see the contract, and to see the conditions. // Therefore, let's wait another couple of days. //

What do you want with the Musikverein? // Copying and practicing take a great deal of time. // The Verein is undertaking that. // Do you want to write to Duport or to the administration? // Don't you also want to write to Sonnleithner? [//] [Blatt 10r]

[**suggesting the wording of a letter:**]

"Since the administration of _____ has invited me, etc., etc., I report that I … [reflexive verb] …. I am keeping the libretto [of Grillparzer's *Melusine*]. I shall report in a few days concerning the time [needed to compose it], the performance, the honorarium, etc." //

JOHANN VAN BEETHOVEN: In any case, I cannot deliver the letter today; not until tomorrow [Tuesday, December 30] after dinner. // He can only be found after dinner. //

Before the symphony is sold, the Mass must be sold. //

[**presumably reading the *Beobachter* of December 29:**]

The theater in Graz has burned down.[46] //

[possibly general conversation:]

Kalkbrenner has arrived here to give several concerts.[47] [//]

[Blatt 10v]

NEPHEW KARL [late evening of Monday, December 29]: He [Johann?] doesn't believe that we will ever have an orderly household, but we will want to convince him to the contrary. // The housekeeper who was first here writes that time hangs heavy on her hands, and [she] seeks a position. //

Ehlers has become vice-director in Berlin. // Subject to terms of 6 weeks, because he is known as a hothead. //

You should reclaim the copy of the *Weihe des Tempels* [*Weihe des Hauses*] because he [Johann] hopes to sell it.[48] // They don't do that. [//] [Blatt 11r]

The Overture to *Fidelio* was done today [Monday evening, December 29]. // Kärntnertor [Theater].[49] //

He can do little or nothing at Duport's because he doesn't understand Duport and, himself, can say even less. // He says nothing except "C'est charmant!" [It's charming!]. //

UNKNOWN [at Beethoven's apartment, representing an applicant for the housekeeper's position; presumably ca. 2 p.m. on Tuesday, December 30]: Please be so kind as to tell me the conditions. [//] She is 40 years old. [//] An official's widow. [//] 150 fl. C.M. as Imperial pension. [//] Will she have someone else [to help] in the kitchen? [//] [Blatt 11v] Will she have her own room? [//] She is a little delicate;

---

[46] The *Österreichischer Beobachter*, No. 323 (December 29, 1823), p. 1644, reported: "In Graz, the provincial theater and Redoutensaal [ballroom] were destroyed by flames in the night of December 24 and 25. The origins and further details are not yet known."—KH

[47] This conversational segment does not seem based on any one specific newspaper report, because the "Arrivals" notice in the *Wiener Zeitung* would not have indicated Kalkbrenner's purpose.

The pianist Friedrich Kalkbrenner arrived in Vienna from London (via Berlin) on December 26, 1823, accompanied by François Joseph Dizi (1780–ca. 1840), and lodged in the Hotel *Zum Erzherzog Carl* in the Kärntnerstrasse No. 968. On January 25, 1824, at the midday hour [12:30 p.m.], both artists gave a concert in the Kleiner Redoutensaal. See the *Wiener AmZ* 7, No. 105 (December 31, 1823), cols. 837–838; Bäuerle's *Allgemeine Theater-Zeitung* 17, No. 2 (January 3, 1824), p. 7; *Beobachter*, No. 25 (January 25, 1824), p. 110; Guetjahr, p. 44; *Wiener Zeitung*, No. 298 (December 30, 1823), p. 1214 (Arrivals).—KH/TA

[48] Beethoven had signed proprietary rights to the Overture to *Die Weihe des Hauses*, Op. 124, among others, over to brother Johann as repayment of a loan. After several vain attempts to get it published, the work appeared from Schott in Mainz in 1825, and Johann received 130 ducats. See Kinsky-Halm, pp. 354–356, and various references in Beethoven's correspondence.—KH

[49] The Overture to *Fidelio* was performed as part of a half-evening concert at the Kärntnertor Theater on Monday, December 29, 1823. See *Allgemeine musikalische Zeitung* 26, No. 3 (January 15, 1824), col. 45.—KH/TA

HEFT 51 (DECEMBER 27, 1823 – CA. JANUARY 3, 1824), BLATT 12R   167

therefore the front room will not do. [//] Have I the good fortune of speaking with the famous composer Beethoven? [//] Plain-cooking on the table? [//] [Blatt 12r] Augartenstrasse No. 160, in the 1st floor [2nd floor, American], von Steinius.[50] //

HOUSEKEEPER APPLICANT MAYER [**at Beethoven's apartment; probably ca. 2:15 p.m. on Tuesday, December 30**]: I am here because of a job that I saw in the newspaper, and am asking about the conditions and my duties. [//] I have a 400 fl. pension, and ask for time until tomorrow to consider it. [//] [Blatt 12v] Mayer in the Schottenhof, [apartment] no. 10; [up] the stairway in the 3rd floor [4th floor, American] at Frau v. Herrwies's.[51]

[Blatt 13r]

NEPHEW KARL: We'll want to figure up what she[52] gets [paid] right away. When did she begin?

[first, Karl multiplies the salary of 36 kr. for 16 days:][53]

36 [kr. per day]
16 [days]
―――
216 [kr.]
36
―――
576 [kr.]

[next, he long-divides 576 by 6(0) kreuzer per florin:]

6 | 576 = 9 fl. 36 kr.
54
―――
36   9 fl. 36 kr.
                          8 fl. 24
                          ―――
                             60

---

[50] Augartenstrasse runs in front of the large park in suburban Leopoldstadt. No. 160 was almost directly across the street from the gate leading to the pavilion that served as home to Vienna's summer concerts. The names given here cannot be located in surviving Conscriptions-Bögen (census records). See Guetjahr, p. 83.—KH/TA

[51] The Schottenhof, on the Freyung at its intersection with Herrengasse, numbered 136 in 1823, is a large building complex with several courtyards and many rental apartments (some quite luxurious), attached to the front of the Schotten Church and its Benedictine monastery. See Groner (1922), pp. 434–435; Guetjahr, p. 8.—KH

[52] This evidently concerns the outgoing temporary housekeeper-cook, employed since December 16 (see Heft 49, Blatt 12r). They waste no time in dispatching her.—TA

[53] Beethoven had had little or no instruction in multiplication and division in his own school days, and so he may have been confused by Karl's arithmetical computations (with both functions in a single undivided column) here.—TA

[NEPHEW KARL, *continued*]

[second, Karl multiplies the salary of 36 kr. for 14 days:]

36 [kr. per day]
14 [days]
―――――
144 [kr.]
36
―――――
504 [kr.]

[next, he long-divides 504 by 6(0) kreuzer per florin:]

6 ⟋ 504 = 8 fl.
  48
―――――
    24 fl. [*sic*]   //

For the 14 days, she has to get exactly 18 fl. [//] [Blatt 13v]

[third, Karl multiplies the salary, now at 24 kr., for 14 days:]

24 [kr. per day]
14 [days]
―――――
96 [kr.]
24
―――――
336 [kr.]

[next, he long-divides 336 by 6(o) kreuzer per florin:]

6 ⟋ 336 = 5 fl. 36 kr. //

23 fl. 36 kr.[54] //

[The housekeeper-cook collects her pay and leaves.]
She is gone with all her things. [//] [Blatt 14r]

[writing largely on behalf of a visitor, possibly named Wolf;[55] probably later on Tuesday, December 30, or possibly the next day:]
Also an acquaintance of Schuppanzigh's. // Recently saw you in the concert.[56] // He knows him very well. // Do you know the violinist Lafont?[57] // He thinks a

---

[54] Evidently represents 18 fl. and an additional 5 fl. 36 kr. owed to the housekeeper-cook.—TA

[55] If the visitor's name was Wolf, and if he was an open admirer of Moscheles, he may have been Jewish. He must have been at least in his mid-40s if he (presumably) had heard Beethoven play in ca. 1798. If so, it could have been in Vienna or possibly in Prague. The visitor was seemingly well-traveled; he had been to Paris and seemingly London and had seemingly lived in Paris for three years.—TA

[56] From the later reference to Moscheles, the visitor probably saw Beethoven at one of the pianist's concerts at the Kärntnertor Theater on December 15 and 17. See Heft 50, Blatt 1r.—TA

[57] Charles Philippe Lafont (1781–1839), significant French violinist.—KH

great deal of Moscheles as a pianist. // Do you know Cramer?[58] // He has already been acquainted with you for 26 years, and also heard you play. [//] He was there 2 times.[59] [//] In Paris for 3 years. //

His name is Wolf.[60] //
You should go to London; you would be treated like a god. //
[presumably the end of the visit.] [Blatt 14v]

[Karl writes for himself; possibly Wednesday, December 31:] I request only the address. // At the grocer's. [//]

BEETHOVEN: + Paper
+ <Hensler>
+ Staudenheimer[61] //

SCHINDLER **[presumably at Beethoven's apartment; probably already just before or during midday dinner on New Year's Day, January 1, 1824 (as below)]:** It is certainly unheard of in Vienna that a *Rentierer* [person of private means; rentier] would give a concert for his own benefit. // A short time ago, Kalkbrenner bought himself an estate near Paris, and is therefore a *Rentier*.[62] //

The two girls [singers Sontag and Unger] will visit [you] within the next few days; they are requesting your most gracious ear.[63] I spoke with Unger today. // I am not making any house calls, but I took her my New Year's card today. [//]

[Blatt 15r]

---

[58] Johann Baptist Cramer (1771–1858), pianist composer, pedagogue, and music publisher; member of the Royal Philharmonic Society in London. See Frimmel, *Handbuch*, I, p. 100.—KH

[59] Possibly Prague; Beethoven played there in 1798.—TA

[60] It is remotely possible that this refers to pianist Joseph Wölfl (1772–1812), also called "Wolf" in France, who lived in Vienna from 1795 and engaged in competition with Beethoven but went to Paris in 1801 and London in 1805.

It is also quite possible that this visitor's own name was Wolf, but his name does not appear among the musicians or musical enthusiasts listed in Böckh (1822) or Ziegler's *Addressen-Buch*.

See Thayer-Deiters-Riemann, II, pp. 66–68; Thayer-Forbes, pp. 204–208; Wurzbach, vol. 57, pp. 216–218.—KH/TA

[61] Dr. Jacob Staudenheim (1764–1830), Beethoven's sometime physician, later personal physician to the duke of Reichstadt, lived in the palace of Count Harrach on the Freyung No. 239. Unless there were any pressing health problems, Beethoven probably intended to send him (as well as Josephstadt Theater director Hensler) New Year's greetings. Beethoven and Karl always called him "Staudenheimer." See Conscriptions-Bogen, Stadt No. 239, Wohnpartei 4 (Wiener Stadt- und Landesarchiv); Frimmel, *Handbuch*, II, pp. 250–252; Wurzbach, vol. 27, pp. 250–251.—KH

[62] The "Arrivals" notice for December 26 in the *Wiener Zeitung*, No. 298 (December 30, 1823), p. 1214, listed Friedrich Wilhelm Kalkbrenner as a *Rentierer*. See also Blatt 10r above.—KH

[63] Concerning the projected visit, see also Heft 50, Blatt 5v, and Heft 52, Blätter 2r–3v.—TA

NEPHEW KARL [**present with Schindler**]: I just now encountered another housekeeper [applicant], but I sent her away, all the more because she didn't appear to be anything special. //

Saturday.[64] //

SCHINDLER [**present with Karl**]: As [they] left, they told me that I should not come until today. //

NEPHEW KARL: On the piano are a New Year's card and a letter from my mother [Johanna]. //

SCHINDLER [**at Beethoven's apartment; probably midday dinner, ca. 2 p.m., on Thursday, January 1, 1824**]:[65] Is she old already? // How many cooks must also polish boots? Therefore .... [//] [Blatt 15v]

You probably know already that Kalkbrenner is here. He has come to Vienna as a *Rentierer* [person of private means; rentier] and not as an artist, with which he has also gone far! //

We are giving it [a concert] for the benefit of a poor, very sick member of our orchestra,[66] // in Krause's Institute in the Josephstadt.[67] // Tietze[68] is a lawyer in his fourth year, and sings a very sonorous tenor. [//]

[Brother Johann and his wife, Therese, seemingly make a New Year's visit to Beethoven's apartment, but it remains essentially undocumented.][69]

[Blatt 16r]

---

[64] Saturday refers to January 3, 1824, but its meaning is unclear. This entry would probably have been made on Thursday, January 1, 1824, or earlier.—TA

[65] See the reference to this dinner with Schindler and nephew Karl on Blatt 16r below. The entries immediately above may be from this dinner as well.—TA

[66] New Year's Day would be a good time for such a benefit concert by the Josephstadt Theater's orchestra, but it does not seem to be reported in the literature. Perhaps Beethoven's Symphony No. 2 in D appeared on the program.—TA

[67] Friedrich Krause's Teaching and Educational Institute for Lutheran Boys, founded in 1817, in suburban Josephstadt, *Zum schönen Garten*, Florianigasse No. 52. Krause had originally partnered with Joseph Blöchlinger, but because they mixed boys of two religions (which was not permitted), Blöchlinger moved his Catholic boys to the old Strozzi-Czernin Palace in the Kaiserstrasse, where nephew Karl went to boarding school through August 1823. The building at Florianigasse No. 52 still stands, is well kept, and still has a beautiful courtyard. See Böckh (1822), p. 533; Guetjahr, p. 313; Hans Rotter, *Die Josefstadt* (Vienna, 1918), p. 161.—KH

[68] Ludwig Tietze/Titze (1798–1850), in later years a beadle at the University of Vienna, was also a tenor in the Imperial Court Chapel from 1832 to 1850. A frequent performer of Schubert's Lieder, he was considered an especially gifted dilettante and participated in many concerts. See Wurzbach, vol. 45, p. 149; *Österreichisches Musiklexikon*, 5, p. 2418.—KH/TA

[69] A visit the previous day is implied in nephew Karl's entries farther down on Blatt 16r.—TA

NEPHEW KARL [at Beethoven's apartment; before midday dinner, ca. 1:30 p.m. on Friday, January 2]: We shall see what kinds of widows apply. //

She [a new housekeeper] is asking whether the fish is to be baked, since we don't have any lemon for it otherwise. // Hot boiled.—Frogs.—Draw straws.

How do you like the last sentence in the letter: "*My wife* has expressed the wish that *we might visit you*"? She herself has bought *Macaronen* [chestnuts][70] in order to show that the ones yesterday were bad. //

You should always have a whole pound [of coffee] roasted at one time; that would make far less bother; plus it is also that way in other houses. // That settles it. // It takes less time than counting them out every time.[71] //

The High German language is different from the common way of speaking, to the extent that I almost believe that many people really don't understand it.[72] Thus, for example, you told the maid yesterday [Thursday, January 1] that she should bring more *Brühe* [broth]; she didn't know that word. Schindler had to translate it into the common language: *lautre Suppe* [clear soup]; that she understood. In this way she may also have confused *aufdecken* [uncover] with *aufbetten* yesterday evening, because she set about making the bed. Also, the housekeeper did not appear to understand when you asked for a strand of *Garn* [thread]; she only knew [the word] *Zwirn*. //

As a rule, people write the way they speak, instead of speaking the way they write. //

Jurende's *Vaterländischer Pilger* [Patriotic Pilgrim] is very voluminous this year; I think, though, that it's the best calendar.[73] [//] [Blatt 16v]

The music for today's play is by Gläser,[74] who, just as he earlier borrowed all of his music from *Der Freischütz*, now does so from *Euryanthe*, so that a person gets to hear all of the choruses, dances, etc., from there, all over again. //

---

[70] The German word *Macaronen* might mean macaroni but would not make sense in context. It is more likely that Karl meant *Maronen*, roasted chestnuts, very popular in the Christmas season.—TA

[71] Beethoven was accustomed to counting out 60 coffee beans for each cup. See Schindler-MacArdle, pp. 386–387.—KH/TA

[72] See Karl's similar comments, specifically about *Wienerisch* (the Viennese dialect), on September 2 and 13/14, 1823 (Heft 40, Blatt 3r, and Heft 42, Blätter 15r–15v).—TA

[73] From 1809, Karl Joseph Jurende (1780–1842) had published the *Mährischer Wanderer* [Moravian Wanderer] calendar, which, from 1814, bore the subtitle *Jurende's vaterländischer Pilger in dem Kaiserstaate Österreich* [Jurende's Patriotic Pilgrim in the Imperial State of Austria]. See Goedeke, VII, pp. 7 and 33.—KH

[74] Franz Gläser, conductor of the Theater in der Josephstadt, furnished music for many of the light theatrical pieces that were performed there. He often imitated idioms by other composers, in these cases Weber. Karl is probably referring to *Arsenius, der Weiberfeind*, that had opened on December 20, 1823, and had virtually a continuous run through January 15, 1824, as well as a number of other performances through the end of February. See Heft 50, Blatt 2v.—KH/TA

I have stomach cramps; in the long run it doesn't have anything to do with the cooking. //

The building door is closed. // Perhaps because of the payment. //

BEETHOVEN [presumably at his apartment; possibly the morning of Saturday, January 3, 1824, probably projecting a shopping trip that day]:
+ The street directly up from the Franziskanerplatz, pens, wine, wine vinegar, etc., all the best products.

Capons and chicken at the Marketplace.

Another kitchen cabinet at the Augustiners.[75]

End of Heft 51

---

[75] This probably meant the Augustiners in the Landstrasse, on the west side of the Hauptstrasse, just south of the Rochus Church, rather than the Augustiners in the walled City.—TA

Heft 52

(ca. January 5, 1824 – ca. January 7, 1824)

[Blatt 1r]

SCHUPPANZIGH [presumably at Beethoven's apartment in the Ungargasse; ca. Monday, January 5, 1824]:[1]

In the 1000 [fl.] they dispatch.[2] //

Leidesdorf isn't asking him [= you] to add new pieces that are long, but rather short.[3] // In every volume, a new short piece that wouldn't take him [= you] too much time [to compose]. // His [= Your?] earnings always increase. //

If he'd [= you'd] like, I'll write to him [Berlin music director Henning], but it would be better if he himself [= you yourself] would write to [Berlin manager] Bethmann, although I am convinced that the money will come one of these days. [//] [Blatt 1v] Henning is known in Berlin as a very upright man. // His composition isn't bad, but there's no sense in it.[4] // 25 fl. // Every 3 years, [he gets] a coat and trousers.[5] // On a journey, he cannot be paid. //

The housekeeper hasn't come to see my wife yet. [//] [Blatt 2r] It is always better to employ a person who has been recommended. // I thought that there was another room that led off from the kitchen. //

Is his [= your] brother still here? // Then did she [Johann's wife, Therese] have a great deal of money? // He [Johann] must have made a great deal of money, though, because the purchase [of the estate in Gneixendorf] costs a great deal. // He is a

---

[1] Schuppanzigh's first visit in Heft 52 seems to follow shortly upon Heft 51. Schindler's remarks come after a day of seemingly not seeing Beethoven, and his entries concerning Unger and Sontag are surely within a couple of days after the close of Heft 51. The contents of brief Heft 52 could not represent more than three or four days.—TA

[2] Possibly the amount promised by Berlin for an opera.—TA

[3] Max Joseph Leidesdorf (1787–1839), composer and partner of the music publishing house of Sauer & Leidesdorf, Kärntnerstrasse No. 941. This modest-sized press, devoted largely to popular music, was not prepared to publish major scores. See Frimmel, *Handbuch*, I, p. 333; Clive, pp. 304–305; and Alexander Weinmann, *Wiener Musikverleger*, p. 31.—KH/TA

[4] Schuppanzigh had performed a work by Henning on one of his subscription quartet concerts.—TA

[5] As part of his salary from the theater in Berlin.—TA

big talker. [//] [Blatt 2v] It is said that he was under investigation <because of his medicines.> //

A little girl, 7 years old. // She said so specifically that she knows us, that my wife didn't ask about where she lived at all. [//]

[Blatt 3r]

SCHINDLER [presumably at Beethoven's apartment; possibly early afternoon on Tuesday, January 6 (Epiphany), 1824]: Did she behave *steyrisch* [in an uncouth way]?[6] //

Wouldn't it be good if you/they take Karl's mother for a short time? Please consider it. // I tried to meet her two times, but failed.[7] //

You are going to get a friendly visit today.[8] [Caroline] Unger and [Henriette] Sontag will probably drop by your place at 3 p.m. They were saying so yesterday in the theater. [//] [Blatt 3v] They will surely not stay long. // In the mornings, they always have one rehearsal or another, and then, in the afternoons, they have to make early preparations for the theater [performances]. //

We can go to the coffee house later. //

It would be good if Grillparzer would discuss it [setting the libretto *Melusine*] with you. You could perhaps still give him many indications [of] how he is to act. [//] [Blatt 4r] But he would probably prefer that you first specify all the conditions. // He would probably not accept that if the directorship did its duty. // And always finds his sincere supporter and his renown in your company. //

It should also say only "with the participation of the Verein," not "the Verein" by itself, because only the most prominent members of the Verein will add to it.[9] [//] [Blatt 4v]

Also invite the girls [Unger and Sontag] for a pipe [of tobacco]. // Both of them are too clever and intelligent to abandon themselves indifferently, but enough—they don't have any unpleasant reputation in the least. //

Sontag came from Prague.[10] // I hear that, with her mother, who is [at the Theater]

---

[6] Steyr is an Upper Austrian town between Vienna and Linz; the adverb *steyrisch* was probably meant in the pejorative sense here. My thanks to Dr. Helmut Weihsmann (Vienna). Additionally, Birthe Kibsgaard (Aarhus, Denmark) and Mark S. Zimmer (Madison, Wisconsin) have also contributed many refinements in translation.—TA

[7] Schindler's intentions here are not entirely clear, but he may not have known about Johanna van Beethoven's illegitimate daughter, now three and a half years old.—TA

[8] The visit had been projected in Heft 51, Blatt 14v. There is no hard and fast way to date this entry, but for two busy singers, Epiphany (*Dreikönigstag*/Three Kings), a religious and national holiday, would be a good time to project a social visit. Even so, through Schindler, they had laid the groundwork for a short visit, in case it proved awkward.—TA

[9] This concerns adding the best amateur performers from the Gesellschaft der Musikfreunde to Beethoven's projected Akademie, ultimately on May 7, 1824.—TA

[10] Henriette Sontag (b. Koblenz, January 3, 1806; d. Mexico City, June 17, 1854) lived with her actress mother in Prague from 1816 to 1823. From July 22 to August 17, 1822, she made her debut in

[SCHINDLER, *continued*]
an der Wien,[11] she gets a grand total of 17,000 fl. W.W. // The benefit performance is already included in that figure. [//] [Blatt 5r] They live very simply and appear to be thinking of the future [by saving their money]. // I never had time before, but now I have an opportune moment and will visit them. //

I must frankly confess to you <(but please don't laugh)> that I don't like to hear your Quartets there [at Schuppanzigh's concerts],[12] because they are performed in a manner that is far too affected, and I am convinced that you did not intend to instruct them in such a way. This has been strongly censured in the review. [//] [falsified entries begin→] <You did not teach it to Schuppanzigh in this way.> [←falsified entries end] [//] [Blatt 5v] One can say that, although all the Quartets are performed very precisely and neatly, they are often very out of tune and raggedy. // I shall bring you the publicly available review of these concerts; it concerns your Quartets, says exactly what I said, and is correct. // They want to make it too beautiful, but that defeats the purpose. [//] [Blatt 6r] In the *Theater-Zeitung*. //

She [presumably the new housekeeper] wants to show you her pension sheet. // She appears to be dissatisfied with her lodging. // Otherwise, she has no other thought than the lodging. // She acts more arrogantly than the previous one. // Not everything is gold, etc. // All of the women who look like that are not suitable for you. // So where is she living? [//] [Blatt 6v] If you wish, I'll go … to see her.

Vienna, and, from spring 1823 was contracted, along with her mother, to the two united Viennese theaters (Kärntnertor and an der Wien) for a combined sum of 18,000 fl., a benefit performance, and six weeks of leave for touring. See Stümcke, pp. 7–9; for her baptismal certificate, noting that she was born at 6 a.m., see Emil Pirchan, *Henriette Sontag: Die Sängerin des Biedermeier* (Vienna: Wilhelm Frick Verlag, 1946), p. 7; and Clive, pp. 343–345.—KH/TA

[11] Franziska Sontag, *née* Markloff (b. Heddernheim, north of Frankfurt, January 12, 1788/89; d. Dresden, April 10, 1865), daughter of an electoral Mainz official, acted in the amateur theater in the Rhenish city before becoming professional and spending a season or two in several German cities. Arriving in Prague in 1816, she succeeded Sophie Schröder in dramatic roles as a heroine or love interest. She gave guest performances in Vienna in November 1817. Early in 1823, she moved to the Theater an der Wien, and her young daughter, Henriette, to the Court Opera in Vienna. By 1825, Franziska was engaged at the Königstädtisches Theater in Berlin. See Eisenberg, p. 977; Stümcke, p. 21; Clive, p. 343.—KH

[12] Schindler's potentially divisive discussion concerns Schuppanzigh's series of six Quartet concerts from October 22 to November 28, 1823. Bäuerle's *Allgemeine Theater-Zeitung* 16, No. 150 (December 16, 1823), p. 599, reported: "Although Herr Schuppanzigh proved himself to be a tasteful and insightful artist every time, he especially gave pleasure in the performance of Haydn's compositions. His flowery style of invigorating the performance through humor and mood, to make his individuality felt, even to be a little coquettish with his violin, was the most effective with these naive compositions, in which the humor is the thing that stands out almost every time. Mozart's charm suffers through garish colors, and Beethoven is too individual for anyone to add things that might appear quite strange and disturbing." For a detailed list of Schuppanzigh's current series (December 28, 1823, through January 25, 1824), see Schickh's *Wiener Zeitschrift* 9, No. 15 (February 3, 1824), p. 128.—KH/TA

[SCHINDLER, *continued*]
// Is she already old? // So it is terrible that one cannot be concerned about these servant women. // They make excuses, one for another. // It will already be dry. //

I saw him in the theater. // [Blatt 7r]

Gänsbacher is here and, as I hear it, has the most hope for [the Kapellmeister's position] at St. Stephan.[13] // But the position pays a great deal. // Where did Preindl[14] get his wealth? // He bequeathed 72,000 fl. to his relatives, and his wife still gets 12,000 fl. // In addition, he had a large cellar full of wine. // I believe that he only received 600 fl. in salary, but the *Stola*[15] pays for the rest. //

Weigl is obviously covered for his entire salary, which he receives after the first year. [//] [Blatt 7v] Because he has served for 40 years. // He will then receive his salary as his pension when he wants to retire. // His benefit performance has also brought him 2,000 fl. W.W. // 5,000 fl. // You don't need this,[16] and in fact you don't need to go to England where you are considered to be a god. // Then you would *also* come back to Vienna as a *Rentierer* [person of private means; rentier]![17] Good God! // [Blatt 8r]

[still waiting for Unger and Sontag; after 3 p.m.[18] on Tuesday, January 6 (Epiphany):]

If they don't come, then it is merely because of jealousy, because Unger told me that she would also come *alone*, but then I replied that she should certainly bring only Sontag with her, that it would give you double the pleasure. Now I am anxious to know whether it will come to pass. // Well, I only expressed the wish that the both of them should come together.[19] // Very beautiful and gentle. //

Perhaps I can bring you news concerning the housekeeper tomorrow afternoon [presumably ca. Wednesday, January 7] in the coffee house.[20] [//] [Blatt 8v]

---

[13] Johann Baptist Gänsbacher (1778–1844). See Heft 50, Blatt 2r.—TA

[14] Joseph Preindl (1756–1823), Kapellmeister at St. Stephan's Cathedral, had died on October 26, 1823. See Heft 50, Blatt 3r.—TA

[15] The *Stolgebühren* (or Jura stolae), named for the stola (surplice) worn by the Catholic clergy in performance of their duties. In this case it refers to fees paid to the clergy (and, by extension, lay officials) for such liturgical services as baptisms, weddings, and funerals.—KH

[16] Even at this late date, Beethoven occasionally considered applying for positions in the Court's musical establishment.—TA

[17] Schindler is chiding Beethoven that he does not want to follow the example of Kalkbrenner's financial success. Of course, Haydn had done essentially the same thing in the early and middle 1790s.—TA

[18] The time of their loosely projected visit is noted on Blatt 3r above.—TA

[19] Beethoven must have suspected that Schindler may have spoiled the prospects of the visit by seeming to insist that Unger come only if she brought Sontag with her, and Schindler is quickly making excuses here. The visit ultimately took place—not without mishap—on Sunday, March 14, 1824. See Heft 59, Blätter 11v–13v.—TA

[20] This would have taken place later on ca. Wednesday, January 7, probably after Schuppanzigh's visit on Blätter 9v–10v, and not covered in this conversation book.—TA

What kind of information have you provided? //

[giving up waiting for Unger and Sontag:]

The girls are probably not coming anymore. // By the way, *Mamsel* Unger will now be reproached as a liar. // I'll encounter her in the street, and she'll say that she's sorry that she couldn't come. // She'll say that it is better for her. The cold.[21] //

[Schindler presumably departs; Beethoven presumably stays home and does not go to the coffee house.]

[Blatt 9r]

ANNA SEISSER [at Beethoven's apartment; presumably the afternoon of the next day, possibly Wednesday, January 7]: I am the widow of the deceased Criminal Court Commissioner Seisser.[22] [//] I live from my pension. [//] I ask you for 2 days to think it over. [//] I would only wish for a regularly employed fine manservant. [//]

[Blatt 9v]

BEETHOVEN: + Barber's razor. [//]

NEPHEW KARL [at Beethoven's apartment, writing for Schuppanzigh; possibly the afternoon of Wednesday, January 7]: He [Schuppanzigh] was at Kalkbrenner's [presumably Hotel *Zum Erzherzog Carl*] and heard him play; he [Kalkbrenner] pleased him better than Moscheles. //

SCHUPPANZIGH [continuing the conversation, now writing for himself]: Kalkbrenner has more feeling in his execution. //

In his compositions, [Ferdinand] Ries copies entire passages from Beethoven. //

In Russia, one eats very well, but in Prussia very poorly. // In Prussia, everyday life is very miserable, but with money, one can procure everything for himself. //

---

[21] On January 3 and 4, the temperatures at 3 p.m. had been ca. 39 and 35 degrees Fahrenheit, respectively. On January 5, the temperature dipped to 27, and on Epiphany, January 6, it was again ca. 27 degrees at 3 p.m. The next day, however, the afternoon temperature rose to 41 degrees. See, among other issues, the *Wiener Zeitung*, No. 6 (January 9, 1824), p. 27 (reporting January 6 and 7).—TA

[22] Franz Joseph Seisser (b. Vienna, ca. 1772), criminal court commissioner with the Viennese Magistrat, living in the City, Rother Thurm No. 688 [renumbered as 646 in 1820], had died of a stroke at the hospital of the Barmherzige Brüder on August 20, 1817. He and his wife, Anna, were legally separated when he died (his property totaled 488 fl. 38 kr); she lived in the new Wieden, Grosse Neugasse, at the *Grünes Dach* No. 263 [renumbered as 329 in 1821 and 542 in 1830]. In 1815 (or by 1817), Anna (b. 1774) shared an apartment with another woman (b. 1789), and Anna's own son, Joseph (b. 1799), a munitions soldier. See Verlassenschafts-Abhandlung (Sperrs-Relation), Fasz. 2: 4485/1817; Exhib. Nr. 353 (Wiener Stadt- und Landesarchiv); *Hof- und Staats-Schematismus*, 1816, p. 593; *Wiener Zeitung*, No. 195 (August 25, 1817), p. 780; Conscriptions-Bogen, Wieden, 542, Wohnpartei 16, later 15 [new collation 542/13] (Wiener Stadt- und Landesarchiv).—KH/TA

[SCHUPPANZIGH, *continued*]

[Blatt 10r] Zelter[23] was indeed here; did he make him [= you] a little visit? // They [the Berlin *Singakademie*] sing with accompaniment of piano and contrabass. // In Russian churches, they sing without accompaniment and very correctly.[24] //

This wine is very healthy for him [= you]; he [= you] can drink a lot of it. It is a present, costs nothing. //

My brother-in-law[25] has a daughter who plays the piano very well; she only hopes to be so fortunate to be able to play something for him [= you]. [//] [Blatt 10v] At every moment, Rehatzek is prepared to do anything he can for Beethoven. [//] Frau Linke is not my wife's sister, but instead her cousin.[26] // In the same time, she has been engaged as [sentence ends].

End of Heft 52

N.B. Another conversation book, possibly begun in a coffee house, late on the afternoon of Wednesday, January 7, and possibly continued through January 16, 1824, is now missing.

---

[23] Schuppanzigh calls him "Zeltner" but refers to Karl Friedrich Zelter (1758–1832), composer, director of the Berlin *Singakademie*, founder of the *Liedertafel*, friend of Goethe, and teacher of the young Mendelssohn. On September 12, 1819, during his stay in Vienna, Zelter had met Beethoven briefly on the road to Mödling. See Frimmel, *Handbuch*, II, pp. 470–472; Clive, pp. 403–404; Thayer-Deiters-Riemann, IV, p. 163; Thayer-Forbes, p. 738.—KH/TA

[24] Schuppanzigh is speaking from personal observation during his travels from early 1816 through mid-April 1823: first through Germany and Berlin, and then to Russia, where he spent most of that period, dividing his time between St. Petersburg and Lemberg (Lvov/Lviv).—TA

[25] Franz Rzehaczek, Court document drafter at the United Court chancellery, accomplished amateur violinist, member of the Gesellschaft der Musikfreunde and owner of a collection of stringed instruments by makers including Stradivarius and three Amati family members. He placed these instruments at Beethoven's disposal for the Akademie on May 7, 1824. His daughter, Anna (b. ca. 1809), had already given a public concert in 1821 and occasionally participated in Schuppanzigh's concerts. The Rzehaczek family lived in the City, Kleine Schulerstrasse No. 846. See *Wiener AmZ* 8, No. 30 (May 12, 1824), pp. 117–118; Böckh, 1822, pp. 360 and 377; Ziegler, *Addressen-Buch*, pp. 139 and 225.—KH/TA

[26] Presumably Barbara Linke, *née* Pirkner (b. Vienna, ca. 1788; d. Vienna, May 9, 1847), married since 1811 to Joseph Linke (1783–1837), violoncellist in Count Rasumovsky's Quartet (1807–1816), principal violoncellist at the Theater an der Wien and cellist since June 1818, and now also cellist in Schuppanzigh's Quartet. See Linke's Verlassenschafts-Abhandlung, Fasz. 2: 5201/1837 (Wiener Stadt- und Landesarchiv).—KH/TA

Heft 53

(January 16, 1824 – January 21, 1824)

[Blatt 1r]

BEETHOVEN [**presumably with nephew Karl at a restaurant, possibly Spöttl's** ***Zum grünen Fassl***, **on the Kohlmarkt; early afternoon of Friday, January 16, then joined by brother Johann**]:[1]

Rother Igel, Wildprett Markt, zur wilden Ente [Red Hedgehog, Wild Game Market, At the Wild Duck], Authentic wild boar, from the surplus of young boar; in general, all types of fresh game at 24 kr., the best for 30 kr., etc. Truffle and everything else.[2] [//]

+ Heubner, Bauernmarkt No. 590: Doussin-Dubreuil, J.L., *Ausführl[iche] Darstellung* [Blatt 1v] *der Ursachen, etc. der in unsern Tagen so häufigen Verschleimungen*, etc., translated from the 8th original edition, etc., by Dr. J.H.W. Schlegel. Octavo. Ilmenau, 1823. 1 fl, C.M.[3] [//]

[Blatt 2r]

[presumably joined by brother Johann:]

---

[1] Because Beethoven's destination afterward was Mathias Artaria's shop in the Kohlmarkt, he and Karl may have had some refreshments and possibly bought some veal to take home at the Spöttl Grocery and Wine Shop, perhaps a hundred feet east of Artaria's. By the same token, the similar shop *Zum schwarzen Kameel* (At the Black Camel) in Bognergasse, only five minutes away, would have been an equally convenient meeting place for Beethoven, Karl, Johann, and Schuppanzigh as they read the sundry newspapers and went their sundry ways. For these two businesses, see also Heft 45, Blatt 19v.—TA

[2] See the *Intelligenzblatt*, No. 12 (January 16, 1824), p. 94 (Advertisements). The retail shop *Zum rothen Igel* of the wild-game dealer Joseph Metzger was located at Wildpretmarkt No. 550; the house shield was *Zur Wildänte* [*Wildente* = Wild Duck]. The same advertisement also appeared in No. 13 (January 17, 1824), p. 104, and many issues through the end of February 1824. The advertisement had not yet appeared in No. 11 (January 15, 1824).—KH

[3] J[acques] Doussin-Dubreuil, *Ausführliche Darstellung der Ursachen, Wirkungen und Heilmittel der in unsern Tagen so häufigen Verschleimungen*, translated from the eighth French edition, with preface and annotations by J[ulius] H[einrich] G[ottlieb] Schlegel. Ilmenau, 1823. See the *Intelligenzblatt*, No. 8 (January 12, 1824), p. 68. Courtesy Prof. Scott Messing, emeritus, Alma College, Michigan (June 4, 2023).—KH/TA

NEPHEW KARL [**writing, in part, on behalf of Johann**]: He [Johann] has spoken with S[chuppanzigh], and he said that he would come here [presumably the restaurant] himself. //

JOHANN VAN BEETHOVEN [**continuing for himself**]: The [theatrical] pieces are the best, but they don't immediately [*gleich*] set the world on fire.[4] //

NEPHEW KARL: Your brother was in a social group where they spoke of Gleich's poetry, and viciously tore them to pieces. He himself recently attended his *most recent* piece [at the Theater] an der Wien.[5] //

The coffee costs	2 fl. 40 [kr.]
Sugar	1 fl. 36
Veal	48
	5 fl. 24 kr
To the waiter	6 kr.
	5 fl. 10 kr.
	1 fl. 30 kr. [//]

[**presumably joined by Schuppanzigh; Karl possibly goes home to Beethoven's apartment with the veal, possibly driven by brother Johann; Schuppanzigh and Beethoven go to Leidesdorf's:**]

[Blatt 2v]

LEIDESDORF:[6] [**presumably at Leidesdorf's shop, Kärntnerstrasse No. 941, with Schuppanzigh; midafternoon on Friday, January 16**]: Do you want to speak with

---

[4] Johann's phonetic spelling (*Stöck* [sticks] instead of *Stücke* [plays]) and whether those sticks catch fire right away may be intentional, but in any case he seems to be making a pun on the name of the playwright Gleich, mentioned in Karl's next entry.—TA

[5] Joseph Alois Gleich (1772–1841) wrote numerous penny dreadfuls and theatrical pieces with folk subjects, which were performed in the Viennese suburban theaters to great public acclaim. The comic-tragic magic-play *Die Elfen-Insel* had first been performed as a "selected prize play" at the Theater an der Wien on January 3, 1824, but was removed from the repertory after its fifth performance. See Bäuerle's *Allgemeine Theater-Zeitung* 17, No. 8 (January 17, 1824), pp. 30–31; Wurzbach, vol. 5, pp. 214–216.—KH

[6] Max Joseph Leidesdorf (1787–1840), composer and partner in the music publishing firm of Sauer & Leidesdorf, Kärntnerstrasse No. 941. See Frimmel, *Handbuch*, I, p. 333; and Clive, pp. 304–305. On the basis of an annotation by Schindler, these passages were originally thought to be in the hand of publisher Matthias Artaria (1793–1835), but a comparison with two autographs (Handschriften-Sammlung, Österreichische Nationalbibliothek, Vienna, Autogr. 52/184; and Staatsbibliothek zu Berlin, mus. ep. M.J. Leidesdorf), confirmed the entries here to be Leidesdorf's handwriting. See Heft 92, Blatt 6r (annotation).—KH/TA

[lawyer] Dr. Bach about it? // The earlier, the better. // I hope that you will be satisfied. //

SCHUPPANZIGH: The main point is about the earlier works, with which one would then begin. [//]

[Blatt 3r]

LEIDESDORF: We would begin with the compositions for pianoforte alone, then the Variations, then with accompanying instruments, and so forth. [//] There will be time before it gets to these works. // I would think one volume of ca. 30 sheets every two months. For example: 9 solo Sonatas, supplements. [//] [Blatt 3v] I certainly know everything that you have written, but this would be very good. Be sure not to forget it. //

SCHUPPANZIGH: Dear Beethoven, just think of business and start working on something. [//]

LEIDESDORF: Doctor [Bach] will explain everything to you exactly. [//] [Blatt 4r]
[Opus] No. 1 is 3 Piano Trios; we can begin with them. [//] I would have all the variations copied and, in general, would have one page left empty for optional variations. [//] I would have all the overtures engraved in score. [//] 4 symphonies. Should the ballet [*Die Geschöpfe des Prometheus*] also appear in score?[7] [//] That can be derived from the parts. [//] [Blatt 4v]

SCHUPPANZIGH: How does it look with the Quartet in A minor?[8] //
In the Kleiner Redoutensaal, because he is a fool.[9] [//]

LEIDESDORF: Reason alone is of no use!! [//] <Owl has ....> [//] Therefore I ask you please don't forget it! [//] [Blatt 5r] I have played it. [//]
[Beethoven walks home, possibly by way of Wildpretmarkt and Bauernmarkt.]

---

[7] Beethoven must have replied that *Prometheus* was currently available only in orchestral parts.—TA

[8] Beethoven's String Quartet in A minor, Op. 132. Sketches for its finale appear already in the midst of those for the finale of the Ninth Symphony. See Robert Winter, "The Sketches for the 'Ode to Joy,'" in *Beethoven, Composers, and Critics* ... (Detroit: Wayne State University Press, 1980), p. 198; and Douglas Johnson, Alan Tyson, and Robert Winter, *The Beethoven Sketchbooks* (Berkeley: University of California Press, 1985), p. 410.—TA

[9] Probably a reference to Kalkbrenner, who, with the harpist Dizi, gave a concert in the Kleiner Redoutensaal on Sunday, January 25, 1824. See the *Allgemeine musikalische Zeitung* 26, No. 8 (February 19, 1824), cols. 124–125.—TA

HOUSEKEEPER APPLICANT [at Beethoven's apartment, writing in French;[10] possibly late morning of Saturday, January 17, possibly with Schindler present]:

I have heard it said that *Monsieur* is seeking a housekeeper, thus I come to present myself. I understand enough German to explain myself to the domestic servants, to maintain the linens in cleanliness, but I do not understand about the kitchen. I understand how to sew well. [Blatt 5v] Sewing, ironing, reckoning with the cook. I prefer going there, if *Monsieur* will put on a kitchen maid who is skillful enough, the rest may ask for a recommendation. I will not fail, but as I am without a position, I wish to be accepted [Blatt 6r] in two or three days. I understand sewing very well; I am able to demonstrate my work. //

SCHINDLER [at Beethoven's apartment; possibly late morning of Saturday, January 17]: She [the French-speaking applicant?] says 25 fl. in all. //

The last time, I was there at 9 o'clock, [but] did not meet her; I believe, however, that it only foreshadowed things to come. // I never went there except when I had to buy something. [//] [Blatt 6v]

Today, Diabelli[11] asked me to visit him and he told me the following: Through [Leopold] Sonnleithner, he heard the results concerning your Mass. Therefore he is making you a proposal that he have the *Mass* as well as the symphony copied (to the extent that it is necessary), in return for which you allow him to have a piano reduction of the symphony made.[12] [//]

Of course, [Blatt 7r] [Johann] has a very natural, benevolent, and also understanding woman [servant], // who has also been waiting for a position since last March. // Right now you need a capable woman, who can bring order to this old disorder with linens, etc.; the old woman [former housekeeper Barbara Holzmann] has done a lot of harm in this respect. *Requiescat* [*in pace*]![13] // If you had seen him [Johann] today, driving with his horse and carriage in the Prater with his family, you wouldn't ask again *where he is!!!* [//] [Blatt 7v]

Nonetheless, I like the king [of Prussia]. Because nothing else would happen to you. The king shows—as does no other monarch—love and respect for the artist. // Neither here nor in Paris has the Court taken any particular notice of him. //

---

[10] While the applicant's French is not perfect, it is relatively better than the German literacy of many of the German-speaking applicants whom Beethoven fielded. She returned briefly, probably on Wednesday, January 21; see Heft 54, Blatt 1v.—TA

[11] Anton Diabelli (1781–1858), composer and music publisher, located on the west side of the Graben No. 1133 (corner of Untere Breuner Strasse). See Frimmel, *Handbuch*, I, p. 107; Clive, pp. 89–91; Alexander Weinmann, *Wiener Musikverleger*, pp. 14 and 26–27.—KH/TA

[12] To be used in the projected choral-vocal rehearsals.—TA

[13] May she rest in peace!—TA

Here in Vienna, Frau von Chezy[14] has been terribly unlucky with her dramatic products, which no one wants to understand. //

[Blatt 8r]

NEPHEW KARL: There is not very much behind it. [//]

BEETHOVEN [**presumably at his apartment, making a shopping list; possibly the late morning of Saturday, January 17**]:
+ *Shaving mug.*
+ Wash hand towel and shaving rags. + Vests.
+ Writing pen.
+ Lobk[owitz].[15]

[Blatt 8v]

NEPHEW KARL [**at Beethoven's apartment; presumably early afternoon of Saturday, January 17**]: Your brother now spends nothing more on his wife's wardrobe; she must make her dresses herself. //

The short woman who was also a housekeeper for you at one time and later was a kitchen maid—and always writes you *letters*—well, I ran into her in Erdberg; she can't understand that you haven't summoned *her*, and [she] told those women who *were* here that you certainly would have wanted to have her. // There appear to be temporary lodgings there, because we are finding all of them there. // The woman who was here today said that she had a position, but that there was a [male] cook there, and therefore she didn't want to go there. [//]

[Blatt 9r]

SCHINDLER [**at Beethoven's apartment; the afternoon of Saturday, January 17**]:[16] It will always be better if you take care of yourself in part, just as [you have] until now. //

This beautiful wintertime is proving to be very useful for you.[17] // Matters with

---

[14] Helmina von Chezy (1783–1856), librettist of Weber's *Euryanthe* and Schubert's *Rosamunde*.—KH

[15] This unclear entry could also refer to one of Karl's textbooks, Joseph Calasanz Likawetz, *Elementa philosophiae*; see Heft 45, Blatt 16r.—TA

[16] Schindler's reference to Kalkbrenner on Blatt 10r essentially dates this entry, assisted by references to the weather, and, ultimately, Unger's reference to Sontag's singing that day (Blatt 10v below).—TA

[17] Weather reports in the *Wiener Zeitung* for January 16–25 (published on January 19–27) indicate a period when daytime temperatures were above freezing, with an occasional sunny day. Also, on Blatt 11v below, Unger suggests driving to the *Lusthaus* in the Prater and walking back, indicating relatively mild weather; and indeed, the day was sunny and the temperature roughly 32 degrees Fahrenheit. See the *Wiener Zeitung*, No. 15 (January 20, 1824), p. 68.—TA

the stove are not yet in order, as I see it. In the end it will not repay you either the trouble or the money to install another one, because the largest part of the winter has passed anyway. // This is the same old story. // I fear that the stove will infest the whole apartment with smoke, because the place for it is really not suitable.[18] [//] [Blatt 9v] You are acting very wisely. She will talk over sleeping without a stove in the room. // At least you are sparing yourself annoyance about this trifle. [//] She says the same, that it is not necessary. // She appears to be somewhat hardened. // This woman takes Augsburger sausage[19] and will make them in a way different from the usual. // I've had more than enough. [//] [Blatt 10r]

A week from tomorrow [Sunday, January 25], Kalkbrenner and Dizi are giving their concert.[20] The *Berliner Zeitung* declared the former to be the greatest piano player under the sun; the *Theater-Zeitung* reprinted the report.[21] // Dizi is said to play his harp so beautifully that one believes that he is hearing an Italian violin.[22] // The mechanism on his harp is said to be remarkable to see. // I really believe that he has done it. // I have never read such pompous praise as the aforementioned, but … it comes from Berlin! // [Blatt 10v] The one in the Leipzig [*Allgemeine musikalische*] *Zeitung*. // I have not read it. [//]

UNGER [at Beethoven's apartment; possibly midafternoon of Saturday, January 17, presumably with Schindler present]:[23] *Dlle* Sontag greatly regrets that she cannot come today, but she has to sing.[24] I could not resist my desire to see our

---

[18] Even though he had not been among Beethoven's circle at the time, Schindler may have known about Beethoven's problems with stoves and maintaining heat in his apartment on the Josephstadt Glacis in winter 1819–1820; see Heft 6, especially Blätter 7v–8v.—TA

[19] An inexpensive sausage, Augsburger was roasted, then cut lengthwise to be eaten.—KH

[20] For Friedrich Kalkbrenner and the French harpist François Joseph Dizi, see Heft 51, Blatt 10r. Their concert took place on Sunday, January 25, 1824, at the midday hour (12:30 p.m.) in the Kleiner Redoutensaal. See the *Allgemeine musikalische Zeitung* 26, No. 8 (February 19, 1824), cols. 124–125; and the *Wiener AmZ* 8, No. 13 (January 29, 1824), p. 52.—KH

[21] Schindler refers to an article, "Opinion of a Much-Read Berlin Journal about the Concert There," that appeared in Bäuerle's *Allgemeine Theater-Zeitung* 17, No. 7 (January 15, 1824), p. 26, praising Kalkbrenner and saying that he "made the incredible come true" and that he was the "hero of all heroes on the pianoforte."—KH/TA

[22] Dizi played on a pedal harp whose mechanism he himself had improved, but Beethoven would not have believed Schindler's hyperbole. In the event, the Viennese correspondent for the Leipzig *AmZ* said that Dizi "aroused little sensation." See *Allgemeine musikalische Zeitung* 26, No. 2 (January 8, 1824), cols. 22–24; No. 8 (February 19, 1824), col. 125; and the *Sammler*, No. 27 (March 2, 1824), p. 108.—KH/TA

[23] On Blatt 21r below, Schindler will speak of details concerning Unger's conversation with Beethoven.—TA

[24] Henriette Sontag sang the title role in Weber's *Euryanthe* at the Kärntnertor Theater on the evening of Saturday, January 17, 1824. Unger's references to and quote from *Euryanthe* on Blatt 12v below may stem from this fact. See the Theater-Zettel, Österreichisches Theatermuseum (courtesy of librarian Othmar Barnert).—TA

dear great Master again. [//] Why haven't you visited us in so long? // Laziness, nothing but laziness. [//]

Will you give us a new opera soon? [//]

Saturday is *Der Taucher*;[25] Friday is the dress rehearsal; are you coming? [//] [Blatt 11r] [I am singing] the *Taucher* [diver] himself.[26] // The opera is composed in a considerate way[27] and has a pleasant story; I believe that it will please you. // Sympathy. // Very nice. // I have to sing 3 arias, 3 duets, 3 trios, and two Finales. // [Sontag is singing] my beloved. //

Forti—the King.
Sontag—his daughter.
Preisinger[28]—his exiled brother.
Unger—his son.
Heitzinger[29]—a rejected prince.

If only the dear God would sometime inspire you so graciously, so that you would soon write something for me, then [Blatt 11v] I would spare no trouble, because it would surely be repaid. // **[At this point, Beethoven may have promised Unger the alto parts in the *Missa solemnis* and Ninth Symphony.]** Then I'll come out every day. //

SCHINDLER **[humorously interrupting Unger]**: Engage her as housekeeper. // She can cook well. [//]

---

[25] Conradin Kreutzer's romantic opera *Der Taucher* premiered in the Kärntnertor Theater on Saturday, January 24, 1824. The cast included Anton Forti (Duke Lorenzo of Messina), Henriette Sontag (his daughter, Alphonsine), Joseph Preisinger (Lorenzo's exiled brother, Alphonso), Caroline Unger (Alphonso's son, Ivo), and Anton Haitzinger (Duke Anton of Calabria). See the *Allgemeine musikalische Zeitung* 26, No. 8 (February 19, 1824), cols. 122–124; and Bäuerle's *Allgemeine Theater-Zeitung* 17, No. 15 (February 3, 1824), p. 60.—KH/TA

[26] Unger was to sing the pants role of the foolishly heroic (but supernaturally protected) Ivo, who dives into the dreaded abyss to retrieve a golden cup in order to win the hand of Alphonsine, sung by Henriette Sontag. See the *Allgemeine musikalische Zeitung* 26, No. 8 (February 19, 1824), cols. 122–124.—TA

[27] That is, considerate to the singers and their voices.—TA

[28] Joseph Preisinger (1792–1865) was still a dilettante pianist and singer when Ziegler assembled his *Addressen-Buch* in fall 1822, but on December 2, 1823, he debuted in Rossini's *La gazza ladra* at the Kärntnertor Theater. See the *Allgemeine musikalische Zeitung* 26, No. 3 (January 15, 1824), col. 40; Eisenberg, p. 792; and Ziegler, *Addressen-Buch*, p. 38.—KH/TA

[29] Anton Haitzinger (1796–1869) was a tenor at the suburban Theater an der Wien, lived in that building's apartments, Laimgrube No. 26, and would sing at the premiere of Beethoven's Symphony No. 9 on May 7, 1824. See Eisenberg, p. 388; Ziegler, *Addressen-Buch*, p. 82.—KH/TA

UNGER [**resuming**]: You must hurry, because I am going to Germany in December.[30] [//]

Go with me to the *Lusthaus*.[31] We'll drive there and walk back. Fulfill my request. // The carriage awaits below. [//] God very much blesses me with patience. [Blatt 12r] *Libussa*.[32] [//] Sometimes. Now perhaps he [Bernard] will have more industry and passion, because he was married a short time ago.[33] You should also marry. Perhaps you would become more industrious.[34] [//] Forgive my somewhat satirical remark. // I swear on Vesta's Altar, until I think about nothing else. [//]

I have been very happy to see you again. [//] How can anyone who knows your *Fidelio* and your symphonies not acknowledge you! If you only knew how often I sing your Lieder![35] [//] That is difficult to decide, since I love [Blatt 12v] them all. [//]

Have you heard *Euryanthe* by Weber?[36] [//] How do you like it? [//] Some of the things appeal to me, but not everything. The poetry is atrocious.

> Nim hin die Seele mein
> Lass mich ganz *du* nur seyn
> Ganz bin ich dein.
> Seufzer wie Flammen wehn

---

[30] Caroline Unger did not give her farewell concert to Vienna until March 10, 1825, in the Kleiner Redoutensaal. After that, she left for Naples with the Italian Opera's impresario, Domenico Barbaja. See the *Allgemeine musikalische Zeitung* 27, No. 15 (April 13, 1825), cols. 241–242.—KH

[31] The pagoda-shaped Imperial *Lusthaus* (pleasure house), a former hunting pavilion in the southern part of the Prater, at the end of the long boulevard, a favorite destination, especially in the spring. See Groner (1922), pp. 284–285; Czeike, vol. 4, p. 118; Pezzl, pp. 174–175.

A drive there would probably be followed by some refreshments. After that, a walk back to Beethoven's apartment (probably across the Danube by means of the Franzens-Brücke or a ferry near the Rasumovsky Palace) would have taken more than an hour, and they probably would have arrived after sunset. The temperature at 3 p.m. was 32 degrees Fahrenheit with sunny skies that remained clear at 10 p.m. See the *Wiener Zeitung*, No. 15 (January 20, 1824), p. 68.—KH/TA

[32] Conradin Kreutzer's *Libussa*, libretto by Joseph Carl Bernard, had been in the Kärntnertor Theater's repertory since December 1822. See *Wiener Allgemeine musikalische Zeitung* 6, No. 99 (December 11, 1822), cols. 790–791.—KH/TA

[33] Beethoven's sometime friend, Joseph Carl Bernard (1786–1850), editor of the *Wiener Zeitung*, had married Magdalena Grassl (b. ca. 1797; d. March 11, 1829) in the Paulaner Church on November 25, 1823. In 1823–1824, they lived in the Wieden, Untere Schleifmühlgasse No. 533 [renumbered as 784 in 1830], in the second block west of the aforementioned church. See Pfarre Wieden (Paulanerkirche), Trauungs-Register, Tom. 5 (1817–1826), fol. 137. My gratitude to Msgr. Franz Wilfinger and secretary Frau Monika Bauer. Also Verlassenschafts-Abhandlung (Magdalena), Fasz. 2: 3758/1829 (Wiener Stadt- und Landesarchiv).—KH/TA

[34] This was obviously the wrong thing to say, and Beethoven may have told her so, or at least given her an angry eye.—TA

[35] Beethoven may have suspected this to be empty flattery and probably asked Unger *which* of his lieder was her favorite. Her evasive reply follows.—TA

[36] Beethoven must have replied in the affirmative.—TA

kühlend um Lindrung flehn
Lass mich in Lust und Wehn,
an deiner Brust vergehn.³⁷ [//]

How do you like these German verses? [//] [Blatt 13r]

You already have a libretto; is it nice? // Is there a role for me? // I would like to read Grillparzer's libretto [*Melusine*], but must renounce the idea, because I believe that you would not permit me to do so. [//] I swear by my honor. [//] I shall bring it back myself and with gratitude.³⁸ [//]

He who believes is blessed, says Jesus. [//]
I'm at your service, in the afternoon.³⁹ [//]
The libretto to *Der Taucher* is very nice. //

I must go now; a fond farewell, and keep your promise soon and come to visit your servant C[aroline] Unger. [//]

[Unger departs.]

[Blatt 13v]

SCHINDLER **[after Unger's departure]**: She is a devil of a girl; full of passion and candor. [//]

BEETHOVEN **[possibly at a coffee house; possibly late afternoon of Saturday, January 17]**:

Sistem der Logik by Dr. Esser. Elberfeld, 1823, Buschler'sche Buchhandlung. Size, octavo. Price 1 Th[ale]r, 12 gr.⁴⁰ [//] [Blatt 14r]

---

³⁷ Unger is citing the love duet between Euryanthe and Adolar (No. 13 in act 2), reprised at the opera's end. Even though she herself did not sing in *Euryanthe*, her recall (except for one omitted line) is remarkably accurate. The lines actually read:
"Hier nimm die Seele mein! / Atme mein Leben ein! / Lass mich ganz du nur sein, / Ganz bin ich dein! / Seufzer, wie Flammen weh'n, / Selig und Lind'rung fleh'n, / Lass mich in Lust und Weh'n / An deiner Brust vergeh'n! (Take my own soul! / Breathe my life's breath! / Let me become your very self, / I am all yours! / Sighs waft like flames; / Blissful it is to beg for relief; / Let me in joy and pain / Die on your breast!)." See the unattributed libretto translation in Weber, *Euryanthe*, Staatskapelle Dresden, etc., cond. Marek Janowski (EMI AVC-30467 [1975/1986]), pp. 25 and 34.—TA

³⁸ Beethoven evidently allows Unger to borrow Grillparzer's libretto to *Melusine*.—TA

³⁹ Unger may imply an intended meeting to return Grillparzer's libretto to *Melusine*.—TA

⁴⁰ Wilhelm Esser, *System der Logik* (Elberfeld: Buschler, 1823), size octavo. See Kayser, II, p. 163. The book was reviewed in the *Jenaische Allgemeine Literatur-Zeitung*, No. 153 (August 1825), cols. 257–264, confirming Esser's title of "Dr." and the German (rather than Viennese) price of the book as noted by Beethoven. His source for the citation remains unclear.—KH/TA

[crossed out; partially legible:]

00	1 [fl.] 42 [kr.]
50	2
5	1 [fl.] 18
5	

NEPHEW KARL [at Beethoven's apartment; presumably midday on Sunday, January 18]: [Ferdinand] Ries has written [from London] that he ardently looks forward to your symphony. // Magdeburg, Prussian Silesia.[41] // 15 months in prison. // He wrote to you from prison. // A letter to his cousin Drever[42] was enclosed, which he received. // 1823. // [written vertically→] You wanted to give it to Drever; was the content [←written vertically] [Blatt 14v] Drever received it from you. [//]

[writing on behalf of a waitress or maid:]
Side dish of vegetables, meat, brandy, roast. //
[resuming:]
At the Elbe, Napoleon had all of the wounded French [soldiers] thrown in, so that they would not be brought back to France, where people could have seen his loss.[43] // Because I am such an extraordinary man, that means that I am as good as 10 [men]. [//] [Blatt 15r]

[writing on behalf of a waitress or maid:]
She understood that you wanted *Two Kreutzer*. //
[resuming:]
His [Ries's] father and Drever's mother are brother and sister. //

---

[41] From the context, this is probably a reference to Magdeburg, Lower Saxony (not Silesia), on the Elbe River, roughly halfway between Braunschweig and Potsdam.—TA

[42] Ferdinand Ries (living in London) and his younger brother, Joseph Franz (a piano maker in Vienna), had a cousin, also living in the Habsburg capital, presumably a son of Madame Anna Maria Drewer, *née* Ries, a soprano employed at the Electoral Court in Bonn in 1790. This cousin was Franz Drewer (b. Bonn, 1777; d. Vienna, June 9, 1830), a musician living in the Kärntnerstrasse No. 1072, apartment 4. His wife, Viktoria (b. Pressburg, ca. 1780), had died on November 18, 1827, and in his testament of February 15, 1830, the childless Drewer bequeathed to the *Tonkünstler-Societät* a sum of 6,000 fl. W.W. that would not go to the society until after the deaths of his relatives. See Verlassenschafts-Abhandlungen, Fasz. 2: 3182/1827 and 1284/1830; Conscriptions-Bogen, Stadt, 1072 [new collation 1072/3 and 1072/10 (as Treber)]; and Totenbeschauprotokoll, 1827, D/T, fol. 33r; and 1830, D/T, fol. 21v (Wiener Stadt- und Landesarchiv); Gustav Gugitz, "Auszüge über Persönlichkeiten des Wiener Kulturlebens" (typescript, Wiener Stadt- und Landesarchiv, 1952), p. 63; and Gugitz, "Auszüge aus den Conskriptionsbögen" (typescript, Wiener Stadt- und Landesarchiv, ca. 1952), p. 285 (as "Treber"); Pohl, *Tonkünstler-Societät*, p. 27; Ludwig Schiedermair, *Der junge Beethoven* (Bonn, 1951), p. 40.—KH/TA

[43] On October 19, 1813, during a disastrous rout of the French by the Allies at the end of the four-day Battle of Leipzig, thousands of Napoleon's troops drowned in the Elster River (swollen by floodwaters), southwest of the city. See David G. Chandler, *The Campaigns of Napoleon* (New York: Macmillan, 1966), p. 936.—TA

He [Ries's younger brother Joseph Franz?] gives lessons to 13 children each day. // He says that he gives instruction in houses where it is necessary to have a stick in his hand, because he will not tolerate any discourteous words from the boys. //

[preparing to pay the current (temporary) housekeeper:]
An officially stamped sheet isn't available any more. [//] [Blatt 15v]
From December 24 to January 18:

24 days	6 fl. 40 kr.
Bread money	36 kr.
14 days board	5 fl. 36
14 days salary	3 fl. 44
[Total]	16 fl. 36 kr. //

If it should not work out with the coming housekeeper, I would advise placing the advertisement in the *Zeitung* again, but using the phrase *Professionisten-Wittwen* [handworkers' widows]. [//] It is not the same platter. [//]

The candle has come to its end. // [Blatt 16r]

The maid gets 16 fl. 36 kr. //

SCHUPPANZIGH **[presumably at Beethoven's apartment; possibly late morning or early afternoon of Monday, January 19]**: Radziwill is now in Posen. He [= You] can surely write directly to him. //

Write to [Frau] Schulz[44] in Berlin; she will take up the matter right away. // At the same time, she will be very pleased if he says [= you say] that you remember her. //

Radziwill is very captivated by him [= you]. [//] Sometimes he doesn't have his money. // Just do it sometime; this is lucrative.[45] [//] [Blatt 16v]

They are not having it engraved if he doesn't [= you don't] have them engraved. // Jews find everything. // A written contract must be made for it. // Otherwise it is a business deal that offers him [= you] a lifetime revenue of 300 ducats. [//] [Blatt 17r]

Then how can this work impede him [= you] when the only thing required is a short new piece every 2 months?[46] //

Now he is [= you are] healthy, he [= you] could work a great deal, but his [= your] domestic affairs take too much time away from him [= you]. //

---

[44] Josephine Schulz, *née* Killitschky (1790–1880), a sister of Schuppanzigh's wife, Barbara, sang *Ah! perfido* on Beethoven's Akademie of December 22, 1808. Since 1812, she had been married to a Justice Councillor Schulz and had been a prominent singer in the Royal Opera in Berlin. See Eisenberg, pp. 939–940; Ledebur, p. 537; Schilling, vol. 4, p. 86; Wurzbach, vol. 32, pp. 181–182.—KH/TA

[45] The possibility that Radziwill might commission a string quartet.—TA

[46] Schuppanzigh may have been referring to the potential business deal with Mathias Artaria (Blatt 2v–4v above) or possibly an earlier discussion with Leidesdorf (who was Jewish) about the publication of Beethoven's songs and other short pieces.—TA

Yesterday, I played his [= your] String Trio in C Minor; it pleased a great deal.[47]

[musical notation][48] [//]

Minuet. //

He [= You] should also be thinking about the Akademie, because the singers must have time to learn their parts.[49] [//] [Blatt 17v] He [= You] must do that; write to him, because otherwise people are telling it around in the city. // It is enough that it is newly composed by him [= you]. //

To Madame Schulz, Royal Court Singer, Berlin.[50]

NEPHEW KARL [at Beethoven's apartment, writing, in part, on behalf of a housekeeper applicant and others; ca. 2 p.m. on Monday, January 19, continuing sporadically into the evening]: She can cook everything up to fine pastries, gruel, etc., which she cannot; because she is from Saxony, where they don't eat such things. // Widow. [//] [Blatt 18r] 15 years. // Sophie Trion, Wollzeile No. 782, in the mezzanine, No. 45, the door.[51] // *Wawi* [old woman].[52] //

There is a washerwoman here, who will wash for 1 fl. 45 kr., 1 *Seidl* of wine at breakfast, midday dinner, and bread. [//] 12 kr. for a Seidl.[53] // She wants [sentence ends]. //

Frau Schlemmer[54] will come herself, to thank you. // She is coming today at 6 with the copyist. //

[probably commenting on Frau Trion's trial:]

---

[47] Schuppanzigh's Quartet played Beethoven's String Trio in C Minor, Op. 9, No. 3, on Sunday afternoon, January 18, 1824. Before it was Haydn's Quartet in A (Tost No. 4), [Op. 55, No. 1]; after it was a Mozart Quintet in D. See Schickh's *Wiener Zeitschrift* 9, No. 15 (February 3, 1824), p. 128.—KH/TA

[48] The German editors failed to identify this brief example.—TA

[49] Presumably the vocal parts to the *Missa solemnis* and Ninth Symphony.—TA

[50] A reminder of his sister-in-law's mailing address in Berlin.—TA

[51] In 1824, Frau Sophie Drion (b. Leipzig, 1773), a chamber servant's widow, lived in the Wollzeile, Haus No. 782, Wohnpartei 8. See Conscriptions-Bogen, Stadt, No. 782; Fremden-Tabelle of 1824 [new collation 782/29] (Wiener Stadt- und Landesarchiv).

By 1825, the *fremde* occupant was a maid, Franziska Rowaz (b. Bohemia, 1794). Both Trion and Rowaz may have worked for Johann Held (b. 1770), an economic councillor to a noble house; his wife, Rosalia (b. 1769); and son, Johann (b. Margareten, 1796), an official in the War Office and unmarried [new collation 782/19].—KH/TA

[52] Probably a variant of the Viennese *Wabn* (from the Czech *baba*), an old woman. See Peter Wehle, *Sprechen Sie Wienerisch?* (Vienna: Verlag Carl Ueberreuter, 1981/2003), p. 297.—TA

[53] A Seidl (usually used as a measure for beer rather than wine) is 0.35 liter.—TA

[54] Josepha Schlemmer (b. 1781; d. November 4, 1828), widow of Beethoven's long-time favorite copyist Wenzel Schlemmer, who had died on August 6, 1823. After he husband's death, she continued his copying services, aided by his former colleague Mathias Wunderl (1771–1833), but seemingly on a reduced scale. On ca. May 29, 1824, she told nephew Karl that if her staff of copyists had done the

The rice is too hard. // [Blatt 18v]

[resuming:]

Professor Schneider is one of the foremost Greek specialists now alive. [//] In a foreign country. I have his Greek dictionary.[55] //

[presumably after 6 p.m.:]

Frau Schlemmer was happy. // He [presumably the copyist] is having a hard time with his work. // Therefore you don't need to negotiate with the copyist about what he is to receive, because she pays him. // That is one person who can copy the whole day long. //

Schuppanzigh doesn't believe that he will be employed at the Kärntnertor [Theater].[56] //

I saw the maid standing on the bridge with her suitcase. [//] The [Blatt 19r] housekeeper said that *today* she already found a position where she can begin immediately. // The housekeeper is surprised about the terrible pay. // Where she is now, she only gets 6 fl. // A housekeeper gets 15 fl. // The washerwoman initially earns 3 fl. // Only *today* did she tell me that the maid always rummaged around and read in my *books*; she had been silent the *whole time* afterward. // We can have her every day. [//]

[Blatt 19v]

BEETHOVEN [**at a coffee house; possibly in the evening of Monday, January 19**]:[57]

Newly invented shaving razor, as well as the legally patented razor strop; across from the Sailerstätt Gate at the end of Weihburggasse No. 804.[58]

---

sloppy work for Schlemmer that they did for her, he would have torn everything up. See *Wiener Zeitung*, No. 262 (November 12, 1828), p. 1092; Heft 38, Blätter 25r and 28r; Heft 39, Blatt 22r; Heft 40, Blatt 10v; Heft 44, Blätter 4v–5r; and Heft 71, Blätter 1v–2r, among others.—TA

[55] There were many philologists with the name Schneider. Karl possibly means Johann Gottlob Schneider (1750–1822), professor in Frankfurt/Oder from 1776 and director of the library at the University of Breslau since 1814. In 1797, he had published a two-volume *Kritisches griechisch-deutsches Handwörterbuch*. In 1802/1804, Fr. W. Riemer published a shorter version as *Kleines griechisch-deutsches Handwörterbuch*, which reached its fourth printing in 1823. See *Allgemeine Deutsche Biographie*, vol. 32, pp. 125–127; Kayser, vol. 5, p. 131; Heft 45, Blatt 32r; and Appendix B.—KH/TA

[56] Schuppanzigh finally became a violinist in the Hofkapelle in 1827 and concertmaster at the Kärntnertor Theater in 1828. See Köchel, *Hof-Musikkapelle*, p. 97; Wurzbach, vol. 32, p. 217; and Clive, pp. 329–331.—KH/TA

[57] There are four advertisements here on two successive pages. It is possible that Beethoven copied the first two (for a razor and potatoes) while visiting a coffee shop on the evening of Monday, January 19, as proposed above. This seems probable, given his own addition of two shopping items following them. It is also possible, however, that all four advertisements were copied in a single coffee-house visit on Tuesday, January 20.—TA

[58] See the *Intelligenzblatt*, No. 14 (January 19, 1824), p. 109 (Advertisements). The same advertisement also appeared on January 21 and 23, 1824. The above-mentioned gate was also called the "Carolinentor."—KH/TA

Potatoes of sundry varieties, Wipplingergasse No. 365 at the porter's.[59]
+ Wine spirits.
+ Straw.
[Blatt 20r]

[possibly another visit to the coffee house; this one late in the afternoon of Tuesday, January 20:]
+ Authentic wax candles, 5 pounds, as one batch, for 3 fl.; *Fortuna* Grocery Shop, Schwertgasse.[60]
+ Linen Shop, Graben, Schoberlechner, at the White Cat; the prices are specified.[61]
+ Boot polish. [//]

[Blatt 20v]

FRAU SCHLEMMER'S COPYIST **[at Beethoven's apartment; possibly at ca. 6 p.m. on Tuesday, January 20]**:[62] If I could copy it alone, then I would do it well, but others cannot easily accommodate it. [//] Written out or ✗. [//]

[Blatt 21r]

SCHINDLER **[presumably at Beethoven's apartment; probably the afternoon of Wednesday, January 21 (through the end of the Heft)]**: Unger will not be here at the time when the opera [Beethoven's projected *Melusine*] reaches performance, because, as she herself said, she will undertake a tour next fall. // It is even better in November, when you yourself would no longer be inconvenienced because of your summer stay [in the country]. // I believe, though, that in *Melusina*, a soprano is altogether more necessary than a mezzo-soprano.[63] // She sings up to an E. //

---

[59] See the *Intelligenzblatt*, No. 14 (January 19, 1824), p. 110 (Advertisements), where the house number appeared as "363." House No. 365 was in the Passauer Gasse, across from the church Maria am Gestade; No. 363, as noted in the advertisement, was in the Wipplingergasse, at the corner of Stoss im Himmel, around the corner from the church. The same advertisement also appeared on January 21, 1824.—KH/TA

[60] See the *Intelligenzblatt*, No. 15 (January 20, 1824), p. 118 (Advertisements). Schwertgasse connected Wipplingergasse and Passauer Gasse at the northwest front of the church Maria am Gestade. The same advertisement appeared on January 22 and 24, 1824.—KH/TA

[61] See the *Intelligenzblatt*, No. 13 (January 17, 1824), p. 102 (Advertisements). The linen merchant Johann Georg Schoberlechner had his shop in the house *Zur weissen Katze*, on the Graben No. 620; see Heft 25, Blatt 35v. The same advertisement appeared on January 20 and 22, 1824. It seems likely that Beethoven saw this advertisement with the one that he noted immediately above on Tuesday, January 20.—KH/TA

[62] Since Josepha Schlemmer and her copyist seemingly visited Beethoven at ca. 6 p.m. on Monday, January 19, the copyist may have returned the next evening at the same time.—TA

[63] Caroline Unger was a mezzo-soprano.—TA

[SCHINDLER, *continued*]

We have *Aschenbrödl* by Isouard.[64] You really should honor us and attend the performance. We are as successful as possible with it. // Yesterday [Tuesday, January 20] it went very well, to the satisfaction of all. [//] [Blatt 21v] Yesterday there was a fine audience, but not full. //

I can still hear her [Unger] say today that she would send it [the libretto to *Melusine*] back to you right away. // At least she didn't say, the other day, that she actually wanted to sing the leading role. //

Last Sunday [January 18], Schuppanzigh played your Trio in C Minor wondrously beautifully, so that it created the most brilliant sensation possible. Next Sunday [January 25], your Septet.[65] // *Gaudeamus igitur!* // Not to me, and also not to the world.[66] //

<Now is indeed ....> That will change in a few months when you move into an apartment that has sun.[67] [//] [Blatt 22r]

You allow everything to concern you too much, even things that are not very important. And all of the things that aren't good for you. You need peace! Peace! Peace! In order to be wholly that to which Nature has destined you here on earth. // Get rid of a lot of this and consider it beneath your dignity, so that you can concentrate your efforts, and you [will] already gain a great deal. //

Have you decided what kind of arrangements you want to make for the Akademie? The time is approaching when it will be necessary to take care of it. It ought not to

---

[64] The opera *Aschenbrödel* [Cinderella] by Niccolò Isouard (1775–1818) was performed for the first time (in this production) at the Theater in der Josephstadt on Tuesday, January 20, 1824, with further performances on January 21 and 31. See Bäuerle's *Allgemeine Theater-Zeitung* 17, No. 14 (January 31, 1824), p. 56; No. 15 (February 3, 1824), p. 50; and No. 17 (February 7, 1824), p. 69.—KH

[65] Ignaz Schuppanzigh performed Beethoven's Septet in E-flat, Op. 20, on Sunday, January 25, 1824. The performers included Schuppanzigh, violin; Franz Weiss (1778–1830), viola; Joseph Linke (1783–1837), violoncello; Joseph Melzer/Mölzer (1763–1832), contrabass; Joseph Friedlowsky (1777–1859), clarinet; August Mittag (1795–1867), bassoon; and Michael Herbst (1778–1833), horn. The performance of the Septet was so successful that it had to be repeated with the same personnel on March 14, 1824. See the *Wiener AmZ* 8, No. 12 (March 27, 1824), p. 45; and Schickh's *Wiener Zeitschrift* 9, No. 15 (February 3, 1824), p. 128.—KH/TA

[66] Beethoven must have made a comment that the ever-popular Septet was tiresome to him, resulting in Schindler's defense of the work.—TA

[67] Beethoven's apartment on the first floor [second floor, American] of Landstrasse No. 323, the northeast corner of Ungargasse and Bockgasse [today's Beatrixgasse], had windows looking west over the courtyard, with afternoon light coming from above. Beethoven did most of his writing during the mornings, and so—with his chronic eye problems owing to smallpox as a child, and especially since his eye inflammation in 1823—he needed strong daylight, as long as possible, from the east. It is possible that Beethoven's apartment did not extend to the east side of the building; but in any case, it would have looked out into a narrow walkway between his building and the next building to the east, allowing only limited light two stories below roof level, even on sunny days. On January 21, only a month after the winter solstice, Beethoven's apartment would have been relatively dark. His next rental terminus would be St. George's Day (April 23), 1824. See Behsel, p. 78.—TA

[SCHINDLER, *continued*]

give you any trouble; [//] [Blatt 22v] if you will place your trust in several men, who will arrange everything on your behalf, you need only say how you wish it. // I myself didn't know it; but Sonnleithner knew it somehow—I learned it in this way. //

Kiesewetter and Sonnleithner only have to make a preliminary inquiry about the idea at the Verein, so that you already know how and what you want to request *before* you write to the Verein, and I consider that to be very good. [//] [Blatt 23r] Now it only depends upon your arranging the finer details so the Verein can determine what it would actually have to do for it. // I now ask you most urgently to write soon to the Verein, so that you are relieved of the first concern. You will receive the answer right away. //

The [Kärntnertor] Theater will provide the [Grosser Redouten-] Saal without further ado; likewise the Verein [will give] the stage scaffolding which is already there. [//]

Thus you must try to get the copying work finished by a specified time; and I just hope that you should not pay and that this would already be arranged. [//] [Blatt 23v] Did your brother tell you, then, that he [Diabelli] would take care of the copying expenses, if you would agree to his wishes?[68] // He wants to have it that a duet or quartet from the opera [unwritten *Melusine*] be performed, which he then would immediately sell to the administration; and in this way a part of the copying costs is already covered. // You can see from this that he is a better speculator than your great exalted brother [Johann]! // I have encountered this. //

Schup[panzigh] has a large and also a fine audience; he must make a profit from it. // Just the same way, Piringer[69] wants to continue the *Concert spirituelle*[70] and try it with 2 Akademies.

End of Heft 53

N.B. Heft 54 appears to follow directly after Heft 53, probably continuing the same conversation.

---

[68] See Blatt 6v above, but also nephew Karl's entries on behalf of brother Johann (December 28, 1823) in Heft 51, Blatt 4r.—TA

[69] Ferdinand Piringer (1780–1829), official in the registry office of the Imperial Court Commerce Commission and member of the representatives of the Gesellschaft der Musikfreunde, lived in the City, Schlossergasse No. 598. He was a violinist and often played in or even conducted concerts. Piringer numbered among Beethoven's circle of friends. See Böckh (1822), p. 376; Frimmel, *Handbuch*, II, pp. 21–23; Clive, pp. 267–268; *Hof- und Staats-Schematismus*, 1823, I, p. 255; Ziegler, *Addressen-Buch*, pp. 115 and 138.—KH/TA

[70] Vienna's *Concerts spirituelles* were initiated in 1819 by Franz Xaver Gebauer (see Heft 50, Blatt 18v), Kapellmeister at the Augustiner Church. After his death in 1822, they were revived, in 1824, by Ferdinand Piringer and Johann Geissler, Lower Austrian knighthood agent and violoncellist, as "private undertakings," i.e., without the public character that they had had under Gebauer. In 1824, there were four concerts (March 4, March 18, April 1, and April 8, all within Lent) that took place in the Saal of the Lower Austrian *Landstände*, to the east of the Minoriten Church. See the *Wiener AmZ* 6, No. 103 (December 25, 1822), col. 822, and 8, No. 6 (March 13, 1824), pp. 21–22; Gräffer-Czikann, I, pp. 586–587.—KH/TA

Heft 54

(January 21, 1824 – February 2, 1824)

N.B. All the entries in this Heft are presented in roughly chronological order; see footnote 1 below.

[Blatt 1r]

SCHINDLER [presumably at Beethoven's apartment in the Ungargasse; the afternoon of Wednesday, January 21, continuing from Heft 53]:[1] Duport is also fortunate now with the new ballet,[2] in that it pleases very much and is also said to be visually very beautiful. They say the most beautiful in many years. //
    You are a Hat Tyrant![3] //

---

[1] In this Heft 54, Blätter 1r–35v were basically written in chronological order from Wednesday, January 21 (continuing directly after Heft 53), through Monday, February 2 (Candlemas, a holiday).
    All of the Blätter after 35, however, seem to have written on various dates between January 22 and 26. As the German editors noted, Blätter 36–43 were entered in reverse chronological order, and so they presented them in correct chronological order (Blätter 43–36), a practice followed here.
    Blätter 43v–41r were probably filled on the afternoon of Saturday, January 24, while Blätter 40v–36v were filled during the evening of Sunday, January 25, after Schuppanzigh's concert. It is not clear whether the next entries on Blätter 36v–36r were made on Sunday night or, instead, were made on Monday, January 26.
    Thereafter, Blätter 44–46 may all have been made on Thursday, January 23, or it is possible that Blatt 44r was entered on the late afternoon of Wednesday, January 22, while Blätter 44v–46r were entered on the late afternoon of Thursday, January 23.
    Fortunately, the time periods now determined for the various entries on Blätter 36–46 (in normal or reverse chronology, as appropriate) correspond to chronological gaps in Blätter 1–35 (and especially Blätter 4–8) and allow a roughly more continuous chronological order than was possible in the German edition.—TA
[2] These entries concern the *Die Fee und der Ritter* [The Fairy and the Knight] by the ballet master Armand Vestris, with music from the works of Gioacchino Rossini, Giovanni Pacini, and Pietro Romani, first performed at the Kärntnertor Theater on December 31, 1823, and repeated frequently thereafter. See Bäuerle's *Allgemeine Theater-Zeitung* 17, No. 6 (January 13, 1824), p. 23, and following issues.—KH
[3] Original German: "Sie sind Hut-Tyrann!" Schindler is humorously accusing Beethoven of cruelly abusing his hat, implying that the hat was not in good condition and needed replacement. This situation reached a crisis on Sunday, February 15, when brother Johann told Beethoven that people were talking about how bad his hat looked. The composer subsequently went shopping with Schindler and bought a new one. See Heft 56, Blätter 10v and 17v–18r.—TA

It has been known since yesterday that Weigl has been named as Kapellmeister at St. Stephan's, but the decree has not been prepared yet. In the event, he has fought a significant victory, in that his competitors had <such> great patronage.[4] [//]

If you have the time, come with Karl to the Josephstadt today;[5] any later and Karl may have less time because of his approaching examination. //

[Schindler probably departs for the Josephstadt.]

[Blatt 1v]

NEPHEW KARL [**initially following up on Schindler's conversation**]: How do you like Gläser's conducting? // Phlegmatic. // Rossini's music to *Aschenbrödl*[6] cannot be compared with today's. //

What did you pay? // She already wrote that earlier:

4 fl. 56 [kr.]
3 fl. 15
1 fl. 41
<u>   29</u>
   30 [//]

HOUSEKEEPER APPLICANT [**at Beethoven's apartment, writing in French; presumably late afternoon of Wednesday, January 21**]:[7] I am not able in the kitchen, but I also know a bit about music. [//]

BEETHOVEN [**presumably at his apartment; possibly morning of Thursday, January 22**]:[8]
    Flour
    Wine spirits
    Vinegar
    Sugar
    Eyeglasses

[Blatt 2r: No writing; crossed through with red pencil.]

---

[4] Actually, Joseph Weigl lost the position to Johann Baptist Gänsbacher, who had the favor of the Imperial family and the support of Vienna's Archbishop Firmian. See Heft 50, Blätter 2r–2v, as well as Blatt 12v below.—TA

[5] This presumably concerns the second performance of Isouard's opera *Aschenbrödel* [Cinderella] at the Theater in der Josephstadt (where Schindler was concertmaster) on Wednesday, January 21, 1824. See Heft 53, Blätter 21r–21v.—KH/TA

[6] Rossini's opera *La cenerentola* (1817).—KH

[7] This is the same woman whom Beethoven interviewed on Saturday, January 17 (Heft 53, Blätter 5r–5v).—KH/TA

[8] This shopping list is difficult to read; it is written with red pencil through "Sugar."—KH

[Blatt 2v]

NEPHEW KARL [at Beethoven's apartment; the afternoon of Thursday, January 22]:[9] For each *Krapfen* [filled donut or apple fritter], 4 kr. //

[written vertically→] It is to be decided this week. // It is being litigated; the archbishop doesn't want Weigl.[10] //

Your Septet will be done. Everyone has asked him [Schuppanzigh] for it.[11] //

Salieri is declaring that he poisoned Mozart.[12] [←written vertically] [//] [Blatt 3r]

She paid the fish-seller woman 1 fl. 15 kr. instead of 45 kr.; and therefore wanted to let us know that it is 2½ pounds. // A blustering old woman. //

Mylord[13] often likes to have his cross.[14] //

I saw Langer today. He now lives almost entirely from his essays in the papers.[15] //

When I went to the bank this morning, I encountered Frau Kudlich,[16] who was shopping all alone with a basket on her arm. //

Leyermann [organ grinder]. [//] [Blatt 3v]

S[chuppanzigh] has been engaged in Berlin.[17] //

---

[9] On Blatt 3r, Karl reports what he did "this morning"; therefore, it is now afternoon.—TA

[10] Since 1822, the archbishop of Vienna had been Count Leopold Maximilian von Firmian (1766–1831). See *Hof- und Staats-Schematismus*, 1824, II, p. 3; Wurzbach, vol. 4, pp. 234–235.—KH/TA

[11] Schuppanzigh performed Beethoven's Septet, Op. 20, on his subscription concert of Sunday, January 25, 1825. See several references below, but especially Blätter 40v–39v. See also Heft 53, Blatt 21v.—KH/TA

[12] Salieri's physical and mental health had declined sharply in ca. October 1823. See also Heft 50, Blatt 13r.—KH/TA

[13] Because of his corpulence, Ignaz Schuppanzigh was called "Mylord Falstaff" within Beethoven's circle, and probably for that reason adopted the habit of addressing Beethoven in the third person, as a lord might address a vassal.—KH/TA

[14] The *Kreuz* (cross) mentioned here is probably Karl Holz (1799–1858), whose name means "wood" and who was often humorously called after Christ's Cross made of wood. As a talented amateur, he usually served as second violinist in Schuppanzigh's String Quartet during this period. Between mid-July 1825 and early December 1826, Holz essentially replaced Schindler as the composer's unpaid secretary. See Clive, pp. 168–169—TA

[15] Johann Langer (1793–1858), author. He wrote poetry and stories for numerous periodicals and had been a writer for Bäuerle's *Allgemeine Theater-Zeitung* since 1816. See Böckh (1822), p. 30; Wurzbach, vol. 14, pp. 113–115.—KH

[16] Presumably the wife of Johann Kudlich. Karl had attended Kudlich's Educational Institute in suburban Landstrasse, Erdberggasse No. 91, in 1818–1819. See Böckh (1822), p. 533; Frimmel, *Handbuch*, I, pp. 308–309 and 452–454; and Clive, p. 198; as well as Heft 2, Blatt 4r, among many other references.—KH/TA

[17] While this appears to be an exaggeration, Schuppanzigh may well have been discussing a guest appearance (or perhaps even a permanent position) with Henning and Bethmann, the visitors from Berlin. Since Bethmann had arrived back in Vienna on January 21 (see Blatt 45v below), the subject may have been especially current.—TA

Jeckl[18] is said to have been engaged at the Hofkapelle; S[chuppanzigh] went to see Dietrichstein,[19] who said that no one had been selected yet. [//]

Everyone is coming to S[chuppanzigh] to ask him to conduct in concerts, but he says that he doesn't want to stand in anyone's light, and that they should ask at the [Musik-]Verein. // At the Court Theater. //

[written vertically→] How is it going with the housekeeping? [←written vertically]

[Blatt 4r]

SCHINDLER [presumably at Beethoven's apartment; at an undetermined time between Thursday, January 22, and Saturday, January 24]: I am to bring you sincere thanks. It very much pleased her.[20] //

It would also benefit Jeckel, who is poverty-stricken and has 6–8 children. // Last year, they [the Burgtheater] retired him with a very small pension. //

No longer as much as before, because his wife cannot earn anything more, since she is old and ugly.[21] //

He is presently on a tour to Munich, Stuttgart, etc.[22] //

The role of Bertha [in Grillparzer's libretto *Melusine*] is not insignificant at all; Unger may take offense, but it appears to be made for her. [//] [Blatt 4v] She has enough to do throughout the piece. // I especially like the 3rd act, because it is full

---

[18] Anton Jeckel (b. Silberberg, Silesia, ca. 1764; d. Vienna, February 11, 1834), violinist. He worked in Moravia in 1808, entered Court service on September 23, 1810, and had played in Beethoven's benefit concerts in 1813–1814. He was a first violinist in the Kärntnertor Theater's orchestra in 1814, concertmaster of the Burgtheater's orchestra by 1817 and through 1821, but was pensioned by the end of 1822. When his wife, Juliane (b. ca. 1776/77), died on February 17, 1823, there were three surviving children: Joseph (b. ca. 1799), a soldier; and daughters Antonia (b. ca. 1808) and Vinzenzia (b. ca. 1810). When Anton died, his estate amounted to 65 fl. From at least 1823 until his death, he lived in the City, Obere Bäckerstrasse No. 764. See *Wiener AmZ* 6, No. 86 (October 26, 1822), col. 688; Verlassenschafts-Abhandlung (Antonia), Fasz. 2: 2011/1829, and (Anton), Fasz. 2: 3902/1834; Conscriptions-Bogen, Stadt 764/3 [new collation, 764/13] (all three in the Wiener Stadt- und Landesarchiv); and Ziegler, *Addressen-Buch*, p. 24.—KH/TA

[19] Count Moritz Dietrichstein-Proskau-Leslie (1775–1864), *Hofmusikgraf* (administrator of the Court's musical establishment, including the *Hofmusikkapelle*) and amateur song composer. See Frimmel, *Handbuch*, I, p. 111; Clive, pp. 91–93; and *Hof- und Staats-Schematismus*, 1824, I, p. 5.—KH/TA

[20] It is not clear whom Schindler means here. Possibly he took something to Unger.—TA

[21] This paragraph seems not to concern the violinist Jeckel, whose wife had died on February 17, 1823. See Blatt 3v above.—TA

[22] Probably violinist Franz Pechatschek (b. Vienna, 1793; d. Karlsruhe, 1840), who had reportedly studied violin with Schuppanzigh in his early years. He joined the Theater an der Wien's violin section in 1809 and by December 1820 had become second concertmaster. On April 9, 1820, he conducted a concert of the Gesellschaft der Musikfreunde, including Beethoven's Symphony No. 5 and the final chorus from *Christus am Ölberge*. From August 1821 to ca. September 1822, he had toured through Germany to Paris and back. Shortly thereafter, he was called to the ducal Court in Stuttgart, remaining until 1826, before moving to Karlsruhe. See also Heft 9, Blätter 5r–5v.—TA

[SCHINDLER, *continued*]
of power and action. // Hard-sounding words here and there, don't you think? // I found too many elisions that have a hard sound. // Also I honestly don't know how you will treat the [role of] Troll, because he is often inconsiderate and crude.[23] //

Weigl was therefore really designated. // He [Archbishop Firmian?] has taken Gänsbacher under his wing, because he taught the children of his brother. // The administration makes the appointment. [//] [Blatt 5r]

But poor Grillparzer[24] is to be pitied; his *Ottokar* will not be performed because the censor has treated it terribly. The stage directors wanted to perform it for their *own* benefit. // I also hear that he himself was at the Kaiser's. It will soon be made clear what actually is to be done with it. //

Let it [the stove] go entirely; that is the best thing; the cold [weather] will soon come to an end anyhow. //

Was Herr Kalkbrenner gracious enough to honor you with a ticket to his concert? Otherwise, he has not given any out. // They say that he is leaving already on Tuesday [January 27].[25] //

So how did you like *Aschenbrödl*?[26] [//] [Blatt 5v] *You* are not what he seems to be. // Haven't you made note of it to him? // Despite his conceit, he [presumably Gläser] is a thousand times more manageable than Herr Drechsler, who is the most miserable conductor that I have ever seen. //

---

[23] The characters in Grillparzer's three-act libretto to *Melusine* (which would ultimately be set to music by Conradin Kreutzer in 1832) include Count Emerich von Forst; his sister Berta; Raimund, a knight; Troll, a servant; the fairies Plantina, Meliora, and Melusina; as well as hunters, knights, nymphs, and spirits. Its sources included folk legend, Friedrich de LaMotte Fouqué, and Ludwig Tieck, but its opening hunting scene is somewhat reminiscent of the prologue to Goethe's *Faust*. Berta has instructed the servant Troll to protect Raimund in the forest, but instead, Troll leads him to the three fairies, including Melusina, who enchants him and, in a final scene with the conflicting forces of the count and Berta versus the supernatural powers of the fairies and spirits, lures him to his death. See Grillparzer, *Werke*, ed. Friedrich Schreyvogel (1958), vol. 2, pp. 973–1000.—TA

[24] On November 25, 1823, Grillparzer had submitted his new tragedy, *König Ottokars Glück und Ende*, to the Viennese Censorship Board, which, on January 20, 1824, issued a prohibition of its performance "on political grounds." After the intercession of several influential persons, permission to publish it was granted on June 5, 1824, and the first performance took place on February 19, 1825. See Franz Grillparzer, *Sämtliche Werke*, ed. August Sauer, continued by Reinhold Backmann (Vienna, 1939), I/18, pp. 13–15.—KH/TA

[25] Kalkbrenner and the harpist Dizi departed Vienna for Munich on Saturday, January 31, 1824. Presumably the illness of Moscheles (in Prague) was the reason for his hasty departure, because Kalkbrenner had to cover his colleague's projected concert dates in London. See the *Wiener AmZ* 8, No. 3 (March 6, 1824), p. 10; *Wiener Zeitung*, No. 27 (February 4, 1824), p. 123. See also Blatt 23v below.—KH/TA

[26] The second performance of Isouard's opera at the Josephstadt Theater took place on Wednesday, January 21, so this entry was probably written on Thursday, January 22.—TA

But he [Seyfried][27] has been sickly the entire winter, and has not been in the orchestra [of the Theater an der Wien] for four months. // But unfortunately he has already emptied his coffers, because healthy thoughts no longer come to mind. // He won't write anything substantial for the theater again, but he can probably do this now for the church. // His always sickly condition contributes a great deal to it. [//] [Blatt 6r] 50–60 fl. for a piece. [//]

It's going very badly for Salieri again. He is completely deranged. He constantly fantasizes that he is to blame for Mozart's death and that he supplied him with poison. // This is the truth—because he wants to confess it as such. // Thus it is true again that everyone gets his reward. //

[Blätter 44–46 (Thursday, January 22, and Friday, January 23) as well as Blätter 43v–41r (Saturday afternoon, January 24) follow here.]

[Blatt 44r]

BEETHOVEN [**at his apartment, writing in ink; ca. Thursday, January 22**]:
Pencil.
Cash in a bank share. //

NEPHEW KARL [**possibly at a coffee house; possibly ca. Thursday, January 22**]:
She [probably the departing maid] maintains that she got no money to go to the market, because you didn't have any small denominations [of money]. // Because she didn't understand what you said, she didn't make any vegetable soup. // She says that you forgot it. //

[Karl copies a newspaper advertisement from Thursday, January 22:]
House officer's widow seeks employment as a housekeeper. Wollzeile No. 783, in the *Zwirn* [thread/yarn] shop *Zum Schmetterling* [At the Butterfly].[28] [**Thursday, January 22**] //

[Blatt 44v]

---

[27] Ignaz von Seyfried (1776–1841), composer and first Kapellmeister at the Theater auf der Wieden/an der Wien from 1797 to 1825; he suffered from a severe stomach illness. See Böckh, 1822, p. 381; Clive, pp. 334–335; and Wurzbach, vol. 34, pp. 176–178.—KH/TA

[28] See the *Intelligenzblatt*, No. 17 (January 22, 1824), p. 134 (Advertisements). The same advertisement appeared on January 24 and 27, 1824. The deceased *Hausoffizier* may have served in the Imperial house.—KH/TA

BEETHOVEN [presumably in a coffee shop, copying newspaper advertisements and notices; possibly all on Friday, January 23]:

+ At Mörschner und Jasper's: *Was hat ein verständiger Hausvater, etc. zu wissen nötig? etc. etc.*; size octavo; Kaschau, 1824; stiff binding; 1 fl. 40 kr. C.M.[29] **[January 21]** //

+ Limburger and Strachin cheese, Weihburggasse No. 908.[30] **[January 21 and 23]** //

[Blatt 45r]

+ Study and work lamps, 14 fl. W.W. each; Plankengasse No. 1063.[31] **[January 23]** //

+ Large apartment in Ober St. Veit, No. 78.[32] **[January 23]** //

+ For rent: 3rd floor [4th floor, American], Ferdinands Brücke, Leopoldstadt No. 589.[33] **[January 23]** //

+ Potatoes of the best varieties, Graben No. 1121.[34] **[January 23]** [//]

[Blatt 45v]

Bethmann, arrived here on January 21, living at City No. 852.[35] **[January 23]** //

+ Cream
+ Shaving mug, razor
+ Blotting sand
+ Shoe-cleaning brush

[Blatt 46r]

---

[29] Excerpt from an advertisement in the *Intelligenzblatt*, No. 16 (January 21, 1824), p. 132 (Advertisements). The book was a comprehensive "how to" about cooking and household economy, assembled from the writings of many authors. The same advertisement had already appeared in No. 1 (January 2, 1824) but did not appear on January 22 or 23.—KH/TA

[30] See the *Intelligenzblatt*, No. 16 (January 21, 1824), p. 127 (Advertisements). The same advertisement appeared on January 23, 1824.—KH

[31] See the *Intelligenzblatt*, No. 18 (January 23, 1824), p. 143 (Advertisements). The same advertisement appeared on January 29 and February 12, 19, and 26, 1824.—KH

[32] See the *Intelligenzblatt*, No. 18 (January 23, 1824), p. 142 (Advertisements). The same advertisement had already appeared in No. 16 (January 21, 1824). Ober St. Veit, an old village perhaps a mile west of Schönbrunn, is now part of the 13th *Bezirk* (Hietzing). Beethoven was already thinking of lodgings for summer 1824, but this one was excessive: 8 rooms, a kitchen on the ground floor, a large *Saal* upstairs, servants' quarters, and a stable for three horses.—KH/TA

[33] See the *Intelligenzblatt*, No. 18 (January 23, 1824), p. 142 (Advertisements). The same advertisement appeared on January 26, 1824.—KH

[34] See the *Intelligenzblatt*, No. 18 (January 23, 1824), p. 142 (Advertisements). The same advertisement would appear again in No. 20 (January 26, 1824), p. 160, and No. 22 (January 28, 1824), p. 177.—KH/TA

[35] Berlin theater director Heinrich Bethmann had arrived back in Vienna on January 21, 1824, and was staying in *Zum ungarischen König*, Grosser Schullerstrasse No. 852. See the "Arrivals" in the *Wiener Zeitung*, No. 18 (January 23, 1824), p. 81.—KH

+ Mälzel's brother[36] about the <time-bea…> metronome
+ Ask about wax candles, as opposed to
+ Tallow candles
+ Sugar //

NEPHEW KARL [presumably at Beethoven's apartment; possibly the evening of Friday, January 23]: I'm eating in the City tomorrow; will you eat at home? If not, perhaps you can come into the City to eat (if you would like to), and I would also come to the *Wirtshaus* [restaurant]. // Certainly it is better at the *Birne*[37] than in most of the *Gasthäuser* [restaurants] in the City.

[Blatt 46v: No writing; not crossed out with red pencil.]

* * * * *

[Blatt 43v]

JOHANN VAN BEETHOVEN [presumably at Beethoven's apartment; possibly early/midafternoon on Saturday, January 24]:[38] But you should [compose] an opera, because this would work in Paris, London, and St. Petersburg. //
A capon.[39] //
But you should certainly write to Duport concerning the opera [*Melusine*]. //
If you make a contract with Duport, you must also make it a condition to obtain

---

[36] Leonhard Mälzel (1783–1855), like his elder brother Johann Nepomuk Mälzel (1772–1838), inventor and maker of mechanical musical instruments. He had also been instrumental in making Beethoven's ear trumpets. Since 1823, he had lived in the suburb of Jägerzeil, No. 20 on the south side of the street of the same name, six buildings away from the Prater. For Leonhard's birth in Regensburg on March 27, 1783, see Rita Steblin, "Mälzel's Early Career to 1813: New Archival Research in Regensburg and Vienna," in *colloquium collegarum: Festschrift für David Hiley zum 65. Geburtstag* (Tutzing: Hans Schneider, 2013), pp. 161–210. See also Frimmel, *Handbuch*, I, pp. 378–380; Gräffer-Czikann, III, p. 526; Alfred Orel, "Mälzel," *MGG*, vol. 8, cols. 1456–1458; Redl (1823), p. 157, and (1824), p. 139; Wurzbach, vol. 16, pp. 250–252; Clive, pp. 224–225.—KH/TA

[37] The restaurant *Zur goldenen Birne* (At the Golden Pear), No. 52 on the east side of Landstrasse Hauptstrasse, a long half-block south of Bockgasse/Beatrixgasse. Beethoven had frequently visited it when he lived virtually across the street from it from October 1817 through October 1819 (except for summers) and seems to have done so (although perhaps less frequently) now, after his move to the corner of Ungargasse and Bockgasse three months before. See Frimmel, *Handbuch*, I, p. 160; Groner (1922), p. 42; Pezzl, p. 241; Klein, *Beethovenstätten in Österreich*, pp. 100–102, 132–133.—KH/TA

[38] On Blatt 42v, he writes that "today" is Kreutzer's *Der Taucher* (premiered on Saturday evening, January 24, with a second performance on Monday, January 26), and on Blatt 43r, he writes that he will attend Kalkbrenner's and Schuppanzigh's concerts on Sunday, January 25. Therefore, "today" is Saturday, January 24.—TA

[39] Johann writes *Ein Kapauner*, possibly referring to the main course of a meal (see Heft 55, Blatt 2r, where the subject of nephew Karl's conversation is a capon), but just as possibly referring (in context) to the former ballet dancer (now resident manager) Duport disparagingly as someone who was castrated. Some question remains, because Johann was often unclear in his writing.—TA

an evening in the Grosser Redoutensaal. // Everyone wants a concert in the evening; at midday, everyone is walking on the promenades.[40] [//] [Blatt 43r] The [Musik-] Verein does not receive permission in the evening. // Also, all the members want to participate without pay. // An aria and quartet from your new opera.[41] //

I am going to Kalkbrenner's Akademie. // And in the afternoon to Schuppanzigh's, to hear your Quartet.[42] // [Blatt 42v]

You absolutely can't believe how much everyone is hoping for and talking about your Akademie. // There is such a great need for German composers. // Today [Saturday, January 24] is *Der Taucher* by Kreutzer.[43] //

I wasn't here. //

Have you thoroughly read the libretto [to *Melusine*] by Grillparzer? // He will gladly make changes in it. // No person other than you can [Blatt 42r] provide a good *German* opera; all the Germans are saying so.[44] //

He should draft the letter to Duport tomorrow. // He [Schuppanzigh] also sent one [ticket] to me. // It [Beethoven's presence] will make him happy. //

NEPHEW KARL [**continuing; early/midafternoon on Saturday, January 24**]: Dizi became quite silly at the Quartet concert and cried out when your Quartet [*sic*] was played.[45] //

You should read Lichnowsky's letter to Duport. [//] [Blatt 41v] They ask. // What you do not know, we do not need. //

JOHANN VAN BEETHOVEN [**continuing**]: Do you already have somebody to copy the Symphony [No. 9]? // This woman [Frau Schlemmer] will probably marry another copyist. //

I want to go the 2nd or 3rd time [that *Der Taucher* is performed] to see whether anyone is in there. // [Henriette] Sontag is very fine. //

---

[40] Favorite areas to walk included the *Bastei* (scenic paths along the top of the City walls, with views out over the *Glacis*), the *Augarten*, and the *Prater*.—TA

[41] Johann is assuming that Beethoven will have two such numbers from *Melusine* finished by the time that he gives his Akademie in spring 1824.—TA

[42] Both Kalkbrenner's concert with the harpist Dizi and Schuppanzigh's Quartet performance took place on Sunday, January 25, 1824, at 12:30 p.m. and 4:30 p.m., respectively. Schuppanzigh's concert actually included Beethoven's Septet in E-flat, Op. 20, as well as a Quartet in C major by Joseph Haydn. See Schickh's *Wiener Zeitschrift* 9, No. 15 (February 3, 1824), p. 128.—KH/TA

[43] Conradin Kreutzer's *Der Taucher* was premiered in the Kärntnertor Theater on Saturday, January 24, 1824, with further performances on Monday, January 26; Wednesday, January 28; Friday, January 30; and so on, into late February. See Blatt 6r above.—TA

[44] This refers to the tensions between Rossini enthusiasts and supporters of German-Austrian operas.—TA

[45] This embarrassing episode could have taken place at any of Schuppanzigh's recent Sunday concerts on January 4, 11, or 18. See the *Allgemeine musikalische Zeitung* 26, No. 8 (February 19, 1824), col. 120.—TA

If it's all right with you, I'll go with Karl to see *Aline* at the Josephstadt [Theater].[46]
[//] [Blatt 41r]
One *never* gets anything beautiful with one pound alone. //
Dizi is not extraordinary on his harp. //

NEPHEW KARL [**continuing; writing, in part, on Johann's behalf**]: Your brother is asking when the two sonatas that are lying out there on the piano will be engraved.[47] //

Tobias [Haslinger] was very courteous to your brother. // He is now paying for his ticket. //

[**Seemingly the end of this group of entries on Saturday, January 24.**]

* * * * *

NEPHEW KARL [**presumably at Beethoven's apartment; late morning or early afternoon of Sunday, January 25, seemingly writing, in part, on behalf of brother Johann**]:
Galitzin is to designate a place [in St. Petersburg] where the concert is to be given.[48] //

---

[46] Henri Berton's opera *Aline, reine de Golconde* had already been performed in Vienna under the title *Aline, Königin von Golkonda* in the Kärntnertor Theater (1804) and the Theater an der Wien (1812). Adolph Bäuerle parodied it in a comical magic-opera libretto, *Aline, oder Wien in einem andern Weltteile*, set to music by Wenzel Müller, premiered at the Leopoldstadt Theater on October 9, 1822. It was further adapted as *Aline, oder Wien und Baden in einem andern Weltteile*, premiered at the Josephstadt Theater on January 22, 1824, with further performances daily from January 23 to 27, January 29, and February 3–6 as well as 8, 9, 12, 13, and 25. See Bäuerle's *Allgemeine Theater-Zeitung* 17, No. 15 (February 3, 1824), p. 59, and following numbers; Franz Hadamowsky, *Das Theater in der Wiener Leopoldstadt, 1781–1860* (Vienna, 1934), p. 93; O. Rommel, *Die Alt-Wiener Volkskomödie* (Vienna, 1952), pp. 784–786; and Rudolph Angermüller, *Wenzel Müller und "sein" Leopoldstädter Theater* (Vienna: Böhlau, 2009), pp. 26–27.

Therefore, if Johann did not attend the premiere of Kreutzer's *Der Taucher* in the Kärntnertor Theater on Saturday, January 24, he would have been free to attend the third performance of *Aline* in the Josephstadt Theater with nephew Karl.—KH/TA

[47] Beethoven's last three Piano Sonatas, Opp. 109, 110, and 111, had already been published in Paris by Schlesinger in 1821 and 1822 and in Vienna by 1823. See Kinsky-Halm, pp. 312–313, 315–316, and 319–320.—TA

[48] Prince Nicolas Borisovich Galitzin (December 8, 1794 – October 22, 1866, Old Style). On November 9, 1822 (New Style), Galitzin had written to Beethoven, offering to commission "one, two, or three new quartets" (ultimately, Opp. 127, 130, and 132) and, in spring 1823, was instrumental in the purchase of a manuscript copy of the *Missa solemnis* in St. Petersburg, where its first complete performance took place on April 18 (April 6, Old Style), 1824, nearly three weeks before Beethoven's *Akademie* of May 7. See Frimmel, *Handbuch*, I, p. 158; Clive, pp. 357–359; and Albrecht, *Letters*, No. 299.—KH/TA

Wouldn't you like to go to your brother's for a turkey dinner?[49] // He heard that Kreutzer's *Der Taucher*[50] went fairly well.[51] // [Blatt 6v]

My good fellow! You learn a great deal from me. // You'll become an all-around philosopher. //

She is orderly. //

Sontag's voice continues to improve. // [Fräulein] Beisteiner is also very fine.[52] [//]

Schuppanzigh, Haslinger, Diabelli, Mayseder, Leidesdorf, [Abbé] Stadler,[53] and Streicher with his wife[54] were there.[55] //

JOHANN VAN BEETHOVEN [at Beethoven's apartment, continuing the conversation; late morning or early afternoon of Sunday, January 25]: Last Thursday [January 22], Hummel's Septet was performed at the small [hall of the] Musikverein;[56]

---

[49] Original German: *Calecutischer Hahn* (literally, Calcutta chicken), meaning a *Truthahn* (turkey); see Campe, *Wörterbuch*, II, p. 868. See the final entry on Blatt 6v and following below.—KH/TA

[50] Conradin Kreutzer's opera *Der Taucher* was premiered in the Kärntnertor Theater on Saturday, January 24, 1824, and was repeated often in the following weeks (January 26, 28, and 30; February 2, 4, 11, 13, 16, 18, and 23). See Bäuerle's *Allgemeine Theater-Zeitung* 17, No. 13 (January 29, 1824), p. 51, and following issues.—KH

[51] On Blatt 15r below, Johann himself provided a similar opinion.—TA

[52] Elise Beisteiner (later married name, Pohl), mezzo-soprano (born in 1805 or 1806), was a member of the Kärntnertor Theater from 1823 to 1825 and then became a Court Opera singer in Kassel. See *Portrait-Katalog*, p. 361; Wurzbach, vol. 23, pp. 27–28.—KH

[53] Abbé Maximilian Stadler (1748–1833), honorary canon of the cathedral, organist, and composer. See Hilde Hellmann-Stojan, "Stadler," *MGG*, vol. 12, cols. 1122–1126; Wurzbach, vol. 37, pp. 60–62; Clive, pp. 347–348; and Ziegler, *Addressen-Buch*, p. 50.—KH

[54] Johann Andreas Streicher (1761–1833), friend of Schiller's in their youth, now a famous piano maker. Since 1802, he had led, in conjunction with his wife, Nannette (1769–1833), daughter of Augsburg piano maker Johann Andreas Stein, the Viennese piano firm of "Nannette Streicher, née Stein." Since 1823, their son Johann Baptist (1796–1871) was a partner in the firm; also in 1823, he [Johann Baptist] had patented a mechanism striking from above. See Clive, pp. 357–359; Frimmel, *Handbuch*, II, pp. 262–264; Folker Göthel, "Streicher," *MGG*, vol. 12, cols. 1515–1517; and his "Stein," *MGG*, vol. 12, cols. 1230–1234.—KH/TA

[55] Presumably at a performance of Kreutzer's *Der Taucher*.—TA

[56] Johann Nepomuk Hummel's Septet in D Minor, Op. 74 (scored for piano, viola, violoncello, contrabass, flute, oboe, and horn) was performed on Thursday, January 22, 1824, at a "*Musikalische Abendunterhaltung*" (Musical Evening of Entertainment), held from 7 to 9 p.m. at the hall of the Gesellschaft der Musikfreunde. The performers included Fräulein Franziska Biehler (piano), Joseph Kaufmann (viola), Friedrich Gross (violoncello), Joseph Nowak (contrabass), Ferdinand Bogner (flute), Joseph Khayll (oboe), and Michael Herbst (horn). Bogner, Khayll, and Herbst were professors at the Gesellschaft's *Conservatorium*; Nowak played bassoon at the Kärntnertor Theater but, like many bassoonists, also doubled on contrabassoon/contrabass to play a "ninth voice," when needed, in an octet *Harmonie*. All the rest were amateurs associated with the Gesellschaft; Kaufmann was also a frequent amateur violinist.

See programs of the Musikalische Abendunterhaltungen (Archiv, Gesellschaft der Musikfreunde, Bd. 2697/32). First names and instruments confirmed in Böckh (1822) and Ziegler, *Addressen-Buch*, both passim. For general background of the Thursday *Abendunterhaltungen*, established in 1818, and running from September to March, see Richard von Perger, *Geschichte der k.k. Gesellschaft der Musikfreunde in*

I am looking forward to today; [Blatt 7r] I am curious to learn what they say about yours today.[57]

That cannot harm him. //

That is the money from the wine. //

Let's write to Duport this evening; if it's all right with you, I'll come here. //

I didn't come on account of the dinner [invitation].[58] //

He's an idiot. [//]

[Blatt 7v]

BEETHOVEN:
2
1 fl. 30 kr. //

NEPHEW KARL [presumably at Beethoven's apartment, after Johann leaves; afternoon of Sunday, January 25]: The housekeeper said that the rabbit is so small that it cannot be roasted, but instead can only be eaten as an ingredient [in a mixed dish]. // The cheese was inexpensive; it cost only 7 kr. //

Just today, he [Johann] told me that he is hot on the trail, that he even found her lover with her [Therese] recently. // He says that he has thrashed her soundly, along with her daughter [Amalie Waldmann]. Whether it's true, I don't know.[59] [//]
[Blatt 8r]

1 pound coffee	2 fl. 40 kr.
2 pounds ordinary sugar	2 fl. 30
1 pound white sugar	1 fl. 36
	6 fl. 46

100
10 //

Wien, 2 vols. (Vienna, 1912), I, p. 19; Pohl, *Gesellschaft der Musikfreunde* (Vienna, 1871), pp. 12 and 99–101.—KH/TA

[57] The comparison was not so direct: Beethoven's Septet, Op. 20 (dating from 1799/1800), was scored for violin, viola, violoncello, contrabass, clarinet, horn, and bassoon (a significantly different instrumentation from Hummel's Septet, dating from 1816). The Beethoven Septet was performed on Schuppanzigh's concert at 4:30 p.m. on Sunday, January 25, 1824. See Heft 53, Blatt 21v.—KH/TA

[58] Beethoven must have answered Johann's proposal by saying that he didn't have much on hand for a supper; thus Johann's reply here.—TA

[59] This entry and most of Karl's entries through the end of Blatt 8r concern Johann van Beethoven's wife, Therese, *née* Obermayer (1787–1828), and her illegitimate daughter, Amalie Waldmann (1807–1831). See Heinrich Rietsch, "Nochmals Johann van Beethoven und anderes," in *Neues Beethoven-Jahrbuch*, ed. Adolf Sandberger, vol. 3 (Augsburg: Benno Filser, 1927), pp. 42–50.—KH/TA

HEFT 54 (JANUARY 21 – FEBRUARY 2, 1824), BLATT 40V

But, as I see it, he doesn't live with her on any married basis now; they often don't speak 10 words with each other all day long. // I presume that she brought property [into the marriage]. // I still remember quite well how she sold pastries[60] on the *Schanzl*.[61]

[End of entries of the late morning/early afternoon, Sunday, January 25.]

[Blätter 40v–36v (evening of Sunday, January 25) as well as Blätter 36v–36r (late on Sunday, January 25, or early Monday, January 26) follow here.]

[Blatt 40v]

NEPHEW KARL **[at Beethoven's apartment, returning with brother Johann after Schuppanzigh's concert; probably ca. 7:30 p.m. on Sunday, January 25]**:

Schuppanzigh's septet and quartet concert wasn't out until a quarter to 7;[62] then *Fratello* [brother Johann] read the newspapers, but was prevented from going by a few falling drops, so that his new coat would not be ruined.[63] The Quartet by Haydn went first and was applauded. Then followed the Septet; it would be in vain, however, to paint the impression that was manifest in everyone; the performance was splendid, and everyone was delighted. // In several days. // Many music dealers were there: Tobias, etc. // It has never been as full as today. [//] [Blatt 40r] The people had to stand outside the doors. //

Herr Schindler was also there and sends his *very most obedient* regards.[64] //

He[65] was never there and came only because of the Septet. //

---

[60] Original German *Kipfel*, Austrian word for small pastries, especially croissants. Therese probably sold pastries on behalf of her brother, the baker Leopold Obermayer (1784–1841), whose bakery and shop were in the western suburb of Windmühle. Karl was born in 1806, and Johann and Therese were married in 1812, so Karl may be remembering a time when he was very young.—KH/TA

[61] The *Schanzl* or *Schanzel*, an area outside the eastern walls, along the banks of the Danube Canal, essentially at today's Morzinplatz at the foot of Rotenturmstrasse. See Groner (1922), p. 419.—KH/TA

[62] On January 25, 1825, the Schuppanzigh Quartet played a Quartet in C major by Haydn and (with guest musicians; see Heft 53, Blatt 21v) Beethoven's Septet in E-flat, Op. 20. Beethoven's Septet takes roughly 40 minutes to perform. The Haydn Quartet in C was unspecified, but the four most likely candidates are Op. 76, No. 3 ("Emperor," ca. 22 mins.); Op. 74, No. 1 (ca. 32 mins.); Op. 64, No. 1 (ca. 26 mins.); and Op. 54, No. 2 (ca. 20 mins.). Because the concert began at 4:30 p.m. (as Schuppanzigh had indicated for this series in Heft 46, Blatt 30v) and lasted until 6:45 (possibly exaggerated by Karl), the lengthier Quartet, Op. 74, No. 1, seems the most likely, giving a total of ca. 72 minutes of music.—KH/TA

[63] On Sunday, January 25, the temperature had reached ca. 46 degrees Fahrenheit under cloudy skies in the afternoon and, by 10 p.m., had gone down to 39 degrees with overcast skies. Thus the raindrops reported by Karl at ca. 7 p.m. seem plausible. See the *Wiener Zeitung*, No. 21 (January 27, 1824), p. 97.—TA

[64] There seems more than a little sarcasm in Karl's reference to Schindler's unctuousness.—TA

[65] This sentence probably does not refer to Schindler.—TA

The solo of the horn[66] <and flute> was[67] very much applauded. //

Dilettantes asked your brother whether the Akademie would take place. // Dilettantes spoke with your brother about the Akademie.[68] [//] [Blatt 39v]

Do you want to write the letter to Duport? That way your brother will go tomorrow [Monday, January 26] and give it to him himself. //

Wolfmayer was also there with his wife [Josepha] and acquaintances. // Tuscher was also there. //

Tell me what I am to get [from the restaurant on the ground floor].[69] // Veal.[70] //

[Karl departs for the restaurant.]

JOHANN VAN BEETHOVEN [**left alone with Beethoven, who may also have been trying to write a letter to Duport**]: And in the .... //

The Septet pleased the audience as much as if it were being performed for the first time. // They didn't play; instead they merely sang with their instruments. // Schuppanzigh sang so infinitely beautifully [through his violin], that [Blatt 39r] he was often interrupted by general applause while he was playing. //

Now you are also getting the money for the Symphony. // With an Akademie, you can pay Steiner, and there will still be 2,000 fl. in paper money left over for you for the summer. //

Give it to me; I'll guarantee it. // At least 4,000 fl. in paper money will remain. // [Blatt 38v] Leidesdorf will also take it over for 4,000 fl. // But he told me that you must give it [the Akademie] in the evening. // All the ladies will come then because they all want to be beautiful in the evening, and they will be. // Leidesdorf told me so. //

---

[66] There is a horn solo in Beethoven's Septet, second movement, Adagio cantabile, bars 68–73; see the *Gesamtausgabe*, p. 16. The performer was Michael Herbst (1778–1833), "solo hornist" at the Theater an der Wien.—KH/TA

[67] The verb was originally plural to match the originally plural subject, probably until Beethoven informed Karl that the Septet was not scored for flute.—KH

[68] There must be some differentiation in these nearly identical sentences. In the first, the dilettantes (probably meaning dedicated music lovers) asked Johann whether there would be an Akademie. Johann may have told them about Beethoven's hopes for a concert at the Kärntnertor Theater, but also his current quandary concerning a commission from that theater for *Melusine* (about which he probably had great misgivings), and his possible solution of simply trying to move the premiere of the Ninth Symphony to Berlin. If these dilettantes then continued to discuss the matter with Johann (as implied in the second sentence), *this* may have accounted for the lateness of their departure from the Musik-Verein—they may already have been conspiring to write the petition to Beethoven (probably finalized in the third week of February 1824) to keep the premiere of the Ninth Symphony in Vienna. Virtually everyone mentioned as attending these concerts (except Schindler) were among the signers of that petition. For the text of the petition, see Albrecht, No. 344.—TA

[69] For the context of this request, see Blätter 30r–30v in this Heft (below, under February 1, 1824).—TA

[70] The word "veal" is covered by brother Johann's fumbling start, "And."—KH

In the Congress [of Vienna].[71] //
It will be quite easy for Duport to schedule it in the evening. //

[Blatt 38r]

NEPHEW KARL [**probably returning from the restaurant**]: Does the Symphony last longer than the *Sinfonia heroica*?[72] //

JOHANN VAN BEETHOVEN [**continuing**]: Is the tenor [part] …. // It would be best if everyone understood and comprehended it. // If two more vocal pieces were added, then the Akademie's program would be complete. //

But Grillparzer's poetry must also be good. //

There are now fine men and women singers at the Kärntnertor Theater: 2 tenors, 2 fine basses, and [Blatt 37v] 3 or 4 fine women singers. //

Leidesdorf told me that Weber has horribly lost his way in his opera [*Euryanthe*], and thereby did even more to harm [the cause of] German opera than to advance it. //

NEPHEW KARL: Half of *Fidelio* is in it. // No one understood it. [//]

Who is she? // Kalkbrenner is giving lessons to [Leopoldine] Blahetka.[73] // Money. [//] [Blatt 37r] She is giving lessons. //

JOHANN VAN BEETHOVEN [**continuing, as they eat the food (presumably veal) that Karl has brought**]: Hufeland[74] says that, in the evening, one should not eat a great deal, and especially little meat. // Often an egg dish. //

My cook gets 100 fl. [annually]. // The old woman [Beethoven's former housekeeper Barbara Holzmann] would probably like to come back to you. [//]

---

[71] The context is unclear; possibly a reference to how beautifully the ladies dressed during the Congress of Vienna in 1814–1815.—TA

[72] Beethoven's Symphony No. 3 ("*Eroica*") takes ca. 50–55 minutes in performance; the yet-unperformed Symphony No. 9, ca. 65–70.—TA

[73] Leopoldine Blahetka (b. Guntramsdorf, 1809; d. Boulogne-sur-Mer, 1885), pianistic wunderkind, daughter of Joseph Blahetka, student of Joseph Czerny (no relation to Carl), who survived early notoriety to become a mature pianist and teacher of some repute. See Frimmel, *Handbuch*, I, p. 50; Clive, p. 36.—KH/TA

[74] Christoph Wilhelm Hufeland (1762–1836), famous physician, author of popular books on health matters, including *Makrobiotik, oder die Kunst, das menschliche Leben zu verlängern* (Berlin, 1805). See Kayser, III, p. 208.—KH

NEPHEW KARL [**probably calculating the money paid at the restaurant**]:

   1 fl. 98
       56
 ―――――
[1 fl.] 42

[written vertically→] Does the maid also get paid for *today*?

38
16
――
54 [←written vertically]

[Blatt 36v]

[**seemingly after brother Johann's departure; late evening of Sunday, January 25:**]

My good fellow! I didn't know that he had said anything, and I also didn't know that I laughed about anything. I only said, "Adieu, Herr Uncle!" as he left. I smiled about it because I am not accustomed to calling him that, and it was merely a [humorous] repetition, because Schindler had addressed him that way at the quartet concert today. //

BEETHOVEN [**at his apartment; late on Sunday, January 25, or early on Monday, January 26**]:[75]

  + Coffee
  + Sugar
  + Shaving mug
  + Razor
  + Pens
  + Locksmith: doors; Karl's
  + Eyeglasses[76] //

---

[75] Beethoven usually made his shopping and errand lists during the course of the morning, but this one, followed by Karl's entries that seem to have been made late in the evening, could have been jotted while Beethoven sat alone after the irritable exchange with Karl about joking with Johann.

Karl probably went into his room afterward but may have returned after a few minutes to write the reference letter for the maid, still on Sunday, before the beginning of the week of classes on Monday.—TA

[76] Beethoven runs this shopping list together on four lines.—TA

NEPHEW KARL: Anna Stolizka, Rauchfangkehrergasse, at the *Greissler* [shop].⁷⁷ //
Near Erdberg.

[written vertically→] 3 fl. 54 kr. [←written vertically]

[Blatt 36r]

NEPHEW KARL [**at Beethoven's apartment; seemingly very late on Sunday, January 25, or possibly early on Monday, January 26**]: I still want to write the testimonial for the maid today,⁷⁸ so that we are not delayed tomorrow. With the *Drangeld* [money on account] she would get 5 fl. 8 kr.; without *Drangeld*, 3 fl. 38 kr. //

On the way [presumably from Schuppanzigh's concert], your brother turned the conversation to the 50 ducats from Berlin, but said that it wouldn't bother him if he still had to wait a long while. //

He [Johann] would be happy if he could get loose from both of them [his wife, Therese, and her daughter, Amalie Waldmann], but he lacks the courage. //

[in the right margin, figuring the maid's payment:]

4 fl. 68 kr. [= 5 fl. 8 kr.]
<u>1 fl. 30 kr. [*Drangeld*]</u>
3 fl. 38 kr.

[written vertically→] The maid told the housekeeper that she would be happy if you would let her go, even before the two weeks were over. // It's over on Sunday. [←written vertically]

* * * * *

[Blatt 8v]

SCHINDLER [**at a coffee house, possibly the *Kameel*;⁷⁹ probably late morning or early afternoon of Monday, January 26**]: Grillparzer sends you manifold greetings.

---

⁷⁷ Beethoven lived at the intersection of Ungargasse and Bockgasse (today's Beatrixgasse). Rauchfangkehrergasse joined with Landstrasse Hauptstrasse from the east, a long block south of its western intersection with Bockgasse, and across the street from the Rochuskirche. At its far eastern end was the Rasumovsky Palace and, across from it, the piano shop of (Mathias) Andreas Stein at No. 78. See Ziegler, *Addressen-Buch*, p. 253. The location of the *Greissler* (a small-wares or possibly grocery shop) cannot be determined but may have been at the point where Rauchfangkehrergasse joined the Hauptstrasse, a building or two north of Erdberggasse.—KH/TA

⁷⁸ This wording argues for Karl's having made the entry late on Sunday, January 25, supported by the following entries summarizing some of the issues raised on that day.—TA

⁷⁹ These entries might have been made at a favorite coffee house near Beethoven's apartment. The entry following, however, notes a book for which there seems to be no corresponding newspaper advertisement. Therefore, Beethoven probably saw it at Haass's shop in Unter den Tuchlauben, which is conveniently near *Zum schwarzen Kameel* in the Bognergasse.—TA

He will visit you one of these days. His *Ottokar* has not only been stricken, but also completely forbidden. He is completely taken aback. // He is already as much as lost here, both as a poet and as an official. // He already feels it himself. // He can never leave the office before 3 o'clock and consequently cannot accept any [midday dinner] invitations.[80] If he doesn't find you at home, he will look for you *here* [at a coffee house].[81] //

He was extremely glad when I assured him that you will compose <his libretto into> an opera.[82] [Blatt 9r] He had been convinced that the opposite was true, and that was the reason why he didn't come to visit you, because he didn't want to press you about it. //

BEETHOVEN [**probably at Haass's shop, Unter den Tuchlauben No. 561**]:[83]
+ *On Some Severe Afflictions of the Eyes*, by Dr. Th. von Sömmering; 5th printing; size Octavo; sewn binding; 24 kr., at Haass, Unter den Tuchlauben, *Kühfuss*, No. 561.[84] [//]

[Blatt 9v]

SCHINDLER: Now I have a big question for you. [Carl] Czerny wants to get together a *Cirkel* [circle] of good singers soon and perform your Mass [in C] with the German text, accompanied by 2 pianos. Would you be so accommodating as to lend him the Mass, as H[err] Schulz translated it into German, for the performance? I ask you very urgently for it, if you have no other purpose for it. // It would be advisable if you were to write to Breitkopf und Härtel about it; perhaps it went there. [//] [Blatt 10r] If only Breitkopf didn't protest that it was another [translation] than the one that they published; they aren't too good about such things. // Schulz [*sic*]. // At Warmbrunn

---

[80] Franz Grillparzer was employed as a salaried document drafter in the office of the minister of finance, Count Johann Philipp Stadion, Himmelpfortgasse No. 964. See *Hof- und Staats-Schematismus*, 1824, I, p. 249. The implication here is that, while most people would have their breaks for midday dinner at 1 or 2 o'clock in the afternoon, Grillparzer usually could not get free until 3. After dinner, he would have to return to the office and work until 6 or 7 p.m.—KH/TA

[81] Grillparzer had a long conversation with Beethoven a week or so later, in Heft 55, Blätter 2v–5v.—TA

[82] Beethoven was probably angry at this misrepresentation of his intentions, but (unlike September 7, 1823) seemingly did not betray his emotions.—TA

[83] The address noted was one block behind the Peterskirche, at the intersection of *Unter den Tuchlauben*, on the south side of the street.—TA

[84] This concerns Samuel Thomas von Sömmering, *Über einige wichtige Pflichten gegen die Augen*, 5th printing (Frankfurt am Main, 1819), octavo. See Kayser, V, p. 272. The German editors did not find a newspaper advertisement for this book, and it seems likely that Beethoven saw it at the Haass shop while he was walking through town. The topic was of great interest to him, given his recent (and possibly lingering) eye inflammations.—KH/TA

in Prussian Silesia. // Countess Schaffgotsch brought it [the translation] and also took possession of your letter again, because Schulz lives on her estate.[85] //

NEPHEW KARL [**possibly at Beethoven's apartment; possibly later on Monday, January 26**]: Gossiper.[86] //

Frau St[reicher] was surprised that you didn't come.[87] //

[written vertically→] What should I say in the reference letter?[88] [←written vertically] [//] [Blatt 10v]

$$\frac{\begin{array}{r}25\\12\\\hline50\\25\end{array}}{300}\ [//]$$

[**continued on Blatt 11r:**]

SCHINDLER [falsified entries begin→] Fräulein [Bettina] von Brentano and Goethe. // Sometime I would like to hear from you yourself something about that lady and your meeting with her.[89] // Count [Moritz] Lichnowsky told me some things, but he no longer remembered for sure when they happened. [←falsified entries end]

[Blatt 11r][90]

NEPHEW KARL [**continuing from Blatt 10v**]: 25 fl. per month makes 300 fl. per year. // The question is whether it will be better at her place. // She says that she doesn't want to stay here any longer; it is worse here than in the prison. [//]

---

[85] The German translation of the text for Beethoven's Mass in C, Op. 86, made by Benedict Scholz (ca. 1760–1824) from Warmbrunn early in 1823. For further details, see Heft 32, Blätter 5v–7r (and footnotes).—KH/TA

[86] Probably a reference to Schindler.—TA

[87] This could refer to Beethoven's not hearing Hummel's Septet on Thursday, January 22, or his own Septet, Op. 20, on Sunday, January 25 (see Blätter 6v–7r above).—TA

[88] Presumably a testimonial on behalf of a departing domestic servant, possibly the latest housekeeper.—TA

[89] Bettina von Brentano (1785–1859), whom Beethoven had met in early summer 1810. She and poet Clemens Brentano were the slightly unstable half-siblings of the solid Frankfurt banker Franz Brentano (whose wife was the former Antonie von Birkenstock). See Frimmel, *Handbuch*, I, pp. 61–63; and Clive, pp. 47–51.—KH/TA

[90] Various doodles and stenographic jottings on the page (largely covered by the other entries), along with the arithmetical computation:

$$\frac{\begin{array}{r}1\text{ fl.}56\\34\end{array}}{1\text{ fl.}22}\text{—KH}$$

BEETHOVEN [presumably at his apartment; probably the morning of ca. Tuesday, January 27]:
+ Candles
hodie [today][91] [//]

[Blatt 11v]

SCHUPPANZIGH [presumably at Beethoven's apartment; possibly the afternoon of ca. Tuesday, January 27]: Has Bethmann [from Berlin] paid already? [//]
I was at his place once, but I didn't want to say anything about it[92] the *first time*, but now I shall speak directly with him. // He [= You] must write to Radziwill himself [= yourself]; that will be the best; he is now in Posen. //

He can find himself compromised by it because he believes that his sister-in-law knows about it. [//] [Blatt 12r] He [= You?] will certainly pay. // From the grand duke of Tuscany. // Who is Odelga, then? // *Agent*.[93] //

He is a miserable fiddler. // But I cannot wait much longer; I have an offer from Berlin. // Duport is an ass. // But he [= you?] could still speak with Duport; perhaps something could be done. //

Katter[94] himself told me that he could not hold out much longer, after which he also got the ballets. [//] [Blatt 12v]
He [= You] can write to him that I am on the point of leaving [Vienna]. //
I get along very well with Forti and Gottdank.[95] // Even Weigl is not against me. //

He [Weigl] has now gotten the Kapellmeister's position at St. Stephan's;[96] his

---

[91] Original Latin *hodie*, meaning "today." In Heft 56, Blatt 25v, Beethoven would write the German counterpart *heute* at the end of an errand list for Wednesday, February 18, 1824, the date on which his advertisement for a housekeeper appeared in the *Intelligenzblatt*. Perhaps he initially intended that such an advertisement would appear on ca. January 27, but no such notice appears in the publication week of January 26–31, 1824.—TA

[92] This concerns either the payment for the music to *Consecration of the House* or a subscription to the *Missa solemnis*.—TA

[93] Carl von Odelga represented the Viennese legations from both Tuscany (in Italy) and Nassau (in Germany)—not as incongruous as it seems, because both regions were ruled by one noble house at this time—and was the contact for soliciting subscriptions to the *Missa solemnis*.—TA

[94] Joseph Katter (ca. 1771–1841), Court violinist and concertmaster of the Court Opera and Court Ballet. See also Heft 49, Blatt 10r.—KH/TA

[95] Anton Forti (1790–1859), baritone, had replaced Michael Vogl as Pizarro on July 18, 1814, to Beethoven's satisfaction. See Clive, p. 113.
Joseph Gottdank (1779–1849), singer and staff administrator at the Kärntnertor Theater. See Verlassenschafts-Abhandlung, Fasz. 2: 6637/1849 (Wiener Stadt- und Landesarchiv); Ziegler, *Addressen-Buch*, p. 73.—KH/TA

[96] As noted previously and confirmed in Heft 55, Blatt 6r, Joseph Weigl ultimately lost the position to the politically influential Gänsbacher. See also Blatt 1r above.—TA

stomach is very fitting for this position. [//] [Blatt 13r] It is also not necessary; he has nothing to do; for compositions, nothing at all already.[97] // 4th floor [5th floor, American]. // But a beautiful apartment.[98] // I was already at his place today, but he wasn't at home.[99] //[100]

He[101] is staying here another two weeks. //

Why doesn't he [= why don't you] do something with [publisher] Leidesdorf? //

A propos: Kalkbrenner is leaving tomorrow.[102] [//] [Blatt 13v]

Young Schmutzer[103] copies beautifully in score. // He does copying work every day at Mechetti's shop;[104] if he passes by [= if you pass by] there, then he [= you] can see him. // I have watched him; he doesn't copy slowly, but wondrously beautifully. // I shall speak with him. [//]

[Blatt 14r]

JOHANN VAN BEETHOVEN [presumably at Beethoven's apartment; probably Wednesday, January 28]: I was at Frau Schlemmer's. She hopes to bring everything by Sunday [February 1].[105] //

I came yesterday [probably Tuesday, January 27] with the carriage in order to take you for a drive in the beautiful weather.[106] //

---

[97] After a distinguished career earlier, Weigl had recently suffered several failures with his theatrical compositions.—TA

[98] These are references to Weigl's seemingly former apartment in the Jägerzeil No. 17. It was perhaps two stories higher than customarily desirable (given the number of stairs to walk for both tenant and servants) but had good sun in the morning and midday, therefore light conducive to composing. See Blätter 18v–19r below.—TA

[99] At this time, Weigl was living in the City, Seilerstätte (or Seilergasse) No. 805; see Ziegler, *Addressen-Buch*, p. 73.—TA

[100] In the right margin, above the dividing line, the notes C-E-G, B-E-G in sixteenth-notes.—KH

[101] Possibly Heinrich Bethmann, theater director from Berlin, arrived on January 21 and was still in Vienna on February 1, 1824. See Blatt 29v below.—TA

[102] Kalkbrenner and the harpist Dizi did not leave Vienna until Saturday, January 31, 1824. See the *Wiener Zeitung*, No. 27 (February 4, 1824), p. 123 (Departures).—KH/TA

[103] Probably Niklaus Schmutzer (b. 1807), musician at the St. Laurenz Church in the western suburb of Schottenfeld and son of the widowed music copyist Leopold Schmutzer (b. 1779). Since 1820, both of them had lived in the northwestern suburb of Alsergrund, Herrngasse No. 83, only two blocks inside the *Linie* (today's Gürtel). See Conscriptions-Bögen Altlerchenfeld, No. 108, and Alsergrund, No. 83 (Wiener Stadt- und Landesarchiv); Behsel, p. 198.—KH/TA

[104] The Art and Music Shop of Pietro Mechetti, formerly Carlo Mechetti, on the Michaelerplatz, in the "new" Michaelerhaus No. 1153. See Redl, 1824, p. 72.—KH/TA

[105] Josepha, widow of Beethoven's longtime copyist Wenzel Schlemmer, continued the family business after her husband's death on August 6, 1823. At this time, she was working on subscription copies of the *Missa solemnis*.—TA

[106] Vienna's temperature had risen to 54 degrees Fahrenheit on the afternoon of Monday, January 26, but the skies were cloudy. On the afternoon of Tuesday, January 27, however, the temperature had fallen to 46 degrees Fahrenheit, but the skies were sunny and clear, therefore a good day for a recreational

But he says that it must have been very smoky with the other 3 stoves; besides, he believed that this stove will change the arrangement of the entire room, and winter will soon be over.[107] // [Blatt 14v]

With Leidesdorf, there is nothing to be done with the Bagatelles and the 2 songs;[108] in short, there is absolutely nothing to do here for Art. // It will be best to write immediately to Schlesinger in Paris.[109] // I was at Leidesdorf's at least 6 times, but it appears to me that the Jews have no money.[110] // [Blatt 15r]

Kreutzer's opera pleased the audience. They say that there is nothing great and absolutely nothing new in it, but he put the pieces together well, and now, when there is nothing better to be found, one is quite satisfied with it. // There is also a bit of *Fidelio* in it. //

[Blatt 15v]

BEETHOVEN [at a coffee house, reading the day's newspapers; probably the late afternoon of Wednesday, January 28]:

Die wiener Köchin wie sie seyn sollte, etc. [The Viennese Cook, as She Should Be], by Theresia Ballauf, married name Muck, etc.; size octavo; Vienna, 1822; 2nd enlarged edition; <unbound, 2 fl.> in stiff covers, 2 fl. 12 kr. C.M.; at Wimmer's in the Dorotheergasse, next to the *Goldenes Jägerhorn*.[111] [//] [Blatt 16r]

Cream and milk products of the Freyer Waffenhof in Biedermannsdorf; Untere Breunerstrasse 1131; a measure of very good cream unboiled, 48 kr. W.W.; double cream 1 fl. 36 kr. in sealed bottles.[112] //

---

carriage ride in the Prater. On Wednesday, January 28, the temperature had fallen again, and the skies were foggy; and the next day, Vienna had rain mixed with snow. See the *Wiener Zeitung*, No. 23 (January 29, 1824), p. 105, and adjacent issues.—TA

[107] See further entries about the stove on Blatt 17v below.—TA

[108] The Six Bagatelles for Piano, Op. 126; the *Opferlied*, Op. 121b; and the *Bundeslied*, Op. 122. Beethoven had ceded the proprietary rights for these works (which would appear from Schott in Mainz in 1825) to his brother Johann in exchange for a loan that Johann had made to him. See Heft 51, Blatt 10v; and Kinsky-Halm, pp. 354–356.—KH

[109] Maurice (originally Moritz) Schlesinger (1798–1871), son of Berlin publisher Adolph Martin Schlesinger (1769–1838), opened his own music publishing house in Paris in 1821. He had visited Vienna in 1819 and would do so again in September 1825 to buy the String Quartet, Op. 132. See Rudolf Elvers, "Schlesinger," *MGG*, vol. 11, cols. 1813–1815; and Clive, pp. 316–318.—KH/TA

[110] The music publishing firm of Sauer and Leidesdorf was indeed a modest enterprise. See Clive, pp. 304–305.—TA

[111] See the *Intelligenzblatt*, No. 22 (January 28, 1824), p. 183 (Advertisements). The same advertisement also appeared on February 6 and 12, 1824. This Blatt is illustrated in Martella Gutiérrez-Denhoff, *Die gute Kocherey: Aus Beethovens Speiseplänen* (Bonn: Beethoven-Haus, 1988), p. 15, with transcription (Dorotheergaße as Dorotheegaße) on p. 16.—KH/TA

[112] See the *Intelligenzblatt*, No. 22 (January 28, 1824), p. 177 (Advertisements). The same advertisement also appeared on January 30 and February 3, 1824.—KH

Potatoes of the best quality; Graben 1121, at the building superintendent's.[113] //

[Blatt 16v]

JOHANN VAN BEETHOVEN [**presumably at Beethoven's apartment; probably late afternoon or evening of Wednesday, January 28**]: There are no opportunities. //

Moscheles is ill in Prague; he lies in bed, suffering from "sand and stone" in the urinary passage.[114] //

I spoke with *Dobias* [publisher Tobias Haslinger]; he sends his most obliging regards and will visit you soon. //

It is generally unanimous here that Kalkbrenner plays much better than Moscheles. [//] [Blatt 17r]

Have you already written to Duport?[115] // When the contract [presumably for composing *Melusine*] is drawn up, you should stipulate 2 free tickets in the parterre for yourself; everyone has them, even Bernard.[116] //

Quite simply like last year; I believe that you still have the receipt. // One writes, "This year, I have the same amount to pay as last year, namely 23 fl." // [Blatt 17v] I wrote it that way for you last year. //

After dinner, you drink too much water at the coffee house.[117] //

NEPHEW KARL [**presumably at Beethoven's apartment; possibly late morning on Thursday, January 29**]: He says that the chimney sweep said that the stove can probably be installed, which the building superintendent, who was present, also conceded; but no person would be able to endure it because of the smoke. Otherwise

---

[113] See the *Intelligenzblatt*, No. 22 (January 28, 1824), p. 177 (Advertisements). The same advertisement had already appeared on January 23 and 26, 1824.—KH

[114] The phrase "sand and stone" refers to the biblical Luke 6:47–49, comparing houses built on foundations of sand and of stone. Emil Smidak translated Moscheles's malady as peritonitis; see his *Isaak-Ignaz Moscheles*… (Brookfield, Vermont: Scolar Press, 1989), p. 33. Mark Kroll's more recent *Ignaz Moscheles and the Changing World of Musical Europe* (Woodbridge, UK: Boydell Press, 2014), pp. 53–55, does not specify the illness. Given brother Johann's experience as a pharmacist, he probably reckoned, even from afar, that Moscheles's malady was most likely kidney stones.

See further references to Moscheles's kidney stones by secretary Schindler on January 30 (Blatt 23v below) and by nephew Karl on February 2 (Blatt 32r below) and again on February 29 (Heft 57, Blatt 16v; similar pagination coincidental).—TA

[115] Presumably Beethoven had written to Duport, as Unger conveyed his assent to Beethoven's conditions on Blatt 19v below.—TA

[116] Joseph Carl Bernard, editor of the *Wiener Zeitung* and a formerly close friend of Beethoven's, had recently married, but in his bachelor days had prided himself on being invited for dinner at wealthy homes and receiving free tickets to the theaters.—TA

[117] Schindler confirms that Beethoven's favorite drink was "fresh spring water, which he drank in large quantities in the summertime" (Schindler-MacArdle, p. 337).—TA

there is no opposition here; the building superintendent will even install it, [Blatt 18r] if you want.[118] //

You should give him the receipt for the *Classensteuer* [graduated income tax]. // Venison. [//]

BEETHOVEN [presumably at his apartment, drawing up shopping/to-do list following his conversation with Karl; late morning of Thursday, January 29]:
+ Candles.
+ Locksmith.[119]
+ Mälzel Metronome.[120]
+ Blotting sand.
+ Apartment Weigl. [//]

[Blatt 18v]

SCHINDLER [presumably at Beethoven's apartment; possibly the early afternoon of Thursday, January 29]: Difficulties for Weigl are piling up lately. The archbishop, who was not consulted when Weigl was appointed, complained about it to the emperor. He claims that he must also be consulted. Summoned by Saurau,[121] Weigl has to explain how he would combine the church duties with the theater. Therefore the administration confirmed him, and that he is excused from the theater when he has duties in the church. // And other irritations that say nothing, and Weigl still remains the person appointed. //

He [Leonhard Mälzel] lived in the Jägerzeil No. 17;[122] he must have moved out of there only a short time ago.[123] One might ask him about it. // On the right side [coming out from the City], the 5th or 6th house from the Prater. [//] [Blatt 19r]

---

[118] This concerns Beethoven's apartment in the Ungargasse.—TA

[119] The locksmith was on Beethoven's errand list on Blatt 36v above (ca. Monday, January 26). He seemingly performed his services on the afternoon of January 29 (see Blatt 19r below).—TA

[120] This refers to Leonhard Mälzel, not his brother Johann Nepomuk; see Blatt 18v above.—TA

[121] Count Franz Joseph von Saurau (1760–1832), state and conference minister, high chancellor and minister of the interior, living in the Wipplingerstrasse No. 384. See *Hof- und Staats-Schematismus*, 1824, I, p. 231; Wurzbach, vol. 28, pp. 279–281.—KH

[122] At that time, Jägerzeil was both a small suburb in the southern part of the island of Leopoldstadt but also the extension of Praterstrasse (the street) as it neared the Prater. Thus, Jägerzeil No. 17 was almost exactly as Schindler described it: in the suburb of Jägerzeil, in the street Jägerzeil, on the right side when coming from the City, actually the fourth building before arriving at the Prater. Schindler is dealing in the old house numbers of 1795; Jägerzeil No. 17 was renumbered as 20 in 1821 and as No. 44 in 1827 (Behsel, p. 55).—KH/TA

[123] Beethoven and Mälzel finally met on February 15, 1824, when Mälzel told him of his upcoming trip to Prague. Therefore, he might have moved out of Jägerzeil No. 17 at the most recent rental terminus, ca. October 1, 1823. See Heft 56, Blatt 12r.—TA

Weigl's apartment is positioned well.[124] The sun in the morning and at midday,[125] but—isn't the 4th floor [5th floor, American] too high for you? // You sprint up stairs too much,[126] and that might hurt you very much in the long run. //

NEPHEW KARL: Have you already been out?[127] //

SCHINDLER [**probably continuing at Beethoven's apartment; possibly ca. 2 p.m. on Thursday, January 29**]:[128] In yesterday's *Beobachter* [January 28], Kalkbrenner received a letter of patent as the foremost and greatest pianist.[129] Truly a rare distinction. //

NEPHEW KARL: The ham is probably not to be eaten raw. //

SCHINDLER: It just needs to be boiled a little bit. //
  A girl is outside.[130] //

NEPHEW KARL: The locksmith has done everything and gets 4 fl. 45 kr.[131] //

[Blatt 19v]

---

[124] The three buildings in the City where Weigl is known to have lived are all appropriately close to the Court Theaters: Prince Paar's building in the Riemerstrasse No. 795, apartment 4; and Himmelpfortgasse No. 950, apartment 7 (where his cellist father lived in apartment 12).
  At least since 1821, Weigl had lived at Seilerstätte (Seilergasse) No. 805, apartment 1, across from the southwest bastion. See Böckh (1822, reflecting 1821), p. 383 (calling the building *Beim Türkenkopf* [At the Turk's Head]); Ziegler, *Addressen-Buch* (reflecting late 1822), p. 83; Gugitz, "Auszüge … Conscriptionsbögen," p. 300.—KH/TA

[125] Beethoven's preoccupation here (and perhaps through most of his life in Vienna) was to find an apartment with good light during his customary working hours of morning and midday.—TA

[126] The operative German word here is *laufen* (to sprint). In Bonn, Beethoven's father, Johann, had been known as "Johann der Läufer" (Johann the Sprinter), a pun on "Johann der Täufer" (John the Baptist), the good-natured humor of which was missed by Maynard Solomon, *Beethoven* (1977), p. 10.—TA

[127] Presumably Beethoven had gone out and, following his list on Blatt 18r above, had contacted the locksmith to come.—TA

[128] Beethoven's newspaper advertisement had directed applicants for the housekeeper's position to apply at his apartment at 2 p.m., and "a girl" comes, possibly to apply, on Blatt 19r, unless it is Caroline Unger, who begins entries on Blatt 19v.—TA

[129] The *Österreichischer Beobachter*, No. 28 (January 28, 1824), p. 130, reported about Kalkbrenner's concert: "Without making a thorough comparison with other virtuosos on the piano … we believe that, in sentimental expression and inner delicacy of playing, Herr Kalkbrenner must unconditionally belong to the first echelon among the living masters of the instrument. He incomparably achieved the highest goal of the instrumentalist … to make his playing sound like singing …."—KH/TA

[130] Schindler may be passing along information brought by a servant, who would not have known a potential applicant from Caroline Unger.—TA

[131] Contacting the locksmith was on Beethoven's to-do list on Blatt 18r above, presumably late morning of Thursday, January 29.—TA

UNGER [**at Beethoven's apartment, arriving in a coach owned by the Kärntnertor Theater;**[132] **presumably the afternoon of Thursday, January 29**]:[133] The woman who is accompanying me is *Baronesse* Lirveeld,[134] who fanatically admires you. Sontag could not come on account of the poor weather,[135] which, however, could not prevent me [from coming]. [//]

We made a sensation in *Der Taucher* yesterday [Wednesday, January 28].[136] [//]

The *Fräulein* is unmarried.[137] [//]

Duport asked me to tell you that your conditions concerning *Melusine* are all right with him.[138] Now he would also like to know Grillparzer's [conditions], in order to unify them. [//]

My friend here and I will make you a bell rope [Blatt 20r] worthy of you. [//] How can Beethoven have a bell rope like *that*? If your hand didn't make it holy, one would have to declare that it would be hung <from> a <common string> a hanging cord. [//]

Are you going to get married? An old bachelor is an idle citizen of the State. *Dixi et salvavi animam meam* [Speak and save my soul]. [//]

We regret that you took so very much trouble and, meanwhile, have sung your *Lied an die Ferne*.[139] //

---

[132] See Blatt 21v below.—TA

[133] Alto singer Caroline Unger had previously visited Beethoven on Saturday, January 17, 1824; see Heft 53, Blätter 10v–13r.—TA

[134] The German editors could not locate any further information concerning the Baroness Lirveeld, whose first name seems to be Mathilde (not a common name in Vienna), and who seems to have lived or lodged in the *Igel* in the Tuchlauben; see also Blätter 21v–22r below. The present editor has considered a possible reading of "L" as a "B," as well as several alternative phonetic spellings, and has not been able to locate any similar names in the lists of performing members in the Gesellschaft der Musikfreunde, as given in Böckh (reflecting 1821) and Ziegler (reflecting fall 1822). It is possible that she was not actually a resident of Vienna but a visitor from elsewhere. The "Arrivals" in the *Wiener Zeitung* from December 1, 1823, through January 30, 1824, do not indicate anyone by this name, although such lists were often selective.

A survey of the Conscriptions-Bögen for the *Roter Igel* (Stadt 550 and 558) and *Blauer Igel* (Stadt 557), including the *Fremden-Tabellen* from 1824 for 550 and 557, has failed to reveal any woman named Mathilde or any surname resembling Lirveeld. She may have been a brief visitor to Vienna from northern Germany or even England (where the name could have been something like Deerfield).

Perhaps coincidentally with the name Mathilde, an advertisement in the *Wiener Zeitung*, No. 51 (March 3, 1824), p. 228: "At Wallishauser's: *Unterhaltungs-Bibliothek* (anthology), 15 vols; Part 2 including an item by Vienna's Johanna Franul von Weissenthurn, and also *Mathilde von Merwald* by K.L. Woltmann."—KH/TA

[135] At 3 p.m. on Thursday, January 29, Vienna experienced rain mixed with snow and a temperature of 37 degrees Fahrenheit. See the *Wiener Zeitung*, No. 25 (January 31, 1824), p. 115.—TA

[136] The third performance of Kreutzer's *Der Taucher* took place on Wednesday, January 28, 1824; see Blatt 6r above.—TA

[137] Presumably Baroness Lirveeld, to whom Schindler refers as "Fräulein v. Lirveeld" in his annotation on Blatt 21v below.—TA

[138] See Blatt 17r above.—TA

[139] Probably Beethoven's *Lied aus der Ferne*, WoO 137, dating from 1809 and published by Breitkopf & Härtel in 1810. See Kinsky-Halm, pp. 603–604.—KH

What answer should I give Duport? When are you giving your Akademie? If one has the Devil *once*, then he can be satisfied. [//] [Blatt 20v] It would be best on a *Norma* Day[140] during Lent, when 3–4 [concerts] take place. [//] If you give the concert, I guarantee that it will be full. [//] You have too little self-confidence; haven't the ovations from the whole World made you just a little proud? [//] Who, then, speaks of objections? [//] Then won't you come to believe that people are longing to worship you in new works again? O Obstinacy! [//]

I have *none*—How many Beloveds do *you* have? [//] <Shall I [no verb] Frau v. S>[141] [//]

[Blatt 21r]

SCHINDLER [**possibly diverting everyone's attention from the previous subject**]: She will get sick from the black coffee. [//]

UNGER [**seemingly bringing the conversation and the visit to a discreet close**]: Tomorrow [Friday, January 30].[142] //

It [presumably the coffee] is too good and makes young girls too hot. Also, the beautiful eyes of my neighbor here[143] could become too dangerous to you. // But don't make any fuss over your friends.

But he [Kreutzer] is leading the whole [performance] very well;[144] we are all

---

[140] German *Norma Tag*, high feast days in the Catholic Church, with a solemn celebration of the Mass and a prohibition of public revelry.—KH

[141] Beethoven may have teasingly asked Unger how many beloveds she had, and she answered in the present tense, "I have none," and then asked him in return how many he had. At this point, he may have mentioned a woman, possibly noble, with a surname beginning "S."

From ca. 1804 to ca. 1807, and even later, Beethoven had been romantically involved (though without any hope of marital fulfillment) with the widowed Countess Josephine von Deym (*née* Brunsvik), who was born in 1779 and died on March 31, 1821. In 1810, she married Baron Christoph von Stackelberg (1777–1841); the marriage was seemingly unhappy. In several scholarly circles, she is thought to have been Beethoven's "Immortal Beloved" in the summer of 1812.

In this case, Beethoven might have mentioned a Frau von Stackelberg, to which Unger might playfully have intended to write something like, "Shall I speak to Frau v. S.?" (with different word order in German), and Beethoven might have replied (possibly curtly) that she was dead, even before Unger finished writing the sentence.

Thus, this conversational gambit came to an end, with Schindler awkwardly rescuing the situation.

See Rita Steblin, "'Auf dieser Art mit A geht alles zu Grunde': A New Look at Beethoven's Diary Entry and the 'Immortal Beloved,'" *Bonner Beethoven-Studien* 6 (2007), pp. 147–180.—TA

[142] The fourth performance of Kreutzer's *Der Taucher* took place on Friday, January 30, 1824; see Blatt 6r above.—TA

[143] Unger refers to her *Nachbarinn*, meaning the baroness sitting next to her, reflected in the translation above.—TA

[144] Presumably the composer of *Der Taucher*, Konradin Kreutzer, now on the Kärntnertor Theater's conducting staff.—TA

satisfied. [//] He is very skillful and treats the whole company with the greatest respect and tact. [//]

Do you also love the French as I do?[145] A hearty farewell; we shall come again soon. [//]

[Blatt 21v]

SCHINDLER: The coachman doesn't want to wait any longer; he belongs to the theater. [//]

LIRVEELD [departing Beethoven's apartment with Unger; presumably the afternoon of Thursday, January 29]: I shall mark the day that good fortune brought me to make your acquaintance.[146] *Mathilde L.* //

SCHINDLER **[after the women depart]**: She is a baroness, but I don't know what her name is.[147] // As Unger says, she is supposed to be a good singer. [//] [Blatt 22r] At the *Igel*, Unter den Tuchlauben, 1st floor [2nd floor, American].[148]

BEETHOVEN [at a coffee house; late afternoon of Thursday, January 29]:
+ Mörschner u. Jasper:[149]

Der fertige Orgelspieler, oder Casualmagazin für alle Fälle im Orgelspiel[e], edited by C. Güntersberg; First Part, and 1st Division of the Second Part; [size] quarto; Meissen. Together, 4 fl. C.M. //

Das Wichtstigste über Einricht[ung] u. Beschaffenh[eit] der Orgel u. über das

---

[145] Unger would later marry a Frenchman.—TA

[146] This sentiment seems more typical of visitors from afar who met Beethoven than of residents of Vienna.—TA

[147] It appears that Beethoven had asked Schindler what the visitor's name was, and that neither of them could make sense of the surname as Unger had written it on Blatt 19v above.—TA

[148] In this street, there were two, and even *three*, buildings by this name: Tuchlauben No. 557, *Zum blauen Igel* (At the Blue Hedgehog); and immediately west of it, No. 558, *Zum rothen Igel* (At the Red Hedgehog), which was connected to No. 550 behind it, which *also* bore the name *Zum rothen Igel* but actually faced the Kammerhof.

Unter den Tuchlauben No. 558 contained not only a well-known restaurant but also the Gesellschaft der Musikfreunde's concert hall and the Born and Baumgartner boardinghouse. See Guetjahr, p. 26; Pohl, *Gesellschaft der Musikfreunde*, p. 12; and Behsel, p. 17.

It is possible that Baroness Lirveeld did not occupy an apartment of her own but may have been a foreign visitor staying with friends. It seems that Beethoven *was* taken by her eyes, as Unger observed, and that he was momentarily smitten with her.—KH/TA

[149] Mörschner und Jasper, book dealers, Kohlmarkt, Count Clary's House, No. 257, had earlier advertised these two organ books, published in Meissen, in the *Wiener Zeitung*, No. 7 (January 10, 1824), p. 32 (Advertisements); and now, No. 23 (January 29, 1824), p. 107; and later in No. 40 (February 19, 1824), p. 178. The organization of the Güntersberg book is somewhat unclear, but Beethoven (as usual) copied the two consecutive advertisements with remarkable accuracy. He copied the second advertisement again on March 5, 1824; see Heft 57, Blatt 33r.—KH/TA

zweckmässig[e] Spiel derselb[en], by W.A. Müller; with 3 illustrations;   [Blatt 22v] [size] octavo; Meissen. 30 kr. C.M. [//]

+ Small matches; candles, etc., with Karl.

+ Blotting sand. [//]

[Blatt 23r]

NEPHEW KARL [**presumably at Beethoven's apartment; the early afternoon of Friday, January 30**]: The locksmith already appeared to be vexed about having to write out what the work cost. He already wanted to be paid yesterday,[150] but I said that his master was only to send the bill for the work that was done, which, however, did not happen, because he only wrote it out when he was *here*. // The housekeeper says that you only instructed her to bring the slip back with her. //

I saw Langer. He is writing a great deal in the journals.[151] // He is no longer studying now. [//] For beginners. [//]

4 fl. 80 kr.   [=] 5 fl. 20 kr.
2 fl. 30
―――――――
2 fl. 50 //

Thursday.[152] [//]

[Blatt 23v]

SCHINDLER [**at Beethoven's apartment; probably ca. 2 p.m., over midday dinner, Friday, January 30**]: When you come from here, the first *Gasse* [street] to the left, into the *Grosse Schullerstrasse*, and the house is right there, the first one on the left.[153] //

The soup should have simmered longer. //

Just don't rub your eye a great deal; otherwise it may get bad again. //

---

[150] The locksmith came on Thursday, January 29 (Blatt 19r above), before Caroline Unger's visit.—TA

[151] Johann Langer (1793–1858); see Blatt 3r above.—TA

[152] Beethoven may have asked Karl what day of the week yesterday was.—TA

[153] This concerns the house in the City, Kumpfgasse No. 825. Schindler describes walking from Beethoven's apartment across the Glacis, then through the Stubentor, turning left one block into the Grosse Schullerstrasse, walking one street north, then turning left into Kumpfgasse. In the first floor [second floor, American], apartment 7, lived the piano teacher and composer Franz Pfeiffer (b. 1772), who is discussed as a copyist. In apartment 13 lived the violoncellist Friedrich Wranitzky (ca. 1796/98–1840), member of the Kärntnertor Theater's orchestra since summer 1822. See Conscriptions-Bögen, Stadt, No. 825 (Wiener Stadt- und Landesarchiv); Böckh (1822), p. 384; Frühwirtscher Grundriss; Guetjahr, p. 38. For the same address, also inconclusive, see Heft 57, Blatt 21r.—KH/TA

Kalkbrenner is supposed to leave today.[154] // He carried the victory in it [the comparison with Moscheles]. //

Moscheles lies in bed in Prague, dangerously ill with "sand and stone."[155] //

Don't be annoyed with these people because they are lacking in goodwill. The old woman [former housekeeper Barbara Holzmann], when she comes, will be better in all respects. // [Blatt 24r] The building superintendent was perhaps solely to blame. // I consider the old woman to be much better than the maid, who comes from the lowest dregs. // The most common. // The main point, though, is that you can entrust everything to her, even if the cooking is not always what you'd like. // They don't [get] more than 80 fl. [annually] in any house. [//] [Blatt 24v]

Hensler[156] inquired about your health and asked me to ask you if you could do without the score to the *Ruins [of Athens]*, that you send it to him, because he wants to use the Overture from it soon. // Today you will probably have the pleasure of seeing him at your place, or he will seek you out in the coffee house.[157] He was already out here the other day, but he couldn't find your apartment because he had forgotten the number. //

Grillparzer is now quite healthy again. //

Will you have the whole score copied? It would be good if you could always have a copy at home. [//] [Blatt 25r] Afterward, don't forget *Fidelio*, which is especially recommended, because it is especially necessary that you have it at home.[158] [//]

BEETHOVEN [possibly at a coffee house; late afternoon of Friday, January 30, reading a two-week-old newspaper]:

+ At Bauer's: Bald (Jac.), *Carmina*, etc.; 4 fl. 15 kr.[159] //

---

[154] Kalkbrenner and the harpist Dizi did not leave Vienna until Saturday, January 31, 1824. See the *Wiener Zeitung*, No. 27 (February 4, 1824), p. 123 (Departures).—KH/TA

[155] Brother Johann had already reported essentially the same malady (probably kidney stones) on Wednesday, January 28 (Blatt 16v above). Nephew Karl would do so on February 2 (Blatt 32r below) and again on February 29 (Heft 57, Blatt 16v; similar pagination coincidental).—TA

[156] Manager of the Theater in der Josephstadt, where Schindler was concertmaster.—TA

[157] This places the time of Schindler's present visit in midafternoon or earlier, since Beethoven customarily went to a coffee house late in the afternoon.—TA

[158] On ca. November 21, 1823, Schindler had told Beethoven that twelve operas were missing from the Court Theaters' library, and that, fortunately, *Fidelio* was not among them. Even so, he had recommended that Beethoven should have a copy made for himself. See Heft 46, Blätter 6v–7r.—TA

[159] Excerpt from an advertisement in the *Intelligenzblatt*, No. 12 (January 16, 1824), p. 100: "Appearing at B. Ph. Bauer, book dealer, on the Freyung, in the Schottenhof: Balde (Jac.), *Carmina selecta*, edited by Franc. Rohn, Professor of classical humanities in the Imperial Royal Gymnasium at the Schottenstift; large octavo; Vienna, 1824; 4 fl. 15 kr." The advertised volume was a collection of annotated poems by the author Jacobus Balde (1604–1668). A Jesuit priest, Balde wrote in modern Latin rather than German. He lived and taught in Innsbruck, Ingolstadt, Munich, Landshut, and Neuburg on the Danube.

Bauer did not advertise every day in the *Intelligenzblatt*, but his advertisement in No. 24 (January 30,

JOHANN VAN BEETHOVEN [at Beethoven's apartment; possibly early afternoon of Saturday, January 31]:

I want to go shopping for you with Karl. //

Lichnowsky was at my place; he will come to see you. You should write the letter to Count Neuberg [Neipperg] right away, and then he [Lichnowsky] can send it.[160] [//]

[Blatt 25v]

SCHINDLER [at Beethoven's apartment; possibly late afternoon of Saturday, January 31]: At dinner [*Tische*], you stuck a gulden bill in your pocket [*Tasche*]; it might get lost if you forget about it. //

JOHANN VAN BEETHOVEN [at Beethoven's apartment; possibly returning after shopping on Saturday afternoon, January 31]: You should send word to Grillparzer to come and visit you; if you want, I'll go to see him. //

I spoke to Kanne[161] today; he sends greetings and will come to visit you soon. //

Hasn't Schuppanzigh brought you any reply concerning Bethmann yet? //

If you want to, we could go to the Theater in the Josephstadt. [//]

[Blatt 26r]

NEPHEW KARL [presumably at Beethoven's apartment; late afternoon of Saturday, January 31]: I am leaving earlier. // Tomorrow is too full; plus, on Sundays they present only popular spectacles.[162] // It's not a half hour's walk from the City out there;[163] otherwise, it's good if I get the exercise. //

[possibly ca. midday on Sunday, February 1:]

When I came, they were screaming outside; I asked what was going on, and they said that you had been out and had made a terrible row. // Without a doubt, the housekeeper alarmed the maid by her gossip. Now, what shall we do? Do you still want to retain *her*? [//] [Blatt 26v]

Right at the beginning, I was also not for taking the old woman [former housekeeper Barbara Holzmann] on again, because I remembered the kinds of tricks that

---

1824), p. 202, featured an entirely different book. Therefore, Beethoven was, for some reason, reading a copy that was two weeks old.—KH/TA

[160] See Lichnowsky's visit on Blätter 33r–34v below.—TA

[161] Friedrich August Kanne (Johann spells his name "Kani"), editor of the *Wiener Allgemeine musikalische Zeitung*, whose publication was suspended during January and February 1824.—KH

[162] This entry may be determined to be on Saturday, January 31, 1824. On this day, the Josephstadt Theater presented Isouard's *Aschenbrödel*, and on Sunday, Meisl and Gläser's *Arsenius*.—KH

[163] Karl's estimate is accurate. From St. Stephan's Cathedral, for instance, to the Theater in der Josephstadt is roughly a half-hour's walk.—TA

[NEPHEW KARL, *continued*]

she played, and that it was *impossible* to retain her if the conduct of the housekeeper who followed her led us, to some extent, to miss the old woman [housekeeper Barbara Holzmann]. She would probably be better than the one we've had up till now, and if (having learned her lesson over several months that, presumably, were not exactly pleasant)[164] she perhaps ceased her grumbling, it would be the best. //

Do you want to take on the old woman [Holzmann]? It must probably be decided by Tuesday [February 3]. //

I did not tell you that they complained to *me*; rather they were silent—on the contrary *quiet*—when I came. // As often as you have some [problem] with the domestic servants, I must bear the guilt for it; I don't know how it comes to that. [//] [Blatt 27r]

If you had been more accessible, everything would have been different long ago. If you place so much confidence in the merchant's wife or whoever *she* is, why haven't you taken her on long ago? //

How would it be if you were to take the maid to the old woman [Holzmann]? We have already seen sufficiently that the housekeeper and maid only seldom got along well; because either the maid was herself already a cook (as is the case here) and doesn't want to be ranked below another cook, or the maid is young and untidy and doesn't like it if the housekeeper nags. It would be entirely different if the maid were to come to the old woman, hoping to succeed her at some time in the future, and therefore treat her as if she were her mother to a certain extent, and everything would be better than with *new* maids of that type. [//]

What is she doing *now* as a maid? [//] [Blatt 27v] I'll learn everything tomorrow. // Saffron.

14 [the number of rolls for two days] //

2 for breakfast
3 for midday dinner
2 for the evening
---
7 rolls[165] [//] [Blatt 28r]

The maid just told me that the housekeeper is gossiping with all the people in the building and is telling everything that happens here. Recently the housekeeper had the superintendent's wife taste the venison that we gave away, and asked her if it wasn't good enough for any nobleman's table. But the building superintendent who installed

---

[164] Beethoven had presumably dismissed Barbara Holzmann (or she had resigned) by the end of September 1823. See Heft 44, Blatt 1r.—TA

[165] Karl uses the Austrian term *Semmel* rather than the German *Brötchen*. The amounts are sufficient for Sunday and Monday (Candlemas, a national holiday).—TA

the stove was sensible enough that he said that it did not concern *him*, and that she should stop with her stupid gossip.—The maid said this. //

The building superintendent is here. //

[Brother Johann also probably arrives; Karl writes, in part, on his behalf:]

Your brother says that the old woman [Holzmann] looked very happy when she learned that she was to come back; I believe so, *too*. // You will probably have told her to come on Monday. // I believe that she has work [on that day]. // She didn't say anything that she wanted to stay here; but the both of them certainly know that the other one isn't coming, because all of this is connected. [//] [Blatt 28v]

I don't think that she is complaining; only the old woman always complains; the maid, however, absolutely never gets along with her. It seems curious to me that Schindler doesn't want to write down *what she said*; I must admit to that. // Who knows why he wrote the whole thing to you? // Therefore one should not hold her accountable. //

At the theater, he [Schindler?] told your brother: "There was heavy weather in the Landstrasse today," and then added as an explanation that you were very monosyllabic and vexed. //

She says that you hadn't ordered anything. She therefore believed that you would get something from the restaurant.[166] //

Your brother told me terrible stories about him. // [Blatt 29r]

Do you believe in "sympathetic cures"? // A new book has come out, discussing sympathetic cures for various ills, among them deafness. Also, there is a reminder in the announcement that people who are afflicted with such problems should only make an *attempt* [at these cures], so that no *harm* might be done. // It was in the *Zeitung*.[167] //

You must have slammed the cupboard too forcefully when shutting it a while back, because everything is loose. The housekeeper wanted to get some apples from it for the herring that we brought,[168] and everything came apart. //

[Blatt 29v]

JOHANN VAN BEETHOVEN **[returning to Beethoven's apartment, seemingly with nephew Karl, after Schuppanzigh's concert; ca. 7 p.m. on Sunday, February 1]**:[169] The third Quartet was one of your last ones;[170] it not only overwhelmed the first two [works

---

[166] Then, as now, there was a restaurant on the street floor of the apartment building where Beethoven lived (corner of Ungargasse and Bockgasse/Beatrixgasse). See Blatt 30v below.—TA

[167] Original German *sympathetische Curen*, "sympathetic cures" or hypnosis.—TA

[168] They are projecting a herring salad made with the fish, apples, onions, pickles, and other ingredients, mixed with a cream or yogurt sauce.—TA

[169] The ensuing conversation seemingly lasts through the beginning of Blatt 32r.—TA

[170] Therefore, either Beethoven's Op. 74 or his Op. 95.—TA

on the concert], rather the whole audience was just as delighted as with your Septet last Sunday [January 25]. I am not in a position to say which of the two aroused more enthusiasm.[171] // Schuppanzigh told me that the money is secure. //

Give me the letter from Bethmann[172] and I'll go with Karl or alone, and assure you that I'll bring the money within 3 days. //

[Blatt 30r]

NEPHEW KARL [seemingly writing for himself]: Kirchhoffer[173] was also at the quartet concert; Kalkbrenner has left.[174] Also Schickh[175] was there, along with Tuscher,[176] Piringer, Wolfmayer,[177] and many others whom you know. //

What should I order at the restaurant? //

JOHANN VAN BEETHOVEN [presumably while Karl was away at the restaurant]: If it is too difficult for you, you can get half of the money from the Berliner [Bethmann]; I'll still wait with the other one until you can. But you should also write to Schlesinger in Paris concerning the [*Consecration of the House*] Overture and *Bagatelles* and Lieder,[178] because *now* there is absolutely nothing to be done with them here. //

---

[171] This concerns the Schuppanzigh Quartet's sixth concert in its third subscription series, which took place at the Gesellschaft der Musikfreunde on Sunday, February 1, 1824, at 4:30 p.m. The precise content of the program is unknown, since the *Allgemeine musikalische Zeitung* (as usual with Schuppanzigh's concerts) merely reported that it had taken place; the *Wiener AmZ* did not appear during January and February 1824; Schickh's *Wiener Zeitschrift*, although reviewing the first five concerts of this series, did not report on the sixth; and a copy of the program (even handwritten) does not survive in the files of the Gesellschaft der Musikfreunde.—KH/TA

[172] Berlin theater director Heinrich Bethmann had arrived back in Vienna on January 21, 1824, and was staying in the Hotel *Zum ungarischen König*, Grosse Schullerstrasse No. 852; see the *Wiener Zeitung*, No. 18 (January 23, 1824), p. 81.—KH/TA

[173] Franz Christian Kirchhoffer (1785–1842), Beethoven's sometime financial adviser in his business dealings with Ferdinand Ries in England. See Clive, pp. 185 and 265.—TA

[174] Kalkbrenner and the harpist Dizi departed Vienna for Munich on Saturday, January 31, 1824. See the *Wiener Zeitung*, No. 27 (February 4, 1824), p. 123 (Departures).—KH/TA

[175] Johann Schickh (1770–1835), editor of the *Wiener Zeitschrift für Kunst, Literatur, Theater, und Mode*. See Frimmel, *Handbuch*, II, pp. 103–104; Clive, p. 208.—KH/TA

[176] Mathias Tuscher, Magistrat's councillor, member of the representative body of the Gesellschaft der Musikfreunde and a performing member (as a singer). He had served as nephew Karl's guardian from March 26 to July 5, 1819. See Böckh, 1822, p. 353; *Hof- und Staats-Schematismus*, 1824, I, p. 668; Thayer-Deiters-Riemann, IV, pp. 139–140 and 144; Thayer-Forbes, pp. 723–724 and 726; and Clive, 373–374.—KH/TA

[177] Johann Nepomuk Wolfmayer, Viennese cloth dealer and music lover; admirer and supporter of Beethoven and his music. In later years, he hoped to commission a *Requiem* from the composer. Karl spells his name Wolfmeyer. Wolfmayer and Tuscher will be mentioned in close proximity again on Blatt 39v below and Heft 57, Blatt 24. See Clive, p. 401.—KH/TA

[178] See also Blatt 14v above. For a good summary of the odyssey of these pieces, see Barry Cooper, *Beethoven*, pp. 302–304.—TA

NEPHEW KARL [**returning from the restaurant**]:
3 portions of roast veal at 24 kr. per portion   1 fl. 12 kr. [W.W.]
[Tip] to the waiter, 3 kr.   3 kr.
                                                    1 fl. 15 kr.

3 fl. 45 kr. left over.[179] [//] [Blatt 30v] We may be happy that we have the restaurant.[180] // There are apples as well.[181] // The meat is about 1 kr. C.M. more expensive. 8 kr. C.M. = 20 kr. W.W. //

[**writing, in part, on Johann's behalf:**]
The Russian czar with his whole Court are coming here at the beginning of Lent and going to Italy at the beginning of March. This could be good for your *Akademie*. // Galitzin is also coming.[182] [//] [Blatt 31r]
Your brother is laughing about counting the coffee beans.[183] //

JOHANN VAN BEETHOVEN: My coffee is always measured and always the same. //

NEPHEW KARL: Don't you want to send him the ham tomorrow morning? You'll get it back, boiled, by midday. //

JOHANN VAN BEETHOVEN: She makes soup too much. // The whole year, I don't worry about the kitchen. // She gets 200 fl. every month.[184] // She must pay extra for everything that comes from Krems.[185] [//] [Blatt 31v]

---

[179] Beethoven must initially have given Karl 5 fl.—TA

[180] This seems to confirm that Karl went to a restaurant within their building, Ungargasse No. 323, and implies that Beethoven might occasionally have been *un*happy that the establishment was present. Even today, there is a busy neighborhood restaurant, *Bierteufl*, at that location. In November 2004, Harvey Sachs sensationalistically described "reeking, rotting garbage, overflowing from bins" in the courtyard of the building (presumably generated largely by the restaurant), and that may have been a source of dissatisfaction for Beethoven in 1824, as well. Today the food and drink are excellent, and the waste is well controlled. See Sachs, *The Ninth: Beethoven and the World in 1824* (New York: Random House, 2010), p. 9; and Rudolf Klein, *Beethovenstätten in Österreich*, p. 133.—TA

[181] The apples would already have been in Beethoven's kitchen, possibly used in a herring salad, proposed on Blatt 29r above.—TA

[182] In the event, neither Czar Alexander nor Prince Galitzin came to Vienna in early 1824.—KH/TA

[183] Beethoven customarily counted out 60 coffee beans for each cup. See Schindler-MacArdle, pp. 386–387; Heft 51, Blatt 16r.—KH/TA

[184] This is probably the budget for the kitchen in Viennese currency (W.W.), equal to 80 fl. C.M.—TA

[185] Johann van Beethoven's estate, *Wasserhof*, in Gneixendorf was roughly two miles northeast of Krems, on the left bank of the Danube, ca. 35 miles northwest of Vienna. See Raffelsperger, II, p. 734, and III, p. 1224.—KH/TA

Do you want to give me the letter to Unger to take along? I know where she lives.[186] // If you order it, it will be harnessed and driven at your command. //

NEPHEW KARL: The maid bids her farewell. How much money on account has she received? // The maid has been here 17 days, so would get 4 fl. 52 kr.; after subtraction of the money on account,[187] 3 fl. 22 kr. [//] [Blatt 32r] She asks whether she shouldn't take 1 partridge for roasting? // What kind of roast? //

[at Beethoven's apartment, returning from Czerny's recital; possibly early afternoon of Monday, February 2 (Candlemas):]

The [kidney] stone is preventing Moscheles from getting to London;[188] so he'll come back here. //

He [Czerny] is said to have admitted that he didn't entirely understand your [Diabelli] *Variations*.[189] // But should they have removed the gentleman who disturbed everyone's pleasure by his unruly applause and pointing out the beauties that each person himself feels? // He wanted to demonstrate that he took the Variations very much to heart, and said (*during the playing*): "Pay attention to what's coming up; it's even more beautiful." [//] [Blatt 32v] How did you like the Waltz? //

Fratello [brother Johann] has promised to come. // [Blatt 33r]

Is the letter [to Neipperg] begun?[190] // He wants to write to him, but you must address him as *Your Excellency* and approach him very gently, because he is very proud. // Marie Louise[191] should agree and therefore take care of it. //

LICHNOWSKY **[at Beethoven's apartment; probably the early afternoon of Monday, February 2 (Candlemas)]**: For matters concerning the grand duke of Tuscany, let's turn to Odelga, to whom I shall go myself. //

NEPHEW KARL **[writing, in part, on Lichnowsky's behalf]**: Count Neuberg [Neipperg] has no influence on Tuscany. It concerns M[arie] Louise only; therefore, [Blatt 33v] the content of the letter is roughly this: "I have completed a *Mass*, to which so-and-so have subscribed; I hope that Your Majesty, the Empress M[arie] L[ouise],

---

[186] In Heft 55, Blatt 13v, Johann reports that he has delivered the note to her father, because she was at a rehearsal; and in Heft 56, Blatt 1r, Unger visits Beethoven and thanks him for the letter. Her address is given in Heft 56, Blätter 22v–23r.—TA

[187] German original *Drangeld*, an advance payment, or payment on account.—KH

[188] See the earlier references to Moscheles's kidney stones by pharmacist brother Johann on January 28 (Blatt 16v) and by secretary Schindler on January 30 (Blatt 23v). Karl would mention them again on February 29 (Heft 57, Blatt 16v; similar pagination coincidental).—TA

[189] Beethoven's *33 Variations on a Waltz by Anton Diabelli*, Op. 120.—KH

[190] See also Blatt 25r above.—TA

[191] Marie Louise (1791–1847), archduchess of Parma; see Heft 50, Blatt 10r.—KH/TA

might subscribe." // You will give the letter to the count to take with him, and he will then enclose it. //

Everything [in Kreutzer's *Der Taucher*] ends happily because of the protection by a fairy. // [Blatt 34r]

He [Lichnowsky] says that he is as happy as a child about the opera and the Akademie. // The count says that you are so indifferent, even though everything is ready and waiting for you. //

His little one[192] has a teacher whom [Carl] Czerny sent; he himself will take over with her in April. //

[Blatt 34v]

LICHNOWSKY [**continuing**]: Czerny hears her play every two weeks and the teacher must teach her entirely according to Czerny's method. // She already has a much better hand position. //

[Blatt 35r]

NEPHEW KARL [**similarly continuing, in part, on behalf of Lichnowsky and brother Johann**]: The king [of England] is singing duets with Rossini.[193] //

[**Brother Johann evidently stops by, presumably in his carriage:**]

Your brother would like to go to Streicher's to see the newly invented pianos; according to him, Czerny is also there.[194] //

[**The maid presumably brings food from the restaurant downstairs, enough for Beethoven, Karl, brother Johann, and Lichnowsky; probably ca. 2 p.m. on Monday, February 2 (Candlemas). Karl continues:**]

$$\begin{array}{r} 4 \text{ fl. } 52 \text{ kr.} \\ \underline{16} \\ 4 \text{ fl. } 68 \end{array}$$ [=] 5 fl. 8 kr. // The maid gets 5 fl. 8 kr. //

Your brother said that the old woman [former housekeeper Barbara Holzmann]

---

[192] Presumably Lichnowsky's young daughter, Josepha Maria; see Heft 44, Blatt 10, and Heft 48, Blatt 2r.—KH

[193] On the occasion of his visit to England in January 1824, Rossini was received by King George IV. Vienna's *Der Sammler*, No. 8 (January 17, 1824), p. 32, reported: "The king advanced to meet him, shook his hand very vigorously, and led him into his chamber, where Rossini enjoyed the distinction of having breakfast personally with His Majesty."—KH

[194] Streicher's piano shop and showroom were located at Ungargasse No. 371, perhaps a ten-minute walk south of Beethoven's apartment; see Behsel, p. 80, and Blatt 6v above. For a follow-up on the possible visit, see Heft 55, Blatt 1r.—TA

would very surely come tomorrow, and that she also told him that she is quite happy to be employed again, etc.[195] [//]

[After eating, Karl, Johann, and Lichnowsky go to Streicher's to see the new inventions, possibly demonstrated by Czerny. Beethoven remains at his apartment alone when Schindler arrives.]

[Blatt 35v]

SCHINDLER **[at Beethoven's apartment; presumably late afternoon of Monday, February 2 (Candlemas)]**: [written vertically→] Czerny was so obliging and gave me a preliminary hearing of your *33 Variations* [*on a Waltz by Diabelli*] on Sunday [February 1].[196] As a layman, I may not make any eulogy to you, but I was completely taken by the greatness and sublimity of this work, which probably won't be completely understood for several years, as Moscheles and Kalkbrenner (who don't understand it) have themselves said so; and Czerny has only now consecrated them [the *Variations*] in that way.

I want to invite Karl to go with me to Czerny's next Monday [*sic*][197] and also hear it, if you'll allow it. //

It is a holiday.[198] //

He will also play the last 3 Sonatas for us.[199] [←written vertically]

The Chronological Entries in Heft 54 End Here.[200]

---

[195] As a point of continuity, Barbara Holzmann is the subject of conversation in Heft 55, Blatt 1r.—TA

[196] Czerny gave weekly recitals to small audiences in his apartment in the City, Krugerstrasse No. 1006, and he seemingly did so on Candlemas morning, Monday, February 2. As a preliminary to that recital, he also seems to have played the *Diabelli Variations* for Schindler on Sunday, February 1. Schindler had evidently not seen Beethoven since Saturday, January 31, so was just now reporting the prehearing to Beethoven. See Ziegler, *Addressen-Buch*, p. 8.—TA

[197] Schindler probably means next *Sunday*, because the recital at Czerny's apartment described in Heft 55, Blätter 6v–8r, took place on Sunday morning, February 8, 1824.—TA

[198] Probably a reference to the day on which these entries were written: Candlemas, Monday, February 2, 1824. There is not another major holiday during the period under consideration.—KH/TA

[199] This would imply the three Sonatas, Opp. 109, 110, and 111. In fact, at his weekly recital on Sunday morning, February 8, 1824, Czerny reportedly played Beethoven's Piano Sonatas, Op. 106 ("Hammerklavier"), Op. 110, and Op. 111, as well as the *Diabelli Variations*. Schindler, nephew Karl, and Lichnowsky were in the audience at Czerny's apartment. See Heft 55, Blätter 6v–8r.—TA

[200] Two recent topics of conversation are followed up, probably within a day or so, in Heft 55: Streicher's new pianos and the potential reemployment of former housekeeper Barbara Holzmann, here in Heft 54, Blatt 35v, are again subjects of conversation in Heft 55, Blatt 1r, suggesting a relatively close continuity.—TA

Blätter 36–43 (Saturday, January 24 – ca. Monday, January 26), in their actual chronology (Blatt 43v – Blatt 36r), appear above in chronological sequence for those dates.

Blätter 44–46 (Thursday, January 22 – Friday, January 23) appear above in the chronological sequence for those dates.

End of Heft 54

Heft 55

(ca. February 3, 1824 – ca. February 12, 1824)

[Blatt 1r]

NEPHEW KARL [**presumably at Beethoven's apartment in the Ungargasse; possibly early afternoon, probably Tuesday, February 3**]:[1] I'll ask him how he found the pianos with Streicher's new invention.[2] [//]

She [former housekeeper Barbara Holzmann] is too old. // 70.[3] // There must be another cook by her side. // Granddaughter. //

I am no eye doctor. // Which doctor did you have last winter? // [Blatt 1v]

---

[1] As noted in Heft 54, two recent topics of conversation are followed up, probably within a day or so, in Heft 55: Streicher's new pianos and the potential reemployment of former housekeeper Barbara Holzmann (ca. February 2, 1824) in Heft 54, Blatt 35v, are again the subjects of conversation in Heft 55, Blatt 1r, suggesting a relatively close continuity. In addition, a capon is common to conversations in Heft 54, Blatt 43v (ca. January 24), and Heft 55, Blatt 2r. Frau Holzmann seemingly returns on/by March 5 (Heft 57, Blatt 32r).

While these entries may have been made after the return from Streicher's on the evening of Monday, February 2 (the Candlemas holiday), they were more likely made at about the midday dinnertime on Tuesday, February 3, 1824.—TA

[2] Johann Baptist Streicher (1761–1833); see Heft 54, Blätter 6v and especially 35r.—TA

[3] Barbara Holzmann (b. Vienna, 1755; d. Vienna, October 25, 1831) initially became Beethoven's cook and housekeeper in June 1822. By this time, she would have been ca. 68. If she were actually 69 (a possibility, given the inaccuracies of age in the Conscriptions-Bögen), then one could say that she was in her 70th year. Her son (d. 1822) had been a Court (or municipal) gilder, who had fallen upon bad times. See Heft 17, Blätter 15v–16r; and Rita Steblin, "Beethoven's Name in Viennese Conscription Records," *Beethoven Journal* 24, No. 1 (Summer 2009), pp. 9 and 13.

At first, Holzmann (who was at least phonetically literate) seemingly brought some order to Beethoven's household. Karl and others seldom humanized her by referring to her by her name; usually she was simply "*die Alte*" ("the old woman"); the appellation *Frau Schnaps* that unfairly characterizes her in earlier literature is based on one or two isolated references (Heft 35, Blatt 15r). By the middle of 1823, she may have suffered from some memory loss or was simply misunderstanding Beethoven's confusing instructions. In any case, Karl developed a certain dislike for her, and either Beethoven dismissed her or she resigned at the end of September 1823. Since then, however, Beethoven's household had never run as well as it had when she managed it. It seems that now (projecting a return) she is asking for some help, presumably her granddaughter (possibly the daughter of her son, the gilder), in the kitchen.—TA

It is only a question of whether sliding from a higher tone to the lower one without lifting the finger is allowed.[4] //

She asked you, but you gave her no answer. // Tomorrow in the *Zeitung* [newspaper].[5] // She told her that she wanted to come into our service. // The other woman asked the maid whether she had been here long, how things go here, etc., whereupon she replied. // [Blatt 2r]

He [possibly the building superintendent][6] prefers to come tomorrow. // That isn't necessary if he comes tomorrow. // How long? He has to do it. // At 2 o'clock. [//] He would prefer 1 o'clock. //

Is she to take a capon? One doesn't get them under 6 pounds or even 7–8 pounds. // For the evening? // It is one capon. //

Lichnowsky was also at Czerny's today.[7] // He looks worn out.[8] //

[It is possible that no datable entries were made in this Heft on Wednesday, February 4; Thursday, February 5; or Friday, February 6.]

[Blatt 2v]

GRILLPARZER **[at Beethoven's apartment; possibly Saturday, February 7]**:[9]
The censor's office has forbidden my tragedy *Ottokar*. // They won't even allow

---

[4] This question of the application of *portamento* in string playing was probably the result of hearing Schuppanzigh's Quartet concert on late Sunday afternoon, February 1 (Heft 54, Blatt 29v). Karl would raise it again after Schuppanzigh's Quartet concert of February 8 (see Blatt 8r below).—TA

[5] The *Wiener Zeitung* was not published on Monday, February 2 (Candlemas), a national holiday. No advertisement for the housekeeper's position at Beethoven's appeared in the *Wiener Zeitung*'s *Intelligenzblatt* during the remainder of this week, through Saturday, February 7. The advertisement (with a revised wording to include "a *Professionist*'s widow who can read, write, and cook well") would appear for one day *only*, on Wednesday, February 18, 1824.—TA

[6] By January 22–24, 1824, Beethoven was having problems with smokiness or improper ventilation in his apartment, and the building superintendent seemingly examined the stove several times and proposed various solutions. This may be one of those instances, although there seem to be no surviving conversational entries for the next day. See Heft 54, Blätter 5r, 14r, and 17v; as well as Heft 56, Blatt 4v.—TA

[7] Schindler wrote essentially the same thing on Blatt 8r below. This remark might pertain to Czerny's recital on Sunday, February 1 (and, if so, it is misplaced), but it may simply concern a visit by Lichnowsky on any day of this week to see his daughter's future teacher.—TA

[8] Original German *abgelebt* (worn-out, decrepit). Heft 57, Blatt 20v, confirms that Lichnowsky looked bad on Sunday, February 29, 1824.—TA

[9] The poet Grillparzer worked for the Imperial treasury and seldom got away for midday dinner before 3 p.m. on business days. Thereafter, he might have been free or he might have had to return to his duties until 6 or 7 p.m. This long visit (seemingly without feeling pressed to return to work) lasts through the middle of Blatt 5v and may have occurred on Saturday, February 7, 1824.—TA

[GRILLPARZER, *continued*]
it to be printed. // It is calculated too much for Austrian audiences.[10] // Who is concerned with Austria? // Unfortunately it is actually patriotic. // No one can understand why it should be forbidden. //

You have taken up *Melusine* again? // I have already turned to the directorship twice, but have received no reply. // I have already stated that I had to request 100 ducats for it. // [Blatt 3r] Because all the profit from an opera libretto is actually limited to that theater where it is first performed. // From the same material I could have made a spoken drama that would have paid me more than 3 times as much. // I *must* ask that much in order to fulfill my obligations to Wallishauser.[11] // They pay up to 300 fl. C.M. for usual opera libretti. //

Have you already begun to compose [*Melusine*]?[12] // Would you simply write out for me where you want changes? [//] [Blatt 3v] Because the piece must begin with a *hunt*. // Perhaps if the last tones of a rousing hunters' chorus just mixed in with the introduction, without the hunters themselves appearing onstage. // To begin with a chorus of nymphs would perhaps weaken the effect of this chorus at the end of the first act.[13] // I really don't understand opera texts. // You want to deliver it to the theater by September? // The directorship wants to raise its reputation with the public. [//] [Blatt 4r] Does the text of the opera also appear to be too long? //

To whom are you thinking about giving the role of Raimund? // People are talking about a young tenor, who is said perhaps not to have appeared onstage yet. I believe that his name is Cramolini,[14] and, in addition to a fair figure, is said to have a very beautiful voice. // They say that the directorship is having him instructed. // [Bass Anton] Forti is somewhat heavy, though. //

I therefore await your suggestions for changes *in writing*. Perhaps soon? // I am not busy now. [//] [Blatt 4v] I am ready to do everything. //

He [possibly Bernard] is somewhat prosaic. // An oratorio can also be *too dramatic*.

---

[10] Beethoven must have asked Grillparzer why he simply did not send *Ottokar* out of the country (perhaps to Berlin) to be performed. By the end of the conversation (Blatt 5v), Grillparzer indicates that he will consider it.—TA

[11] For a similar reference to the publisher, see Heft 50, Blatt 5v.—KH/TA

[12] Beethoven was often embarrassed or even irritated by such questions but seems to have replied gracefully that he had not begun to compose and that he was still looking through the libretto.—TA

[13] A rousing hunting scene at the beginning of the opera might have rendered much that followed as anticlimactic (as occurred later in Boito's *Mefistofele*), so Beethoven must have suggested opening with a less dramatic chorus of nymphs.—TA

[14] Ludwig Cramolini (1805–1884), tenor, made his debut at the Kärntnertor Theater on February 25, 1824, in the opera *Joconda* by Niccolò Isouard. Cramolini reported on his personal relationship with Beethoven in a memoir not published until long after his death. See the *Allgemeine musikalische Zeitung* 26, No. 12 (March 18, 1824), col. 187; *Beethoven-Jahrbuch*, ed. Theodor Frimmel (Munich and Leipzig, 1909), pp. 373–375; Eisenberg, p. 167; Kopitz and Cadenbach, I, pp. 191–197.—KH/TA

// If too much *action* that the audience doesn't see and therefore doesn't comprehend is presumed. //

<At Ha's. I have always [thought ends]> [//]

Actually, *can't* one portray Jesus Christ musically? // The music must portray *human* pains; then what does one do with *God*? [//] [Blatt 5r] I have always considered *Judith* as good material for an oratorio. //

Drahomira. // A great deal of variety, great characters, effects. // <Read the> The mother of the sainted Duke Wenzel of Bohemia.[15] // One of her sons killed the other. She herself is heathen; her better son is a Christian. // In Prague, they still show the place where she, along with her carriage and horses, were swallowed up by the earth. // [Blatt 5v]

If my hopes have entirely disappeared *here*, I'll send it [*Ottokar*] to Berlin. //

He [Archduke Rudolph?] is witty, but only for those who are his equals. At most, also for his *servants*. [//]

BEETHOVEN:

6	6
6	6
6	6
6	6
6½[16]	6½

[Blatt 6r]

SCHINDLER [at Beethoven's apartment; probably the early afternoon of Sunday, February 8]:[17] I recently encountered her [Unger], just as I left your place; she told me then that she would pay you a little visit, perhaps today or tomorrow.[18] //

The belief in Salieri's confession is also to be judged in that light. // It is absolutely no proof, it only strengthens the belief.[19] //

Was Grillparzer at your place? //

---

[15] The son of the heathen Drahomira (877/90 – after 935), Duke Wenzel I (Václav, "Good King Wenceslas") was born in ca. 907. He was raised as a Christian by his grandmother Ludmila (St. Ludmila) and was murdered by his brother Boleslav, leader of the heathen nobility, on September 28, 935.—KH/TA

[16] The first column is crossed out.—KH

[17] Schindler arrived after attending Carl Czerny's Sunday-morning recital. His entries, beginning here, seem to flow (alternating with Karl's) directly to their departure together for the Schuppanzigh Quartet's Sunday-afternoon concert on February 8, 1824.—TA

[18] Alto Caroline Unger seems not to have visited Beethoven again until Friday, February 13, 1824; see Heft 56, Blätter 1r–2r.—TA

[19] This concerns the rumor that Salieri had confessed to poisoning Mozart. See Heft 50, Blätter 13r–14r; Heft 54, Blätter 2v and 6r; and Thayer, *Salieri, Rival of Mozart*, pp. 153–154.—KH/TA

Weigl's lot has now been decided. Who would believe it? Gänsbacher is Kapellmeister [at St. Stephan's]. The archbishop really rammed it through.[20] [//]
[Blatt 6v]

His *Ottokar*? // They [artistic works] go to Schweiger,[21] but he is not here; therefore it may lie there a long time. // Is it the reply to the one that I delivered to the post office?[22] // I doubt it, because Hubertus[23] never comes here, so why should he pay for an apartment? //

So, how did I come by the title of Town Cryer [gossip]—*je vous en prie* [I ask you]? //

Today [Sunday, February 8], Czerny played us your B-flat, A-flat, and C Minor Sonatas, and, by *request*, the *Variations* again.[24] The B-flat Sonata gives him plenty to do. [//]

[Blatt 7r]

NEPHEW KARL: <They will ....>

SCHINDLER [**continuing**]: The fugue of all fugues is the Devil's; he [Czerny] had to take a rest.[25] // He was already tired, because he had already played a great deal. //

He[26] is certainly coming, and very certainly this morning, as he so dearly assured me, because he has the commission and will give it to you himself. // You'll rip off his head, if you take the little one by the ear. //

Perhaps the archduke will pay instead of his brother.[27] [//]

---

[20] In December 1820, it had been decided that Joseph Weigl would be the next Kapellmeister at St. Stephan's; but by ca. December 20, Archbishop Firmian announced his support for Johann Baptist Gänsbacher and got the earlier decision overturned, creating an awkward musical-political situation for the next several months. See, among others, Heft 50, Blätter 2r–2v, and Heft 54, Blatt 2v.—TA

[21] Presumably Baron Joseph von Schweiger-Lerchenfeld, Imperial royal major, treasurer of Cardinal Archduke Rudolph, who had departed for Prague on February 2, 1824. See *Hof- und Staats-Schematismus*, 1824, I, p. 194; *Wiener Zeitung*, No. 28 (February 5, 1824), p. 127; and Wurzbach, vol. 32, p. 358.—KH

[22] This letter does not seem to have survived.—TA

[23] Dr. Johann Hubertus (b. 1752), staff physician and personal physician to Archduke Rudolph, lived in the fashionable *Bürgerspital* apartment complex, City No. 1100. Carbon wanted an option on his apartment. See Conscriptions-Bögen, Stadt, No. 1100 (Wiener Stadt- und Landesarchiv); Groner (1922), p. 60; *Hof- und Staats-Schematismus*, 1824, I, pp. 120 and 195, and II, p. 126; as well as Blätter 19r–19v below.—KH/TA

[24] The semiprivate recital at Czerny's apartment consisted of Beethoven's Piano Sonata in B-flat, Op. 106 ("*Hammerklavier*"); Piano Sonata in A-flat, Op. 110; and Piano Sonata in C minor, Op. 111; as well as his *33 Variations on a Waltz by Anton Diabelli*, Op. 120.—KH/TA

[25] Beethoven's *Hammerklavier* Sonata in B-flat features frequent fugues of great difficulty.—TA

[26] Probably Schuppanzigh; see Blätter 10r–9r below. Schindler's sarcastic tone suggests that he has little affection for the violinist.—TA

[27] Seemingly a reference to Archduke Rudolph, perhaps in reference to the Kapellmeister's position at St. Stephan's.—TA

[Blatt 7v]

NEPHEW KARL: S[chindler] ate at your brother's yesterday [Saturday, February 7]; he has received unfortunate letters from Linz, in default of the money owed him from his apothecary shop. //

[presumably with all sitting down to midday dinner, ca. 2–3 p.m.:]
It [wine] only cost 16 kr. [//] From the same barrel. //

SCHINDLER: But it is roasted well. //

NEPHEW KARL: He [Schindler] is telling how your brother fought with his wife yesterday [Saturday, February 7]. //

SCHINDLER: They [Johann and Therese] never learn. // Now he is buying a house for 9,000 fl. C.M. in Linz, where he will open the apothecary shop. //
I don't want to hear any more music today, not even Schuppanzigh's Quartet concert; I still have the Sonatas in my head too much. [//] [Blatt 8r]
She will wash it out.[28] //
Lichnowsky was also at Czerny's.[29] // Czerny deserves all respect, because, among all the pianists, he is the only one who still loves *classical* music and especially studies your works with diligence and love, and really acknowledges openly that any success that he has in composition is owed only to the study of your works. //

[After dinner, Schindler and Karl depart on foot by ca. 3:45 for Schuppanzigh's 4:30 p.m. concert.]

NEPHEW KARL **[at Beethoven's apartment, returning from Schuppanzigh's concert; ca. 6:45 p.m. on Sunday, February 8]**: Piringer also played in the C-major Quintet, [Op. 29].[30] //
Something peculiar that I noticed at Schuppanzigh's is that he is accustomed to sliding with the finger on the string from one tone to another, so that, for example, he plays the tones [music notation], one hears the tones between [music notation] short and fast, like an unclear scale. Is that right?[31] [//]

---

[28] Something must have spilled at dinner.—TA
[29] Nephew Karl wrote essentially the same thing on Blatt 2r above.—TA
[30] On its concert of Sunday afternoon, February 8, 1824, Schuppanzigh's string quartet played Haydn's "Tost" Quartet in B-flat, Op. 55, No. 3; Mozart's Quartet in E-flat, K. 428; and Beethoven's String Quintet in C, Op. 29. As always when Schuppanzigh programmed quintets, Ferdinand Piringer (see Heft 53, Blatt 23v) played second viola. See *Wiener AmZ* 8, No. 12 (March 27, 1824), p. 45.—KH/TA
[31] On Blatt 1v above, Karl raised a similar question pertaining to the use of *portamento* at Schuppanzigh's Quartet concert of Sunday, February 1.—TA

[Blatt 8v]

UNKNOWN [possibly while Beethoven is running errands in the City; presumably the morning of Monday, February 9]: When will you be at home? I have a package from Herr von Schickh.[32] [//]

[Blatt 10v][33]

NEPHEW KARL [at Beethoven's apartment; in the late evening, possibly of Monday, February 9]: [written vertically, through Blatt 9r→]

$$\begin{array}{r} 1 \text{ fl. } 36 \text{ kr.} \\ \times 2 \\ \hline 3 \text{ fl. } 12 \text{ kr.} \end{array}$$ [//]

This evening I encountered [Maria] Pamer;[34] she looked destitute and tried to avoid me when she saw me, and I naturally also did the same. //
    Ham instead of *Kaiserfleisch*.[35] //
    It always takes several days until it [an advertisement] comes out in the *Zeitung*. It would be good if it were typeset, if not today, then *tomorrow*, so that it appears on Monday [February 16].[36] //
    Now have it sewn by the maid. //

[Blatt 10r]

SCHUPPANZIGH [presumably at Beethoven's apartment; possibly Tuesday, February 10]: 20 fl. W.W.   5 Thaler [=] 1 Friedrich[37] //
    Yes, there is nothing more now. [//]

---

[32] Johann Schickh was the editor of the *Wiener Zeitschrift*, which was publishing reviews of Schuppanzigh's concerts, and Beethoven might have dropped by its offices. The unknown writer was relatively literate and may have been an assistant on the journal's staff. The package may have contained complimentary copies of the *Zeitschrift*, whose subscription price was otherwise relatively expensive.—TA

[33] Blätter 9 and 10 were bound in reverse order. The entries on all four pages were written vertically.—KH/TA

[34] Maria Pamer (b. 1807), daughter of the popular dance band leader Michael Pamer (1782–1857), had been a young maid in Beethoven's employ before June 1822 but left or was dismissed, and occasionally expressed a desire to return, especially in late September 1823. See Heft 31, Blatt 52r; Heft 42, Blatt 24v; and Heft 43, Blatt 19r.—TA

[35] *Kaiserfleisch*: young, delicately smoked pork. See Loritza, p. 70. For an earlier conversational reference with anecdotal origins of the dish, see Heft 7, Blatt 41r.—KH/TA

[36] The advertisement appeared (one day only) in the *Wiener Zeitung*'s *Intelligenzblatt* on Wednesday, February 18, 1824. See Heft 56, Blatt 25v.—TA

[37] *Friedrichs d'or*: Prussian gold coins (1750–1855), corresponded in value between 5 and 5⅔ silver *Taler*.—KH

BEETHOVEN:
  12 fl. 30
    2   30
    2   30
  <2   30>
    2   30

SCHUPPANZIGH [in a column next to Beethoven's]:
  8 fl. 30 kr.
  10 fl.   C.[M.]
  24 fl.   W.W.
  16
    4
  ―――
  20   21. 15

SCHUPPANZIGH [**continuing**]: <I advis ….> Bethmann told me that they would forever preserve this work [the Overture and incidental music to *The Consecration of the House*] as a treasure. // [Blatt 9v] [entries written vertically→] They have no thought of giving out any part of it; on the contrary, Bethmann says that he wants to arrange it in such a manner that this music can be done at every ceremony. //

Herr Bethmann has had it calculated at the bank, and it comes to 87 Thalers. // Herr Bethmann is hesitating concerning the term used for the opening of the theater.[38] [//] [Blatt 9r]

Where is the document? // He [= You] must give it back to the Gesellschaft [der Musikfreunde]. // He [= You] must write that he [= you] received the amount. [//] [←end of entries written vertically]

[Blatt 11r]

NEPHEW KARL [**possibly at Beethoven's apartment; possibly Wednesday, February 11**]:

Herr S.[39] says that any proposal is certainly *better* than *this one*. // Or //

SCHICKH [**probably at the office of the *Wiener Zeitschrift*; probably late morning or early afternoon of Wednesday, February 11**]: Why then aren't you composing the Grillparzer opera yet? If you compose the opera first, then people can only hope that you will write a *Requiem*! // <You know ….>

Children and fools speak the truth. // [Blatt 11v] There are 100 to 1 odds that

---

[38] This is unclear; perhaps the northern Germans did not feel comfortable with the term *Weihe* (consecration).—TA

[39] It is not clear whether Karl means Schuppanzigh or Schickh (or even Schindler).—TA

Salieri's confession statement is true! // Mozart's manner of death confirms this statement! [//]

[Blatt 12r]

SCHINDLER [**presumably at Beethoven's apartment; probably early afternoon of Wednesday, February 11**]: But it astonishes me very much that you feel troubled about me on that account, since you see, though, what kind of <crossed-out> -stomach I have. //

NEPHEW KARL [**at Beethoven's apartment; probably early afternoon of Wednesday, February 11**]:[40] I encountered your brother in the City; he is still coming out here today. //

SCHINDLER [**seemingly continuing**]: You are so somber again, sublime master. What's wrong? Where has your cheery mood been for some time?[41] // Don't take it so much to heart; it is largely the fate of great men! // Many people are alive who can testify how he [Mozart] died, and whether there were symptoms. // He [Salieri] will have damaged Mozart more through his disapproval, than Mozart did to him.[42] [//] [Blatt 12v]

Do you know about Weigl's case as it stands now? // As is known, the archbishop protested against the government's decision. The documents had to be submitted to him, and he laid them out before the consistory which, quite naturally of the same mind as the archbishop, overturned the government's decision. Now the affair is dawdling along and will take a long time. //

NEPHEW KARL: <He wants the ....> //

---

[40] If brother Johann is coming yet that day, and if Johann (Blatt 13v below) says that there is a performance of *Der Taucher* "today," then today is Wednesday, February 11.—TA

[41] The German editors have not designated these entries as "falsified," but their unctuous tone is consistent with entries made after Beethoven's death.—TA

[42] By the mid-to-late-1780s, the popularity of Mozart's Advent and Lenten concerts may have threatened Salieri's two gigantic benefit concerts each season with the *Tonkünstler Societät*, and the elder composer may have reacted in a politically territorial manner. Such covert activities seldom leave a great deal of evidence, but Salieri may have reacted negatively to Beethoven's competing concerts at the Theater an der Wien on April 5, 1803, and *especially* on December 22, 1808.

After the latter occasion, Beethoven wrote to Breitkopf and Härtel on January 7, 1809, concerning "intrigues and cabals and meannesses of all kinds," adding: "The promoters of the concert for the widows, out of hatred for me, Herr Salieri being my most active opponent, played me a horrible trick. They threatened to expel any musician belonging to their [Court Theater] company who would play for my benefit" (Anderson, No. 192; Brandenburg, No. 350).

Thus, in 1824, Beethoven was still painfully aware of Salieri's reaction against his own activities and would have perceived parallel reactions against Mozart's successes in the 1780s.—TA

SCHINDLER [continuing]: Then the archbishop is said to have alleged that his [Weigl's] wife[43] would be much too arrogant to deal suitably with the *Sängerknaben* [Singing Boys], as necessary, and treat them [suitably]. [//] [Blatt 13r] Chambermaid to the late Empress Marie Therese.[44] //

NEPHEW KARL: They [simply] want Gänsbacher. //

SCHINDLER [continuing]: What would he [Haydn] have said, if you had brought him a sonata like the B-flat ["Hammerklavier"]? He would have had a stroke, because this would certainly be over his head.[45] // If Haydn had not lived, Mozart and you would have become exactly what you are. //

Böhm has returned from Paris.[46] He is bringing a package of music from Schlesinger[47] with him; he will deliver it to you himself one of these days. [//]

[Blatt 13v]

JOHANN VAN BEETHOVEN [at Beethoven's apartment; possibly at midday dinnertime, ca. 2 p.m., Wednesday, February 11]: It was boiled at my place. // Maybe it was boiled a little too long. //
To her father; she [Unger] was in rehearsal.[48] //

---

[43] Since 1805, Joseph Weigl had been married to Elisabeth Bertier, who had been listed in the Court directory of 1802 as a "chambermaid" to Archduchess Leopoldina. See *Hof- und Staats-Schematismus*, 1802, p. 421; Franz Grasberger, "Weigl," *MGG*, vol. 14, col. 379; Clive, pp. 391–392.—KH/TA

[44] This reference to Weigl's wife seemingly associates her with the wrong member of the Imperial family (see immediately above). Maria Theresia, generally called "Marie Therese" (1772–1807), daughter of Ferdinand I, was, from 1790, the second wife of Emperor Franz I. She had been an active advocate for music, and her early death was felt throughout the remainder of Franz's long reign. See John A. Rice, *Empress Marie Therese and Music at the Viennese Court, 1792–1807* (Cambridge: Cambridge University Press, 2003).—KH/TA

[45] Despite their reputed differences (upon which Schindler surely seeks to capitalize), Beethoven may have defended Haydn vigorously here and after the next entry, especially since, recently, he had probably modeled the third movement of his Symphony No. 9 after the slow movement (interrupted by fanfares) in Haydn's Symphony No. 60 (*Il distratto*), which the older composer might have shown him in June 1803 (see Landon, *Haydn: Chronicle and Works*, vol. 6, pp. 262–263).—TA

[46] Joseph Michael Böhm (1795–1876), violinist, professor at the Gesellschaft der Musikfreunde's *Conservatorium*, member of the Hofkapelle, and later a teacher of Joseph Joachim. On February 1, 1824, he had returned from a concert tour to Paris and Munich, where, on New Year's Day 1824, he had participated in a Court Akademie and, on January 22, had given a grand concert of his own. See Frimmel, *Handbuch*, I, p. 53; Clive, p. 38; Schickh's *Wiener Zeitschrift* 9, No. 46 (April 15, 1824), p. 392; *Wiener Zeitung*, No. 27 (February 4, 1824), p. 123.—KH/TA

[47] Maurice Schlesinger (1798–1871), music publisher in Paris; son of Adolph Martin Schlesinger, music publisher in Berlin. Young Schlesinger had visited Vienna (and Beethoven) in the summer of 1819 and would do so again in September 1825. The later visit is well documented in the conversation books for the period. See Clive, pp. 316–318.—KH/TA

[48] In Heft 54, Blatt 31v (Sunday, February 1), Johann offered to deliver Beethoven's letter to Unger; in Heft 56, Blatt 1r, she visits Beethoven and thanks him for it.—TA

Today [Wednesday, February 11] is *Der Taucher*,[49] so we should probably go to the loge. //

SCHUPPANZIGH [presumably at Beethoven's apartment; probably midafternoon of Wednesday, February 11]: He [= You] must sign this, and tomorrow morning, by 9 o'clock, send his [= your] nephew with the document and this receipt, [Blatt 14r] and then he gets the money.[50] // He is to go there after 10 o'clock or 10:30. // He is staying at home the entire morning. // He said at 9 o'clock; otherwise send him at 8 o'clock; that is all the same. // He is coming home late,[51] and therefore he might still be sleeping at 8 o'clock. [//] [Blatt 14v]

Bethmann tells me that he would have this form letter copied by another person, or might write it himself; it's all the same thing, only his [= your] signature is necessary. //

Has he [= Have you] already been at his place? // I was at his place concerning the story at Court,[52] and then I told him that I was coming to see him [= you], [Blatt 15r] so that he immediately committed himself to go with me. // He is very effective at Dietrichstein's, where it was clear that *nothing* will come out of this engagement. // Jekel[53] isn't getting anywhere; Jansa,[54] a prodigy of Worcziczek's.[55] // He is taking all possible pains, but Dietrichstein says that he proposed me, but that he doesn't know whom the emperor will choose. [//] [Blatt 15v] Baron Löhr[56] told

---

[49] Comparing the pacing of the entries with performances of Kreutzer's *Der Taucher* places this particular entry on Wednesday, February 11, 1824. See Heft 54, Blatt 6r (second half) for a list of all the performances in February.—TA

[50] Schuppanzigh's custom of addressing Beethoven in the third person becomes irritatingly cumbersome here, when dealing with instructions for Karl (also in third-person form) to run the composer's errands, but his meaning emerges nonetheless. Abbott and Costello could not have written it better.—TA

[51] If Karl is planning to see *Der Taucher* with brother Johann that evening (Wednesday, February 11), he will not be home until late.—TA

[52] Ignaz Schuppanzigh (1776–1830) had applied for a violinist's position in the Hofkapelle left vacant by the death of Zeno Franz Menzel on November 19, 1823. As noted here, it was given to young Leopold Jansa (1795–1875). Schuppanzigh would finally receive a position in the Hofkapelle in 1827. See Köchel, *Hof-Musikkapelle*, pp. 93 and 97; Clive, pp. 329–331.—KH/TA

[53] Anton Jeckel (ca. 1764–1834) had already been pensioned from the Burgtheater's orchestra at the end of 1822 but now sought this virtually tenured position with benefits; see Heft 54, Blatt 3v.—KH/TA

[54] Leopold Jansa (b. Wildenschwert, Bohemia, March 23, 1795; d. Vienna, January 24, 1875), violinist, came to Vienna to study law in 1817 but soon added composition to his unofficial studies. In 1823, he became a chamber virtuoso in Count Brunsvik's *Hauskapelle* but was appointed to the Imperial Hofkapelle in 1824 (replacing Menzel). He would become a major figure in Vienna's musical life in the next generation. See Köchel, *Hof-Musikkapelle*, pp. 93 and 97; Schilling, III, pp. 697–698 (for his correct employment in 1823, confirmed on Blatt 15v); and Ziegler, *Addressen-Buch*, p. 136.—KH/TA

[55] Jan Hugo Voříšek/Worzischek (1791–1825), Czech composer, held by Beethoven in high esteem and, from 1823, first Court organist. See Frimmel, *Handbuch*, II, p. 469; Clive, p. 382.—KH/TA

[56] Presumably Baron [*Freiherr*] Franz von Loehr, Court councillor, chancellery director of the I.R. high steward's office. See *Hof- und Staats-Schematismus*, 1824, I, p. 90.—KH

me this much: that, in his recommendation,[57] the count [Dietrichstein] praised Jansa extraordinarily. // [Jansa is] a young man of 20 years, engaged at Count Brunsvik's.[58] // I've really had enough of it here already. //

[Blatt 16r]

SCHINDLER [presumably at Beethoven's apartment; possibly late in the afternoon of Wednesday, February 11]: It [the matter of the Swedish Academy's diploma] is now at Minister Saurau's,[59] in the office. // This gentleman also works at Court and has done a great deal, so that it has finally been passed along; it is Herr Oberleitner, the well-known mandolinist.[60] //

NEPHEW KARL [presumably at Beethoven's apartment; presumably mid-to-late morning, Thursday, February 12]:
[arithmetical computations:][61]

1 # [ducat] : 4½ fl. = 87 # : X
1 : 9/2 [4½] = 87 [#] : X
2 : 9 = 87 [#] : X

$$2 \overline{\smash{)}783} 391 \text{ fl. C.M.}$$
$$\,\,9$$
$$18$$
//

We only need to know whether she is a *Professionistenwittwe* [widow of a

---

[57] Such memoranda, discussing and recommending individuals for Court appointment, would mention the names and qualifications of the foremost candidates. Drafted by the office of the *Hofmusikgraf* (the count in charge of music), they were endorsed by the *Obersthofmeister-Amt* (office of the high steward) and forwarded to the emperor. With many annotations and endorsements, the document was then returned to the originating office for action.—TA

[58] Count Franz von Brunsvik (1777–1849), a longtime friend of Beethoven's. See Frimmel, *Handbuch*, I, pp. 79–81; Clive, pp. 63–64.—KH/TA

[59] Count Franz Joseph von Saurau (1760–1832), high chancellor and minister of the interior; see Heft 54, Blatt 18v.—KH/TA

[60] Andreas Oberleitner (b. 1786), at that time Court cellar servant, in later years Court silverware and banquet inspector; in addition, a virtuoso guitar and mandolin player, who also composed several pieces for these instruments. See *Hof- und Staats-Schematismus*, 1824, I, p. 99; Schilling, V, p. 192; Wurzbach, vol. 20, p. 454.—KH

[61] Arithmetical computations based on discussions on Blätter 13v–14r, probably reflecting funds received from Berlin for *The Consecration of the House*: seemingly 87 ducats at 4½ fl. per ducat, calculated in several ways to arrive at 391 fl. (actually 391 fl. 30 kr.).

Beethoven had evidently learned very little of multiplication and division at school in Bonn, and Karl's rhetorically based computations such as these cannot have helped the composer's comprehension of the process.—TA

handworker].[62] [//] [Blatt 16v] If possible you should decide today whether you are going to hire the one you have *seen* or have it [the advertisement] placed in the *Zeitung*, because otherwise it will be too late.[63] //

LICHNOWSKY [**presumably at Beethoven's apartment; possibly the afternoon of Thursday, February 12**]: I encountered Baron Schweiger's[64] brother, who gave me a letter to you from Archduke Rudolph; since his brother is in Prague, he could not send it to you himself. // [Blatt 17r][65]

The directorship agrees to everything that you wish concerning the opera and, at the moment, is making arrangements with Grillparzer. // [Blatt 17v] On my part, you can certainly be convinced that I value your honor above everything. [//] [Blatt 18r]

My advice is that if you wish the participation of the [*Musik-*] *Verein*, you speak directly with Kiesewetter, in order not to concede to its gentlemen too much of the profit that could escape you. // [Blatt 18v] This time, in general, you must go to work *more economically* with the concert. //

<It is> I am going to see Saurau myself.[66] //

I'll come for sure in a few days. [//]

[Blatt 19r]

CARBON[67] [**at Beethoven's apartment; probably still on the afternoon of Thursday, February 12**]: Do you believe that I should write something to Dr. Hubertus himself,[68] since I am referring to what you are sending? // Perhaps he will answer more swiftly. // If there could be a reply, I ask [you] for a few lines; for this purpose I have noted my address. [//] [Blatt 19v] I am making so much trouble

---

[62] *Professionist* is an Upper German term for a handworker. See Heft 53, Blatt 15v, for the same term.—KH/TA

[63] As noted elsewhere, the advertisement for a *Professionist*'s widow appeared (one day only) in the *Wiener Zeitung*'s *Intelligenzblatt* on Wednesday, February 18, 1824. See Heft 56, Blatt 25v.—TA

[64] For Baron Schweiger, see Blatt 6v above. It could possibly refer to his brother, Baron Eduard von Schweiger. See *Hof- und Staats-Schematismus*, 1824, I, p. 77; *Wiener Zeitung*, No. 66 (March 20, 1824), p. 292.—KH

[65] Only the top half of Blatt 17 survives.—KH

[66] See Schindler's mention of Saurau on Blatt 16r above.—TA

[67] The author of these entries was initially unknown to the German editors, but see Heft 20, Blatt 5r, for their later identification of Franz Ludwig Carbon, landowner in Mödling who seems to have obtained some sort of a position in Vienna.—TA

[68] Dr. Johann Hubertus (b. 1752) was Archduke Rudolph's personal physician, who now spent most of his time with Rudolph in Olmütz and wherever his clerical duties took him, rather than in Vienna. Carbon had been coveting Dr. Hubertus's apartment in Vienna's fashionable *Bürgerspital* apartment complex for several months and had already tried to persuade Beethoven to intercede on his behalf in November 1823. This time, it seems that he succeeded. See Heft 45, Blätter 4v–5r.—TA

for you—please, if I can ever be of service to you, just ask me. // I shall surely remain, because I am employed here. // *Cataster* [land registry]. [//]

[Blatt 20r]

NEPHEW KARL [**at Beethoven's apartment, possibly arriving with Johann; possibly the afternoon or early evening of Thursday, February 12**]: Grillparzer is coming tomorrow. //

JOHANN VAN BEETHOVEN [**seemingly continuing**]: This certainly doesn't concern you at all. // You have certainly written the directorship that they are to come to an agreement with the poet, and therefore they are also satisfied; likewise, Grillparzer must also come to an agreement with them. //

If Streicher cannot make it,[69] he will surely take pains on behalf of your [piano]. //

NEPHEW KARL [**continuing**]: Streicher would also do it in vain. // [Blatt 20v]

He[70] is not a licensed *physician*. Merely a *surgeon*. // He may absolutely not treat *internal* illnesses as a physician. //

End of Heft 55

---

[69] Probably a device to enable Beethoven to hear the piano better. Stein had earlier attempted to make and attach such a device. Indeed, the reference in this sentence might be to Stein, with the reference in the next clause to Streicher.—TA

[70] Possibly Dr. Carl von Smetana (1774–1827), doctor of surgery, administrative physician, who operated on Karl for a hernia at Giannatasio del Rio's Institute in 1816 and later became Beethoven's physician for a while. See Frimmel, *Handbuch*, II, p. 185; Clive, p. 340.—KH/TA

Heft 56

(ca. February 13, 1824 – ca. February 20, 1824)

[Blatt 1r]

UNGER [at Beethoven's apartment in the Ungargasse; possibly late morning or early afternoon, presumably Friday, February 13]:[1] Please don't be angry with me if I disturb you, but I could no longer hold back my desire to see you and to ask whether you remember me.[2] [//] I thank you for your dear kind note;[3] I shall preserve this letter as a relic; it is only too bad that I don't deserve the title.[4]

I tried everything, but Duport can do nothing, since Hildebrand has the first claim.[5] [//] Weigl also hoped in vain, and Gänsbacher has become director at St. Stephan. [//] [Blatt 1v]

Do you have anything ready yet for *Melusine*? // [Bass Anton] Forti has read it [the libretto] and is delighted by it; I believe that he would be the most suitable person to sing the role of the *Ritter* [Knight]. [//] Shouldn't he [tenor Ludwig Cramolini?] be able to sing a lover with more skill than anyone else?

The Opera is said to be coming to the Burg. [//] They say that the Theater at the Kärntnertor will be newly built. [//] Twice as large. The decision will be made by the end of next month [March].[6] [//]

---

[1] Heft 55 had seemingly gone through Thursday, February 12, 1824. If Blatt 15 of Heft 56 was entered on February 15, there are enough breaks and shopping lists before that to indicate that this Heft was begun two or three days before. Similarly, the entries in Heft 56 seem to go through a Friday; therefore, February 20.—TA

[2] What Unger means in this context is whether Beethoven will "remember" her with a composition.—TA

[3] In Heft 54, Blatt 31v (evening of Sunday, February 1), Johann offered to deliver a note that Beethoven had written to Unger; in Heft 55, Blatt 13v, he reported that he had delivered it to her father (because she was in a rehearsal).—TA

[4] Since the letter was being delivered by brother Johann, Beethoven probably loaded the address with at least one inflated title.—TA

[5] Johann Hildebrand (b. 1790), second concertmaster at the Kärntnertor Theater; see Heft 49, Blatt 10r.—KH

[6] After a fire, the Kärntnertor Theater (the Court's second theater after the Burgtheater) had been rebuilt in 1763 but was subject to closure in times of economic difficulty (including the Balkan Wars from March 1788, to November 1791). By October 1810, the Burgtheater was in such disrepair that the

Why is your associate Herr Schindler absent today? [//] [Blatt 2r]

I want to tour all of Germany; do you believe that I dare risk it? [//] If I were to go in such company,[7] I would surely be received with open arms. [//]

I must now depart from your dear company, because I have stolen the time in order to come and see you. A hearty farewell; I'll come back soon and bring the beautiful [Henriette] Sontag to see you. [//]

BEETHOVEN:

$$\begin{array}{r} 45 \\ \underline{95} \\ 130 \\ 130 \\ <3> \\ I^8 \end{array}$$

[Blatt 2v]

NEPHEW KARL [**at Beethoven's apartment; probably early afternoon, before 2 p.m., Friday, February 13**]: Herr Schindler sends his deepest respects. // Your brother doesn't want to come for midday dinner, because he fears misconduct during his absence. //

From silk. //

It is really too bad about Schuppanzigh.[9] //

Your brother will already have told you that Duport is having Grillparzer's libretto [to *Melusine*] translated into French, so that he can study it thoroughly. [//] [Blatt 3r] Barbaja.[10] //

Court Opera was moved permanently to the Kärntnertor. Here it remained until the 1860s, when it was replaced by the much larger Court (presently State) Opera building, across the street to its southwest. See Groner, 1922, pp. 340 and 499–500.—KH/TA

[7] Beethoven probably said that he was contemplating such a journey.—TA

[8] The meaning of this is unclear.—TA

[9] Schuppanzigh had lost a violinist's position in the Hofkapelle to the young Leopold Jansa; see Heft 55, Blätter 14v–15v (ca. February 8).—KH

[10] Domenico Barbaja (1778–1841), Italian impresario and leaseholder for the Kärntnertor Theater through March 31, 1825. When Barbaja was in Italy, Louis Antoine Duport was his resident manager in Vienna. See Ziegler, *Addressen-Buch*, p. 71; Clive, pp. 96–97.—KH/TA

BEETHOVEN:

```
31 [fl.]
31
_____
62          38 fl.
            62
            _____
            100 [fl.]

  2 fl. 23 [kr.]
    40
    12
```

NEPHEW KARL [continuing]: But use the receipt that you received from Graz.[11] // Today is the W.[12] // Leschen, Ries.[13] // He was surely skilled. [//]

[Blatt 3v]

KIRCHHOFFER[14] [at Beethoven's apartment; the afternoon of Friday, February 13]: He[15] will wait for me. //

For my part, it ought not to come to a standstill. // We'll wait for 100 subscribers before we begin.[16] // I'll also get you a guarantee [of a minimum payment?], if you'd like. // Speak. // But we can wait until the end with that. //

[Blatt 4r]

NEPHEW KARL [possibly at a coffee house; possibly late afternoon of Friday, February 13]: I believe that that was a correspondent's report [about the theater in Berlin]. I read the same thing already on Saturday [February 7]; it also struck *me* the same way. //

This way, we come to the *best* and *least expensive* of the veal. // What kind of basis does he have for his opinion? //

---

[11] This may be a reference to subscriptions for a Schiller edition, to be published in Graz, noted on Blätter 4v–5r below.—TA

[12] "Today" was Friday the 13th, as well as a *Norma* Day in the church, but they do not fit into either custom or context here. Therefore, Karl's reference remains unclear.—TA

[13] Karl mentions two piano makers, Joseph Franz Ries (City, Alter Fleischmarkt), younger brother of Ferdinand Ries, and Wilhelm Leschen (Wieden, Alleegasse). For Ries, see Heft 51, Blatt 2r; for Leschen, see Heft 49, Blatt 10v, and Blatt 36v below.—KH/TA

[14] The German editors had previously identified this writer as the publisher Maximilian Joseph Leidesdorf but later determined that it was Franz Christian Kirchhoffer (1785–1842), Beethoven's liaison with Ferdinand Ries and sometime financial adviser. See *Konversationshefte*, vol. 3, p. 324, note <>21; Heft 34, Blatt 8v; Clive, pp. 185 and 255.—KH/TA

[15] Probably a coachman, given the brevity and singular subject of this visit.—TA

[16] Probably a reference to a projected collected edition of Beethoven's works.—TA

[The following entries on this page seem to deal with a visit to or by a tailor, also mentioned on Blatt 5v:]

$$\begin{array}{r} 44 \\ \underline{44} \\ 6\,|\,\underline{484}\,|\ 8\ \text{fl.}\ 4\ \text{kr.} \\ \underline{48} \end{array}$$

With today's 44 kr., [it totals] 8 fl. 48 kr. //
[written vertically→] He has no tape measure with him. [←written vertically]
[written vertically with scribbles→] Thursday [←written vertically]

BEETHOVEN:

$$\begin{array}{r} 44 \\ \underline{44} \\ 1\ \text{fl.}\ 28 \end{array}$$

[Blatt 4v]

BEETHOVEN [at his apartment; possibly the morning of Saturday, February 14]:
+ Mirror.
<+ Tailor.>
+ Stovepipe.[17]
<+ Glassmaker and locksmith.>
+ Blotting paper.
+ Blotting sand.
+ About the Schiller edition still at Meyer's, the copperplates, on domestic [Blatt 5r] vellum paper, 2 fl. C.M.[18] //

NEPHEW KARL [probably at Beethoven's apartment, after attending a late-morning rehearsal at the Theater in der Josephstadt; ca. 3 p.m. on Saturday,

---

[17] References to excess smoke and poor ventilation in Beethoven's apartment appear two or three weeks before, in Heft 54, Blätter 5r, 14r, and 17v.—TA

[18] Excerpt from an advertisement in the *Intelligenzblatt*, No. 35 (February 13, 1824), p. 294: "At Jacob Mayer and Co., book dealer, Singerstrasse, Deutsches Haus, subscriptions will be taken for the Copperplate Gallery for Schiller's Collected Works, Graz Pocket Edition in XXX volumes … subscription price valid until the end of March, 1824. Printed on domestic vellum paper for the ordinary edition, 2 fl. C.M.; English vellum paper … 3 fl. C.M."

The same advertisement had appeared in No. 27 (February 4, 1824), p. 230, and, most recently, No. 33 (February 11, 1824), p. 280. Judging from his insertion of *noch* (still), Beethoven may have responded to (or at least noticed) the advertisement earlier. A bookshop remains at that location even today. See also the remark about Graz on Blatt 3r above.—KH/TA

[NEPHEW KARL, *continued*]

February 14]: Gläser took great pains with the Overture;[19] they had a morning rehearsal until 2 o'clock; Schindler says that tomorrow it will go even better.[20] // If only the wind instruments were better! // The soldiers play horribly wrong.[21] // The notes were right already, but badly phrased.[22] // It [the Overture] must also make its effect *in this way*. //

At least it does no harm if it were to come out in the *Zeitung*, because nothing is to be done with the old woman [Barbara Holzmann] anyway.[23] // [Blatt 5v]

The tailor is here. Tomorrow. // One can pay him the money. [//] 2 fl. 30 kr.

[probably during a shopping trip in the City; mid-to-late afternoon of Saturday, February 14:]

Your brother was at [Carl] Czerny's. He told him that you have a concerto in the works[24] and (whether at your behest or not—I don't know) that Czerny was to play it in your Akademie. //

We will have to go back to the Kohlmarkt,[25] though. //

---

[19] Franz Joseph Gläser (1798–1861), son of copyist Peter Gläser, who would soon copy parts for Beethoven's Ninth Symphony. See Clive, p. 130.—KH/TA

[20] Beethoven's *Consecration of the House* Overture, Op. 124, was probably used as an overture to Hensler's *Der Feldtrompeter*, a half-evening play performed on February 15, 1824. See Bäuerle's *Allgemeine Theater-Zeitung* 17, No. 26 (February 28, 1824), p. 103.

The play dated from 1798. It had been arranged as a Singspiel by Joachim Perinet, with music by concertmaster Ferdinand Kauer at the Leopoldstadt Theater in 1808 (published Vienna: Wallishauser, 1808). Its first performance at the Theater in der Josephstadt took place on May 24, 1823, and it may have been performed there on December 6, 1823, with Beethoven's Symphony No. 2 (or excerpts from it), conducted by Schindler. See the *Allgemeine Theater-Zeitung* 16, No. 151 (December 18, 1823), p. 604; and Bauer, *Theater in der Josephstadt* (1957), p. 207.—TA

[21] In addition to the Josephstadt Theater's customary orchestral personnel, Beethoven's *Consecration of the House* Overture calls for an additional pair of horns and 3 trombones, evidently employed as extras from an army band, presumably stationed at the nearby *Alserkaserne*, where several of Vienna's most prominent regimental bands were quartered. Such bands were usually made up of civilians (rather than actual soldiers) who were at least relatively competent on their instruments.—TA

[22] Even today, most performances of the *Consecration of the House* Overture include tentative playing by the trombone section, who fail to sustain their notes with full intensity, even in the relatively easy opening march, where they provide the important structural continuity between the phrases elsewhere in the orchestra, and a strong transition to the fanfares that follow. One major exception is Otto Klemperer's recording with London's Philharmonia Orchestra on EMI.—TA

[23] Therefore, by this time, Beethoven (perhaps influenced by nephew Karl) had evidently decided not to reemploy former housekeeper Barbara Holzmann (though Blatt 19v below contradicts that); the advertisement would appear in the *Intelligenzblatt* on Wednesday, February 18 (see Blatt 25v below).—TA

[24] Ultimately, and at the last minute, Beethoven would request Czerny to play the Piano Concerto No. 5, Op. 73, on the varied repeat of his Akademie on May 23, 1824; see Albrecht, *Letters to Beethoven*, No. 366 (ca. May 20, 1824).—TA

[25] This probably refers to the Grocery Shop of Ignaz Spöttl's Late Widow's Son [!] on the Kohlmarkt, *Zum grünen Fassel* [At the Little Green Barrel], No. 260; on the north side of the street, two buildings west of Wallnerstrasse. See Groner, 1922, p. 102; as well as Heft 45, Blatt 19v.—TA

I really believe that Czerny would play the Concerto well under your leadership. Indeed, he has already played in the Grosser [Redoutensaal].[26] [//] [Blatt 6r]

There was nothing here but roast lamb, but since I know that you don't like to eat it, I didn't want to take it, all the more so since he said that the roast veal would be fresh. //

When she [Karl's mother, Johanna] wrote for the *first* time about money, I would and could raise no objection to it, but I can say that I immediately thought that we would find ourselves in a disagreeable situation again, because she doesn't rest. [//]

BEETHOVEN:

48
48
48 //

+ Blotting sand.
+ Carrying case.
Pencil.[27]
At the saddler's.
24
30

[Blatt 6v]

SCHINDLER [**at Beethoven's apartment, probably coming from the concert at the Josephstadt Theater; early afternoon of Sunday, February 15**]:[28] We struggled valiantly with the Overture yesterday [Saturday, December 14], but the *trombones* were not completely clean.[29] // The ones [trombonists] that we had in the past; some other ones had to play yesterday.[30] //

---

[26] Although Beethoven had played the Piano Concerto No. 5 in private at Prince Lobkowitz's Palace with members of the Theater an der Wien's orchestra before sending it off to Breitkopf und Härtel for publication, Czerny had played Vienna's first public performance at a benefit concert at the Kärntnertor Theater on February 12, 1812. He had also played it on Kärntnertor hornist Friedrich Hradetzky's own benefit concert at the Kleiner Redoutensaal on April 12, 1818. See the *Allgemeine musikalische Zeitung* 14, No. 13 (March 25, 1812), col. 210; and 20, No. 21 (May 27, 1818), pp. 388–389.—TA

[27] At some time before February 20, Karl bought a dozen pencils from an itinerant peddler at a beer house; see Blatt 32r below.—TA

[28] Although interrupted by Karl, who takes care of visits from the locksmith and woodcutter, Schindler's basic conversation lasts through Blatt 10r below.—TA

[29] At this point, Schindler added "(Op. 124)," which the German editors did not identify as falsified, although the opus number for the *Consecration of the House* Overture had probably not been determined by February 1824.—TA

[30] Saturday morning's rehearsal lasted until 2 p.m. See the brief account on Blatt 5v above.—TA

NEPHEW KARL [**seemingly interrupting**]: The locksmith. 1 fl. 30 [kr.] //

SCHINDLER [**continuing**]: Did you buy the wood yourself?[31] //
One can certainly get a good *Thaler* of [Styrian] wine at the *Birne*,[32] but for 2 fl. it's too expensive. //

NEPHEW KARL [**continuing**]: Schindler says that he doesn't understand why your brother doesn't give you an *Eimer*[33] of wine, since he has so much of it. //

[Blatt 7r]

SCHINDLER [**continuing**]: But you don't know that, at home, he [Johann] allows his wine to be guzzled by the baker's apprentices who open the barrels for him.[34] //
They have even unsealed sealed barrels. //
Then don't you want to take the housekeeper from the Leopoldstadt? // This is one person who has some brains and who really knows and esteems you <for what you really are> probably through her nieces. // She is very delicate and fragile. [//]
[Blatt 7v]
She really doesn't appear to care about a beautiful room. She told me that she only wished to be able to stay in Karl's room during the day when she has time. //

NEPHEW KARL: *Aline, Queen of Golconda*. // Müller.[35] //
They [the woodcutters] will come up when they are finished.[36] //
[at some time early in the following conversation with Schindler, Karl notes the money to be paid to the woodcutters on the top of Blatt 8r:]

---

[31] From additional stray references on Blätter 7v and 8r, it becomes clear that woodcutters have come to deliver the wood and receive payment.—TA

[32] The restaurant *Zur goldenen Birne* (At the Golden Pear), Landstrasse Hauptstrasse No. 52. See Groner, 1922, p. 42.—KH/TA

[33] *Eimer*, an old measure of capacity. One Austrian *Eimer* consisted of 40 Viennese *Mass* (measures), equaling 56.589 liters.—KH

[34] Johann van Beethoven's Viennese apartment in suburban Windmühle, Kothgasse No. 61, was located in the building owned by his brother-in-law, the master baker Leopold Obermayer. See Frimmel, *Handbuch*, I, p. 465; Clive, pp. 24–26.—KH/TA

[35] The current parody version of *Aline, oder Wien und Baden in einem andern Weltteil* (libretto by Adolf Bäuerle, music by Wenzel Müller) had opened at the Josephstadt Theater on January 22, 1824, and enjoyed considerable success. In the broad period under discussion here, it was performed on February 8, 9, 12, 13, and 25, 1824. Karl and Johann had evidently seen it on ca. Saturday, January 24; see Heft 54, Blatt 41v.
On February 14 and 15, *Die Schlangenkönigin* was performed; on February 15, it was performed along with *Der Feldtrompeter*, with the *Consecration of the House* Overture included as part of the latter. See Bauer, *Theater in der Josephstadt* (1957), p. 208.—KH/TA

[36] Presumably the woodcutters who brought the wood mentioned on Blatt 6v.—TA

        <Cutting twice   3 fl.
        <u>Splitting and stacking 3 fl.</u>
                                  6 fl.>

SCHINDLER [**continuing**]: Because [Emperor] Franz cannot tell how he said to Weigl: "Don't you have enough yet?" etc. // Weigl is said to be very disconcerted. //

    This [*Consecration of the House*] Overture is a monster of a work, and I yearn to hear it well played by a large orchestra someday.[37] [Blatt 8r] The effect would have to be extremely grand and splendid. //

    I would gladly be guilty of such a bad thing a second or third time. [falsified entries begin→] I, guilty for this Overture? [←falsified entries end] //

    The many elisions make setting the French language to music too difficult. //

    That is really the <goddamned> business with Weigl. As Unger told me, he is said to have committed the folly and just recently boasted in her presence [Blatt 8v] that the emperor said that he would most certainly get the position, and now is ashamed, since Gänsbacher received the *Decret* [decree of appointment] already the day afterward. //

    Every hawker woman[38] may chat him up. //

    Every Thursday. //

    That was the summary law. //

    Send her away as soon as possible; that is the best thing, because she is a beast, but don't anger yourself about it. [//] [Blatt 9r]

    In the Harrach shops on the Freyung;[39] only somewhat *expensive*—but *very good and beautiful*. //

---

[37] Beethoven would program it with the Kärntnertor Theater's orchestra and supplemental musicians on May 7 and 23, 1824, to complement the premiere of his Ninth Symphony. He seems already to have made that decision; see Blatt 15r below.—TA

[38] Original German *Fratschlerweib*, also *Fratschlerin*, a Viennese expression for a *Hökerin* (street hawker). At the beginning of the nineteenth century, there were said to be over 3,000 of them in Vienna, with many of them known around the city for their ready wit and their coarseness. See Groner, 1922, pp. 117–118; Loritza, p. 45; Realis, I, p. 450.—KH

[39] Market huts or booths, erected on the Freyung [open square] in front of the Harrach Palace [Freyung No. 239 in the 1821 numbering]. During legally regulated seasonal markets, one could obtain, among other items, Bohemian and Linzer linens offered for sale. Even today, farmers from Burgenland (the area bordering Hungary, and near the Harrach lands where Haydn was born) bring their produce to these markets, including delicately flavored, consistently textured radishes as large as small plums. As Schindler noted, they are also "somewhat expensive, but very good and beautiful." See Paul Harrer, "Wien: Seine Häuser, Menschen und Kultur," typescript, ca. 1951–1957 (Wiener Stadt- und Landesarchiv), II/1, p. 153; Redl, 1824, pp. 228–229.—KH/TA

[SCHINDLER, *continued*]

One is also assured that it [the shop] is not out of the way, because the turnover is almost the largest on the square here.[40] //

The linens are also reputed to be good in a shop on the Graben,[41] but I don't know the house sign, but I can find out very easily. // If you'd like I can investigate where one can get such things that are good, beautiful, and reasonably priced. [//] [Blatt 9v]

Unger was indisposed for several days,[42] otherwise she would surely have visited you. // She exercises too little caution for herself, both in terms of eating and drinking. // Sontag is more cautious. // Unger is too much of an unstable person[43]—therefore she gambles with her health and has already lost often. //

Alla breve is probably the best. //

Grillparzer will probably have another copy.[44] //

If you can do without it, it probably doesn't make any difference. [//] [Blatt 10r] Grillparzer says that he has not given it to them for that reason, so as not to want to force the matter. // The reply from Naples can be here in two weeks; by then, one can perhaps also know what the censor says. // Grillparzer doesn't believe that the censor will strike out one word. //

There is splendid scenery in *Aline*, among other things, Nussdorf, the palace of Archduke Karl's wife in Helena [the *Helenental* near Baden], another rocky region in Helena, and a lake harbor.[45] [//]

---

[40] If by "here," Schindler means suburban Landstrasse, then the marketplace was and remains today in front of the parish's St. Rochus Church, a long block south on the Hauptstrasse from Beethoven's apartment, beyond the *Birne* restaurant and coffee house that he frequented.—TA

[41] This concerns either the linen dealership of the Wladislaw Brothers, *Zum lustigen Bauern*, on the Graben, at the corner with the Kohlmarkt, No. 569, or the newly opened linen-goods dealership of Johann Georg Schoberlechner, *Zur weissen Katze*, on the south end of the Graben No. 620. Beethoven himself had already made note of Schoberlechner's *Katze* (see Heft 53, Blatt 20r). See *Frühwirtscher Grundriss*; *Intelligenzblatt*, No. 13 (January 17, 1824), p. 102; Redl, 1824, p. 71.—KH/TA

[42] Unger had visited Beethoven on January 17, January 29, and February 13 (see Heft 51, Blatt 10v; Heft 54, Blatt 19v; and Heft 56, Blatt 1r above. Since February 1, Unger had sung in *Der Taucher* (February 2 and 4); *Richard und Zoraide* (February 7 and 9); and again in *Der Taucher* (February 11 and 13). There is no discernable indisposition on the part of either Unger or Sontag from January 29 to February 15. See Theaterzettel, Kärntnertor Theater, Bibliothek, Österreichisches Theater-Museum; courtesy librarian Othmar Barnert.—TA

[43] Original German *Schuss* (or *Schussbartel*), a designation for unstable or shiftless people. See Loritza, p. 119.—KH

[44] Perhaps Unger has not yet returned the libretto to *Melusine* that Beethoven lent her on ca. Saturday, January 17, 1824; see Heft 53, Blatt 13r.—TA

[45] Bäuerle and Müller's magic opera *Aline, or Vienna in Another Part of the World* was being performed at the Josephstadt Theater with somewhat altered scenery. One scene in act 1 showed Nussdorf, a wine-growing village north of Vienna (between Heiligenstadt and the Danube). Scenes from act 2 showed the Weilburg, the palace of Archduke Carl and his wife, Henriette (*née* von Nassau-Weilburg), in the Helenental near Baden, and a rocky region in the area (instead of Brühl near Vienna, as prescribed by the libretto). The lake harbor is the prescribed location of the final scene. See the printed libretto of

[Schindler seemingly departs.]

[Blatt 10v]

BEETHOVEN **[starting an errand list; afternoon of Sunday, February 15]**:
+ Wax stick.
+ Penknife.
+ Hat.[46] //

NEPHEW KARL **[at Beethoven's apartment; still probably the afternoon of Sunday, February 15]**: A decisive word from Duport will come soon now; in it, all the conditions will be accepted and the opera will be commissioned. //
The apartment of an actor.[47] //
Schindler often goes to Czerny's now.[48] [//] [Blatt 11r]
A Bohemian woman. // It doesn't look good for comprehension. //

46 kr.
   18
   16   58
―――――
14 fl. 24 kr.   51 //

14 fl. 24 [kr.]   //

He said yesterday[49] that, several years ago, he was a member of a Gesellschaft [society] that still exists under the name the *Ludlamites*,[50] where, among others,

---

Aline, n.p., n.d. (Bibliothek, Österreichisches Theatermuseum); Bäuerle's *Allgemeine Theater-Zeitung* 17, No. 15 (February 3, 1824), p. 59; Franz C. Weidmann, *Wiens Umgebungen* (Vienna, 1823), pp. 247–248; as well as Heft 54, Blatt 41v.—KH/TA

[46] On January 21, 1824 (Heft 54, Blatt 1r), Schindler called Beethoven a "hat tyrant" for reasons that are unclear. On the evening of Sunday, February 15, brother Johann will advise Beethoven to buy a hat; see Blätter 17v–18r below.—TA

[47] Possibly a reference to where Caroline Unger and her father might be living; see Blätter 22v–23r below.—TA

[48] A reference to Czerny's weekly salon recitals, largely of Beethoven's music.—TA

[49] Karl is probably reporting a conversation that took place on Saturday, February 14, when he attended a morning rehearsal of the *Consecration of the House* Overture at the Josephstadt Theater. Even surveying the list of members provided in Castelli's autobiography (see below), it is not clear with whom Karl conversed, although it may have been Schindler. See Blatt 5r above.—TA

[50] *Ludlamshöhle*, a convivial, loosely organized society of Viennese artists, authors, and businessmen, including similarly minded individuals visiting from abroad. They took their name from Oehlenschläger's play *Ludlams Höhle*, given its Vienna premiere at the Theater an der Wien on December 15, 1817, and met in the restaurant of J. Haidvogel in the Schlossergasse. Their idiosyncrasies eventually aroused suspicion, and in 1826, they were banned because of alleged dangers to the state. See Ignaz Franz Castelli, *Memoiren meines Lebens, Gefundenes und Empfundenes*, 4 vols. (Vienna: Kober & Markgraf, 1861), II, pp. 174–176; new, heavily abridged edition, ed. Josef Bindtner (Munich, 1913), II, pp. 1–3.—KH/TA

Moscheles was accepted [as a member], and every one of them received his own name; thus Moscheles was called *Tasto der Kälberfuss*.[51] [//] [Blatt 11v] The *purpose* was to entertain themselves for a couple of hours after the theater.[52] //

She [a domestic servant] says that she has been here for a week now, and that she is leaving in a week. // She also wants to go tomorrow. //

BEETHOVEN [continuing an errand list; afternoon of Sunday, February 15]:
Meissner Brothers.[53]
Apartment.
+ Oil.
+ With the wine.
A machine that can be pushed to fit the pianos.[54] //

[Blatt 12r]

LEONHARD MÄLZEL[55] [presumably at Beethoven's apartment; still the afternoon of Sunday, February 15]: I am now going to Prague; when I return, I am making a mechanical trumpeter with 50 tones, so that [sentence ends]. // Leonhard Mälzel, Jägerzeil No. 20. [//]

---

[51] *Tasto*, because he made his living playing the *Tasten* (piano keys); *Kälberfuss*, because calves' feet were his favorite dish, and he ate them almost daily. Other members (with fraternity names based on various wordplays) included government official and amateur cellist Vincenz Hauschka (Greif von am Katzendarm); poet and physician Alois Jeitteles (Glazo Barbirmidi Lanzetta); Grillparzer (Saphokles der Istrianer); poet Christian [*sic*] Kuffner (Lord Plautil Plauting); Castelli (Eif Charon der Höhlenzote); Theater an der Wien oboist Joseph Sellner (Hochholz von Sanct Blasius); peripatetic flute virtuoso Johann Sedlatscheck (Sedl von Latscheck); composer Adalbert Gyrowetz (Notarsch Sakramensky); banker Joseph Biedermann (Pipo Canastro); Salieri (Don Tarar di Palmira); poet, biologist, and censor Johann Baptist Rupprecht (Van der Gumpendorf); and Joseph Blahetka (Der neue Jephta), among others, including Carl Maria von Weber. See Castelli, *Memoiren* (1861), II, pp. 198–213, especially p. 201; ed. Bindtner (1913), II, p. 28.—KH/TA

[52] Even with his fondness for puns, Beethoven must have found the *Ludlamshöhle* group strange and asked what its purpose might be. For a sympathetic history of such societies, see Rita Steblin, *Die Unsinnsgesellschaft: Franz Schubert, Leopold Kupelwieser und ihr Freundeskreis* (Vienna: Böhlau, 1998).—TA

[53] Presumably the wholesale (banking) business of the Meisl Brothers, owned by Andreas Meisl, in the City, Rauhensteingasse No. 949, through whom Beethoven occasionally settled monetary transactions. See Redl, 1824, p. 26; and Blatt 19v below.—KH

[54] For some time, Beethoven had been working with piano maker Matthäus Andreas Stein about solving this problem; see also Heft 55, Blatt 20r.—TA

[55] On ca. January 23, 1824, Beethoven had made a note to himself to contact Leonhard Mälzel about the metronome. In 1825, Mälzel constructed a mechanical *Orchestrion*, consisting of 50 clarinets, horns, trumpets, and trombones. On January 29, 1824, Schindler gave Beethoven the address of Jägerzeil 17, but that was the old numbering; the current numbering since 1821 was "20." See Heft 54, Blätter 18v and 46r; and Wurzbach, vol. 16, pp. 250–252.—KH/TA

[Blatt 12v]

GLÖGGL [?]⁵⁶ [**presumably at Beethoven's apartment; still the afternoon of Sunday, February 15**]: I have inquired about you a thousand times. // But you look very well. //

We play your quartets very diligently. //

But when I speak loudly, you understand me. //

Fuchs is also a man whom you know.⁵⁷ // Knows nothing of the world. // The [= My] cousin is still living in Linz.⁵⁸ [//] [Blatt 13r]

I would be very happy if you would have some kind of music for my daughter, who already plays very well. She is 13 years old. She sends you hand-kisses. [//] There may be a great deal that she could play; everything; she has already played Variations of yours. [She takes lessons] twice every week. //

Quartets. [//] [Blatt 13v]

I am staying here perhaps until Thursday [February 19];⁵⁹ my profession is shoemaker. If you would be so gracious, you need only deliver it to the Prince's porter. [//]

It is a healthful region there [possibly Eisenstadt or Esterház]. //

Again I ask you most sincerely. Please don't forget my dear cousin. My daughter's soul depends upon your music, by the greatest man [Blatt 14r] on earth. [//] I shall write to you occasionally. [//]

---

⁵⁶ From various elements in his conversation, it may be possible to narrow the identity of this previously "unknown" writer. He is a professional shoemaker, possibly ca. 38–50 years old, but is seemingly an accomplished amateur string player. He and Beethoven both know a Fuchs (possibly Johann Nepomuk Fuchs, 1766–1839, in the Esterházy employ). He has a ca. 13-year-old daughter who plays piano; he has a cousin who is "still living in Linz" (possibly Domkapellmeister Franz Xaver Glöggl, 1764–1839, for whom Beethoven composed his *Equale* for Trombones, WoO 30, for All Souls' Day in 1812); writes with phonetic but not semiliterate spelling; takes delivery in the City through his prince's [Esterházy's] porter.

On the basis of the above, the writer might be a son of Franx Xaver Glöggl's brother Joseph (b. 1759), a musician who had also been active in Linz earlier but who had moved to Budapest in 1810 and died there in 1821. See also Andrea Harrandt, "Glöggl, Familie," *Österreichisches Musiklexikon*, II, pp. 594–595.—TA

⁵⁷ Probably Johann Nepomuk Fuchs (1766–1839), who joined the Esterházy orchestra as a violinist in 1788, became vice-Kapellmeister in 1802, and officially succeeded Haydn to the title of Kapellmeister in 1809. Given the surrounding context, Johann Nepomuk Fuchs is more likely than the Theater an der Wien's hornist Benedict Fuchs (1765–1828) or the Court orchestra's violinist Peter Fuchs (1753–1831). See Max Rudolf, "Johann Nepomuk Fuchs," *Journal of the Conductors' Guild* 11, Nos. 3/4 (Summer/Fall 1990), p. 120.—TA

⁵⁸ The German editors identify this as a reference to Beethoven's brother Johann.—KH/TA

⁵⁹ No one remotely resembling this writer is listed among the selected "Departures" between February 15 and 25, 1824, as published in the *Wiener Zeitung*.—TA

I have not begun yet. //
Until your bill[60] comes. //

JOHANN VAN BEETHOVEN [at Beethoven's apartment, presumably with his carriage to take Karl to Schuppanzigh's concert; Sunday, February 15, ca. 4 p.m.]:[61]

We must speak with [lawyer] Dr. Bach first, before we go to the *Magistrat*, because all of this must be done in writing at the Magistrat's. // He'll have this raised through the legal representative. [//] [Blatt 14v]

Schindler told me at dinner that he knows of a *fine* municipal craftsman's widow [as housekeeper] for you, so take her; because that is what Schindler understands. // She can wash and write very well. // He knows her and will attest to her loyalty—that is quite a lot. // He told me at dinner that you must make your decision quite soon, otherwise she'll get another job. // Because he already told you earlier. [//] [Blatt 15r] You must certainly expect that with everyone. // Because you often get many bad ones [job applicants] because the good ones soon get a job. //

Your Overture went very well [at the Theater] in the Josephstadt this time;[62] it will certainly please a great deal in your Akademie.[63] // You should now be concerned about the copying of 2 movements of your Mass [*Missa solemnis*]. // Schuppanzigh spoke with me today; he has not been engaged at the Court Theater; they don't want to [Blatt 15v] engage him until December. // As it appears, he still doesn't want to do that; because it is too long for him, and he cannot live that long without income. //

That is the very worst thing; the woman is already here again. //

[**Johann and nephew Karl depart for the 4:30 concert; Johann resumes the conversation after their return to Beethoven's apartment; probably ca. 6:45 p.m.:**][64]

---

[60] German original *Reinichung*, which could be a phonetic spelling of *Reinigung* (cleaning), but is more likely *Rechnung* (bill), assuming that Beethoven will pass the costs of copying piano music on to the writer.—TA

[61] The concert began at 4:30. Beethoven's apartment was only a 5–10-minute drive away, and Johann seemingly arrived there early enough to have a conversation beforehand.—TA

[62] On Saturday, February 14, there had been a difficult rehearsal of the *Consecration of the House* Overture (presumably used in the play *Der Feldtrompeter*) at the Theater in der Josephstadt, lasting until 2 p.m. Johann had probably attended a second rehearsal earlier on Sunday, February 15. See Bäuerle's *Allgemeine Theater-Zeitung* 17, No. 26 (February 28, 1824), p. 103; and Blätter 5r and 6v above and 19r below.—TA

[63] Therefore, Beethoven had already decided to use the *Consecration of the House* Overture on his concerts that would premiere the Ninth Symphony, ultimately May 7 and 23, 1824.—TA

[64] The Haydn Quartet takes ca. 20 minutes in performance; the Beethoven Quartet, ca. 26; and the Mozart Quintet, ca. 29. With breaks, the concert would not have been finished before 6:15 p.m., and, after postconcert conversation, Karl and Johann might have returned to Beethoven's apartment by ca. 6:45—TA

[JOHANN VAN BEETHOVEN, *continued*]

There was a guitar virtuoso[65] who heard your Quartet today [Sunday, February 15];[66] he comes from Paris and is said to be the greatest. He has regards to bring you [Blatt 16r] from Paris; Lichnowsky will introduce him to you. //

Has Grillparzer already sent you a poem for your Akademie?[67] // I believe that you should send the libretto [Grillparzer's *Melusine*] to Duport, partly so he can look through it, partly so he can give it to the censor. // So give it to me; I'll give it to him right away, tomorrow. // Duport knows that already. // But you must first see whether the censor lets it pass, [Blatt 16v] and whether Duport and Barbaja then accepted this book for their theater, and all of this can only be decided if the libretto is delivered to them quickly. //

Young people are all like that. // [Sign] of the times. //

If you want, I'll look Schindler up at the Theater [in der Josephstadt] and tell him that he is to bring the housewife.[68] [//] [Blatt 17r] He says that she is very fine and can cook well—you can't wish for more. //

Have you given any further thought to Prince Galitzin?[69] // If only he had one. // You cannot undertake a tour without 2 new works. //

With one concert here, you would also make at least 3,000 fl. // The *net* amount remaining would be 3,000 fl.; [the publisher] Leidesdorf will guarantee it. [//] [Blatt 17v]

---

[65] Probably the guitar virtuoso Carl von Gärtner from Kassel, who spent a considerable time in Vienna on his way back from a tour to St. Petersburg and gave a concert "on a very large guitar" in the Saal of the Lower Austrian *Landstand* on March 19, 1824. See *Wiener AmZ* 8, No. 12 (March 27, 1824), p. 47; Bäuerle's *Allgemeine Theater-Zeitung* 17, No. 46 (April 15, 1824), p. 184; *Wiener Zeitung*, No. 65 (March 19, 1824), p. 288.—KH

[66] The second concert of Ignaz Schuppanzigh's fourth subscription series of string quartet concerts, held at the hall of the Gesellschaft der Musikfreunde, took place on Sunday, February 15, 1824. The program consisted of the Haydn's String Quartet in D minor, Hob. III/76; Beethoven's String Quartet in G, Op. 18, No. 2; and Mozart's Quintet in A, K. 581, for clarinet and string quartet.

The clarinettist was the Czech-born Joseph Friedlowsky (1777–1859), principal clarinettist at the Theater an der Wien since 1802, for whom Beethoven had written exposed passages in Symphony No. 4, the Violin Concerto, and Symphony No. 8, among others. Schubert would later compose the clarinet part in *Der Hirt auf dem Felsen* for him. Protected by Archduke Rudolph through his chamberlain Count Troyer (an amateur clarinettist), Friedlowsky was the only Bohemian appointed to the faculty of the Gesellschaft's *Conservatorium* in 1821/1822.

See the *Wiener AmZ* 8, No. 12 (March 27, 1824), p. 45; Böckh, 1822, p. 367.—KH/TA

[67] Poets, largely amateurs, often wrote poems of praise to be distributed during operas or concerts; these poems were sometimes published afterwards in such newspapers as Schickh's *Wiener Zeitschrift* or Bäuerle's *Allgemeine Theater-Zeitung*.—TA

[68] Mentioned on Blatt 14v above, as a potential housekeeper.—TA

[69] Galitzin in St. Petersburg had instigated a subscription to the *Missa solemnis* and would conduct a complete performance of it there in April, 1824. He also commissioned Beethoven's late String Quartets, Opp. 127, 130, and 132. See Clive, pp. 135–137.—KH/TA

If you had followed my advice then, I would have accepted him [presumably Karl], and he would be a fine apothecary now, and could soon be a professor of chemistry.[70] //

I nearly froze my feet on my last trip to my estate [in Gneixendorf], so that I am suffering greatly now. //

[A maid seemingly interrupts the conversation:]

NEPHEW KARL: She is asking for a candle. //

JOHANN VAN BEETHOVEN [**continuing**]: You must buy yourself a hat right away,[71] tomorrow; people are talking about the fact that you have such a bad hat. [//] [Blatt 18r] You can get a good hat now for about 12–13 fl. in the Landstrasse, next to the coffee house.[72] //

One figures ½ pound of meat for every adult person; otherwise a soup is *never* good. // I almost never eat anything in the evening because I don't eat my midday meal until 3 o'clock. [//]

[Blatt 18v]

NEPHEW KARL [**continuing**]: They did a quartet with obbligato clarinet; the clarinettist was extraordinarily good, but I don't know his name.[73] //

He [Johann] says that in summer he is not here anyway. // He says that that is the first *authentic*[74] wine that he has found at our place. // He says that he will send us some of his authentic mountain wine, which is healthier than all the wines. He wants to look after the horses and coachman. [//]

[Blatt 19r]

---

[70] On July 27, 1823, Karl had told Beethoven that he wanted to become a French language teacher with additional areas in Latin and Greek. Beethoven, his family, and acquaintances repeatedly ignored Karl's wishes. This frustration and other factors led to his suicide attempt in Summer, 1826. See Heft 36, Blatt 15r (July 27, 1823).—TA

[71] In Heft 54, Blatt 1r, Schindler had called Beethoven a "hat tyrant." Beethoven had already noted a hat on his shopping list on Blatt 10v above, and he bought one below.—TA

[72] There was no actual hat shop in the Landstrasse; hat businesses were among the upper-class shops located exclusively within the walled City. There were, however, shops, each with a variety of wares, located in the suburbs, such as Joseph Graff's mixed-wares shop in the Landstrasse Hauptstrasse, No. 44, in the second building south of the coffee house at Landstrasse Hauptstrasse No. 42 (corner of Gärtnergasse). See Behsel, p. 71; Pezzl, pp. 557–558; Redl, 1824, p. 59.—KH/TA

[73] As noted above (Blätter 15v–16r), Joseph Friedlowsky had joined the Schuppanzigh Quartet in Mozart's Clarinet Quintet, K. 581. Karl's failure to recognize Friedlowsky (1777–1859) was unfortunate, because Beethoven would surely have remembered his name in a most positive light. It also confirms that there were no printed programs at Schuppanzigh's concerts and that handwritten programs (if they were passed around) were few and far between.—TA

[74] Authentic (*ächt* or *echt*) possibly understood as "unadulterated." With assistance from William R. Meredith (December 14, 2022).—TA

JOHANN VAN BEETHOVEN [continuing]: But he [Gläser] rehearsed the [*Consecration of the House*] Overture well.[75] //

NEPHEW KARL [continuing]: He says that she [Johann's wife Therese] doesn't deserve it. //

JOHANN VAN BEETHOVEN [concluding the postconcert conversation on Sunday night, February 15; making an appointment for the next morning]: On the Stephansplatz, at the coffee house;[76] precisely 11 o'clock. //

[seemingly at Beethoven's apartment, having failed to appear for the 11 a.m. appointment on Monday, February 16:]

Malie [Therese's daughter Amalie Waldmann] has a sore throat, and I was with her at Herbeck's,[77] a superb man. //

NEPHEW KARL [seemingly at Beethoven's apartment; probably noon or early afternoon of Monday, February 16]: He is also not an eye doctor. // Herbeck is not an eye doctor. //

[Blatt 19v]

BEETHOVEN: + Meissl Brothers.[78]

NEPHEW KARL [probably continuing]: Therefore 1 fl. 48 kr. //

The maid also always laughs with the old woman [housekeeper Barbara Holzmann], and when I came today, both of them were in the room and laughed with one another. Even when I had already sat down, the maid still laughed with her, so that I told them to go outside. The old woman had to mend some underpants. [Blatt 19a-r]

He [Johann] says that she [Therese] *herself* would like to get away from *him*, so as to be even more independent, but she doesn't go unless he gives her her part of the assets, which amounts to about 80–100,000 fl. (because half of his assets is her property), and he doesn't want to do that. // Reproaches are no longer of any use, since it [the situation] cannot be changed; also he regrets it, though too late. // She does not embarrass him too much, because she is out of the house the whole day; having hardly eaten, she already rushes off again. // The way it was settled afterward. // The child's [Amalie's] father is also here, but does nothing for the girl. // He doesn't acknowledge

---

[75] See the rehearsals on Blätter 5r and 6v above.—TA

[76] Joseph Benko's coffee house in the Brandstatt No. 628, a building facing directly onto Stephansplatz. See Gustav Gugitz, *Das Wiener Kaffeehaus* (Vienna, 1940), pp. 213–215.—KH

[77] Dr. Joseph Franz Herbeck, I.R. surgeon and member of the Medical-Surgical Akademie, lived in the former Imperial Hospital on the Ballhausplatz. See *Hof- und Staats-Schematismus*, 1824, I, p. 120, and II, pp. 126 and 405.—KH

[78] Bankers in the Rauhensteingasse No. 949; see also Blatt 11v above.—KH

the girl. [Blatt 19a-v] Their similarity certainly confirms it.[79] // He has given 300 fl. [in support], but now he doesn't want to do anything more. //

Piringer was also at [Schuppanzigh's] Quartet concert [on Sunday, February 15] and sends you his respects. //

BEETHOVEN [at a coffee house, reading newspapers; late afternoon of Monday, February 16]:

+ Potatoes, white, of the best kind, at 5 pecks; in the Jägerzeile No. 527, at the building superintendent's.[80] [//] [Blatt 20r]

+ Double flannel ties for the old vest,

+ and then only one more flannel pants and vest.

+ Kitchen garden for sale, consists of a portion of land, 508 square miles [sic],[81] also usable for building lots; Landstrasse <6a> No. 46, at the end of Gärtnergasse and beginning of Marxer Gasse.[82] [//] [Blatt 20v]

+ Ungargasse No. 400: a garden for rent.[83] //

NEPHEW KARL [at the coffee house or Beethoven's apartment; possibly evening of Monday, February 16]: He [presumably Czerny] expressed the greatest joy over it and said that he would take all possible pain to play it in your spirit. // Lichnowsky was also there.[84] // Czerny has now gotten a noble student, a princess, who was entrusted to him by Her Majesty the empress. // He gives lessons from 8 in the

---

[79] Beethoven must have suggested that Amalie Waldmann might not have been the biological daughter of the presumed father, to which this was Karl's reply.—TA

[80] See the *Intelligenzblatt*, No. 37 (February 16, 1824), p. 307, col. 1 (Advertisements). The advertisement specified German white potatoes from Gersthof (a farming community at the end of Währinger Strasse, about a mile northwest of the *Linie*) and Pötzleinsdorf (farther northwest of Vienna); at 5, 10, or more pecks, but the seller would prefer a lot of more than 100 pecks. The same advertisement had appeared in No. 35 (February 13, 1824), p. 290.—KH/TA

[81] The original German (as transcribed in the *Konversationshefte*) reads *Meilen* (miles), and indeed Beethoven may have had a rare slip of the pencil when copying the advertisement (he was paraphrasing more in these two advertisements than he usually did). The copy in the *Intelligenzblatt* itself (see below), however, reads *Klafter* (a fathom or ca. 6 feet).—TA

[82] See the *Intelligenzblatt*, No. 36 (February 14, 1824), p. 302 (Advertisements). The advertisement did not appear in the February 16 issue but did appear again on February 17, 19, 24, 26, and 28, 1824.—KH/TA

[83] The advertisement used *verlassen*, an Austrian term for *vermieten*, rent. A corresponding published advertisement cannot be located, but given the location's proximity to Beethoven's apartment, it was probably posted on the bulletin board of the coffee house or some similar location.—KH/TA

[84] Karl may be reporting about a private recital at Czerny's apartment in the Krugergasse. Lichnowsky's daughter would soon begin lessons with Czerny. Karl may also have seen Czerny at Schuppanzigh's concert.—TA

morning to 8 in the evening. // He played a *Romanze* of yours with Steiner, which he had arranged for 2 pianos and 4 hands.[85] [//]

[Blatt 21r]

SCHINDLER [presumably at Beethoven's apartment; possibly early afternoon of Tuesday, February 17]: I've just come from Madame Lehmann. She already has a position, but will leave there if you take her. She'll come to see you tomorrow [presumably Wednesday, February 18] or Thursday [February 19]. // I must confess that I think very highly of Lehmann. Wait till she shows you what she can accomplish with cooking. // At least she shows herself to be knowledgeable and clever.[86] //

NEPHEW KARL [interjecting]: We encountered him once on the Glacis, when I was still at Blöchlinger's [Institute]. [//]
  [Publisher Sigmund Anton] Steiner. [//]

[Blatt 21v]

SCHINDLER [presumably continuing]: Hensler sent your new Overture [*Consecration of the House*] to Pressburg today. I certainly expressed my opinion against old Gläser.[87] It will not be pleasant for you, because it was done against your wishes, but there is nothing to be done with old Hensler.—In this way, it [the Overture] will be copied before it ever gets published. // If you wait, then it's too late. // Last time, he really didn't have the trombones taken as well, because they cost 5 fl. //
  Wasn't [Caroline] Unger here yet? //
  [falsified entries begin→] *Eh bien*, so I am to blame that you composed this Overture! *Bravo!* The world will admire it. [←falsified entries end] [Blatt 22r]

---

[85] Steiner published this arrangement of Beethoven's Romance in F for violin and orchestra, Op. 50, under the title "*Romance favorite* by Louis van Beethoven, Oeuvre 50; arranged as a *Rondo brilliant* for pianoforte, 4-hands, by C. Czerny, Op. 44." See Kinsky-Halm, p. 118.—KH

[86] She is probably the woman whom Beethoven will interview on Wednesday, February 18 (Blätter 26r–26v below).—TA

[87] Peter Gläser (1776–1849), father of the composer and conductor Franz Gläser, became one of Beethoven's principal copyists after Schlemmer's death in August 1823. Among others, Gläser prepared the performance parts of the Ninth Symphony used at its May 7, 1824, premiere. Wenzel Rampl made the presentation copy of the score of that symphony to be sent to Friedrich Wilhelm III in Berlin. Gläser lived in suburban Altlerchenfeld, Kaiserstrasse No. 24 [today, south side of Josefstädter Strasse, roughly one building east of the Gürtel]. See Conscriptions-Bogen, Altlerchenfeld, No. 24 (Wiener Stadt- und Landesarchiv); Frimmel, *Handbuch*, I, pp. 169–171; Frimmel, *Studien*, II, p. 11; Clive, pp. 130–131.—KH/TA

[SCHINDLER, *continued*]

She [Unger] told me that she is really going to Berlin in December, and [Henriette] Sontag, to Kassel. // But Sontag isn't leaving until Easter of next year.[88] //

Things are going terribly in the Josephstadt right now, because no one can tolerate Herr Hensler's scandalous treatment. [//] 7–8 members, among them the painter, machinist, pantomimists, first dancer, first singer, etc. // Hensler was always known as a rude fellow, but he makes more progress in this art every day. He doesn't treat anyone with respect. He recently told Drechsler in public [Blatt 22v] that he cursed the hour when he engaged him.[89] //

[presumably hat shopping with Beethoven:]

Since you now have a new hat,[90] be sure to get rid of the old one; therefore, I ask you to give it to me as a remembrance, as a <hol> relic. // That way you will always have it. //

[possibly walking in the Herrengasse near Rosengassel/Hintere Schenkenstrasse No. 55; probably mid-to-late afternoon of Tuesday, February 17:]

Unger lives here at the *Tor* [gate].[91] You should surprise her; she is usually at home alone at this time. [//] [Blatt 23r] Immediately in the street to the right.[92] //

But that is not good for you.[93] Better to buy something that is already at hand than to wait and see how it turns out. //

[seemingly walking back out to the Landstrasse:]

You would not believe what building a small house costs; it's always better to buy one that's already built. [//] [Blatt 23v] It's better to stay there [in the apartment in the Landstrasse] for now. Houses here are imposed with enormous taxes. // For the fun of it, have a landlord show you his list of expenses sometime; it is not to be

---

[88] Caroline Unger did not leave Vienna to go to Naples until March 1825 (see Heft 53, Blatt 11v). Henriette Sontag gave her farewell concert in the Grosser Redoutensaal on April 17, 1825, then gave guest appearances in Leipzig, and debuted at the Königsstädtisches Theater in Berlin on August 3, 1825, in Rossini's *L'Italiana in Algeri*. See the *Allgemeine musikalische Zeitung* 27, No. 21 (May 25, 1825), col. 347; Stümcke, pp. 31–32 and 42; Clive, pp. 375–376.—KH/TA

[89] This sounds familiar.—TA

[90] In Heft 54, Blatt 1r, Schindler had called Beethoven a "hat tyrant." References to Beethoven's need for a new hat appear on Blätter 10v and 17v–18r above.—TA

[91] Caroline Unger lived in the Rosengassel, corner of Hintere Schenkenstrasse No. 55. The address in Ziegler oriented the reader to Teinfaltstrasse, to the north. The *Tor* (gate) here may refer to the building's *Tor* (most likely), although the location was near two gates in the City's walls, the Schottentor, and, especially (at the end of Teinfaltstrasse), the newer pedestrian Franzentor (opened in 1817). The area is a ca. 30-minute walk from Beethoven's apartment. See *Neuester Grundriss der Haupt- und Residenzstadt Wien* (1825); Behsel, p. 2; Ziegler, *Addressen-Buch*, p. 75; and Blatt 10v above.—KH/TA

[92] Beethoven, who probably did not appreciate surprise guests himself, seems to have resisted Schindler's suggestion that he surprise Unger.—TA

[93] Beethoven might have been waxing enthusiastic over a hat or the prospects of buying a parcel of land and building his own house on it. See the advertisement that he had copied on Blatt 20r above.—TA

believed. // This suburb has too many unhappy associations for you;[94] it's always better on the other side, such as the Wieden,[95] etc. [//] [Blatt 24r]

One Herr Jansa, a young man of 23–24 years,[96] has gotten the vacant position in the [Hof-]Kapelle. [//] Again, proof that merit goes absolutely unrecognized here. //

How is it going with Schuppanzigh? Is he really going to Berlin? // Dietrichstein [the Court musical administrator] was supposed to have chosen him, unless Jansa petitioned about it. // If one knows [the situation], it is believable that [Abbé] Stadler and Kiesewetter are his protectors. [//] He [Jansa] is employed in Pest.[97] [//] [Blatt 24v]

It is always enough as a pension for one's old age, and <now> as long as one is active, there is also other income in addition. // Jeckel would certainly have deserved it, because he is old and has 6 small children.[98] // So he [Schuppanzigh] should go there [Berlin?] right away, because there is really nothing here. // Schuppanzigh is already accustomed to living in a foreign country. [//]

[Blatt 25r]

NEPHEW KARL [**at Beethoven's apartment; probably late afternoon or evening of Tuesday, February 17**]: If you like her [housekeeper interviewee Lehmann?], you should take her. // I would like to see the woman. //

---

[94] Original German: *Diese Vorstadt ist zu traurig für Sie*. Rasumovsky's burned palace was in suburban Landstrasse; Antonie Brentano's family lived farther out in the Erdberggasse; Giannatasio del Rio's school (which Karl had attended) faced the Glacis, not far from Beethoven's present apartment; and Kudlich's school was in the same neighborhood as the Birkenstock/Brentano house. All of these (and more) may have held bittersweet memories for Beethoven. Antonie Brentano is one of the candidates for being the "Immortal Beloved" of 1812. See a drawing of her in Frankfurt am Main in 1820 as the frontispiece of this volume. Susan Lund, the dedicatee of this volume, is one of the strongest advocates for Antonie Brentano's "candidacy." For general background on the Birkenstock and Brentano families, see Clive, pp. 34–36 and 47–51.—TA

[95] Wieden was Vienna's oldest suburb, lying immediately south of the Kärntnertor and to the east of the River Wien. Long after Schikaneder's company at the Theater auf der Wieden moved across that river to the Theater an der Wien in 1801, Beethoven's circle continued to refer to the new location as the Wiedener Theater. Thus, Schindler possibly confused the terminology of suburban Wieden with suburban Laimgrube an der Wien, "on the other side" of the River Wien. See Groner, 1922, pp. 544–545.—KH/TA

[96] Violinist Leopold Jansa had been born on March 23, 1795, and was therefore 28 years old at the time. See Heft 55, Blatt 15r.—KH/TA

[97] His employer was Count Franz von Brunsvik; see Heft 55, Blatt 15v.—TA

[98] Now ca. 60 years old, Jeckel had three surviving children: a son in the army and two daughters, ages ca. 16 and 14; see Heft 54, Blatt 3v.—TA

I also don't believe that the wine is authentic.⁹⁹ // It was written. // But I have examined it carefully. The inscription read: *Zu den 3 Löwen*.¹⁰⁰ // When they believe that they have someone as a repeat customer, then they immediately start sending bad wine; only they are careful about it at the *beginning*. [//] [Blatt 25v] But everyone who understands the matter has to be on the watch, because one can be horribly cheated with wines. //

<If> There are certainly other places where students are taken in for room and board for extremely reasonable prices. [//]

BEETHOVEN [at his apartment; probably the morning of Wednesday, February 18]:¹⁰¹
+ Shaving soap.
+ Washing soap.
+ Razor.
today.¹⁰² [//]

[Blatt 26r]

FRAU LEHMANN¹⁰³ [at Beethoven's apartment; ca. 2 p.m. on Wednesday,

---

⁹⁹ Authentic (*ächt* or *echt*) possibly understood as "unadulterated." With assistance from William R. Meredith (December 14, 2022).—TA

¹⁰⁰ Probably Anton Schneider's wine and grocery dealership, *Zu den drei weissen Löwen* [At the Three White Lions], in the walled City, Kärntnerstrasse No. 1073, on the north side of the street, across from its intersection with Weihburggasse, and therefore within Beethoven's customary walking routes.

A less likely candidate would Johann Bäcker's grocery dealership *Zu den drei Löwen* in the near western suburb of St. Ulrich, behind the church, Entengasse (today's Burggasse) No. 42. See Pezzl, p. 244; Redl, 1824, pp. 38 and 57; and the *Intelligenzblatt*, No. 45 (February 25, 1824), p. 357 (Advertisements).—KH/TA

¹⁰¹ Beethoven writes this shopping list over this preexisting computation in his hand:
   30
   40
   16
   112—KH

¹⁰² Original German *heute*; see also Heft 54, Blatt 11r, where Beethoven wrote the Latin *hodie* to remind himself that something would happen "today."

In this case, it might refer to his advertisement for a housekeeper in the *Intelligenzblatt*, No. 39 (Wednesday, February 18, 1824), p. 320: "A Professionist's [handworker's] Widow—who can read and write and cook well, and who has already been in service as a cook in good houses, will be employed as a housekeeper under advantageous conditions. Further information available daily at 2 o'clock in the Ungargasse No. 323, rear stairway, on the 1st floor [2nd floor, American], door No. 12."

The advertisement appeared only once this week, and *not* on February 17, 19, 20, or 21.—TA

¹⁰³ This is presumably the same potential applicant whom Schindler discussed with Beethoven on Blatt 21r above. She writes relatively well.—TA

February 18]:[104] Because I have a position at this time, I could not come until two weeks from Monday, because I must first give notice. Otherwise, concerning the kitchen, it is merely a matter of my getting to know your tastes. // But perhaps it is better if the time is short; I shall therefore give notice right away tomorrow, so it would be two weeks from tomorrow. [//] [Blatt 26v] At 6 o'clock on Sundays. //

NEPHEW KARL [at Beethoven's apartment; some while after 2 p.m. on Wednesday, February 18]: Have you hired her? // I am surprised that none have applied up to now. // It is even rarer that a *Professionisten*'s [handworker's] widow has already cooked in [someone's] house. // At least no baronesses will come.[105] //

I know the treasury's payments office.[106] //

anima
anim-
anm
âm-e[107] // [Blatt 27r]

You can still retain her for a couple of days; it isn't worth the trouble to employ still *another* woman. //

The one [presumably grocery and wine shop] on the Kohlmarkt is better.[108] //

BEETHOVEN [at a coffee house; presumably the late afternoon of Wednesday, February 18]:

+ *astronomische Berechnungs Tabellen des Jahres 1824* [Astronomical Calculation Tables for the Year 1824] by Johann Veyhelin, lithographed by Jos. Trentsensky, general store, No. 868, Zwettelhof, also at Artaria's, Kohlmarkt.[109] [//]

[Blatt 27v]

---

[104] The entries on this page are written over some earlier computations in Beethoven's hand:

12		3	6
6	6	2	
2½		3	6
2½			2
2		17	
2½—KH			

[105] Beethoven and Karl had recently interviewed some applicants who behaved in an aristocratic way.—TA

[106] The *k. k. Universal Cameral-Zahlamt*, located in the City, Singerstrasse No. 886, was one of four state payments offices. See *Hof- und Staats-Schematismus*, 1824, I, p. 276.—KH

[107] For similar linguistic scribblings, presumably written in between interviews with potential housekeepers, see Blatt 32r below.—TA

[108] Probably the Grocery Shop of Ignaz Spöttl's Late Widow's Son [!] on the Kohlmarkt, *Zum grünen Fassel* [At the Little Green Barrel], No. 260; see also Blatt 5v above.—TA

[109] Excerpt of an advertisement in the *Intelligenzblatt*, No. 34 (Thursday, February 12, 1824), p. 286. As usual, Beethoven copied the advertisement (or the elements that interested him) with relative

SCHUPPANZIGH [**presumably at Beethoven's apartment; possibly midafternoon of Thursday, February 19**]:[110] I've made a proposition to Duport: he is to give me compensation up to now, with the condition that, when they want to, they can turn the director's [concertmaster's] position over to me, but I still don't have an answer. [//] Until December. // There is no income in the summer. // He [=You] can write to the Archduke [Rudolph], that even [Blatt 28r] his recommendation was of no use, because I was rejected. // They engaged Jansa. // [Abbé] Stadler, who took very much interest in this, has become ill because of this mess. // He has his own group [of supporters]. // Just believe me that he [= you] can't make a better deal. // [Blatt 28v]

It is already time to think about the concert [to perform the Ninth Symphony and *Missa solemnis*] because the people have to study their vocal parts. // For a greater number of performers, one must have many dilettantes; there are very good dilettantes here. // That is the bad thing about these people, that they take bread out of the mouths of [professional] artists. [//] [Blatt 29r]

That's easy to say, but what then am I supposed to live on? It is 9 months until December [1824] and possible employment.[111] // If Duport were concerned about keeping me here, believe me that he would certainly make sacrifices for me, but nothing worries these people. [//] [Blatt 29v] What does it matter to the administration to sacrifice a couple of 200 fl., when they often engage a singer who doesn't perform until a half year later?[112] // I wrote to Duport the day before yesterday, but he hasn't answered me yet. [//] [Blatt 30r]

Gottdank, the stage director, told me that he will give Duport no rest until he hires me. [//] Duport asked Weigl about me; Weigl said that it would be very good to engage me; however he hopes that they don't get too near to Katter, because he is his relative. //

Weigl was also rejected at St. Stephan's. [//] [Blatt 30v] The *Decret* for Weigl had already been written, if he himself had gone there to get it; thus he would not be able to hire one person more. All of a sudden came the command from the emperor to hold up the *Decret*. [//]

[Blatt 31r]

accuracy, although not always in the order that they appeared in the advertisement. The same advertisement had also appeared in No. 24 (Friday, January 30, 1824), p. 201. It did not appear in any issues from Monday, February 16, through Friday, February 20, 1824.—KH/TA

[110] In his *Intelligenzblatt* advertisement of Wednesday, February 18, Beethoven had committed to being at home at 2 p.m. on that day and for a reasonable number of days afterward to interview potential housekeepers. Karl sat with him during this time on Wednesday and Friday; perhaps Schuppanzigh visited at the corresponding time on Thursday.—TA

[111] After being away in Germany and then largely in Russia since 1816, Schuppanzigh arrived back in Vienna on ca. April 15, 1823. On February 15, 1824 (Blätter 15r–15v, above), Karl mentioned that the Theater did not want to engage Schuppanzigh until December, 1824. Courtesy Mark S. Zimmer (Madison, Wisconsin) and Birthe Kibsgaard (Aarhus, Denmark).—TA

[112] The tenor Ludwig Cramolini (1805–1884) seems to fit this profile. See Clive, p. 79.—TA

NEPHEW KARL [at Beethoven's apartment; long conversation, starting at ca. 2 p.m., then going into the evening on Friday, February 20]:

[discussing, then interviewing Franziska Hirschmann, an applicant for the housekeeper's position:] From the country. [//] She doesn't know from where. [//] Austrian; [from] Austria. [//] The vegetable dealer.[113] // She's had to do everything—carrying wood, etc. // A surgeon's widow // Leopoldstadt, Herrngasse No. 297, at the landlord's. Frau Hirschmann.[114] // She has children, but they do not live with her. // [Blatt 31v]

I encountered Schuppanzigh this morning. He went to [Abbé] Stadler to learn from him how they had given preference to a slovenly and even, as he expressed it, drunken young man, not yet 20 years old, since Dietrichstein, who was to award the position, had him summoned and told him that *now* he should apply; *now* is the time, when he hopes to be useful to him; and though it was precisely Dietrichstein who first suggested this Jansa (which is the young man's name) and did everything to get him the position before all the other applicants. //

You demanded it from me. // [written vertically→] Karlsbad. [←written vertically] [Blatt 32r]

[written previously in the right margin→] lamina-lamin-lamn-lam-lâme; Hieronymus-Hieronym-Hieronm-Hierom-Jerôme; bestia-beste-bête; asinus-asin-asne-âne[115] [←written previously in the right margin]

I bought pencils on the day that I went to the theater with your brother in the evening.[116] Someone brought them into the beer house and several people bought some; also the price seemed very inexpensive to me and so I bought a bunch and, what's more, for 30 kr. Then I didn't go shopping anymore, and therefore forgot about them. As you can see, there's still the full dozen. //

[interviewing a second applicant, Juliane Gneisel:]
Her husband was a chamber servant [to the nobility]. // She is strong in cooking because she has served in several houses of the nobility. // Juliane Gneisel, Breitenfeld

---

[113] Original German *Kräutlerin*. Beethoven must have asked where the applicant (presumably minimally literate) had learned that they had a vacancy, and the answer was from a woman working at one of Vienna's many vegetable stalls.—TA

[114] Franziska Hirschmann (b. 1770), a surgeon's widow, living at Leopoldstadt No. 297, in the house of the soapmaker Adam Wolfinger. In February 1824, she had had the following advertisement placed in several issues of the *Intelligenzblatt*: "A citizen's widow from the country, about 40 years old, wishes to become a housekeeper for a lady or a gentleman or even a parish rectory under reasonable conditions. Submit addresses, designated 'N.H.,' to the house owner at Leopoldstadt No. 297." See Conscriptions-Bogen, Leopoldstadt No. 297 (Wiener Stadt- und Landesarchiv).—KH

[115] These scribblings are similar to the linguistic development that Karl traced on Blatt 26v above and demonstrate how interested he was in languages and philology; and that these should have been his area of concentrated study at the university.—TA

[116] A pencil was on Beethoven's shopping list on Blatt 6r above; on Blatt 7r above, Karl mentions the opera *Aline*.—TA

[NEPHEW KARL, *continued*]

No. 81, 1st floor [2nd floor, American].[117] // [Blatt 32v] She says that lard is absolutely out of the question, because no lard may be used at the homes of the aristocracy; everything must be cooked well; as a result she is very strong in cooking. // She said that the housekeeper didn't want to tell her, but instead said that one [applicant] was here already anyway. //

6½ pounds. //

In other respects he is diligent. //

The old Papa died quite a long while ago. What a difference between *you* and *him*!!!![118] [//] [Blatt 33r]

At 8:30. //

We can try it for 2 fl. // 24 kr. must be added for the bottles, and the cheese costs 36 kr. *Quod erat demon[strandum]*. //

36 and 24 [kr.] make	1 fl.
The wine	1 fl. 30
	2 fl. 30 [W.W.] is 1 fl. C.M. //

In mathematical proofs, the proven proposition is developed; in the end, one repeats the *thesis* (or the proposition to be proven) and says *Quod fuit demonstrandum*—that which was to be proven. [//] [Blatt 33v]

That was Lafontane [*sic*].[119] //

The ball lasted 8 full hours.[120] //

[interviewing a third applicant, Frau Sartory:][121]

She is satisfied with the conditions. Although she has never been in a servant's position

---

[117] Breitenfeld was a Viennese suburb, immediately west of the Josephstadt and north of Kaiserstrasse (today's Josephstädter Strasse), but still inside the *Linie* (today's *Gürtel*), and now incorporated into the Josephstadt. The location would be on the west side of Bennogasse, between Bennoplatz and Laudongasse. Juliane Gneisel's name cannot be found among the surviving Conscriptions-Bögen in the Wiener Stadt- und Landesarchiv, but the survival and retrieval rate for census records in this part of Vienna are inconsistent in this period. See Groner, 1922, p. 50; Behsel, p. 207.—KH/TA

[118] Karl may have been referring to Leopold [?] Radoux's oil portrait of Beethoven's grandfather Ludwig (1712–1773), which the composer kept until his death.—TA

[119] The French poet of fables Jean de La Fontaine (1621–1695).—KH

[120] Court *Fasching* [or *Carneval*] balls in the weeks before Ash Wednesday (March 3 in 1824) were held in the two Redoutensäle on Sundays, Tuesdays, and Thursdays and lasted from 9 p.m. until 5 a.m. In addition, there were private or commercial balls at the *Mehlgrube* on the Neuer Markt, at the *Sperl* in the Leopoldstadt, and other locations, some on Mondays and Wednesdays, starting as early as 7 p.m. and frequently advertised in the *Intelligenzblatt* during this season.

Karl does not seem to have made any conversation-book entries on Thursday, February 19, so it is quite possible that he attended a ball that evening.—TA

[121] Frau Sartory was the wife of a schoolteacher. For further references to her as late as ca. January 28, 1825, see Heft 79, Blatt 10r; and Heft 83, Blatt 20v.—TA

[NEPHEW KARL, *continued*]
before, she can cook, wash, etc., *more* than well. // Her handwriting.[122] // [written vertically→] You should not be shocked by her clothing. She has never been a domestic servant, [because of] her circumstances. [←written vertically] // [Blatt 34r] She says that you should not consider that. What's more, she wanted to go to a nobleman, and so was *not* a domestic servant. // Josephstadt, at the *Hirsch*, Platzl No. 1; Sartory, 2nd floor [3rd floor, American], door 34.[123] [//] Hungarian noble['s?] widow; a Hungarian woman. // [written vertically→] Through [legal] trial. [←written vertically] // [Blatt 34v] She was satisfied with the room. // In any case she doesn't receive visits. // If it [sentence ends] // We have made good progress [in interviewing candidates]. // It is not about the informal way that she *walks*, but about her breasts that it would not be advisable.[124] // If you want, I shall speak with the Greek teacher.[125] [//] [Blatt 35r]

[seemingly writing in part on behalf of a currently employed domestic servant:]
She sent the mail. // She is going to the restaurant across the way. //

She has already thrashed her sweetheart by going to the ball without him. She just said so. // Because he believed that they must first be married. // Unaccompanied. // She promenaded around for a long time before some man invited her to dance. // [Blatt 35v]

We won't get one like Mamsell Pamer so soon anymore.[126] // Because he will reply: "I am Herr von Echsner."[127] //

---

[122] Beethoven may have asked for a sample of her handwriting, and she seemingly wrote on another sheet of paper or a chalkboard.—TA

[123] This address was actually in the suburb of Neubau, not the Josephstadt, but is easily confused. The numbering of Neubau started with the *Goldener Hirsch* (Golden Stag), at the west end of "Am Platzl" (now part of Neustiftgasse), just northwest of the St. Ulrich Church, and continued around the corner and north on the east side of Schottenhofgasse for a block, and then east on the south side of Roverani/Rofranogasse (today's Lerchenfelder Strasse). Unfortunately, the *Grundobrigkeit* (sacred-secular administrative authority) is *Stift Schotten* (the Schotten Monastery) (as is true for several of the near western suburbs of Vienna—for which the *Conscriptions-Bögen* (census sheets used for military conscription) do not begin until 1830. No one named Sartory remains in the main series or *Fremden-Tabelle* in 1830. See Behsel, p. 159.—TA

[124] Unlike most applicants for domestic positions, this applicant must have been personally attractive and attractively dressed. Karl had had trouble with a maid's carelessly exposing herself to him the previous summer, and he and Beethoven had frequently discussed the advisability of hiring women domestics who were unattractive or sufficiently along in years that there would be no gossip.—TA

[125] On Friday, February 27, Karl noted that he would go to see the Greek teacher the next day to try to get a seat in his class. See Heft 57, Blatt 13v. Karl's Greek teacher at Blöchlinger's Institute had been Paul Pulay (1777–1836), a baptized Jew. His Greek teacher at the University was Anton Joseph Stein (1759–1844); see Clive, pp. 351–352.—TA

[126] Maria Pamer (b. 1807), a domestic servant who had left Beethoven's employ prior to June 1822 and was still frequently mentioned in conversation with a certain degree of nostalgic fondness. Her father was the popular dance orchestra leader, Michael Pamer. See Heft 42, Blatt 24v; Heft 55, Blatt 10v; and several references in between. See further on Heft 78, Blätter 11r and 36r; and Heft 79, Blatt 25r. They considered hiring her again as late as March 23, 1825 (Heft 85, Blatt 46r).—TA

[127] The German editors index him as Carl Exner (Echsner), but with no further identification. No other individuals named Exner, Echsner, Öchsner, or Öxner seem to appear in either Beethoven's

[NEPHEW KARL, *continued*]

[Karl writes, in part, on behalf of visiting Johann:]

He [Therese's lover] doesn't dare. // He doesn't come anymore; she goes to him. // Your brother has forbidden him to come to the house. // But she answers: "Good, then I'll go to him now, if he is not to come *here* any longer." [//] [Blatt 36r]

Schumlauer, 2 bottles	1 fl. 30 [kr.]
Karlowitzer, ditto, 2 bottles	1 fl. 30
	3 fl. //

He hangs on to anyone who gives him something. //

Your brother also said already that Lichnowsky still goes to his _____ every day,[128] but that if he notices a similar deviation from the rule on [the part of] his wife, he gets horribly enraged and doesn't permit it. //

Your brother would really *like* to get loose from her, and *she* would like the same, so there must be *something* that's holding the *both of them* from it. [//] [Blatt 36v]

Do you want a piece of cheese? //

She [one of the day's applicants] would like to come here, but otherwise appears not to be in pleasant circumstances, as near as I can tell. // An Austrian woman; I forget the town. //

[Johann departs; it is clearly a Friday evening, presumably February 20:]

Your brother had to go because he has promised to go and visit a family where they play cards every Friday. [//] 18 //

Leschen said that he would be very reasonable, because he has the greatest esteem for you as an artist.[129] [//]

End of Heft 56

N.B. There are only three or four days (over a weekend) between Hefte 56 and 57—possibly enough for a small conversation book, now missing.

---

conversation books or his correspondence. A musician, Franz Exner (b. ca. 1772), had been taken from Count Harrach's house and died of consumption at the Barmherzige Brüder in Vienna on April 15, 1808 (see Gugitz, "Verlassenschafts-Abhandlungen," V324/1808, p. 68).—TA

[128] Presumably Count Moritz Lichnowsky kept a mistress whom he saw daily.—TA

[129] Wilhelm Leschen, piano maker in suburban Wieden; see Heft 49, Blatt 10v.—TA

Heft 57

(February 25, 1824 – March 9, 1824)

[Blatt 1r]

NEPHEW KARL [**at Beethoven's apartment in the Ungargasse (or possibly already in a coffee house or restaurant in the City); probably early afternoon of Wednesday, February 25**]:[1] They [the domestic servants] did not receive any candles today.[2] //

All of a sudden, today, the maid started in about wanting to leave, that she gave you notice two weeks ago. [written vertically→] She just started two weeks ago Monday. [←written vertically] [//]

[Blatt 1v]

SCHUPPANZIGH [**seemingly greeting Beethoven and Karl, possibly on his way upstairs at a two-storied coffee house or restaurant in the City;[3] possibly approaching midday dinnertime, ca. 2 p.m., on Wednesday, February 25**]: In any case, I am coming here tomorrow [Thursday] morning. [//]

NEPHEW KARL: 2 fl. 30 [kr.][4] //

[discussing items for the maid's recommendation:]
Perhaps she wishes that you also indicate her birthplace, and then that she is still a virgin, and things that are said in the other testimonial. If she'll bring a *Stempelbogen*,[5] I'll be happy to write it; she only asks that more [information] be included there. [//]

---

[1] Heft 56 probably ended on the evening of Friday, February 20, 1824. Heft 57 may begin as early as Tuesday, February 24, when the report about the *Componium* (turned into a joke concerning Gelinek on Blatt 3r below) appeared in the *Beobachter*; but probably the day after, on Wednesday, February 25.—TA

[2] On Blatt 10r below, Beethoven reminds himself to buy candles.—TA

[3] For a reference to Schuppanzigh's being "upstairs," see Blatt 3v below. Schuppanzigh was fond of a multi-storied coffee house/restaurant on the southeast corner of Dorotheergasse and Plankengasse. The upper floor was more exclusive and featured its own table settings and silverware.—TA

[4] This sum is duplicated (or replicated) on Blatt 4r below, possibly at the end of this extended encounter in the coffee house or restaurant.—TA

[5] A prepaid, stamped sheet of paper for writing official documents.—TA

[Blatt 2r][6]

LEOPOLD SONNLEITHNER [?][7] **[presumably accompanied by Castelli, encountering Beethoven in the coffee house or restaurant; continuing]**:

<You will surely do well, and [illegible: the income] will be great. Schuppanzigh, [Ferdinand] Piringer, and I shall take care of everything.[8] [//]

He[9] eats at the *Stern* in the *Brandstatt*[10] every Sunday.> [//]

There is also nothing in the Hofkapelle; [Leopold] Jansa, a young man who

---

[6] The crossed out areas on Blätter 2r, 2v, and most of 3r are badly smudged, with many words on Blatt 2r illegible. Thus there are ambiguities in the German transcriptions and, as a result, the English translations.—KH/TA

[7] In 1981, Shin Augustinus Kojima identified the author of these entries as Leopold Sonnleithner (1797–1873), nephew of Joseph Sonnleithner (1766–1835), the initial German librettist of Beethoven's *Fidelio* in 1804–1805. A lawyer by profession (as were many of the men in his family), Leopold was an amateur musician who grew up in a household where his father, Ignaz, sponsored a successful semiprivate salon from ca. 1813 through the mid-1820s. By 1824, if Piringer was considered the primary contact for the Gesellschaft der Musikfreunde's instrumental amateurs, then Sonnleithner occupied the same unofficial position with respect to its choral forces. One must remember, however, that he was essentially the same age as Schubert. By the 1860s, he was considered one of Vienna's grand old men in music and, indeed, looking back on this era with considerable nostalgia and authority, he had also become a proverbial "legend in his own mind."

Sonnleithner is literate, even quoting Latin, as an educated jurist would, but nonetheless refers to "Brandstadt," "Schupanzigh" (twice), and "Linovsky" here. In any case, because the paper is smudged, these entries are difficult to read, even illegible.

See Kojima, "Die Aufführung der Neunten Symphonie Beethovens—einige neue Tatsachen," in *Bericht über den Internationalen Musikwissenschaftlichen Kongress, Bayreuth, 1981*, ed. Christoph Hellmut Mahling and Sigrid Wiesmann (Kassel: Bärenreiter, 1984), pp. 390–392; and Albrecht, *Letters to Beethoven*, No. 344, footnote 2.

Leopold von Sonnleithner, "Musikalische Skizzen aus 'Alt-Wien,'" in *Recensionen und Mittheilungen über Theater, Musik und bildende Kunst*, six installments, from 7, No. 47 (November 24, 1861), pp. 737–741, through 9, No. 21 (May 24, 1863), pp. 322–325 (including a chapter on the Sonnleithner family by Wilhelm Böcking); repr., with introduction by Otto Erich Deutsch, in *Österreichische Musikzeitschrift* 16 (1961), pp. 49–62, 97–110, 145–157; fully translated and edited in Alexandra Vago, "Musical Life of Amateur Musicians in Vienna, ca. 1814–1825," M.A. thesis, musicology (Kent State University, December, 2001), pp. 130–189. See also Clive, pp. 341–343.—TA

[8] Encouraging Beethoven to give a concert, probably anticipating the *Ludlamshöhle* Petition that would probably be delivered the next day. Sonnleithner may have let the cat out of the bag already on Blatt 3r below but may also have crossed the question out before Beethoven read it. For confirmation of the petition's delivery, see Blatt 11v below. In any case, Sonnleithner does not mention Schindler among his organizational group.—TA

[9] Probably Ignaz Schuppanzigh, who had just been mentioned, and who would call a concert-organizational meeting at the *Stern* on Sunday, March 7, at 1 p.m. (see Heft 58). It could possibly be poet Franz Grillparzer, Sonnleithner's cousin, who also had a known association with that restaurant. See *Der grosse Groner*, ed. Czeike, 1974, pp. 141 and 787.—TA

[10] The restaurant *Zum Stern* [At the Star] in the *Brandstatt* No. 629, which was located across the courtyard from Leopold Wanner's beer house *Zur Eiche* [At the Oak] in the Brandstatt No. 631. See *Frühwirtscher Grundriss*; Pezzl, p. 242.—KH

absolutely doesn't take no for an answer, has been employed as a violinist in the Hofkapelle. [//]

[Blatt 2v]

IGNAZ FRANZ CASTELLI[11] [**presumably accompanying Sonnleithner**]: Müller's trumpets and timpani.[12] [//] Always annoyed about money. [//] He paid over 35,000 [fl.] [//]
   [**introducing himself:**]
   Castelli. //
   He gives quartet concerts, but only of your [works].[13] [//]

[Blatt 3r]

SONNLEITHNER [**continuing**]: <Have you received the invitation[14] that I signed?> [//] Count Lichnowsky[15] sent it to me, and 100 of your friends signed it.[16]> [//]
   Abbé Jelinek[17] has been transformed, in a way, into a machine. *Qualis, quantus clamor* [What kind of outcry, and how great]. //

---

[11] A comparison of these entries with those in Heft 97, Blätter 57r–58v, and in turn with an autograph letter in the Handschriften-Sammlung (Manuscript Collection), Austrian National Library, reveals that they are by Ignaz Castelli. See Heft 68, Blatt 21v; and Heft 97, Blatt 57r.
   Ignaz Franz Castelli (1781–1862), Viennese poet and theatrical author, was among the signers of the Petition to Beethoven that Sonnleithner mentions on Blatt 3r below. See Wurzbach, vol. 2, pp. 303–306; Clive, pp. 68–69.—KH/TA

[12] Possibly used in Müller's parody *Aline*, premiered at the Theater in der Josephstadt on January 22, 1824. See Heft 56, Blatt 7v.—TA

[13] Possibly a reference to Schuppanzigh, many of whose string quartet concerts consisted of one work each by Haydn, Mozart, and Beethoven.—TA

[14] The so-called *Adresse* or Petition to Beethoven, written in extremely flowery language, requesting him to reconsider the possibilities of premiering his newest works, the Ninth Symphony and *Missa solemnis*, in Berlin and instead keep the performances in Vienna. It was signed by 30 prominent (mostly wealthy) amateur music lovers and music publishers, with a few professional musicians like Czerny (who catered to the wealthy) but no professional orchestral musicians. It was dated merely "Vienna, in February, 1824." Later entries reveal that it was a product of the *Ludlamshöhle*, a loose organization of writers and music lovers hoping to promote German culture and lessen the current Italian influence in Vienna. Beethoven was aware of the humorous or silly names that the participants often gave themselves, and he did not approve. Later references may call the document the "*Ludlamshöhle* Petition." See Albrecht, *Letters to Beethoven*, No. 344; and, with modified translation, Albrecht, *Beethoven's Ninth Symphony: Rehearsing and Performing Its 1824 Premiere* (Woodbridge, Suffolk: Boydell and Brewer, 2024), Appendix B.—TA

[15] Beethoven's current friend Count Moritz Lichnowsky was among the signers, as was his nephew, Prince Eduard Lichnowsky (son of Beethoven's friend Prince Karl Lichnowsky, who had died in 1814). See Clive, pp. 202–205.—KH

[16] Actually, as noted above, the document was signed by 30 individuals, suggesting that Sonnleithner, already holding a doctorate in law, was not above stretching the truth to suit his purposes.—TA

[17] Abbé Joseph Gelinek/Jelinek (1758–1825), Bohemian-born priest and composer, active in Vienna since about 1790, at first with the Kinsky family and later in the Esterházy employ. He composed and

NEPHEW KARL [**presumably still at the restaurant**]: [written vertically→] Dinner?[18] What otherwise? Roast? [←written vertically]

[Blatt 3v]

SONNLEITHNER [**continuing**]: Do you want to see Schuppanzigh? I'll take you to him in the room upstairs. [//]

BEETHOVEN:[19]
    50 [kr.]
    50
    30
    30
  ─────
3 [fl.] 40 [kr.]

SCHINDLER [falsified entries begin→] Mylord[20] complains about everything that takes place where he is not present with his bow. Therefore don't believe him in this respect. [←falsified entries end]

NEPHEW KARL [**presumably still at the restaurant; ca. 2 p.m. on Wednesday, February 25**]: [written vertically→] Vegetable soup. Soup horseradish. Blue cabbage. Roast? Loin of beef. [←written vertically] //

[Blatt 4r]

---

published an extraordinary number of variations for piano, and, as a result, was often derisively called the "Variation Hero" or "Variation Smith."

The joke here implies that, just as Gelinek cranked out variations like a machine, a machine had now been invented that cranked out variations like Gelinek. It refers to the *Componium* or *Musical Improviser*, an invention that had been introduced in Paris in January 1824 by the mechanic Dietrich Nikolaus Winkel from Lippstadt, Westphalia. The *Österreichischer Beobachter*, No. 55 (February 24, 1824), p. 526, reported: "For the past few weeks in Paris, there has been exhibited for an admission fee, a mechanical-musical instrument named a *Componium* by its inventor, because it appears to compose a theme on its own (or takes one given to it) and then proceeds to play endless variations on it, without any further touch by the human hand."

See also the *Wiener AmZ* 8, No. 1 (March 3, 1824), pp. 3–4, No. 7 (March 17, 1824), pp. 25–26, and following issues; the *Beobachter*, No. 55 (February 24, 1824), p. 526; *Wiener Zeitschrift* 9, No. 35 (March 20, 1824), p. 297; Clive, pp. 124–125; and Wurzbach, vol. 5, pp. 128–129.—KH/TA

[18] Seemingly trapped in an unexpected social encounter, Karl and Beethoven may have resigned themselves to staying at this restaurant for dinner. The situation is recognizably Viennese, even today.—TA

[19] The sum here is actually 2 fl. 40 kr. The sum on Blatt 4r is correct.—TA

[20] After Beethoven's death, Schindler must have spied violinist Schuppanzigh's name among these entries and succumbed to the temptation to belittle him.—TA

BEETHOVEN:
2 [fl.] 30 [kr.]
$\underline{50}$
3 [fl.] 20 [kr.] //

[probably the end of an unexpectedly prolonged social situation in a restaurant in the City.]

NEPHEW KARL **[upon returning to Beethoven's apartment; later in the afternoon of Wednesday, February 25]**: The maid says that while you were gone today, a gentleman was here who appeared very vexed to find no one [at home].[21] // How did they behave themselves?

Beer   46 [kr.]
$\underline{1\text{ fl. }12}$
1 fl. 58 [kr.] [//]

[Blatt 4v]

SCHUPPANZIGH **[probably at the same restaurant, as promised; the morning of Thursday, February 26; presumably joined by Karl]**: I recently played at a performance of *Der Freischütz*;[22] it is a shame how the orchestra played.[23] // How is it looking for his [= your] concert? // It's getting late; Lent doesn't last long.[24] // He [= You] can give 3 movements from it [the *Missa solemnis*].[25] [//] Only no piano piece. [//] [Blatt 5r] There is no pianist here.[26] //

He [= You] need Piringer to take care of the best [instrumental] dilettantes,

---

[21] This observation lends credence to the idea that Beethoven may have spent longer in the City than originally planned.—TA

[22] Weber's *Der Freischütz* had been performed at the Kärntnertor Theater on January 22 and February 6, 1824. See Bäuerle's *Allgemeine Theater-Zeitung* 17, No. 15 (February 3, 1824), p. 58; and No. 19 (February 12, 1824), p. 75.—KH

[23] The Viennese correspondent for Leipzig's *Allgemeine musikalische Zeitung* 26, No. 8 (February 19, 1824), cols. 121–122, likewise confirmed that "the old, well-established reputation of this orchestra … became a joke."—TA

[24] Lent began on Ash Wednesday, March 3; Easter Sunday was on April 18 in 1824.—TA

[25] In the Akademie of May 7, 1824, the Kyrie, Credo, and Agnus Dei were performed. Beethoven (or brother Johann) seems initially to have projected the Sanctus (with its extensive violin solo for Schuppanzigh) as the third excerpt. See Blatt 18v below.—KH/TA

[26] Schuppanzigh may have forgotten about Carl Czerny or did not consider him to be a viable performer in public. The latter view was evidently shared by Czerny himself, who turned down Beethoven's invitation to perform the Piano Concerto No. 5 at the repeat of his Akademie on May 23, 1824. See Albrecht, *Letters to Beethoven*, No. 366.—TA

Sonnleithner to take care of the [choral] singers, and Blahetka to take care of the announcements and fliers.[27] // He offered to do it. //

Also Preisinger.[28] // <not> One must not overlook [bass singer] Forti; he is skillful. // Rauscher.[29] [//] [Blatt 5v] Haitzinger. // Jäger has the most beautiful voice.[30] //

Young [Leopold] Sonnleithner has all the singing dilettantes under his command. // Sonnleithner knows them very well, and he understands it. //

It would be very good if he [= you] might sometime make a visit to Duport, in order to speak about me again. [//]

[Schuppanzigh presumably departs, leaving Beethoven and Karl alone.]

[Blatt 6r]

BEETHOVEN **[seemingly still at the restaurant in the City; morning of Thursday, February 26]**:
Otherwise ask Grillparzer very quietly.
+ Shoe wax.[31]
+ Letter paper. //

NEPHEW KARL **[continuing]**: I can certainly say without bragging that I was diligent in *French*, can understand *any* book, and am also able to *write* it without errors. But to compose *poetry* in it demands fluency akin to what we have in our *mother tongue*. And now in English, in which I am a beginner! But—Schiller [Blatt 6v] has already been completely translated into English, and it wouldn't be difficult to adapt the translation of this chorus.[32] //

If you aren't going to eat anything more, you could have the bill made out *right now*, since I am still here.

---

[27] Joseph Blahetka (1783 – after 1847), manager of a paper factory in Guntramsdorf, ca. 2 miles south-southeast of Mödling and ca. 12 miles south of Vienna. He had married Barbara Sophia Traeg (b. 1787), a niece of the Viennese music publisher Johann Traeg. Their daughter Leopoldine (1809–1885) was a talented pianist, and Beethoven was well acquainted with the family. In ca. 1821, Blahetka was also noted as an author and professor of stenography, living in the Josephstadt, Florianigasse No. 52. See Böckh, 1822, p. 8; Deutsch, *Schubert-Dokumente*, p. 69; Ziegler, *Addressen-Buch*, p. 5; and Clive, p. 36.—KH/TA

[28] Joseph Preisinger (1792–1865); see Heft 53, Blatt 11r.—KH/TA

[29] Jacob Rauscher, singer at the Theater an der Wien, living in suburban Wieden, Waag Gasse No. 294, one block west of the Paulaner Kirche. See Ziegler, *Addressen-Buch*, p. 83.—KH/TA

[30] Franz Jäger, singer at the Theater an der Wien, living in the theater's apartment building, Laimgrube No. 26. See Ziegler, *Addressen-Buch*, p. 82.—KH/TA

[31] See Beethoven's old loyalty to Franz Spar's wax polish on Blatt 13r below.—TA

[32] Beethoven had promised London's Philharmonic Society a manuscript copy of the Ninth Symphony, which it received in December 1824. An English translation of Schiller's "Ode to Joy, in the same meter" appeared from Beresford (Berlin, 1810). See Kayser, V, p. 82.—KH

9 fl. 60
4 fl. 22
5 fl. 38 come back. [//]

[Blatt 7r]

BEETHOVEN: Inheritance tax on bank shares and bank obligation notes from the times of the testator.—O Misery! //

NEPHEW KARL [**possibly at Frau Schlemmer's copying shop in the Kohlmarkt; late morning or early afternoon of Thursday, February 26**]: How many copyists are working here? // Has it already been determined in which *place* she is located? [//]

[Blatt 7v]

SCHINDLER [**joining Beethoven in the City as Karl goes his own way; probably early afternoon of Thursday, February 26**]:
Are you going home from here now? //
[**possibly partly on the walk home, then partly after arriving at Beethoven's apartment:**]
Yesterday [Wednesday, February 25], with your brother, we notified the police about the business with his wife, and if he is smart and follows the advice that was given him, he—as he assures me by his honor—can rescue capital of 50,000 fl. C.M. (as he himself states it) for you and Karl. It will cost him little. // He will soon show how he thinks. // It is happening in the greatest silence and circumspection. [//] [Blatt 8r] If he doesn't consider a few hundred gulden for it, he will easily be censured. // But he now sees for himself how much he has wronged you and himself. // It has begun so well that it now depends solely upon him as to how the matter will be resolved. // Only one witness is necessary, but this [person] must be able to give evidence about it officially. // This will also be done, once the investigation takes place. [//] [Blatt 8v] One must now come to his aid, because he is really serious about it, otherwise I would absolutely never have gotten mixed up in it. But he assures me so sincerely that he owes it to himself and especially to you. // If he can only keep his mouth shut and speak nowhere about it, because this will spoil it otherwise. // Someday soon a police official will introduce him to the police director, who will certainly make it his concern [Blatt 9r] if your brother doesn't want to have everything done in vain. // I told him bluntly what he must do in this regard. He promised to do it, so now we shall see. // He cannot let it go, because she is now saying that he is to pay her half to her. // He declares that she brought nothing to him. But in the marriage contract, he pledged half of the entire property that exists now to her, and therefore she is citing that. // [Blatt 9v]

[at Beethoven's apartment, looking through his bookshelves:]
I would really like to read through the *Mythologie* again. If you have a copy of it, please lend it to me for just a little while.[33] [//]

[Schindler seemingly grabs a roll to eat, a book to read, and sits with Beethoven during the following interview:]

KATHARINA KUMMER[34] **[at Beethoven's apartment; 2 p.m. or shortly thereafter on Thursday, February 26]**:[35] Excuse me, I have Learned From a Woman That You Wish to have a Housekeeper.[36] [//] [I live] in the Tiefer Graben No. 167, 2nd floor [3rd floor, American]. // <Tomorrow.>[37] Friday [February 27], at about 5:30 in the evening in Hietzing.[38] [//]

[Schindler presumably borrows a book and departs after the applicant does.]

[Blatt 10r]

BEETHOVEN **[at his apartment, possibly as it grows darker; mid-to-late afternoon of Thursday, February 26]**:
+ Small candles.[39] //

NEPHEW KARL **[possibly at a coffee house or at Beethoven's apartment; the evening of Thursday, February 26]**:
Not much will come from the action that Herr S[chindler] has begun.[40] // Who is included in the term "we"? //

---

[33] Presumably Moritz's *Götterlehre*, also noted by Karl on Blatt 10r below.—TA

[34] According to a Conscriptions-Bogen (census sheet) of 1824, a Frau Katharina Kumer (b. 1778), widow of a former tavern keeper, along with her son Franz (b. 1797), a business bookkeeper, and her daughter Rosalia (b. 1809), lived in the City at Tiefer Graben No. 167, Wohnpartei 4. There had been two other widows (Anna Hödl, b. 1776, and Rosalia Stubler, b. 1794) earlier in Wohnpartei 3, but Kumer (probably Kummer) fits the requirements much better. See Conscriptions-Bogen, Stadt, No. 167 [new collation, 167:4] (Wiener Stadt- und Landesarchiv).—KH/TA

[35] Beethoven's advertisement in the *Intelligenzblatt* on Wednesday, February 18, had specified that interviews would be conducted at 2 p.m. daily. The advertisement had not appeared more recently. See Heft 56, Blätter 25v and 27v.—TA

[36] At least in this sample, the applicant writes with a few phonetic spellings and more capitals than usual, but reasonably well otherwise.—TA

[37] Presuming, from the surrounding chronology, that "tomorrow" will be Friday, February 27.—TA

[38] Hietzing, an old village on the western edge of the Schönbrunn Palace park, today part of the 13th *Bezirk*. Lichnowsky lived in Hietzing during the summer of 1823. See Groner, 1922, p. 168; and Heft 36, Blatt 1r.—KH/TA

[39] Original German *Lichter*; Karl's note on Blatt 1r above suggested the need to buy candles; Beethoven's additional note on Blatt 11r confirms it.—TA

[40] In July 1823, Schindler had visited brother Johann's apartment and reported to Beethoven about Therese's misconduct with her lover while Johann lay ill (see Albrecht, *Letters to Beethoven*, Nos. 326–328; and Heft 35, Blätter 5r–19r). At that time, there was a threat of police action that never took place,

HEFT 57 (FEBRUARY 25 – MARCH 9, 1824), BLATT 10V

Also some Bratwursts. //

I seriously doubt the truth of this tale. //

He [Schindler] asked me for Moritz's *Götterlehre*.[41] //

This evening, the old woman [housekeeper Barbara Holzmann] asked me to tell you that S[chindler] ate a Semmel [roll], so that you wouldn't think that she had reckoned too much for them. [//] [Blatt 10v] She meant it well, [but] she knows that you notice immediately if too much gets charged for something; so she asked me to let you know about this. //

They are trying to find out when the end of *Fasching* is.[42] //

1 fl. 51 [kr.][43] //

SCHINDLER [falsified entries begin→]:

I anticipated [*anticipirt*] one roll, because I was hungry; the extra expense must be given to the housekeeper and charged to my bill. //

Orestes is clever; otherwise Pylades[44] again gives you lessons that you prefer not to hear.[45] [←falsified entries end]

[Blatt 11r]

BEETHOVEN [probably at his apartment; probably the morning of Friday, February 27]:

+ Candles.

+ Measure 2 supports for the chicken coop and afterward show them to the carpenter. //

and Karl as much as says that the same thing will happen now; see Blatt 25v below for Schindler's own reference to this "action." In both cases, no matter how serious Johann's situation seemed to be, Schindler's meddling threatened to make it worse.—TA

[41] Karl Philipp Moritz (1757–1793), author, professor of ancient studies at the Berlin Academy of Art from 1789. In 1791, he published *Götterlehre oder mythologische Dichtungen der Alten* (Manual of the Gods, or Mythological Poems of the Ancients), a book that later appeared in several editions. See Schindler's search for it on Beethoven's shelves, Blatt 9v above. See *Allgemeine Deutsche Biographie*, vol. 22, pp. 308–310; Kayser, IV, p. 143.—KH

[42] In 1824, the *Fasching* (or Carneval/Carnival) season ended with Ash Wednesday, March 3. The *Fastenzeit* (Lent) then lasted until Easter Sunday and Monday (April 18 and 19).—KH/TA

[43] This may have been the cost of the Bratwursts noted above, possibly ordered as takeout from the restaurant on the street floor of Beethoven's apartment building.—TA

[44] Just as Schindler's first falsified entry refers to the roll that he ate, this second refers to characters that he might have expected to find in Moritz's book on mythology. Orestes and Pylades were close friends, and many writers interpret it as a homosexual relationship. Schindler may possibly have been homosexual; Beethoven was not.—TA

[45] The references to "you" here are in the familiar *du* form, used for family members, close friends, children, animals, and poetic address. Schindler was never on a *du* basis with Beethoven (though he might have implied here that he was), and he would have had little reason to write such entries to Karl (to whom they otherwise seem to be directed), because, unlike Beethoven, Karl could *hear* Schindler in a normal conversational tone.—TA

NEPHEW KARL [**adding to Beethoven's errand list**]:

Wipplingerstrasse. Go straight ahead from the Hoher Markt, then turn to the right into Herr Mayer's shop. Candles. // Molded variety, 8 for 36 kr. Kitchen candles, 10 for 30 kr.[46] //

BEETHOVEN [**possibly while out shopping; probably early afternoon of Friday, February 27**]:

17	14
17	<14>
8½	20
42½	8½

+ Sugar

2½
2½
2½
2½

[Blatt 11v]

NEPHEW KARL [**at Beethoven's apartment, presumably before and during midday dinner; ca. 2 p.m. on Friday, February 27**]:

Have you read through the letter[47] that was sent to you yesterday [Thursday, February 26]? //

He [Lichnowsky?] may have over 200,000 fl. in property. //

---

[46] This refers to the housewares shop of Johann Mayer in the City, Wipplingerstrasse No. 386. See Redl, 1824, p. 48.—KH

[47] The Petition, dated "Vienna in February 1824" and signed by thirty music lovers, asking Beethoven, in embarrassingly flattering language, to retain the premieres of the *Missa solemnis* and, especially, the Ninth Symphony in Vienna. The previous Tuesday morning (February 24), Leopold Sonnleithner had already asked Beethoven whether he had received it.

On Thursday, February 26, Beethoven and Karl met Schuppanzigh in the City in the morning (Blatt 4v above). Then they seemingly visited a copying shop around noon (Blatt 7r). Thereafter, Schindler may have met Beethoven and accompanied him home (Blatt 7v) and possibly remained while Beethoven interviewed a potential housekeeper at 2 p.m. (Blatt 9v).

Schindler (Schindler-MacArdle, pp. 275–276) says that Court Secretary Felsburg and Dr. Johann Nepomuk Bihler (or Biehler) brought the document "just after the noon meal." Beethoven's customary time to eat that meal was ca. 2 p.m., but he had also reserved that time to interview housekeeper applicants. Schindler may have been present when the two signers of the Petition delivered the document (we have no other indication who did so), but in any case, the delivery itself left no entries from anyone in Beethoven's conversation book, nor did Schindler read it until Monday, March 8 (Blatt 39v below). See also Albrecht, *Letters to Beethoven*, No. 334; and Blatt 3r above.—TA

Mozart's fingers were so bent from his incessant playing that he couldn't cut meat by himself. //

Did you also learn a wind instrument?[48] //[49] [Blatt 12r]

3 pounds [pound sign] make 1 fl. 48 [kr.]; therefore 12 kr. remain. // The vinegar is used up. // That is 50. //

She [Barbara Holzmann or housekeeper applicant Kummer][50] says that the tooth is decayed, but she cannot have it pulled. //

He [Schindler] is eating at your brother's today. //

She [Barbara Holzmann or housekeeper applicant Kummer] says that the kitchen is warmer than the room, even when it isn't heated. // [Blatt 12v]

Your brother serves his cause badly, because he carries on about it everywhere he goes; and if the matter is not held in strict secrecy, then everything is done in vain. //

Presumably people have often misled her about how painful it is to have a tooth pulled. I think that she'd rather die than try to do it. //

The ancients must have been great lovers of lentils. For a lentil stew, Esau sold his right of the firstborn to his younger brother. [//] [Blatt 13r] Jacob at his cousin [*sic*] Laban's.[51] //

Is she [Barbara Holzmann or housekeeper applicant Kummer] also to bring *Sallat* [lettuce]? // She says that she made 6 pieces from the whole fish. Two are here; one was on the lentils, and three are still being boiled out there [in the kitchen]. // Judging from the head, it [the fish] was fairly large. // Blessed are they who believe without having seen. //

BEETHOVEN [at a coffee house; late afternoon of Friday, February 27]:

+ Spar's wax polish factory, am Hof, Färbergasse No. 334.[52] [//]

[Blatt 13v]

---

[48] Beethoven may have answered that he had studied horn with Bonn's senior but low-registered hornist Nikolaus Simrock (1751–1832) and that he too was more adept in the instrument's low register.—TA

[49] Above and below the dividing line are calligraphic scribbles: "Karl," "Popper," "Pipes," and "Pidoll."—KH

[50] Katharina Kummer, the housekeeper applicant who wrote on Blatt 9v above—TA

[51] This discussion was surely prompted by the presence of lentils on Beethoven's dinner table on a meatless Friday with fish as the main dish, accompanied by lentils and a salad.

In Gen. 25:30–34, Esau and Jacob are twin sons of Isaac, with Esau the elder of the two. Esau finds himself famished and trades his birthright to Jacob for a bowl of lentil stew. By Gen. 28:2–5, Jacob flees a now-angry Esau, going to a distant land to work for his maternal uncle Laban. Western myths tell that, eventually, the two brothers reconcile and cultivate vast acres of lentils in Idaho's Palouse.—TA

[52] The shoe- and leather-wax factory of Franz Spar. Over the years, Beethoven had also bought shoe or boot polish made by Spar at a shop in the Kärntnerstrasse. See the *Intelligenzblatt*, No. 47 (Friday, February 27, 1824), p. 369 (Advertisements). The same advertisement, proclaiming Spar's fifteen years in business, had already appeared in No. 32 (February 10, 1824), p. 265; and No. 39 (February 18, 1824), p. 319.—KH/TA

NEPHEW KARL [probably at Beethoven's apartment; probably the evening of Friday, February 27]:

Since I'm eating tomorrow [Saturday, February 28] in the City anyhow, I'll go to the Greek teacher[53] and speak with him. I believe that he will be quite happy to find a place [for me]. //

[seemingly at a restaurant, presumably in the City, after running errands; probably midday dinner[54] on Saturday, February 28:]

The cashier who paid me the stipend from Archduke Rudolph has also become deaf.[55] //

Grinzing[56] is also a beautiful location. //

Since it needs no bill.[57] [//] [Blatt 14r]

Soup, 2 portions	14 [kr.]
Beef, 2 portions	48
Pastry, 2 portions	48
Wine	1 fl. 30 [kr.] //

7
24
24
3
—
58 kr., the amount I have consumed. I can already pay it. //

Soup, beef, and accompanying dishes. // On average, 2 fl. are enough. // For me, the pastry is almost too strong. There is <coffee> *rum* as well. [//]

---

[53] Possibly Anton Joseph Stein (1759–1844), professor of Latin literature and Greek philology at the university; see Heft 60, Blatt 30r. Possibly Karl has not given up his hopes, expressed on July 27, 1823, of becoming a French-language teacher with secondary areas in Latin and Greek; see Heft 36, Blätter 15r–15v.—TA

[54] It seems as though Beethoven may have joined Karl for that aforementioned dinner in the City.—TA

[55] This entry concerns the annual stipend, totaling 4,000 fl., awarded to Beethoven by Prince Lobkowitz, Prince Kinsky, and Archduke Rudolph early in 1809, to keep the composer in Vienna after he had received an offer from Kassel. Of the three guarantors, only Archduke Rudolph had been dependable with his payments. Within Rudolph's staff were Andreas Martini, director of the high steward's office, privy paymaster, and head cashier; Joseph Nitsche, official and cashier's comptroller in the high steward's office; and Johann Protivinsky, official in the head cashier's office. See Frimmel, *Handbuch*, I, p. 87; and *Hof- und Staats-Schematismus*, 1824, I, p. 194.—KH/TA

[56] Grinzing, a village to the west of Heiligenstadt, four hilly miles northwest of Vienna, since 1892 in the 19th *Bezirk*. See Groner, 1922, p. 139.—KH

[57] Karl uses the term *Rechnung* here, possibly interchangeable with *Quittung*, in any case probably referring to the statement that the intended recipient of a stipend was actually alive, usually signed by the recipient's parish priest.—TA

[Blatt 14v]

BEETHOVEN [presumably at a coffee house; probably late afternoon of Saturday, February 28]: Live in the [Landstrasse] Hauptstrasse, at the *Barmherzige* [*Brüder*] (Brothers of Mercy), since it [the sunshine] is bright enough in the first [American, second] floor and everything is secure.—Apartment right there, No. 272, first floor.[58] [//] [Blatt 15r]

+ Pepper, however Pepp[er] .... //

NEPHEW KARL [at Beethoven's apartment; probably late Sunday morning, February 29]: Your brother spoke again about his wish to get away [from Therese] entirely. Schindler had then taken him to a young man who is with the police. The case is progressing very slowly now, because they vigorously defend themselves against every charge made against them. // One wants to prevent that just now; because one knows that she would oppose it. // He said that he has to catch her in the act, [but observed] by *another* witness. [//] [Blatt 15v] He doesn't want to pay the money just now, because he now contributes only as much per month as he receives from the estate [in Gneixendorf]. [//]

Also she [presumably Therese] has to support the girl [daughter Amalie] herself. // Up to now, he [Johann] is still Master of His Money. // I don't think that the girl would have gotten such a thought into her head if the old woman [housekeeper Barbara Holzmann] hadn't always encouraged her to leave, because *she* herself must go. //

[before midday dinner; the afternoon of Sunday, February 29:]
What have you given [= paid] today? [//] [Blatt 16r] What kind of vegetables, soup? //

[at Beethoven's apartment; the afternoon of Sunday, February 29:]
Tobias [Haslinger] sends you greetings. // He presumably believes that it will

---

[58] Presumably an announcement on a poster. Beethoven may have visited the St. Rochus Parish office to get verification that he was alive for Karl to take to Archduke Rudolph's cashier (see Blätter 13v–14r above). He may even have stopped in to see an apartment in the nearby building. On Thursday, March 4, Beethoven would enter something similar on Blatt 29v below.

The monastery of the shoe-wearing Augustinian monks in suburban Landstrasse was secularized in 1812. Their buildings, south of the monastery church of Sts. Rochus and Sebastian, were transformed into several rental buildings that, in the numbering of 1821, bore the conscription numbers 270 to 273 and the majority of which belonged to one Joseph Schwarzel. No. 272 was on the west side of the Hauptstrasse, two buildings south of the Rochuskirche.

At the same time, the *Barmherzige Brüder* (Brothers of Mercy), a service order that likewise followed the Rule of St. Augustine, maintained a convalescents' home one long block south of the former Augustinian monastery, at Landstrasse Hauptstrasse No. 228.

See Guetjahr, pp. 146–148; Wilhelm Kisch, *Die alten Strassen und Plätze von Wiens Vorstädten* (Vienna, 1888), I, pp. 397–398; Pezzl, pp. 138, 144, and 468; Realis, I, p. 115.—KH/TA

[NEPHEW KARL, *continued*]
probably take another month before the copying work is finished. He will hasten with the letter of yesterday.[59] //

Today your Herr Brother gave me a pair of gloves that were too small for him. // He asked me to meet him at Czerny's. //

Is the *Stern* across from the beer house where you were to have come? // [Blatt 16v]

Your brother was at the ball, the day before yesterday [seemingly Friday, February 27].[60] //

The building superintendent's wife came up here again with a sheet that I was to sign, but I didn't write anything and told her that she was to come when you are at home. // From the *Classensteuer* [graduated income tax] and *Erwerbsteuer* [profits tax]. She said that if it didn't pertain to you, which she knew, it still must be signed to the effect that the sheet had been shown to you, so that the landlord doesn't get into trouble. [//]

They say that Moscheles is very ill. // He is dying from a [kidney] stone.[61] [//] [Blatt 17r]

The maid has asked me whether today you might allow her make a *Mehlspeise* [pastry], at least for herself, because no meat may be eaten today; [the same] as on Ash Wednesday.[62] // Without meat. //

From today on, there are examinations until mid-April, and I get a turn every week. // The Easter holidays [Sunday and Monday, April 18 and 19]. // In these functions, they must presumably be dressed in black. [//]

[Blatt 17v]

---

[59] Any letter of ca. February 28, 1824, has not survived. Possibly Karl is referring to the famous Petition received on February 25 or 26 (see Blatt 11v above).—TA

[60] Balls at the Court *Redoutensäle* took place on Sunday, Tuesday, and Thursday nights from 9 p.m. until 5 a.m. Other private balls took place on Monday and Friday nights and so forth and were advertised in the *Wiener Zeitung* or its *Intelligenzblatt* at various times during Lent. At this time, however, only a public ball at the *Mehlgrube* on the Neuer Markt on Thursday, February 26, was advertised in the *Wiener Zeitung*, No. 46 (February 26, 1824), p. 203. That does not preclude Johann's having attended a ball somewhere on Friday evening, February 27, 1824.—TA

[61] See other references to Moscheles's malady, which struck him when he arrived in Prague in early January 1824, in Heft 54, Blatt 16v (by pharmacist brother Johann on January 28); in Heft 54, Blatt 23v (by secretary Schindler on January 30); and in Heft 54, Blatt 32r (by nephew Karl on February 2), similar pagination coincidental. In any case, Moscheles recovered and lived until 1870.—TA

[62] For dating this entry, the maid does not say that today *is* Ash Wednesday itself; she says that it is meatless, "as on" Ash Wednesday. Today is actually *Quinquagesima* or "Estomihi" Sunday (sometimes called Hall [Hallows] Sunday in English), the Sunday before Ash Wednesday, and treated as an early extension of Lent. *Quinquagesima* refers to ca. 50 days before the Passion; "Estomihi" refers to "Esto mihi in Deum protectorem" (Be unto me a protector in God) from Psalm 3:3, used as a Proper for the day. Observance as a meatless day was by no means universal, as exemplified by Karl's qualifying the maid's request as "at least for herself."—TA

SCHINDLER [falsified entries begin→] Again you allow yourself to be wheedled too much. // I am not afraid of your anger, because I am right, which will become evident by tomorrow. [←falsified entries end]

BEETHOVEN [presumably at his apartment; late afternoon of Sunday, February 29, while nephew Karl and brother Johann attend Schuppanzigh's Quartet concert]:[63]
· Coffee.
 Wiping rags.

SCHINDLER [falsified entries begin→] Karl and your brother make everybody suspicious of you, which you have already experienced so often, and yet you always believe them again. // What kind of interest in it should S.[64] have? [←falsified entries end]

[Blatt 18r]

NEPHEW KARL [continuing from Blatt 17r, returning to Beethoven's apartment with brother Johann; ca. 6:45 p.m. on Sunday evening, February 29]: Sonnleithner told him that everyone must have his part at home and study it, so that everything will go together neatly. // Tomorrow he is reserving [Frau] Schlemmer [as copyist]. // Schuppanzigh is coming tomorrow or the day after tomorrow;[65] he said that people are already giving him no rest, and that now is high time [to give the concert]. //
 Kohlmarkt. // [Blatt 18v]
 Next time, you should go to a coffee house. There you give the waiter[66] a couple of groschen, and you will be comfortable and not in danger of catching cold. //

[writing, in part, on behalf of Johann:][67]
 Your brother was of the opinion that first the Overture [should be performed], <then the Mass> then the Gloria. After that an aria or a duet, then the Dona nobis pacem and Sanctus.[68] And the Symphony for last. // [Blatt 19r]

---

[63] On Sunday, February 29, Schuppanzigh gave one of his subscription concerts in the hall of the Gesellschaft der Musikfreunde. The program consisted of Haydn's "Apponyi" Quartet in C, Op. 74, No. 1 (the finale of which had to be repeated); Beethoven's Quartet in F, Op. 18, No. 1; and Mozart's String Quintet in E-flat, K. 614. See the *Wiener AmZ* 8, No. 12 (March 27, 1824), p. 45.—TA

[64] Schindler might mean Schuppanzigh or Sonnleithner. In any case, the reference carries little validity, because the entry is falsified.—TA

[65] This would place his projected visit on Monday, March 1, or Tuesday, March 2. In the event, there are no conversational entries by Schuppanzigh until Saturday, March 8 (see Blatt 34v below).—TA

[66] Karl uses the term *Marqueur*, meaning *Markör*, technically a referee at a billiard game but used in Austria to designate a waiter.—KH

[67] For confirmation of Johann's presence, see Blätter 20v–21r below.—TA

[68] Beethoven had written an extensive solo for Schuppanzigh in the Sanctus/Benedictus of the *Missa solemnis*, but for the performance on May 7, 1824, the three movements would be the Kyrie, Credo, and Agnus Dei; see also Blatt 35v below.—TA

He says that *Mamsell* Sontag would be grateful for an aria, even if she didn't receive it until the last day. //

Piringer said that he'll undertake the number of instrumental musicians [from the Verein]; Sonnleithner the choruses; Schuppanzigh the orchestra,[69] Blahetka the announcements, tickets, etc., and therefore everything is taken care of. //

You can give 2 Akademies.[70] [//] [Blatt 19v] Linke[71] said today [at the Schuppanzigh concert] that if the poster for the 2nd concert said, "Beethoven will improvise," they would storm the house. // He will take over everything that needs to be done. // When do you want to have it announced? //

Schuppanzigh is coming tomorrow.[72] //

One cannot give two symphonies on the same concert. [//] [Blatt 20r] Instead, then, one movement of a new piano concerto. // Where is that printed? // Better are some vocal numbers, for which the public is so eager. // In just this way, a couple of arias or duets should be there. // There is a new bass singer there, Preisinger,[73] then [tenor] Haitzinger, Unger and Sontag. [//] [Blatt 20v]

In a few days, he [Grillparzer] will call again to pick up the libretto. //

JOHANN VAN BEETHOVEN [at Beethoven's apartment, writing for himself; evening of Sunday, February 29]: Have you already hired the new cook? //

NEPHEW KARL [continuing]: It will be picked up. //
Lichnowsky was at your brother's place; he looks bad.[74] //

JOHANN VAN BEETHOVEN [continuing]: He [Grillparzer] will come and get it one of these days. // Sonnleithner. [//]

[Blatt 21r]

---

[69] For Beethoven's concert of February 27, 1814, Schuppanzigh had worked with orchestral contractor Anton Brunner to obtain the independently contracted orchestral musicians, and he witnessed the bill that Brunner presented to Beethoven. See Albrecht, *Letters to Beethoven*, No. 181.—TA

[70] After considerable indecision, these concerts took place in the Kärntnertor Theater on Friday, May 7, and (with variants in the program, though no improvisation on Beethoven's part) at the Grosser Redoutensaal on Sunday, May 23, 1824.—TA

[71] Joseph Linke (b. Drachenberg, Prussian Silesia, June 8, 1783; d. Vienna, March 26, 1837). Violoncellist in Count Rasumovsky's String Quartet (with Schuppanzigh as leader) from 1807 to early 1816. Beethoven wrote his Violoncello Sonatas, Op. 102, for Linke, who became principal cellist at the Theater an der Wien in June 1818. When Schuppanzigh returned to Vienna in mid-April 1823, he reconstituted his quartet with Linke as cellist. In 1828, Schubert wrote the pizzicato second violoncello part for him in the slow movement of his String Quintet in C, D. 956. Linke later moved to the Court Opera at the Kärntnertor Theater until his death. See Frimmel, *Handbuch*, I, pp. 364–366; Wurzbach, vol. 25, pp. 215–217; Clive, pp. 208–209.—TA

[72] See Blatt 18r above and Blatt 34v below.—TA

[73] This would ultimately be the solo quartet that sang on May 7 and 23, 1824.—TA

[74] This confirms that Lichnowsky may have been in bad health; see Heft 55, Blatt 2r.—TA

HEFT 57 (FEBRUARY 25 – MARCH 9, 1824), BLATT 21V

NEPHEW KARL [continuing]: I just derived the word "Apotheke" from the Greek for him [Johann].[75] //

[City] No. 825, in the 1st floor [2nd floor, American], but I don't know the door number.[76] [//]

[End of entries for Sunday, February 29.]

UNKNOWN[77] [at Beethoven's apartment; possibly late morning or early afternoon of Monday, March 1]: If one can already wash a few things, then she can wash everything. //

BEETHOVEN [at his apartment, dealing with the aforementioned wash; before going out on Monday, March 1]:
6 napkins.
3 tablecloths.
2 vests.

[Blatt 21v]

NEPHEW KARL [at Beethoven's apartment; early afternoon of Monday, March 1]: Today I ask you for the tuition for the first course—9 fl. W.W. This is the last day that is designated for payment; it will no longer be accepted later. //

Yesterday [Sunday evening], as I came out here with your brother,[78] the idea occurred to him to watch the people dancing at the restaurant across from here. I went with him. There, sitting on a special bench, was our former kitchen maid, without anyone accompanying her, and waiting for someone to dance with her. [//]
[Blatt 22r]

[possibly at ca. 2 p.m., the designated interview time:]
A housekeeper wants to be employed, but she is already in a gentleman's service.— // She could have knowledge of the apartment. // Another woman. // She is with a patient and cannot get away. // <She> He is only to tell the apartment. // Naglergasse No. 289, 1st floor [2nd floor, American], last door to the right. Eidner.[79] [//]

[After the inquirer departs, Karl probably does likewise, to go to classes and pay his university tuition bill.]

---

[75] Karl scribbled such derivations for his own amusement in Heft 56, Blatt 32r (q.v.), among other places.—TA

[76] For the same address, with a similarly inconclusive association, see Heft 54, Blatt 23v.—TA

[77] The German editors presume the writer to be a man; his brief entry is phonetically spelled (even slurred), unpunctuated, uncapitalized, circular, and unclear.—TA

[78] See Blätter 18r–18v above.—TA

[79] According to a Conscriptions-Bogen (conscription/census sheet) of 1821, Magdalena Eigner [not Eidner], a municipal goldworker's widow (b. Vienna/Fünfkirchen, 1776, 1778, or 1781) lived at Naglergasse No. 289, Wohnpartei 6, in the City. See Conscriptions-Bögen, Stadt, No. 289, new collation

[Blatt 22v]

SCHINDLER [at Beethoven's apartment, after Karl departs; as early as ca. 2:30 p.m. on Monday, March 1]: Isn't Karl at home? //

I have hemorrhoids, a vein of gold in my backside rather than in my coin purse.[80] //

Hasn't the archduke [Rudolph] answered your last letter yet?[81] // So you also don't know whether he is coming here [from Olmütz] during Lent? // In case he does, I will have a most humble request to submit on behalf of a good friend. // For many years, he [this friend] has been a regiment's chaplain and belongs to his diocese. He [Rudolph] promised him a parish long ago; therefore here [in Vienna] would be the place where one could ask him about it again.[82] [//]

[Blatt 23r]

NEPHEW KARL [returning home; later on Monday, March 1]: I don't think that his improvisation tired him out very much. // It was less a *Phantasie* than a kind of *potpourri* that tickles the ears, but also permits many allusions [to other works].[83] [//]

BEETHOVEN [possibly somewhere where he might not want to be heard; continuing on Monday, March 1]: As soon as the ideas are right, nothing more stands in the way of working them out.[84] //

SCHINDLER [falsified entries begin→] But the working out doesn't create the *moment*. Do you remember the two themes that I gave you to improvise on, two years

---

289/3; 289/15; and 289/36 (Wiener Stadt- und Landesarchiv). She had lived with her husband, Johann Georg Aigner (b. 1755), in the same building since at least 1805. He seems to have died around 1820. She was still living in the building in 1830.

Thus it seems that Magdalena Eigner could not leave her present duties to apply but sent a man to make inquiries on her behalf. She may already have been acquainted with Beethoven's apartment or one similar to it. For instance, the composer's former friends, the Janschikh family, had lived somewhere in this building four years earlier, so it might have been known in servant's circles.—KH/TA

[80] The German term used here was *Goldene Ader*, literally the golden vein, a term for hemorrhoids. Nephew Karl will make a sarcastic wordplay on it on Blatt 29r below.—KH/TA

[81] Beethoven's most recent surviving letter to Archduke Rudolph (beginning, "Yes, yes, I am a windbag"), from December 7, 1823, contains some newsy chatter before getting to the main point, recommending Schuppanzigh for the late Zeno Menzel's violinist position. See Albrecht, *Letters to Beethoven*, No. 339; Brandenburg, No. 1756.—TA

[82] Schindler continues this subject, presumably on Ash Wednesday (Blatt 25r below).—TA

[83] Presumably a reference to the Viennese concerts in December 1823, when Ignaz Moscheles improvised on Beethoven's Broadwood piano, lent for the occasion. See also Heft 49, Blatt 4v.—KH

[84] Probably another reference to Moscheles's improvisation, but also Beethoven's own procedure when improvising.—TA

ago in Mödling?[85] *Erano due Sogetti*, and then your instructions about the procedure. [←falsified entries end]

[Blatt 23v]

NEPHEW KARL [**at Beethoven's apartment; possibly still on the afternoon of Monday, March 1**]: [At the concert on Sunday,] a number of people told your brother that you should still make haste with the Akademie, and have it announced in the *Zeitung* as a certainty, so that people would have hope about it. // Schuppanzigh stood with us in the street for a half hour, and talked about the Akademie. Everything is in readiness to serve you; all of them have already taken up their places.[86] //

Your brother is to reserve the copyists. // [Frau] Schlemmer. // Gloria and Credo. [//] [Blatt 24r] The younger son is apprenticed to a merchant.[87] [//]

BEETHOVEN [**at his apartment; possibly Tuesday, March 2**]:
+ Mustard
+ Olive oil.[88]

[**Ash Wednesday, March 3, is a national holiday. Beethoven probably stays at home and works before going to the coffee house.**]

[**at a coffee house; late afternoon of Ash Wednesday, March 3:**]
+ Müller's *Organ*, 2nd enlarged edition, octavo, Meissen, 1823. Sewn binding. 45 kr. C.M. at Mörschner, etc. on the Kohlmarkt.[89] //

---

[85] Beethoven had spent parts of the summers of 1818, 1819, and 1820 in Mödling, ca. 9 miles southwest of Vienna. Schindler tells of visiting Beethoven in Mödling in 1819 or 1820, possibly as a law clerk for lawyer Dr. Johann Baptist Bach. This entry does not correspond to otherwise authentic events of those years and, in any case, is falsified.—TA

[86] Karl seems to be reporting about a more recent occasion, but much the same thing may have taken place after Schuppanzigh's Quartet concert on Sunday, February 1, when Karl and Johann arrived back at Beethoven's apartment considerably later than usual. See Heft 54, Blätter 29v–30r.—TA

[87] When copyist Wenzel Schlemmer died on August 6, 1823, he left his widow, Josepha, and two children: Anna (b. ca. 1810) and Alexander (b. ca. 1815). Alexander was apprenticed to a master tailor, Schehak (Tuchlauben, Blauer Igel, No. 557), by 1831; Anna became an actress. See Verlassenschafts-Abhandlung/Sperrs-Relatition, Fasz. 2: 4682/1823: enclosure (Wiener Stadt- und Landesarchiv).—TA

[88] Beethoven uses the term *Baumöl*.—KH/TA

[89] Excerpt from an advertisement in the *Intelligenzblatt*, No. 51 (March 3, 1824), p. 396; Beethoven copied it accurately. During this period, the advertisement appeared only on Wednesday, March 3, 1824. Beethoven had copied out an earlier version of it in Heft 54, Blätter 22r–22v.—KH/TA

NEPHEW KARL [at Beethoven's apartment, after the *Concert spirituel*; possibly ca. 6:30 p.m. on Thursday, March 4]:[90]
She says loin of beef.[91] [//] [Blatt 24v] The small coffeepot broke as the maid washed it, or, as she says, it fell to pieces. She therefore brought a different one in here. //

Tuscher[92] sends you greetings. // I think that there is no musical event where Wolfmayer[93] would not attend. He is a great music lover. //

Who is going to receive [the money] that comes in from this concert? // It was fairly full, but probably not many *paid* tickets.[94] [//]

[Blatt 25r]

SCHINDLER [at Beethoven's apartment; probably early evening of Thursday, March 4]: I owe him [the Moravian priest][95] many thanks, because he was also the person who enabled me to study. // There is a law that says that any [priest] who serves [in the army] for 10 years can apply for a parish. But this one has served more than 12 years. // In such a large diocese as Olmütz there are many vacant benefices each year. // The archduke should have a man who is as educated as this around his High Person, because he is a man of letters and is very musical. [//] [Blatt 25v] He is presently with Wallmoden's *Cuirassiers* in Hungary.[96] //

I <beseech> ask you to let me read the memorandum[97] that you received from

---

[90] The first in the series of four *Concerts spirituels*, held in the *Saal* (hall) of the Lower Austrian *Landstand* (Assembly), in midafternoon (probably ca. 4 p.m.) on Thursday, March 4, 1824. The all-Haydn program consisted of his Symphony No. 103 ("Drumroll") and the oratorio version of his *Seven Last Words*. The symphony, probably Haydn's longest, lasts ca. 30–35 minutes; the oratorio, ca. 60–65 minutes. Unless brother Johann drove him home, Karl's walk would have taken ca. 30 minutes. See *Allgemeine musikalische Zeitung* 26, No. 18 (April 29, 1824), col. 281; and *Wiener AmZ* 8, No. 6 (March 13, 1824), pp. 21–22.—TA

[91] *Nierenbraten*. For this cut of meat, see Heft 47, Blatt 22v; courtesy Styra Avins and Josef Eisinger.—TA

[92] Mathias Tuscher, Magistrat's councillor, amateur singer, and member of the representative body of the Gesellschaft der Musikfreunde; see also Heft 54, Blatt 30r; and Clive, pp. 373–374.—KH/TA

[93] Johann Nepomuk Wolfmayer, wealthy Viennese cloth dealer and enthusiastic supporter of Beethoven and his music; see also Heft 54, Blatt 30r; and Clive, p. 401.—KH/TA

[94] Karl's report on the concert continues the next day on Blatt 31r below.—TA

[95] Schindler continues a topic that he had begun a couple days before (Blatt 22v above).—TA

[96] Count Ludwig Georg Thedel von Wallmoden-Gimborn (1769–1862), owner of the "k.k. Cuirassier-Regiment No. 6." Cuirassiers were mounted horse soldiers, protected by breast- and backplates and helmets, and armed with razor-sharp swords that could often slice an enemy in half with one blow. See the *Hof- und Staats-Schematismus*, 1824, I, p. 337.—KH/TA

[97] The Petition, dated "Vienna in February 1824," and signed by thirty music lovers, asking Beethoven, in flowery language, to perform the premieres of the *Missa solemnis* and, especially, the Ninth Symphony in Vienna. It seemingly originated with the *Ludlamshöhle* group. Beethoven seems to have received the Petition on Thursday, February 26 (see Blatt 11v above), but this is the first time

a number of friends of art. But forgive me for my ... not curiosity ... but instead, sincerest interest. //

He [Johann] was already to have decided upon this action [with the police against Therese] if he could still get something from it. //

In our orchestra [at the Josephstadt Theater], the other day, a veritable revolt broke out. Tired of the abuse by the great [conductor] Gläser, the orchestra as a body wanted to leave, and we[98] had to call the police to prevent them. However, [Blatt 26r] the winds are all going away until [or: by] Easter.[99] // Everything that these men permit themselves must now be considered, because they no longer seek their subsistence there. // We really had every reason to be satisfied with them, because they were all capable and experienced members. // The cause of the outbreak was that the clarinettist asserted that he could not play what Gläser wrote, and he boorishly complained to him that he didn't want to do it—and that began the baiting. [//] [Blatt 26v] He [Gläser?] has more calm, security, and consequence in his performances than his predecessor. [//]

BEETHOVEN [**humorously reacting to the last anecdote**]: + *Die Befreiung* [The Liberation], poem by g.u., s[et] to m[usic] by B[eethoven]. //

SCHINDLER [falsified entries begin→] *Pathetique Sonata*—please give me an explication about it again, especially about the thoughts in the central section. // It is very difficult to have the 2 principles [*2 Principe*] to appear next to one another in such a way as you wish it, and as it certainly must be.[100] // Czerny plays all of that also in tempo. [←falsified entries end]

[Blatt 27r]

SCHINDLER [**continuing, with authentic entries; early evening of Thursday, March 4**]: It[101] was drafted without the omission of one single thing, of which you will

---

that Schindler seems to have seen it, nearly a week after it was delivered. He would not read it until Monday, March 8 (Blatt 39v below). See also Albrecht, *Letters to Beethoven*, No. 334; and Blätter 3r and 11v above.—KH/TA

[98] As the orchestra's concertmaster (rather than actual solo violinist), Schindler at least partially identifies with the administration here.—TA

[99] Original German is *bis Ostern*. It is not clear whether Schindler means "until Easter" or "by Easter," because they performed Cherubini's *Der Wasserträger* (requiring winds in the orchestra) on March 9. Easter Sunday was April 18 in 1824. The events reported by Schindler are not reflected in Bäuerle's *Allgemeine Theater-Zeitung* of this period.—TA

[100] Schindler's famous falsified entries about the *Pathétique* Sonata, Op. 13, and the "zwei Principe" also appear in Heft 35, Blatt 9r, supposedly reflecting July 5, 1823.—TA

[101] The following discussion pertains to the diploma (dated December 28, 1822) sent by the Royal Swedish Musical Academy on January 31, 1823, naming Beethoven as an honorary member. Acceptance of this honor required the approval of the emperor, who did so on April 21, 1824, only after several

[SCHINDLER, *continued*]

be convinced later. So much work is said to be piled up in the cabinet that 6,000 items await dispatch by the emperor, and there are many among them that have been up there for 2 years. But if you have inquired about it through a different person, then you will certainly be convinced. // They were certainly up there around 2 years already. //

He [Emperor Franz] now wants to have Archduke Rainer[102] come to help him. Franz is going to Italy as viceroy.[103] [//] [Blatt 27v]

I know—you have already entrusted Lichnowsky with this. I am very happy that you have become convinced that I am not responsible for it. // The actual reason for the delay is only the cabinet officials who have already intimated to me several times that it is settled—and when I inquire more specifically about it, I hear that it still lies in the cabinet. // As soon as he [the emperor] has it, it won't be held up there. // Court Councillor Martin.[104] [//] [Blatt 28r] Kutschera[105] already spoke to Martin about it in the summer, but this Herr Martin wants to be persuaded, or so it appears. //

Stein[106] believes that Leschen would have leathered the parts [of the Broadwood piano] that had suffered damage.[107] // Stein wants to look at it, and if you can do without it, he wants to leather it for you. Then, he believes, it will be just as it was before. // He is afraid of leathering it the way that the English do—but I don't believe that's a concern. It gives him pleasure to be able to be accommodating to you. [//] [Blatt 28v] He is the only one who understands the mechanics; one must grant him that. [//]

---

interventions with the cabinet director on its behalf. See Albrecht, *Letters to Beethoven*, Nos. 301, 306, and 354.—KH/TA

[102] Archduke Rainer (1783–1853), the younger brother of Emperor Franz, was viceroy of the Kingdom of Lombardy-Venetia from 1814 to 1848. His unpopular regime in Milan was one of the focal points of the Italian *Risorgimento*. See Wurzbach, vol. 7, pp. 125–128.—KH/TA

[103] Presumably Archduke Franz Karl (1802–1878), son of the reigning Emperor Franz, who was married to Princess Sophie of Bavaria on November 4, 1824. They were the parents of the future Emperor Franz Josef.—TA

[104] I.R. Cabinet Director Anton Martin, one of the highest state officials, living on the Graben No. 618. See *Hof- und Staats-Schematismus*, 1824, I, p. 202.—KH

[105] Baron Johann von Kutschera (1766–1832), lieutenant field marshal and adjutant general of Emperor Franz I. See *Hof- und Staats-Schematismus*, 1824, I, p. 310.—KH

[106] Matthäus Andreas Stein (1776–1842), son of the Augsburg piano maker Andreas Stein, brother of Nannette Stein Streicher, and brother-in-law of piano maker Johann Baptist Streicher. From 1802, he had an independent piano building firm in Vienna, in which his son Karl Andreas (1797–1863) was also active. Stein lived in suburban Landstrasse, Rauchfangkehrergasse No. 78, near the Rasumovsky Palace. In previous years, he had occasionally visited Beethoven on Sunday mornings to perform maintenance on his Broadwood piano and to try to develop a sound-enhancing device for it. See Frimmel, *Handbuch*, II, p. 253; Ziegler, *Addressen-Buch*, p. 253; and Clive, p. 351.—KH/TA

[107] This may refer to Moscheles's recital on December 15, 1823, when he played on both a Leschen and Beethoven's Broadwood piano. Leschen evidently provided transportation for both instruments. See Heft 49, Blatt 3r.—TA

[Having probably overstayed his welcome, Schindler seemingly leaves.]

BEETHOVEN **[commenting to himself]**:
70 fl. for nothing; from Streicher nothing.
To Graf[108] *concerning my English piano.* [//]

[Blatt 29r]

NEPHEW KARL **[at Beethoven's apartment; resuming in the evening of Thursday, March 4]**: He [Schindler] could probably use a *vein of gold*.[109] //

Blahetka has indeed offered to affix seals to the tickets, etc., but I believe that all these matters should be left to your brother. It really would be safer. //

But if it were advertised for the 2nd concert that you would improvise, then I believe—as do Schuppanzigh, Piringer, and everybody who's spoken about it recently—that the hall would be too small. //

Earlier I believed that one should not have the scales examined, <because> so it could be watched all the better in secret. [//] [Blatt 29v] It would be best, though, if one knew his servants; and then he could make sure un̲noticed. //

BEETHOVEN **[probably copying a poster on a wall near the Rochuskirche, while running errands; late morning or early afternoon of Friday, March 5]**: No. 272: apartment at the Augustiners.[110]

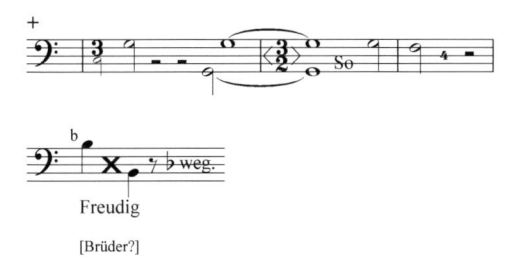

Freudig

[Brüder?]

---

[108] Conrad Graf (1782–1851), Viennese piano maker, living in suburban Wieden, Wiedener Hauptstrasse No. 182, directly south of the Paulanerkirche. On ca. January 24, 1826, he took Beethoven's Broadwood piano in for repairs and lent him one of his own newer models as a replacement. This Graf piano remained in Beethoven's apartment (but not as his actual possession) until just before he died. See Breuning, *Aus dem Schwarzspanierhause*, p. 58; Breuning-Solomon, pp. 63, 72, and 113; Frimmel, *Handbuch*, I, pp. 179 and 268–269; Thayer-Deiters-Riemann, V, pp. 252 and 498; Ziegler, *Addressen-Buch*, p. 251; Heft 102, Blätter 34r and 44v; Albrecht, *Letters to Beethoven*, Nos. 460 and 477; and Clive, pp. 138–139.—KH/TA

[109] The *goldene Ader* (literally golden vein), a regional term for hemorrhoids (from which Schindler suffers at this time), but here probably used in a sarcastically crude wordplay that means something akin to "Somebody should shove a golden stick up his ass." See also Blatt 22v above.—TA

[110] Presumably copied from a poster and not a newspaper. For an earlier reference on Saturday, February 28, see Blatt 14v above.—TA

SCHINDLER [falsified entries begin→] What does this mean?[111] [←falsified entries end]

[Blatt 30r]

NEPHEW KARL:

13	53
2	2
26	106
6½	26
32½	60/132 = 2 fl. 12

34 fl. 13 kr.

BEETHOVEN:

1 fl. 38 kr.
19
1 fl. 57 kr. //

NEPHEW KARL [at Beethoven's apartment; ca. 2 p.m. on Friday, March 5]: If a servant has not been in one position for one year, one can take away all payments that one has had outside the specified salary. //

The woman is fat, sluggish, and—if I am not very mistaken—pregnant. [//] [Blatt 30v] Recently there was an advertisement in the *Zeitung*, seeking a housekeeper for 200 fl. [per year]. We pay far more. 200 fl. per year makes only 15 fl. 40 kr. per month [*sic*].[112] // At a Court war councillor's. //

Even now, Köferle[113] still doesn't have any salary. //

Wrong. // He had Niemetz's[114] mother pay a few ducats, in order to have her sons considered.

[preparing for midday dinner after the applicant leaves:]

What do you want to eat? [//] [Blatt 31r]

An entirely new wine dealer, in the Wollzeile, No. 777; the least expensive wine

---

[111] Schindler might have asked *himself* precisely this, when he was surveying the conversation books after Beethoven's death.—TA

[112] Actually, a salary of 200 fl. per year, if divided by 12, yields 16 fl. 40 kr. per month.—TA

[113] Joseph Köferle, teacher of geography, history, and religion at Blöchlinger's Institute. See Frimmel, *Handbuch*, I, pp. 282–283; Frimmel, *Studien*, II, 116–117; Thayer-Deiters-Riemann, IV, p. 193.—KH

[114] Karl's former fellow student and close friend at Blöchlinger's Institute, Joseph Niemetz (b. January 20, 1808), came from a relatively poor family. Beethoven made no pretense of liking him. See also Heft 49, Blätter 5r–5v; and Clive, p. 249.—KH/TA

[NEPHEW KARL, *continued*]
costs 28 kr.; the best, 1 fl. W.W. In the last category, one can also get prorated half-bottles for 30 kr. W.W.[115] // At least one can try it, and if the wine doesn't appear good enough even to be table wine (which I don't believe, since it has been advertised everywhere that they have received several lots of very unadulterated wine), it would still be good enough for the servants. //

[continuing the concert report from the previous evening,[116] at Beethoven's apartment, probably at dinner; after 2 p.m. on Friday, March 5:]

Right after the *Concert* [*spirituel*],[117] your brother went to the small [hall of the] Musik-Verein.[118] // He wants to acquire taste. [//] [Blatt 31v] He always cries *Bravo*. // At Schuppanzigh's,[119] he enjoyed himself so loudly during the quartets that people shush him with *psst*! // He himself says, "I have nothing to do, the whole day long." //

Do you want wine?

Do you still remember the woman violin and clarinet player, whom we encountered with her husband (an oboist, as far as I can remember), and who toured to Russia? [//] Well, she was at the *concert*, [Blatt 32r] but very plainly clothed, in the same cloth overcoat in which I saw her previously. I think that her name is Pfeiffer.[120] [//]

---

[115] The wine shop of the brothers Heinrich and Franz Sturm was located in the City, Wollzeile No. 777. For several years, they had sold all kinds of domestic wines. See Pezzl, p. 244; Redl, 1823, p. 243, and 1824, p. 220.—KH

[116] Karl had begun the report on Blatt 24v above.—TA

[117] Karl (having been interrupted by Schindler the previous evening) gradually continues his report about the *Concert spirituel* of mid-to-late afternoon on Thursday, March 4.—TA

[118] Also on March 4, 1824—at the customary time between 7 and 9 p.m.—was the 17th *Musikalische Abendunterhaltung* (Musical Evening Entertainment) in the 1823–1824 season of the Gesellschaft der Musikfreunde. These performances took place at the Verein's hall in *Zum rothen Igel*, Tuchlauben No. 558 (ca. 10 minutes from the Landstand, if Johann went on foot). The program consisted of works by Mayseder, Rossini, Czerny, Schubert, and Pechatschek. See "Programme der musikalischen Abendunterhaltungen" (Archiv, Gesellschaft der Musikfreunde, Bd. 2697/32).—KH/TA

[119] Schuppanzigh's latest string quartet concert had been the previous Sunday, February 29, at 4:30 p.m. See Blätter 17v–18v above.—TA

[120] Karl's memory was close: Caroline Schleicher was born in Stockach, near Konstanz, on December 17, 1794, the daughter of a professional bassoonist. She studied clarinet and violin from age nine. After her father died in 1819, she toured extensively, arriving in Vienna on February 3, 1822, already making appearances on February 15 and 27. She met Ernest Krähmer, principal oboist at the Burgtheater, and married him in the Stephansdom on September 19, 1822.

Ernest (as he signed himself, rather than "Ernst") Krähmer was born in Dresden on March 30, 1795, became a city musician there in ca. 1810, but came to Vienna and entered the Burgtheater's orchestra on February 1, 1815 (replacing Elssler/Esslair). He was playing chamber music and concerts at Court by fall 1822 and entered the Hofkapelle upon the death of Joseph Khayll (January 23, 1829). Meanwhile, he had met and married Caroline Schleicher (1822), and they went on tour to Russia (fall 1822) and Hungary (winter 1823), among others.

Ernest and Caroline Krähmer would, themselves, give a concert in this same hall of the Landstand

BEETHOVEN: 88 //

NEPHEW KARL [at Beethoven's apartment; probably ca. 3:30–4:00 p.m. on Friday, March 5]: The old woman [housekeeper Barbara Holzmann] wants to go now.[121] [//]

BEETHOVEN [at home or after going out]:
6 handkerchiefs.
1 pair of foot-warmers. //

NEPHEW KARL [at a coffee house, reading the *Wiener Zeitung*; late afternoon of Friday, March 5]:
New *animals* have arrived—lions, tigers, and more like them.[122] // Have you already seen a crocodile? // [Blatt 32v]

---

on the next Sunday, March 7, 1824. He would play oboe and *czakan* (a walking-stick flute); she would play clarinet and violin; and together they would play duet variations for oboe and clarinet (composed by Caroline). In addition, Mozart's *Marriage of Figaro* Overture would open the concert, and Madam Grünbaum would later sing a scene and aria. It seems likely that Ernest played oboe in this *Concert spirituel*, that Caroline was in the audience, and that they also took the opportunity to examine the hall in advance of their own concert. For their advertisement with their complete program, see the *Wiener Zeitung*, No. 54 (Saturday, March 6, 1824), p. 242. Nephew Karl and brother Johann attended the concert and reported about it briefly to Beethoven in Heft 58, Blätter 3r–3v.
    Ernest Krähmer continued at the Burgtheater and Hofkapelle until his death on January 16, 1837. Of ten children born to him and Caroline, five survived infancy. Caroline remained in Vienna as a performer and teacher into the 1840s but had left the city for a time by 1859. She was reputedly still teaching in Vienna in the 1870s and died in suburban Fünfhaus on April 19, 1873 (courtesy Michael Lorenz, Vienna, December 2020).
    See Schilling, IV, pp. 211–213; Böckh, 1822, p. 371; Ziegler, *Addressen-Buch*, pp. 65 and 68; *Wiener Allgemeine musikalische Zeitung* 6, No. 20 (March 9, 1822), col. 158, and No. 89 (November 6, 1822), cols. 705–706; *Allgemeine musikalische Zeitung* 26, No. 18 (April 29, 1824), cols. 281–282; and Theodore Albrecht, "Ernest Krähmer and His Wife Caroline (geb. Schleicher), Musical Pioneers in Vienna's Biedermeier Period," trans. Ernst Kobau, *Journal der Gesellschaft der Wiener Oboe* 56 (March 2013), pp. 3–10. My thanks to Stephansdom archivist Reinhard Gruber and Michael Lorenz of the University of Vienna for their assistance.—TA

[121] If Beethoven and Karl ate a somewhat late midday dinner after ca. 2 p.m., Barbara Holzmann (seemingly working for them again) would probably have had the kitchen cleaned up and would have been ready to leave by 3:30 or 4 p.m.—TA

[122] On Friday, March 5, 1824, the following advertisement appeared in the *Wiener Zeitung*: "Announcing the Grand Menagerie of Herren van Acken and Martin. One of the largest menageries in Europe, in which are … three living lions and five various kinds of tigers, has arrived in Vienna and will be opened in a few days. Posters will provide more specific information." See the *Wiener Zeitung*, No. 53 (March 5, 1824), p. 236. The advertisement appeared again in No. 54 (Saturday, March 6, 1824), p. 242; and No. 55 (Monday, March 8, 1824), p. 246; but no longer ran on Tuesday, March 9, 1824.
    Beethoven and nephew Karl visited the traveling Van Aken Menagerie on Friday, May 14, 1824. It remained in Vienna, probably set up "at the end of the Jägerzeil [today's Praterstrasse], first *Hütte* [pavilion] on the right," through June 30, 1824. See the *Intelligenzblatt*, No. 143 (June 24, 1824), p. 1015 (specifying Hermann van Aken as the comanager). See also Heft 67, Blätter 28v, 30v–31r, 35v–36r;

HEFT 57 (FEBRUARY 25 – MARCH 9, 1824), BLATT 33R 303

I like this mustard better than all the French ones and the kinds of names that they always have—expensive and nothing to them. //

The [shoemaker's] bill comes to 15 fl. and a few kreuzer. //

1 pair of upper leathers	9 fl.
1 pair boots, made over	5 fl.
1 pair of heels	1 fl.
	15 fl. //

When you need something again, you might want to have him do the work. [//] [Blatt 33r] Schindler told him that he should make the boots quite large; I don't know why. // 2 fl. // He had to take the boots with him. //

BEETHOVEN [also at the same coffee house, reading the *Intelligenzblatt*; late afternoon of Friday, March 5]:

+ Silver writing pens for travelers; Plankengasse No. 1061; write for 5 hours without new ink, which itself is available. Price 5 fl. C.M.[123]

[Blatt 33v]

+ At Mörschner, etc., Kohlmarkt 257: *Der fertige Orgelspieler*, etc., etc., by C. Güntersberg; 1st and 2nd volumes, 4 fl. 45 kr. C.M.

+ Fleck, *7 Festchoräle* [7 Festive Chorales] for organ with 4 trombones, 2 trumpets, and timpani, etc., quarto, pamphlet sewn binding; 24 kr. C.M.[124]

[Blatt 34r]

NEPHEW KARL [continuing]: Piringer has enough with the choruses. //

Piringer is surely very good, but he isn't what Schuppanzigh is. In any case, it would be unjust to neglect S.,[125] since he is the one who has taken the most pains [on your behalf], and spurred the other people on. //

Tomorrow? // But it would also be possible tomorrow.

6 | 276 4
    36

[Blatt 34v]

Heft 72, Blatt 22v; and (for more extensive background on this Rotterdam-based venture) Heft 83, Blätter 25r–25v.—KH/TA

[123] See the *Intelligenzblatt*, No. 53 (March 5, 1824), p. 404 (Advertisements). The same advertisement had already appeared in No. 48 (February 28, 1824), p. 374.—KH/TA

[124] Excerpts from an advertisement in the *Intelligenzblatt*, No. 53 (March 5, 1824), p. 406. Beethoven had already copied the advertisement for Güntersberg's *Der fertige Orgelspieler* on January 29, 1824; see Heft 54, Blatt 22r. The chorales by C. Fleck were new here.—KH/TA

[125] This initial surely refers to Schuppanzigh.—TA

LICHNOWSKY [**probably at Beethoven's apartment; possibly late morning or early afternoon of Saturday, March 6**]: It[126] is not at Saurau's; I'll follow through on it. // I'll talk it over with Dietrichstein. // I am going to see Baron Lehr.[127] //

SCHUPPANZIGH [**presumably at Beethoven's apartment; afternoon of Saturday, March 6**]: What, then? // But [copying] must be begun with the Overture. //

Is the Symphony copied already? [//] [Blatt 35r] It's more than high time. // One week of Lent has already passed, and in the final week nothing may be given. // <One must> He [= you] must have the Symphony copied in your apartment. //

<20> 12 each [upper string] part;

10 <8> Violoncelli;

8 Contrabasses.

In that respect, one must consider that the *Ripieno* parts will be cared for. // One must mark "Solo" in the parts where only single players in the winds are to play. [//] [Blatt 35v]

Let me see the Mass [*Missa solemnis*] a little bit. // In which part is the most extensive fugue? // The double fugue is in the *Credo*. // The *Kyrie* is not long. // We should begin with the *Kyrie*, then the *Credo*, and after that the *Sanctus*.[128] // [**continues directly on Blatt 36r.**]

SCHINDLER [**falsified entries begin→**]: Our opinions are too much at odds again; where can that lead? // Good, I hear it—but [does] Falstaff?[129] [←falsified entries end]

[Blatt 36r]

SCHUPPANZIGH [**continuing directly from Blatt 35v**]: Does the entire chorus sing in the *Kyrie*, or are there solo parts in addition? // I believe that we should perform the *Dona nobis* [*Agnus Dei*] instead of the *Sanctus*.[130] // The count [Lichnowsky] is also of my opinion. //

---

[126] Beethoven's petition for permission to accept a foreign honor, in this case the honorary membership from the Royal Swedish Musical Academy.—TA

[127] Presumably Baron [*Freiherr*] Franz von Loehr, Court councillor, chancellery director of the I.R. high steward's office. See *Hof- und Staats-Schematismus*, 1824, I, p. 90; and Heft 55, Blatt 15v.—KH

[128] If the *Sanctus* had been included, as projected here, Schuppanzigh would have had an opportunity to play the extensive violin solo in the following *Benedictus* that Beethoven had surely written for him as a pun: "Benedictus qui venit in nomine Domini" (Blessed is he who comes in the name of the Lord), in this case "Mylord," that is, Mylord Falstaff (Schuppanzigh's nickname).—TA

[129] In several authentic discussions, it seems apparent that Schindler is not fond of Schuppanzigh, though not on the confrontational level implied here in entries made after Beethoven's and (presumably) Schuppanzigh's deaths.—TA

[130] Even with the violin solo for Schuppanzigh in the *Benedictus*, there is little evidence that Beethoven opposed this substitution, which, in the end, took place.—TA

Just be sure to come to the *Stern* tomorrow [Sunday, March 7] at 1 o'clock.[131] //

For this reason, preparations for the Akademie must be hastened, because it will certainly lead to a second Akademie. [//]

[Blatt 36v]

BEETHOVEN [at a coffee house; late afternoon of Saturday, March 6]:

At Tendler und Manstein: *Die Aufgeklärte Wiener Haushält[erin]*, etc., etc., etc., edited by Magdalena Lichtenegger,[132] stiff binding, 3 fl. 54 kr. W.W.

Also there: *Praktisches Urfahr Linzer Kochbuch*, etc., etc., [Blatt 37r] by Franziska Probst, stiff binding, 2 fl. W.W.[133] //

[The next authentic entries are found at the beginning of Heft 58.]

SCHINDLER[134] [falsified entries begin→]: *Rhythm*. // Aristotle asked: Why do many people sing better in rhythm than fewer?[135] // The Greeks defined rhythm as a certain mutual relationship of a part to the whole; that whole may exist in time, in space, or in both at the same time. [//] [Blatt 37v] It is uncontestably the most necessary thing for the understanding of music. // The protracted rhythms in your works lie not in the calculation, but rather in the nature of the melody and oftentimes even in the harmony—am I right? // I'm glad. One can observe rhythm by the beat of the pulse, on the flight of birds, etc. // Arsis and Thesis. // Many birds begin their flight in Arsis—I have observed that. // The eagle? Waterbirds? Proof! [←falsified entries end]

[Heft 58 goes here chronologically. It covers from 1 p.m. on Sunday, March 7, through the early afternoon of Monday, March 8. It then leads directly back to authentic entries on Heft 57, Blatt 38r below.]

[Blatt 38r]

---

[131] This meeting at the *Goldenes Stern*, Brandstadt No. 629, to plan Beethoven's upcoming Akademie is covered in Heft 58.—TA

[132] Instead of "egger," Beethoven originally wrote "berger," then corrected it.—KH/TA

[133] Urfahr is a region north of the Danube, across from Linz. The cookbook's original edition (Linz, 1821) gave the author's surname with the feminine suffix (Probstin), and Beethoven copied it as such; it had reached a third edition by 1837.

No advertisement for the Tendler und Manstein bookshop appears in the *Intelligenzblatt* from February 25 to March 10, 1824. The dealer had advertised the Probst cookbook as early as the *Intelligenzblatt*, No. 46 (February 25, 1822), p. 386, and again on March 6 and 14, 1822 (two years before this). Courtesy Prof. Scott Messing, emeritus, Alma College, Michigan (June 5, 2023).—TA

[134] After Beethoven's death, Schindler found the remainder of Blatt 37r and all of Blatt 37v blank. He then supplied falsified entries that have nothing to do with Beethoven's copying of advertisements on Blatt 37r or a potential housekeeper and news from the Josephstadt on Blatt 38r.—TA

[135] Aristotle, *Problema physica*, Nos. 22 and 45.—KH

SCHINDLER [at Beethoven's apartment; probably early afternoon of Monday, March 8, continuing the entries begun at the end of Heft 58]: I expect very many good things from this woman, because she really has a special inclination and esteem for you. //

<I would gladly have inquired about your health last week, but we were too occu-> pied with rehearsals. Tomorrow [Tuesday, March 9] we are having—don't be alarmed—*Der Wasserträger* [The Water Carrier] by Cherubini. // We even have a guest water carrier—one Herr Gned—who, however, will not make any difference.[136] //

[falsified entries begin→] I only had rehearsals of *Wasserträger*. [←falsified entries end] // [Blatt 38v]

I heard with sincerest pleasure that the Akademie has already been resolved. I am extraordinarily happy with your decision. // It must happen in that way. // Don't get any extraordinary ideas in your head; it will go quite splendidly, because everyone is already happy about it. [//] On the contrary, you are obligated to the contemporary world to do it—to the better world, that is. //

[falsified entries begin→] [Henriette] Sontag—I spoke with her about it today. [←falsified entries end] // [Blatt 39r]

<I believe that> Unger sings <alto.> She sings G [to] F. // I'll ask her specifically about it [her range]. // She learns everything on her own. // Everything will go excellently; don't worry so much about it. // A fresh, healthy voice is better than one that is already rather worn out. // [Madame] G[rünbaum] is now so neglectful that she appears unable to participate; [I] made this observation at the *Schöpfung* performance.[137] [//] [Blatt 39v]

Have you also decided already who will conduct? // and <the whole thing.>[138] [//]

---

[136] On Tuesday, March 9, 1824, Cherubini's opera *Les deux journées, ou Le porteur d'eau* (commonly called *Der Wasserträger* in German) was given under its alternate German title *Graf Armand, oder die Tage der Gefahr* at the Theater in der Josephstadt, where Schindler was concertmaster. The correspondent to Leipzig's *Allgemeine musikalische Zeitung* wrote: "Herr Gned portrayed the Water Carrier, and, in fact, all the Muses lamented it from the depths of their hearts! And Cherubini's superb creation itself was assaulted quite unmercifully by the orchestra."

Gned (probably Georg Gned, b. Vienna/Wieden, 1789) was a member of the Kärntnertor Theater from May 9, 1814, to 1816; he was a singing actor at the Theater an der Wien in 1817 and toured later that year. He returned to the Kärntnertor Theater from 1820 to 1827. See *Allgemeine musikalische Zeitung* 26, No. 18 (April 29, 1824), col. 282; Bäuerle's *Allgemeine Theater-Zeitung* 17, No. 35 (March 20, 1824), p. 139; *Portrait-Katalog*, p. 353.—KH/TA

[137] Soprano Therese Grünbaum (1791–1876), called "the German Catalani," was a daughter of the Leopoldstadt Theater's composer Wenzel Müller. From 1818 to 1828, she was a Court singer and member of the Kärntnertor Theater, appearing frequently in opera and concert. Haydn's oratorio *Die Schöpfung* had recently been performed on the *Tonkünstler-Societät*'s two Advent concerts on December 22 and 23, 1823. See Eisenberg, p. 360; *Hof- und Staats-Schematismus*, 1824, I, p. 110; *Portrait-Katalog*, p. 356; Wurzbach, vol. 5, p. 393; *Wiener AmZ* 7, No. 101 (December 17, 1823), col. 808; Clive, p. 344.—KH/TA

[138] The conductor would be Michael Umlauf (1781–1842), the Kärntnertor Theater's staff conductor with whom Beethoven had worked successfully as early as his (Beethoven's) benefit concert of January 2,

HEFT 57 (FEBRUARY 25 – MARCH 9, 1824), BLATT 40r

Just believe, with certainty, that everyone will highly treasure this honor to participate. //

Let me finally read the memorandum today, pretty please.[139] // The Württemberg Court councillor André,[140] who edits the *Hesperus*, has asked me for correspondence articles from here, which I promised to supply to him. But can I, about that? [//]

[Blatt 40r]

People are saying out loud that Palffy[141] will (indeed, has to) go bankrupt soon. [//] This much is certain: that as of Saturday the 6th [of March], the orchestra [of the Theater an der Wien] had still not been paid their salaries. // It is known that Duport pays the alliance with Palffy, which continues until this April, 10,000 fl. W.W. per month. Now, however, he no longer pays this sum in cash, but instead pays for Palffy's old debts in connection with the theater, and sends him the account statements rather than money.—Good!—but the box office doesn't take in anything, and therefore cannot pay anything. // [Blatt 40v]

[End of Schindler's authentic entries of Monday, March 8.]

[falsified entries begin→] Hasn't Ries written in a long time? [←falsified entries end] //

BEETHOVEN **[at his apartment; probably the morning of Tuesday, March 9]**:
+ Ink. [//]

SCHUPPANZIGH **[at Beethoven's apartment; late morning or early afternoon of Tuesday, March 9, bringing a copyist with him]**:
The solo parts with bass line underneath.[142] // Give him money. // Does he [= Do you] also need the organ? // He *expects* two more copyists *today*. //
<Maschek[143] says that he cannot bring the score into the house.> [//]

1814, and who had conducted *Fidelio* many times since then. If Beethoven had scored the Ninth Symphony with the orchestra of the Kärntnertor Theater in mind, then he probably already envisioned Umlauf as a potential conductor. There was some discussion later about Beethoven's possibly conducting the *Consecration of the House* Overture, but common sense prevailed. See Clive, pp. 374–375.—TA

[139] See earlier references to the *Ludlamshöhle* Petition on March 4, 1824 (Blatt 25v above). Several days later, Schindler had not yet read it, but this time, he apparently did so, leading to his apparent offer to send it to the *Hesperus*, which Beethoven probably rejected.—TA

[140] Christian Karl André (1763–1831), pedagogue, had edited the magazine *Hesperus*, published in Stuttgart since 1809; in 1822, it added the subtitle *Encyclopedic Journal for Educated Readers*. Since 1821, he had been secretary of the Provincial Society in Stuttgart, with the title of a Court councillor. See *Allgemeine Deutsche Biographie*, I, pp. 432–433; Schilling, I, p. 198; Eduard Bernsdorf, *Neues Universal-Lexikon der Tonkunst* (Dresden, 1856), I, pp. 233–234; Kayser, III, p. 127.—KH

[141] Count Ferdinand von Palffy (1774–1840), owner of the Theater an der Wien. See Frimmel, *Handbuch*, II, pp. 6–8; and Clive, pp. 257–258.—KH/TA

[142] Such a reduced score would have been needed for the solo singers to learn and rehearse their parts.—TA

[143] The meaning is unclear. Paul Maschek (1761–1826), composer, piano teacher, well-known glass harmonica player. From 1813 to 1820, he was secretary of the *Tonkünstler-Societät* and later occasionally

COPYIST [MASCHEK?]: I've [copied] 80 *Bögen* [sheets] in one night. [//]

[Blatt 41r]

SCHUPPANZIGH [**continuing**]: [whole page, written vertically→] That depends upon him [= you]. // It is more than high time. Sontag is more beloved [by audiences] than Grünbaum. [←written vertically] [//]

[Blatt 41v]

NEPHEW KARL [**at Beethoven's apartment; late morning or early afternoon of Tuesday, March 9**]:
"Spring is already beginning to sprout," says Voss.[144] [//] She [the housekeeper] is afraid that the Schnitzel has already somewhat spoiled, because she had to wait longer and it was already ready at 9 [o'clock].

Two new operas are coming to the stage next week. *Das Schloss Lowinsky, oder Repressalien* ([Theater] an der Wien)[145] and *Der Schnee* (at the Kärntnertor).[146] // The music to the *Schnee* is by a Frenchman. //[147]

HOUSEKEEPER[148] [**at Beethoven's apartment, offering choices for midday dinner; ca. 1 p.m. on Tuesday, March 9**]: Lamb
Veal   Vegetable soup
Green cabbage   Rice
Veal with salad

End of Heft 57

served as a copyist for Beethoven, who initially considered employing him for the upcoming concert on May 7, 1824. From his entries in Heft 59, Blätter 10v–11v, etc., he seems both reasonable and literate. By March 23, however, Beethoven had determined to use the Josephstadt Theater's Peter Gläser instead (Heft 60, Blätter 18r–18v). See Böckh, 1822, p. 373; Pohl, *Tonkünstler-Societät*, p. 99; Wurzbach, vol. 17, pp. 78–79.—KH/TA

[144] Johann Heinrich Voss (1751–1826), poet and philologist, eldest member of the Göttingen *Dichterbund* (Poets' League).—KH

[145] *Das Schloss Lowinsky, oder: Repressalien*, a comic opera in two acts, freely from the Italian by Joseph von Seyfried, with music by Hartmann Stunz, first performed at the Theater an der Wien on Thursday, March 18, 1824. Joseph Hartmann Stunz or Stuntz (1793–1859), former student of Peter von Winter and Antonio Salieri, was now vice-Kapellmeister in Munich. For Franz Oliva's frank discussion of him on April 5, 1820, see Heft 11, Blätter 24r and 38r–39r. See also Bäuerle's *Allgemeine Theater-Zeitung* 17, No. 40 (April 1, 1824), p. 159.—KH

[146] An opera in four acts by (Daniel) François (Esprit) Auber, in an adaptation by the Viennese Ignaz Franz Castelli, first performed at the Kärntnertor Theater on Friday, March 19, 1824. See Bäuerle's *Allgemeine Theater-Zeitung* 17, No. 42 (April 6, 1824), pp. 166–167.—KH

[147] Under the line, Karl's calligraphic doodles: *Schneemann* (snowman) and *Schneeball* (snowball).—KH

[148] This may be a new housekeeper. The last specific reference to Barbara Holzmann's presence is on March 5, 1824 (Blatt 32r above). Karl encounters Holzmann again on April 15, 1824, after she had left Beethoven's employ (see Heft 62, Blatt 2r).—TA

Heft 58

(March 7, 1824 – March 8, 1824)

N.B. Heft 58 belongs chronologically between Heft 57, Blatt 37r, and Heft 57, Blatt 38r.

Beethoven initiated blank Heft 58 at a prearranged concert-planning meeting with violinist Ignaz Schuppanzigh, publisher Tobias Haslinger, patron Count Moritz Lichnowsky, and (incidentally) violinist Joseph Böhm at the *Goldenes Stern* restaurant, Brandstatt No. 629, across from the front of St. Stephan's Cathedral, on Sunday, March 7, 1824, at 1 p.m. He then used it until the next day.

[Blatt 1r]

SCHUPPANZIGH [sitting next to Beethoven and writing, in part, on behalf of others present, at a meeting at the *Goldenes Stern* restaurant in the City; 1 p.m. on Sunday, March 7]:[1]

Was [copyist Frau] Schlemmer at his [= your] place yesterday?[2] [//]

Does he [= Do you] want red [wine]?[3] [//] That is also here. // Does he [= Do you] want beef? //

[For solo singers,] I believe [baritone] Forti, [tenor] Jäger, and [soprano] Grünbaum,[4] because she is the most musical. //

---

[1] Schuppanzigh had established the location and time with Beethoven in Heft 57, Blatt 36r. Later investigators misread the surrounding chronology and placed this meeting on March 9 (a Tuesday), but my pacing of the entries, based on Beethoven's known daily habits, places the meeting on Sunday, March 7, a more logical meeting day for at least six individuals, some of whom otherwise led very busy lives.—TA

[2] If Schlemmer's widow, Josepha (who continued his copying business), had visited Beethoven on Saturday, March 6, after Schuppanzigh departed, she left no entries at that point in Heft 57, so Beethoven's reply was probably "no."—TA

[3] Schuppanzigh (and possibly others) seem to have arrived at the *Stern* before Beethoven did and had already ordered their drinks and perhaps something to eat.—TA

[4] Therese Grünbaum (1791–1876), singer, daughter of composer Wenzel Müller, and a member of the Kärntnertor Theater from 1818 to 1828. See Wurzbach, vol. 5, p. 393; Clive, pp. 325 and 344; and Heft 57, Blatt 39r.—KH/TA

Does he [= Do you] know Böhm[5] personally? He is sitting next to the count [Lichnowsky]. //

Is the new Symphony already copied, that is, the score? //

We need 40 choral parts, namely 10 of each voice. // Haslinger is of the opinion that one could have the choral parts engraved for less cost. // [//]

[Blatt 1v]

BEETHOVEN [**writing, so as not to be overheard**]: <Say nothing more about engraving the Mass [*Missa solemnis*]; I am about to send it off.> //

SCHUPPANZIGH: On the morning of the day after tomorrow [Tuesday, March 9], 10 copyists of the best sort will come to his [= your] place. //

Tobias [Haslinger] will have a circular issued to the dilettantes on stringed instruments; but you'll need to sign your name to it yourself. [//] [Blatt 2r]

Are the parts to be lithographed? // Tobias would do that *without interest*. // The vocal parts must first be copied out to be lithographed. // Every one of the choral parts must be copied 10 times. //

In the Symphony:
    6 1st Violin [parts]
    6 2nd Violin [parts]
    4 Viola [parts]
    5 Violoncello [parts, also for contrabasses]
    Doubled Winds[6] [//] [Blatt 2v]

---

[5] Violinist Joseph Böhm had been born on March 4, 1795, in Pest, where his father was concertmaster at the theater. He began instruction with his father at age four. In ca. 1806, he went on tour with his father to Poland, where the elder Böhm worked for four years. In 1808, young Joseph met the French violinist Pierre Rode on his way home from a concert tour to Russia and seemingly had a few lessons with him, a decisive factor for his career. At some time between 1813 and 1815, he went to Vienna, where he is said to have played at the Burgtheater before the emperor. From Schuppanzigh's remark on Blatt 2v below, it appears that Böhm might have been his student up to early 1816, when he himself left Vienna for seven years, mostly in Russia, and probably with Schuppanzigh there (see Blatt 2v below). In 1818, Böhm toured to Italy, and, as noted elsewhere, he had recently returned from a tour to Paris. As professor at the Gesellschaft der Musikfreunde's Conservatorium, Böhm would have many prominent students, among them Joseph Joachim, and would become (along with Schuppanzigh) a champion of Beethoven's late string quartets. He died in Vienna on March 28, 1876.

See Schilling, vol. 1, p. 697 (article signed by "18"); and Heft 55, Blatt 13r.

Violinist Joseph Böhm does not appear in any of the surviving Burgtheater records of 1814–1817, nor is he identical with Franz Böhm, who served as the orchestra's stagehand during this period. See Status der k.k. Hof-Theater (ca. November 1814); Hoftheater, General-Intendanz; Karton 6: No. 131/1814, Beilage 6; and Consignation (March 1817); Hoftheater, G.I., K. 8: 197/1817; k.k. Hoftheater, Personal-Stand; G.I., K. 10: 318/1819 (Haus-, Hof- und Staatsarchiv).—TA

[6] The term used here is *Harmonie*, used to designate an ensemble of 2 oboes, 2 clarinets, 2 horns, and 2 bassoons, sometimes with a single contrabassoon or contrabass viol. In this case, the doubling

Do you still need Rampl[7] for the score of the Symphony? // I'll go and see him tomorrow [Monday, March 8]. // He also has a poor appearance. //

This is a wooden student of mine; his name is Holz [= Wood].[8] // This [seemingly Böhm] was a more intelligent one.[9] [//]

[The meeting ends.]

[Blatt 3r]

NEPHEW KARL **[probably with brother Johann, returning to Beethoven's apartment after the Krähmers' concert; probably at ca. 2:30 p.m. on Sunday, March 7]**:[10]

The enthusiasm with which everyone offered to participate is astonishing; it would be a shame if this would be in vain. //

---

probably extends to flutes (that is, 2 first flute and 2 second flute parts, etc.) but not to trumpets and trombones.—TA

[7] Wenzel Rampl/Rampel (1783–1851), "musical copyist in the Imperial Theater," often served as Beethoven's copyist in the years 1823–1826. Alan Tyson designated him as "Copyist B." He was the son of copyist Peter Rampl and, in 1811, married the much older Anna Ettmann (1768–1826), a cook, and, after her death, the chambermaid Anna Maria Kugler (b. 1794). At his wedding in 1811, one of the witnesses was the copyist Wenzel Schlemmer (1768–1823). Rampl lived in the northern suburb of Rossau, Grüne Torgasse No. 145, across from the back of the Servitenkirche.

See Conscriptions-Bogen, Rossau No. 145; and Altlerchenfeld, No. 95 (Wiener Stadt- und Landesarchiv); Pfarre Rossau (Servitenkirche): Taufbuch, 1783, fol. 16, No. 121; Sterbebuch, 1826, fol. 326; Dompfarre St. Stephan: Trauungsbuch, 1811, fol. 438; Pfarre Schotten: Trauungsbuch, Tom. 44, fol. 78; Frimmel, *Handbuch*, II, pp. 49–50; Frimmel, *Studien*, II, pp. 15 and 17; Alan Tyson, "Notes on Five of Beethoven's Copyists," *Journal of the American Musicological Society* 23, No. 3 (Fall 1970), pp. 439–471; and (for biographical details and further sources) Heft 21, Blatt 1r.—KH/TA

[8] Karl Holz (b. Vienna, March 3, 1799; d. Vienna, November 9, 1858), cashier's officer in the Lower Austrian Provincial Income Office and a performing member of the Gesellschaft der Musikfreunde. In 1824, Holz was second violinist in Schuppanzigh's String Quartet. This may have been Beethoven's first meeting with the man who would replace Schindler as his unpaid secretary from late July 1825 until early December 1826. Even here, Schuppanzigh is making puns on his name, just as Beethoven would do later on. See Thayer-Forbes, pp. 942–943; Clive, pp. 168–169 (with correct dates); Heft 91, Blatt 3v.—KH/TA

[9] Schuppanzigh's use of two tenses ("this one *is*" versus "this one *was*") suggests the presence of two students. If Holz was the present student, then Joseph Böhm (see Blatt 1r above) was surely the past one, revealing a teacher-student relationship previously unreported in the encyclopedic literature.—TA

[10] Nephew Karl had mentioned seeing Caroline Krähmer, *née* Schleicher, at the *Concert spirituel* (where her husband, Ernest, was presumably performing) on Friday, March 5 (see Heft 57, Blätter 31v–32r). Now he and brother Johann presumably attended their benefit concert at the *Landständischer Saal* at 12:30 p.m. on Sunday, March 7. Therefore, they were not present at Beethoven's meeting at the *Stern* at 1 p.m.

The Krähmers' typical potpourri program (with a vocal soloist and a small orchestra) consisted of Mozart, *Marriage of Figaro* Overture; Joseph Panny, Oboe Concerto, first movement and Adagio (Ernest); Danzi, Potpourri for clarinet (Caroline); Mercadante, recitative and aria from an unnamed opera (Therese Grünbaum); Ernest Krähmer, new Concert-Polonaise for the czakan (Ernest); Viotti, Violin Concerto (otherwise unidentified), first movement (Caroline); Caroline Krähmer, Double Variations for clarinet and oboe (both players). The seven pieces, with applause in between, might

They say that the waltzes were by Tobias.[11] //

The copyist's name was Gebauer.[12] // The best and most dependable. // But it must be copied out one time. Also, only the choral parts will be lithographed. // You don't have to undertake the proofreading all by yourself. Schuppanzigh can also do it, if he has the score. //

Grünbaum. [//] [Blatt 3v] The public doesn't like her. //

[impatient about getting some midday dinner:]

I'm going to the *Birne* myself to get a capon. Only I want to order a salad. // She [the maid] wants to look around for a salad. I'm going to the *Birne*.[13] //

JOHANN VAN BEETHOVEN [**placating Karl**]: She [the maid] has gone for a salad. //

NEPHEW KARL [**returning from the *Birne***]: When I came home, the maid stood down there at the house gate with her lover, who quickly left; then the maid ran up here. //

There was nothing but *poularde* [hen] there. // I took 9 kr. along with me; <since I ....> [//] [Blatt 4r] The .... 6 kr. // another 6 kr. for a salad without dressing. //

[Violoncellist] Linke and he [Böhm] quarreled with one another, and Linke told him that if he could play something, he (Linke) could certainly also play it. // Böhm was the injured party. //

[writing on brother Johann's behalf:]

have lasted a total of 75–90 minutes. After some social chatting, the drive (in Johann's carriage) to Beethoven's apartment probably took another 10–15 minutes. If Beethoven was walking back from the Stephansplatz (ca. 25 minutes), the three probably arrived within minutes of each other.

See the *Wiener Zeitung*, No. 54 (Saturday, March 6, 1824), p. 242; *Allgemeine musikalische Zeitung* 26, No. 18 (April 29, 1824), cols. 281–282.—TA

[11] Publisher Tobias Haslinger (1787–1842), with whom nephew Karl is obviously on informal terms. See Clive, pp. 151–152.—KH/TA

[12] Benjamin Gebauer (b. Fischstein, Silesia, ca. 1758; d. Vienna, September 20, 1846), copyist and former oboist at the Theater an der Wien/auf der Wieden, at least since 1795. He copied substantial parts of the score of Beethoven's Symphony No. 3 (*Eroica*) that is preserved in the archive of the Gesellschaft der Musikfreunde. The composer always had a checkered working relationship with Gebauer, but friends periodically suggested him as an alternative. Now that Schlemmer was dead (August 6, 1823), they were evidently eager to do so again. See Theodore Albrecht, "Benjamin Gebauer: The Life and Death of Beethoven's 'Copyist C,'" *Bonner Beethoven-Studien* 3 (2003), pp. 7–21.—TA

[13] Karl is not being selfish here. Beethoven had presumably eaten at the *Stern* at 1 p.m. (see Blatt 1r above), and Johann had said in an earlier conversation-book entry that he preferred his main meal late in the afternoon. Therefore, Karl was the only one of the three needing dinner at a time when most restaurants had already run low on midday preparations (as indeed happened here). The *Birne* (Pear) restaurant was located on Landstrasse Hauptstrasse, a 5–10 minute walk from Beethoven's apartment.—TA

He [Johann] says that he got his second apothecary's shop for free with the help of a handwritten letter from the emperor; it is worth 20,000 fl.[14] // [Blatt 4v]

He says that there is a difference between *living* together and *being* together. // He says that he does what he wants, and lets her [Therese] do what she wants. //

SCHUPPANZIGH [**at Beethoven's apartment; presumably late morning or early afternoon on Monday, March 8**]: Does he [= Do you] want them [the solo vocal parts] with underlaid bass? //

SCHINDLER [**at Beethoven's apartment; sometime after Schuppanzigh's departure on Monday, March 8**]: Then has he brought something for me? // Let's go together to see him, or allow me to go alone. [//] [Blatt 5r]

It is impossible for the housekeeper to cook at home, because of the washing.[15] // She believes that the washerwoman will want much more. [//] But they need nearly 3 days for this washing anyway. //

Then do you know the address of this handsome youth?[16]

[falsified entries begin→] I advise you to go to Berlin in any case. Lichnowsky will say, "wait, wait," but I no longer believe that it will develop, because many of our ideas conflict. I am losing my patience. [←falsified entries end]

N.B. Schindler's authentic entries at the end of Heft 58 lead directly to his entries in Heft 57, Blatt 38r.

End of Heft 58

---

[14] On March 13, 1808, Johann van Beethoven acquired the apothecary shop *Zur goldenen Krone*, also called the "Water Apothecary," in Linz, House No. 601. He sold this apothecary on December 30, 1816, and immediately founded the apothecary *Zum goldenen Adler* as the first apothecary shop in Urfahr, across the Danube from Linz, on the *Platzl* there. Whether he had obtained these apothecary shops "in vain" through a document in the handwriting of the emperor could not, up to 1970, be traced. See Alfred Marks, "Die alten Linzer Apotheken in 'Oberösterreich,'" *Linzer Zeitschrift* 9, Heft 1–2 (1959), p. 61; Otto Zekert, "Apotheker Johann van Beethoven," special publication from *Pharmazeutische Monatshefte* (Vienna, 1928), pp. 8–11.—KH/TA

[15] They are concerned that cooking smells might get into the wash, possibly while it is drying.—TA

[16] Possibly a reference to either Joseph Böhm or Karl Holz, whom Schuppanzigh had introduced the day before as potential copyists or proofreaders.—TA

Heft 59

(March 9, 1824 – March 16, 1824)

N.B. Heft 59 seemingly follows directly after the end of Heft 57 (not 58).

[Blatt 1r]

SCHUPPANZIGH [**presumably returning to Beethoven's apartment; probably the afternoon of Tuesday, March 9**]:[1] Is the date of the concert determined already? // What does his [= your] brother say? // <It is> The best day is April 8.[2] // I know it. // When does he [= do you] see his [= your] brother? //

It would be better if he [= you] were to get the theater tickets from [resident manager] Duport, because tickets cause hellacious[3] confusion, [Blatt 1v] and by doing so, much confusion is spared. // And it is certain that, with these tickets, no one can make a *mess*[4] of it. // You don't have to pay anyone else; even without them, he [= you] will bring in a great deal. //

Except for the Imperial Court, no one.[5] [//] [Blatt 2r]
This is done in half an hour. //
Now I must go and earn some bread again;[6] send his [= your] brother to see me. //

NEPHEW KARL [**at Beethoven's apartment; still on the afternoon of Tuesday, March 9**]: The best thing is that neither the maid nor the housekeeper be on this

---

[1] Working back from Schindler's arrival at Beethoven's apartment on Blatt 11v below, and assuming that those entries were made on Sunday, March 14, suggests strongly that these entries in Heft 59 follow those in Heft 57, Blatt 41v. Schuppanzigh had apparently been at Beethoven's apartment in the late morning of Tuesday, March 9, but now returned later in the afternoon.—TA

[2] In 1824, April 8 was the Thursday before Palm Sunday. The date would therefore avoid conflicts with the *Tonkünstler-Societät*'s Lenten benefit concerts on Sunday, April 11, and Monday, April 12. See Pohl, *Tonkünstler-Societät*, p. 71.—TA

[3] Schuppanzigh uses *höllisch* here. In Heft 63, Blatt 2r, Schindler quotes Schuppanzigh as being "*ganz höllisch*" glad, suggesting that Schindler's delivery of Schuppanzigh's message in that instance is accurate.—TA

[4] Schuppanzigh uses the term *Balavatsch* (more commonly *Palawatsch*), an eastern Austrian word for *Durcheinander, Wirrwarr*—confusion, chaos, or a mess.—TA

[5] Beethoven may have asked who would automatically receive complimentary tickets.—TA

[6] Probably by giving violin lessons in the homes of his students.—TA

footing, because servants' gossip does a great deal. // Up to now, we always came to a clear understanding in the first 3 days about the suitability, honesty, etc., of our housekeepers. In *her* case it will also not take long until we are *completely certain*; up to now, better to say very little. [//]

[Blatt 2v]

SCHINDLER [**at Beethoven's apartment; still on the afternoon of Tuesday, March 9**]: Unger regrets very much that she now has many rehearsals in the mornings and afternoons, and cannot visit you. To participate in the concert would be the greatest honor that she could ever hope for. She sings from F to A/B-natural. For the bass part, Herr Preisinger, instead of Herr Forti, recommends himself to you as better for such compositions than Forti. //

It [Cherubini's *Der Wasserträger*] has been shamefully maltreated, and people in general are dissatisfied. The reason is primarily *Drechsler*,[7] who doesn't know the *spirit* of this composition, as well as the strengths of the entire personnel. He took all the tempi [Blatt 3r] absolutely wrong; in this way, especially the Finale of act I went to the devil. I cannot forgive it. //

It would doubtless go according to your wish, if Unger invited Sontag and Herr Preisinger in your name, something that she is willing to undertake. Who is to sing tenor? Herr Haitzinger or someone else? // Jäger is better for such a large work. // I very often socialize with Jäger; if you'll permit me, I'll acquaint him with your wish. [//] [Blatt 3v]

Have you decided yet to write something special for the 2 girls for this occasion? // Will it [the concert] take place at night? That is very much to be hoped. //

It would merely be a matter of reaching an agreement with Duport. If he gives a ballet, the concert won't hurt him a bit. // It's more a question of from where the good orchestral players who depart in this way are replaced.[8] // It merely depends upon talking it over with him; then he will make the arrangements in the way you want them and need them.[9] [Blatt 4r] Just appear on stage once again; it is time

---

[7] Joseph Drechsler (1782–1852), composer and conductor at the Theater in der Josephstadt since October 1822. In a review of Cherubini's opera *Der Wasserträger* in the Josephstadt on March 9, 1824, Vienna's correspondent to the *Allgemeine musikalische Zeitung* noted: "Herr Drechsler is a most inconsistent conductor, and only too often cannot make up his own mind. *Regis ad exemplum* [according to the example of the king]." See the *Allgemeine musikalische Zeitung* 26, No. 18 (April 29, 1824), col. 282; Clive, pp. 161 and 232; and Heft 51, Blatt 3r.—KH/TA

[8] For instance, the Kärntnertor Theater's senior low hornist, Friedrich Hradetzky (ca. 1769/72–1846), who had played there since ca. 1797, had been dismissed effective the end of January 1824. Beethoven had written the solo for him in the *Fidelio* Overture of 1814 and now had written the extensive low-horn solo for him in the third movement of the Ninth Symphony.—TA

[9] Beethoven may indeed have negotiated reengaging Hradetzky for his two Akademies (the documents do not indicate one outcome or another), but legends surrounding the premiere say that

and it is necessary. What is the purpose of the folding screen? // To your friends and admirers, however, it cannot be indifferent to know what is ready and what, [owing to] your unpardonable reticence, cannot be heard. It would be just as unpleasant to see your works being performed first in foreign countries—Enough!

NEPHEW KARL [**at Beethoven's apartment; later in the afternoon of Tuesday, March 9?**]:
A kitchen candle burns 2–2½ hours. // [Blatt 4v] They must be lit until 11:30 [p.m.]. // Because of the washing. // Washing must actually be done in the evenings. // One must *inquire*. [//] *Inquire*.

```
C.M. 3 + 1 = 10 W.W.            50
                                 4
        4 = 10                  54
          30                    10
           1                    31
          ──                    ──
          41                    95  1 fl. 35 kr. [W.W.]
           4
          ──
          45
          50
          ──
         <95>   1 fl. 35 kr. [W.W.]
```

JOHANN VAN BEETHOVEN [**at Beethoven's apartment; probably late morning or early afternoon of Wednesday, March 10**]: I have already spoken with Schuppanzigh. Following that, [I] went to see Duport yesterday [presumably Tuesday]; he is very taken with you and your Akademie, but he told me that it is not in his power, but rather Count Dietrichstein's. Therefore, you must [Blatt 5r] write a courteous letter to Count Dietrichstein right away,[10] asking that he give you approval, so that you can have the Grosser Redoutensaal for your Akademie on the evening of

---

he composed the horn solo for principal hornist Eduard Constantin Lewy (1796–1846), who played it at the premiere. Lewy, however, had probably arrived in Vienna only in late November 1823 and so was not present when Beethoven orchestrated the third movement. As noted below, Beethoven probably did not meet the talented Lewy until May 2, 1824, when he also met the theater's new principal bassoonist, Theobald Hürth. Hürth was originally from the Pfalz near Mainz, Lewy from Zweibrücken and St. Avold, but Kärntnertor Kapellmeister Conradin Kreutzer had lured both of them to Vienna from Switzerland. See Heft 64, Blätter 22v and 27v.

Another musician (traditionally associated with the Theater an der Wien) whom Beethoven seemingly attempted to hire for his upcoming concerts was principal clarinettist Joseph Friedlowsky (1777–1859); see Heft 64, Blatt 27r.—TA

[10] A Beethoven letter to Dietrichstein; see Anderson, No. 1273, and Albrecht, *Letters to Beethoven*, No. 348.—TA

[Thursday,] April 8,[11] because you know that it depends upon him alone. I'll do the rest with him in person. [//] [Blatt 5v]

[A concert in] the evening is worth 1500 fl. more [than one during the day]. // But he [Duport] may not, without the count. // We'll try, [but] if it doesn't work, then the midday hour [12:30 p.m.] certainly remains to us.[12] // Duport told me that he would then give an old opera or an old ballet in the evening. [//] [Blatt 6r]

I just spoke to the copyist[13] on the way. He told me that I should tell you that the copying would go much faster and better, if he can have his people under his supervision at home at his place, because it is so far to come out here to your place that the people would be tired out if they come to you, and they don't want to do that; and then they would also start to copy at 4 o'clock in the morning at his place, which they couldn't do at your place.—[//]

[Blatt 6v]

NEPHEW KARL [after Johann's departure; probably the afternoon of Wednesday, March 10]: Your brother was here? //

Is the Redoutensaal therefore to be the location of the performance? // There was talk about the Theater an der Wien. // I think that the Redoutensaal is the best. //

On Sunday, you should go with me to the [Musik-]Verein.[14] It's good when the people see you. //

How expensive are you thinking about making the tickets? For the gallery and the *Parterre* (in the Redoutensaal). //

---

[11] The Thursday before Palm Sunday and Holy Week.—TA

[12] Beethoven's letter to Dietrichstein, dated March 21, 1824; see Anderson, No. 1272.—TA

[13] This concerns the copyist Paul Maschek, who lived in the Wieden No. 454 (the corner of Ziegelofengasse and Neuwieden Strasse [today's Margareten Strasse]); see Böckh, 1822, p. 373. Relatively speaking, Maschek himself lived fairly distant out into suburban Wieden. Walking from his place to Beethoven's would have taken ca. 45 minutes. See also Blatt 8r below and Heft 57, Blatt 40v.—KH/TA

[14] The third concert in the Gesellschaft der Musikfreunde's 1823–1824 season took place in the Grosser Redoutensaal at 12:30 p.m. on Sunday, March 14, 1824. Two works by Mozart were on the program: a Symphony in D Major [possibly the "Prague" Symphony No. 38, K. 504] and the cantata *Davidde penitente*, K. 469. With intermission, it would have lasted until around 2 p.m. See Perger, *Geschichte der k.k. Gesellschaft der Musikfreunde* (Vienna, 1912), I, p. 288; *Wiener Zeitung*, No. 59 (March 12, 1824), p. 264.

The concert to which Karl referred, however, was at the *Musikverein*'s own hall in the *Rother Igel* (Tuchlauben): the twelfth of violinist Ignaz Schuppanzigh's subscription concerts, this one featuring Schubert's new String Quartet in A Minor, D. 804, and Beethoven's popular Septet in E-flat major, Op. 20. It began at 4 p.m., two hours after the end of the Gesellschaft's own larger-scaled concert at the Redoutensaal. See the *Allgemeine musikalische Zeitung* 26, No. 18 (April 29, 1824), cols. 282–283.

In any case, on Tuesday, March 9 (see above), Beethoven had already asked Schindler to explore the possibility of inviting soprano Henriette Sontag and alto Caroline Unger to dinner (presumably at 2 p.m.) on that coming Sunday, March 14.—KH/TA

The shoemaker is here. //

She didn't know yet that she was to come at *one* ring of the bell. [//]

[Blatt 7r]

BEETHOVEN [**possibly at his apartment; Thursday, March 11, or early on Friday, March, 12**]:

Superfine f[lour]	1 fl. 18 [kr.]
Baking flour	1 fl. 48 [kr.]
Semolina	1 fl. 44 [kr.] //

SCHINDLER [falsified entries begin→] So Count Brunsvik[15] is coming; perhaps his wife, as well. // A small child at home. // I look forward to this phlegmatic *Teremtette*.[16] Yes indeed, a rare and noble person! // He doesn't want to play in the performance; therefore he is bringing 4 ears along, so as not to miss anything. // After the concerts, he wants to take you with him to Hungary. // Very good for your eyes. // And in the fall, we'll journey to England. [←falsified entries end]

[Blatt 7v]

NEPHEW KARL [**at Beethoven's apartment, seemingly accompanied by brother Johann and writing, in part, on his behalf; possibly the afternoon of Friday, March 12**]:

They are copying in *their* residences. While she [presumably Beethoven's maid] was there, one of the copyists just then brought him [Maschek] the copied parts. //

<Today, the bank shares are at 1015 fl.>[17] // If only a person knew everything beforehand! //

Up to now, he [Johann] has not brought it about, but [publisher] Steiner asked him whether he still had the works, and whether he wanted to credit him, because it would be troubling to him to pay immediately. He now wants to discuss this with him very seriously. // Not until October 1. // He spoke with [violinist Joseph] Böhm, who told him that [Paris publisher Maurice] Schlesinger would pay you very

---

[15] Count Franz von Brunsvik (1777–1849), a longtime friend of Beethoven's, probably mentioned here, after the composer's death, in connection with violinist Jansa; see Heft 55, Blatt 15v; and Clive, pp. 63–64.—KH/TA

[16] A Hungarian word for blusterer. In Heft 63, Blatt 1v (in another falsified entry), the German editors provided a different translation. *Both* falsified entries reflect a period during or *after* Schindler had lived in Buda-Pest (1827–1829).—KH/TA

[17] On Saturday, March 13, 1824, the bank shares stood at 1,014$^{1}/_{10}$ fl. in C.M. Otherwise, the rate for bank shares between March 10 and 18 had fluctuated between 999 and 1,013 fl., averaging about 1,006 fl. See *Wiener Zeitung*, No. 61 (March 15, 1824), p. 271.—KH/TA

[NEPHEW KARL, *continued*]
well for the Symphony.[18] [//] [Blatt 8r] Therefore, you don't have to worry; it will make that [amount]. //

He [Johann] believes that you should trust Schindler to get the *winds* and other instruments from the [Josephstadt] Theater, because, first, he knows the people, knows where they live, and said that most of them would come without payment.[19] Schuppanzigh, on the other hand, is not as well known, because he was gone for so many years. // Schuppanzigh is too easygoing. //

Maschek told your brother that the people [copyists] didn't want to come here because it's too far. // It depends upon where *they* live. // When she [presumably Beethoven's maid] was there, he sat there, still in his sleeping shirt, and copied. // [Blatt 8v]

Schlesinger will be very happy to take it [the Symphony]. He is doing very well. [//] *Sign it!*[20] //

He [Johann] believes that the housekeeper appears fine to him. She shows enthusiasm, though. //

Schindler ate a whole bowl of *Fritatten*[21] yesterday [presumably Thursday], but otherwise he didn't get much else. Only soup, beef, and side vegetables. //

Will it be necessary to give tickets to the participants? I don't think so. // To the more prominent ones.[22] //

I've got a dissertation about the undigestibility of cheese, since Herr Apothecary [Johann] [Blatt 9r] asserted that he had chemically analyzed it, and had found all the elements that partially decompose in wine spirits, water, etc. // Only you should say it, but your brother says that the eye doctor can do nothing here, and that "cures and coins" are useless. It is self-evident. // I want to account for it. //

He says that a thousand people are already going there [Beethoven's concert] just to see you. Don't even think about an empty house.

---

[18] Böhm had recently returned to Vienna from a tour that had taken him to Paris.—TA

[19] Beethoven was aware that the Josephstadt Theater's orchestra had recently experienced personnel problems and, in any case, did not want to assign any increased responsibility for personnel to Schindler, who did not have the respect of Vienna's most experienced professionals. A week later, on March 20, Schindler and Lichnowsky would go a step further and, without Beethoven's authorization, approach Count Palffy about holding the Akademie at the Theater an der Wien and using that theater's orchestra as the core personnel; see Heft 60, Blätter 3r–8r.—TA

[20] A letter to Schlesinger, written by Karl on ca. March 11, 1824, and signed by Beethoven, has seemingly not survived.—TA

[21] *Fritatten*: thin egg and flour crepes; also cut up into flat noodles and eaten in a beef-broth soup (still a popular light meal in Vienna).—KH/TA

[22] It is not clear whether this means complimentary tickets to the more prominent musicians or to the more prominent music lovers.—TA

Given	5 fl.
Bill	2 fl. 52 kr.
Remains	2 fl. 8 kr. [//]

[Blatt 9v]

SCHINDLER[23] [falsified entries begin→] Yesterday [conductor Michael] Umlauf and Schuppanzigh were very much surprised that, contrary to earlier years, you now deviate so notably from the quicker tempos in your works, and everything is now too fast for you. // Master, may your little disciple and little son say what he feels about this?[24] //

At the rehearsal yesterday, I wanted to embrace you as you gave all of us the reasons why you now feel *differently* about your works than you did 15–20 years ago. I honestly confess that, in earlier years, I did not agree with this or that tempo, because I felt the *meaning* of that music differently. //

Also at the rehearsals at the [Theater in the] Josephstadt,[25] it was clearly plain to see that you wanted all the Allegros slower than you did earlier. I noted the reasons well. // A tremendous difference! Things in the middle voices that had been inaudible or confused earlier now came out clearly. // [Blatt 10r]

Master, you grieve too much; let yourself be persuaded by a poor sinner. Do you really have so little knowledge of people? How often have you yourself said that you perceive that your brother always seeks to ruin you, and your nephew denies you, and yet you always believe them. Don't you see how Karl seeks to slander everyone around you who appears dangerous to him?[26] Also we will still be divided about this because I no longer abandon myself to your mistrust.[27] //

Why? Because it is only too clear that, through this irrational deliberation,[28] we have only gone from one dilemma to another. [←falsified entries end]

---

[23] Schindler found two pages (Blätter 9v and 10r) completely empty after Beethoven's death and filled them with falsified entries.—TA

[24] Language such as this is quite inconsistent with Schindler's authentic conversation-book entries.—TA

[25] Rehearsals for concerts at the suburban theater that included Beethoven's Symphonies, supposedly led by Schindler after consultation with the composer about them. In fact, Schindler was concertmaster in the Josephstadt, and most concerts during this period would have been conducted by Gläser. See Schindler, 2nd ed. (1845), p. 283.—KH

[26] There is an element of truth in Schindler's accusations. Brother Johann considered Ludwig incapable of running his own financial affairs, and Karl's complaints were often the source of Beethoven's dissatisfaction with various domestic servants, including housekeeper Barbara Holzmann and several of the maids. Similarly, Karl probably (and with some justification) regarded Schindler as an intrusive pest.—TA

[27] Here is the increasingly resentful side of Schindler writing after Beethoven's death.—TA

[28] This retrospectively concerns Beethoven's indecision over the location of the upcoming concerts, probably *quite* rationally based on the orchestral musicians available at any given location.—TA

[Blatt 10v]

COPYIST MASCHEK[29] **[at Beethoven's apartment; probably Saturday, March 13]**:
Am I to leave space here? [//]

My writing is good, but I cannot copy everything myself. [//] For the most part. [//] The parts that have already been proofread are already duplicated. [//] Please give me the violas and basses now. [//] The tenor and bass parts of the Credo and Agnus are missing. [//]

Are these already proofread? Now I'll have them duplicated. [//] [Blatt 11r] So I'll bring it. [//]

The violins of the Kyrie were proofread.[30] // I have returned these 4 parts for proofreading yesterday [Friday, March 12]. //

But we could duplicate the parts, in order not to be held up, and afterward deliver a part for proofreading, and then correct all the others after that, since no substantial mistakes will be there anyhow. [//] [Blatt 11v] I ask only for the 4 parts. //

But we won't be finished otherwise. //

SCHINDLER **[at Beethoven's apartment; probably late morning of Sunday, March 14]**:[31]

Unger and Sontag are free to come to dinner today. Then one sings: <"[Struck out] hung from a tree.">[32] // She didn't let me know until today. // It is still early in the

---

[29] Paul Maschek was copying the orchestral and choral parts for the *Missa solemnis*. He seems to have been far more literate than most of Beethoven's copyists, especially the deceased Wenzel Schlemmer. See Heft 57, Blatt 40v.—TA

[30] At this point, the observant copyist begins writing dividing strokes between conversational elements to indicate when he is finished.—TA

[31] The date can be determined through several pieces of evidence, documented more fully below. It snowed in the morning and afternoon of Sunday, March 14. Sunday would have been a logical time to invite dinner guests (as Beethoven seemingly did, through Schindler, who failed to report their acceptance). With shops closed on Sunday, Beethoven's housekeeper managed to scrape together a meager meal by combining leftovers from a nearby restaurant with a few items already at home. To these, Beethoven added more wine than the food could offset. According to Schindler's subsequent report to Beethoven (which proved greatly exaggerated), Sontag was sick through the night after the visit, had difficulty attending a rehearsal at Court on Monday, March 15, at 10 a.m., and had to cancel a performance of Kreutzer's *Der Taucher* at the Kärntnertor Theater that night.

Moreover, in Heft 60, Blatt 37b, Schindler refers to the visit as having taken place on a Sunday and says that he did not learn until 9 a.m. that day that Sontag could come. He further said that her illness that night was not due to anything that happened at Beethoven's but instead to a vinegar salad that she ate at home that night.—TA

[32] It seems that, three or four days previously, Beethoven had commissioned Schindler to invite singers Caroline Unger (who had visited him before) and Henriette Sontag to join him for dinner on this day (thus a Sunday seems the best choice). Schindler never got back to him about whether they could or not, and now—evidently while Beethoven was shaving (as becomes apparent below)

HEFT 59 (MARCH 9 – MARCH 16, 1824), BLATT 12R

day; therefore have Spanish partridges [= potatoes][33] soft-boiled. [//]
[Schindler departs, to return later with Unger and Sontag.]

[Blatt 12r]

HOUSEKEEPER **[at Beethoven's apartment; returning from an attempted shopping expedition; probably shortly after noon on Sunday, March 14]**: Everything is already closed. [//] Hen and two portions of meat from the restaurant, in addition. // How many persons?[34] // We have salad and a *Gugelhupf* for a pastry. [//] 2 < ½ > [//]

[Blatt 12v]

UNGER[35] **[arriving at Beethoven's apartment with Sontag and Schindler; ca. 1–2 p.m. on Sunday, March 14]**: Fräulein Sontag joins me in rejoicing that you

and without letting him know ahead of time—showed up with the two young women in tow. Thus Beethoven found himself in a socially embarrassing situation: he was left hanging, so to speak, a parallel to the idiom that Schindler invokes in his quote.—TA

[33] When discussing this conversation in his biography of Beethoven, Schindler explained, "By Spanish partridges one understood *potatoes*, in a joking way." See Schindler, 2nd ed., p. 286; not included in the 3rd ed. or Schindler-MacArdle.—KH/TA

[34] Probably four for dinner: Caroline Unger, Henriette Sontag, Anton Schindler, and Beethoven. On Sunday, March 14, nephew Karl, possibly with brother Johann, attended Schuppanzigh's twelfth and final subscription concert for the season at the Musikverein's hall in the *Rother Igel*. The program, beginning at 4 p.m., consisted of Schubert's String Quartet in A Minor, D. 804 (its premiere), and Beethoven's popular Septet in E-flat, Op. 20. It would have lasted until ca. 5:30 p.m. Eighteen months later, Karl recalled the Quartet: "It was very pretty, but no spoken account can describe it. In all, it is *his own spirit*, but one sees how you always strive further." See Heft 97, Blatt 8r (September 14, 1825).

At 12:30 p.m., Karl may also have attended the Gesellschaft der Musikfreunde's concert (with Mozart's Symphony in D ["Prague"?] and *Davidde penitente*) in the Grosser Redoutensaal. For both concerts, see the *Allgemeine musikalische Zeitung* 26, No. 18 (April 29, 1824), cols. 282–283.—TA

[35] In 1873, Unger wrote to Ludwig Nohl with an account of her acquaintance with Beethoven and this visit. Unger attributed Beethoven's kindness to her, overall, as an extension of his friendship with her father and said that they would occasionally encounter Beethoven taking a walk in Dornbach or some other location and that he would encourage her to continue her studies in music. Concerning this particular visit, she wrote:

"I can still see the simple room in the Landstrasse, where a piece of cord served as a bellpull, and where a large table stood in the middle, on which good roast beef was served to us with fine sweet wine. I see the second room next to it, filled to the ceiling with orchestral parts. In the middle of it stood the piano that Field (if I am not mistaken) had sent to Beethoven from London. Jette Sontag and I entered into this room as if into a church, and we attempted (unfortunately in vain) to sing for the esteemed master.

"I remember my presumptuous remark that he did not understand how to write for the voice because a note in my part in the Symphony lay too high for my voice. To that he answered, 'Just learn it, and the note will come!' To this day, that phrase has remained a byword in my work."

The piano, of course, had been a gift of the maker John Broadwood, but the pianist John Field was not among those English pianists who signed the instrument. See Ludwig Nohl, *Mosaik* (1881),

were so kind to invite us. We're coming from a rehearsal; therefore please excuse us that we've come so early. // We had a rehearsal of today's weather[36]—that is, of the opera *Der Schnee* [The Snow].[37] [//]

SONTAG [**continuing**]: I haven't come to eat well,[38] but rather to make your valued acquaintance, which I have so long awaited. [//]

UNGER: Schindler told us that, to the delight of all, you have finally decided to give a concert. We will be grateful [Blatt 13r] if you find us worthy to sing on it. [//]

May we go into the other room to sing something?[39] Don't you have *Fidelio* at hand? //

[Unger and Sontag go into the next room:]

Do the Benedictus, though, [at the concert]. [//] How could the public find one of *your* works to be long? //

[Possibly with the two singers otherwise engaged, the embarrassed Beethoven seemingly pulls Schindler aside to ask him why he brought them out for dinner without sufficient advance notice. Schindler replies in writing, but then the singers join in excusing the action:]

SCHINDLER [**continuing**]: I did not find Fräulein Unger at home yesterday, therefore I could not find out until today; therefore, it's not my fault. //

UNGER: He knew the day before yesterday [Friday, March 12] that *I* would *surely* come, but it was only Dlle Sontag about whom he didn't know for certain, although I had promised to bring her with me.[40] [//]

[Blatt 13v]

---

p. 282; reprinted in Friedrich Kerst, *Die Erinnerungen an Beethoven*, 2 vols., 2nd ed. (Stuttgart: Julius Hoffmann, 1913), II, pp. 77–78.—TA

[36] In Vienna (during the period from March 10 to 19, 1824), it snowed in the morning and afternoon of Sunday, March 14, and again on the afternoon of Tuesday, March 16. In both cases, the temperatures were such that little of it remained on the ground for long. See *Wiener Zeitung*, No. 62 (March 16, 1824), p. 276; and No. 64 (March 18, 1824), p. 283.—TA

[37] Auber's *Der Schnee* (adapted by Castelli) premiered at the Kärntnertor Theater the next Friday, March 19, 1824.—KH/TA

[38] Beethoven had evidently made apologies that he was not prepared to entertain.—TA

[39] This suggests that Beethoven's apartment had a room for eating and entertaining, another where he had his Broadwood piano and presumably worked, and (as he designated much earlier), a room where Karl slept. In addition, there was a kitchen and presumably a pantry of some sort.—TA

[40] Unger had visited Beethoven on at least two previous occasions, and had promised to bring Sontag on at least one of those, without her actually coming, so such an assurance on Unger's part now was not entirely credible.—TA

SCHINDLER: Yes, I knew that, but what I could not learn yet yesterday [Saturday] was whether Sontag would come for certain. //

SONTAG: As we arrived, you were in the midst of shaving. When I saw that, we turned aside and waited, so as not to disturb you. //
  Why are you going so far from the City? Take [summer] quarters nearer the City, then we can visit you quite often.[41] [//]
  [Schindler, Unger, and Sontag all depart.]

BEETHOVEN [at his apartment; probably the morning of Monday, March 15]:
  + Only the bass parts.[42]
  + Only the parts. //

SCHINDLER [falsified entries begin→] <I just gave Sontag a lecture, which she understood very well. She recently made a [wrong turn?], like Falck [?], and so [badly?] that she didn't find the right path again, [illegible line].> [←falsified entries end]

[Blatt 14r]

BEETHOVEN [**at a coffee house; the late afternoon of Monday, March 15**]:
  Wallishauser, Hoher Markt No. 543: Iwan Simonow's etc. *Beschreibung einer neuen Entdeckungsreise in das Südliche Eismeer*, etc., Preface by Litrow; size 8vo; Wien, 1824; bound in a wrapper; 1 fl. 30 kr. W.W.[43] [//]

[Blatt 14v]

NEPHEW KARL [**at Beethoven's apartment; probably the morning of Tuesday, March 16**]:
  Shoulder. //
  She[44] says that the redness comes from laying it on something made of iron. // The wash should remain until the day after tomorrow, otherwise it won't be ready

---

[41] Beethoven spent at least the early part of the summer of 1824 in Penzing, ca. 3 miles southwest of the City. See Albrecht, *Letters to Beethoven*, No. 362.—TA

[42] The German original is unclear and could be read as *B. g.* or *B. j.* or *B. s.* This edition has opted for the last, as possibly meaning *Bass-stimmen* (the bass parts mentioned on Blatt 10v above).—KH/TA

[43] Excerpt from an advertisement in the *Wiener Zeitung*, No. 61 (March 15, 1824), p. 272. Other than his spelling of Littrow as Litrow, Beethoven copied this advertisement for a book about new discoveries in the Antarctic Ocean accurately. The advertisement also included a 13-line description of the book that Beethoven did not copy. The same advertisement had also appeared in the *Wiener Zeitung*, No. 55 (Monday, March 8, 1824), p. 246; and No. 58 (Thursday, March 11, 1824), p. 260.—KH/TA

[44] Seemingly a new housekeeper. The most recent reference to Barbara Holzmann occurred on Friday, March 5, 1824 (Heft 57, Blatt 32r).—TA

tomorrow. Also, she has only a few things to be soaked today, and that is not good for the wash. //

I think that she's going to the Lichtensteg. // At the Lugeck, where all the meat booths are. // Not far from the university.[45] [//]

<pre>
4 fl. 19 kr.   [=]   3 fl. 79 kr.
     50   50
                       3 fl. 29   //
</pre>

How much should I pay? //

SCHINDLER [falsified entries begin→] The rehearsal went well today, but there is still too much trouble with the difficult passages in the Chorus, especially with the high passages for the soprano. // I maintain that no chorus in the world can sustain this high tessitura, because the tuning of the orchestra is now too high. [←falsified entries end]

[Blatt 15r]

SCHINDLER [**authentic entries, at Beethoven's apartment; probably late morning of Tuesday, March 16**]: To whom are you to give it now, since it is so pressing? I cannot advise. // If we had the string parts[46] soon, then we wouldn't have to be in such a hurry with the wind instruments. //

I'm coming in the afternoon; maybe by then he'll have brought it. //

I must remain *ex officio* at your brother's today, because he has a great deal to say to me before his departure [for Gneixendorf?]; therefore I beg your pardon, [falsified entries begin→] dear Master.[47] [←falsified entries end] //

Now an unpleasant piece of news from Sontag, which will certainly trouble you. The few drops of wine from the first pressing also caused a great explosion in her, so that the performance of *Der Taucher* had to be canceled yesterday.[48] [//] [Blatt 15v]

---

[45] Lichtensteg, a narrow street between the southwestern corner of the Hoher Markt and Bischofsgasse. Because many meat vendors had erected their sales booths here, the Lichtensteg was later called *Unter den Fleischbänken*. Lugeck is a square across the Bischofsgasse, just south of the point where it intersects with Lichtensteg. The area is, at most, a 5-minute walk north of the old university. See Groner, 1922, p. 273.—KH/TA

[46] Schindler uses the term *Quartetten*, that is, the four string parts (Violin I, Violin II, Viola, and Violoncello/Contrabass parts), that would presumably be copied before the wind parts were begun.—TA

[47] Schindler seldom engaged in such flattering forms of address while Beethoven was alive.—TA

[48] Saturday, March 13, and Sunday, March 14, were ballet evenings at the Kärntnertor Theater. Monday, March 15, was Conradin Kreutzer's opera *Der Taucher* with Sontag and Unger; Tuesday, March 16, was a ballet evening; and Wednesday, March 17, was *Der Taucher* with Sontag and Unger. The performances began at 7 p.m. No performances were seemingly canceled owing to any indisposition on

The night before last, she vomited 15 times. Yesterday evening, however, it was better. Unger's reaction was just exactly the opposite.[49]—They are heroines! //

They are not accustomed to drinking wine; it's even worse wine than it says. // Sontag was supposed to have gone to a rehearsal of a Court concert yesterday [Monday, March 15] morning. As she would have lost the 24-ducat fee, she sent word that she was already feeling better and would come.[50] //

SCHINDLER [falsified entries begin→] The two beauties send their regards and ask for better, more healthy wine in the future.[51] [//] Quite right, both of your dinner guests would otherwise become too expensive. [←falsified entries end]

End of Heft 59

Sontag's part. See Kärntnertor Theater, Zettel; Bibliothek, Österreichisches Theatermuseum (courtesy Othmar Barnert); confirmed in Bäuerle's *Allgemeine Theater-Zeitung* 17, No. 36 (March 23, 1824), p. 143; and No. 40 (April 1, 1824), p. 159.—TA

[49] In Heft 60, Blatt 37v, Schindler reports that Sontag's illness was actually due to a vinegar salad that she ate at home on Sunday night. This could also explain why Unger evidently did not get sick.—TA

[50] In preparation for a *Hof-Concert* in the Imperial Ceremonial Hall, scheduled for 11 a.m. on Tuesday morning, March 16, 1824, a rehearsal was projected for Monday morning, March 15, at 10 a.m. Sontag and Unger were to sing a duet from Rossini's *Semiramide* and in the finale to act 1 of Rossini's *Maometto Secondo*. In addition, Sontag was to sing an unidentified opera aria by Mercadante and participate in a Quintet with chorus from Rossini's *Zelmira*. The 24-ducat fee mentioned here is consistent with the 108 fl. soloists' fees found in contemporary documents (a ducat was equivalent to 4½ fl.).

In the event, however, the concert was postponed two weeks, to Tuesday, March 30, with the rehearsal for it rescheduled to Monday, March 29.

Therefore, there was no rehearsal at Court on Monday morning, March 15, and there was no canceled performance of *Der Taucher* at the Kärntnertor Theater that evening. Schindler's falsehoods would surely have troubled Beethoven. It seems likely, then, that Schindler manipulated the facts to repay the composer for his anger over the confused dinner invitation.

See Hof-Musikkapelle, Karton 13, 1824, fols. 22, 49–51, and 63 (Haus-, Hof- und Staatsarchiv).—TA

[51] In this falsified entry after Beethoven's death, Schindler compounds the falsehood of his entries on Blätter 15r–15v.—TA

Appendix A

Descriptions of the Conversation Books in Volume 5

N.B. The brief descriptions here are based on the full physical descriptions preceding each Heft in the German edition. All Hefte are understood to be in the Staatsbibliothek zu Berlin—Preussischer Kulturbesitz, except for Hefte 1 and 95, which are in the Beethoven-Haus, Bonn.

Virtually all of the Hefte, except for 1 and 95, bear either annotations or an inserted slip by Anton Schindler or Alexander Wheelock Thayer. Most Hefte also contain librarians' cataloging numbers, often in ink.

Many of these originally blank booklets have paper shields pasted on to the exterior of the front covers (probably standard at the time of manufacture) for the purchaser to write a title, date, or some other identifier.

Heft 44 (ca. October 29/30, 1823 – ca. November 2/3, 1823): 22 Blätter; all the pages contain writing. Format 20.3 x 12.5 cm.

Heft 45 (ca. November 4, 1823 – ca. November 20, 1823): 42 Blätter, including some light blue in color; all the pages contain writing. Format 20 x 12.4 cm.; 17.4 x 11 cm.; and 20 x 11.3 cm.

Heft 46 (ca. November 21, 1823 – ca. November 26, 1823): 40 Blätter; Blatt 9v contains no writing (crossed out with red pencil); all the other pages contain writing. Format 19.3 x 12.5 cm.

Heft 47 (ca. November 29, 1823 – ca. December 6/7, 1823): 43 Blätter; all the pages contain writing. Schindler's pagination skips Blatt 20. Format 19.8 x 12 cm.

Heft 48 (December 7, 1823 – December 13, 1823): 34 Blätter; Blatt 12v contains no writing (crossed out with red pencil); all the other pages contain writing. Format 20.3 x 12.5 cm.

Heft 49 (December 13, 1823 – December 16, 1823): 12 Blätter; all the pages contain writing. Format 20 x 12.3 cm.

Heft 50 (December 20, 1823 – December 25, 1823): 20 Blätter; all the pages contain writing. Format 20.5 x 12.4 cm.

Heft 51 (December 27, 1823 – ca. January 3, 1824): 16 Blätter; all the pages contain writing. Format 20.2 x 12.5 cm.

Heft 52 (ca. January 5, 1824 – ca. January 7, 1824): 10 Blätter; all the pages contain writing. Format 20.6 x 12.7 cm.

Heft 53 (January 16, 1824 – January 21, 1824): 23 Blätter; all the pages contain writing. Format 20.5 x 12.6 cm.

Heft 54 (January 21, 1824 – February 2, 1824): 46 numbered Blätter and one unnumbered cover sheet; cover sheet and Blatt 46v contain no writing; Blatt 3r contains no writing (crossed out with red pencil); all the other pages contain writing. Format 20.5 x 12.5 cm.

Heft 55 (ca. February 3, 1824 – ca. February 12, 1824): 20 Blätter; only the top half of Blatt 17 is present; all the pages contain writing. Format 20.4 x 12.3 cm.

Heft 56 (ca. February 13, 1824 – ca. February 20, 1824): 37 Blätter. When making the pagination, Schindler skipped a Blatt after 19; another hand numbered the skipped Blatt as 19a. All the pages contain writing. Format 20.1 x 12.3 cm.

Heft 57 (February 27, 1824 – March 9, 1824): 41 Blätter; all the pages contain writing. Format 20.3 x 11.7 cm.

Heft 58 (March 7, 1824 – March 8, 1824): 5 numbered Blätter, 1 unnumbered cover sheet, and 2 unnumbered concluding Blätter. Blätter 1r to 5r contain writing; Blatt 5v crossed out with red pencil; the two concluding Blätter contain no writing. Format 20.5 x 12.5 cm.

Heft 59 (March 9, 1824 – March 16, 1824): 15 Blätter; all the pages contain writing. Format 20.3 x 11.7 cm.

Appendix B

Nephew Karl's Language Teachers: Pleugmackers and Pulay

Peter Joseph Pleugmackers (1774–?)

Pleugmackers was born in Eupen in Limburg/Liège (today's east Belgium), 17 miles west of Aachen, Germany, in 1774. Eupen is a German-speaking city within a French-speaking region. His father was Peter Pleugmackers, of independent means, and his mother Anna Maria, *née* Römer, likewise of independent means. By January 23, 1804, when he married at St. Stephan's Cathedral in Vienna, his father had died and Peter Joseph was now a captain in the Imperial Army—possibly in one of Archduke Karl's Regiments—and living in the Alster-Kaserne, No. 172, immediately east of the *Allgemeines Krankenhaus* [General Hospital].

His new wife was Anna Sophia Gombault, born in Troyes in Champagne, France, 70 miles southeast of Paris, and baptized on November 3, 1778. Her parents were Niklas Remy Gombault, deceased, of independent means, and his wife Maria Carolina, *née* Thuyelle. At the time of her marriage to Peter Joseph (who went by Joseph), she was living in the Weihburggasse No. 975 [renumbered as 919 in 1821].[1]

In February, 1820, Pleugmackers (as "Pleugmackers, Prof.") advertised in the *Wiener Zeitung*'s *Intelligenzblatt* that he was approved by the Lower Austrian Government to give German, French, English, and Italian instruction in courses of 70 lessons, or by the month, and also as individual lessons devoted to difficult grammatical passages. This and Karl's description of Pulay's Greek teaching on September 11, 1820 (below), may provide insights into language instruction at Blöchlinger's Institute during this period: Pleugmackers's "course of 70 lessons" could be a semester of 14 weeks at 5 days per week. Pleugmackers could be reached until 10 a.m. each day at his apartment in

---

[1] Pfarre St. Stephan, *Trauungs-Buch*, 1804–1807, fol. 11.

the Bauernmarkt, Münzerstrasse No. 622, 3rd floor [4th floor, American], door to the right.[2]

In 1824, as "J. Pleugmackers, language teacher," he spent the summer in Baden, living at Pfarrgasse No. 41, not far from Beethoven.[3]

On May 20, 1826, he was living in the city, Dorotheergasse No. 1112, second stairway, second floor [third floor, American], and announced his intention to give French instruction in Hietzing (west of Schönbrunn) and the surrounding area during the summer months.[4]

On May 1, 1830, Sophia Pleugmackers was included in a list as having contributed 2 fl. C.M. to help the victims of the Danube flood, three months earlier.[5] This seems to confirm that the family still had a reasonably substantial income and was in a financial position to make charitable contributions.

In the next generation, Joseph Pleugmackers (presumably born ca. 1815–1820) was also a member of the Austrian Army. In 1843, he was promoted from *Oberleutnant* [First Lieutenant] to *Kapitän-Leutnant* [low-ranking Captain] in the Archduke Carl Infantry Regiment No. 3,[6] and in 1845, was promoted to *wirklicher Hauptmann* [full Captain],[7] the same rank that his father had held when he married in 1804. In 1848, as captain, he was appointed as *curator absentis* in a dispute over the nearest relatives of a soldier who had died in 1817.[8] In June, 1849, Pleugmackers was promoted to Major, still in the Archduke Carl Infantry Regiment No. 3.[9] In May, 1854, as a major, he was transferred to the prestigious Hoch- und Deutschmeister Infantry Regiment No. 4.[10] This regiment was stationed in Vienna in 1854, but moved to [Buda-]Pest in 1855, Debrezin [Debrecen] in 1858, and Pressburg [Bratislava] in 1859.

While stationed in Budapest, young Pleugmackers (now ca. 37–42) may have retired from the Army and followed in his father's footsteps with an advertisement:

---

[2] *Intelligenzblatt*, No. 36 (February 15, 1820), p. 251.

[3] *Cur- und Fremden-Liste der Curortes Baden*, Heft 74 (1824), p. 1.

[4] *Intelligenzblatt*, No. 114 (May 20, 1826), p. 774. Hietzing was a village with the summer residences of many wealthy Viennese, including the banker Bernhard Eskeles, with whom Beethoven was friendly.

[5] *Wiener Zeitung*, No. 99 (May 1, 1830), p. 1.

[6] *Oestreichische* [sic] *Militärische Zeitschrift* 2 (Vienna, 1843), p. 210.

[7] *Oestreichische* [sic] *Militärische Zeitschrift* 8 (Vienna, 1845), p. 224.

[8] *Wiener Zeitung's Amtsblatt*, No. 34 (February 3, 1848), p. 88, col. 2; repeated No. 36 (February 5, 1848), p. 94; and No. 39 (February 8, 1848), p. 100. The Edict itself was dated Brünn, January 19, 1848.

[9] *Wiener Zeitung*, No. 132 (June 3, 1849), p. 1557, col. 3.

[10] The extensive list of promotions and transfers was first published in the *Wiener Zeitung*, No. 19 (May 6, 1854), p. 1239, and then reprinted nationwide in the *Ost-Deutsche Post* (Vienna; May 7, 1854), *K.k. Schlesische-Troppauer Zeitung* (May 9, 1854), *Agramer Zeitung* (May 10, 1854), *Klagenfurter Zeitung* (May 11, 1854), *Vereinigte Laibacher Zeitung* (May 12, 1854).

"Professor PLEUGMACKERS, language teacher, res. Hatvauergasse No. 5, second floor [third floor, American]."[11]

Paul (Wolfgang) Pulay (1777–1836)

Paul Pulay, a baptized Jew, was a teacher of Latin and Greek at Blöchlinger's Institute from ca. February, 1820, to ca. March, 1823, and possibly beyond. Pulay had been born in Kanischa (Kanizsa) in southwest Hungary, ca. 80 miles southeast of Graz, in 1777. The town's full name is Nagykanizsa, but is known colloquially as Kanizsa (rendered phonetically in German as Kanischa).

Kanischa's education was in the hands of the progressive Piarist Order, and its teachers may have suggested that Pulay go to Vienna to attend or teach at the Piarist *Gymnasium* [high school], only three blocks from Blöchlinger's Institute. Blöchlinger was on friendly, collegial terms with the Piarists, and they occasionally ate dinner together.

Probably before he left Kanischa, Pulay converted to Catholicism and took the baptismal name of Wolfgang, after St. Wolfgang (ca. 934–994), who had converted the Hungarians to Christianity. In the Viennese *Conscriptions-Bögen*, he seems to have been noted as Paul Pulay, but the documents pertaining to his death in 1836 specify his name as Paul Wolfgang Pulay.

After retiring as a *Kindererzieher* [children's teacher], Pulay died, aged 58, of *Durchfall* [diarrhea], at his apartment in the Viennese suburb of Alsergrund, No. 127, on July 1, 1836.[12] The apartment where Pulay died was on the north side of Alserstrasse, two blocks west of the *Allgemeines Krankenhaus* (General Hospital).[13] Looking ahead to 1826 (below), this location was only a ten-minute walk from Beethoven's apartment at the time.

Pulay joined the faculty in ca. February, 1820. Initially he did not live at the Institute, but came for lessons between 10 and 12 every weekday morning. Young Karl studied Greek with Pulay and seems to have made good progress.[14] Karl may have begun Greek under Joseph Bergmann (1796–1872), who was supplemented and then replaced by Pulay when he (Bergmann) left to finish his own studies at the

---

[11] *Pesth-Ofner Localblat und Landbothe*, No. 173 (July 31, 1857), p. 4. The same advertisement appeared on August 2, 1857. Though improbable, this advertisement may have been posted by the elder Joseph Pleugmackers, now ca. 82 or 83, had he survived.

[12] See Vienna, Magistrat, Totenbeschauprotokoll, 1836, B/P, fol. 37v; death on July 1 (Wiener Stadt- und Landesarchiv); and *Wiener Zeitung*, No. 152 (July 6, 1836), p. 860. Further routine notices concerning his estate appeared in the *Wiener Zeitung* or its *Intelligenzblatt* on August 26 and 31, September 3, December 16 and 19, 1836; and April 12, 1837.

[13] See Behsel, p. 199.

[14] See Heft 8, Blätter 1r and 19v.

University of Vienna. Bergmann eventually became director of the Imperial Coin and Antiquarian Collections.

On September 11, 1820, Karl reported to Beethoven: "My Greek teacher gives me two hours each day and gets 600 florins [gulden]."[15] In Spring, 1822, Pulay evidently bought something—probably a book—on Karl's behalf for 26 *groschen*, and (after repeated reminders) Beethoven finally reimbursed him in June.[16] The amount was equal to 78 *kreuzer* or 1 *florin/gulden* 18 *kreuzer*, a reasonable price for a textbook or modest literary work.

Like several part-time teachers, Pulay eventually roomed at Blöchlinger's. More than a year after he had graduated from Blöchlinger's Institute, Karl told Beethoven that when Pulay could not sleep, he would come and wake Karl up, so they could talk.[17] Karl told this story to Beethoven after they had toured the Heiligenkreuz Monastery on October 10, 1824. Possibly Karl associated the nocturnal prayers and chants of the monks with Pulay's wakefulness, but there was no hint of any homosexual intent on Pulay's part.

On February 27, 1823, Beethoven had a conversation with Cajetan Giannatasio del Rio (1764–1828), director of the school where Karl had studied and boarded from February, 1816, through December, 1818. With a chuckle, Giannatasio told Beethoven that he had recently met Pulay, who attributed all of Karl's good progress to himself.[18] By March 25, 1823, however, Pulay had had a falling out with Blöchlinger and was spreading rumors that Blöchlinger's Institute was teaching ideas that were against religion and the government.[19] Pulay prophesied that "The Institute carries within itself the seed of its own destruction," as quoted by Karl on June 22, 1823.[20] In September, 1823, Karl encountered Pulay twice (both times very enthusiastically) while running errands in Vienna on Beethoven's behalf,[21] and Pulay later reconciled with Blöchlinger,[22] although we do not know when or under what circumstances.[23]

Within a few days after Karl attempted suicide on August 6, 1826, Pulay visited Beethoven, offered his condolences and even offered to serve as Karl's private tutor in exchange for room and board,[24] but by this time it had tentatively been determined that Karl would join the Army.

[15] See Heft 16, Blatt 74r.
[16] See Heft 17, Blatt 19v.
[17] See Heft 77, Blatt 5v.
[18] See Heft 25, Blätter 31v–32r.
[19] See Heft 27, Blätter 26v–28v.
[20] See Heft 34, Blatt 25v.
[21] See Heft 42, Blätter 6r and 17v.
[22] See Heft 117, Blatt 20r,
[23] Karl's Greek teacher at the University of Vienna, from Fall, 1823, was Anton Joseph Stein (1759–1844); see Heft 60, Blatt 30r.
[24] See Heft 117, Blätter 20r–20v.

Bibliography

Albrecht, Theodore. "Anton Grams: Beethoven's Double Bassist." *Bass World* 26 (October, 2002), pp. 19–23.

Albrecht, Theodore. "Anton Schindler as Destroyer and Forger of Beethoven's Conversation Books: A Case for Decriminalization." In *Music's Intellectual History*. Ed. Zdravko Blažeković and Barbara Dobbs Mackenzie. New York: RILM, 2009, pp. 169–181.

Albrecht, Theodore. "Beethoven and Shakespeare's *Tempest*: New Light on an Old Allusion." *Beethoven Forum* 1 (1992), pp. 81–92.

Albrecht, Theodore. "Benjamin Gebauer, ca. 1758–1846: The Life and Death of Beethoven's Copyist C." *Bonner Beethoven-Studien* 3 (2003), pp. 7–22.

Albrecht, Theodore. "Bribe, Borrow, and Steal: Johann Herbeck's Conducting Activities in Vienna, 1852–1877," *Journal of the Conductors' Guild* 4 (Fall, 1983), pp. 129–132.

Albrecht, Theodore. "Elias (Eduard Constantin) Lewy and the First Performance of Beethoven's Ninth Symphony," *Horn Call* 29, No. 3 (May, 1999), p. 27–33, 85–94, and cover.

Albrecht, Theodore. "Die Familie Teimer—sowie eine neuere (überarbeitete) Datierung der zwei Trios für zwei Oboen und Englischhorn (op. 87) und der Variationen WoO 28 von Ludwig van Beethoven." *Wiener Oboen-Journal*, no. 24 (December, 2004), pp. 2–10; no. 25 (March, 2005), pp. 3–9; no. 27 (October, 2005), pp. 6–7.

Albrecht, Theodore. "'First Name Unknown': Violist Anton Schreiber, the Schuppanzigh Quartet, and Early Performances of Beethoven's String Quartets, Op. 59." *Beethoven Journal* 19, no. 1 (Summer, 2004), pp. 10–18.

Albrecht, Theodore. "The Fortnight Fallacy: A Revised Chronology for Beethoven's *Christ on the Mount of Olives*, Op. 85, and the Wielhorsky Sketchbook." *Journal of Musicological Research*. Ed. F. Joseph Smith, 11 (1991), pp. 263–284.

Albrecht, Theodore. "The Hearing Beethoven: Demythifying the Composer's Deafness." *Beethoven Journal* 34, No. 2 (Winter 2019), pp. 44–56. Published simultaneously as "Der hörende Beethoven." Trans. Ernst Kobau. *Journal der Gesellschaft der Wiener Oboe* 85 (March 2020), entire issue, pp. 3–23.

Albrecht, Theodore. "Hyperbole and High Drama: The Chronology and First Performance of Beethoven's Oratorio Christus am Ölberge, Op. 85," *Bonner Beethoven-Studien* 13 (2021), projected.

Albrecht, Theodore, trans. and ed. *Letters to Beethoven and Other Correspondence.* 3 vols. Lincoln: University of Nebraska Press, 1996.

Albrecht, Theodore. "Otto Heinrich Graf von Loeben (1786–1825) and the Poetic Source of Beethoven's *Abendlied unterm gestirnten Himmel*, WoO 150." *Bonner Beethoven-Studien* 10 (2012), pp. 7–32.

Albrecht, Theodore. "Picturing the Players in the Pit: The Orchestra of Vienna's Kärntnertor Theater, 1821–1822." *Music in Art* 34, nos. 1–2 (2009), pp. 203–213.

Albrecht, Theodore. "Time, Distance, Weather, Daily Routine, and Wordplay as Factors in Interpreting Beethoven's Conversation Books." *Beethoven Journal* 28, no. 2 (Winter, 2013), pp. 64–75.

Allgemeine Deutsche Biographie. Ed. Rochus von Liliencron. 56 vols. Leipzig: Duncker & Humblot, 1875–1912.

[*AmZ.*] *Allgemeine musikalische Zeitung.* Leipzig: Breitkopf und Härtel, 1798–1848.

Allgemeine musikalische Zeitung mit besonderer Rücksicht auf den Österreichischen Kaiserstaat. Ed. Ignaz von Seyfried and Friedrich August Kanne. Vienna: S.A. Steiner, 1817–1824. (Commonly called the *Wiener Allgemeine musikalische Zeitung* or *Wiener AmZ.* Often cited with mention of editor Kanne to avoid confusion.)

Allgemeine Theater-Zeitung [title varies]. Ed. Adolf Bäuerle. Vienna, 1806–1860.

Amtsblatt. Separately titled supplement to the daily *Wiener Zeitung* (q.v.). Vienna, 1818–1827.

Anderson, Emily, trans. and ed. *The Letters of Beethoven.* 3 vols. London: Macmillan/ New York: St. Martin's Press, 1961. Customarily cited as Anderson.

Anderson, Emily, trans. and ed. *The Letters of Mozart and His Family.* 3rd ed. New York: W.W. Norton, 1985.

Arnim, Bettina von. *Goethe's Briefwechsel mit einem Kinde.* 2 vols. Berlin: Ferdinand Dümmler, 1835.

Bartlitz, Eveline. *Die Beethoven-Sammlung in der Musikabteilung der Deutschen Staatsbibliothek: Verzeichnis.* Berlin: Deutsche Staatsbibliothek, 1970.

Bauer, Anton. *150 Jahre Theater an der Wien.* Zürich: Amalthea Verlag, 1952; revised as *200 Jahre Theater in der Josefstadt, 1788–1988,* ed. Gustav Kropatschek. Vienna: Verlag Anton Schroll, 1988.

Bauer, Anton. *Opern und Operetten in Wien: Verzeichnis ihrer Erstaufführungen.* Graz and Cologne: Böhlau, 1955.

Bauer, Anton. *Das Theater in der Josefstadt zu Wien.* Vienna: Manutiuspresse, 1957.

Beer, Gretel. *Austrian Cooking and Baking.* London: Andre Deutsch, 1954. Repr., New York: Dover Publications, 1975.

Beethoven im Gespräch. Ein Konversationsheft vom 9. September 1825. Facsimile. Ed. Grita Herre. Trans. Theodore Albrecht. Bonn: Verlag Beethoven-Haus, 2002. (Heft 95.)

Beethoven, Ludwig van. *Beethoven: Drei Skizzenbücher zur Missa solemnis. II: Ein Skizzenbuch zum Credo, SV 82. Teil 1: Übertragung.* Transcription. Ed. Joseph Schmidt-Görg. Bonn: Beethovenhaus, 1970.

Beethoven, Ludwig van. *Entwurf einer Denkschrift an das Appellationsgericht in Wien vom 18. Februar 1820.* Ed. Dagmar Weise. Bonn: Beethoven-Haus, 1953.

Beethoven, Ludwig van. *Missa solemnis, Opus 123, Kyrie: Faksimile nach dem Autograph.* Ed. Wilhelm Virneisel. Tutzing: Hans Schneider, 1965.

Behsel, Anton. *Verzeichniss aller in der kaiserl. königl. Haupt- und Residenzstadt Wien mit ihren Vorstädten befindlichen Häuser.* Vienna: Carl Gerold, 1829. (Annotated copy in the Wiener Stadt- und Landesarchiv.)

[Beobachter.] *Der Oesterreichische Beobachter.* Vienna, 1818–1827.

Biba, Otto. "Beethoven und die 'Liebhaber Concerte' in Wien im Winter 1807/08." In *Beiträge '76–78. Beethoven Kolloquium 1977: Dokumentation und Aufführungspraxis.* Ed. Rudolf Klein. Kassel: Bärenreiter, 1978, pp. 82–93.

Biba, Otto. *"Eben komm' ich von Haydn": Georg August Griesingers Korrespondenz mit Joseph Haydns Verleger Breitkopf & Härtel, 1799–1819.* Zürich: Atlantis, 1987.

Böckh, Franz Heinrich. *Merkwürdigkeiten der Haupt- und Residenzstadt Wien und ihren nächsten Umgebungen.* Vienna: Bernhard Philipp Bauer, 1822–1823 [reflecting 1821]; Supplement, 1823 [reflecting 1822–1823].

Böckh, Franz Heinrich. *Wiens lebende Schriftsteller, Künstler und Dilettanten im Kunstfache.* Vienna: Bernhard Philipp Bauer, 1822.

Bory, Robert. *Ludwig van Beethoven.* Zürich: Atlantis, 1960. (Available in several languages.)

Brandenburg, Sieghard. "Johanna van Beethoven's Embezzlement." Trans. Mary Whittall. In *Haydn, Mozart, and Beethoven: Studies in the Music of the Classical Period. Essays in Honour of Alan Tyson.* Ed. Sieghard Brandenburg. Oxford: Clarendon Press, 1988, pp. 237–251.

Brandenburg, Sieghard, ed. *Ludwig van Beethoven. Briefwechsel: Gesamtausgabe.* 7 vols. Munich: G. Henle, 1996–1997.

[Breitkopf & Härtel, *Gesamtausgabe.*] *Ludwig van Beethovens Werke: Vollständige kritisch durchgesehene überall berechtigte Ausgabe.* Ser. 1–25. Leipzig: Breitkopf und Härtel, 1864–1890. Repr., Ann Arbor, Mich.: J.W. Edwards, 1949.

Brown, James D. *Biographical Dictionary of Musicians.* London: Alexander Gardner, 1886.

Brummitt, Eric. "The Writings of Antonio Tosoroni: Promoting the Early Valved Horn as an Orchestral Instrument in 19th-Century Italy." Paper. Early Brass Festival, New Orleans, July 24–27, 2008.

Campe, Joachim Heinrich. *Wörterbuch der Deutschen Sprache.* 5 vols. Braunschweig: Schulbuchhandlung, 1807–1811.
Castelli, Ignaz Franz. *Memoiren meines Lebens.* 2 vols. Ed. Josef Bindtner. Munich: Georg Müller, 1913.
Clive, Peter. *Beethoven and His World: A Biographical Dictionary.* Oxford/New York: Oxford University Press, 2001.
Clive, Peter. *Schubert and His World: A Biographical Dictionary.* Oxford: Clarendon Press, 1997.
Comini, Alessandra. *The Changing Image of Beethoven.* New York: Rizzoli, 1987.
Conversationsblatt: Zeitschrift für wissenschaftliche Unterhaltung. Ed. Franz Gräffer and Ignaz Franz Castelli. Vienna: Wallishausser & Gerold, 1819–1821.
Costenoble, Carl Ludwig. *Aus dem Burgtheater, 1818–1837.* 2 vols. Vienna: Konegen, 1889.
Cooper, Barry. *Beethoven's Folksong Settings: Chronology, Sources, Style.* Oxford: Clarendon Press, 1994.
Czeike, Felix, ed. *Historisches Lexikon Wien.* 6 vols. Vienna: Kremayr & Scheriau, 1992–2004.
Davidis, Henriette. *Praktisches Kochbuch.* Ed. Gertrude Wiemann. Berlin: W. Herlet Verlag, 1907. Repr., Augsburg: Bechtermünz Verlag, 1997.
Davies, Peter J. *Beethoven in Person: His Deafness, Illnesses, and Death.* Westport, Conn.: Greenwood Press, 2001.
Deutsch, Otto Erich. *Alt-Wiener Verduten: 25 Feuilletons über Stadt und Leute.* Ed. Gritta Deutsch and Rudolf Klein. Vienna: Österreichischer Bundesverlag, 1986.
Deutsch, Otto Erich. *Beethovens Beziehungen zu Graz.* Graz: Leykam, 1907.
Deutsch, Otto Erich. *Schubert: Memoirs by His Friends.* Trans. Rosamond Ley and John Nowell. London and New York: Macmillan, 1958. Originally: *Schubert: Die Erinnerungen seiner Freunde.* Leipzig: Breitkopf und Härtel, 1957.
Deutsch, Otto Erich. *The Schubert Reader/Schubert: A Documentary Biography.* Trans. Eric Blom. London: Dent, 1946/New York: W.W. Norton, 1947. Originally: *Schubert: Die Dokumente seines Lebens.* Munich: Georg Müller, 1914. (See also under Waidelich.)
Deutsch, Otto Erich. *Schubert: Sein Leben in Bildern.* Munich/Leipzig: Georg Müller, 1913. (Never translated or reprinted.)
Deutsches Literatur Lexikon. Ed. Lutz Hagested. 35 vols. to date. Berlin: De Gruyter, 1999–.
Dorfmüller, Kurt, ed. *Beiträge zur Beethoven-Bibliographie: Studien und Materialien zum Werkverzeichnis von Kinsky-Halm.* Munich: G. Henle, 1978.
Dorfmüller, Kurt, ed. *Ludwig van Beethoven: Ausstellungs-Katalog der Bayerischen Staatsbibliothek.* Tutzing: Hans Schneider, 1977.

Eisenberg, Ludwig. *Grosses biographisches Lexikon der deutschen Bühne im XIX. Jahrhundert.* Leipzig: P. List, 1903.
Faber, Elfriede M. *300 Jahre Kunst, Kultur & Architektur in der Josefstadt.* Vienna: Holzhausen, 2000.
Ferguson, Niall. *The House of Rothschild: Money's Prophets, 1798–1848.* New York: Viking, 1998.
Filek, Egid. *Komm mit in der Wienerwald.* Vienna: Wiener Verlag, 1949.
Fischmann, Nathan L. "Das Moskauer Skizzenbuch Beethovens aus dem Archiv von M.J. Wielhorsky." In *Beiträge zur Beethoven-Bibliographie ....* Ed. Kurt Dorfmüller. Munich: G. Henle, 1978, pp. 61–67.
Fischmann, Nathan L. "Die Uraufführung der Missa solemnis." *Beiträge zur Musikwissenschaft* 12 (1970), pp. 274–280.
Fortuna: Taschenbuch des kais. kön. privil. Josephstädter Theaters für das Jahr 1824. Ed. Franz Xaver Told. Vienna: Leopold Grund, [1824].
Frimmel, Theodor [von]. *Beethoven-Handbuch.* 2 vols. Leipzig: Breitkopf und Härtel, 1926. (Abbreviated version in English as Paul Nettl, *Beethoven Encyclopedia*, 1956.)
Frimmel, Theodor [von]. *Beethoven im zeitgenössischen Bildnis.* Vienna: Karl König, 1923.
Frimmel, Theodor [von]. *Beethoven-Studien.* 2 vols. Munich: Georg Müller, 1905–1906.
Garland, Henry, and Mary Garland. *The Oxford Companion to German Literature.* 2nd ed. New York: Oxford University Press, 1986.
Gay, Ruth. *Unfinished People: Eastern European Jews Encounter America.* New York: W.W. Norton, 1996.
Giannoni, Karl. *Geschichte der Stadt Mödling.* Mödling: Stadtgemeinde, 1905.
Ginsburg, Lev. "Ludwig van Beethoven und Nikolai Galitzin." *Beethoven Jahrbuch* 4 (1959–1960), pp. 59–65.
Gluck, Franz. "Prolegomena zu einer neuen Beethoven-Ikonographie." In *Festschrift Otto Erich Deutsch zum 80. Geburtstag.* Ed. Walter Gerstenberg, Jan La Rue, and Wolfgang Rehm. Kassel: Bärenreiter, 1963, pp. 203–212.
Goedeke, Karl. *Grundriss zur Geschichte der deutschen Dichtung.* 2nd ed. 18 vols. Dresden: L. Ehlermann, 1884–1998.
Goethe, Johann Wolfgang von. *Faust.* Trans. Walter Kaufmann. New York: Anchor Books, 1963.
Goldschmidt, Harry. *Franz Schubert: Ein Lebensbild.* Leipzig: Henschel, 1960.
Goldschmidt, Harry. *Um die Unsterbliche Geliebte.* Beethoven Studien 2. Leipzig: VEB Deutscher Verlag für Musik, 1977.
Gräffer, Franz. *Kleine Wiener Memorien.* Ed. Anton Schlossar and Gustav Gugitz. 2 vols. Munich: G. Müller, 1918.
Gräffer, Franz, and Johann Jacob Heinrich Czikann, eds. *Oesterreichische National-Encyklopädie.* 6 vols. Vienna: Michael Schmidl's Witwe & Ignaz Klang, 1835–1837.

Grandaur, Franz. *Chronik des Königlichen Hof- und National-Theaters in München.* Munich: Theodor Ackermann, 1878.

Grillparzer, Franz. *Grillparzers Werke.* Ed. August Sauer. 20 vols. Vienna: Gerlach & Wiedling, 1914–1916.

Grimm, Jacob, and Wilhelm Grimm. *Deutsches Wörterbuch.* 33 vols. Leipzig: Hirzel, 1854–1971.

Groner, Richard. *Wien, wie es war.* Vienna: Waldheim-Eberle, 1922.

Groner, Richard. *Wien, wie es war.* Rev. ed., ed. Felix Czeike. Vienna: Verlag Fritz Molden, 1965.

[Groner-Czeike.] *Das Grosse Groner Wien Lexikon.* Ed. Felix Czeike. Vienna: Verlag Fritz Molden, 1974. (Includes biographical entries. For later editions, see under Czeike.)

Guetjahr, Mathias. *Vollständiges Verzeichniss aller in der k.k. Haupt- und Residenzstadt Wien und ihren Vorstädten befindlichen Strassen, Gassen, Plätze und Häuser.* Vienna: Carl Gerold, 1816–1821.

Gugitz, Gustav. *Das Wiener Kaffee-Haus.* Vienna: Jugend und Volk, 1940.

Gugitz, Gustav. See also Archival Documents (below).

Gundacker, Felix. *Generalindex der katholischen Trauungen Wien.* Vienna: Gundacker, 1998.

Gurk, Joseph, and Eduard Gurk. *Wien's Umgebungen, nach der Natur gezeichnet.* Vienna: Mollo, 1827. Repr., ed. Robert Wagner. Graz: Akademische Druck- und Verlagsanstalt, 1988.

Gutiérrez-Denhoff, Martella. *"Die gute Kocherey": Aus Beethovens Speiseplänen.* Bonn: Beethoven-Haus, 1988.

Haberl, Dieter. "Beethovens erste Reise nach Wien—Die Datierung seiner Schülerreise zu W.A. Mozart." *Neues Musikwissenschaftliches Jahrbuch* 14 (2006), pp. 215–255.

Hadamowsky, Franz. *Wien, Theatergeschichte: Von den Anfängen bis zum Ende des Ersten Weltkriegs.* Vienna: Jugend und Volk, 1988.

Hadamowsky, Franz. *Die Wiener Hofoper (Staatsoper), 1811–1974.* Vienna: Georg Prachner, 1975.

Hadamowsky, Franz. *Die Wiener Hoftheater (Staatstheater) 1776–1966. Teil 1: 1776–1810.* Vienna: Georg Prachner, 1966.

Hagested, Lutz, ed. *Deutsches Literatur Lexikon.* 35 vols. to date. Berlin: De Gruyter, 1999–.

Hamm, Wilhelm. *Das Weinbuch.* 3rd ed. Ed. A. von Babo. Leipzig: Weber, 1886.

Hanslick, Eduard. *Geschichte des Concertwesens in Wien.* Vienna: Wilhelm Braumüller, 1869.

Hess, Willy. *Verzeichnis der nicht in der Gesamtausgabe veröffentlichten Werke Ludwig van Beethovens.* Wiesbaden: Breitkopf und Härtel, 1957.

Hilmar, Rosemary. *Die Musikverlag Artaria & Comp.* Tutzing: Hans Schneider, 1977.

Hof- und Staats-Schematismus des österreichischen Kaiserthums [title varies]. Vienna, 1800–1848.

Hollender, Martin. "Joachim Krüger Alias Dr. Krüger-Riebow: Bücherdieb, Antiquar und Agent im Kalten Krieg." *Bibliothek* 30, no. 1 (2006), pp. 69–75. (Detailed account of the theft of the conversation books, 1951–1961.)

Hopfner, Rudolf. *Wiener Musikinstrumentenmacher, 1766–1900: Adressenverzeichnis und Bibliographie*. Vienna: Kunsthistorisches Museum/Tutzing: Hans Schneider, 1999.

Hüffer, Eduard. *Anton Felix Schindler*. Münster: Aschendorff, 1909.

Hummel, Walter, and the Internationale Stiftung Mozarteum Salzburg. *W.A. Mozarts Söhne*. Kassel: Bärenreiter, 1956.

Humphries, John. *The Early Horn: A Practical Guide*. Cambridge: Cambridge University Press, 2000.

Husslein-Arco, Agnes, and Sabine Grabner, eds. *Ferdinand Georg Waldmüller (1793–1865)*. Vienna: Christian Brandstätter Verlag, 2009.

Hutchings, Arthur. *Mozart: The Man, the Musician*. New York: Schirmer Books, 1976.

Intelligenzblatt. Separately titled supplement to the daily *Wiener Zeitung* (q.v.). Vienna, 1818–1827.

[Israelitische Kultusgemeinde, Vienna.] *Die ersten Statuten des Bethauses in der Inneren Stadt. Facsimile of By-Laws, 1829*. Ed. Bernhard Wachstein. Vienna: Israelitische Kultusgemeinde, 1926.

Ivanov, Georgi Konstantinovich. *Notoizdatel'skoe delo v Rossii: Istoricheskaya spravka* [Music Publishing in Russia: Historical Survey]. Moscow: Sov. Kompozptor, 1970.

Johnson, Douglas. "The Artaria Collection of Beethoven Manuscripts: A New Source." In *Beethoven Studies*. Ed. Alan Tyson. New York: W.W. Norton, 1973, pp. 174–236.

Johnson, Douglas. "Music for Prague and Berlin: Beethoven's Concert Tour of 1796." In *Beethoven, Performers, and Critics: International Beethoven Congress, Detroit, 1977*. Ed. Robert Winter and Bruce Carr. Detroit: Wayne State University Press, 1980, pp. 24–40.

Jones, Charles Howard. "The Wiener Pianoforte-Schule of Friedrich Starke: A Translation and Commentary." D.M.A. diss., University of Texas at Austin, 1990.

Kagan, Susan. *Archduke Rudolph, Beethoven's Patron, Pupil, and Friend: His Life and Music*. Stuyvesant, N.Y.: Pendragon Press, 1988.

Kayser, Christian Gottlob. *Vollständiges Bücher-Lexicon enthaltend alle von 1750 bis zu Ende des Jahres 1832 in Deutschland und in den angrenzenden Ländern gedruckten Bücher*. 6 parts. Leipzig: L. Schumann, 1834–1836.

Kaznelson, Siegmund. *Beethovens Ferne und Unsterbliche Geliebte*. Zürich: Standard-Buch Verlag, 1954.

Kerst, Friedrich. *Beethoven: The Man and the Artist, as Revealed in His Own Words*. Trans. and ed. Henry Edward Krehbiel. New York: B.W. Huebsch, 1905. Repr., New York: Dover Publications, 1964.

Kerst, Friedrich, ed. *Die Erinnerungen an Beethoven*. 2 vols. Stuttgart: Julius Hoffmann, 1913.

Kinsky, Georg. *Das Werk Beethovens: Thematisch-bibliographisches Verzeichnis*. Completed by Hans Halm. Munich: G. Henle, 1955.

Kisch, Wilhelm. *Die alten Strassen und Plätze von Wien*. 3 vols. Vienna: Frank, 1888–1895.

Klein, Rudolf. *Beethovenstätten in Österreich*. Vienna: Verlag Elisabeth Lafite, 1970.

Klusacek, Christine, and Kurt Stimmer. *Josefstadt: Beiseln, Bühnen, Beamte*. Vienna: Mohl, 1991.

Koch, Bertha. *Beethovenstätten in Wien und Umgebung, mit 124 Abbildungen*. Berlin: Schuster & Loeffler, 1912.

Köchel, Ludwig von. *Die kaiserliche Hof-Musikkapelle in Wien von 1543 bis 1867*. Vienna: Beck'sche Universitäts-Buchhandlung, 1869.

Köhler, Karl-Heinz. "The Conversation Books: Aspects of a New Picture of Beethoven." In *Beethoven, Performers, and Critics: International Beethoven Congress, Detroit, 1977*. Ed. Robert Winter and Bruce Carr. Detroit: Wayne State University Press, 1980, pp. 147–161.

Köhler, Karl-Heinz. *"... tausendmal leben!": Konversationen mit Herrn van Beethoven*. Leipzig: VEB Deutscher Verlag für Musik, 1978.

[Köhler et al.] *Ludwig van Beethovens Konversationshefte*. Ed. Karl-Heinz Köhler, Grita Herre, and Dagmar Beck. 11 vols. Leipzig: VEB Deutscher Verlag für Musik. Vol. 1 (1972), vol. 2 (1976), vol. 3 (1983), vol. 4 (1968), vol. 5 (1970), vol. 6 (1974), vol. 7 (1978), vol. 8 (1981), vol. 9 (1988), vol. 10 (1993), vol. 11 (2001).

Kopitz, Klaus Martin. "Wer schrieb den Text zu Beethovens Chorphantasie? Ein unbekannter Bericht über die Uraufführung." *Bonner Beethoven-Studien* 3 (2003), pp. 43–46.

Kopitz, Klaus Martin, and Rainer Cadenbach, eds. *Beethoven aus der Sicht seiner Zeitgenossen*. 2 vols. Munich: G. Henle, 2009.

Kos, Wolfgang, ed. *Wiener Typen: Klischees und Wirklichkeit. Katalog. Wien Museum*. Vienna: Christian Brandstätter Verlag, 2013.

Kramer, Waldemar. *Frankfurt Chronik*. 2nd ed. Frankfurt am Main: Waldemar Kramer, 1977.

Krammer, Otto. *Wiener Volkstypen*. Vienna: Wilhelm Braumüller, 1983.

Kysselak, Franz. See Archival Documents (below).

Landon, Howard Chandler Robbins. *Beethoven: A Documentary Study*. New York: Macmillan, 1969. (As much a pictorial as documentary biography of the composer.)

Landon, Howard Chandler Robbins. *Mozart and Vienna*. New York: Schirmer Books, 1991. (Much of the volume is devoted to Pezzl, *Skizze von Wien*, 1786–1790, q.v.)

Ledebur, Carl von. *Tonkünstler-Lexicon Berlin's von den ältesten Zeiten bis auf die Gegenwart*. Berlin: Ludwig Rauh, 1861.

Leitzmann, Albert, ed. *Ludwig van Beethoven: Berichte der Zeitgenossen, Briefe und persönliche Aufzeichnungen*. 2 vols. Leipzig: Insel-Verlag, 1921.
Lexikon für Theologie und Kirche. 2nd ed., ed. Josef Höfer and Karl Rahner. Freiburg im Breisgau: Herder, 1963.
Liess, Andreas. *Johann Michael Vogl: Hofoperist und Schubertsänger*. Graz: Hermann Böhlau, 1954.
Loewenberg, Alfred. *Annals of Opera, 1597–1940*. 3rd ed. Totowa, N.J.: Rowman & Littlefield, 1978.
Lorenz, Franz. "Franz Gläser: Autobiographie." *Die Musikforschung* 31 (1978), pp. 43–45.
Loritza, Carl. *Neues Idioticon Viennense*. Vienna/Leipzig: Josef Stöckholzer v. Hirschfeld, 1847.
Ludwig van Beethoven: Ausstellungs-Katalog der Bayerischen Staatsbibliothek. Ed. Kurt Dorfmüller. Tutzing: Hans Schneider, 1977.
Lund, Susan. "Beethoven: A True 'Fleshly Father'?" *Beethoven Newsletter* 3, no. 1 (Spring, 1988), pp. 1 and 8–11; 3, no. 2 (Summer, 1988), pp. 25 and 36–40.
Lütge, Wilhelm. "Waldmüllers Beethovenbild." *Der Bär* (1927), pp. 35–41.
MacArdle, Donald W. *An Index to Beethoven's Conversation Books*. Detroit: Information Coordinators, 1962. (Index to names in Schünemann and Prod'homme editions.)
MacArdle, Donald W. "Anton Felix Schindler, Friend of Beethoven." *Music Review* 24, no. 1 (1963), pp. 51–74.
Macek, Jaroslav. "Beethovens Freund Karl Peters und seine Frau." In *Beethoven und Böhmen*. Ed. Sieghard Brandenburg and Martella Gutiérrez-Denhoff. Bonn: Beethoven-Haus, 1988, pp. 393–408.
Maiski, Ivan Michailovich. *Neuere Geschichte Spaniens 1808–1917*. Berlin: Rütten & Loening, 1961.
Mansfeld, Herbert A. *Index Nominum: Ex Libris Copulatorum Vindobonensis*. Vienna: Mansfeld, 1964, 1987.
Marek, George R. *Beethoven: Biography of a Genius*. New York: Funk & Wagnalls, 1969.
Mayer, Anton. *Wiens Buchdrucker-Geschichte, 1482–1882*. 2 vols. Vienna: Wilhelm Frick, 1885–1887.
Mendel, Hermann. *Musikalisches-Conversations-Lexicon: Eine Encyclopädie der gesammten musikalischen Wissenschaften*. 10 vols. Ed. August Reissmann. Berlin: Robert Oppenheim, 1877–1883.
Messner, Robert. *Die Innere Stadt Wien im Vormärz: Historisch-topographische Darstellung auf Grund der Katastralvermessung*. 3 vols. Vienna: Verein für Geschichte der Stadt Wien, 1996–1998.
Messner, Robert. *Die Josefstadt im Vormärz*. Vienna: Verein für Geschichte der Stadt Wien, 1972. (Similar one-volume suburban studies for Leopoldstadt [1962], Alsergrund [1970], Wieden [1975], and Landstrasse [1978]).

Meusel, Johann Georg. *Das gelehrte Teutschland, oder Lexikon der jetzt lebenden teutschen Schriftsteller*. 5th ed. 23 vols. Lemgo: Meyersche Buchhandlung, 1796–1831.

[*MGG*.] *Die Musik in Geschichte und Gegenwart*. 17 vols. Ed. Friedrich Blume. Kassel: Bärenreiter, 1949–1986. (Individual articles cited under authors' names in footnotes.)

Militär-Schematismus des österreichischen Kaiserthums. 2 vols. Vienna: K.k. Hof- und Staats-Druckerei, 1819–1820.

Morton, Frederic. *The Rothschilds: A Family Portrait*. Rev. ed. New York: Collier-Macmillan, 1991.

Moscheles, Charlotte, ed. *Aus Moscheles' Leben: Nach Briefen und Tagebüchern*. 2 vols. Leipzig: Duncker & Humblot, 1872–1873.

Nettl, Paul. *Beethoven Encyclopedia*. New York: Philosophical Library, 1956. (English-language condensed edition of Frimmel, *Beethoven-Handbuch* [1926], q.v., and articles from Wurzbach, q.v. Largely the work of his students at Indiana University.)

Neuwirth, Joseph. *Die k.k. Technische Hochschule in Wien 1815–1915*. Vienna: Gerold, 1915.

Nichols, Irby Coghill, Jr. *The European Pentarchy and the Congress of Verona, 1822*. The Hague: Martinus Nijhoff, 1971.

Nohl, Ludwig. *Beethoven's Leben*. 4 vols. Leipzig: Ernst Julius Günther, 1867–1877.

Nohl, Ludwig. *Eine stille Liebe zu Beethoven: Nach dem Tagebuch einer jungen Dame*. Leipzig: Ernst Julius Günther, 1875. (Excerpts from the Diary of Franziska [Fanny] Giannatasio del Rio [1790–ca. 1873/74].)

Nohl, Ludwig. *An Unrequited Love: An Episode in the Life of Beethoven (from the Diary of a Young Lady)*. Trans. Annie Wood. London: Richard Bentley & Son, 1876. (Includes excerpts from the diary of Franziska [Fanny] Giannatasio del Rio [1790–ca. 1873/1874].)

Nohl, Walther. "Beethovens 'Konversationshefte': With Other Essays." *Athenaion Blätter* (Potsdam) 4, no. 1 (1935), pp. 2–28.

Nohl, Walther, ed. *Ludwig van Beethovens Konversationshefte*. Munich: O.C. Rech/Allgemeine Verlagsanstalt, 1923–1924.

Österreichisches Biographisches Lexikon 1815–1950. 17 vols. to date. Ed. Leo Santifaller et al. Vienna/Graz: Böhlau, 1957–2015.

Palla, Rudi. *Verschwundene Arbeit: Ein Thesaurus der untergegangenen Berufe*. Illustrations selected by Christian Brandstätter. Vienna: Christian Brandstätter Verlag, 1994. Repr., 2010.

Parkinson, Roger. *The Hussar General: The Life of Blücher, Man of Waterloo*. London: Peter Davies, 1975. Repr., Ware, Hertfordshire: Wordsworth Editions, 2000.

Perkins, Charles C. *History of the Handel and Haydn Society of Boston*. Boston: Alfred Mudge, 1883.

Perger, Richard, and Eusebius Mandyczewski. *Geschichte der k.k. Gesellschaft der Musikfreunde in Wien*. 2 vols. Vienna: Alfred Holzhausen, 1912.

Pezzl, Johann. *Beschreibung von Wien*. 7th ed. Ed. Franz Ziska. Vienna: Carl Armbruster, 1826.

Pezzl, Johann. *Skizze von Wien*. 6 vols. Vienna: In der Kraussischen Buchhandlung, 1786–1790. (Extended excerpts in Landon, *Mozart and Vienna* [1991], q.v.)

Pfeiffer, Martina. "Franz Xafer [*sic*] Gebauer: Sein Leben und Wirken." Ph.D. diss., University of Vienna, 1995.

Phillebois, Anton, ed. *Verzeichniss aller in Wien practicirenden Doctoren der Arzney und Wundarzney, dann der bürgerlichen Wund und Zahnärzte*. Vienna, 1824.

Pichler, Caroline. *Denkwürdigkeiten aus meinem Leben*. 2 vols. Ed. Emil Karl Blümml. Munich: Georg Müller, 1914. First published Vienna: A. Pichlers sel. Witwe, 1844.

Picture of Vienna, Containing a Historical Sketch of the Metropolis of Austria, a Complete Notice of All the Public Institutions, Buildings, Galleries, Collections, Gardens, Walks, and Other Objects of Interest or Utility, and a Short Description of the Most Picturesque Spots in the Vicinity, with a Map of the Town and Suburbs. Vienna: Braumüller und Seidl, 1844.

Pohl, Carl Ferdinand. *Denkschrift aus Anlass des hundertjährigen Bestehens der Tonkünstler-Societät*. Vienna: Carl Gerold's Sohn, 1871.

Pohl, Carl Ferdinand. *Die Gesellschaft der Musikfreunde des österreichischen Kaiserstaates und ihr Conservatorium*. Vienna: Wilhelm Braumüller, 1871.

Pope, Stephen. *Dictionary of the Napoleonic Wars*. New York: Facts On File, 1999.

[Portrait-Katalog.] *Katalog der Portrait-Sammlung der k. u. k. General-Intendanz der k.k. Hoftheater. Zugleich ein biographisches Hilfsbuch auf dem Gebiet von Theater und Musik*. Vienna: Adolph W. Künast (Wallishausser'sche Hofbuchhandlung), 1892. (Not all of the personnel listed are represented by actual surviving portraits.)

Prod'homme, Jacques Gabriel, trans. and ed. *Les cahiers de conversation de Beethoven, 1819–1827*. Paris: Éditions Corréa, 1946.

Raffelsperger, Franz. *Allgemeines geographisches statistisches Lexikon aller Österreichischen Staaten*. 2nd ed. 6 vols. Vienna: Typo-geographische Kunstanstalt/Ignaz Klang, 1845–1853.

Redl, Anton. *Adressen-Buch der Handlungs-Gremien und Fabriken der kaiserl. königl. Haupt- und Residenzstadt Wien dann mehrerer Provinzialstädte*. Vienna: Redl, 1818–1824.

Regier, Willis Goth. *In Praise of Flattery*. Lincoln: University of Nebraska Press, 2007.

[Reichardt.] *Johann Friedrich Reichardts Vertraute Briefe, geschrieben auf einer Reise nach Wien*. Ed. Gustav Gugitz. Munich: Georg Müller, 1915.

Rietsch, Heinrich. "Aus Briefen Johanns van Beethoven." *Neues Beethoven Jahrbuch* 1 (1924), pp. 115–127.

Rietsch, Heinrich. "Nochmals Johann van Beethoven und anderes." *Neues Beethoven Jahrbuch* 3 (1927), pp. 44–50.

Rollett, Hermann. *Neue Beiträge zur Chronik der Stadt Baden bei Wien*. 13 vols. Baden: Ferdinand Schütze, 1880–1900.

Rotter, Hans. *Die Josephstadt*. Vienna: Rotter, 1918.

Russell, John. "'Vienna.' Chapter 5 of the 1828 Edition of John Russell's *Tour in Germany*. Facsimile." Introduction by William Meredith. *Beethoven Journal* 29, no. 2 (Winter, 2014), pp. 66–83. From *A Tour in Germany and Some of the Southern Provinces of the Austrian Empire in 1820, 1821, 1822*. Edinburgh: Constable, 1828.

Sachs, Curt. *Real-Lexikon der Musikinstrumente*. Berlin: Julius Bard, 1913. Repr. Hildesheim: G. Olms, 1964.

Sachwörterbuch der Geschichte Deutschlands und der deutschen Arbeiterbewegung. 2 vols. Ed. Horst Bartel. Berlin: Dietz Verlag, 1969–1970. (Used for the East German edition.)

Der Sammler, ein Unterhaltungsblatt. Vienna: Schaumburg/Anton Strauss, 1809–1846.

Sandberger, Adolf. "Zum Kapitel: Beethoven und München." In *Ausgewählte Aufsätze zur Musikgeschichte*, vol. 2. Munich: Drei Masken Verlag, 1924, pp. 258–265.

Sauer, August, ed. *Grillparzers Gespräche und die Charakteristiken seiner Persönlichkeit durch die Zeitgenossen*. 5 vols. Vienna: Literarische Verein, 1904–1911.

Schilling, Gustav, ed. *Encyclopädie der gesammten musikalischen Wissenschaften, oder Universal-Lexicon der Tonkunst*. 6 vols. and suppl. Stuttgart: Franz Heinrich Köhler, 1835–1842.

Schindler, Anton. *Beethoven in Paris*. Münster: Aschendorff, 1842.

Schindler, Anton. *Biographie von Ludwig van Beethoven*. 3rd ed. 2 vols. Münster: Aschendorff, 1860.

[Schindler-MacArdle.] Schindler, Anton. *Beethoven as I Knew Him*. Trans. Constance S. Jolly. Ed. Donald W. MacArdle. Chapel Hill: University of North Carolina Press, 1966. Reduced repr., New York: W.W. Norton, 1972. (Annotated translation of *Biographie*, 3rd ed. [1860].)

[Schindler-Moscheles.] Schindler, Anton. *The Life of Beethoven, Including His Correspondence with His Friends, Numerous Characteristic Traits, and Remarks on His Musical Works*. 2 vols. Ed. Ignaz Moscheles. London: Henry Colburn, 1841. Altered repr., Boston: Oliver Ditson, [1840s]. (Only Moscheles's name appeared on the title page.)

Schirmer, Wolfhart. "Standortberichtigung zu Beethovens Wohnstätte in Hetzendorf (1823)." *Mitteilungsblatt der Wiener Beethoven-Gesellschaft* 12, no. 1 (1982), pp. 1–3.

Schmidl, Adolf. *Wiens Umgebungen auf zwanzig Stunden im Umkreise: Nach eigenen Wanderungen geschildert*. 3 vols. Vienna: Carl Gerold, 1835–1839.

Schmidl, Adolf. *Wien wie es ist*. Vienna: Carl Gerold, 1833.

Schmidt, Friedrich August. *Neuer Nekrolog der Deutschen*. Vols. 1–19. Ilmenau/Weimar: Voigt, 1824–1843.
Schmidt, Otto. *Wiener Typen und Strassenbilder*. Ed. Helfried Seemann and Christian Lunzer. Vienna: Album Verlag Seemann & Lunzer, 2000.
Schmidt-Görg, Joseph. *Beethoven: Die Geschichte seiner Familie*. Bonn: Beethoven-Haus, 1964.
Schmidt-Görg, Joseph, and Hans Schmidt. *Beethoven*. Bonn/Hamburg: Deutsche Grammophon Gesellschaft, 1969/New York: Praeger, 1970.
Schönfeld, Johann Ferdinand von. *Jahrbuch der Tonkunst von Wien und Prag*. Vienna: Schönfeld Verlag, 1796. Repr., ed. Otto Biba. Munich: Musikverlag Emil Katzbichler, 1976.
Schreyvogel, Joseph. *Josef Schreyvogels Tagebücher, 1810–1823*. 2 vols. Ed. Karl Glossy. Berlin: Gesellschaft für Theatergeschichte, 1903.
Schünemann, Georg, ed. *Ludwig van Beethovens Konversationshefte*. 3 vols. Berlin: Max Hesses Verlag, 1941–1943.
Schwarz, Heinrich. "Die Anfänge der Lithographie in Wien." Diss., University of Vienna, 1921; published Vienna: Böhlau Verlag, 1988.
Seyfried, Ferdinand von. *Rückschau in das Theaterleben Wiens seit den letzten 50 Jahren*. Vienna: Selbstverlag des Verfassers, 1864.
Seyfried, Ignaz von. "Journal." See Archival Documents (below).
Slezak, Friedrich. *Beethovens Wiener Originalverleger*. Vienna: Franz Deuticke, 1987.
Slezak, Friedrich. "Zur Firmengeschichte von Artaria & Compagnie." *Beethoven Jahrbuch* 9 (1973–1977), pp. 453–468.
Slovenski biografski leksikon. 16 vols. Ed. Izidor Cancar *et al.* Ljubljana: Zadružna gospodarska banka, 1925–1991.
Smidak, Emil F. *Isaak-Ignaz Moscheles*. Aldershot: Scolar Press, 1989.
Smolle, Kurt. *Wohnstätten Ludwig van Beethovens von 1792 bis zu seinem Tod*. Bonn: Beethoven-Haus; Munich: G. Henle, 1970.
Solomon, Maynard. *Beethoven*. New York: Schirmer Books, 1977.
Solomon, Maynard. *Beethoven*. 2nd, rev. ed. New York: Schirmer Books, 1998.
Solomon, Maynard. "Beethoven's Tagebuch." In *Beethoven Essays*. Cambridge, Mass.: Harvard University Press, 1988, pp. 233–295 and 351–353. (One of several publications of essentially the same material.)
Solomon, Maynard. "Beethoven: The Nobility Pretense." *Musical Quarterly* 61, no. 2 (1975), pp. 272–294; rev. in *Beethoven Essays*. Cambridge, Mass.: Harvard University Press, 1988, pp. 43–55 and 310–314.
Sonneck, Oscar George, ed. *Beethoven: Impressions by His Contemporaries*. New York: Schirmer, 1926. Repr., New York: Dover Publications, 1967.

Sonnleithner, Leopold von. "Musikalische Skizzen aus Alt-Wien." *Recensionen und Mittheilungen über Theater und Musik* 7, no. 47 (November 24, 1861)–9, no. 20 (May 17, 1863).

[Sonnleithner-Vago.] Vago, Alexandra. "Musical Life of Amateur Musicians in Vienna, ca. 1814–1825: A Translated Edition of Leopold von Sonnleithner's *Musikalische Skizzen aus Alt-Wien* (1861–1863)." M.A. thesis, Kent State University, 2001.

Spohr, Louis. *Lebenserinnerungen*. Unabridged ed., ed. Folker Göthel. Tutzing: Hans Schneider, 1968.

Sporschil, Johann Chrysostomus. "Musikalischer Wegweiser." *Allgemeine Theater-Zeitung* 16, no. 137 (November 15, 1823), p. 548. (Probably documents loss of conversation books, ca. November 1, 1822.)

Stadler, Maximilian. *Abbé Maximilian Stadler: Seine Materialien zur Geschichte der Musik unter den Österreichischen Regenten: Ein Beitrag zum muzikalischen Historismus im vormärzlichen Wien*. Ed. Karl Wagner. Kassel: Bärenreiter, 1974.

Steblin, Rita. "'Auf diese Art mit A geht alles zu Grunde': A New Look at Beethoven's Diary Entry and the 'Immortal Beloved.'" *Bonner Beethoven-Studien* 6 (2007), pp. 147–180.

Steblin, Rita. *Beethoven in the Diaries of Johann Nepomuk Chotek*. Bonn: Verlag Beethoven-Haus, 2013.

Steblin, Rita. "Beethoven's Name in Viennese Conscription Records." *Beethoven Journal* 24, no. 1 (Summer, 2009), pp. 4–13. (Biographical details on housekeeper Barbara Holzmann, pp. 9 and 13.)

Strömmer, Elisabeth. *Klima-Geschichte: Methoden der Rekonstruktion und historische Perspektive, Ostösterreich 1700 bis 1830*. Vienna: Franz Deuticke, 2003.

Suppan, Wolfgang. *Steirisches Musiklexikon*. 2 vols. Graz: Akademische Druck- und Verlagsanstalt, 1962–1966.

Szmolyan, Walter. "Beethoven-Funde in Mödling." *Österreichische Musikzeitschrift* 26 (1971), pp. 9–16.

Tausig, Paul. *Die Glanzzeit Badens: Ein Kulturbild aus den Jahren 1800–1835. Nach Akten, teilweise neuen Literaturquellen und unveröffentlichten Tagebüchern. Mit einem Stadtplane aus dem Jahre 1812*. Baden: Wladarz, 1914.

Thayer, Alexander Wheelock. *Ludwig van Beethoven's Leben*. 3 vols. Trans. Hermann Deiters. Vol. 1, Berlin: Ferdinand Schneider, 1866; vols. 2–3, Berlin: W. Weber, 1872–1879. (Coverage only to 1816.)

[Thayer-Deiters-Riemann.] Thayer, Alexander Wheelock. *Ludwig van Beethovens Leben*. 5 vols. Ed. Hermann Deiters and Hugo Riemann. Leipzig: Breitkopf und Härtel, 1901–1911.

[Thayer-Forbes.] Thayer, Alexander Wheelock. *Thayer's Life of Beethoven*. 2 vols. Ed. Elliot Forbes. Princeton, N.J.: Princeton University Press, 1964–1967. (Updated version of Thayer-Krehbiel, still with portions of Thayer's original text omitted.)

[Thayer-Krehbiel.] Thayer, Alexander Wheelock. *The Life of Ludwig van Beethoven.* 3 vols. Trans. and ed. Henry Edward Krehbiel. New York: Beethoven Association/G. Schirmer, 1921. Reduced repr. London: Centaur, 1960. (Omits portions of Thayer's original text.)

[Thieme-Becker.] *Allgemeines Lexikon der bildenden Künstler von der Antike bis zur Gegenwart.* Founded by Ulrich Thieme and Felix Becker. 37 vols. Leipzig: E.A. Seemann, 1907–1950.

Thomas, Georg Sebastian. *Die Grossherzogliche Hofkapelle, deren Personalbestand und Wirken unter Ludewig I., Grossherzog von Hessen und bei Rhein.* Darmstadt: G. Jonghaus, 1858.

Trost, Alois. "Über einige Wohnungen Beethovens." In *Ein Wiener Beethoven-Buch.* Ed. Alfred Orel. Vienna: Gerlach & Wiedling, 1921, pp. 206–208.

Tyson, Alan. "Notes on Five of Beethoven's Copyists." *Journal of the American Musicological Society* 23, no. 3 (Fall, 1970), pp. 439–471.

Ullrich, Hermann. "Franz Oliva: Ein vergessener Freund Beethovens." *Jahrbuch des Vereins für Geschichte der Stadt Wien* 36 (1980), pp. 7–29.

Volkmann, Hans. "Beethoven und Sporschil." In *Neues über Beethoven.* Berlin: Hermann Seemann Nachfolger, 1904, pp. 62–64.

Waidelich, Till Gerrit, Renate Hilmar-Voit, and Andreas Mayer, eds. *Franz Schubert: Dokumente, 1817–1830.* 2 vols. Tutzing: Hans Schneider, 1993–2003.

Walden, Edward. *Beethoven's Immortal Beloved: Solving the Mystery.* Lanham, Md.: Scarecrow Press, 2011. (Promotes Bettina Brentano as the "Immortal Beloved.")

Walker, Alan. *Franz Liszt.* Vol. 1, *The Virtuoso Years, 1811–1847.* New York: Alfred A. Knopf, 1983.

Wegeler, Franz Gerhard. *Nachtrag zu den biographischen Notizen über Ludwig van Beethoven: Bei Gelegenheit der Errichtung seines Denkmals in seine Vaterstadt Bonn. Mit einem von Beethoven componirten, zum erstenmale bekannt gemachten Liede.* Koblenz: Bädeker, 1845.

[Wegeler-Ries.] Wegeler, Franz Gerhard, and Ferdinand Ries. *Biographische Notizen über Ludwig van Beethoven.* Koblenz: Bädeker, 1838.

[Wegeler-Ries-Kalischer.] Wegeler, Franz Gerhard, and Ferdinand Ries. *Biographische Notizen über Ludwig van Beethoven.* Ed. Alfred Christlieb Kalischer. Berlin: Schuster & Loeffler, 1906.

[Wegeler-Ries-Noonan.] Wegeler, Franz Gerhard, and Ferdinand Ries. *Beethoven Remembered: The Biographical Notes of Franz Wegeler and Ferdinand Ries.* Trans. Frederick Noonan. Arlington, Va.: Great Ocean Publishers, 1987. (Translation of Kalischer, 1906, edition.)

Wehle, Peter. *Sprechen Sie Wienerisch?* Vienna: Ueberreuter, 1981. Repr., 2003.

Weidmann, Franz Carl. *Die Umgebungen Wiens.* Vienna: Mayer, 1839.

Weinmann, Alexander. *Beiträge zur Geschichte des Alt-Wiener Musikverlages, Verlagsverzeichnis Giovanni Cappi*. Vienna: Wiener Urtext-Ausgabe, 1967.

Weinmann, Alexander. *Wiener Musikverleger und Musikhändler von Mozarts Zeit bis gegen 1860*. Vienna: Österreichische Akademie der Wissenschaften, 1956.

Weinzierl, Stefan. *Beethovens Konzerträume: Raumakustik und symphonische Aufführungspraxis an der Schwelle zum modernen Konzertwesen*. Frankfurt am Main: Verlag Erwin Bochinsky, 2002.

Weise, Dagmar. See Beethoven, Ludwig van, *Entwurf einer Denkschrift*.

Weston, Pamela. *Clarinet Virtuosi of the Past*. London: Novello, 1971.

Wiener Allgemeine musikalische Zeitung (1813). Ed. Ignaz Franz v. Schönholz. Repr., ed. Othmar Wessely. Vienna: Hermann Böhlaus Nachfolger, 1986.

[*Wiener AmZ.*] See *Allgemeine musikalische Zeitung mit besonderer Rücksicht, 1817–1824* (above).

Wiener Zeitschrift für Kunst, Literatur, Theater, und Mode. Ed. Johann Schickh. Vienna, 1816–1835. (Often cited with mention of editor Schickh to avoid confusion.)

Wiener Zeitung. With supplements *Intelligenzblatt* and *Amtsblatt*. Vienna, 1818–1827.

Wlassack, Eduard, ed. *Chronik des k.k. Hof-Burgtheaters zu dessen Säcular-Feir im Februar 1876*. Vienna: L. Rosner, 1876.

Wurzbach, Constant von. *Biographisches Lexikon des Kaiserthums Oesterreich*. 60 vols. Vienna: K. k. Hof- und Staatsdruckerei, 1856–1891. (Volumes cited with arabic numbers to avoid confusion.)

Załuski, Iwo, and Pamela Zaluski. *Mozart in Italy*. London: Peter Owen, 1999.

Ziegler, Anton. *Addressen-Buch von Tonkünstlern, Dilettanten, Hof- Kammer- Theater- und Kirchen-Musikern ... in Wien*. Vienna: Anton Strauss, 1823. (Contents generally reflect Fall, 1822.)

Archival Documents

Gugitz, Gustav. "Abhandlungen Schotten [1783–1850]." Typescript. Vienna: Stadt- und Landesarchiv, ca. 1952.

Gugitz, Gustav. "Auszüge über Persönlichkeiten des Wiener Kulturlebens, 1783–1850." Typescript. Vienna: Stadt- und Landesarchiv, ca. 1952.

Gugitz, Gustav. "Auszüge aus den Conscriptions-Bögen." Typescript. Vienna: Stadt- und Landesarchiv, ca. 1952.

Hofmusikkapelle. Akten. Haus-, Hof- und Staatsarchiv, Vienna.

Hoftheater. Generalintendanz. Akten. Haus-, Hof- und Staatsarchiv, Vienna.

Kysselak, Franz. Todesnachrichten aus Zeitungen 1814–1870. Wiener Stadt- und Landesarchiv, Handschriften 3.4.A.112.1–8 (cited as "Memorabilien Österreichs, Verstorbene" in the German edition).

Portheim Katalog. Biographical index on manuscript cards. Wiener Stadt- und Landesbibliothek.

Program files. Archiv, Gesellschaft der Musikfreunde, Vienna.

Seyfried, Ignaz von. "Journal … Theater an der Wien, 1795–1829." Manuscript. Handschriften-Sammlung, 84958 Jb. Wiener Stadt- und Landesbibliothek.

Theater-Zettel (Burgtheater; Kärntnertor Theater; Theater an der Wien). Bibliothek, Österreichisches Theatermuseum, Vienna.

Vienna church records (baptisms, marriages, deaths), 1783–1850. Cited in footnotes by parishes.

Vienna. Magistrat. Conscriptions-Bögen, 1805–1856. Wiener Stadt- und Landesarchiv.

Vienna. Magistrat. Totenbeschauprotokoll. Wiener Stadt- und Landesarchiv.

Vienna. Magistrat. Verlassenschafts-Abhandlungen (Sperrs-Relation). Wiener Stadt- und Landesarchiv.

Index of Writers of Conversational Entries

N.B. This index includes the names of individuals (including Beethoven himself) who wrote entries in Hefte 44–59 of Beethoven's Conversation Books. In addition, when one writer writes entries on behalf of another who is present, both conversationalists are listed here. Unknown writers are indexed under U, often with a descriptor. Writers who were still "Unknown" in the German edition, but who have been identified here, are entered under the identity ascertained for them. Unknown writers whose occupations are clear and pertinent to their entries are entered by their occupations (e.g., Tailor). Beethoven's often anonymous domestic staff (often with indeterminate duties) may be found under Housekeeper, Cook, and Maid, or their names, when known.

Artisan (unknown)   31–32

Bauer, Nannette (housekeeper applicant)   8
Beethoven, Johann van (brother)   102–103, 108–110, 112, 114, 127, 133–134, 136, 147–151, 160–161, 165–166, 180, 202–206, 208–209, 215–217, 227–231, 244–246, 248, 261–264, 275, 291–292, 312–313, 317–320
Beethoven, Karl van (nephew)   1–8, 10–15, 18–20, 24–40, 42–52, 53, 58–67, 69–73, 75, 77–79, 81–85, 88–92, 98–102, 104–106, 107–121, 123–125, 127, 131–142, 143, 147–149, 151, 153, 157–172, 177, 180, 188–191, 196–198, 200, 202–211, 213, 217–219, 223, 225–232, 235–236, 239–244, 246–248, 250–256, 258–259, 263–266, 268–270, 272–275, 277, 280–296, 299–303, 308, 311–313, 315–321, 325–326
Beethoven, Ludwig van (composer)   5, 9, 15, 21, 24–25, 28–31, 34–37, 43–46, 48, 51–52, 53–54, 59, 64–66, 76–77, 80, 84, 87, 89–92, 99–102, 105, 112, 114, 118, 122, 134, 139, 141, 147, 150, 156, 157, 164, 169, 172, 177, 179, 183, 187–188, 191–192, 196, 200–202, 206, 210, 212, 214, 216–217, 218, 222–224, 238, 242, 250–252, 254, 258–259, 264–265, 269–270, 280–287, 289, 291, 293–295, 297, 299–300, 302–303, 305, 307, 310, 319, 325
Beethoven, Ludwig van (copying book advertisements, etc.)   25, 29–30, 36, 45, 51, 53, 77, 164, 179, 187, 201, 212, 216, 222–224, 252, 270, 295, 297, 303, 305, 325
Böhm, Joseph (violinist)   310–311

Carbon, Franz Ludwig (Mödling official)   20–21, 247–248
Castelli, Ignaz Franz (poet, journalist)   279
Cook (domestic)   141, 149, 168
Copyists   66–67
    Maschek, Paul   307–308, 322
    Rampl, Wenzel   66–67
    Schlemmer, Josepha   106, 192
    Wunderl, Matthias ("Copyist E")   66–67

Eigner, Magdalena (housekeeper applicant)   293

Frank, Frau (housekeeper applicant)   102

Glöggl (family relative, shoemaker)   260–261

INDEX OF WRITERS OF CONVERSATIONAL ENTRIES 353

Gneisel, Juliane (housekeeper applicant) 272–273
Gottschedt, Anna (housekeeper applicant) 161, 163–164
Grillparzer, Franz (poet, playwright) 236–238
Gross, Leonore (housekeeper applicant) 163–164

Halm, Maria Theresia (from Trier) 121
Haslinger, Tobias (publisher) 309–311
Henning Carl Wilhelm (violinist, Berlin) 21–23, 76–77
Hirschmann, Franziska (housekeeper applicant) 272
Holz, Karl (violinist, future secretary) 311
Housekeepers and applicants 48, 296, 308
    Applicants (gen.) 102, 114, 166–167
    Bauer, Nannette 8
    Eigner, Magdalena 293
    Four candidates 163–164
    Frank, Frau 102
    French-speaking 182, 196
    Gneisel, Juliane 272–273
    Gottschedt, Anna 161, 163–164
    Gross, Leonore 163–164
    Hirschmann, Franziska 272
    Krupka, Susanna 163–164
    Kummer, Katharina 284
    Lehmann, Frau 266, 269–270
    Mayer 167
    New (January 2, 1824) 171
    New (March 9, 1824) 308, 323
    Paid 168
    Sartory, Frau 273–274
    Seisser, Anna 177
    Trion, Sophie 190–191
    Unsuitable, pregnant 300
    Widow from Prague 161–162

Kirchhoffer, Franz Christian (business advisor) 37–38, 40–41, 147, 251
Krupka, Susanna (housekeeper applicant) 163–164
Kummer, Katharina (housekeeper applicant) 284

Lachner, Franz (composer, organist) 125–127
Lehmann, Frau (housekeeper applicant) 266, 269–270
Leidesdorf, Max Joseph (publisher) 180–181
Leschen, Wilhelm (piano maker) 139

Lichnowsky, Moritz (Count) 9–10, 33, 67–68, 107, 109, 150–151, 230–231, 247, 304, 309–311
Lirveeld, Baroness (friend of Unger) 220–222

Maid (domestic) 119, 151, 188, 263, 274
Mälzel, Leonhard ("mechanic," like elder brother Johann Nepomuk) 259
Maschek, Paul (copyist) 307–308, 322
Mayer (housekeeper applicant) 167
Moscheles, Ignaz (pianist, composer) 93–97, 140

Piano maker (Leschen?) 139

Rampl, Wenzel (copyist) 66–67
Ries, Joseph (piano maker) 41–42, 158
Rinn, Anna (housekeeper applicant) 163–164

Sartory, Frau (housekeeper applicant) 273–274
Schickh, Johann (journalist) 241, 242–243
Schindler, Anton (all entries) 28, 54–58, 62, 85–88, 92, 97–98, 103–105, 115, 118–123, 127–129, 131–132, 140–141, 143–147, 151–156, 164, 169–170, 174–177, 182–185, 187, 192–194, 195–196, 198–200, 211–213, 218–219, 221–225, 232, 238–240, 243–244, 246, 254–258, 266–268, 280, 283–285, 291, 294–300, 304–307, 313, 316–317, 319, 321–327
Schindler, Anton (falsified entries) 28, 85, 119–120, 123, 164, 175, 213, 266, 280, 285, 291, 294–295, 297, 300, 304–307, 313, 319, 321, 325–327
Schlemmer, Josepha (copyist) 106, 192
Schulz, Andreas (Vienna-Mödling bookkeeper) 117–118
Schuppanzigh, Ignaz (violinist) 21–23, 69–71, 100–101, 111, 173–174, 177–178, 181, 189–190, 214–215, 241–242, 245–246, 271, 277, 281–282, 304–305, 307–308, 309–311, 313, 315
Seisser, Anna (housekeeper applicant) 177
Sonnleithner, Leopold (lawyer) 278–280
Sontag, Henriette (soprano) 324–325
Stein, Matthäus Andreas (piano maker) 116

Trion, Sophie (housekeeper applicant) 190–191

Unger, Caroline (mezzo-soprano) 184–187, 220–222, 249–250, 323–324
Unknown
   Artisan 31–32
   Housekeeper applicant's representative 166–167
   Lachner, Franz (?) 125–127
   Man (concerning washing) 293
   Schickh's representative 241
   Widow applicant 161–162

Waitress/Maid 188
Wildfeyer, Wilhelm (Count Kollowrat's tutor) 25–26
Wolf (visitor, admirer of Moscheles) 168
Wunderl, Matthias ("Copyist E") 66–67

Index of Beethoven's Compositions

This Index of Beethoven's Compositions is arranged under three primary topics—Instrumental, Vocal, and Miscellaneous. Within these topics, the bold-print subheadings should make locations of specific genres and works fairly clear. Sub-headings under such works as Symphony No. 9 and the *Missa solemnis* tend to be diverse and even chaotic, and so the researcher is advised to survey all of the subordinate entries for potentially useful information. For the most part, the language used to identify works will follow common practice in English-speaking countries: *The Creatures of Prometheus* in English, but the *Abendlied unterm gestirnten Himmel* in German.

Proposed, incomplete, or unset works are generally placed within the genres most appropriate to the work, if completed. Therefore, the unset operatic idea of *Melusine* is placed among the dramatic works, and the unset libretto for *Der Sieg des Kreuzes* among the choral works.

Instrumental

SYMPHONIES

Symphonies, general   186
Symphony No. 1 (Op. 21), mistaken identification   154
Symphony No. 2 (Op. 36)
   1st movement on Moscheles concert   24, 63, 96
   Entire symphony at Josephstadt Theater (Schindler conducted)   103–104, 253
   Gesellschaft der Musikfreunde (December 14)   123, 132–133
   Josephstadt Theater (ca. December 12)   123, 170
   Kanne misidentified key   154
Symphony No. 3, *Eroica* (Op. 55)
   Gebauer copied; Beethoven dissatisfied   312
   Length   209
Symphony No. 5 (Op. 67)
   Pechatschek conducted (1820)   198
   Piccolo part   108

Symphony No. 6   164
Symphony No. 9 (Op. 125)   9, 56, 64, 68, 94, 111, 116, 136–137, 160, 165, 185, 256
   Alto part   185
   Composed with Kärntnertor Theater in mind   307
   "Copied already?" (March 5)   304
   Copies by Gläser and Rampl   266
   Copy for Moscheles   152
   Copy for Philharmonic Society of London (arrived December 1824)   282
      Possible English translation   282
   Copying   182, 190, 203
      Solo parts with bass line   307, 313
      Solo/ripieno passages in wind parts   304
   Division of labor for Akademie   194
   First performance never intended for London (ca. December 4/5)   94
   Gesellschaft der Musikfreunde, potential participation in Akademie   247
   "High income from Akademie" (Johann)   208

Symphony No. 9 (*continued*)
    Historical string instruments lent by
        Rzechaczek   178
    Hornists Hürth and Lewy   143–144
    "Longer than *Eroica*?" (Karl)   209
    Need to work economically   247
    Orchestration   112
    Plates to Haslinger   163
    Presentation copy for Friedrich Wilhelm
        III   266
    Publish by subscription   163
    Piano reduction for rehearsals   182
    Ries looks forward to receiving   188
    "Score copied yet?"   310
        Rampl needed?   311
    Sketches for Finale   181
    Tessitura (choral) and tuning (falsified)
        326
    Trombones, horns   112
    Violin parts   102
    Vocal parts, need time for study   271
    Vocal quartet personnel   292
    Vocal soloists suggested at Christmas,
        1823   155
    Wind parts (*Harmonie*) doubled   310
    3rd movement
        Horn solo for Hradetzky   316
        Influence from Haydn Symphony No.
            60   244
    4th movement
        "Freude" theme sketched   82, 101
        Note too high for Unger   323
        Piccolo part   108
        Schiller, *An die Freude*   30
        "Seid umschlungen"   112
            Sketch   299
        türkische Musik, sketch   108
        Violoncello recitatives   59, 101
        Work on   142

CONCERTOS AND CONCERTED WORKS

Piano Concerto, new (February 1824)   292
    For Czerny to play May 7   253–254
    Johann told Czerny   253–254
    Karl mentions   292
Piano Concerto No. 5 (Op. 73)
    Beethoven asked Czerny for May 23
        Akademie   253–254
        Czerny declined to play   281

Piano Concerto No. 5 (*continued*)
    Beethoven played in private (1809,
        Lobkowitz)   254
    Hradetzky concert (1818)   254
    Performances by Czerny   254
    Written for Theater an der Wien orchestra
        254
Romance in F for Violin and Orchestra (Op.
    50)
    Czerny arrangement for piano, 4 hands
        266
    Played with S.A. Steiner   266

OTHER ORCHESTRAL WORKS

Namensfeier Overture (Op. 115)   93–94, 95
    Called *Jagd-Overtüre*   128, 140
    Moscheles concerts   128, 135, 140, 154–155
    Rehearsal for Moscheles   140
    Relative difficulty   94–95, 128, 140
Wellington's Victory (Op. 91)   86, 93

STRING QUARTETS

String Quartets, general
    Played by Glöggl family members   260
    Played by Lachner at Tabor, Bohemia
        125
    Played by Radziwill   76–77
    Possible commission   189
    Request by Raigersfeld   87
    Review   75
        Haydn, Mozart, Beethoven   175
    Schuppanzigh's performances "too
        affected"   175
String Quartets (Op. 18)   126–127
    Förster advised   126
    Performed at Tabor   127
    Op. 18, No. 1   291
    Op. 18, No. 2   261–262
    Op. 18, No. 5   9
String Quartets (Op. 59)   69–70
    Op. 59, No. 3   69–70
String Quartet (Op. 74)   227–228
String Quartet (Op. 95)   227–228
String Quartet (Op. 127)   40–41
String Quartet (Op. 130)   40–41
String Quartet (Op. 132)   40–41
    Sketches   181
String Quartets, late, for Galitzin (Opp. 127,
    130, 132)   262

INDEX OF BEETHOVEN'S COMPOSITIONS

OTHER CHAMBER MUSIC

Piano Trios (Opp. 1 and 3) 181
String Trios (Op. 9) 65, 67, 70
   Op. 9, No. 3 190
      On Schuppanzigh concert 190, 193
String Quintet (Op. 4) 160
String Quintet (Op. 29) 240
Septet (Op. 20) 193, 206, 207
   Flute not included 208
   Performance (January 25, Schuppanzigh) 193, 197, 213, 228
      Johann wants reaction 206
      Solos applauded 208
   Popularity tiresome to Beethoven 193
   Repeat performance (March 14) 193, 203, 318, 323

PIANO WORKS—GENERAL

Works, general 240
   In Czerny's recitals 258
   In *Gesamtausgabe* 181
   Lachner's 10-year-old female cousin plays 126
   Revised (updated) versions 71
   Variations, appropriate for young players 260

PIANO SONATAS

Piano Sonata (Op. 2, No. 1; falsified) 120
Piano Sonata (Op. 10, No. 3; falsified) 85, 120
Piano Sonata, *Pathétique* (Op. 13; falsified) 120, 297
   Czerny plays in tempo 297
   2 *Principe* 297
   Schindler wants explanation again 297
Piano Sonata (Op. 22) 65
Piano Sonata (Op. 31; falsified) 120
Piano Sonata, *Hammerklavier* (Op. 106) 232, 239–240
   Haydn's supposed "opinion" (Schindler) 244
Piano Sonatas (Opp. 109, 110, 111) 204
   Czerny plays in weekly private recitals 232
   Schindler and Karl attended (February 8) 232
   Opp. 110 and 111 239–240
Piano Sonatas
   In *Gesamtausgabe* 181
   In minor keys (falsified) 120
   Schindler's falsified interpretations 120

SONATAS WITH OTHER INSTRUMENTS

Violin Sonata (Op. 23) 120
Violoncello Sonatas (Op. 102), for Linke 292

OTHER PIANO MUSIC

Bagatelles (Op. 126) 216, 228
Romance favorite, piano 4 hands (Op. 44), Czerny arrangement of Violin Romance in F (p. 50) 266
Variations, *Diabelli* (Op. 120) 230, 232
   Czerny
      Does not understand fully 230
      Private performance for Schindler (February 1) 232
      Semi-private recital (February 8) 239–240
   Unruly audience approval 230
Variations, *Eroica/Prometheus* (Op. 35) 107
   Moritz Lichnowsky, dedicatee 107

Vocal (and Dramatic, Non-Vocal)

DRAMATIC WORKS

Consecration of the House, Overture and incidental music (Op. 124)
   For Berlin 21–22, 69, 76, 111, 113–114, 144–145, 164
      Bethmann, payment 214
"To be done at every ceremony" 242
   Karl to collect payment 245
Overture 22, 93, 128
   Beethoven to conduct? 307
   "Copied before it ever gets published" 266

Consecration of the House (continued)
    Copying (March 6)   304
    Copy for Johann   113
    In *Gesamtausgabe*   181
    Johann advises for Akademie   291
    "Monster of a work; hope to hear with a large orchestra"   256
    Performance (February 15, Josephstadt Theater) "went very well"   261, 263
    Phrasing in opening March needs to be effective   253
    Pressburg, sent to (February 16)   266
    Publication rights ceded to Johann   91, 166, 228
    Rehearsal (February 14), Josephstadt Theater   258, 261
        Gläser conducted   264
    Schindler involved in composition   266
    Solo/ripieno wind parts   304
    Successful in London   93, 105
    Used for *Der Feldtrompeter*   103–104, 253–255
    Will please in Akademie   261
    Treasured in Berlin (Bethmann)   242
    "Will unser Genius" (aria with horns)   112
    "Wo sich die Pulse" (chorus)   22
    Wunderl as copyist   113
Creatures of Prometheus, ballet (Op. 43), in score in *Gesamtausgabe*   181
Egmont, Overture and incidental music (Op. 84)   49, 128
    Gesellschaft der Musikfreunde (December 14)   123, 132–133, 134
Fidelio (1814)   22–23, 64, 67–68, 137, 186, 209, 214
    "Abscheulicher," cuts made   22–23
    Beethoven lacks a copy   57
    Compared to *Freischütz*   7–8
    Copy in Kärntnertor Theater library   57
    Dresden   22
    "Gut, Söhnchen, gut"   99
    Influenced Kreutzer's *Taucher*   216
        Wordplay on Gneixendorf   99
    Librettist Joseph Sonnleithner   278
    Overture (November 15)   5, 23, 67–68
        Horn solo for Hradetzky   316
        For mechanical clock   99
        Performance, Kärntnertor Theater concert   166

Fidelio (continued)
    Overture *(continued)*
        Performance, Josephstadt Theater   104
    Piano score by Moscheles   92
    Prisoners' Chorus   3
    Revival (November 1822)   7–8
    Score copy needed at home   224, 324
    To be performed with Sontag (1824)   156
    Umlauf conducted many times   307
    Weber imitates   83
Leonore Prohaska, incidental music (WoO 96)   76
Ruins of Athens, Overture and incidental music (Op. 113)   11, 22, 96, 129, 144
    Hensler wants to borrow/use Overture   224
    Copied whole score?   224
    Published by Steiner   96, 129
    "Will unser Genius"   112
Opera subjects/projects, discussed or planned
    Faust, suggested by Henning   77
    Grillparzer, *Melusine* (unset)   10, 33, 55, 67, 83, 85, 103–105, 146, 148–150, 160, 165, 174, 185, 237, 242, 257, 262
        Beethoven to write to Duport   202, 217, 220
        Casting, potential   237, 249
        Censor, possible revisions   257
        Passes (February 15)   262
        Conditions concerning   220–221
        Duport to decide (ca. February 15)   258
        Commissions French translation   250
        Estimated completion date   150
        Estimated income 12,000 fl. W.W.   150
        Excerpts for May 7 Akademie   160, 194, 203, 291–292
        Grillparzer coming to get libretto   292
        Grillparzer's own musical ideas   237
        Kärntnertor Theater approves it   247
        Lichnowsky happy with it   231
        Negotiations with Duport   165
        Plot summary   198–199
        Setting by Conradin Kreutzer (1832)   199
        Soprano vs. mezzo-soprano roles   192–193
        Unger wants to read libretto   187
        Has not returned it?   257

Opera subjects/projects (*continued*)
  Grillparzer, *Melusine* (*continued*)
    Unger and Forti want roles   249
  Opera, new
    People's hope for   113
    Potential   202

CHORAL WORKS

Der glorreiche Augenblick, cantata (Op. 136),
    piccolo part   108
Bundeslied (Op. 122)   216, 228
Choral Fantasy (Op. 80)   82
Christus am Ölberge (Op. 85)
  Chorus "Welten singen" (1820)   198
  Influenced by Salieri's *Les Danaïdes*   83
  Rehearsal (April 4, 1803)   107
Germania, Wie stehst du jetzt (WoO 94),
    final chorus from Treitschke, *Die gute
    Nachricht*   164
Mass in C (Op. 86)   79–80
  Augustiners, St. Cecilia's Day (November
      23)   67
  "Came together badly"   67
  Czerny to organize performance in
      German   212
    Wants to borrow Scholz translation
        212–213
  Gloria   90
Missa solemnis in D (Op. 123)   55, 86, 104,
    111, 160, 185, 204
  Akademie
    3 movements of *Missa*; no piano work
        (Schuppanzigh)   281
    Johann advises programming   291
    Unger and Sontag want the Benedictus
        324
  Alto part   185
  Copy to Frankfurt   91
  Copy for Saxon court   113
  Copying   160, 182, 190, 215
    2 movements (February 15)   261
    For performance   160
    Progress report, Maschek (March
        13)   322
      Credo and Agnus: tenor/bass parts
          missing   322
      Kyrie: violin parts already
          proofread   322
    Schuppanzigh looks at score for
        copying   304

Missa solemnis (*continued*)
  Copying (*continued*)
    Security   106
    Solos with bass line   307, 313
  Copyists
    Maschek   322
    Rampl   24, 66–67
    Schlemmer, Josepha   106, 215
    To copy Gloria and Credo   295
  Esterházy, Nikolaus, not a subscriber   147
  Gloria   90
    Copying   5
  Johann advises Leidesdorf publication
      114
  Karl delivers copy to Rampl?   20
  Kiesewetter advises on performers for
      Akademie   155
    Schuppanzigh as concertmaster   155
    Weigl as conductor   155
  Marie Louise (Parma), offer to   150,
      230–231
    Neipperg   230–231
  Marketing
    Areas and prices   114
    Galitzin suggests   114
  No figured bass   127
  Odelga (Tuscany)   230–231
  Publication
    Proposed   103
    Ready to send for publication   310
    By subscription   163
      Mass before symphony   165
  Public awaiting it   55
  Public performance?   55
  Radziwill   132
  Sanctus, solo for Schuppanzigh in
      Benedictus   281, 291
    Pun on "Milord"   304
  St. Petersburg, performance   204
  Tessitura (chorus) and timing (falsified)
      326
  Tuscan legation   49–50
  Tuscany and Sweden   132
  Violin part(s)   102
  Vocal parts, need time for study   271
  Wind parts, solo/ripieno marking   304
Opferlied (Op. 121b)   216, 228
Unrealized/Incomplete
  Die Befreiung, humorously suggested
      cantata   297
  Mass for Court and Emperor Franz's
      conservative taste   13, 90, 127

Unrealized/Incomplete (*continued*)
   Requiem
      Grillparzer hopes for one   242
      Wolfmayer wanted to commission
         101, 228
   Passion music, Judas Iscariot   100
   Der Sieg des Kreuzes (Bernard)   39, 42, 242
      Grillparzer's opinion   237–238
      Schindler advises returning libretto   56

SONGS

Abendlied unterm gestirnten Himmel (WoO 150)   54, 102

An die ferne Geliebte, cycle (Op. 98), Jeitteles   26
Das Blümchen Wunderhold (Op. 52, No. 8)   149
Gellert *Lieder* (Op. 48)   65
Lied aus der Ferne (WoO 137)   220
Seufzer eines Ungeliebten and *Gegenliebe* (Bürger, WoO 118)   82, 101

MISCELLANEOUS VOCAL WORKS

Ah! Perfido (Op. 65)   189

Miscellaneous

Equale for Trombones (WoO 39)   260
Gesamtausgabe/Collected Works, projected   129
   Manuscript copies in Haslinger's collection   129
   Order of publication   181
   Plans for   180–181
   To Rudolph and Gesellschaft der Musikfreunde   129
   Wait for 100 subscribers   251
Guitar compositions   26
New (periodical) piece every month   189
Vocal work (alto) for Unger   185
Works ceded to Johann   319

General Index

N.B. This General Index includes people, topics, activities, and concepts that were part of Beethoven's conversations during this period. It does not include entries that appear in the Index of Writers of Conversational Entries or the Index of Beethoven's Compositions, although the Index of Writers is often cross-referenced here to remind the reader to look there as well.

While the General Index attempts to be comprehensive and thorough, it cannot be a concordance. If all members of a family appear in an entry in a footnote, the General Index will customarily list the father, probably the mother, but no children unless they appear to be important. Beethoven and his acquaintances seldom referred to the domestic staff (housekeepers, cooks, maids) by name and so identifying and indexing them accurately remains a problem.

This General Index contains no entries under "Beethoven, Ludwig van," with subheadings such as "Deafness." Instead, such entries will simply be listed under "Deafness."

Entries concerning nephew Karl van Beethoven occur frequently, and so, like composer Ludwig, may occasionally be entered under subject: "Vests, Karl."

Internal references to Beethoven's family (otherwise listed under Beethoven) are often identified by their given names: Johann (brother), Karl (nephew), Therese (sister-in-law).

Entries concerning Beethoven's unpaid secretary Anton Schindler become increasingly frequent from November, 1822, and include numerous subheadings to specify their characteristics and the subjects of their conversations.

Information concerning books that Beethoven copied from newspapers, etc., is generally indexed under author's surname and a short title.

Those seeking Schindler's infamous and strangely elusive *Zwei Prinzipe* will find them in Volume 4 under Heft 35, Blatt 9r.

Ableidinger, Silvia   xxiii
Accompaniment: piano/contrabass in Berlin
   178
Address   223, 293
   Ungargasse (full)   269
Adelung, J.C., *Kleines Wörterbuch*   25
Ader, golden (hemorrhoid)   294, 299
Advent charities   85, 102
Aigner, Magdalena. *See* Eigner
Albrecht, Carol Padgham   xxi, xxv
Albrecht, Theodore, *Letters to Beethoven*   xxii
Albrechtsberger, (Johann) Georg   xii, 7
   Biographical sketch   7
   "Gänsbacher, his best student"
      (Lichnowsky)   151

Alcoholic beverages. *See* Beer; Wine
Alexander I (Russia), coming to Vienna
   (Lent, 1824)   229
   Galitzin coming too   229
   Neither came   229
   Presence good for upcoming Akademie
      229
Alexander, Franz (Gneixendorf lessee)   97
Aline, opera (Berton), Johann and Karl attend
   204
All Souls Day   13
   Grand Requiem service   13
   Mozart, *Requiem*   13
   Veni, Sancte Spiritus   13
Allgayer-Kaufmann, Regine   xxiv

Allgemeine Theater-Zeitung (Bäuerle)   26–27, 44
   Address, Leopoldstadt   45
   Langer, contributor   197
   Reviews of Beethoven's Quartets   175
   Sporschil article   26–27
Almonds   73
Alms   2, 92. *See also* Advent charities; Blind woman; Charity
Alserkaserne
   Army bands, civilian members   253–254
   Hornists and trombonists at Josephstadt Theater   253–254
Amateurs, weak but good-natured   3–4
Amazonen (ballet)   135
Amenda, Carl   ix
American Beethoven Society   xxiv
Amitay, Moshe   xxv
Amsterdam   127
Amundsen, Roald   4
Anderson, Emily, attitudes   xx, xxii
André, Christian Carl (Württemberg Court Councillor), asks Schindler for articles   307
Animal plays   98–99
   Eagle, dog, frog, bear, apes, etc.   98
   Vienna's theaters (Fall, 1823)   98
Antarctic Ocean (Simonow)   325
Antiochus   72
Anti-Semitism   26
   Remarks   71
Apartment hunting   59, 65, 162, 201, 259
   Augustiners in Landstrasse   299
   Barmherzige Brüder (Landstrasse)
      Bright sunlight   289
      Secure   289
   January, 1824   218–219
   Leonhard Mälzel's apartment   218–219
   Weigl's apartment   218–219
   See also Light
Apothecary, Johann wanted Karl to become   263
Apotheke (in Greek), Karl and Johann   293
Appel, Bernhard   xxiii
Applause, interrupting music   208
Apples, salad   227
   At restaurant below   229
Aristotle, on rhythm   305
Arithmetic   188
   Beethoven, little instruction   167
   Karl's   246
      Consecration funds from Berlin   246

Arithmetic (*continued*)
   Karl's (*continued*)
      Not a clear math teacher   246
      Multiplication/division   167
      Schuppanzigh's   242
Armchair Journeys   82–83
Arsenius (play)   157
Arsis and Thesis (Schindler)   305
Artaria (music publishing firm)   96
Artaria, map (1824)   xxix
Artaria, Mathias   180, 189
Ash Wednesday   290
Asinus-âne   272
Asioli, Bonifazio, *Easiest Way to Tune Keyboard Instruments*   52
Astronomical Tables for 1824, Vehelin   270
Auber, *Der Schnee*   308, 324
   Corresponding weather (March 14)   324
Auer, Leopold (archivist)   xxiii
Augarten concerts   167
Augustiner Church (Vienna)   144, 194
   Concerts spirituels   155
   Karl attends Christmas Mass there   153–154
   Mass by Gänsbacher   144
Augustiners (Landstrasse)   172
Austrian National Bank   xvii
Austrian National Library   xvii
Avins, Styra   89

Bach, Johann Baptist (lawyer)   xxxi, 31, 88, 180–181, 261
   Friend of Schönauer   88
   Negotiations with Duport   165
   Negotiations with Magistrat   261
   Rude at inauguration of Rector   88
Bach, Johann Sebastian   xx, 118
Bach, Wilhelm Friedemann
   Fugues   151
   Lichnowsky mentions   151
Bachelor, old (Beethoven) is idle citizen   220
Bäcker, Joseph (coffee house)   161
Baden (1822)   xiii
Baden (Summer residence, 1823), tobacco   3
Baker. *See* Obermayer
Balance, orchestral, middle voices clearer (falsified)   321
Balde, Jacob, *Carmina selecta*   224–225
   Modern songs in Latin   224
Ballauf-Muck, Theresia, *Wiener Köchin*   216
Ballet, Court
   Amazonen   135
   Paired with Moscheles concert   135

Ballet, Court (*continued*)
   As good as Paris 88
   Conductor Katter 214
   Die Fee und der Ritter (Italian pastiche) 195
Balls, Fasching (Carnival; February 27)
   Johann attended 290
   See also Fasching balls
Bank shares 200, 283, 319
   Cash in (January 22) 200
   Inheritance tax on 283
   Value (March 12) 319
Banker/wholesaler, formerly grocer 84
Bankers, Jewish. *See* Rothschild; Wetzlar
Banking and financial matters 64, 111, 116, 118, 150, 241, 264–265
   Payment from Berlin for *Consecration* 246
   Projected earnings in Russia 262
   Projected income from Akademie (Johann) 208
Barbaja, Domenico 33, 54, 160, 250, 262
   Administration "defrauded the Court" 87–88
   Dismissed Kärntnertor Theater orchestra members 54
   Lease to end 87
   Now in Naples 69
   Terms of lease 87–88
   Would pay Beethoven well for an opera 105
Barber's knife (razor) 27, 48, 177. *See also* Razor (barber)
Barnert, Othmar xxiv, 24, 94, 133, 184
Barometer maker 31
Barrel, green. *See Fassl*
Basket, shopping (new) 66
Bass parts (voice) 325
Bassoon
   Mittag (Theater an der Wien) 205
   Nowak (Kärntnertor Theater) 205
Bauer, Caspar (Esterházy courier to England) 87, 93
   Beethoven to visit (falsely informed) 87
Bauer, Monika xxiv, 186
Bauer, Nannette (housekeeper applicant) 80–85, 89, 98, 111–112, 116
   Address (Ledergasse) 112
   Attitudes 112
   Cooking samples 82–83, 85

Bauer, Nannette (*continued*)
   Cooking trial (December 9–10) 112, 116–117
     Bitter (everything) 116
     Water not hot enough 116
   "Heiress" 89
   Impertinent 123
   Lady of the house 112
   Leaves (December 5) 98
   Literate 80
   Makes salad with vinegar 112
   Meets Holzmann 124
     Knows her from Obere Pfarrgasse 125
   No trial period 91
   Past her sexual prime 84
   Predicts short term of employment 124
   Qualifications 80
   Rubs out stain for Karl 131
   Sister teaches music 85
   Trial period (possibly 4 weeks) 85
   Washing 89
   Worked for Hungarian noble 112
Bauer's bookshop 224–225
Bäuerle, Adolf. *See Allgemeine Theater-Zeitung*
Baumeister, Joseph (Rudolph's librarian) 145–146
Baumgarten (Vienna), wife of Captain. *See* Boarding house
Baumgarten and Born. *See under* Boarding house
Beans, prohibited 27
Beck, Dagmar xvii
Bed-making 171
Bednarik, Josef xxi, xxiv
Beef 48, 124, 288, 309, 320
   Cost 8, 87
   Loin of 8, 89–90
     Cooking time 89
   Preferred to roast lamb 254
   Roast 91, 188
   Schnitzel 48
   With potatoes 161
   See also Boeuf à la mode; Veal
Beefsteak, pronunciation 65
Beer 32, 53, 76
   English 51
   Ordinary 51, 90
Beer house 254, 272
   Karl bought pencils in 254, 272
Beethoven, Carl van (brother) x, xx, 2, 13, 73

Beethoven, Carl van (*continued*)
    Letter from Treasury   2
    Schönauer his executor   88
    Son Karl goes to confession   32
Beethoven, Johann van (brother)   100–101, 113, 147, 153, 160–161, 164–166, 179–180, 207
    Advice concerning publication of *Missa solemnis*   114
    Advises publisher Leidesdorf   114
    Advises Beethoven on hat   258, 263
    Advises program order for Akademie   291
    Akademie, projects upcoming   102
    Analyzed "undigestible" cheese   320
    Apartment in Vienna   255
    Apothecary
        Investigation about medicine   173–174
        Wanted Karl to become   263
    "Apotheke" from Greek   293
    Asks about new cook   292
    Attends *Aline*   204
    Attends *Consecration Overture* rehearsal   264
    Attends Czerny's home recitals   253
    Attends Fasching Ball   290
    Attends Schuppanzigh concert (January 25)   211
    Attends Schuppanzigh's quartet concert (February 29)   291
    Attends *Taucher* (February 11)   245
    Beethoven blames him for loss of trunk   70
    Beethoven drinks too much water   147, 217
    "Better to compose an opera"   202
    "Big talker" (Schuppanzigh)   173
    Cards, goes to play   275
    Carriage   112, 114
    Coachman to Musik-Verein concert   132
    Coffee beans, Johann laughs at Beethoven's counting   229
        Johann's coffee is measured   229
    Coming to dinner   114
    Cook
        Boils ham for Beethoven   229
        Makes soup too much   229
        Salary   209
    Copyright ethics   102
    "Country is best medicine"   83
    Criticizes Beethoven's household   166

Beethoven, Johann van (*continued*)
    Delivers letter to Duport (January 26)   208
    Drives to Lichnowsky's   108–110
    Drives in Prater   108–110, 182
    Eats midday dinner at 3 p.m.   263
        Seldom eats in evening   263
    Embarrassment at concerts   301
    Evening meal   109–110
    Finances, money from Berlin   211
    Forbids Theresia's lover to visit   275
    "Fratello"   230
    Gives Karl gloves   290
    Gneixendorf (estate)   173
        Goes to (ca. March 17)   326
        Installment payments   91
        Karl's wordplay on name   98
        Nearly froze feet on trip to   263
    "Great exalted brother" (Schuppanzigh)   194
    Grillparzer's negotiations with Kärntnertor Theater   248
    Hair dyed black   149
    Ham, boiled by Johann's cook   229
    Health   83
        Not healthy   2
    Housekeeper, knows a good one   104, 127
    Humorous reference (Karl, Schindler)   153
    Investigation about medicines   174
    Invites Beethoven for a drive   83, 215
    Invites Beethoven to *Figaro* and *Fassl*   133, 136–137
    Invites Beethoven and Karl to Josephstadt Theater   225
    Invites Beethoven to see *Euryanthe*   83
    Jealous (potentially) of Beethoven's celebrity   68
    "Jews have no money"   216
    "Johann der Läufer" (pun)   219
    Lichnowsky, visits with   148–149
    Linz
        Payment from Pharmacy   240
        To buy home there (9,000 fl.)   240
    Looks after horses and coachman   263
    Lost correspondence (Beethoven's), has (?)   26
    "Makes everybody suspicious of Beethoven" (Schindler; falsified)   291

Beethoven, Johann van (*continued*)
    Makes noises at concerts   301
    Manages his household   68
    Marital problems   10, 105, 110, 113, 147, 264–265, 275, 283–285, 287, 289, 297, 313
        Cannot seek divorce   105
        Considers police intervention   283
        Lives independently of Therese   105
        Wants to separate from Therese   211, 289
    Marriage contract   283
    Meddling/muddling plans for Akademie   192, 194, 203, 208–209, 253
    Meeting at coffee house (February 16)   264
    Meets with Schindler (March 16)   326
    Missa solemnis, advocates publishing   103
    Moscheles, saw him at Artaria's   96
    Moscheles's kidney stones   217
        "Sand and stone"   217
    Musical dealings   217
    Negotiations w/ Duport re *Melusine*   165
    Newspapers, read after Schuppanzigh's concert (January 25)   207
    Not in Vienna in summer   263
    "Nothing to do, all day long"   301
    Offers to deliver letter to Unger   244
    Opera
        About him (by Karl)   153
        Advocates composing   102, 202
        Valid internationally   202
    Operas, negative opinion of   83, 85
    Payment from Pharmacy in Linz   240
    Personal relations (nice) with all   182
    Possible marital problems (February 13–15)   250, 264
    Predicts specific earnings from Akademie   208
    Preparations for Akademie   202–203
    Property to Therese, potential   10
    Protects property   283
    Provides tickets for Akademie   299
    Recommends Schlesinger in Paris   216
    Reports on January 25 concert   208
    Schindler ate with him (February 7)   240
    Schindler calls him "Uncle"   210
        Karl does too   210
    Schindler encounters   85
    Second apothecary shop for free   313
        Recommendation from Emperor   313
        Worth 20,000 fl.   313

Beethoven, Johann van (*continued*)
    Sends regrets (February 13)   250
    Shopping for Beethoven   225
    Speaks loudly with Beethoven   137
    Spends on Therese's wardrobe   183
    Spoke with Forti   147, 149–150
    Spoke to Haslinger   217
    Therese, fought with (February 7)   240
    Ticket, received from Schuppanzigh   203
    Tightwad   110
        Puts paper in his shoes   110
    Told Czerny that Beethoven was writing a concerto   253
    Trusts Schindler to get extra pros from Josephstadt Theater   320
    Visits Beethoven (February 11)   243
    Visits Duport (March 9)   317–318
    Wanted Karl to become an apothecary and professor of chemistry   263
    Wants to improve "taste"   301
    Wants to see new Streicher pianos   231
    Wife Therese, extramarital affairs   206
        Found Therese with her lover (ca. January, 1824)   206
        "Hardly married to her" (Karl)   207
    Wine
        Allows apprentices to guzzle   255
        Has/produces   255
        Money from wine sales   205
        Will send authentic mountain wine   263
    Wordplay   180
    Works ceded to him   319
        Consecration Overture   91
    See also Beethoven, Johann van in the Index of Writers
Beethoven, Johann van (father), pun: "der Läufer"   219
Beethoven, Johanna (Reiss) van
    Karl does not deal with   124
    Letter to Beethoven (January 1)   170
    Ludovika (illegitimate daughter)   174
    New Year's card   170
    Potential conflict   254
    Schindler tries to meet   174
    Wrote about money   254
Beethoven, Karl van (nephew)   x, xiii, 20–21, 157–172, 179
    Academic interests (languages, philology)   272, 288
    Advises divorce for Johann   113

Beethoven, Karl van (*continued*)
  Advises no meat in evenings 4
  Advises tip for seat in coffee house 291
  Advocates for opera 104–105
  Against rehiring Holzmann 225–227, 235
  Anticipates Beethoven's old age 32
  Apartment hunting 162
  "Apotheke" in Greek 293
  Arguments with Beethoven xl, 12, 137
    Almost has argument 73
  Arithmetic 167–168
  Attends *Aline* with Johann 204
  Attends *Aschenbrödel* at Josephstadt Theater 196
  Attends Krähmer concert (March 7) 311
  Attends Schuppanzigh concert (January 25) 211
  Attends Schuppanzigh concert (February 29) 291
  Bank, goes to (January 22) 197
  Beethoven blames him for various things 124
  Bernard cold to him 42
  "Blessed are they who believe" (humorous) 287
  Blöchlinger, visits 61–62
  Book, buys 58
  Bought a dozen pencils at beer house 254, 272
  Breakfast in a restaurant with Beethoven 282
  Brings Schindler's regrets (February 13) 250
  Calligraphy, doodling 104
  Calls Schindler "gossiper" 213
  Capon and salad 312
  Chestnuts, will bring 119
  Cinderella (Isouard) compared to Rossini 196
  Clothes, stained 131
  Coffee houses, students not allowed 37
  Confession, goes to 32
  Consecration Overture, gets compensation for 245–246
  Copies for Beethoven in Court (?) Library 148
  Declines Johann's invitation to Josephstadt Theater (January 31) 225
  "Devoted to Beethoven" 44
    "Today, tomorrow, forever" 49
  Dinner in City (February 24) 202

Beethoven, Karl van (*continued*)
  Eating in the City 288
  Education
    Essay at Blöchlinger's Institute 2
    Pleugmackers 331–333
  English
    Class 20
    Easy to translate "An die Freude" into English 282
    Language 65, 282
  Epithet 113
  Exam, approaching 196
  Exams, in mid-March to April 290
  Expresses himself authoritatively 112
  Fidelio, compares it to *Freischütz* 7
  Flegeljahre (awkward age) 132
  French, describes his abilities in 282
    But not in poetry 282
  French teacher, wanted to become xl, 263, 288
    Additionally Latin and Greek 288
  Friedlowsky's name, did not know 263
  German language, comments on 100
  Gläser's conducting 196
  Grateful to Beethoven 137–138
  Greek study 8, 10, 11
    Will visit Greek professor (Anton Joseph Stein) 288
  Grocery shopping 60
  Heroes 40
  "Honor and money, one can have" 58
  Hope, Sir Thomas (anecdote) 153
  Housekeeper advertisement, delivers to Police 123
  Housekeepers, helps interview 272
  Humor 75
    Swordfish 75
  Instruction, religious, in Mödling 59
  Interviews housekeeper applicant 161–163
    Sent applicant away 170
  Italian class 91
  Italian music, describes 7
  Johann brings carriage 112
  "Johann, der arme Onkel" (hypothetical opera title) 153
  Johann gives him gloves 290
  Johann not usually called "Uncle" 210
  Johann sends coachman 132
  Johann wanted him to be an apothecary and professor of chemistry 263

Beethoven, Karl van (*continued*)
  Johanna (mother), no dealings with   124
  Johann's marriage, on   207
  Kitchen problems, notes   120
  Köferle (teacher)   20, 300
  Kudlich, Frau   197
  Language study   91, 263, 282, 288
  Lichnowsky inquires about   68
  Linguistic scribblings   270, 272
  Linke (cellist), describes   101
  Littrow's "Kepler's Life," reads   53–54
  Logic textbooks   42
  Loves Beethoven more than own father   73
  Ludlamshöhle Petition   286
  Maid
    Bared her chest to him   30, 59
    Insolent to him   65
  "Makes everybody suspicious of Beethoven" (Schindler)   291
  Mass, attends on All Souls Day   13
  Mathematics, study
    Divides   167
    Multiplies   167–168
    Not a clear mathematics teacher   246
    Short division   303
  Meals   19
    At Born and Baumgarten boarding house   30, 33, 46
    Dinner schedule   53, 69, 84, 90–92, 139
    Schedule at home   29
  Misunderstanding   73
    Due to Beethoven's hearing   210
  Money, called to account for spending   272
  Moscheles
    Evaluates his performance   137–139
    Hears   111
    Negative opinion of   111
    Neutral toward   25
    Opinion   61
  Napoleon, O'Meara's book about   146
  Niemetz, Joseph (friend), Karl takes him to *Figaro*   136
  "Nobleman thinks … partridges"   26
  On human nature   29
  On Napoleon   11–12
  On Schiller's works   251
  Opera, wants to write   153
  Operas, would prefer to write   6

Beethoven, Karl van (*continued*)
  Pamer, Maria (former maid), encounters   241
  Pension, testimonial for requires parish priest   34
  "People dreadfully naïve"   11
  "People, mediocre … rich"   5
  Philosophy curriculum   12
  Philosophy tutor, Socher   135–136
  Pleugmackers (influential teacher)   39–40, 331–333
  Prays for Beethoven   73
  Prefers Redoutensaal   318
  Psychology textbook   119
  Pulay (Greek teacher)   39–40, 274, 333–334
  Recommends copyist Gebauer   312
  Regards Schindler as "pest"   321
  Reinlein family, friends   60
  Reprimand for food   161
  Room in Beethoven's apartment   255
  Rooming in City (possibly part-time)   19, 71, 75
  Ruins of Athens, will write sequel   11
  Runs errands   65
  Schiller, quotes *Erwartung*   61–62. See also Schiller, Works
  Schindler
    Characterizes Karl kindly   132
      Sincere, quiet   132
    Fingiert (falsified) remarks   321
    To pay   42
  Schneider's Greek dictionary, has   191
  Schubert or Vogl: "very vulgar fellow"   146
  Schubert's *Rosamunde*, notes   146
  Schuppanzigh
    Reminds Beethoven concerning recommendation   101
    Will visit   100
  Self-evaluation, humorous   63–64
  Shakespeare
    Parodies   75
    Quotes, concerning Schuppanzigh   72
  Shopping for Beethoven   225
  Sleeps in on Saturday   60
  Speaks loudly with Beethoven   137
  Sporschil article's author (speculates)   44–45
  Steiner, S.A., opinion of   112
  Stockings, shops for   53

Beethoven, Karl van (*continued*)
　Stomach cramps　172
　Symphony No. 9; notes "beautiful Andante"　xli
　Take-out from restaurant, below (February 1)　228–229
　　Tip for waiter　229
　Teaches Beethoven. *See* Mathematics (above)
　Tells Bible story (Esau)　287
　Testimonials. *See* Pension (above)
　Testimonials, for maid (January 26)　211, 213
　Textbooks, University　42
　Theater, attended *Hund des Aubri*　99
　"Truth … white beard?"　6
　University
　　Attitudes　121–122
　　Excuse for class absence　119
　　Karpe textbook a "blemish"　122
　　Tuition　293
　　Walked to with Prof. Stein　72
　University schedule　12, 19–20, 37, 53, 84, 91, 115, 119, 139
　　New semester　19
　Unpacking Beethoven's apartment　1, 12
　"Vienna … best place in world"　108
　Visits Lichnowsky　107
　Visits Optical Armchair Journeys　82–83
　Walking times　225, 296
　"We are fortunate"　4
　"Well-read," self description　62
　Wisdom, demonstrates　149
　Wordplay
　　On Gneixendorf　98
　　On hemorrhoids　294, 296
　Wunderl (copyist), encounters　115
　See also Beethoven, Karl van, in the Index of Writers
Beethoven, Ludwig van. *See* Beethoven, Ludwig van, in the Index of Writers
Beethoven, Ludwig van (grandfather)　273
Beethoven, Therese van (Obermayer), Johann's wife　83, 92, 110
　Assets: 80,000–100,000 fl.　264
　Becoming old　113
　Beethoven avoids her　83
　Community property　10
　Daughter. *See* Waldmann, Amalia
　Does what she wants　313
　Dresses, must make her own　183

Beethoven, Therese van (*continued*)
　Fought with Johann (February 7)　240
　Friends with Lichnowsky's wife　10
　Household squanderer　68
　Illegitimate daughter. *See* Waldmann, Amalia
　Infidelity　110
　Johann would like freedom from her　211
　Lover　275
　　Johann caught her with (ca. January, 1824)　206
　Marital problems　297, 313
　Money, has her own　173
　Morals reported by servant　147
　Must lead her own life　105
　Pastries, sold before marriage　207
　Sister-in-law of Stockhammer　153
　Undeserving　264
　Would like freedom from Johann　264, 289
Beethoven-Haus, Bonn　xvii, xix
Behsel, Anton　xxix
Beisteiner (Pohl), Elise, singer　205
Bell (servants)　59, 220
　Bell pull　323
Bellonci, Camillo (hornist)　29
Beloveds, "How many?" (Unger)　221
Benda family　12
Benedict, Julius, in Vienna with Weber　1, 7
Benko, Joseph (coffee house, Brandstatt)　264
Berbiguier, Concerto for 2 flutes　39
Berg, Heinrich　xxiii
Berlin
　Arts and sciences flourish　76
　Complete freedom　76
　Königliche (Staats-) Bibliothek　xi–xviii
　König(s)städtisches Theater　21–23, 24. *See also* Bethmann; Henning; *and Consecration of the House* Overture in the Index of Compositions
　Kreutzer's *Libussa* performed　148
　Royal Insurance Society　23
　Royal Opera House　189
　Royal Theater　23
　Schindler advises Beethoven to go　313
　Schuppanzigh possibly going there　197, 268
　Singakademie, piano/contrabass accompaniment　178
Berliner Zeitung, praise of Kalkbrenner　184

Bernard, Joseph Carl   148
   Anti-Semite   26
   Beethoven avoids him   39
   Beethoven distances himself   38, 42
   Biographical sketch   186
   Cold to Karl   42
   Complimentary tickets to *Melusine*   217
   Mother-in-law owns home   128
   Residence   186
   Sieg des Kreuzes (libretto), Beethoven
      refuses to set   194
      Grillparzer's opinion of *Sieg*   237–238
   Unger's opinion of his "industry"   186
   Wife Magdalena Grassl   128
Bernard-Peters-Janschikh circle   25
Berton, Henri, *Aline*   204
Bestia-bête   272
Bethmann, Heinrich Eduard (Berlin theater
   manager)   22–23, 69–70, 76, 164, 197
   Address   201
   Back in Vienna (January 21)   201
   Biographical sketch   22
   Consecration Overture as "treasure"   242
   Has he paid (for *Consecration*)   214
   Letter from (February 1)   228
   Reply through Schuppanzigh (payment)
      225
   Schuppanzigh sees re *Consecration* (ca.
      February 11)   245–246
   In Vienna (January 21–ca. February 14)
      215
Beyde, August Johann Friedrich, trumpet and
   horn maker   157
Biba, Otto   xxiii
Bible
   Esau, sold birth rights to Jacob   287
   "Sand and stone"   152
Biedermann, Joseph (banker), *Ludlamshöhle*
   259
Biedermannsdorf   216
Biehler, Franziska, pianist   205
Bierteufl restaurant   229
   Counterpart in Beethoven's day   229
   Good food and beer   229
   Hof clean   229
   One-pan meals   229
Bihler, Johann Nepomuk (co-author of the
   Ludlamshöhle Petition)   286
Billiards   63
   Referee   291
Bingham, Nick   xxv
Birkenstock house (Erdberg)   268

Birne, Zur goldenen ("Golden Pear,"
   Landstrasse)   xi, 110, 255
   Capon and salad (Karl)   312
   Poularde (hen)   312
   Restaurant better than City   202
Birthday (Beethoven's)
   Actual date   137–138
   Johann invites him to *Figaro*   133, 136–137
   Letter from Duport (December 14)   133
Bischofhof, people cheat maid   60, 64
Bjelik, Martin   xxiv
Bjelik, Rosemarie   xxiv
Blahetka, Joseph (father)
   Announcements and fliers for Akademie
      282, 292
   Ludlamshöhle   259
   Offers tickets for Akademie   299
   Pianist daughter Leopoldine   282
Blahetka, Leopoldine (pianist)
   Biographical sketch   209
   Studying with Kalkbrenner   209
   Teaching   209
"Blemish" (philosophy textbook)   12
Blind woman   2, 92
Blöchlinger, Henriette (wife)   20
Blöchlinger, Joseph   20
   Former Catholic partner of Lutheran
      Krause   170
   Has book on Napoleon   14
   Karl visits   61–62
Blöchlinger's Educational Institute   2, 266,
   274, 300
   Food   20
      Coffee with sugar   20
      Greek and Latin study, Greek teacher
         Pulay   274
   Niemetz lives there   136
   Niemetz's mother paid bribe   300
   Teachers   39–40
Blotting paper   252
Blotting sand   201, 223, 252, 254
Blumauer, Aloys, *Travestied Aeneas*   108, 110
Blutwurst, no butter or fat in it   149
Boar, wild (food)   179
Boarding house   151
   Born and B/Paumgarten   30, 33–34, 78, 87
   Referred housekeeper applicants   38, 46
   See also Housekeeper, Search
Boeuf à la mode (beef or ox)   134
Bogner, Ferdinand (flute)   205
   Applauded in Septet   208
   Professor, Conservatorium   205

Böhm, Franz (Burgtheater stagehand)   310
Böhm, Joseph (violin)   309–313
    Biographical sketch   244, 310
    Brings package from Schlesinger   244
    Quarreled with violoncellist Linke   312
    Returned from Paris   244
    Smarter than Holz   311
    Tells of Parisian publication terms
        319–320
Boisterousness (Beethoven), late in evening
    72
Boito, Arrigo, *Mefistofele*   237
Bones, weight added to meat   42
Bonn, electoral orchestra   xxxiv
Bookbinder   24, 66, 84, 90, 134
Books
    Karl buys   58
    "Old German"   58
    Theft   35
Books, conversation (blank).
    See Conversation Books
Bookshops, Vienna. *See individual shops*
    Gerold; Mörschner & Jasper;
    Wallishauser; Wimmer
Bootjack   65
Boots
    Made over   303
    Make larger   303
    New soles (Karl)   13
    Polish   192
    Polished by cook   170
    See also Shoe-cleaning brush
Born, Baroness. *See* Boarding house
Bottles, charge   151
Bourbons: rule again   145–146
Boydell & Brewer   xix, xxiii, xxv
Brachmann, Luise (1777–1822)
    "Best German woman poet" (Beethoven)
        30
    Biographical sketch   30
    Drowned herself   30
Brandenburg, Sieghard   xxiii
Brandstatt, coffeehouse   264
Brandy   188
Bratwurst   285
    Ordered as take-out from restaurant below
        285
Brauneis, Vera   xxiv
Brauneis, Walther   xxi, xxiv
Bread   33
    Rye   6
    Washer-woman   190

Bread money   81
Breitkopf & Härtel   xix, xxiii
Brentano, Antonie (*née* Birkenstock)
    frontispiece, 78, 91, 213, 268
    Biographical sketch   268
    Drawing (Frankfurt am Main, 1820)   268
    Frontispiece   268
    "Immortal Beloved"   268
    See also Frontispiece
Brentano, Clemens and Franz   213
Brentano, Franz (banker)   Frontispiece, 66,
    78, 91
    Financial intermediary   66
    Medium (shipping) for *Missa solemnis*
        78, 91
Breuning, Stephan von   xiv, 161
    Family   161
Brilliant (Ira F.) Beethoven Center   xxiv
Brixi, Franz Xaver
    Family   126
    Masses   126
Broadwood Piano. *See* Piano, Broadwood
Broom   84
Brosche, Günter   xvii
Broth   149, 171
"Brother, great exalted" (Schmid on Johann)
    194
Brotsitzer (bread for a profit)   33
Browne, Johann Georg (Count)   65
    Dedicatee   65
Bruder (brother). *See* Beethoven, Johann van
Brühl (Mödling)   68
Brunsvik, Franz (Count)   246
    Blusterer   319
    Coming to Akademie with family
        (falsified)   319
    Employed violinist Jansa   246, 268
    "Rare and noble"   319
Brunsvik, Josephine (Countess)   82–83, 221
    Candidate for Immortal Beloved   82–83,
        221
Brush, shoe-cleaning   201
Bürde, Samuel Gottlieb   149
    Librettist for Kreutzer's *Taucher*   149
Bürger, Gottfried August   82
    Blümchen Wiederhold (Beethoven's Op.
        52/8)   149
    Iliad   82
    Seufzer and *Gegenliebe*   82
Bürgerspital   20–21. *See also* Holzmann;
    Zmeskall
Burgtheater, opera moving there   249

GENERAL INDEX

Business matters. *See* Banking and financial matters
Butter   149, 156
Buttmann, Philipp Carl (Greek grammar)   11
Byron, George Gordon (Lord)   11

Cabbage
   Blue   280
   Green   308
Cabinet (*Kasten*/*Schrank*)   162–163, 172
   Kitchen (at Augustiners, Landstrasse)   172
Cabinet-maker   162–163, 172
Cake pan, borrowed   65
Calendar, for scheduling
   For 1824   40, 141
   Household   171
Calendar (Jurende)   171
Calligraphy, experiments (Karl)   287
Candle maker   36–37
Candlemas (holiday)   226
Candles   36, 42, 48, 189, 214, 223
   And soap   36, 43, 48
   Beethoven reminds himself to buy   277
      Preisach   36
   Hodie (buy them today)   214
   Kitchen   72, 119, 286
      Burns 2–2½ hours   317
      To help dry washing   317
      Until 11:30 p.m.   317
   Maid asks for   263
   Mayer's shop   286
   Servants did not receive   277
   Small candles   277, 284, 285–286
   Tallow   19, 37, 65
      Harmful   19
   Various kinds   286
   Wax   202
      As opposed to tallow   202
   Wax (Fortuna, grocer)   19, 192
Candy, sugar-drop   20
Capon   202, 235–236, 312
   Karl's *Birne* take-out   312
   At Marktplatz   172
   Reference to Duport (?)   202
   Styrian roasted   59
Capuchin Church, graves of emperors   89
Carafa, Michele, *Gabriela di Vergi*   160
Carbon, Franz Ludwig von (Mödling)   51
   Asks favor re apartment   20–21, 58

Carbon, Franz Ludwig von (*continued*)
   Employed in Vienna (Land Registry)   247–248
   Inquires about Karl   21
   Wants Hubertus's apartment in Bürgerspital   247–248
      Wants Beethoven to intercede for apartment   247–248
   Wife recovers   20
   See also Carbon in the Index of Writers
Card games, every Friday   275
Carl, Karl Friedrich (theater manager)   23
Carnival (Fasching) balls. *See* Balls; Fasching balls
Caroline, Empress (Austria)   14
Carp   5
Carpenter and carpentry shops   38, 48, 162–163, 285
   Chair, price   48
   Fees   48
   Tools   44
Carpet   59
Carriages, fares   110. *See also under individual carriage styles*
Carrying case, from a saddler (?)   254
Castelli, Ignaz Franz
   Biographical sketch   88–89
   Introduces himself   279
   Ludlamshöhle   258–259
   Poem on Emperor Joseph II   88–89
Cauliflower   153
Censorship   45
   Politics   45
   Religion   45
Censorship Office, lets *Melusine* pass   262
Chair, third (?)   85
Chairs, price   48
   Breakable wood, varnished, without cushions   48
Charity   2, 92
   Advent   85
   Overseer of poorhouse   85, 92, 102
Cheese   275
   Limburger and Strachin   201
   Inexpensive   206
   Parmesan   80
   Prices   273
   Undigestible   320
      Johann chemically analyzes it   320
Chemistry, professor, Johann's wish for Karl   263

Cherubini, Luigi
    Aging   32
    Lodoiska Overture   24, 57
    Wasserträger   57
        Maltreated at Josephstadt Theater
            306, 316
        Required winds   297
Chest, maid bared all to Karl   30
Chestnuts   119, 139, 171
Chezy, Wilhelmine von   50–51, 146
    Biographical sketch   50
    Dramatic works unsuccessful   183
    Poor libretto for *Euryanthe*   50–51, 149
    "Atrocious"   186–187
    Review in her defense   68
Chicken
    At Marktplatz   172
    Spring (*Polakel*)   141
Chicken coop   90, 285
    Supports for   285
Chimney sweep   217–219
    Re stove   217
Choral accompaniment
    Berlin   178
    Russia   178
Choral parts
    Engraved/lithographed   310, 312
    Every part copied 10 times   310
    Need total of 40 (10 x 4)   310
Chorales, accompanied   303
Chorus tessitura too high (falsified)   326
Choruses organized by Piringer   303
Christmas Eve dinner, restaurant (?)   151
Church attendance (Beethoven)   xxxi
Church, castigates people   152
Church services
    Beethoven almost never   13
    Karl seldom   13
Churchill, Neville   118
Churgin, Bathia   xxv
Cicero, "O tempora, o mores!"   78
"Citizen without uniform" (Karl)   58
Clarinet. *See* Friedlowsky; Krähmer, Caroline
Clarinets, mechanical   259
Clarinettist, Josephstadt Theater, started
        orchestra revolt against Gläser   297
Classensteuer (graduated income tax)   290
Clementi, Muzio   96
    Conspired with Härtel   97
    Lachner's female cousin plays   126
Clergy, Catholic, noblemen   50
Clothing, flannel, not warm enough   46

Coachman   251
    Johann's   263
Coat
    Coats, theft at University   35
    Dress   5
Cockney (London)   xix
Coffee   5, 6, 20, 105, 111, 171, 180, 210, 288,
        291
    Beans   171, 229
        Johann laughs at Beethoven's counting
            229
        Johann's is measured   229
        Sixty beans   171
    Black for Unger   221
    At Blöchlinger's   20
    Cost   180, 206
    Makes girls too hot   221
    Pound, roasted   171
Coffee brewer's widow   163
Coffee cups   15, 48
Coffee house(s)
    At a coffee house (*Kameel?*)   211–212
    Bill   27, 321
    First Coffee House (Landstrasse)   45, 121
        Halm residence   121
    Landstrasse   263
    New (Josephstadt, Joseph Bäcker)   161
    Stephansplatz (Benko's, Brandstatt)   264
    Tip for private room   291
    Two stories, corner Plankengasse and
            Dorotheergasse   277, 280
Coffee machine, iron   31
Coffee mill   15
Coffee pot (small, broke)   296
Cold, avoiding a   291
Collet, Rosa (countess), née Galler   162–163
    Half dead   162
Collin, Heinrich von, *Regulus* (Burgtheater)
        146
Cologne, to cover toilet odor   12
Componium (instrument)   280
Compositional process (Beethoven)
        294–295
Concerts
    1808 (December 22)   ix
    1813 (December 8)   ix
        Jeckel in violins   198
    1814 (February 27)   x
        Jeckel in violins   198
    1818 (April 12), Hradetzky, horn; Piano
            Concerto No. 5   254
    1823 (October 31)   9

Concerts (*continued*)
    1823 (November 6), Gesellschaft der
        Musikfreunde (GdMf)   39–41, 48
        Beethoven did not attend   39
        Hauschka conducted   39, 48
        Karl attends with guest   39–40
        Not well attended   42
        Program   39, 49
    1823 (November 15), Charity, *Fidelio*
        Overture   67
    1823 (November 21), Schuppanzigh,
        program   67, 70
    1823 (November 22)   24
    1823 (November 28), Schuppanzigh   21, 76
        Program   69
    1823 (November 29)   24
    1823 (December 7), Golden Fleece   107
    1823 (ca. December 11), Josephstadt
        Theater   123
        Beethoven, Symphony No. 2   123
    1823 (December 14), GdMf   49
        Forti, "Good job!"   134
        Horns, wrong notes   134
        Johann and Karl attend   132–134
        Kirchhoffer attended   134
        Schmidl conducted   49
        Symphony No. 2 and *Egmont* Overture
            49, 123
    1823 (December 15 and 17), Moscheles
        24, 122, 135
        Beethoven attends   122
        Broadwood piano   122
        Repeat on 17th   122, 140–141
            Beethoven and Karl attend
                140–141, 143
            Review by Kanne   154–155
    1823 (December 21), Schuppanzigh
        147–148
        Series now on Sundays for
            businessmen   148
    1823 (December 25), St. Marx   103
        Weigl conducted   155
    1823 (December 28), Schuppanzigh   68
    1824 (January 18), Schuppanzigh Quartet
        190, 193
    1824 (January 22), Abendunterhaltung,
        GdMf   205
    1824 (January 25), Kalkbrenner and Dizi
        181, 184, 195, 203
    1824 (January 25), Schuppanzigh Quartet
        193, 197, 211, 213
        Attendees (again)   228

Concerts (*continued*)
    1824 (January 25), Schuppanzigh Quartet
        (*continued*)
        Horn and flute applauded   207
        Never as full as today   207
        Not out until 6:45   207
        Report, general (Karl)   207
        Schindler attended   207
        Septet repeated on March 14   197
        Wolfmayer and wife   208
    1824 (February 1), Schuppanzigh at GdMf,
        quartet program unknown   228
    1824 (February 15), Schuppanzigh   261
        Program noted   261, 263
    1824 (February 29), Schuppanzigh   295
        Karl and Johann attend   291
        Program   291
    1824 (March 4), *Concert spirituel*   296,
        301
        Not many paid tickets   296
    1824 (March 7), Krähmer   311
    1824 (March 14), Schuppanzigh   318, 323
        Program   323–324
        Starting time   323
    1824 (March 16), Court   326–327
        Postponed to March 30   327
        Rehearsal, with Sontag, also postponed
            326–327
        Rossini opera excerpts   327
    1824 (May 7), Akademie, planning and
        preparations   55–56, 68, 85, 98,
            102, 111, 113, 116, 147, 153–154,
            190, 193–194, 203, 221, 256, 262,
            281–282, 295
        8 Contrabasses   304
        8 Violoncelli   304
        Advise GdMf to participate   154
        "Allow others to help" (Schindler)
            194
        Arrangements made   306
        Beethoven's doubts   221
        Beethoven does not use winds from
            Josephstadt Theater   320
        Beethoven encouraged to improvise
            111, 292, 299
        Chorus, Sonnleithner to take care
            of   282
        Circular to string dilettantes   110
        Complimentary tickets?   320
        Composition for Sontag and Unger?
            316
        Concert content developing   261

Concerts (*continued*)
   1824 (May 7), Akademie
      Conductor, Umlauf, selected
         (March 8)   306
      Consecration of the House will please
         261
      Copying preparations   326
      Czar's presence could be good   229
      Czerny to play new concerto   253
         Johann's meddling   253
      Date set early   315
      Division of labor   292
      Double winds required   304
      Early division of labor   194
      Estimated income (high)   104
         Johann predicts   208
      Evening, better time and better profit
         203, 208–209, 316, 318
      Extra pros
         Probably will play without pay   320
         Schuppanzigh to contact   320
      Grosser Redoutensaal?   317–318
      Johann's programming advice
         291–292
      Johann visits Duport   317–318
      Kiesewetter suggests performers early
         155
      Leidesdorf will guarantee profit   262
      Location, indecision (falsified)   321
      Melusine (excerpt) on program   194, 203, 209
      Piringer to get dilettantes   281–282
      Planning sessions   304–307, 309–313
      Poem in praise of concert   262
      Popular demand for Akademie
         (February 29)   291
      Projected profits   262, 278–279
      Repeat performance projected   292
      Repertoire   221
      Ripieno/concertino   304
      Schindler attempts preliminary
         arrangements   62
      Schuppanzigh projects three
         movements from *Missa solemnis*,
         but no piano work   281
      Solo vocal parts with bass underlay
         313
      Sonnleithner
         Advises Schindler to help   154
         Chorus   282
         Predicts great profit   278–279
         Time of year   308

Concerts (*continued*)
   1824 (May 7), Akademie
      String numbers (estimated)   304
      Ticket prices   318
      Umlauf to conduct   306
      Unger and Sontag want Benedictus
         324
      Vocal quartet projected   292
      Will be full (1,000 people); worries
         useless   320
      Winds doubled   310–311
      Wish for April 8   317–318
Concerts, Court, soloists' fees   108
Concerts spirituels   144, 155
   Augustiner Church   194
   Gebauer, Franz Xaver, founder   194
   History   194
   To continue   194
Conducting
   Beethoven's own   x
   Hauschka mechanical   48–49
Conductors, "Weigl, Hauschka, Beethoven"
   155. *See also* Drechsler; Gläser, Franz;
   Hauschka; Schindler; Seyfried;
   Umlauf; Weigl, Joseph
Congress of Vienna   x, 76
Conscriptions-Bögen: Fremden-Tabelle   190
Contrabass and piano accompaniment
   (Berlin)   178
Contrabasses/ists
   8 players for Ninth Symphony   304, 310
   Melzer   193
   Nowak   205
Conversation Books
   Destruction myth   xv–xvi
   History   xii–xviii
   Loss (1822)   xiii–xiv, 26–27, 70
   Publication history   xvi–xviii
   Schindler did not destroy   27
   Theft (1951–1961)   xvi–xvii
   "To hell with stuff … useless"   70
Conversations, Beethoven moves from
   uncomfortable topics   56
Conyngham, Elizabeth (George IV's mistress)
   86
Cook/cooks   122, 141, 149
   Bought *Polakel* (spring chicken)   141
   Cooked chicken and rabbit   141
   Eats very little   152
   From fourth floor   65
   Home-cooked better than restaurant   135
   "I'm getting out of here."   112

Cook/cooks (*continued*)
    Male   183
    New   292
    Polishing boots   170
    Search   70, 102
    Trial, portion salty   81
    Uses little/no fat or butter   156
    Worked for Wetzlar and Lichnowsky
        56–57, 62, 68, 78
    See also Housekeeper; Maid
Cook (Johann's)   209
    Has a budget   229
    Pays extra for food from Krems   229
    Salary   209
    Soup too often   229
    To boil a ham   229
Cookbook
    Housekeeper needs   1
    Viennese (Ballauf)   216
Cooking
    And household economy   201
    Maid helped   47
    See also Holzmann
Cooper, Barry   xxv
Copying (Beethoven's own)   xx
    Advertisements accurate   46, 270–271
Copying work   165, 190–192
    8 violoncelli, 8 contrabasses   304
    10 copyists on March 9   310
    In Beethoven's apartment   304
    Complaints   66–67
    Consecration "before it ever gets
        published"   266
    Costs, projected   194
    Diabelli to pay for copying?   194
    Done at Beethoven's apartment (?)   106
    Every choral part 10 times   310
    Fidelio score (to have at home)   224
    Gebauer, Karl recommends   312
    Gläser to copy the Ninth, replacing
        deceased W. Schlemmer   308
    "How many; working where?"   283
    Johann to organize   295
    Lithographed/engraved choir parts   310, 312
    Maschek, progress report (March 13)   322
    Missa solemnis (Schlemmer), two
        movements copied   261
    Overture and Symphony (March 6)   304
    Rampl for score of Ninth Symphony?   311
    Ruins of Athens score (February 24)   224
    Sample   106

Copying work (*continued*)
    Schindler wants string parts soon
        (March 16)   326
    Security measures   5, 106
    Solo/ripieno parts in winds   304, 310
    Solo vocal parts in Ninth Symphony
        190, 291
    Solo vocal parts with bass line   307, 313
    Speed   106
    Symphony No. 9   203
        Gläser to copy   266, 311
        Solo singers' parts   190
    See also Missa solemnis in the Index of
        Compositions
    See also Paper, Music; *and Fidelio* in the
        Index of Compositions
Copyist C (Gebauer). *See* Gebauer, Benjamin
Copyist E (Wunderl). *See* Wunderl
Copyists
    Gebauer, Benjamin   312
    Gläser   266
    Pfeiffer, Franz   223
    Schlemmer, Wenzel, replacement
        Can copy all day long   191–192
        Employed by Josepha Schlemmer
            190–192
        Method   192
        Writes entries   192
    Schmutzer, Niklaus   215
        Copies beautifully   215
    Schwarz, Matthias (Haslinger's copyist)
        129
    See also Gläser, Peter; Rampl; Schlemmer,
        Josepha; Schlemmer, Wenzel;
        Wunderl
Copyright
    Ethics   102
    International   10, 97
Correspondence, lost (Fall, 1822)   26–27
    "To hell with stuff … useless"   70
Court cellar   246
Court hiring practices   246
Court, Imperial, complimentary tickets   315
Court Opera (Italian), to close down   160
Crackers   153
Cramer, John Baptist   95, 169
    Heard Beethoven play   169
Cramolini, Ludwig (tenor), role in *Melusine*
    237
Cream   201, 216
    In salad   227
Crocodile   302–303

Cross (church), sarcasm   151
Cuirassiers, defined   296
Cupboard
    Beethoven slammed door   227
    Everything too loose   227
Cures, sympathetic (hypnosis)   227
Curfman, Scott   xxv
Currency
    Devaluation   xi
    General   xxx
    See also Banking and financial matters; Exchange
Curtains, gray   24
Cushions   48
Customs, harps from England   37, 41
Czermack, Mathias (wine dealer)   150
Czerny, Carl   25, 109
    Arrangement of Beethoven's Romance, Op. 50   266
    Biographical sketch   3
    Concerto No. 5
        Declines to play on May 23   253–254, 281
        Early performances   254
    Concerts, house, largely Beethoven's works   258
    Diabelli Variations, does not understand fully   230
        Private performance (February 1, 1824)   230, 232
    Home recital (ca. February 16)   265–266
    Johann attended recital   253
    Johann told him Beethoven was writing a concerto   253
    Karl and Johann attend together (February 29 or March 1?)   290
    Lesson schedule   265–266
    New noble student   265
    Plays (Sonata, Op. 13?) all in tempo   297
    Schindler often attends recitals   258
    Sees new Streicher pianos   231
    Sunday morning recital (February 8, 1824)   238–239, 240
        Tired him out   239–240
    Visited by Lichnowsky   236
    Wants to organize Mass in C in German   212
    Wants to borrow Schulz translation   212
    Will play Opp. 109, 110, 111; also *Hammerklavier*, Op. 100 (February 8, 1824)   232

Czerny, Joseph   109

Daily schedule. *See* Routine, daily
Dancing at restaurant (*Sklavin*)   293
Davies, Dr. Peter J.   ix
Deafness (Beethoven)   116–118, 137, 210
    Did not hear maid   236
    History   ix–xii
    Misunderstanding with Karl   210
    Public does not mention   113, 116
    Schmidt balm, probably ineffective   118
    Sympathetic cures   227
    See also Hearing
DeBolt, David   xxv
December 15 (Beethoven's birthday?)   137–138
Decorations/awards   76
Degen, Joseph Vincenz (printer), map (1809)   xxix
Del Rio, Giannatasio. *See* Giannatasio del Rio
Dematteis, Phil   xxv
Denk, Erich   xxiii
Deym, Joseph (Count)   82–83
Diabelli, Anton   205
    Copying *Missa solemnis* and Symphony   182
    "Will pay for copying" (Johann)   194
Diarrhea   148
Dietary restrictions   27
Dietrichstein, Moritz (Count of Music)   87, 245–246
    Administrator in charge of Akademie   317–318
    Encouraged both Schuppanzigh and Jansa for Hofkapelle   272
    Schuppanzigh inquires concerning position   198
    Supposed to have supported Schuppanzigh   268
    Swedish diploma   304
    Violin vacancy   70
Dilettantes
    "Deprive professionals of employment" (Schuppanzigh)   271
    String recruiting circular (Haslinger), signed by Beethoven   310
DiMattia, Raymond   xxv
Dinner, Christmas Eve, in restaurant   151
Dinner, midday   300
    December 24, nothing left over   152
    February 28, Soup, beef, pastry, wine   288
        Cost   288

Dinner, midday (*continued*)
    Roast loin of beef, vegetable soup, horseradish soup, blue cabbage 280
Dinner, Sontag and Unger (March 14) 322–326
    Aftermath 326–327
    Confession before 322–325
    Food on hand and bought 323
    Schindler's and Unger's accounts 323
    Uncomfortable in circumstances 322–323
Dinner, spill (February 8) 240
Dinner service (porcelain) 29, 52
    Price for 6 persons 29
Diploma, Swedish Akademie 246–247
Dirzka, Ignaz (bass singer, choral director) 137
"Distrustful," Beethoven about Schindler (falsified) 122
Division (mathematics; Karl) 303
Dizi, François Joseph (harp) 181, 184, 203
    Concert, *Kleiner Redoutensaal* 166
    Departs (January 31, 1824) 199, 215
    Enthused over Beethoven's works 203
    "Not extraordinary" 204
    Sounds like a violin 184
    See also Kalkbrenner
Doberer, Maria xxiv
Dogs, for rat control; not needed 114
Domestic affairs, rob Beethoven of time 189
Doors (Karl's?), locksmith 210
Dornbach, village 161–163
Doussin-Doubreuil, J.L., *Ursache … Verschleimung*, ed. Schlegel 179
Dozes off (Beethoven) 43
Dragonetti, Domenico 95
    London Philharmonic pay dispute 95
    Refused to play Beethoven Ninth 95
Drangeld (advanced money) 211
Drawing 134
Drechsler, Joseph (Josephstadt Theater) 104, 159
    Biographical sketch 316
    Hensler cursed him 267
    "Most miserable conductor" (Schindler) 199
    Wrong tempi at Josephstadt Theater 316
Dressmaker 34–35, 84
Drewer, Franz (musician)
    Bequest to *Tonkünstler-Societät* 188
    Son of Anna Maria Ries 188

Drion, Sophie. *See* Trion
Drowsiness (Beethoven) 43
Du-friends. *See* Hauschka; Kanne
Ducks, wild 60, 179. *See also Ente*
Due Soggetti (*Zwei Principe?*) 294–295, 297
Dufay, Guillaume (1397–1474) 107
Duggan, John xxv
Dumpling forms 80
Dumplings 153
Duncker, Johann Friedrich Leopold 76
    Biographical sketch 76
    Leonore Prohaska 76
    Sends greetings 75
Duport, Louis Antoine (dancer, administrator) 55, 67, 69, 85, 98, 105, 133, 135, 149, 160, 195, 220–221, 262
    Agrees to all for opera 247
    "An ass" (Schuppanzigh) 214
    As "capon" 202
    Birthday letter to Beethoven (December 13) 133
    Can accommodate Beethoven's schedule 318
    Concert, evening: ask for 209
    Details for Akademie 316
    Diligent in his duties 88
    Flattery concerning Beethoven 147
    Hildebrand for concertmaster 249
    "Idiot" (opinion of someone) 206
    Invites Beethoven and Karl to Kärntnertor Theater 86
    Johann visits (March 9) 317–318
    Letter to Beethoven (ca. December 24, 1823) 163
    Letter to (ca. January 25) 206, 208
    Lichnowsky writes 203
    Melusine
        Agreement with Grillparzer concerning *Melusine* 150
        Decision about 258
        Forti advocates *Melusine* 147
        Having *Melusine* translated into French 250
        Negotiations with Johann concerning *Melusine* 165
        Would pay 12,000 for *Melusine* 105
        "Wrote concerning *Melusine*" 202–203
    Provides Kärntnertor Theater and *Grosser Redoutensaal* 194
    Satisfied with Schindler's audition 134
    Says little 166
    Schuppanzigh applies to him 271

Duport, Louis Antoine (*continued*)
    Schuppanzigh asks Beethoven to intercede 282
    To supply tickets 315
    Would give Beethoven complimentary tickets 123

Eagle (Schindler) 305
Ear trumpets ix, 95. *See also* Hearing; Mälzel
Easter (Sunday, April 18) 290
Echsner, Herr von 274–275
Economic matters. *See* Banking and financial matters
Educated people: mathematics, philosophy, psychology 119
Education (Beethoven's), learned wind instrument (horn) 287
Eel 72
Eggs
    Bad smell 70
    "Egg dish in evening" (Hufeland) 209
    Supper 119
Ehlers, Wilhelm (stage director, Berlin) 164, 166
    "Hot head" 166
    Sang in *Die gute Nachricht* 164
Eigner/Aigner, Magdalena (housekeeper) 293–294
    Dates 294
    Goldworker's widow 293–294
    Johann Georg (husband) 294–295
Eimer (measure of wine) 255
Eisinger, Josef 89
Elbe River 188
Elberfeld 187
Elssler family 79
    Fanny (ballet) 79
    Haydn connection 79
    Joseph (oboe) 79
    Kaunitz connection 79
England
    Beethoven's reputation 87, 93
    Monetary values 96
    Potential earnings 105
    Potential tour 126
    Visit, projected (Fall, 1824; falsified) 319
    See also London
English language 65
English Theater (Vienna) 55
Ente, zum wilden (Wild Duck) 179
Erard, Sebastian (piano maker, Paris) 158

Erard piano 41
Erdberg (suburb) 183
    Antonie Brentano 268
    Opposite side of City from Wieden 268
    "Unhappy associations" (Schindler) 268
Erdödy, Anna Maria (Countess) xii
Erlauer wine. *See* Wine, Erlauer
Esau and Jacob (Bible story) 287
Esser, Franz, *System of Logic* 187
Esterházy, Nikolaus II (Prince)
    Degenerate 79–80
    Missa solemnis, did not subscribe 147
Esterházy, Paul Anton (Prince), ambassador 86
"Everyone gets his reward" (Schindler on Salieri) 200
Exchange (monetary) 40–41, 241. *See also* Currency
Exner, Carl (Herr von) 274–275
Exner, Franz (musician) 275
Eybler, Joseph 57
Eye doctor, last winter 235
Eyeglasses (Beethoven's) 48, 196, 210. *See also* Light
Eyesight 319
    "Cures and coins" cannot help 320
    Doctor 320
    "Don't rub eyes" 223
    Eye condition 235
    Inflammation 212
    Needs light 149
    Problems 320
    See also Light, For composing

Falstaff, Mylord. *See under* Schuppanzigh
Fasching balls 273
    Court events in *Redoutensäle* 273
    Friday, February 27 290
    Lasted 8 hours 273
Fasching, end of 285
Fassl, Zum grünen (Kohlmarkt) 133, 179, 253, 270, 291. *See also* Spöttl
Fat (food) 149, 156
"Fat, men that are" (Shakespeare) 72
Feder, Johann Georg
    Logik 42
    Metaphysik 42
    Psychologie 28, 31, 43
Fee und der Ritter, Die (Italian pastiche ballet) 1
Feldtrompeter, with *Consecration* Overture (February 15) 261

Feldtrompeter, Der (Hensler)   253
Felsburg (co-author of *Ludlamshöhle* Petition)   286
Ferdinand III (Tuscany)   132
Financial matters. *See* Banking and financial matters
Fire, danger of   37
Firecrackers in university class   124
Firewood. *See* Wood, fire
Firmian, Leopold Maximilian (Archbishop)   144
    Gänsbacher, forced hiring at St. Stephan   239, 243–244
    Weigl, did not want   196–197, 199
Fischer, Mathias   159
Fish   5, 19, 91
    Baked [fried?]   171
    Boiled   287
    Fridays   91
    Hearing   19
    Piece in lentils   287
    Whole into six pieces   287
    With lemon   171
    See also Carp; Pike
Fish-seller (woman)   196–197
Flannel   46, 65
Flatiron   124. *See also* Iron
Fleck, *7 Festchoräle*   303
Flegeljahren (awkward age), Karl   132
Flour, baking and fine   115, 196, 319
    Semolina   319
Flutist, Bogner   205
Food, bitter like medicine   116
"Fool" (Kalkbrenner)   181
Foot warmers   43, 302
Förster, Emanuel Aloys   126
    Anleitung zum Generalbass   126
    Quintet arrangement of Beethoven symphony   126
Forti, Anton (bass/baritone)   55, 185, 214, 237, 309
    Advocated with Duport for *Melusine*   147
    "Better at comic roles" (Karl)   134
    Biographical sketch   134
    Preisach better for Akademie   316
    Rossini aria (?)   132, 134
    Sarcastic to horns   134
    To sing in Akademie   282
    Violist, Theater an der Wien, when young   134
    Wants role in *Melusine*   249
Fortuna (grocery shop)   192

France, Bourbon rule restored   145–146
Frank, Frau (housekeeper applicant)   102
    Semi-literate   102
Frankfurt am Main   66
    Cäcilienverein   78, 91
        Receives *Missa solemnis*   78, 91
    Postal coach   78
    Postal day and route   78
    See also Brentano, Franz
Frankfurt-Heddernheim   175
    Birthplace of Franziska Sontag   175
Franz I (Emperor)   xi, xxx, 13, 218
    Backlog of documents   298
    Barbaja's lease   88, 105
    Court subsidy for concerts   132
    Grillparzer's *König Ottokar*, decision   199
    Marie Louise, daughter   150
        Married to Napoleon   150
    "Not at fault, instead his servants"   122
    On Stephansdom position   271
    Portrait same as presence   139
    In Vienna (December, 1823)   133
    Weigl
        Reportedly told that he had the Stephansdom job   256
        To Weigl: "Don't you have enough?"   256
    Wants Archduke Rainer to help   298
Franz Josef, future emperor   298
Franz Karl, Archduke, going to Italy as viceroy   298
"Fratello" (brother Johann)   230
Fraud in theater lease   87–88
Freethinker   68
French language
    Karl describes his abilities   282
    Schindler uses   239
French names (mustard)   303
French teacher. *See* Pleugmackers
Freyung, shops   256
Friedlowsky, Joseph (clarinet)   97, 193
    Biographical sketch   262
    "Extraordinarily good" (Karl)   263
    Mozart Clarinet Quintet   261, 263
    Schubert composed for him   262
Friedrich Wilhelm III (Prussia)
    Respect for artists   182
Friedrichs d'or   241
    Conversion rate   241
Fries, Johann Moritz (Protestant banker), wine estates (Vöslau)   4
Fritatten   320

Frogs (boiled)   171
Fröhlich, Johann Baptist (pastor, Mödling)   59
Fuchs, Benedict (horn)   260
Fuchs, Ingrid   xxiii
Fuchs, Johann Nepomuk (Esterházy orchestra)   260
Fuchs, Peter (violin)   260
Führer, Rudolf   xxiv
Funke, L.P., psychology text (Helmstedt)   119

Galitzin, Nicolas Borisovich (Prince)
    Coming to Vienna with Czar (Lent)   229
    Commissions three Quartets   40–41
    Missa solemnis, St. Petersburg venue   204
    Suggests marketing *Missa solemnis*   114
    See also Gallizinberg
Gallizinberg   xxv
Gänsbacher, Johann Baptist   176
    Albrechtsberger's best student   151
    "Without effect or passion"   151
    Mass for Augustiners   144
    Masses and Requiem   151
    New St. Stephan Kapellmeister   144, 196–197, 199, 256
    Tyrol volunteer, political advantage   144
    Wins St. Stephan job over Weigl   214–215, 239, 243–244
"Garbage, reeking, rotting" (Sachs)   229
Garden, for sale   265
Garden, kitchen (lot) for sale   265
Gärtner, Carl von (guitarist from Kassel)   262
    Attended concert (February 15)   261
    Knows Lichnowsky   262
Gaudeamus igitur   193
Gebauer, Benjamin (Copyist C)   312
    Beethoven dislikes his work   312
    "Best and most dependable" (Karl)   312
    Biographical sketch   312
    Copied Eroica Symphony   312
    Oboist and copyist, Theater an der Wien   312
Gebauer, Franz Xaver
    Concerts spirituels   155
    Greatly missed   155
Geissler, Johann, *Concerts spirituels*   194
Gelinek, Joseph (Abbé)   277
    Compositional machine   279–280
    Derisive names   280
Geography (Blöchlinger's Institute)   300

George, William   xxiv
George IV (England)   86
    "Shithead"   86
    Singing duets with Rossini   231
German language
    Beethoven's use   171
    High different from common   171
    Karl comments on gender   100
    Maids' different dialect   171
    Schindler translated   171
    Spoken vs. written   171
German opera   33
    Versus Italian opera   33
Gerold's bookshop   36, 77
Gersthof (near Währing), potatoes   265
Gesellschaft der Freunde der Wiener Oboe   xxiv
Gesellschaft der Musikfreunde   39, 134, 160, 174, 194, 202, 242
    Abendunterhaltung schedule   205–206
    Amateur instrumentalists   292
    Concert (March 14), Mozart: Symphony (Prague), *Davidde penitente*   318
    Eroica Symphony copy in Archiv   312
    Good for Beethoven to be seen there   318
    Library, Haslinger's collection of Beethoven's works   129
    Participation in Akademie   247
    Potentially in Akademie   154
    Scaffolding for Akademie   194
    Sieg des Kreuzes, advance for   194
    To copy for Beethoven   165
Giannatasio del Rio, Cajetan   x, 13
    Wishes Beethoven to visit   61
Giannatasio del Rio, Franziska (Fanny)   x, xi, xiii
Giannatasio del Rio's Institute   248
Gierlichs, Grazyna   xxv
Giuliani, Mauro   128
Gläser, Franz (composer/conductor)   103, 144–145
    Arsenius der Weiberfeind (comic opera)   144–145, 171
    Based on Weber's *Euryanthe*   171
    Counterpart to *Arsenia, Man-Hater*   144–145
    Conceited   199
    Conductor, Josephstadt Theater   98
    Karl asks opinion of his conducting   196
    Better than Drechsler   199
    Politics against Schindler   103–104

Gläser, Franz (*continued*)
   Revolt, Josephstadt Theater 297
   Took pains with *Consecration* Overture
     (February 14–15) 253
Gläser, Peter (copyist, Josephstadt)
   Phlegmatic 196
   Principal copyist, Ninth Symphony 266,
     308
Glass maker 252
Glasses 48
Gleich, Joseph Alois 180
   Biographical sketch 180
   Elfen-Insel 180
   Poetry derided 180
   Theatrical prices 180
Glöggl
   Amateur string player 260
   Related to large musical family 260
   Shoemaker 260
   Visit 260
Glöggl, Franz Xaver (Domkapellmeister,
   Linz) 260
   Beethoven's *Equale* 260
Gloves, too small for Johann 290
   Given to Karl 290
Gned, Georg (Kärntnertor Theater),
   Wasserträger at Josephstadt Theater
   306
Gneiselo, Juliane (housekeeper applicant)
   272–273
   Does not use lard 273
   From Breitenfeld 272–273
   Good cook 272
Gneixendorf (near Krems) 83
   Amount received from estate 289
   Food from Krems 229
   "Gut, Söhnchen, Gut" (wordplay) 99
   Johann back from 85
   Johann's trip (ca. early 1824) 263
   See also Beethoven, Johann van
Godesberg (near Bonn) 62
Godt, Irving xxi
Goethe, Johann Wolfgang von
   And Bettina Brentano 213
   See also Egmont in the Index of
     Compositions
Golden Fleece (Festival) 107–109, 133
   Banquet and concert 107–108
   L'homme armé 107
   Order 107
   Program 107–108
"Gossip" (Schindler) 213, 239

Gottdank, Joseph (singer, stage director,
   Kärntnertor Theater administrator)
   55, 137, 214, 271
Gottschedt, Anna (housekeeper applicant)
   162–163
   Address 162
   Attributes (Piano, Graz) 162
   Karl prefers her 163
Government (Austria) 76
Goya, portrait of Prince Kaunitz 79–80
Graf, Conrad 173, 299
   Biographical sketch 299
   Shop near Paulanerkirche 299
   To repair Broadwood 299
Gräffer's bookshop 19
Grapes 208
Grassl, Magdalena (wife of J.C. Bernard).
   See Bernard
Graz
   Musikverein 162–163
   Theater burned 166
Greek language
   Derivations (Karl) 293
   Pronunciation 10–11
   Use 82
Greek teacher 8, 10, 44–45, 274, 288
   Karl wants place in class 288
   See also Pulay; Stein
Griesinger, Georg August
   Biographical sketch 113
   No Saxon subscription for *Missa solemnis*
     113
Grillparzer, Franz 25, 55, 67, 146, 148,
   211–212, 282
   Agreement, Duport, re *Melusine* 150
   Beethoven
     Visits (February) 225, 236–237
     Will visit (February) 212, 248
   Changes, can make 203
   Drahomira, libretto for Beethoven 238
   Finance Ministry, position, duties 212, 236
   Healthy again (January 30) 224
   Judith (potential subject) 238
   Kärntnertor Theater agrees for opera
     247–248
   König Ottokar 199, 212, 236–237, 239
     To Berlin 238
   Ludlamshöhle 259
   Melusine (unset by Beethoven) 146,
     148–149, 160, 165, 174, 185, 187,
     198–199, 208–209, 220
     Another copy of *Melusine* 257

Grillparzer, Franz (*continued*)
   Melusine (*continued*)
      Coming to pick up libretto   292
      Summary of plot   198–199
      Poem for Beethoven's *Akademie*   262
      Rudolph (Archduke)   238
      Sieg des Kreuzes, opinion of   237–238
      Sonnleithner, Leopold, cousin   278
      Wallishauser (his publisher)   146, 237
      See also Grillparzer in the Index of Writers
Grinzing, potential summer residence   288
Grocery shop (*Fortuna*)   192
Grocery shopping   6, 34, 60
Gröger, Constanze   xxiv
Gröger, Thomas   xxi, xxiv
Gross, Friedrich (violoncello)   205
Grosser Redoutensaal. *See* Redoutensaal, Grosser
Gruber, Reinhard H. (Stephansdom archivist)   xxiv, 302
Gruel   190
Grünbaum, Theresia   25, 108, 309
   Biographical sketch   306
   "German Catalani"   306
   "Public doesn't like her" (Karl)   313
   Schöpfung performance   306
   Sontag is more beloved   308
   Worn out voice   306
Grünne, Countess (court lady to Henriette, wife of Carl)   259
Gugelhupf   323
Guitar   25–26, 117, 246, 262
   Schulz   117
Gumpoldskirchner wine. *See* Wine, Gumpoldskirchner
Güntersberg, C., *Der fertige Orgelspieler*   222–223, 295, 303
Gyrowetz, Adalbert, *Ludlamshöhle*   259

Haass (book dealer, Tuchlauben)   212
Haidvogel, J. (restaurant, Schlossergasse)   258–259
Hair, Beethoven's, haircut   76
Hair, dyed black
   Barbara Holzmann   149
   Brother Johann   149
Haitzinger, Anton (tenor)   24–25, 135, 185, 195, 292
   For Akademie   316
   Jäger is better   316
   To sing in Akademie?   282
Halm, Anton (composer)   121

Halm, (Maria) Theresia (wife)   121
   Address and directions   121
   Biographical sketch   121
   From Trier   121
   Invites Beethoven to visit them   121
Ham
   Beethoven sends to Johann's cook   229
   Boiled too long at Johann's   244
   Not to be eaten raw; needs to be boiled   219
   Returned, boiled   229
Hand towel   183
Handel, George Frideric
   Alexander's Feast, "Wake them"   135
   Keyboard works, Lachner's female cousin plays   126
Handkerchiefs, two   73, 302
   Blue one in breast pocket   73
Handwriting (Beethoven)   xx, 41
   As souvenir   41
Hardie, Nita (Heard)   xxv
Harpist, Dizi   184, 204
Harps, four (from England)   37, 41
   Stumpff, Ries, customs   37, 41
Harrach Palace, Staudenheim   169
Harrach shops, on the Freyung   256–257
Haslinger, Tobias   1, 129, 163, 205, 217, 238, 289–290, 309, 311–312
   Choral parts could be lithographed for less   310
   Circular to string dilettantes   310
   Hand copied works by Beethoven   129
   Personal music library   129
   Sends greetings   289–290
   Waltzes   312
   See also Haslinger in the Index of Writers
Hats   195
   Beethoven's bad hat, comments on   263
   Cost in Landstrasse   263
   Hat tyrant   195, 258
   Johann comments   195
   Johann orders Beethoven to buy   263
   Poor condition   195
   Schindler advises somewhat   267
   Schindler asks for Beethoven's old one as souvenir   267
   Shopping with Schindler   195
   Theft at University   35, 81
Hauffen, Joseph (dressmaker)   34–35
Hauschka, Vincenz (violoncellist, official)   155
   Biographical sketch   49
   Conducting mechanical   39, 48–49

GENERAL INDEX

Hauschka, Vincenz (*continued*)
   Du-friend 155
   Ludlamshöhle 259
Haushälterin, Wiener (method book) 305
Hausmannskost (home cooking) 128
Hawkers, street 256–257
   Wit and coarseness 256
Haydn, Joseph
   Creation/Schöpfung 64
   Elssler (oboe) 79
   Financial success 176
   Hohenadel, Katharina (student) 109
   "Opinion" of Beethoven's Hammerklavier Sonata 244
   Quartet in A, Op. 55/1 190
   Quartet in B-flat, Op. 55/3 ("Tost") 240
   Quartet in C 207
   Quartet in C, Op. 74/1, Finale repeated 291
   Quartet in D minor, Op. 76/2 261
   Quartet in G, Op. 74/3 160
   Quartets 175
   Schöpfung 306
   Seven Last Words (oratorio version) 296
   String quartets played for Salieri 64
   Symphony No. 60's influence on 3rd movement of Beethoven's Ninth Symphony 244
   Symphony No. 103 296
   Trumpet Concerto 157
Health (Beethoven), general
   Avoiding a cold 291
   See also Eyesight; Light; Wine
Hearing 137
   Beethoven hears Glöggl 260
   Did not hear maid 236
   Fish 19
   "Good enough to conduct *Missa solemnis*" (Schindler) 155
   Misunderstanding with Karl 210
   See also Deafness; Ear trumpets; Mälzel
Hearing balm (Schmidt) 113, 117–118
   Ineffective 118
Heating (*Heitzung*) with warmed air 77, 183–184
Heddernheim (Frankfurt), birthplace of Franziska Sontag 175
Heft 1 (subject) xii
Heft 95, *Beethoven im Gespräch* (subject) xvii
Heiligenstadt Testament ix
Heindl, Gertraud xix

Held, Johann, economic councilor 190
   Johann, younger (War Office) 190
   Rosalia (wife) 190
Hell, Helmut xxiii
Hemorrhoids (Schindler) 294, 299
Hen
   Coop 90
   From restaurant in house (March 14) 323
   Poularde, Birne 312
Henikstein, Joseph von (banker, amateur singer), Galitzin's banking contact 40
Henning, Carl Wilhelm 21–23, 69–70, 76–77, 111–114, 164
   Acquired *Consecration of the House* 164
   Biographical sketch 21
   Coat/trousers as salary 173
   Concertmaster, Berlin 21
   No pay when traveling 173
   Obtains Beethoven's music 113, 164
   Quartet played 21, 76–77
   Schuppanzigh played his Quartet 76–77, 173
   Schuppanzigh will see (December 5) 100
   Self-introduction (again!) 76
   Suggests *Faust* 77
Hensler, Carl Friedrich (Josephstadt Theater) 157, 159
   Asks for score of *Ruins of Athens* 224
   Cursed Drechsler 267
   Daughter Josepha (Scheidlin) 104
   Feldtrompeter 103–104, 253
      With *Consecration* Overture 103–104, 253
   Intrigues against 157, 159, 169
   Schindler's evaluation of him 104
   Sent *Consecration* Overture to Pressburg (February 16) 266
   Treatment of painter, machinist, pantomimists, etc. 267
   Treats theater personnel badly 267
   Various performances 266
   Wants to use Overture to *Ruins of Athens* 224
Herbeck, Johann 160
Herbeck, Joseph Franz (Doctor), treated Amalie Waldmann; Johann present 264
Herberstein, Joseph (Treasury), letter to brother Carl 2
Herbst, Michael (hornist) 193, 205
   Applauded in Septet 208
   Professor, Conservatorium 205
   Theater an der Wien 205

Herforth, Harry xxv
Hero, subject for poet 40
Heroes, Greek 4
Herre, Grita xvii–xviii, xxxiii, 17
Herring salad 227
Herrweis, Frau 167
Hesperus (Stuttgart), asks Schindler for articles 307
Heterosexuals, selected. *See* Beethoven, Johann; Beethoven, Karl; Schlemmer, Wenzel
Heubner, bookshop (Bauernmarkt) 179
Hieronymus-Jerôme 272
Hietzing
    Lichnowsky summer residence (1823) 284
    Pleugmackers, language teacher 332
Hildebrand, Johann (assistant concertmaster) 71–72
    Conducts Moscheles concert 95, 140
    Wanted to be concertmaster for Beethoven's Akademie 249
Hirsch, Carl Friedrich (student) xii
Hirschmann, Franziska (housekeeper applicant) 272
    Has children, not living with her 272
    Semi-literate 272
    Surgeon's widow (Leopoldstadt) 272
    Wood, has carried 272
History (Blöchlinger's Institute), Köferle 300
Hodie (Beethoven's use for "heute") 214
Hofkapelle 108–109, 268, 278–279
    Jansa 268
    Political machinations 272
    Schuppanzigh lost to Jansa 250
Hofmann & Goldstein (Kirchhoffer's employers) 37
Hohenadel/Hochenadel, Katharina (Haydn student) 109
Holiday weekend 6
Holtei, Carl von (poet, Berlin) 22, 77
Holz, Karl (violinist) 9, 311, 313
    Biographical sketch 311
    Cross of Wood (wordplay) 197, 311
    Introduced by Schuppanzigh 311
    Schuppanzigh's second violin 197
Holzmann, Barbara (1755–1831, housekeeper) xx, 1–2, 13, 28, 58, 75, 78, 92, 253, 289, 308
    Amends with wine 78

Holzmann, Barbara (*continued*)
    "Better than previous interim housekeepers" (Schindler) 224
    Biographical sketch, brief 235
    Comments on room, kitchen temperatures 287
    Cooks poorly 224
    Did everything herself 78
    Dyed her hair black 148–149
    Granddaughter 235
    Had been dismissed or resigned (end of September 1823) 226
    Indulged Beethoven too much 75
    Johann encountered her 148–149
    Karl against re-hiring her 225–226, 235
    Laughs with maid (February 16) 264
    Meets Nannette Bauer 124
    Mends underpants 264
    Needs a helper 226, 235
    Not present for March 14 dinner 322–323, 325–326
    Predicts short term of employment 124
    Projected return (ca. February 1, 1824) 224
    Returns (by ca. March 4, 1824) 302, 306
    Salary 224
    Schnitzel already spoiled 308
    Serves dinner 287
    Starts February 3, 1824 231–232, 235
        Happy to be employed again 232, 235
    Starts March 5, 1824 235
    "Too old" (Karl) 235
    "Would like to come back" (Johann, January 25) 209
Home cooking (*Hausmannskost*) 128
    "Home-cooked better than restaurant meals" 135
Homer (poet)
    Iliad
        Trans. G.A. Bürger 82
        Translation method 82
    Odyssey 11
"Homer, The People's" (Müller) 149
Homme armé, l' 107
Homosexuality 97, 146
    Allusions (potential), Schindler 285
    Beethoven not homosexual 285
    See also under Jenger; Rudolph; Schindler
Honors, foreign, permission 29
Hope, Thomas (Sir) 153
    Anastasius (novel, humorous) 153
Hopfner, Rudolf xxiv

Hopp, Friedrich Ernst (actor, Josephstadt Theater) 153, 159
Horn
  Beethoven studied with Simrock 287
  Herbst 205
  Hradetzky 254, 316
  Keyed 157
  Low xi
  Middle (Herbst) 205
Horn quartet 112
Hornists 29. *See also* Bellonci; Herbst; Hradetzky; Lewy
Horns, Kärntnertor Theater 134
  Missed notes in *Figaro* 134
  Sarcasm from Forti 134
Horns, mechanical 259
Horseradish 280
Horses, Johann's 263
Höslinger, Clemens xxiii
House hunting
  Building a house 267–268
  High costs 267–268
House numbers (Vienna) xxviii
Household Guide (*verständiger Hausvater*) 201
Housekeeper/housekeepers 60, 75, 77–78, 182, 191, 223, 296, 313
  Advertisement (Beethoven's) 64
  Alarmed maid with gossip 225
  Applicants 31, 47, 306
    Arrogant "baroness" (Karl) 270
    Bohemian, cannot understand 258
    Can cook 141
    Can read and write 100, 102, 127
    December 29 161, 166–168
      Attributes 161
      Bored 166
      Compared 163
      Mayer 166–167
      "Too aristocratic" 163
    Eigner 293
      Washing 293
    From Leopoldstadt 255
    From Silesia 141
    From Vöcklabruck 37
    Gneisel, Juliane 272–273
    "Has brains" 255
    Hirschmann, Franziska 272
    January 19, Sophie Trion (can cook) 190
    Karl sent one away 170
    Kummer, Katharine 284, 287

Housekeeper/housekeepers (*continued*)
  Applicants (*continued*)
    Lehmann 266, 269–270
      Schindler advises for cooking 266, 269–270
      To start ca. March 4(?) 270
    None of them tall 120
    Semi-literate 114
    Served in doctor's house 141
    Wants to use Karl's room during the day 255
  Beethoven reprimands 40
  Brief, 4 days, November, 1823 46–47
    Honest, but careless with money 46–47
  Cook, temporary (ca. December 16–30) 167–168
    Collects pay 168
  Cooking samples 91
  Ca. February 15: "Beast, send her away" 256
  Financial manipulation 64
  French-speaking applicant 182, 196
    Kitchen good, sewing not 182
    Music, knows a little about 196
    Salary: wants 25 fl. 182
  Gossip (December 27) 158
  Gossips about venison given away 226–227
  Housekeeping at Lichnowsky's 158
  "I'm getting out of here" 112
  Maid, new (ca. January 13/14) 198, 230
  Maid, former, writes letters to Beethoven 183
  Morality, perception 84
  Needs cookbook 1
  Needs kitchen knife 49
  Needs to do *more* 153
  New (January 5) 175–176
    More arrogant than previous 175
    Pension sheet 175
  New (ca. March 9) 308
  New (March 12–14) 323, 325–326
    Enthusiastic 320
    Literate 323
    Lugeck 326
    Not Holzmann 322–323
    Not much food (March 14); saves bad situation 322–325
    Seems fine to Johann 320
    Shopping for meat 326
  October–November, 1823 1, 4, 13, 19, 33

Housekeeper/housekeepers (*continued*)
　Paid fishseller woman (January 22)
　　196–197
　Payment (January 18/19)　189
　Perfumed room against toilet odor　12
　Polishing boots?　170
　Potential (January 17)　185
　Pregnant　300
　Rinn, Anna　162–163
　Salary　70, 81, 131, 167, 189, 300
　Scales for　111
　Search　38, 46–48, 56–57, 62, 65, 67, 70, 77, 80–82, 84, 88–89, 92, 98, 102, 104, 111, 114–117, 120, 127, 161, 177, 183, 189, 196, 198, 200, 219, 236, 246–247, 258, 269, 271, 272, 275, 284, 293–294
　　Advertisement (Beethoven's)　116–120, 123, 151–152, 189, 236, 241, 246–247
　　　Beethoven must sign　123
　　　"Can read/write well"　118–120, 123, 151–152
　　　Karl places in newspaper　116–117, 151–152
　　　In *Wiener Zeitung* (February 18)　253, 269
　　Gottschedt, Anna　162
　　Gross, Leonore　163–164
　　Interim woman　270
　　Karl against Holzmann　225–227
　　Krupka, Susannah　162
　　Schindler recommends craftsman's widow　261–262
　　　Can wash and write well　261
　　Seisser (applicant)　177
　　　Biographical sketch　177
　　Shopping　65
　　To see Schuppanzigh's wife　173–174
　　"Too many applicants"　91
　　Uniforms for (proposed)　34–35
　　Widows　171
　　See also Bauer, Nannette; Cook; Frank, Frau; Holzmann; Maid; Neuwirth, Marianne; Pamer, Maria; Seisser; Servants
Housekeeping money　31, 60, 81, 124
Houseplants, green　92
Hradetzky, Friedrich (horn)　254
　Dismissed　316

Hubertus, Johann (Rudolph's physician)　20–21, 239, 247
　Carbon wants his apartment　247–248
　Lived in Bürgerspital　239
Hufeland, Christoph Wilhelm (physician)
　Makrobiotik　19–20
　　In Beethoven's library　19
　　"Small meals; little meat in evening"　209
　　Often an egg dish　209
Hummel, Johann Nepomuk
　Piano Concerto in A Minor　62
　Septet, D minor, Op. 74　205, 213
　　Performed (January 22)　205–206
Humor　2, 41, 63–64, 70, 72, 75, 88–89, 98–99, 102, 108–109, 120, 153, 255–256, 311
　Esau on the Palouse　287
　Hawkers　256
　Karl's proverb ("Blessed are they")　287
　Lost with Karl due to Beethoven's hard hearing　210
　Ludlamshöhle　257
　　Beethoven disapproved　259
　Moscheles' kidney stones　217, 224
　Re Josephstadt Theater revolt　297
　Religion (sarcasm)　152
　Sarcasm　134, 299
　See also Puns; Wordplay
Hungarian Court Chancellery. See Zmeskall
Hürth, Theobald (bassoon)　143–144
Hussites　125, 127
Hut-Tyrann (Beethoven)　195
Hüther, Franz (Musikverlag Pennauer)　102
Hyatt, Mary Sue　xxv

Igel, rother. See Rother Igel
Immortal Beloved. See Brentano, Antonie; Brunsvik, Josephine
Improvisation (Beethoven's)
　At Lichnowsky's　111
　Method　294–295
　At projected Akademie (?)　111
　Public wants Beethoven to improvise　299
Income, annual (Beethoven), guaranteed　101
Inheritance tax, bank shares　51
Ink　307
Inkwell　134
Instrument collection, Rzechaczek (strings)　178
Intestines. *See* Tripe

Iron (pressing clothes)   67
Isouard, Niccolo
   Aschenbrödel   193
   Jaconda   237
Italian class (University)   91
Italian language   10, 43
Italian opera   33
   Coming back in April, 1824   33
   Defrauded the Court   88
   Versus German opera   33
   See also Barbaja; Kärntnertor Theater

Jacket   5
Jäger, Franz (tenor)   309
   Better than Haitzinger   316
   Has most beautiful voice   282
   Socializes with Schindler   316
   To sing on Akademie   282
Jägerhorn, goldenes   216. *See also* Wimmer's bookshop
Jansa, Leopold (violinist)   245–246, 319
   Brunsvik employment, Pest   268
   "Doesn't take no for an answer" (Sonnleithner)   278–279
   Prodigy of Jan Hugo Voříšek/Worzischek   245
   "Slovenly, drunken young man" (Abbé Stadler)   272
   Won Hofkapelle over Schuppanzigh   250, 268, 272
Janschikh
   Beethoven distances himself   38
   Family   294
Janus (periodical), Wähner   137–138
Jeckel, Anton (violinist)   245–246, 268
   Beethoven's concerts (1813–1814)   198
   Deserved pension   268
   Family   268
   Hofkapelle (?)   198
   Kärntnertor Theater and Burgtheater   198
Jeitteles, Alois (physician, poet)   26
   An die ferne Geliebte   26
   Ludlamshöhle   259
Jenger, Johann Baptist
   "Corruption" (homosexuality)   97
   Schubert circle   97
Jesus: "He who believes is blessed"   187
   Portraying musically   238
Jews   26
   Confused name (Mandl)   14

Jews (*continued*)
   "Jews find everything" (Schuppanzigh)   189
   "Jews [publishers] have no money" (Johann)   216
   Make fuss over Moscheles   71
   Steiner, considered to be   71
   Synonymous with "banker"   71, 112, 208
   In Vienna   13–14
   Wolf (medical devices)   168
   See also Henikstein; Hofmann & Goldstein; Jeitteles; Mendelssohn; Moscheles; Pulay; Rothschild; Wetzlar
João (John) VI, Portugal   145–146
Joelson, Carl Joel   58
Johann der Läufer (pun)   219
Joseph II (Emperor)
   Castelli's poem   88–89
   Humorous remark about ancestors   89
   Simple sarcophagus   89
Josephstadt, walking route from City   136
Josephstadt Theater. *See* Theater in der Josephstadt
Josephy, Katharina (maid)   1
Josquin Desprez   107
Judas Iscariot   100
Jurende, Karl Joseph
   Moravian Wanderer (calendar)   171
   Patriotic Pilgrim (calendar)   171

Kagan, Susan   xxv
Kaiserfleisch (smoked pork)   241
Kalkbrenner, Friedrich   94, 215, 228
   "Better than Moscheles" (Schuppanzigh)   177
   Concert with Dizi (January 25)   166, 181, 184, 203
   Departed (January 31)   199, 215, 224
   Financial success   176
   A "fool"   181
   "Greatest piano player"   184
   His hotel   177
   Patent as "greatest pianist"   219
   "Plays better than Moscheles"   217, 224
   "Pompous praise"   184
   Praise in *Berliner Zeitung*   184
   "Rentier"   169–170, 176
   Teaching Leopoldine Blahetka   209
   Ticket, complimentary, to Beethoven (?)   199
Kameel, Zum schwarzen   34, 60, 179, 212

Kanne, Friedrich August
　Du-friend　154
　Journalistic activities　155
　Review of Moscheles's concert　154–155
　Wiener *Allgemeine musikalische Zeitung* suspended　225
　Will visit soon (February 24?)　225
Kant, "Moral law" quote　54
Karl, Archduke, Schloss Weilburg (near Baden)　257
Karlsbad (Bohemia)　272
Kärntnertor Theater　194
　Administration thinks Beethoven written out　143
　Agrees to all for opera　247
　Ballet as good as Paris　88
　Beethoven gets comp tickets　123
　Closed (April, 1825–March, 1826)　160
　Coach for Unger　220–222
　Decline in quality (1823)　55
　Duport invites Beethoven and Karl　86
　Fidelio Overture　166
　Financial oversight (box office)　56
　Franz allows Barbaja to pay　105
　"Free admission for artists, London and Paris" (Moscheles)　86
　History of building and closures　249–250
　Italian operas in Italian　105
　Lease ends; possible closing　87
　　Closed (April, 1825)　88
　Library missing twelve operas　57
　　Fidelio safe in library　57
　Mozart, *Don Giovanni* (December 21)　147–148
　Mozart, *Figaro* (German)　133, 135–137
　　December 14　133–134, 136–137
　　Horns' wrong notes　134
　　"Out by 9 p.m."　133
　Orchestra
　　Auditions　143–144
　　Hradetzky　316
　　Moscheles's concerts　140
　　Played badly (February 1824)　281
　　Relative strength　98
　　Replacing fired members　316
　　Reputation "became a joke"　281
　　String sections　98
　　Violin auditions　143–144
　Politics　271–272
　Rehearsals (Akademie, May 7)　194
　Rehearsals, operatic　185
　Remodeling plans (1825–1826?)　249–250

Kärntnertor Theater (*continued*)
　Schuppanzigh applies　271
　Schuppanzigh plays *Der Freischütz* as substitute　281
　Spoken drama, to be used for　87–88
　Vocal soloists fine　209
　Weber, *Euryanthe*, lost 7,000 fl.　149
　See also Court Opera
Karpe, Franz Samuel, philosophy textbook a "blemish"　122
Katter, Joseph (concertmaster, Kärntnertor Theater)　214
　Related to Weigl　271
　Spoke on Beethoven's behalf　140
Katze, Zur weissen (White Cat), Graben　192
Kauer, Ferdinand (Leopoldstadt Theater concertmaster, composer)　104, 253
Kaufmann, Joseph (amateur violist, violinist)　205
Kaunitz, Aloys Wenzel (Prince)
　Fanny Elssler　79
　Portrait by Goya　79–80
　Russell's description　80
　Sexual relations with ballet girls　79
　Shot himself in Paris (rumor)　79
Kepler, Johannes (astronomer)　53–54
　Biographical sketch　53–54
　Littrow's biographical article　53–54
Keys (door), confusion with　73
Khayll, Aloys (flutist, piccolo player)　71, 99, 108
　Beethoven's piccolo parts for him　108
　Concert fee　108
Khayll, Joseph (oboist)　205
　Professor, Conservatorium　205
Kibsgaard, Birthe (Aarhus, Denmark)　174, 187, 194, 197, 224, 226, 239, 242, 251, 255, 263–264, 271, 277, 287, 313
Kidney stones (Moscheles)　217, 224, 290
Kiesewetter, J.G.C.H.
　Parts of Funke text　119
　Psychology text　119
Kiesewetter, Raphael Georg　119, 153–154, 160, 268
　Advises Beethoven to consult GdMf　154
　Liaison with GdMf　194
　Encounters Schindler at Christmas Mass　153–154
　Partnership with GdMf for Akademie　247
　Politics　268
　Prefers Weigl to conduct Akademie　155
King of Rome　150

Kinsky, Prince (stipend) 288
Kirchhoffer, Franz Christian (bookkeeper) 63, 94
　Advises on subscriptions to a collected edition 251
　Attends GdMf concert 134
　Biographical sketch 37, 63
　Cashier/bookkeeper, Hofmann & Goldstein 37
　Concert (January 25) 228
　Esterházy concerning *Missa solemnis* 147
　Harps from England 37, 41
　Liaison with Ries 37
　See also Kirchhoffer in the Index of Writers
Kitchen (cooking) books 305
Klemperer, Otto, phrasing in *Consecration of the House* Overture 253
Knapp, Edmund xxiii
Knife/knives 44
　Kitchen 49
Knödel 80
　Floury, soft 159
Kobau, Ernst xxi, xxiv
Koch, Bertha xxviii
Köferle, Joseph (teacher) 20, 300
　And sugar 20
　Geography, history, religion 300
　Still without salary 300
Köhler, Karl-Heinz xvi–xviii
Kohlmarkt 291
　Spöttl's *Zum grünen Fassl* 253, 291
Kojima, Shin Augustinus 278
Kollowrat, Franz Xaver 25
　Refused to employ Jeitteles 26
Königstadt Theater (Berlin) 21
　Facing Alexanderplatz 23
　Like Vienna's Josephstadt and Leopoldstadt Theaters 23
Konvikt (educational institution) 141
　Schubert a student 141
　Strict 141
Kosz, Ilse xxiii
Krähmer, Caroline *née* Schleicher (clarinetist and violinist, 1794–1873)
　Attended *Concert spirituel* concert (March 4) 301
　Beethoven remembered her 301
　Biographical sketch 301–302
　Clarinettist, violinist 301–302
　Composer 302
　Concert with husband Ernest (March 7) 301–302, 311–312

Krähmer, Caroline *née* Schleicher (*continued*)
　Death date 302
　Plainly clothed 31
　Toured Russia 301
　Viotti violin concerto 311
Krähmer, Ernest (oboist, 1795–1837)
　Biographical sketch 301–302
　Concert with wife Caroline (March 7) 301–302, 311–312
　Czakan 302, 311
　Principal oboist at Burgtheater, Hofkapelle 302
Krapfen (filled donuts) 197
Krause, Friedrich
　Former partner of Catholic Blöchlinger 170
　Protestant Educational Institute (Josephstadt) 170
Krems, Johann's food from there 229
Kremser, Werner xxv
Kreutzer, Conradin 143–144, 148
　Libussa 148, 186
　Sets Grillparzer's *Melusine* (1832) 199
　Taucher 149, 185, 187, 202–204, 220–221, 243
　　Attended by professional musicians 205
　　Ends happily because of fairy 231
　　Influenced by *Fidelio* 216
　　March 15 performance not cancelled due to illness 326–327
　　Performances led well 220–221
　　Plot 185
　　Rehearsals 185
Krommer, Symphony in D (new) 39, 42
Krueck, Alan xxi
Krug (mug) 222
Krüger, Joachim (conversation books thief) xvi–xvii
Krupka, Susanna 162–163
Kubik, Gerhard xxiv
Kučera, P. Milan xxiv
Kudlich, Johann Baptist (educator) 43, 197
　Wife (shopping alone) 197
Kuffner, Christoph (poet, official), *Ludlamshöhle* 259
Kummer, Katharina (housekeeper applicant) 284, 287
　Comments on temperature 287
　Son Franz (bookkeeper) 284
　Writes reasonably well 284

Kumpfgasse (walking route)   223, 293
Kur (dictionary criterion)   xxi
Kutschera, Johann Nepomuk, Baron
   (General)
   Adjutant to Franz   122, 298
   Dispatched at cabinet   122

Lachner, Franz   125–127
   Biographical sketch   125–126
   Brixi masses (?)   126
   Female cousin, age 10   126
      Her compositions   126–127
      Plays Handel, Haydn, Mozart,
         Beethoven, Clementi   126
Ladenburger, Michael   xxiii, xxxiii
Lafont, Charles Philippe (violinist)   168
La Fontaine, Fables   273
Laichmann, Michaela   xxiii
Lamb, roast   308
   Beethoven did not like   254
Lambskin   46
Lamps   201
Landshut, educator Sailer   126
Landstand   194
   Saal   296
   See also Concerts spirituels
Lang, Johann (author)   197
   Poetry, stories (*Allgemeine Theater-Zeitung*)
      197
Langer, Johann (author)   223
   No longer studying   223
Languages, German, high   171
Lanner, Joseph   xli
Lard, not butter
   Applicant Gneisel does not use   272
   Not used in noble homes   273
Latin (academic subject). *See* Bible;
      Pleugmackers; Pulay
Latin language   78
   Balde, modern songs in Latin   224–225
   Beethoven's use for himself   214
   Pronunciation   10
Latin professor (Stein)   8, 10
Laundry. *See* Washing
Lechner, Ursula   xxiv
Lee, John M.   xxv
Lehmann, Frau (housekeeper applicant)
      266, 269–270
   Already employed   270
   Schindler recommends for cooking   266
   Will start ca. March 4   270

Leidesdorf, Max Joseph (publisher)   102,
      180–181, 189, 205, 215–216
   Address   180
   Biographical sketch   180
   "Jews have no money" (Johann)   216
   Nothing to do with Bagatelles and songs
      216
   On Weber's *Euryanthe*   209
   "Reason alone is of no use"   181
   To get *Missa solemnis* (?)   114
   To take over Beethoven's debt (?)   208
   Wants short pieces   173
   Will guarantee amount for May 7 concert
      261
Leipzig
   Battle of (French retreat)   188
   Businesses/products   118
   Nikolai Church   118
   Schmidt's hearing balm   113, 117–118
Lemon   104
   For fish   171
Lent (Ash Wednesday, March 3)   160
   Concert season   221
   No meat   290
   Religious schedule   290
Lentils   5
   Beethoven eats   287
   Esau story   287
   Piece of fish cooked with them   287
Leo X (pope)   13
Leo XII (Genga), pope   14
Leopoldstadt Theater
   Aline   255
   Interactions with Josephstadt Theater
      253
   See also Bäuerle; Müller, Wenzel
Leschen/Löschen, Wilhelm (piano maker)
      116, 122, 133, 139, 251, 275, 298
   Biographical sketch   116
   Graf jealous   116
   Offers reasonable prices to Beethoven
      275
   Piano on Moscheles's concert   63, 127
   Transports pianos   139–140
Letter paper   282
Letters
   1823 (December 7), to Rudolph   101, 113
   1823 (December 10), to University for
      Karl   119
   1823 (December 13), to Odelga   132
   1823 (ca. December 29), to Duport   163
   1824 (ca. January 1), from Johanna   170

GENERAL INDEX 391

Letters (*continued*)
    1824 (ca. January 20), to Radziwill 189
    1824 (ca. January 20), Lichnowsky to Duport 203
    1824 (ca. January 25), to Duport 206, 208
    1824 (ca. February 1), from Bethmann
        Delivered by Johann 228
        Johann gets payment 228
    1824 (February 1), to Unger 230, 249
    1824 (February 2), to Marie Louise (Parma), re *Missa* (Karl coaches) 230–231
    1824 (February 11), to Unger 244
    1824 (ca. March 11), to Schlesinger 320
        Not survived 320
Lettuce/lettuce salad (*Salat*) 91, 287
Lewy, Elias (Eduard Constantin), hornist 143–144, 317
Leyermann (organ grinder) 197
Library, Beethoven's 12, 19–20
    Inventories 12
    Karl sets up 12
    Moritz, *Götterlehre* 284–285
Library, Kärntnertor Theater, missing 12 operas 57
Lice, combs for 164
License (*Privilegium*) 32
Lichnowsky, Carl/Karl (Prince, Silesia) 107
Lichnowsky, Caroline (Althan), mother 109
Lichnowsky, Eduard Maria (Prince) 109–110
    Literary activity 110
    Parades his knowledge 110
    Poem on Napoleon 110
    Roderich (tragedy) 151
    Signed *Ludlamshöhle* Petition 109
Lichnowsky, Moritz (Count, brother of Carl) 8–10, 13–14, 67–68, 107–109, 158, 165, 213, 247, 298, 309–311, 313
    Advice, often intrusive 33, 150–151
    Agrees with Schuppanzigh 304
    Application for Swedish diploma 298, 304
    Approached Palffy for Theater an der Wien 320
    Bad health (?) 292
    Beethoven improvises 111
    Biographical sketch 107
    Brings letter from Rudolph 247
    City residence/address 9, 105, 107
    Compares Johann and Therese 68

Lichnowsky, Moritz (*continued*)
    Cook (formerly Johann's) 56–57, 62, 68, 78
    Czerny (Carl) to teach daughter Josepha Maria 231, 265
    At Czerny's house recital 265
    Daughter (illegitimate) Jeannette (Josepha Maria) Stummer 9, 109
        Plays piano, needs teacher 109
    Delivery of letter to Neipperg 225
    Departed Beethoven's circle (April, 1824) 156
    Duport
        Letter to (ca. January 20) 203
        Negotiations with 165
    Euryanthe, railed against 8–9
    "*Freischütz* is no opera" 33
    Friend in Greek history 68
    Going to Odelga, re *Missa* 230–231
    Gossip
        About Bettina Brentano 213
        Meddling 105
    Happy with *Melusine* and Akademie 231
    Hosts Beethoven and Karl (December 7) 107
    Housekeeper/housekeeping 158
    Intercedes with Saurau 247
    Invitation (ca. December 6) 102, 105
        Address 105
    Karl, inquires about 68
    Knows Gärtner (guitar) 262
    Knows Neipperg/Neuberg 150
    Letter about publication of Petition 163
    Looks worn out 236
    Ludlamshöhle Petition
        Sent to Leopold Sonnleithner 279
        Signed 109
    May "evaporate" before Akademie (Schindler) 156
        But will attend 156
    Mother Carolina 109
    On Friedemann Bach fugues 151
    On Gänsbacher and Albrechtsberger 151
    On programming movements of *Missa solemnis* 304
    Opera connoisseur 10
        Critical thoughts on opera 32–33
        Kärntnertor Theater for Beethoven opera 67
    Property may be worth 200,000 fl. 286
    Social afternoon 107–108
    Speech impediment in self or servant 105

Lichnowsky, Moritz (*continued*)
   Summer residence in Hietzing (1823) 284
   Uses Pfann's baths 35–36
   Visit to Beethoven 230–231
   Visits Czerny 236
   Visits Johann 225
   Visits his mistress every day 275
      Does not allow his wife the same practice 275
   Wife, second (Josepha/Johanna Stummer, singer) 108–109
   Will visit Beethoven (December 23) 148–149
   Woman teacher 109
   "Work economically" for Akademie 247
   See also Lichnowsky in the Index of Writers
Lichtenberger, Magdalena, *Aufgeklärte Wiener Haushälterin* 305
Light, sun 149, 212, 218–219
   Apartment that has sun 193
   Barmherzige Brüder, Landstrasse, bright 289
   For composing 215
   Days becoming longer 149
   Lamps, study and work 201
      Weigl's apartment 218–219
Lighters, chemical 36–37
Likawetz, Joseph Calasanz 32, 183
   Elementa philosophiae/Elements of Philosophy (textbook) 32, 183
Lindpaintner, Overture to *Abrahams Opfer* 39, 42
Linen shops
   Schoberlechner (Graben) 192, 257
   Wladislaw Brothers (Graben) 257
Linguistic scribblings (Karl) 270, 272
Linke, Barbara 178
Linke, Joseph (violoncellist) 9, 70, 193
   "Beethoven should improvise on repeat Akademie" 292
   "Best cellist in Europe for quartets" 101
   Biographical sketch 101, 292
   Quarrelled with violinist Böhm 312
   Related by marriage to Schuppanzigh 178
   Schubert's Quintet in C, pizzicato 101, 292
   Sounds like a contrabass 101
Linz, Fuchs's cousin 260
Lions (menagerie) 302–303

Lirveeld, Baroness 220–222
   Came with Unger (January 29) 220
   Coffee, black, makes her too hot 221
   Mathilde? 220, 222
Literature, Austrian 3
Littrow, Joseph Johann (astronomer) 53–54
   Article on Kepler 53–54
   Citation of Kant 54
   "Kosmologische Betrachtungen" 54
Llewellyn, Gudrun xviii
Llewellyn, (Robert) Terence xviii
Lobkowitz family 183
   Bankrupt 10
Lobkowitz, Franz Joseph Maximilian (Prince)
   Son Joseph (Pepi) 38
   Stipend for Beethoven 288
Locksmith (doors and fee) 210, 219, 223, 255
   Annoyed to write out bill 223
   Fee 1 fl. 30 kr. 255
Lockwood, Lewis xviii–xix, xxv
Logic (university subject) 31
   Esser, *System of Logic* 187
   Feder, *Logik* 42
   Feder, *Metaphysik* 42
   Textbook 187
Löhr/Loehr, Franz, Baron 245–246
   Re Swedish Diploma 304
Loin of beef (*Lungenbraten*) 296
London 188
   Beethoven, opera in demand 202
   Beethoven, possible journey 169
   Little musical work, March–June 96
   No tour (December, 1823) 87
   Wine mixed with rum 96
Lorenz, Michael xxi, xxiv, 302
Lorenz, Ralph xxv
Löschen. *See* Leschen
Lost items (in Fall, 1822, move), "To hell with stuff … useless" (Schuppanzigh) 70
Lottery 43
   Shop 36
Louis XVIII, King, France 145
   Suppression of Spanish Revolution (1820) 145–146
Love life 221
Löwen, zu den drei (Kärntnerstrasse), wine 269
Lowinsky, Das Schloss (comic opera, Stunz/Stuntz) 308
Lucre, filthy 58
Ludlamshöhle Petition. *See* Petition, Ludlamshöhle

Lugeck
  Meat shop   326
  Not far from University   326
Lund, Susan   dedication page, xviii, xxv, 268
Lung (meat)   47

Ma, Si-Hon   xxv
Ma-Kircher, Klaralinda   xxiii
Macaroni/noodles   80, 139, 153
Macháček, Joseph   xxiv
Magistrat, discussions with   261
Mahler, Gustav
  Montenuovo's support   150
  Symphony No. 4 (*Fisolen*)   xx
Maid/maids (few by name, most semi-literate at best)   4, 8, 28, 30, 43, 59, 89, 119, 151
  About bone make-weight in meat   42
  Angry speech   65
  Applicant (December 14)   135
  Arrived ca. January 13/14
    Alarmed by housekeeper's gossip (February 1)   225
    Alarmed about venison   226
    Departs February 2   230
  Bared her chest to Karl   30, 59
  Beethoven retains   151
  Bell to summon   59, 319
  Broke coffee pot   296
  Came ca. January 14   211
  Can cook   59
  Cheated out of money   60, 64
  Cooking, helped with   47
  Departing (January 22)   210
    Misunderstandings   200
  Errand to copyist Maschek   319, 320
  Exposed herself to Karl (Summer 1823)   274
  (ca. February 8–February 22), wants to leave ca. February 15   259
  (February 15) Asks for candle   263
  (February 25) Servants did not get candles   277
  (to ca. February 25) Wants to leave   277
  (ca. February 29) Wants to make a *Mehlspeise*   290
  From lowest dregs (January 30)   224
  From Vöcklabruck   37
  Found missing item   127
  Got rice   114
  Ill and pregnant   124
  Ill-tempered   78
  Insolent to Karl   66

Maid/maids (*continued*)
  Josephy, Katharina   1
  Laughs with Holzmann   264
  Lazy   59
  Letter to Beethoven (ca. November 19)   47
  Literate   191
  Maid, former, at restaurant   293
    Waiting to dance   293
  Makes Karl's bed   62
  Misunderstandings with Beethoven   73, 200, 236
  Money left on table   91–92
  New (ca. January 13–14)   179–180, 182, 191, 230
    Gets take-out (February 2)   210, 231
    Paid (January 25?)   210
  Pamer, Maria   xli. *See also* Pamer, Maria
  Payment and departure   211
  Potential new   226–227
  Pregnant   300
  Previously with Countess Morzin   65
  Reads Karl's books   191
  Recommendation, asks for   139, 277
    Will bring *Stempelbogen*   277
  Rowaz, Franziska   190
  Rye bread, eat   6
  Salary   64, 77–78
  Sews   241
  Shopping   66
    New shopping basket   66
  Sickly   4, 6, 8, 11–12, 27–28, 30, 36, 59, 83
    Better food allotment   12
    Physician   6, 8, 12, 30, 83
  "Sow"   59
  Stolizka, Anna   211
  Testimonial (January 26)   211, 213
  Was scolded   78
  With her lover   312
  "Worse at Beethoven's than in prison"   213
  Writes lover about education   124
  Zimenska, Anna   1
  See also Cook; Housekeeper
"Mäkler" (operator) Moscheles   87
Makrobiotik. See under Hufeland
Mälzel, Johann Nepomuk   ix–x, 202
  Biographical sketch   93
  Dolls, talking (makes)   93
  Ear trumpets   93
  Moscheles saw him in Paris   93–94
  Wellington's Victory   93

Mälzel, Leonhard x
   Apartment has light   218–219
   Biographical sketch   202
   Ear trumpets   93, 202
   Going to Prague   259
   Jägerzeil No. 20   202
   Mechanical trumpeter with 50 tones   259
   Metronome   202
   Orchestrion (new model)   259
   Renumbered address   218–219
   Schindler's confusion   259
Mandeville, E.C.A.D. (Gen.)   14
Mandolin   246
Manservant   177
Maps (Vienna)   xxix
Maria am Gestade (church)   192
Marie Louise (Parma)   150
Marie Therese (wife of Franz)   244
Market shops on the Freyung   256–257
Marketing/economic areas   114
Marriage, Unger advises Beethoven   186
Martin, Anton, Count/Ritter   298
Martin Menagerie. *See* Menagerie
Maschek, Paul (copyist)   307–308
   Address   318
   Cannot bring score into house   307
   Copied 80 Bögen in 1 night   308
   Copied in his sleeping shirt   320
   Copyists to work from his home   318
   Copyists working from their homes   319
      Could start at 4:00 a.m.   318
   Expects more copyists (March 9)   307
   Literate   322
   Lives 45 minutes from Beethoven   318
   Lives too far from Beethoven's apartment   320
   Progress report (March 13)   322
   Schindler wants string parts soon   326
   Visits Beethoven (March 13)   322
Masić, Dika   xxv
Masić, Leila   xxv
Matches   36–37, 223
Mathematics
   Division   167, 303
   Karl teaches Beethoven   246
   Mathematical proofs   273
   Multiplication   167–168
   "Necessary for an educated person"   119
Mathilde von Merwald (Woltmann)   220
Mattia, Raymond di   xxv
Mayer, Frau [von] (Mariahilf)   163

Mayer, Johann (candles, Wipplingerstrasse)   286
   Not to be confused with Mayer's bookshop in the Deutsches Haus   286
Mayer's bookshop
   Deutsches Haus   29–30
   Schiller, *Works*   29–30, 35
Mayseder, Joseph (violin)   25, 98, 108, 128, 135, 205
   Biographical sketch   3, 138
   Concert (December 27, 1823)   86
   Concert fee   108
   Plays well; piece had no coherence   138
Meals
   Home-cooked versus restaurant   135
   "Small" (Hufeland)   209
Meat   2, 188
   Beef, added bones (makeweight)   42
   Cost of 3 pounds   287
   Half pound for every adult   263
   "Little in evening" (Hufeland)   209
   Lung (2 kinds)   47
   Never eat in evening   4
   No lack   46
   Roast beef from restaurant (March 14)   323
   Roasted at baker's   46
   See also Beef; Rabbit
Mechanical clock (Strauss restaurant)   99
   Owner Wolfgang Reischl   9
Mechanical devices (hearing). *See* Ear trumpets
Mechetti, Pietro and Carlo, music shop (Michaelerplatz)   215
Medicine
   Physician vs. surgeon defined   248
   Sympathetic cures (hypnosis)   227
Medicines   13
   Bitter   116
   Maid got   47
Mehlgrube   xi. *See also* Gebauer, Franz Xaver, *Concerts spirituels*
Mehlspeise. *See* Pastry
Meisl, Carl (playwright, Josephstadt)   98, 144
   Hund des Aubri   98–99
   Männerfeindin   159
Meisl Brothers (bankers)
   Beethoven did business with   259
   Rauhensteingasse   264
Meissner Brothers. *See* Meisl Brothers

Meissner, P.J. (*Heitzung*)   77
Melkus, Eduard   xxiv
Melkus, Marlis   xxiv
Melusine. See under Grillparzer
Melzer, Joseph (contrabassist)   193
Menagerie, Van Aken and Martin   302–303
   Beethoven and Karl visit (May 14)   302–303
   Jägerzeil (March–June 1824)   302–303
   New animals   302–303
Mendelssohn, Felix   94
Menzel, Zeno Franz (violinist)   294
   Death   69, 109
   Position vacant   69–70
Merchant of Venice. See under Shakespeare
Meredith, William R.   xxiv, 263
Messner, Robert   xxix
Metronome   202
Meyer's book shop (Deutsches Haus)   252
Midday dinner   300
Middeke, Michael   xxv
Milk products   216
Minuet   190
Mirror   252
Misar, Edith   xxiii
Misar, Karl   xxi, xxiii
Mistrust (Beethoven's)   47
Mittag, August (bassoonist)   193
Mölzer, Joseph (contrabassist). *See* Melzer
Monetary exchange   75. *See also* Banking and financial matters
Monetary values   75, 116
Money, paper (potential loss)   225
Montegre, A.J., *Hemerrhoiden*   164
Moravian Calendar (Jurende)   237
Moritz, Karl Philipp, *Götterlehre oder mythologische Dichtungen*   284–285
Mörschner & Jasper bookshop (Clary house, Kohlmarkt)   164, 201, 222–223, 295–296
Morzin, Louise (Countess/widow)   28, 65
   Her former servant   28
Moscheles, Ignaz   134, 140
   Admirer named Wolf   168–169
   "Art, not"   69
   Beethoven kindly disposed   25
   Beethoven's *Namensfeier* Overture   128, 140
   Beethoven's Ninth Symphony, wants   152
   Biographical sketch   24, 94
   Borrows Beethoven's Broadwood   25, 115–117, 122, 135

Moscheles, Ignaz (*continued*)
   Brother welcomed by Beethoven   93, 96
   Calves' feet, favorite dish   259
   Concert (Christmas benefit, 1823), appears   103
   Concert, half-evening (November 22)   61, 63, 69, 71, 96
   Concerts   24–25
   Concerts, full evening (December 15/17)   94–95, 135, 138, 140–141
      Beethoven's Broadwood   96
      Enemies hissed   138–139
      Kanne reviews (December 15)   154
      Karl's evaluation   138–139
   Czerny and nephew Karl neutral   25
   Departs Vienna (January 2)   140, 152
   Diary (December 3) does not mention Schindler   92
   Drinks no wine   96
   Dutch Akademie, confirms   122
   Fantasies and variations   61, 63, 69
   Fantasy on *Gott erhalte*   25, 135, 138, 148
   Fantasy on Rossini's *Gazza ladra*   24
   Fantasy on Themes of Mozart and Beethoven   24
   Going to London   38
   Ill, kidney stones
      In Prague   217, 290–291
      Per Karl   230
      Per Schindler   224
   Improvisations
      Facile   294
      Played on Beethoven's Broadwood   294
      Prepared beforehand   111
      "Superficial" (Stein)   116
   "Jew Moscheles" (Schuppanzigh)   71
   "Kalkbrenner is better" (Johann)   217
   "Kalkbrenner is better" (Schuppanzigh)   177
   Kärntnertor Theater orchestra, Hildebrand   140
   Knows Count Troyer   97
   Leaving Vienna   135
   Leschen piano   63, 116–117
   Leschen transports pianos   139
   London
      Names friends   95
      Reaction   115
      Residence (Oxford Street 143)   96
   Ludlamshöhle: Tasto der Kälberfuss   259
   Married Charlotte Embden   94

Moscheles, Ignaz (*continued*)
   Mayseder's concert (December 27) 86
   Means of travel, brags on 94
   Offers to take messages to London 94
   "Only interested in eating" (Karl) 143
   "Operator" (*Mäkler*) 87, 94
   Piano Concerto in E-flat 25, 135
   Piano Concerto in E major 24, 63, 86
   Piano Concerto in G minor 24
   Piano score to *Fidelio* 92
   Pianos: Leschen, Broadwood, Graf 127, 294, 298
   Plays own works 61
   Poster: no mention of Beethoven 135
   Predicts great earnings for Beethoven in England 105
   Publications, simultaneous 97
   Return to London, itinerary 94
   "Routine composer/player" (Schindler) 143
   Saw Johann at Artaria's 96
   Saw Mälzel in Paris 93
   Saw Ries in London 93
   Schindler, conversation with 86
   Schindler falsifies Beethoven's judgment 88
   Schindler falsifies introduction to Beethoven 86–87
   Schindler relays thoughts to Beethoven 122
   Schuppanzigh dislikes him 25, 71
   "Speed" (Karl) 61
   At Steiner's shop 157
   Superficial 71
   Token gift from Beethoven (?) 140
   Translated and plagiarized Schindler's *Biographie* 25
   Truth, self-serving distortion 88, 94–95
   Variations on Alexander March 25, 135, 138
   Variations on Danish Song 138
   Visit to Vienna (October, 1823–January, 1824) 86
   Visits back to Vienna 3
   Visits Beethoven 86, 92–94
Mosel, Ignaz von (librarian, violist, composer), "M." (initial) 87
Mösle's widow, bookshop 25
Mostić, Ana xxv
Mozart, Wolfgang Amadeus (1756–1791) 57
   Beethoven's concern 243
   Clarinet Quintet in A, K. 581 261, 263

Mozart, Wolfgang Amadeus (*continued*)
   Clemenza di Tito 57
   Davidde penitente 318
   Dir, Seele des Weltalls 132
   Don Giovanni 24
      Kärntnertor Theater (December 21) 147–148
   Figaro, Kärntnertor Theater (December 14) 133, 136–137
      Cast 137
      Encores 137
      Horns missed notes 134
      "Out by 9 p.m." 133
   Figaro Overture 311
   Fingers bent by playing 287
   Lachner's cousin plays works 126
   Lent and Advent concerts a threat to Salieri 243. *See also* Salieri
   Quartet in D, K. 465 9
   Quartet in D, K. 499 or 575 160
   Quartet in E-flat, K. 428 240
   Quartets 175
   Quintet in D 190
   Quintet in E-flat, K. 614 291
   Requiem 13
   Salieri declares he poisoned M. 197, 200, 238, 242–243
   Schauspieldirektor Overture 108
   Symphony in D (Prague) 318
Muck. *See* Ballauf-Muck
Mug/cup, shaving. *See* Shaving mug
Mukuna, Kazadi wa xxv
Müller, *Organ* 222–223, 295
Müller, Wenzel (Leopoldstadt Theater) 308–309
   Aline (at Kärntnertor Theater) 255, 257–258
   Scenery 257–258
   "The People's Homer" 149
   Weilburg 257
Müller, Wilhelm August 222–223
Multiplication, not in Bonn's curriculum 167. *See also under* Mathematics
Multiplication in Its Most Complete Form (textbook) 36
   Seen at Gerold's 36
Munich, Beethoven not in 87
Music theory (Schindler) 305
Musik-Verein. *See* Gesellschaft der Musikfreunde
Mussels 72
Mustard 76, 80, 295
   French names 303

Nägele, Hans Georg (Zürich publisher)   120
Nails   31, 134
Napkins   293
Napoleon   11–12, 110
    Battle of Leipzig, conduct   188
    Dinner on battlefield   14
    Education, positive effect   11
    Napoleon in Exile (O'Meara)   146
    Poem about Moscow retreat   110
    Wars, French losses at Leipzig   188
Napping (nodding off), Beethoven   43
Nature   3
Neate, Charles   95
Necktie, flannel   65
Neipperg/Neuberg (Count)   150, 225, 230–231
    No influence in Tuscany   230–231
    See also Marie Louise (Parma); Parma
Nettl, Paul   xxxiv
Neuer Musik-Verlag   102
Neuwirth, Georg and Petronella   84
Neuwirth, Marianne (housekeeper applicant)   84
New Year's cards
    Johanna van Beethoven   170
    Schindler   169
Newlin, Dika   xxv
Niemetz, Joseph (Karl's fellow student)   131, 136
    Beethoven disapproves   136, 300
        Lives at Blöchlinger's   136
        Subject of quarrels   136–138
        Mother bankrupt   131
        Mother paid bribe   300
    Theater (*Figaro*) with Karl   136
Nierenbraten   296
Nohl, Ludwig   323
Nohl, Walther   xvi
Noodles. *See* Macaroni
Norma Tag, definition   221
Nose, viscous humidity   32
Novaja Semlia (Arctic Ocean)   4
Nowak, Joseph (contrabassist)   205
    Bassoonist, Kärntnertor Theater   205
    Doubled for *Harmonie*   205

Oberleitner, Andreas (court cellar servant, guitar and mandolin virtuoso)   246
Obermayer, Leopold (baker)   46, 147
    Apprentices guzzle Johann's wine   255
Oboe, Gesellschaft der Freunde der Wiener   xxiv

Oboists. *See* Bednarik; Khayll, Joseph; Kobau; Krähmer, Ernest
Öchsner, Herr   274–275
Odelga, Carl (Tuscany, Nassau)   132, 214
    Biographical sketch   132
Odysseus (pronunciation)   11
Oehlenschläger, *Ludlams Höhle*   258–259
Oil   259
    Olive oil   295
Oliva, Franz   xii, xxv–xxvi
Olmütz   66
    Benefices   296
O'Meara, Barry, *Napoleon in Exile*   146
Onions   227
Onslow, Quartet No. 11, D minor   9
Opera, German   203. *See also* Rossini
Optical Armchair Journeys   82–83
Orestes and Pylades (potential homosexual allusions)   285
Organ grinder   197
Organ methods   222–223
Organ playing   303
Overcoat thefts, university   81
Owl   181
Oxford University Press   xviii
Öxner, Herr   274–275
Oysters   72, 110
Ozanich, Lois Rova   xxv

Pacini, Giovanni, *Fee und Ritter* (ballet)   195
Palawatsch (mess)   315
Palestrina, Giovanni Pierluigi da   107
Palffy-Erdöd, Ferdinand (Count, Vienna)   307
    Financial problems   307
    Theater an der Wien   307
        Schindler and Lichnowsky approach for Akademie location (unauthorized)   320
Palmieri, Robert   xxv
Palouse (Idaho)   287
Pamer, Maria (b. 1807), former maid   75, 81, 115, 241, 274
    Biographical sketch   241, 274
    Considered her as late as March 1825   274
Pamer, Michael (1782–1857), violin, Theater an der Wien   241
    Dance band leader   241
Pan, sauce   38
Panoramas, projected   82–83

Paper 169
  Blotting 31
  Drawing 134
  Letter 282
  Light blue and ordinary (Heft 45) 17–18
  Music 37, 53
  Ordinary 89
  Printing 141
Paris
  Beethoven opera in demand 202
  Regards from residents 262
  Royalties 152–153
Parma, Marie Louise and Neipperg, solicitation for *Missa solemnis* 230–231
Parry, William Edward (Admiral) 4–5
Partridges 26, 33, 230
  For roasting 230
  Spanish (potatoes) 323
Parts, bass (orchestral or soloists?) 325
Passauer Gasse 192
Pastor, Mödling, Johann Baptist Fröhlich 59
Pastry/pastries 84, 151, 190, 290
  "Almost too strong" (Karl, February 28) 288
Paul, Bernhard xxi, xxiv
Paulaner Church 186, 299
Pauli, Ernst
  Acts well 159
  Weiberfeind 159
Paumgarten, wife of Captain. *See* Boarding house
Pavia, University 34
Pechatschek, Franz (violinist)
  Biographical sketch 198
  Conducted Beethoven Symphony 5 at GdMf 198
  Studied with Schuppanzigh 198
  Theater an der Wien (1809–1820) 198
  Tour (1822) 198
Peddler, itinerant, pencils 254
Pelikan, Zum goldenen xxv
Pencil/pencils 24, 66, 84, 90, 134, 200
  Dozen bought in a beer house 254, 272
  Inexpensive 272
  Red 196
Pencil case, wood 90
Penknife 258
Pennauer, Anton (Neuer Musikverlag) 102
Pens 172, 183, 210
  Large ink supply 303
  Silver, for travelers 303

Pension, Beethoven's (1809). *See* Stipend
Pension Lehrerhaus (Vienna) 55
Pensions xv
  Old age 268
  Weigl 176
"People, medicine … rich" 5
Pesth
  German Theater 22
  Jansa previously employed there 268
Peters, Karl (tutor/guardian)
  Beethoven distances himself 38
  Letters from Italy (1820) 38
Petition, *Ludlamshöhle* (February, 1824) 109, 258–259
  Attempted delivery 281
  Banned (1826) 258–259
  Copying 290
  Delivery 278–279, 286
  Fanciful names of members 258–259
  Haslinger 289–290
  "Have you read it?" (Karl) 286
  Moscheles, Tasto der Kälberfuss 259
  Name from Oehlenschläger play 258
  Purpose 259
  Restaurant of J. Haidvogel 258
  Schindler wants to read (March 4) 296–297
  Schindler reads later (March 8) 286, 307
  Various authors 286
Pfaf, origin of word 50
Pfann, Joseph, baths/springs (Meidling) 35–36
  Admission fees 36
  "Causes coughing" 68
  Lichnowsky patronized 35–36
Pfarrhund, Frau Stella xxiv
Pfeiffer. *See* Krähmer, Caroline
Pfeiffer, Franz (copyist and piano teacher) 223
Pfifficus (sly dog) 64
Pheasant 253
Philharmonic Society (London) 95
  Fees for pianists 95–96
Phillips, Bruce xxiii
Philosophy (University course of study) 12–13, 31–32, 35
  Courses 135–136
  Discussion group 139
  Karpe textbook, a "blemish" 122
  Necessary for an educated person 119
Physician defined 248
Physician for maid 6, 8, 30

GENERAL INDEX

Physics (subject)   121
Pianists, young Viennese *Wunderkinder*.
    See Blahetka, Leopoldine
Piano   45
    Double [Erard?]   90
    English [Broadwood?]   90
Piano, Broadwood   116, 122, 133, 294, 298, 323
    Beethoven paid customs, taxes   135
    Compared to Viennese pianos   135
    Cost   96
    To Graf for repair   299
    Hearing device   259
    Lent for Moscheles concerts   122, 127, 135
    London wants report   115
    Moscheles thanks Beethoven   140
    Parts damaged   298
    Streicher attempts hearing device   248
    Tone good, not enough power   138
    Transportation   139–140
        Cost of   139
Piano, Clementi   96
Piano, English, with Berlin strings   122
Piano, Erard   158
Piano, Graf   116
    Graf jealous of Leschen   116
    For Moscheles   127
Piano, hearing device   259
Piano, Leschen. *See* Leschen
Piano lessons   189, 265–266
    Discipline   189
Piano makers
    Erard   41–42
    Leschen   251, 275
    Ries   251
    See also Graf; Stein, Matthäus Andreas;
        Streicher, Johann Andreas;
        Streicher, Johann Baptist
Piano ("played out"), for sale   46
Piano repairs, Erard   41–42
Piano teacher, for Lichnowsky's daughter   109
Pianos, Viennese, compared to Broadwood   134
    Johann and Czerny see newly invented instruments   231
    New Streicher   231, 235
Piccolo   108
Pickles   227
Pidoll family (Lorraine)   138
Pig, wild, price   34
Pike (fish)   5, 78

Pils, Susanna   xxiii
Pipes (smoking), Beethoven's, repairs   50
Pirate reprinting   97
    Beethoven victim   97
    Härtel conspired with Clementi   97
Piringer, Ferdinand   3–4, 9, 56, 194
    Attended Schuppanzigh's concert (February 15)   265
    Biographical sketch   3–4, 194
    Concert (January 25)   228
    Continues *Concerts spirituelles*   194
    Good violinist   303
    Organizes choruses   303
    Played in Quintet, Op. 29   240
    To get dilettantes for Akademie   281–282, 292
Pistols   45
Platter   189
Pleugmackers, Peter Joseph (language teacher)   39–40
    Biographical sketch   331–333
Pleyel, Camille, pronounced *Play-ELL*   158–159
Pleyel, Ignatz, pronounced *Plile*   158–159
Poet, "best German woman" (Brachmann)   30
Poison. *See* Mozart; Salieri
Polakel (spring chicken)   141
Police, called against orchestra strike at Josephstadt Theater   297
Police direction, must sign Beethoven's housekeeper advertisement   123
Policeman, district   19
Politics, censorship   45
Poorhouse overseer, collecting alms   85
Pork, smoked (*Kaiserfleisch*)   241
Portamento   236, 240
    Negative opinion   236
    Schuppanzigh Quartet   236
Portrait, Radoux (grandfather Ludwig)   273
Portugal, João (John) VI   145–146
Potato sack   15
Potatoes   161
    On the Graben   201, 217
    Quality   217
    Spanish partridges   323
    Sundry varieties   192
        Different advertisement   201
    White, best, from Gersthof and Pötzleinsdorf (Jägerzeil)   265
    With beef   161
Potatoes, mountain   45–46

Pots 5
Pötschner, Peter xvii
Potter, Cipriani 95–96
Pötzleinsdorf, potatoes 265
Poularde (hen), *Birne* 312
Pousain, Maria Margaretha (Staudenheim's housekeeper). *See* Staudenheim
Powder 13
Practising (rehearsing *Melusine*) 165
Prater
   Johann drives there 182
   Unger invites to *Lusthaus* 186
   Walk in 183
Preindl, Joseph (former Kapellmeister, St. Stephan) 145, 176
   Wealth/money bequeathed 176
   Wine cellar 176
Preisach, Salomo, candles and soap 36, 43
Preisinger, Joseph (bass singer) 185
   For Akademie (?) 282, 316
   Better than Forti for Akademie 316
   New bass singer, Kärntnertor Theater 292
"Priest, lawyer, philosopher" 75
Priest, Moravian 294, 296
   Helped Schindler's education 296
   Man of letters and musical 296
   Served in military 296
   With Wallmoden's *Cuirassiers* in Hungary 296
Priests, complaints against 50
Princesses, Imperial, "go to market" 149
Principe, zwei 295
Prison, "Working at Beethoven's is worse than" (maid) 213
Probst, Franziska, *Praktisches Urfahr Linzer Kochbuch* 305
Programs, none printed at Schuppanzigh's quartet concerts 263
Prohsmann, Alfred xxiii
Promberger, Johann (pianist) 62
Proverb 108, 181
   Leidesdorf 181
Proverbs, Old German 58
Prussian legation 36
Psarakis, Brigitte xxiii
Psychology (University courses) 31–32, 43, 119, 121
   Necessary for an educated person 119
   Textbook (Kiesewetter) 119
   University curriculum 121

Publication terms, Paris 319
   Böhm relates 319
   Schlesinger 319–320
Publishers. *See* Artaria; Diabelli; Sauer and Leidesdorf
Pulay, Paul (Latin and Greek teacher) 39–40, 274
   Biographical sketch 333–334
   Converted Jew 39
Punch, cold and warm 29
Puns 2, 8, 219
   "Johann der Läufer" 219
   See also Humor; Wordplay
Pythagoreans, no beans 27

QED (Quod erat demonstrandum) 273
Quartetten (orchestral string parts) 326

Rabbit 3–4, 8, 25, 28
   In a mixed dish 206
   Small 206
   With fur or skinned 60
   Young 141
Radoux, Leopold, portrait of grandfather Ludwig van Beethoven 273
Radziwill, Anton Heinrich (Prince, violoncellist) 8, 132, 214
   Admires Beethoven 189
   Berlin 8, 76–77
   Biographical sketch 132
   Composed music to Goethe's *Faust* 77
   Letter to 189
   Plays Beethoven's Quartets 76
   Posen, city governor 76–77, 189, 214
Rags, wiping 291
Raigersfeld (English sea captain) 87
Rainer, Archduke
   To help with Franz's backlog 298
   Unpopular in Italy 298
Raisins 73
Raizen (Serbs), colony near Baden 51
Rampl, Wenzel ("Copyist B") 20, 40
   Biographical sketch 311
   Copied presentation copy of Ninth Symphony 266
   Copying *Missa solemnis* 24, 66–67
   Poor appearance 311
   Schlemmer as witness to wedding 311
   To copy Ninth Symphony score? 311
   Wife Anna Ettmann 24
Rasumovsky, Andreas (count/prince) 69
Rasumovsky Quartet (ensemble) 178

Rat control   113
    Dogs   114
Rathgeber, Ernestine   xxv
Rauchfangkehrergasse   211
Rauscher, Jacob, to sing in Akademie (?)   282
Razor (barber)   27, 48, 177, 201, 210, 269.
    See also Barber's knife
Razor, shaving   191
Razor strop   191
"Reason alone is of no use" (Leidesdorf)   181
Rebmann, Martina   xxiii
Redoutensaal, Grosser
    For Akademie (May 7, 1824)   194
    For Akademie (May 23, 1824)   202–203
    Czerny played there; did not like it   254
Redoutensaal, Kleiner, Kalkbrenner concert   166, 181
"Reeking, rotting garbage" (Sachs)   229
Rehearsing (*Melusine*)   165
Reinlein, Jacob (Karl's schoolmate)   60
Reischl, Wolfgang (Strauss Restaurant)   161
Religion   187
    Blöchlinger's Institute   300
Religion, censorship   45
Religious holidays. *See* All Souls Day; Easter
Repressalien (Stuntz, comic opera), Theater an der Wien   308
Reprinting, pirate. *See* Leidesdorf; Pirate reprinting
Residences
    Baden (1822)   xiii
    Baden (Summer/Fall, 1823)   10
    Grinzing (Potential Summer 1824)   288
    Hetzendorf (Summer, 1823)   9
    Landstrasse (Ungargasse No. 323)
        Address, directions and location   1–2, 118–120, 269
        Apartment hunting (January–February)   218–219
        Bell rope   220
        Bookshelves   284
            Schindler browses   284
        Building door is closed   172
        Building superintendent   218, 224, 227
            His wife   226, 290
        Classensteuer   290
        Dancing at restaurant   293
        Description of Beethoven's apartment (Unger)   323–324
        Dogs for rat control   114

Residences (*continued*)
    Landstrasse (*continued*)
        Doors, locksmith   210
        Heated too much   23
        Karl sets up library   12
        Locksmith (doors)   219, 223
        Moving in   1–2
        Projected move from   193
        Restaurant below   227, 285, 288, 323
            Beethoven and Karl happy for it   229
            Cost   231
            Karl gets take-out   228
            Maid brings food from (February 2)   231
            Veal, evening takeout (January 25)   208
            Cost   210
        Room/kitchen temperatures   287
        Room off of kitchen   173
        Springs up stairs   219
        Stoves   216–218, 227, 236, 252
            Superintendent comes to fix stove   236
        Sunlight, not enough   193
        Women in building
            Gossips   115
            Made up   115
            Too much perfume   115
            See also Schöne Sklavin
    Mödling (1819, 1820, 1822; falsified)   294–295
    Penzing (Summer 1824)   326
    Sailerstätte 994 (Lamberti)   xi
Restaurants
    Meals (general)   1
    Sklavin (dancing)   293
Reuchlin, Johann   8, 11
Rhythm (falsified discussion)   305
Ribar, Maria   xxv
Rice   114, 308
    None on December 24   153
    Too hard   191
Richter, Jean Paul, *Flegeljahre*   132
Ridler, Johann Wilhelm (history, dean)   122
Riedl, Joseph (publisher)   129
    Transfers products to Steiner   129
Ries, Anna Maria (Drewer)   188
Ries, Ferdinand   ix, xxvii, 62, 93–95, 104
    Business correspondence   228
    "Copies entire passages from Beethoven" (Schuppanzigh)   177

Ries, Ferdinand (*continued*)
  Cousin of Franz Drewer 188
  "Hasn't written in a long time" (falsified) 307
  Letter from him (December, 1823) 134, 147
  Looks forward to getting Symphony No. 9 188
  Moscheles saw him in London 93
  Piano Concerto in C Minor, Op. 115 95
  Piano Concerto in C-sharp Minor, Op. 55 63
  Sends 4 harps 37–38, 41
  Two concertos for Beethoven's inspection 38
  See also Kirchhoffer
Ries, Franz (violinist father, Bonn) 62
Ries, Joseph Franz Nikolaus (violin, piano maker, Vienna) 38, 41–42, 62, 158, 188, 251
  Address 42, 158
  Born 1792 158
  Gives lessons 41–42, 158, 189
    Strict discipline 189
  Piano repairs 41–42, 158
  Piano tuning 41–42
Rifle 45
Rinn, Anna, summer rooms in Dornbach 162–163
Risorgimento, Italian 298
Roast
  Beef (?) 188
  For dinner 280
  Loin of beef with vegetable soup, horseradish, and blue cabbage 280
Roast (beef). *See* Beef
Roasting spit. *See* Spit, roasting
Rochus Church market place 256–257
Rolls (*Semmel*)
  Breakfast (2), dinner (3), evening (2); total 7 226
  Enough for Sunday and Monday (Candlemas) 226
  Holzmann reports Schindler eats 284–285
Romani, Pietro, *Fee und Ritter* (ballet) 195
Romberg, Bernhard (violoncellist), variations on Swedish song 132
Room and board, establishments catering to students 269
Rosiza, Mme (hatmaker) 164

Rospini, Karl Joseph (mechanical instruments, eyeglasses) 31–32
  Barometer maker 31
  Optical instruments 31
  Thermometer 32
Rossini, Gioacchino 7, 159
  "As the Viennese will" 108
  Cenerentola 196
    "Isouard's is better" 196
  Compositions on Golden Fleece concert 108
  Fee und Ritter (ballet) 195
  La gazza ladra 185
  Opera excerpts, Court concert (March 16/ March 30) 327
  Singing duets with George IV 231
  Vocal duet 39
Rossini fever among young 62
Rother Igel 179. *See also* Boarding house
Rothschild, Salomon Mayer 14
Routine, daily (Beethoven) xxvi–xvii, 45, 137
  Concentrated work 142
  Dinner time 312
"Row, terrible" (Beethoven) 225–227
Rowaz, Franziska (maid) 190
Roy, Klaus George xxi
Royal Dutch Academy of Fine Arts, Diploma 122, 127
Royal Swedish Music Academy, Diploma 27
Royalties from Paris (Salieri) 152–153
Royalty (shitheads), "everywhere the same as here" (Schindler) 86
Rudolf (Oberstkellner) xxv
Rudolph (Archduke) 20–21, 97
  Baumeister (librarian) 145
  Bought Haslinger's manuscript Beethoven collection 129
  Collection went to GdMf 129
  Cashier
    Has become deaf 288
    Staff named 288
  Coming at Lent? 294
  Efforts on Schuppanzigh's behalf 109, 113, 135
    Beethoven's letter (December 7) 23, 113
  Letter 69–71, 101, 104
  Homosexuality (?) 97
  Hubertus, physician 20–21
  Letter to 66
  Letter to Beethoven (ca. February 1) 247

Rudolph (*continued*)
    Needs priest like Schindler's benefactor 296
    In Olmütz 21
    Probably in Vienna for Golden Fleece 109
    Recommendation of no use for Schuppanzigh at Kärntnertor Theater 271
    Recommendation for Schuppanzigh 294
    Stipend payment (February 28) 288
    To pay Beethoven, rather than Johann 239
    "Witty, only for equals" (Grillparzer) 238
        "Also sometimes for servants" 238
    Zips (valet), death 145
Rum 96, 288
    Mixed with wine 96
Rupprecht, Johann Baptist (poet, biologist, censor), *Ludlamshöhle* 259
Russell, John, description of Kaunitz 80
Russo, Eugenie xxv
Rzechaczek, Franz (government official)
    Amateur violinist 178
    Extensive string instrument collection 178
    Lent historic instruments for Ninth Symphony 178
    Pianist daughter Anna 178

Sachs, Harvey, "Reeking, rotting garbage" 229
Sack, potato 15
Saddler, carrying case 254
Saffron 226
Sainsbury, John, *Dictionary of Musicians* 97
Salad 312, 323
    Herring, with apples, onions, pickles, mixed with cream or yogurt 227
    With veal 308
    With vinegar 112
    Without dressing 312
Salaries
    Drangeld 211
    Henning's 173
    Housekeeper 189, 191, 224
    Johann's cook 209
    Maid 189, 191, 211, 230
    Sontag's 175
    See also Stipend
Salat, Jacob (professor, philosophy, Landshut) 126

Salieri, Antonio 24
    Beethoven's and Mozart's concerts a threat to him 243
    Biographical sketch 57
    Danaïdes, influenced Beethoven's *Christus* 83
    Declares he poisoned Mozart 197, 200, 238, 242–243
        Beethoven's concern 243
    Declining health 57, 63–64, 152, 197, 200, 238
        Cut his throat 63–64
        Forcefully taken to hospital by daughters 64, 152
        Suicide attempt with table knife 152
    "Deranged, completely" 200
    "Everyone gets his reward" (Schindler) 200
    Harmed Mozart through disapproval 243
    Haydn quartets played for him 64
    Haydn's *Creation*, conducted 64
    Ludlamshöhle 259
    Position not to be filled 57
    Residence 57
    Royalties from *Axur* 152–153
    "Sand and stone" 152–153
Sallat (lettuce) 287
Salon music (history, Sonnleithner) 278
Sand, blotting 201
"Sand and stone," Biblical reference (Luke 6: 47–49) 152
    Re Moscheles 217, 224
Sandra (Alexander?), deaf salesman x
Sängerknaben (St. Stephan) 244
Sarcasm 299
Sartory, Frau (housekeeper applicant) 273–274
    Address 274
    Wife of school teacher 275
Sauce pan 38
Sauer and Leidesdorf (publishers) 102, 173. *See also* Leidesdorf
Saurau, Franz Joseph Count, chancellor 218, 246–247
    Lichnowsky intercedes for Swedish diploma 247
    Re Swedish diploma 246–247, 304
Sausages
    Augsburger (cheap) 184
    Dried 20
Saxony, Court 113

Scales (weight)   91, 111
    Need to be examined   299
Schaffgotsch, Johanna Nepomucena
    (Countess in Prussian Silesia), bought
    Scholz's *Mass* translation   213
Scheidl, Johann Maximilian (bookbinder)
    65
Scheidlin, Sigmund (banker; Hensler son-in-
    law)   104
Scheisskerl (George IV)   86
Scheuch, P. Albin   xxiv
Schicht, Johann Gottfried, *Harmonie* (text)
    126
Schickh, Johann   241–243
    Concert (January 25)   228
    On Mozart's manner of death   242–243
    Sends package   241
    Wiener Zeitschrift (and office)   53–54, 241
        Published Jeitteles   26
Schiesskunst [Art of Shooting] by Thon   45
Schiller, Friedrich   3
    An die Freude   30
        "Easy to translate"   282
    Erwartung (Karl quotes)   61–62
    "Fine Arts breathe life"   7
    Son Ernst, Prussian judge   39
    Son Karl   39
    Taucher   149
    Tonkunst   7
    Works   29–30, 35, 51
        At Doll's   51
        From Vogel (Leipzig)   51
        Graz edition   251
        At Meyer's   251
        Tanzer Bros.   29–30
        Translated into English   282
Schindler, Anton   xii, xxvi, xxxii, 65,
    174–177, 182–184
    About row with servants   227
    Admonition, confidential   131
    Advocates performance of *Missa solemnis*
        55
    Approached Palffy for Theater an der
        Wien   320
    Asks for Beethoven's old hat as souvenir
        267
    Ate at Johann's (February 7)   240
    Attends Czerny's private weekly recitals
        232, 239
    Auditions for Kärntnertor Theater   128,
        134
    Beethoven does not use "du" form   285

Schindler, Anton (*continued*)
    Beethoven as teacher (falsified)   85
    Beethoven's Akademie
        Offers to be concertmaster   56
        Preliminary arrangements   62
    Beethoven's concern for his stomach   243
    Beethoven's good graces, back in   72
    Beethoven's Quartets at Schuppanzigh's
        concerts   175
    Beethoven's Septet, Op. 29 (defends)   193
    Beethoven's Sonata, Op. 10 (not taught)
        85
    Beethoven's tensions with him   72
    Boots   303
    Borrowed books from Beethoven   42
    Calls Johann "great exalted brother"   194
    Characterizes Karl kindly   132
    Chattering   182
    Christmas dinner at Stockhammers'   153
    Christmas Mass at Augustiner Church
        153–154
        Met L. Sonnleithner and Kiesewetter
            153–154
    Concertmaster, Josephstadt Theater
        (duties)   55
    Concertmaster, Kärntnertor Theater
        Qualified to be   55, 70
        Turned down to be   98
        Wants to be   70
    Conductors for Akademies, lists   155
    Conductors, Josephstadt Theater,
        comments on   199
    Conducts Symphony No. 2 (Josephstadt
        Theater)   103–104, 253
        Not allowed on *Zettel*   103
        Several concerts   164
    Consecration of the House Overture
        "A monster;" hopes to hear with a
            "large orchestra" someday   256
        Possible involvement in composing
            266
    Considered intrusive pest   324
    Conversation books, did not destroy   27
    Critical of Kanne   155
    Criticizes Beethoven's pencil (falsified)
        119
    "Cross castigates people"   152
    Curious about Bettina Brentano   213
    Debt to Moravian priest in youth   296
    Duties, Josephstadt Theater   55, 143, 164
    Eats at Johann's (February 27)   287
    Eats a roll   284–285

GENERAL INDEX

Schindler, Anton (*continued*)
   Eats whole bowl of *Fritatten* (March 11) 320
   Falling out with Beethoven (August–November, 1823) 28, 42
      Back in his good graces 17
      Karl to pay him 42
      Wants to reconcile 43
   Falsified entries
      At odds with Schuppanzigh 304
      Beethoven "distrustful" 123
      Discussion of rhythm 305
      Flattering language and terms 326/327
      Impersonates Karl 28
      Not afraid of Beethoven's anger 201
      Note to himself 300
      Peevish 119–120
      Piano Sonata, Op. 13 120, 297
      Piano sonatas, early-middle, minor keys 120
      Symphony No. 2 (for Beethoven's "approval") 123
      Tempos 321
      Zwei Principe (2 Principles; falsified) 297
   Friend of tenor Ludwig Tietze 170
   At Gesellschaft concert (November 16) 42
   Gläser (Franz) politics against him 103
   Go-between with Hensler (February 1824) 224
   Gossip 213, 239, 284–285
      Holzmann reports 285
      See also Chattering (above)
   Hemorrhoids 294, 296, 299
   Hensler, evaluation of 104
   History, those who do not know 152
   Homosexual, potential allusions 285
   Housekeeper candidates, likes 185
      Recommends craftsman's widow 261–262
   Humor 294, 299
   Implied study with Beethoven 164
   "In God's name" (expression) 129
   Insinuates against Ries 307
   Invites Beethoven and Karl to Josephstadt Theater (January 21) 196
   Johann
      Addresses him as "Uncle" 210
      Encounters 85

Schindler, Anton (*continued*)
   "Kalkbrenner victorious over Moscheles" 217, 224
   Kanne, sarcastic comment about 154–155
   Ludlamshöhle Petition
      Not among group 279
      Wants to read Petition
         (March 4) 296–297
         (March 9) 307
   Meets with Johann (March 16) 326
   Melusine, comments on 198–199
   Moscheles concert (December 17) 140–141
   Moscheles, conversation with 86
   Moscheles (falsified introduction to Beethoven) 86, 92
   Moscheles, "routine" 143
   New Year's card 169
   Not afraid of Beethoven's anger (falsified) 291
   Not coming (February 13) 250
   Not malicious, just pitiful 28
   Offers to be concertmaster, Beethoven's Akademie 56
   On Beethoven's improvisational method 294–295
   On Grillparzer's *Melusine* 192–193, 198–199
   On manner of Mozart's death 243
   On Rudolph's staff 239
   Opinion of Unger 187, 192
   "Orestes and Pylades" 285
   Pleads "not guilty" for dinner confusion on March 14 324
   Poetic interpretations for Beethoven works 120
   Potentially divisive 175
   Predicts Lichnowsky's departure 156
   Preservation and editing xiv–xvi
   Promises that Beethoven will compose *Melusine* 212
      Beethoven probably angry 212
   Reads Petition (March 8) 286
   Relays Moscheles's thoughts 122
   Religion (sarcasm) 152
   Reported inaccurately about dinner (March 14) 325
   Requested for *Hesperus* articles 307
   Resented after Beethoven's death 321
   Residence, Josephstadt, Josephsgasse 55
   "Reward, everyone gets his" (on Salieri) 209
   Salieri's decline, news of 238

Schindler, Anton (*continued*)
   Sarcastic prattle re Haydn 244
   Schuppanzigh
      Belittles 280
      Criticizes 175
      Seldom sees 56
      Supportive of 268
   Schuppanzigh's concert (January, 1825) 207
      Sends sarcastic regards 207
   Socializes with tenor Jäger 316
   Sonata, Op. 13, wants explanation again (falsified) 297
   String parts, wants soon 326
   Theater duties 297
   Tries to meet Johanna 174
   Unger misses at Beethoven's (February 13) 250
   Uses French 239
   Wants to borrow *Mythologie* (Moritz, *Götterlehre*) 284–285
   Warns about black coffee for Unger 221
   Witnessed Johann's problems (Summer 1823); reported to police 289
   Zwei Principe/Two Principles (falsified) xxxii
   See also Schindler in the Index of Writers
Schlegel, August Wilhelm 51, 179
Schlegel, (Carl Wilhelm) Friedrich von (translator) 51
   Biographical sketch 44–45
Schlegel, J.H.W. 179
Schleicher, Caroline. *See* Krähmer, Caroline
Schlemmer, Josepha (copyist's wife, widow) 5, 40, 106, 115, 192, 291, 309
   Biographical sketch 190–191, 295
   Copies after Wenzel's death 106, 215
   Copies at her home 106
   Copies *Missa solemnis* xl, xli, 215
   Copyist security 106
   Family 295
      Daughter Anna, actress 295
      Son Alexander, apprenticed to master tailor 295
         Going to orphanage? 106
   Pays assistant copyists 191
   Solo vocal parts 291
   To copy Gloria and Credo 295
   To copy Symphony No. 9 (?) 203
   "Which location?" 283
   Will come to see Beethoven 190
      Will bring copyist 190–191

Schlemmer, Josepha (*continued*)
   "Will marry another copyist" (Johann) 203
   See also Missa solemnis in the Index of Compositions
Schlemmer, Wenzel (copyist) xx, 40–41
   Grammar and phonetic spelling xx
   Widow Josepha kept business 106, 215
   Witness to Rampl's wedding 311
Schlesinger, Adolph Martin (Berlin publisher) 216
Schlesinger, Maurice (Paris) xiv, 216, 319–329
   Better than Leidesdorf in Vienna 216
   Biographical sketch 216
   Publication terms 319–320
   Sends package of music through Böhm 244
   Would pay well for Symphony No. 9 320
Schlögl, P. Matthias xxiv
Schloss Lowinsky, Das, or *Die Repressalien* (Kuntz; trans. Joseph von Seyfried; Theater an der Wien) 308
Schmerling, Joseph (law) 90
   Sons ill-mannered students 90
Schmetterling (Butterfly), sewing shop 200
Schmid, Elisabeth xxv
Schmidl, Johann Baptist 49
Schmidt, G., Dr. (Leipzig) hearing balm 113, 117–118
   Address brought by Andreas Schulz 118
   Probably ineffective 118
Schmidt, Johann Adam (early physician) 118
Schmidt-Görg, Joseph (concealing conversation books) xvii
Schmiedl, Franz-Josef xix, xxiii
Schmutzer, Nikolaus (copyist, church director) 215
   Copies "beautifully" 215
   Father Leopold also copyist 215
   Living in Alsergrund 215
   Works at Mechetti's 215
Schnee, Der (Adam; trans. Ignaz Castelli; Kärntnertor Theater) 308
Schneider, Anton (wine dealer) 269
Schneider, Johann Gottlob (Breslau), Greek dictionary 191
Schnitzel 48, 308
Schoberlechner, Franz (pianist), gifts from Troyer 97
Schoberlechner, Johann Georg (linens, Graben) 192

Scholz, Benedict (Warmbrunn)
    Lives on Schaffgotsch estate   213
    Mass in C, German translation   212
Schönauer, Johann Michael   88
    Executor for brother Carl   88
    Friend of lawyer Bach   88
    Rude at Rector's inauguration   88
Schöne Sklavin (restaurant)   227
    Karl gets take-out   228–229
    See also Residences, Landstrasse
Schöny, Heinz   xvii
School teacher (Sartory)   273
Schools, Piarist   50
Schottenhof   167
Schröder, Sophie (actress, mother),
    biographical sketch   175
Schröder, Wilhelmina   156
    Compared to Sontag   68
    Leonore in Dresden and Berlin   22
    Omitted half of "Abscheulicher"   22
    "Spontini removed apathy"   22
    "Terribly lazy"   22
Schubert, Franz   97
    Der Hirt auf dem Felsen   262–263
        Anton Friedlowsky played premiere
        262–263
        For Joseph Friedlowsky   262–263
    Friend of Schindler   170
    Friend of tenor Tietze   170
    Quartet in A Minor, D. 804   318
        Karl compares to Beethoven   323
    Quintet in C, pizzicato for Linke   101,
        292
    Rosamunde, Theater an der Wien   146,
        183–184
        "Vulgar ... morality" (Karl)   146
        Or reference to Vogl (?)   146
Schultz, Johann Reinhold (London)   5, 95
    Biographical sketch   95
    Visit (September 28, 1823)   95
Schulz, Andreas (bookkeeper)   113, 117–118
    Biographical sketch   117
    Brings address for Schmidt's hearing balm
        113, 117–118
    Sons Eduard (piano), Leonhard (guitar)
        117–118
    Violist, guitarist   117
Schulz, Frau von   65
Schulz, Josephine (*née* Killitschky)   189–190
    Letter to   189–190
    Schuppanzigh's sister-in-law   189–190,
        214

Schünemann, Georg   xvi
Schuppanzigh, Ignaz (violinist)   21–23,
    25, 69–71, 76, 102, 105, 108–109, 111,
    113–114, 160, 173–174, 179–180, 193,
    205, 278–279, 299, 303, 309–311
    "Accustomed to living in a foreign
        country" (Schindler)   268
    Acquaintance   168
    Address (Spenglergasse)   100
    Advises April 8 for concert   315
    Akademie planning session   309–311
    Anti-semitic (mildly)   189
    Applies, concertmaster, Kärntnertor
        Theater   69–98, 109, 113–114, 271
    Arithmetic   242
    Asks Beethoven to intercede with Duport
        282
    Beethoven does not attend concerts   33
    Beethoven entertains   66
    Beethoven *Gesamtausgabe* (projected)   181
    Beethoven recommends him to Rudolph
        113, 135
    Beethoven's annual income (notes)   101
    Beethoven's Quartets   175
        "Schuppanzigh too affected"
            (Schindler)   175
    Beethoven's Septet, Op. 20 (Schuppanzigh
        requests to play)   191
    Berlin
        Inquires about payment   214
        Reportedly engaged   197, 268
    Biographical sketch   9
    Wife (*née* Barbara Killitschky)
        173–174
    Brings Henning   21–23
    Brother-in-law (doctor)   70
    Coffee house   277, 280
    Concert (November 21)   67, 70
    Concert (December 18)   160
    Concert (January 25)   211, 213
        Out late   207
    Concerts to be Sundays (4:30)   69, 148,
        154
    Conductor, requests to be   198
    Dietrichstein, Schuppanzigh visits about
        Court appointment   198
    Eats at *Stern* in the Brandstatt every
        Sunday   278
    Gives advice   242
    Gives lessons in students' homes   315
    Henning, will see (December 5)   100
    Work by   173

Schuppanzigh, Ignaz (*continued*)
   Hofkapelle, rejected for position   198
      Loses to Jansa   250, 268, 272
      Receives position (1827)   191
   Housekeeper/cook, can get for Beethoven   70
   Introduces Holz   311
   Invites Beethoven for dinner   70
   "Jew Moscheles is here"   71
   Kalkbrenner, Friedrich
      "Better than Moscheles" (Schuppanzigh)   177
      Visited   177
   Kärntnertor Theater
      No hope for position   191
      Not engaged at Court Theater   214, 261–262
      Played *Der Freischütz* as substitute (February 1824)   281
      Receives position (1828)   191
   "Kyrie is not long"   304
      Agrees with Lichnowsky   304
   Linke, Joseph (cellist), related by marriage   178
   Maid, present when she was scolded   78
   "Men who are fat" (Shakespeare)   72
   Moscheles, negative opinion of   69
   Mylord Falstaff (nickname)   21
   Negative effect of dilettantes   271
   On copying for Akademie (March 6)   304
   Performances with his Quartet   9 November, 1823   33
   Portamento   236, 240
   Prefers Holz for second violinist   197
   Projects three movements from *Missa solemnis* for Akademie   281
      "Only no piano work"   281
   Pun on "Domine" (*Missa solemnis*)   102, 304
   Quartet concert program (February 8)   240
   Quartet concert (February 15)   263
      No printed programs   263
   Quartet series at GdMf   154
      Large audience   194
   Recommended copyist Schmutzer   215
   Reply from Bethmann   225
   "Ries copies Beethoven"   177
   Rudolph, recommendation from   294
   Rudolph, wants recommendation from   69–71, 101, 104

Schuppanzigh, Ignaz (*continued*)
   Russia   261
   Russian choral accompaniments   178
   Rzechaczek his brother-in-law   178
   "Sang through his violin" (Johann)   208
   Schindler belittles (falsified)   280
   Schindler seldom sees him   56
   Schulz-Killitschky, Josephine (Berlin), sister-in-law   189, 214
   Solo in Benedictus   291
   Steiner: "a damned Jew"   71
   "Taken the most pains" on Beethoven's behalf   303
   Tempos (falsified)   321
   Termed "a good man" (Karl)   72
   Third-person address   244
   Threatens to leave Vienna (February 10)   246
   "Tickets cause hellacious confusion"   315
   To get orchestra for Akademie   292
      Extra pros   320
   To visit Beethoven (March 1)   291–292
   Unger interceded for him   249
   Urgently needs income   261–262
   Visits Beethoven (February 8?)   239
   Zelter, Carl Friedrich
      Berlin *Singakademie* accompaniments   178
      Gives Beethoven some wine   178
      Visits to Vienna   177–178
   See also Concerts
Schütz, Amalie (singer), in Amsterdam   85–86, 127
Schwarz, Matthias (Haslinger's copyist)   129
Schweiger-Lerchenfeld, Joseph, Baron von (Rudolph's treasurer)   239, 247
   Brother Eduard   247
   Gone to Prague   239
Scissors   44
Scott, Jack   xxv
Screen, folding   317
Second-hand shops   49, 53
Security, *Missa solemnis*   106
Sedlatschek, Johann (flute virtuoso), *Ludlamshöhle*   259
Seelig, Heinrich (*Zur Stadt Triest*)   110
Seidl, measure of beer and wine   32, 190
Seidl/Seidel, Joseph von (postal official)   45, 63–64
   Confusion with Scheidl   66
   Essayist   63

Seipelt, Joseph (bass)   24, 108, 155
   Concert fees   108
Seisser, Anna (housekeeper applicant)   177
   Biographical sketch   177
   Manservant, wishes for   177
   Widow of criminal court commissioner Franz Joseph   177
Sellner, Joseph (principal oboist, Theater an der Wien), *Ludlamshöhle* member name   259
Semmel. *See* Rolls
Servants, domestic   46
   (1816)   xi
   Bell for summoning   220
   Characteristics for employment   316
   Claim Beethoven made terrible row   225–227
   Dress like ladies   60
   Duties   1, 12
   Gossip   315–316
   Uniforms considered   34–35, 84
Seyfried, Ignaz von   56
   Financial affairs   200
   Sick for four months   200
Shackleton, Ernest   4
Shakespeare, William
   Julius Caesar (quoted by Karl)   72
   Merchant of Venice (parodied by Karl)   75
Shaving (Beethoven)   325
   Not very well   27, 48
Shaving mug   183, 201, 210
Shaving soap   269
Shithead (George IV)   86
Shoe-cleaning brush   201
Shoe wax   282
   Spar's wax polish (?)   282
Shoemaker   319
   Bill (itemized)   303
Shoes   48
   Heels   303
   Upper leathers   303
Shooting, Art of, by Thon   45
Shotgun   45
Siberia   4
Silken goods   250
Simonow, Iwan, *Antarctic Journey*   325
Simrock, Nikolaus (publisher)   x–xi, xxvii
   Beethoven's horn teacher   287
Simrock, Peter Joseph   x–xi, xxx
Sittl, Weinhaus   xxv
Sketchbooks, lost in move   26–27
   "To hell with stuff … useless"   70

Sketches   181. *See also under* specific works in the Index of Compositions
Slave girl, beautiful. *See* Residences, Landstrasse
Sleeping shirt, Maschek's, worn while he copies   320
Smart, George   95
Smetana, Carl von (surgeon)
   Biographical sketch   248
   May not treat internal illnesses   248
   "Not a physician, merely a surgeon" (Karl)   248
   Operated on Karl's hernia (1816)   248
Smith, F. Joseph   xxv
Smith, Frank Joe. *See* Schmiedl
Smoking   63
Snuff   77
Soap   36, 43, 48
   Maker   272
   Preisach   36, 43
   Shaving   269
   Washing   269
Socher, Friedrich (Karl's philosophy tutor)   135–136
Social gatherings   51
Social situations, unexpected and prolonged (typical Viennese)   280–281
Sogetti, due (Zwei Principe?)   294–295, 297
Soldiers, old, under the skies   4
Sollicitator (justice of the peace)   70
Solstice (winter); Beethoven needs light   149
Sömmering, Samuel Thomas, Afflictions of Eyes   212
Sonnleithner, Leopold von (lawyer, amateur musician, legend-in-his-own-mind)   55–56, 160, 165, 278–280, 292
   Akademie (May 7)
      Predicts great profits from   278
      To take care of dilettante choral singers   282, 292
   Biographical sketch   278
   "Copy mass and symphony"   182
   Cousin of Grillparzer   278
   History of Vienna's salon music   278
   Legend in his own mind   278
   Liaison with GdMf   194
   Ludlamshöhle Petition   278, 279
      Lichnowsky sent him Petition to sign   279
   Vocal parts for study at home   291

Sontag, Franziska, *née* Markloff (mother of Henriette)
   Biographical sketch   175
   Born in Heddernheim   175
   Königstadt Theater, Berlin (1825)   175
Sontag, Henriette (soprano)   1, 24, 135–137, 147, 155, 177, 185, 220, 292, 306
   For Akademie?   316
   Acting needs work   68, 85
   Biographical sketch   174–175
   Came from Prague with her mother   174–175
   Compared to Schröder   68
   Court concert fee: 24 ducats   327
   Dinner (March 14)   318, 322–325
      Aftermath incorrect   326–327
      Did not vomit   327
   Going to Kassel   267
   "Improving" (Karl)   205
   More beloved than Grünbaum   308
   More cautious with eating and drinking than Unger   257
   Poor weather, did not visit   220
   Potential Fidelio   156
   Projects summer visits   325
   Range up to F(?)   192
   Rehearsal/performance schedule   174
   Salary   175
   Tobacco (?)   174
   Unger will bring to visit   250
   "Very fine" (Johann)   203
   Wants aria from *Melusine* for Akademie   292
   Wants to visit Beethoven   147, 156
      Cannot visit; has to sing *Euryanthe*   184
      Will visit   169, 174, 176
Sood, Sushma   xxv
Soup   161, 320
   Amount of meat needed   288–289
   Clear   171
   Johann's cook makes it too much   229
   Needs more simmering   59, 223
   Vegetable   200, 280
   With dried sausage   20
Spanish uprising/revolution (1820)   145–146
Spar, Franz   287
   Spar's boot/shoe wax   282
   Wax polish factory   287
   See also Shoe wax
Speech, loud (Beethoven)   13
   Gossip   13–14

Speech, loud (*continued*)
   Lichnowsky disapproves   13
   Possible lack of patriotism   13
Spelling (Beethoven)   xx
Spelling, phonetic   158, 171. *See also* Holzmann; Schlemmer, Wenzel
Spill at dinner (February 8)   240
Spit, roasting/turning   90, 92
Spitzbergen, Norway   4
"Splint-legs" (Schindler)   99
Spontini, Gaspare   22
   Egotism   76
   Impediment to progress   76–77
Sporschil, Johann Nepomuk   xiv, xxvi, 26–27, 63
   Article with loss of Beethoven's "correspondence"   44–45, 68, 87
   Beethoven blames Johann   70
   Lost items   70
   "To hell with stuff ... useless"   70
Spöttl, *Fassl* Grocery (Kohlmarkt)   34, 60, 133, 179, 253, 270
   Owner deaf in one ear   60
   See also Fassl
Spring (Akademie time) "is beginning to sprout" (Voss)   308
St. Anna Normal School   159
St. Laurenz Church, Schottenfeld   215
St. Leopold's Day (Carl's death day)   35, 67
St. Petersburg, Beethoven opera in demand   202
St. Rochus Church   13
St. Stephan's Cathedral
   Gänsbacher as Kapellmeister   151, 196–197, 199
   Kapellmeister salary   145
   Singing boys (for hire)   145
   Weigl vs. Gänsbacher   144, 176, 196–197, 199, 271
St. Ulrich Church   42
Staatsbibliothek zu Berlin—Preussischer Kulturbesitz   xix
Stackelberg, Josephine von   221
Stadion, Johann Philipp (Finance Ministry), Grillparzer's employer   146
Stadlen, Peter   xvii, xxxii
Stadler, Maximilian (Abbé)   205, 268, 271–272
   Politics   268
Staudenheim, Jacob (Dr.)   43, 169
   Foot warmers as gift   43
   Lived in Harrach Palace   169

Steblin, Rita   xxi, xxiv, 1
   On Immortal Beloved   221
Stegmayer, Matthäus (choral director)   57
Stein, Anton Joseph (Latin, Greek, Philology professor)   8, 10–11, 14, 44–45, 71–72, 274, 288
   Disciplined lectures   79
   Firecrackers in his class   124
   Greek pronunciation   8, 11
   Greek teacher at University   274, 288
   Karl respects and fears   10
   Karl walks to University with him   72
   Pedant   8, 79
   Residence Ungargasse   8
Stein, Matthäus Andreas (piano maker/repairer)   xxxi, 116–117, 298
   Attempts hearing device for Broadwood pianoforte   248, 259
   Attended Moscheles's concert   116
      Negative impression   116
   Broadwood piano   41
   Maintains Beethoven's pianos   41, 298
   Model piano, for Beethoven   116
   Rauchfangkehrergasse (near Rasumovsky Palace)   116
   Sounding board   41
   Sunday mornings   298
   See also Stein in the Index of Writers
Steiner, Sigmund Anton (music publisher/dealer)   96, 157, 163
   "A damned Jew" (Schuppanzigh)   71
   Akademie to earn funds to repay loan   208
   Asks about Johann's ceded works   319
   Beethoven seeks legal recourse   112
   Has "swindled" Beethoven   112
   Haslinger, junior partner   1
   Karl's opinion of   112
   Loaned money to Beethoven   208
   Not Jewish   71
   Nothing good to say about Weber   50
   Plays Romance, Op. 50, as piano 4 hands with Czerny   266
   Profits greatly from Beethoven's works   71
   Rights to *King Stephan* and *Ruins*   129
Steinius (resident in Augartenstrasse)   167
Stempelbogen (document)   277
Stern, *Goldenes*, restaurant (Brandstatt)   278, 290, 305, 309–311
Steyrisch (uncouth)   174
Stier (bull, Taurus)   141

Stipend/annuity/pension, Beethoven's (1809)
   Endorsement by parish priest   288
   Payment from Lobkowitz   288
   Payment from Rudolph   288
Stockhammer, Ferdinand (Count), financial advisor
   Family, Purkersdorf, friends of Schindler   153
   Family sends greetings   153
   Schindler eats Christmas dinner with them   153
   Signed *Ludlamshöhle* Petition   153
   Therese (Johann's wife) is sister-in-law   153
Stockings, sheep's wool (Karl)   53
Stolizka, Anna, Rauchfangkehrergasse (departing maid?)   211
Stomach cramps   172
Stoneware   29
Stovepipe   252
Stoves   44, 199
   Oil it   15
   Prevention of smoke and fire danger   37
   Smoky   183–184, 236
   Ungargasse   216–218, 227
   See also under Residences, Landstrasse
Strauss, *Zum goldenen* (restaurant)   99
   Losing business   161
   Wolfgang Reischl   99
Straw   192
Straw, bundles   46–47
Stregczek, Thomas Mathias (candlemaker, wax)   162
Streicher, Johann Andreas (piano maker)   205, 299
   Johann and Czerny visit (February 2)   232
   New piano models   231–232
   Residence/shop in Ungargasse   231
   To attempt hearing device for piano   248
Streicher, Johann Baptist, "new invention"   235
Streicher, Nannette *née* Stein   205, 213
   Not yet visited Beethoven (November 15)   39
   Not yet visited Beethoven (November 30)   51
String parts
   Estimated numbers (March 6)   304, 310
   Hurry to copy (March 16)   326
Stroh, Patricia   xxiv
Strop, razor   191

Strozzi Palace. *See* Blöchlinger's Educational Institute
Students, room and board   69
Stummer, Josepha Maria (singer)   9
Stumpff, Johann Andreas (harp maker)   xxxiv, 37, 41, 94
Stunz/Stuntz, Hartmann   308
Sturm, Heinrich and Franz (wine shop)   301
Stuttgart, *Morgenblatt*   27
Sugar   5–6, 20, 31, 65, 73, 111, 180, 196, 202, 210, 286
    Ordinary (price)   206
    Price   73
    White (price)   206
Supper, light (evening)   13, 73, 110, 137–138
    Christmas Eve in restaurant   151
    Eggs   13, 119
    Price   73
Surgeon defined   248
Sweden
    Did not subscribe to *Missa solemnis*   132
    Diploma (Royal Music Academy)   27, 29, 297–298, 304
    See also Royal Swedish Music Academy

Tablecloths   293
Tabor, Bohemia
    Lachner's performances of Beethoven's String Quartets   125, 127
    Protestant stronghold   125, 127
Tailor   92, 252, 253
    Needs payment of 2 fl. 30 kr.   252
    No tape measure   252
    Prices   5
    Visits Beethoven   252, 253
Tallow, melting   43
Tandelmarkt   49, 53
Tape measure (tailor's)   252
Taurus   141
Taxes
    Income, graduated   290
    Payment records   217–218
    Receipt   218
Tea   13
Teacher, woman (Lichnowsky?)   109
Teaching (Beethoven)   xxvii
Tempo
    Beethoven's now slower (falsified)   321
    Schuppanzigh and Umlauf on (falsified)   321
Tempora, o mores!   78
Tendler and Manstein (book dealer)   305

Teplitz, visit (1811)   163
Tepperberg, Joachim   xxiii
Textbooks (University)   13, 122
Thayer, Alexander Wheelock   xi, xv, xxxiv
Theater an der Wien   96
    Animals, use of   98
    Copyist C, Gebauer   312
    Orchestra had not been paid (March 6)   307
    Seyfried, conductor   200
Theater in der Josephstadt   144–145, 164, 225
    Aline   204
    Arsenius der Weiberfeind   157
    Beethoven, Symphony No. 2 (ca. December 12)   123
    Conductors   199
    Consecration of the House   22, 253
    Drechsler, Joseph (conductor)
        Finale of *Wasserträger* Act I went to the devil   316
        Wrong tempi   316
    Gläser (Franz) conducts   98
    Hensler's treatment of painter, machinist, pantomimists, first dancer   267
    Intrigues   157
    Isouard, *Aschenbrödel*   193, 199
    New Year benefit concert   170
        Beethoven, Symphony No. 2   170
    Orchestra
        Against Gläser   297
        Capable, experienced   297
        Police called   297
        Revolt   297
        Schindler's duties   297–298
        Size and strength   103
        Winds, potentially unused, for Beethoven's Akademie   320
        Winds on strike   297
        Young players   98
    Personnel treatment and morale problems   267, 320
    Rehearsal schedule   253–254
    Schindler's accomplishments   98
    Schindler's duties   143
    Sundays: only popular spectacles   225
    To use *Ruins of Athens* Overture (ca. February 1824)   224
    Trombones from Alserkaserne   253
    Wasserträger, Cherubini (March 9)   297, 306, 316
    See also Concerts; Schindler
Theater in der Leopoldstadt   76, 253

Theater-in-the-round   82–83
Theater-Zeitung. See *Allgemeine Theater-Zeitung*
Theaters, new, Munich, Frankfurt, Hamburg   102
Theatrical matters
   Politics   159
   Rivalry   159
Theft (conversation books)   xvi–xvii
Thefts, overcoat (university)   81
Theoretician (Tomaschek)   26
Theresianum   50
Thermometer (Rospini)   32
Thiersch, Friedrich, Greek grammar   11
Thon, Theodor (forest commissioner)   45
Thread (yarn)   171, 200
Tickets, Akademie   315
   Complimentary   320
Tiefer Graben   15
Tieftrunk, Johann Heinrich (philosophy professor, Halle)   126
Ties, double flannel   265
Tietze/Titze, Ludwig (tenor)
   Friend of Schindler   170
   Interpreter of Schubert   170
   Law student   170
Tigers   302–303
Time bea[ter], metronome   202
Timpani   112
   Müller's   279
Tip (to waiter)   180
Tobacco   43, 77
   And Lottery shops   36
   Hungarian (in paper)   3
   Product of Baden   3
   Snuffing   77
Toilet
   Odor   12
   Odorless   37
Tomaschek, Johann Wenzel   x, xiii, 25–26
Tonkünstler-Societät   23
Tooth, pulled, painful   287
Tooth powder   120, 125
Tours, Munich and London (false rumor)   87
Towel, hand. *See* Hand towel
Traeg, Johann (music publisher)   282
Travestied Aeneas   108, 110
Treasury, Imperial
   Letter to brother Carl   2
   Payment office   270

Trion, Sophie (housekeeper applicant)   190
   Biographical sketch   190
   From Saxony   190
   "Old woman"   190
Tripe (intestines)   8
Trombones   112
   Beethoven's *Equale*   260
   From an army band   253–254
   In *Consecration* Overture at Josephstadt Theater   253–254, 266
   Mechanical   259
Troyer, Count   97
   Gift to Schoberlechner   97
Truffles   179
Trumpet
   Keyed   157
   Mechanical   259
Trumpeters
   Josephstadt Theater   103
   Müller's   279
"Truth … white beard?" (Karl)   6
Tuning, too high overall (*fingiert*)   326
Türkheim, Ludwig von (physician)   20–21
Turkish music   108
Tuscany
   Grand Duke   214
   Legation   49–50
   For *Missa solemnis*   49–50
   See also Odelga
Tuscher, Mathias (former guardian)   296
   At Schuppanzigh concert (January 25)   208, 228
Two Principles (falsified)   xxxii, 294–295, 297
Tyrol   144

Umlauf, Michael   x, 64
   About tempos (falsified)   321
   Biographical sketch   306–307
   Conducts *Fidelio*   64
   Conducts *Fidelio* Overture   166
   To conduct Ninth Symphony Akademie (March 8)   306–307
   Violinist   64
Underpants (Beethoven's)   73
   Holzmann mends   264
Ungargasse (suburban Landstrasse)
   Beethoven's residence. *See* Residences, Landstrasse
   Stein and Streicher, shop and residence   231

Unger, Caroline (mezzo-soprano)   24, 54,
        108, 155, 177, 185, 198, 257–258, 292, 306
    Answer to Duport   221
    Beethoven's letter (ca. February 11)   230,
        244
    Borrows *Melusine*   257
    Concert fee   108
    "Devil of a girl" (Schindler)   187
    Dinner (March 14)   318, 322–325
        Her account   323–324, 326–327
    Father   244
    German tour, potential   186, 250
    Going to Berlin   267
    Indisposed (mid-February)   257
        Due to eating and drinking   257
    Invites Beethoven to visit her   187
    Learns on her own   306
    Loves the French   222
    Melusine, wants to sing in   187, 192–193
        Borrowed libretto   193
        Role of Bertha   198–199
    No beloveds   221
    Note too high in Symphony   323
    On Beethoven's need to marry   186
    Opinion of J.C. Bernard   186
    Range
        F to A/B-natural   316
        G to F   306
        Up to F   192
    In rehearsal   244
    Rehearsal/performance schedule   174
        Rehearsals mornings and afternoons;
            cannot visit   316
    Residence (with father)   258, 267
    Schindler encountered before (February 8)
        238
    Schuppanzigh, evidently interceded for
        249
    Sick from black coffee   222
    Story about Weigl and St. Stephan   256
    Suggests walk in Prater   183
        Invites to Lusthaus in Prater   186
    Theater's coach   220
    Tobacco (?)   174
    Tour (Fall, 1824?)   192–193
    Visits Beethoven
        (January 17)   184–187
        (January 29)   220–222
        (February 13)   249
    Wants a Beethoven composition   185
    Weber's *Euryanthe*: quotes atrocious
        poetry   186–187

Unger, Caroline (*continued*)
    Will visit Beethoven   169, 174, 176, 238
        Visits (January 17)   184–187
Uniform, domestic servants   84
Universal Cameral-Zahlamt   270
University   135
    Calendar   4
    Curriculum   31
        Logic   31
        Mathematics   45
        Philosophy   31–32, 78
        Psychology   31–32
        Textbooks   32, 122
    Doctoral graduate   139–140
        Received gifts   139–140
    Education good under Napoleon   11
    Karl's general complaints   49
    Lectures, Philosophy
        Classroom discipline   79, 81–82, 124
            Firecrackers   124
        Near Lugeck   326
        Noisy   78–79
        Security   81–83
        Students insolent to faculty   79
        Tuition   293
            9 florins   293
        Materials   73
    Philosophy faculty (Wilde)   81
    Rector election   81–82, 88
    Schedule, Karl's   53–54.
        See also Beethoven, Karl, University
            schedule
    Students   90
        Schmerling sons, ill-mannered   90
    Thefts   35, 81
        Coats, hats, books   35
    Too little ceremony   88
    Young people learn little   121
Unknown (ca. February 9)   241
    Brings package from Schickh   241
Urfahr, across from Linz   305
Urhan, Mehmet   xxiii

Van Acken and Martin Menagerie   302.
    See also Menagerie
Varena, Joseph von (Graz)   163
    Beethoven's unpublished orchestral works
        163
    Charity concerts   163
Veal   59, 134, 180, 254, 308
    24 kr. per portion   229
    "Best and least expensive" (Karl)   251

Veal (*continued*)
    Leg   90
    Take-out from restaurant on ground floor   208, 228–229
    See also Beef
Vegetables   289
    Dealer   272
    Side dish   188, 320
    Soup   200, 280, 308
Veni, Sancte Spiritus (chant)   13
Venison   218
    Given away (January 1824)   226–227
    Haunch   90
    Roast   91
Vests   293
    Old   265
Veyhelin, Johann, *Astronomical Tables for 1824*   270
Vienna, Congress of. *See* Congress of Vienna
Vienna, directions   xxvii–xxviii
Vienna, "merit goes absolutely unrecognized" (Schindler)   268
Viennese dialect. *See* Wienerisch
Viennese vocabulary   158, 171
Vinegar   112, 196, 287
Violin/violinists
    Kaufmann   205
    Violin 1, 12 players   304, 310
    Violin 2, 12 players   304, 310
    See also Böhm, Joseph; Holz; Krähmer, Caroline; Piringer; Schindler; Schuppanzigh
Viola/violists   117
    12 (?) players   304, 310
    Forti (young), Theater an der Wien   134
    Kaufmann (talented amateur)   205
    Schulz   117
    Weiss, Franz   193
Violoncellists
    10 players   304, 310
    Gross   205
Violoncello   59. *See also* Brunsvik, Franz; Hauschka; Linke, Joseph; Zmeskall
Visitors, Beethoven does not like surprise guests   267
Vogl, Johann Michael (bass)   137
    Morality (?)   146
    Salary (?)   146
Vogler, Georg Joseph (Abbé), Mass (?)   155
Voříšek, Jan Hugo (organist)   245
    Chorus   39
Vöslau. *See* Wine, Vöslau

Voss, Johann Heinrich (poet), "Spring begins to sprout"   308

W_____ (physician, suicide and funeral)   32
    Disappointed: not appointed Court Surgeon   32
Wächter, Johann Michael and Theresia (singers)   137
Wagner, Richard, *Mein Leben*   xxi
Wähner, Friedrich   27
    Janus (journal)   137–138
Waiter, restaurant, tip   180
Waitress/maid   188
Waldmann, Amalie/Maly (Therese's illegitimate daughter)   83, 206, 211, 264–265, 289
    Biological father   264–265
    Dr. Herbeck for sore throat   264
    Financial support   264–265
Walking routes to Kumpfgasse traced (Karl)   223, 293
Walking times (Karl)   225, 296
Walks (Beethoven)   xxv
Wallishauser, Johann Baptist
    Bookshop (Hoher Markt)   146
    Published Grillparzer, *Melusine*   146, 237
Wallmoden, Ludwig Georg (Cuirassiers)   296
Walls, wet (varnished)   37
Warmbrunn (Silesia)   22, 213
    Benedict Scholz   213
Warsow, Friedrich (Haslinger's calligrapher)   129
Wash basin (Karl)   21, 65
Washerwoman   4, 67, 190, 313
    Cooking smells get into wash   313
    Plus foods   190
    Prices   190
Washing/laundry   47, 81, 89, 293
    Done in evenings   317
    Hand towel   183
    Soaking   326
    Stains   325–326
Washing soap   269
Wasserhof (Johann's estate)   229
Watch (Schindler's), runs poorly   153
Water   65
    "Beethoven drinks too much" (Johann)   148, 217
    Carrying   47
    Cause of Beethoven's diarrhea   148

Water, Beethoven's favorite drink (Schindler) 217
Water, cooking, not hot enough 116
Water, Viennese 35
    Wieshofer's 35
Waterbirds (Schindler) 305
Watson, Walter, "cursed the hour" 267
Watts, Catherine xxv
Wax, stick of 258. See also Candles, Wax
Weather 108, 112, 177, 183–184, 207, 215–216, 220
    Rain 27
    Snow (March 14) 324
Weber, Carl Maria 3, 94
    "As God wills" 70, 108
    Der Freischütz 7–8, 33, 69, 83, 171
        Kärntnertor Theater (February 24, Schuppanzigh as substitute) 281
    Euryanthe 1, 7–10, 24, 33, 50–51, 54, 56, 67–68, 83, 129, 146, 159, 171, 183–185
        Abbreviated version 83
        Kärntnertor Theater: monetary losses 149
        "Poetry atrocious" (Unger) 186–187
        Imitates *Fidelio* 83, 209
        "Lost his way" (Leidesdorf) 209
    Ludlamshöhle 259
    Visit to Baden 7
Wegeler, Franz Gerhard ix
Weiberfeind (Woman hater) 157
Weidinger, Anton (keyed trumpeter, keyed hornist) 157
    Article in *Intelligenzblatt* 157
    Haydn, Trumpet Concerto 157
Weight values 75
Weigl, Andreas (archivist) xxiii
Weigl, Joseph (younger) 54–55, 57, 62, 144, 176
    Apartment 218–219
    Beethoven maintained distance 54
    Beethoven "never visited" 54
    Bid for St. Stephan 256, 271
    Biographical sketch 54
    Combining church duties with theater 218
    "Don't you have enough?" (Franz) 256
    Kiesewetter's choice 155
    Loses St. Stephan position to Gänsbacher 199, 214–215, 239, 243–244
    Pension 176
        Served 40 years 176

Weigl, Joseph (*continued*)
    Proposed conductor for *Missa solemnis* 155
    Recent failed operas 215
    Related to violinist Katter 271
    Salary 176
    Supported Barbaja's personnel cuts 54
    Supposedly visits Beethoven often 54
    Wife Elisabeth Bertier 244
        Chambermaid to Archduchess Leopoldine 244
        Too arrogant for Sängerknaben (Firmian) 244
    Won Kapellmeister at St. Stephan 196
    Lost Kapellmeister at St. Stephan 197, 199
Weihsmann, Helmut xxi, xxv
Weinhaus Sittl xxv
Weinmann, Ignaz xvii
Weinmüller, Carl Friedrich (bass), as Leporello 24
Weiss, Franz (composer, violist) 9, 70, 193
Weiss, Piero xviii
Wenzel, Saint, of Bohemia 238
Wetzlar (Baron), previous owner of Gutenbrunn 57
    Association with Mozart 57
Wholesaler (formerly grocer) 84
    Mostly financial business 84
Wiener Allgemeine musikalische Zeitung
    Poor success for Kanne 155
    Suspended (January/February 1824) 225
Wiener Beethoven-Gesellschaft xxiv
Wiener Zeitschrift für Kunst.... See under Schickh
Wiener Zeitung, Beethoven's ad 241
Wienerisch (Viennese dialect) xix, 158, 171, 190
    Karl's comments 171
Wieshofer's Viennese Water 35
Wikosch, Martin Johann (history faculty)
    Cannot identify students 79
    Description of his lectures 78–79
    Firecrackers in his classroom 124
    Salary 79
Wilde, Franz Xaver (philosophy faculty) 81
Wilde, Karen xxi
Wildfeyer, Wilhelm (Kollowrat tutor) 25–26, 39–40
    Biographical sketch 26
    Guitar 25–26
Wildpretmarkt (Wild Game Market) 60
Wilfinger, Franz (Msgr.) xxiv, 186

Wimmer's bookshop (Dorotheergasse)   216
Wind parts, no hurry to copy (March 16)   326
Windmühle (suburb)   xiii
Windows, need to oil   15
Winds, doubled   310–311
Wine   134, 172
   Austrian, inexpensive   15
   Authentic (unadulterated)   269
   Bad, sent to repeat customers   269
   Beethoven had too much (?)   72
   At the *Birne*   255
   Bottles   273
   Cypress, at *3 Laufern*   150
   Erlauer   110, 113
   (February 28)   288
   Fine sweet   323
   Frauendorf, at *Birne*   58
   From the City   47
   Gift from Zelter   178
   Glass for Holzmann   78
   Gumpoldskirchner   118
   Hungarian   70
   Inexpensive   118
   Italian, good   72
   Johann, money from sale   206
   Karl, drinks too much   72–73
   Karlowitzer   275
   Less expensive in Italy   34
   London: mixed with rum   96
   Mixtures   4
   Mountain, Johann will send   263
   No longer good   72
   Piccolit, adulterated   34
   Preindl's cellar   176
   Present from Schuppanzigh ("very healthy")   178
   Prices   4, 32, 34, 255, 273
   Red   70, 309
   Schumlauer   275
   Seelig, *Zur Stadt Triest*   110
   Seidl, one   134
   Thaler (Styrian)   255
   Tiefer Graben   118
   Unadulterated   263, 301
      Good enough for servants   301
   Vöslau, Fries   4
   Washerwoman, at breakfast   190
Wine dealer, new (Wollzeile)   300–301
   Low prices   300–301
   Sturm Brothers, proprietors   301
   Unadulterated   301
Wine spirits   28, 60–61, 192, 196, 320

Wine vinegar   172
Winkel, Dietrich Nikolaus, *Componium* (instrument)   280
Winkler, book dealer   29
Winter (unknown, GdMf?)   161
Wiping rags   291
Withalm, Benedict, varnish factory (Graz)   37
Wladislaw Brothers (linens, Graben)   257
Wolf, visitor   168
   Admirer of Moscheles   168
Wolfinger, Adam (soap maker)   272
Wölfl, Joseph   169
Wolfmayer, Johann Nepomuk (cloth dealer, benefactor)   101
   Attends all musical events   296
   Attends concert with wife Josepha (January 25)   208, 228
   Wants to commission Requiem   101, 228
Woman, blind   2, 92
Woman copyist. *See* Schlemmer, Josepha
Women, literate   118–120. *See also* Bauer, Nannette; Holzmann; Housekeeper, Search
Wood, fire   89, 255
   Delivery and cutting   117, 119
   Maid carried   47
   Supply almost gone   89
Woodbin   89
Woodcutting   119, 255–256
   Fee   255–256
   Tallow on saws   119
Woodpile, key   141
Wool   53
Wordplay   8, 75, 109, 270, 272, 280, 294, 311
   Crude   299
   Johann der Läufer (father Johann)   219
   Kreuz (Cross) of wood (Holz)   197
   Pun (Holz)   311
   Pun (Milord, Schuppanzigh) in Benedictus   304
   See also Humor; Puns
Wranitzky, Friedrich (violoncellist)   223
Writing materials (Karl's)   73
"Written out" (Beethoven)   143
Wunderl, Mathias (Copyist E)   5, 8, 40, 106
   Assisting Josepha Schlemmer   115
   Biographical sketch   5
   Copies *Consecration of the House* Overture   5
   Copies *Missa solemnis*   5
   Encounters Karl in street   115

Wunderl, Mathias (*continued*)
    Made errors 115
    Pun on name 8

Yogurt 227

Zechmeister, Gerhard xxiv
Zelter, Karl Friedrich (Berlin *Singakademie*)
    Accompaniment style in Berlin 178
    Met Beethoven 178
Zimmer, Mark S. (Madison, Wisconsin; *The Unheard Beethoven*) 174, 187, 194, 197, 224, 226, 239, 242, 251, 255, 263–264, 271, 277, 287, 313
Zimmerreise (projected light journeys) 82–83
Zips, Franz Joseph (Rudolph's valet), death 145
Zmeskall, Nikolaus (violoncello) 56, 121
    Very weak 69
Zwei Prinzipe (falsified) xxxii, 294–295, 297

Printed in the United States
by Baker & Taylor Publisher Services